Trans-Siberian

Railway

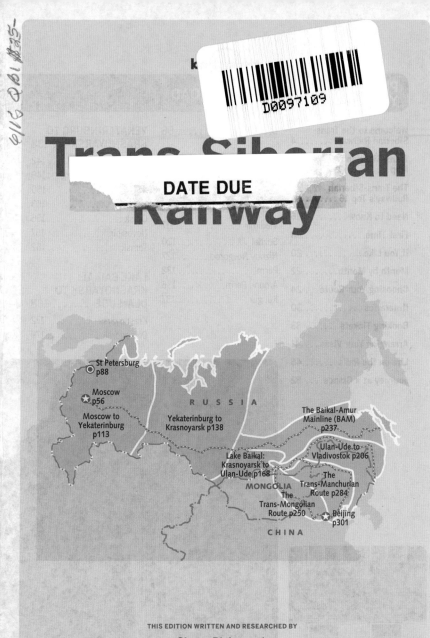

St Petersburg
p88

Moscow
p56

Moscow to
Yekaterinburg
p113

R U S S I A

Yekaterinburg to
Krasnoyarsk p138

The Baikal-Amur
Mainline (BAM)
p237

Ulan-Ude to
Vladivostok p206

Lake Baikal:
Krasnoyarsk to
Ulan-Ude p168

MONGOLIA

The
Trans-Mongolian
Route p250

The
Trans-Manchurian
Route p284

Beijing
p301

CHINA

THIS EDITION WRITTEN AND RESEARCHED BY

Simon Richmond,

Greg Bloom, Marc Di Duca, Anthony Haywood, Michael Kohn, Shawn
Low, Tom Masters, Daniel McCrohan, Regis St Louis, Mara Vorhees

PLAN YOUR TRIP

ON THE ROAD

DAVID FORMAN / GETTY IMAGES ©

MARTIN MOOS / GETTY IMAGES ©

IRKUTSK P179

Contents

LAKE BAIKAL P173

Welcome to the
Trans-Siberian Railway

Snow-dusted or sun-kissed steppe and taiga, the Gobi Desert and the Great Wall – the Trans-Siberian routes unite landscapes and experiences into the journey of a lifetime.

Jewel in the Crown of the Tsars

No other rail journey can compare to the Trans-Siberian Railway, once hailed as 'the fairest jewel in the crown of the Tsars'. Today the name is shorthand for a web of tracks, fanning out from Moscow and European Russia, across seven time zones to the Pacific edge of Asia. Survivor of revolution, wars, natural calamities and extreme weather, this historic iron way provides access to both contemporary metropolises and stuck-in-time villages as well as beautiful landscapes.

Choice of Routes

Trans-Siberian journeys are packed with wow moments. We defy you not to get a kick out of marching across the cobbles of Moscow's Red Square, wandering around Běijīng's Forbidden City or taking in the glorious panorama of Vladivostok's Golden Horn Bay. The more adventurous will certainly want to explore, and possibly plunge into, icy Lake Baikal or ride with nomads across Mongolia's magnificent steppes. There's also the Baikal-Amur Mainline (Baikalo-Amurskaya Magistral; BAM) passing through remote and stunning parts of Siberia.

Slow, Rewarding Travel

The opportunities to alight and explore what was once one of the world's most forbidding and feared destinations are now only limited by your time, budget and imagination. With an average speed of 60kph Trans-Siberian services are not for travellers in a hurry. But there's probably never been a better, more comfortable time to travel with improved train facilities, online ticketing and a proliferation of affordable Western-style hostels and other accommodation along the way.

Cultural Contrast

While aboard the train, embrace the chance to interact with your fellow passengers and learn a little about their respective cultures as you share with them something of your own. Contrary to common conceptions, you'll discover that Russians in particular are among the kindest people you could meet, ever ready to share their provisions and engage in conversation. So whether you're on the Trans-Siberian Railway simply for the sake of the journey or for the access it provides to Russia, China and Mongolia, prepare yourself for a magnificently rewarding experience of changing landscapes and cultures, people, and of life on the rails.

Why I Love the Trans-Siberian Railway

By Simon Richmond, Author

Etched on my memory is the research trip I made for the first edition of this guide, when I was arrested on a platform and separated from my luggage (including computer, notes and nearly all my money) which continued on the train into Siberia. The day was saved by a wonderful collection of Russians who pulled together to reunite me with all my belongings. Awesome engineering feat it may be, but it's this chance to make friends and connect with Russians and other nationalities on the Trans-Siberian Railway that really makes the journey so special.

For more about our authors, see page 432

Above: Trans-Siberian train skirts Lake Baikal (p168)

Trans-Siberian Railway

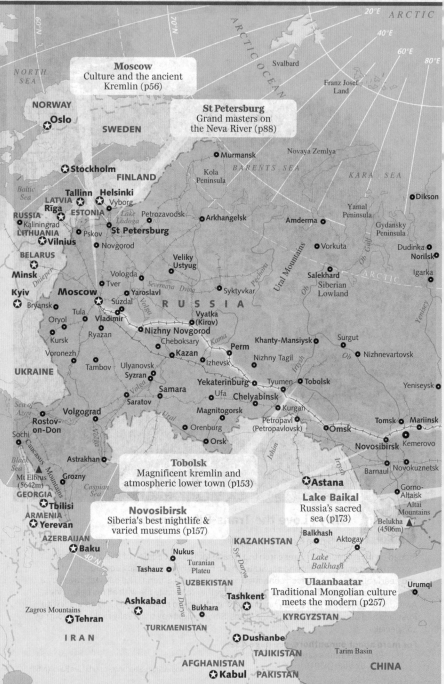

Moscow
Culture and the ancient
Kremlin (p56)

St Petersburg
Grand masters on
the Neva River (p88)

Tobolsk
Magnificent kremlin and
atmospheric lower town (p153)

Novosibirsk
Siberia's best nightlife &
varied museums (p157)

Lake Baikal
Russia's sacred
sea (p173)

Ulaanbaatar
Traditional Mongolian culture
meets the modern (p257)

RAIL ROUTES

Trans-Siberian
Trans-Mongolian
Trans-Manchurian
Baikal-Amur Mainline
Ural
Other

Barguzin Valley
Remote and romantically
timeless valley (p205)

Gorkhi-Terelj National Park
Glorious rock formations and
green valleys (p277)

Olkhon Island
Spellbinding landscapes and
epic myths (p193)

Shānhǎiguān
The Great Wall meets
the sea (p298)

Běijīng
Explore China's capital
by bike (p301)

Vladivostok
Russia's principal city
of the east (p227)

0   1000 km
0   600 miles

Trans-Siberian Railway's
Top 16

Moscow's Kremlin & Red Square

1 This ancient fortress (p58) is the founding site of Moscow and the ultimate symbol of political power in Russia. Within its ancient walls you can admire the artistry of Russia's greatest icon painters, gawk at the treasure trove that fuelled a revolution, shed a tear for Russia's great and tragic rulers, and climb the tower for an amazing panorama. Flanking the northeastern wall of the Kremlin, Red Square is dominated by bold towers and the colourful domes of St Basil's Cathedral. Kremlin and the Moscow River

Life Aboard the Train

2 The great pleasures of Trans-Siberian travel are the on-board rituals of eating, sleeping and simply gazing through the windows at the unfurling landscape. Also getting to know your fellow passengers, invariably Russians, who have a real knack for making the compartments a home away from home. Amble along to the restaurant car, if there is one, and pal up with the *provodnitsa*, the female train attendant who cherishes her carriage as her own little fiefdom.

LONELY PLANET / GETTY IMAGES ©

EDD WESTMACOTT / ALAMY ©

Běijīng by Bike

3 In order to get under the skin of Běijīng (p301), hire a bike and cycle like mad through the city. Navigate twists and turns, thread through alleys, down boulevards and around landscaped parks, and the city will reveal itself as a fascinating mosaic of charming old *hútòng* (narrow alleyways) neighbourhoods and 21st-century architectural wonders. Biking Běijīng puts you at ground level with the locals, and there is a tangible sense of camaraderie as you pull up to an intersection and push off together as if in a massive bike rally. Tiān'ānmén Square (p308)

Russia's Sacred Sea

4 Siberia exile, Old Believer Archpriest Avvakum, found it to be a bountiful paradise where all was larger than life: mountains and rocky gates that rose into the heavens, and pure waters brimming with fish. Lake Baikal (p168), the world's largest freshwater lake, still has the power to amaze whether you glimpse its sapphire waters from the train as it skirts the southern shore or disembark to get an even closer look. For those who like to hike, also consider tramping part of the splendid Great Baikal Trail (p191).

WALTER BIBIKOW / GETTY IMAGES ©

NUTEXZLES / GETTY IMAGES ©

Mongolian Landscapes

5 Mongolia is a beautiful country. Your Mongolian travel mates will croon about the blue waters of Lake Khövsgöl, the singing sand dunes of the Gobi Desert and the glaciated peaks of the Altai Mountains. Closer to Ulaanbaatar, it's easy to make day or overnight trips to Gorkhi-Terelj National Park (p277) amid the glorious rock formations and green valleys. For a wonderful experience that combines natural landscapes and wildlife viewing, visit Khustain National Park, where wild *takhi* horses roam across the pristine grasslands of central Mongolia. Gorkhi-Terelj National Park

Suzdal's Idyll

6 Ding-dong ring the bells of a few dozen churches as you ride your bike through the streets of Suzdal (p120), lined with wooden cottages and lush gardens. This is Russia as it would have been, if not for the devastating 20th century – unpretentious, pious and very laid-back. Some of the best religious architecture is scattered around, but you can just as well spend all day lying in the grass and watching the river before repairing to a *banya* for the sweet torture of heat, cold and birch twigs.

Arts Unleashed in Moscow

7 Moscow's performing and visual arts scenes are a major drawcard. Classical ballet, music and theatre have traditionally been at the heart of Russian culture. Today, exciting and creative artists are experimenting with new forms of theatre, painting, music, sculpture and dance. If you have your heart set on classical opera or ballet at the Bolshoi Theatre (p82), or icons at the State Tretyakov Gallery (p71), you won't be disappointed. But try to catch the experimental cultural scene, too. Dancers at the Bolshoi Theatre

IZZET KERIBAR / GETTY IMAGES ©

THOMAS L. KELLY / GETTY IMAGES ©

St Petersburg's Hermitage

8 Little prepares you for the scale and quality of the exhibits at the State Hermitage Museum (p90). An almost unrivalled history of Western art, the collection includes a staggering number of Rembrandts, Rubens, Picassos and Matisses – the latter two now displayed in new galleries in the General Staff Building. In addition, there are superb antiquities, sculpture and jewellery. If that's not enough, then content yourself with wandering through the private apartments of the Romanovs, for whom the Winter Palace was home until 1917.

Naadam in Ulaanbaatar

9 During Naadam in Ulaanbaatar (p267) you'll see proud examples of Mongolian archery, wrestling, horseracing and *shagai* (anklebone shooting), played out before enthusiastic crowds in traditional dress. National foods *huushuur* (mutton pasties) and *airag* (fermented mare's milk) are consumed in great quantities. Naadam is also a great time to catch a performance of traditional acts including the other-worldly *khöömei* (throat singing), glass-shattering *urtyn-duu* and cringe-inducing *nugaralt* (contortionism).

Great Wall of China

10 There are two opinions about the significance of the Great Wall (p327). For the Chinese the Wall represents a marvellous architectural achievement, accomplished with enormous manpower and advanced technical designs. For Mongolians, it represents nomadic strength, power and determination, for only the fiercest of warriors could force another people to construct such a colossal defensive work. For Trans-Siberian travellers, the Wall is a majestic ending (or starting) point to the long cross-continental journey.

PHOTOGRAPHY BY SPL / GETTY IMAGES ©

Olkhon Island

11 Sacred to the shamanist western Buryats, enchanted Olkhon (p193) sits halfway up Lake Baikal's western shore. It's obvious why the gods and other beings from the Mongol *Geser* epic chose to dwell on this eerily moving island, though today it's more likely to be a bunch of backpackers you meet emerging from a cave. The island's landscapes are spellbinding, Baikal's waters lap balmiest on its western shore and if you're after some Siberia-inspired meditation, there's no better spot.

TAN YILMAZ / GETTY IMAGES ©

Novosibirsk

12 Once viewed as an intimidating monolith, Novosibirsk (p157) has suddenly blossomed into one of Russia's most hip and hospitable metropolises. Siberia's unofficial capital boasts a delightful range of accommodation, an up-and-coming restaurant and bar scene, and noticeably friendly locals. Located about one-third of the way between Moscow and Vladivostok, it's a perfect stop-off for rail-weary souls looking to unwind with a big night out on the town. There are cultural diversions as well, in the form of worthy museums, Siberian wooden architecture and a lively music and arts scene.

Historical Tobolsk

13 The former capital of Siberia, Tobolsk (p153) is today best known across Russia for its magnificent kremlin. Crowds are rare, though, and if you come on a weekday you are likely to have the grounds almost to yourself. The kremlin is perched high above the old town, a part of Tobolsk where you lose track of time as you explore the endless wooden buildings and dramatic churches. Tobolsk is off the main Trans-Siberian route, but its charms are well worth the detour. Kremlin, Tobolsk

Tradition in Siberia

14 The villages and depleted small towns of Siberia may be gradually sinking back into the enormous landscape, but Siberians (Sibiryaki) survive and see themselves as the purer essence of Russia – the way Russians elsewhere used to be. Tradition expresses itself in hospitality and acceptance of strangers (and their odd ways). It means Siberian *izby* (wooden houses) clinging to the railway, hugging the rivers and lakeshores, or hiding deep in the forests. Despite the growth of large, loud cities, Siberian tradition and the Siberian identity survive and thrive. Wooden houses, Irkutsk (p179)

Barguzin Valley

15 The remote and romantically time-less Barguzin Valley (p205) is said to have been the birthplace of Chinggis (Genghis) Khaan's mother. It is one of the Baikal region's most attractive places and, despite the trickle of visitors finding their way into the region these days, remains one of the least visited spots around Lake Baikal. Snow-dusted peaks and curious rock formations gaze down upon a land-scape dotted with salt lakes and fairy-tale wooden villages, where horse carts and sleighs are more numerous than cars.

Vladivostok

16 Vladivostok (p227), capital of Russia's east, has a swagger in its step after being remade for an economic summit in 2012. No longer a remote satel-lite of Moscow, Vladivostok is Asia's rising star, and Golden Horn Bay is its heart and soul. Take it in from one of the city's myri-ad viewpoints, or join the frenzy of activity on the bay with a ferry cruise. Check out the impressive new suspension bridge spanning the bay. Suddenly those San Francisco comparisons don't seem quite so preposterous.

Need to Know

For more information, see Survival Guide (p379)

Currency
Yuán (¥; China), tögrög (T; Mongolia), rouble (R; Russia)

Language
Mandarin (China); Mongolian, Kazakh (Mongolia); Russian (Russia)

Visas
Required for most nationalities for Russia and China and for a handful in Mongolia. Begin organising three months in advance.

Money
ATMs plentiful in Russia and in big cities and towns in China, widely available in Ulaanbaatar and regional capitals of Mongolia.

Mobile Phones
Pre-paid SIM cards readily available in all three countries for unlocked phones. Mongolia has four carriers (two GSM and two CDMA).

Country Codes
China ☏86
Mongolia ☏976
Russia ☏7

When to Go

Moscow
GO May–Jun

Irkutsk
GO Jun

Ulaanbaatar
GO Aug–Sep

Vladivostok
GO Jun

Beijing
GO Sep–early Nov

Desert, dry climate
Warm to hot summers
Mild summers, cold winters
Mild summers, very cold winters
Cold climate

High Season
(Jun–Aug)

➡ China: peak June to August; hot, but rainstorms offer respite

➡ Mongolia: peak June to August; rain late July to August; book everything early around Naadam

➡ Russia: peak June to early September

Shoulder
(May & Sep–Oct)

➡ China: April and May plus September and October; most pleasant weather

➡ Mongolia: May and September some ger (yurt) camps closed, fewer tourists, weather changeable

➡ Russia: beautiful but can get chilly

Low Season
(Nov–Apr)

➡ China: December to February; cold and dry. Fewer tourists, (except around Chinese New Year)

➡ Mongolia: some ger camps and smaller guesthouses closed

➡ Russia: plan indoor pursuits or winter sports; take saunas

Websites

Lonely Planet (www.lonely planet.com) Best for travel planning.

Ctrip (www.english.ctrip.com) Hotel-booking and air ticketing website for China.

Tea Leaf Nation (www. tealeafnation.com) Digesting Chinese social media for the English-speaking world.

Mongolia (http://mongolia. travel) Government travel site.

Way to Russia (www.wayto russia.net) Comprehensive online travel guide.

Important Numbers

China police	110
Mongolia police	102
Russia police	02

Time Zones

Russia has 11 time zones. Times are always given in Moscow time at Russian stations and on Russian trains. Ulaanbaatar and Běijīng are both five hours ahead of Moscow and eight hours ahead of GMT/UTC. When it's noon in Moscow it's 9am GMT/UTC and 5pm in Běijīng and Ulaanbaatar. Each destination heading in the guide tells you how far in advance of Moscow time it is.

Your Daily Costs

Budget: Less than US$50

➡ Dorm beds and meals in simple restaurants, cafes and street stalls

Midrange: US$50–210

➡ Eating in decent restaurants and staying in hotels with private facilities

➡ In Russia expect a maximum midrange of US$210

➡ In Mongolia expect a maximum of US$120

➡ In China expect a maximum of US$160

Top End: Over US$210

➡ Russia is the most expensive (from US$210)

➡ In Mongolia you'll find high-end places (from US$120) in only a few areas

➡ In China dining and higher comforts begin at US$160

Arriving in Russia, China & Mongolia

Moscow

Train – Aeroexpress (www. aeroexpress.ru/en/) trains connect to the city centre from all three airports (from R340, half-hourly 5.30am to 12.30am, 35 minutes).

Taxis – R2000 to R2500. At least an hour to the city centre; varies wildly with traffic.

Běijīng Capital Airport

Subway – Airport Express line (¥25, every 10 minutes, 30 minutes to city centre).

Taxi – ¥100 (incl ¥10 highway toll); 30 to 60 minutes to city.

Chinggis Khaan International Airport, Ulaanbaatar

Buses – inconvenient; **Private taxis** – often over-charge (fare should be US$12 to US$20). Organise pick-up through hotels.

Getting Around

To check train times and make bookings go to the trip planning section of Russian Railways' website (http://pass.rzd.ru/main-pass/public/en).

Train This will be your main way of getting around with many overnight services between far flung cities.

Air To get to your start or end point on the Trans-Siberian or speed up sections of the route. Only book airlines with solid safety records.

Bus For getting to places not covered by the train. Sometimes faster than local *elektrichka* train services.

Car or Taxi Sometimes the only way to get to really remote destinations.

Exchange Rates

		China	Mongolia	Russia
Australia	A$1	¥5.3	T1626	R40
Canada	C$1	¥5.4	T1649	R41
Europe	€1	¥7.6	T2333	R58
Japan	¥100	¥5.3	T1616	R40
New Zealand	NZ$1	¥4.8	T1463	R36
UK	UK£1	¥9.7	T2978	R74
US	US$1	¥6.1	T1870	R46

For current exchange rates see www.xe.com.

For much more on **getting around**, see p394

First Time

For more information, see Survival Guide (p379)

Checklist

➡ Make sure your passport is valid for at least six months beyond the expiry date of your visa

➡ Arrange your visa

➡ Check airline baggage restrictions

➡ Check travel advisory websites

➡ Tell banks and credit card providers your travel dates

➡ Organise travel insurance

What to Pack

➡ Good walking shoes – Trans-Siberian cities are best explored on foot

➡ Phrasebooks, minidictionary or translation apps

➡ Earplugs & eye mask for napping on trains, noisy hotels and during long White Nights

➡ Sense of humour and a bucketful of patience

Top Tips for Your Trip

➡ Consider using a specialist travel agency to arrange visas, make key transport bookings and hire guides. See p38 and p42 for lists of reputable agents.

➡ Treat yourself to a stay at a business or luxury hotel over the weekend when many often drop their rates substantially to cover the shortfall in business customers. Big discounts can also be had on hotel rack rates (the ones we quote in this guide) for online bookings.

➡ Rail tickets can be booked online or at stations 45 days in advance. There are sometimes discounts for advance bookings made online; for more details see p35.

➡ Fixed-price business lunches, common in Russian cities, are a great deal and an ideal way to sample the cuisine at fancier restaurants.

What to Wear

Russians make an effort when they go to the theatre or a posh restaurant – you should do likewise to fit in. If exploring on foot, a comfortable pair of waterproof walking shoes will come in handy, as will an umbrella or rain jacket.

In winter bundle up with several layers before going out and bring a long, windproof coat to stay nicely warm. Hats and coats are always removed on entering a museum or restaurant and left in the cloakroom.

Dress codes are more casual in China and Mongolia.

Sleeping

For major cities it's a good idea to book a night or two in advance. Elsewhere you can usually just turn up and find a room. See p380 for more accommodation information.

➡ **Hotels** Range from unreconstructed edifices of the Soviet era to luxurious and contemporary.

➡ **Hostels, B&Bs and homestays** Plenty of hostels along the Trans-Siberian routes; not so many B&Bs or homestays, but worth trying for a true experience of Russian hospitality.

➡ **Ger camps and homestays** A Mongolian accommodation option.

Money

➡ If prices are listed in US dollars or euros, you will still be presented with a final bill in roubles in Russia.

➡ ATMs linked to international networks can be accessed across Russia, China and Mongolia. Credit cards are commonly accepted in the big cities but don't expect to be able to use them in more off-the-beaten-track spots and rural areas.

➡ Inform your bank and/or credit card provider of the dates you'll be travelling in Russia, China and Mongolia to avoid a situation where the card is blocked.

Bargaining

Prices are fixed in shops, but at souvenir markets, such as Izmailovo in Moscow, polite haggling over prices is a good idea.

Tipping

➡ **When to Tip** In Russia, customary in restaurants, cafes and bars, optional elsewhere. Less common in China and Mongolia.

➡ **Restaurants** Leave small change or about 10%, if the service warrants it.

➡ **Guides** Around 10% of their daily rate; a small gift will also be appreciated.

➡ **Taxis** No need to tip as the fare is agreed either before you get in or is metered.

➡ **Hotels** Only in the most luxurious do you need to tip bellhops, and only if service is good.

DOMINIK STASZOWSKI / GETTY IMAGES ©

Etiquette

Russians are sticklers for formality and can be superstitious; Chinese and Mongolians are a little more relaxed. Follow these tips to avoid faux pas.

➡ **Visiting Homes** In Russia, shaking hands across the threshold is considered unlucky; wait until you're fully inside. Always bring a gift. In all three countries, remove your shoes and coat on entering a house.

➡ **Religion** Dress respectively and conservatively when visiting churches, mosques and Buddhist and Taoist temples in all three countries.

➡ **Eating & Drinking** In China help fill your neighbour's plate or bowl at the dinner table. Vodka toasts are common at shared meals in Russia and Mongolia – it's rude to refuse and traditional (and good sense) to eat a little something after each shot.

Language

In all three countries, English speakers are more common in the big cities than smaller towns and the countryside. Learning Cyrillic script and a few key phrases will help you enormously in being able to decode street signs, menus and timetables – this is also the case for Mongolia where Cyrillic is used, too.

If You Like...

Majestic Landscapes

Tunka Valley Snowcapped peaks send icy streams murmuring into this broad vale where hot springs gush in mineral-hued pools and Buddhist prayer wheels whir in the breeze. (p195)

Gobi Desert Where camels slurp water from wells and lone horsemen gallop alongside the train. (p279)

Northern Mongolia Gers (yurts) dotting the landscape and rushing streams meandering into the distance. (p277)

The Volga River Imbued with history and legend, the Volga's waters loll beneath the main line at Kazan and Nizhny Novgorod. (p127)

Views from the Train

Bratsk Dam One of the most spectacular moments on the 4200km BAM route comes when the train trundles right across the top of the towering Bratsk Dam. (p242)

Lake Baikal No stretch of the Trans-Siberian Railway is more photogenic than that between Slyudyanka and Posolskaya running tight to the shoreline of Lake Baikal. (p195)

Approaching Běijīng Less than one hour outside the Chinese capital the train rolls through a series of 60-odd tunnels, each time emerging with stunning views of mountains, rivers and steep-sided cliffs.

Ulaanbaatar Whichever direction you arrive from, the sprawl, congestion and chaos of Ulaanbaatar make for an engrossing sight. (p257)

Iconic Architecture

St Basil's Cathedral The most internationally recognised and architecturally exquisite building in Russia. (p65)

Forbidden City China's standout imperial residence, home to two dynasties of emperors and their concubines. (p307)

Gandan Monastery Ulaanbaatar's most famous Buddhist monastery is notable for its three-storey Migjid Janraisig Süm. (p262)

Tobolsk A magnificent kremlin looks down upon the city's picturesque old town. (p153)

Severobaikalsk train station Symbolic of the brave new world in concrete the BAM was meant to represent. (p243)

Multicultural Encounters

Tatar Kazan For total Tatar immersion, travel the route to Siberia via Kazan, the capital of Tatarstan, where you'll find a thriving Muslim culture. (p120)

Nomad hospitality On the vast plains of Mongolia hospitality is a time-honoured tradition. Expect to receive endless bowls of tea, snacks and shots of vodka.

Carriage liaisons Often the Chinese can be quite reserved, but on the train they loosen up and are usually thrilled to chat with foreigners. On the Russian trains the art of conversation reaches its highest forms.

Ivolginsky Datsan The epicentre of the Russian Buddhist world is contained within an ever-expanding compound of temples, prayer wheels and monks' quarters. (p203)

Good Food & Drink

Haute-Russe cuisine Splurge on a Russian feast amid 18th-century opulence at **Café Pushkin**. (p79)

Omul This fish is sold smoked to passengers at Slyudyanka station and elsewhere around Lake Baikal. (p190)

GIULIA FIORI PHOTOGRAPHY / GETTY IMAGES ©

Pozy (Buryat dumplings) Filled with a blend of pork and beef; best enjoyed in the authentic setting of a ger.

Chinese delights Dumplings are famed in northern China, or try the scorpions on **Wángfǔjǐng Snack Street**. (p317)

Hikes & Walks

Great Baikal Trail (GBT) Volunteer to help build a path around the world's largest freshwater lake – or hike the parts that have been completed. (p191)

Frolikha Adventure Coastline Trail A challenging 100km GBT section on Lake Baikal's northeast coast – worth every mosquito bite and blister. (p244)

Great Wall Walk over the mighty ramparts of the Great Wall to get a sense of its long history and significance. (p327)

Bogd Khan Mountain Hike from Mandshir Khiid to Ulaanbaatar, through peaceful forests south of the Mongolian capital. (p277)

River Trips & Rafting

Tuul River Paddle a canoe down the Tuul River, outside Ulaanbaatar, for fun day or overnight trips. (p265)

St Petersburg trips Take the *Meteor* hydrofoil from the Hermitage to Peterhof, one of the many river and canal cruises in St Petersburg. (p102)

Moscow river cruise Avoid traffic jams and feel the breeze on your face while you get a new perspective on Moscow's most famous sights. (p73)

Komsomolsk-na-Amure Choose between mellow multiday floats and one-day whitewater whirlwinds in the wilds surrounding this key BAM hub. (p247)

IZZET KERIBAR / GETTY IMAGES ©

Top: Gobi Desert (p279)
Bottom: St Basil's Cathedral, Moscow (p65)

Month by Month

January

Much of Russia, northern China and Mongolia are in deep freeze during this and subsequent months. It's cold outside, but the train will be warm (or stifling hot).

☆ Russian Orthodox Christmas (Rozhdestvo)

A religious fast from morning to nightfall on Christmas Eve (6 January), followed by a feast that includes roast duck and the porridge *kutya*. Special masses at midnight.

☆ Spring Festival/Lunar New Year

The Chinese New Year is family-focused, with dining and gift-giving of *hóngbāo* (red envelopes stuffed with money) and a week-long holiday. In Mongolia it's a good time to be invited to a family celebration.

☆ Hã'ĕrbīn Ice & Snow Festival

In China, Hēilóngjiāng's capital Hã'ĕrbīn (Harbin) is all aglow with rainbow lights refracted through fancifully carved ice statues (www.harbinice.com).

March

Strong winds, sub-zero temperatures, snow and dust storms hit Mongolia. Temperatures are still low in northern China and Russia, but days are significantly longer.

☆ Pancake Week (Maslenitsa)

Folk shows and games are staged to celebrate the end of winter, with lots of pancake eating before Lent in Russia.

April

Slush in Moscow and less savage temperatures in Siberia. Northern China remains cold, and in the Mongolia–China border regions April is like March. Gradually the weather improves.

☆ Easter (Paskha)

Easter Sunday in Russia begins with midnight services. Afterwards, people eat *kulichy* (dome-shaped cakes) and *paskha* (cheesecake), and exchange painted wooden Easter eggs.

May

Everywhere the weather is warming up and the tourist season is getting under way. In Mongolia some ger (yurt) camps open. Snowfall may still occur, especially in the north. All of China is on holiday for the first four days of the month – avoid.

☆ Victory Day

On 9 May, this Russian public holiday celebrates the end of WWII, which Russians call the Great Patriotic War. Big military parades in Moscow and St Petersburg are well worth attending.

🏃 Great Wall Marathon

Experience the true meaning of pain while getting your Great Wall sightseeing done (http://great-wall-marathon.com).

June

Much of China is hot and getting hotter, southern Siberian cities can get sticky, and in Mongolia temperatures are climbing to the pleasant mid- to high 20s (Celsius).

🎆 White Nights

Russia's cultural capital, St Petersburg, hosts a huge party as days lengthen. Events run until late July.

🎆 Dragon Boat Festival

Find yourself the nearest large river and catch all the waterborne drama of dragon-boat racers in this celebration of one of China's most famous poets.

🎆 Roaring Hooves Festival

Often held at a remote location in the Gobi Desert, this international music festival (www.roaringhooves.com) can be staged anywhere in the country.

🎆 Perm White Nights

This cultural and arts festival (www.permfest.com) in the Ural Mountains city runs throughout June.

July

The grasslands of Inner Mongolia turn green; in southern Siberia and elsewhere in Russia temperatures can soar. This is the warmest month in Běijīng. Mongolia gets heat waves, hitting 40°C in the Gobi.

🎆 Naadam Festival

Mongolia's premier summer sports festival erupts in July. The date is fixed in Ulaanbaatar (11 to 12 July) but will change from year to year in other cities and towns. In China the same occurs in Inner Mongolia.

🎆 Kamwa Festival

The 'ethno-futuristic' Kamwa Festival (www.kamwa.ru), in early September in Perm and Khokhlovka, brings together ancient ethno-Ugric traditions and modern culture.

August

Train prices in Russia can spike during this month as many people take holidays – book ahead if you want to travel on particular services along the Trans-Siberian route. Rain storms in Běijīng; less dusty in Mongolia.

🏃 Mongolia Bike Challenge

Mongolia draws serious mountain bikers for this rally. The route of the challenge (www.mongoliabikechallenge.com) varies each year, covering about 1500km through some of the finest Mongolian landscapes.

🎆 Golden Naadam

This late-summer sports festival (usually held 21 August) takes place at Terelj, Mongolia.

September

The fleetingly lovely *tiāngāo qìshuǎng* ('the sky is high and the air is fresh') autumnal season in Běijīng.

🎆 Mid-Autumn Festival

Celebrated in China on the 15th day of the eighth lunar month and also called the Moon Festival. Locals devour cakes stuffed with bean paste, egg yolk, walnuts and more.

December

Short days and long nights keep most people inside for most of this month. If you're prepared it's the best time to see freshly snow-covered landscapes.

🎆 December Nights Festival

Moscow's most prestigious music event, hosted at the Pushkin Fine Arts Museum, features a month of performances by high-profile musicians and accompanying art exhibits.

🎆 Sylvester & New Year

Russians and Mongolians celebrate New Year's Eve enthusiastically, usually with lots of beer, vodka and fireworks (not necessarily in that order).

Plan Your Trip

Choosing Your Route

Contrary to popular belief, the Trans-Siberian Railway follows not a single route but several from European Russian to the Russian Far East and inner Asia. Read on to discover the differences between each of the main lines and a variety of alternatives.

General Online Planning

The Man in Seat 61 (www.seat61.com/Trans-Siberian.htm) Most informative and current site for train travel in Russia, Mongolia and China (and other countries). Also has suggestions on getting to the railheads and on ferry services.

Lonely Planet (www.lonelyplanet.com) Use the Thorn Tree forum.

Railway Timetables

Russian Railways (http://pass.rzd.ru/main-pass/public/en)

Tutu.ru (www.tutu.ru; in Russian)

Yandex (http://rasp.yandex.ru; in Russian)

German National Railways (www.bahn.de) Has an English page for searching timetables.

China Train Guide (www.chinatrainguide.com)

China Highlights (www.chinahighlights.com)

Mongolian Railways (www.mtz.mn/eng/index.php)

Initial Decisions

Start by asking yourself the following questions:

➡ **Do I want to travel only in Russia?** For many travellers, only the classic **Trans-Siberian** route between Moscow and Vladivostok will be of interest. But you can also use part of this route to connect with the **Baikal-Amur Mainline (BAM)** that starts from Tayshet and terminates in Sovetskaya Gavan, or to branch out to other destinations east of Moscow along Russian Railways' vast network.

➡ **Do I want to use the train to get to or from Běijīng?** The two main options are the highly popular **Trans-Mongolian** linking Moscow and Běijīng via Ulaanbaatar in Mongolia, or the Moscow-Běijīng **Trans-Manchurian** service that goes only via Russia and China. Other alternatives involve crossing the Amur River by ferry at either Blagoveshchensk (110km off the main Trans-Sib route) or Khabarovsk and continuing by rail to Hā'ěrbīn (Harbin), which has good rail links with Běijīng. Hā'ěrbīn can also be reached by train or bus from Vladivostok.

➡ **Do I want to extend my rail journey beyond the major termini?** The most popular option here is to start or finish in **St Petersburg**. If you're really going for it, there's nothing stopping you from train hopping into Russia from the Atlantic coast of Portugal and then all the way beyond Běijīng to Vietnam – a journey of over 17,000km!

Trans-Siberian: From Moscow to Vladivostok

This classic route runs between Moscow and Vladivostok mostly following the historic path of Russia's first railway across the subcontinent. Trains roll for 9289km across steppe and through taiga on a journey that takes at least 143 hours (around six full days) from the capital to the Pacific.

Should you stay on the train for the full journey, the experience is like being on a long voyage through the Russian heartland, the scenery alternating between the sublime (along the shores of Lake Baikal) to the monotonous (seemingly endless taiga or the constant clatter of freight trains passing).

During peak travel season in the summer you may find yourself in the company of fellow long-distance passengers (some of whom on the *Rossiya* will be foreign travellers) for several days, if not the whole journey. However, most Russians generally only travel shorter overnight sections of this route, so you'll have a chance to meet a wide range of people.

Trains & Prices

The *Rossiya* (Train 1/2) is the prime-choice *firmeny* (higher quality or premium) train on the route, departing Moscow on odd days and, with exceptions, departing Vladivostok on even days (five days, 23½ hours). It's best used for nonstop travel or for long sections of the route such as Moscow–Irkutsk and Irkutsk–Vladivostok.

The following prices are for the Moscow–Vladivostok journey booked online for mid Aug 2014 through Russian Railways. Prices vary with season and extra comforts.

Platskart (open compartment with bunks) R13,650

Kupe (4-berth compartment) upper/lower berth R19,416/R24,118

SV (also called *lyuks*; 2-berth compartment) R45,338

Train 99/100 This Moscow–Vladivostok service goes via Yaroslavl every other day (six days, 16½ hours). *Platskart* is R9138, *kupe* R15,794.

Flagship Trains for Shorter Hops

Because tickets on the *Rossiya* are among the most expensive on the route, travellers who wish to break the journey along the way are better off using other trains to connect. Other *firmeny* services include:

001 (Г)/**002** (Й) Moscow–Kazan (*Premium*) Has a luxury *myagky* carriage, compartments sleeping two with their own toilet and shower.

15/16 Moscow–Yekaterinburg Goes via Kazan.

29/30 Moscow–Kemorovo (*Kuzbass*) Leaves Moscow usually on odd days, useful for stations as far as Novosibirsk on the Trans-Sib line.

37/38 Moscow–Tomsk (*Tomich*) Leaves Moscow usually on even days, Tomsk on odd.

55/56 Moscow–Krasnoyarsk (*Yenisey*) Leaves Moscow usually on odd days, Krasnoyarsk on even.

Trans-Mongolian: From Moscow to Běijīng via Ulaanbaatar

This route is a popular one because it takes travellers on a coherent journey across three distinct cultures, landscapes and languages – even if not every traveller on the

TRANS-MANCHURIAN/ TRANS-MONGOLIAN BUDGET ROUTES

Trans-Manchurian Budget Route

How? Moscow to Irkutsk (*platskart* €250, three days 14 hours). Stopover in Irkutsk. Irkutsk to Zabaikalsk (*platskart* €110, 31 hours). Zabaikalsk to Mǎnzhōulǐ (bus €20). Stopover in Mǎnzhōulǐ. Mǎnzhōulǐ to Běijīng (hard sleeper €50, 32 hours).

Total cost: Approximately €430.

Trans-Mongolian Budget Route

How? Moscow to Ulan-Ude (*platskart* €270, three days 16½ hours). Stopover in Ulan-Ude. Ulan-Ude to Ulaanbaatar (bus €25, 12 hours). Stopover in Ulaanbaatar. Ulaanbaatar to Èrlián (hard sleeper €45, 12½ hours). Èrlián to Běijīng (sleeper bus €20, 10 hours).

Total cost: Approximately €360.

TOP STOPOVERS

The only practical way to break a journey is to buy separate tickets. Also see Itineraries (p30) for other possible stops to incorporate into a Trans-Siberian journey.

Moscow–Vladivostok

➡ **Nizhny Novgorod** Situated on the Volga River, 'Nizhny' has some good museums and a lively food and culture scene. High-speed Sapsan (seat R1457) and Lastochka (seat from R400) trains run from Moscow; both take four hours and complement conventional services. The nightly premium train 35/36 (kupe R3000, 7¼ hours) has luxury twin berths with shower and toilet (R5580).

➡ **Yekaterinburg** The unofficial capital of the Ural Mountains. Allow three days to explore nearby sights, or at least a week to explore a chunk of the region. The flagship 15/16 service (kupe R4520, 27 hours, daily) travels via Kazan.

➡ **Tyumen** The first of the large Siberian cities after you leave Yekaterinburg has the advantage of being the springboard for an easy side trip off the main line to historic **Tobolsk**, with its magnificent kremlin overlooking the Irtysh River (allow a minimum of three days so you have at least one full day in Tobolsk). The premium service connecting Moscow with Tobolsk, via Tyumen, is the 59/60 Tyumen (kupe R8330, 38 hours).

➡ **Novosibirsk** Russia's 'third city' and the unofficial capital of Siberia. Two to three days will give you a taste of the city. Add a couple of more days if you decide to branch off to nearby **Tomsk**. Anyone with a week or more up their sleeve for an extended side trip should consider bussing to the Altai Republic, as its Mongol-Turkic heritage offers an interesting cultural contrast on this route.

➡ **Krasnoyarsk** An attractive city, situated on the Yenisey River and providing

train is coherent after the 7826km between Moscow and Běijīng! You will need up to three visas.

The major train servicing this route is the weekly Chinese train K3/4 (also appearing on Russian timetables as 33/43), which takes 5½ days between Běijīng and Moscow, travelling via Dàtóng and Èrlián in China, Ulaanbaatar in Mongolia, and Ulan-Ude in Russia. A highlight of the journey is part of the Gobi Desert in Mongolia. Many travel agencies offer stopover packages with a night or two in a Mongolian ger (the traditional collapsible yurt). Between Ulan-Ude and Moscow the train follows the same route as the Trans-Siberian from Vladivostok, crossing European Russia via Nizhny Novgorod. It's the most comfortable of the regular trains and uses Chinese locomotives, carriages and staff.

The cheapest prices as of September 2014 on this route with train K3/4 are US$569 for a 4-berth hard sleeper booked with China International Travel Service (CITS) in Běijīng travelling westwards, and around US$686 for kupe travelling eastwards booked online with an agency in Russia. See p33 for more on prices.

Trans-Manchurian: From Moscow to Běijīng via Manchuria

The weekly Trans-Manchurian train 19/20 goes via Chita to Zabaikalsk, the border town on the Russian side where the bogies are changed before the train crosses to Mǎnzhōulǐ in China. The entire journey is 8988km and takes six days and two hours from Moscow to Běijīng, via Nizhny Novgorod in European Russia.

The two important things to remember about this route are that it uses Russian rolling stock and staff and it does not pass through Mongolia. (You will only need visas for Russia and China.) It can also be combined with a stopover in Hā'ěrbīn. Most of your fellow passengers will be Russians or Chinese doing shorter hops.

Eastbound on train 20 prices start from around US$717 for kupe. Westbound on train 19 is around US$634 for a 4 berth hard sleeper. See p33 for more on buying tickets.

opportunities for extended side trips into **Tuva** – again, offering an ethnic contrast – or north to **Yeniseysk**.

➡ **Irkutsk and Lake Baikal** Irkutsk is easily the most popular of the stopovers, and for one reason: Lake Baikal. If you arrive in Irkutsk during the day and immediately step into a *marshrutka* (collective taxi), you can be sipping a drink on the lapped shores of the world's largest freshwater lake in just over an hour. A three- to four-day stopover is the absolute minimum if you want to at least dip a toe into the Baikal region. Irkutsk is also the base for longer side trips to **Olkhon Island** or the **Tunka Valley**. The most popular pastime during a short Baikal stopover, though, is simply lotus eating (more accurately, smoked-fish eating) in **Listvyanka** or other accessible small towns on Lake Baikal.

➡ **Ulan-Ude** Travellers have been known to stop here just to see with their own eyes the monumentally oversized bonce of Lenin's memorial. Buryat and Buddhist (with doses of shamanism) culture are also drawcards.

➡ **Khabarovsk** Stop here for the flavour of a historic and lively Amur town. The premium train 5/6 *Okean* connects Khabarovsk with Vladivostok (*kupe* R2345, 11 hours), half the price of a similar ticket on the *Rossiya*.

Moscow–Běijīng

In order to break a Moscow–Běijīng journey in, say, Irkutsk, it's best to take a Russian domestic train and then pick up the twice-weekly train 5/6 at Irkutsk for Ulaanbaatar, and then the once- to twice-weekly K23/24 between Ulaanbaatar and Běijīng.

➡ **Ulaanbaatar** Mongolia's capital is the main stopover on the Trans-Mongolian route.

➡ **Hā'ěrbīn** A late 19th-century Russian enclave in Manchuria.

Baikal-Amur Mainline (BAM)

A Soviet-era brainchild, the BAM – a more obscure trans-Siberian route – is entirely within Russia, beginning in Tayshet, a rail junction east of Krasnoyarsk (and almost 4800km east of Moscow). It skirts the northern tip of Lake Baikal at Severobaikalsk and terminates 4287km east of Tayshet at Sovetskaya Gavan. Many travellers exit shortly before this at Vanino, however, as there's a ferry here to Sakhalin Island. Getting to and from the eastern railhead of the BAM can be inconvenient, and your best rail hub is Komsomolsk-na-Amure, 13½ hours before the terminus.

Unlike the other routes, the BAM largely passes towns lacking historic character, as most were founded in order to build the line. This is grubby-window and taiga country. The BAM weaves through dramatic mountain landscapes rising to over 3000m, cuts a swath through seemingly endless taiga that fringes the track and plunges suddenly into the darkness of tunnels up to 15.3km long.

Severobaikalsk is the major stop for relaxing on Lake Baikal. Stops at Bratsk, Tynda and especially Komsomolsk-na-Amure are popular for short breaks from the poetic rattle of rail life.

Invariably, travelling on the BAM involves taking short hops, such as from Tayshet to Komsomolsk-na-Amure, and from Komsomolsk-na-Amure to Sovetskaya Gavan (see p28).

Alternative Routes & Transport

With notable exceptions, such as train 15/16 (which goes via Kazan) and train 99/100 (which goes via Yaroslavl), the major trains cross European Russia via Nizhny Novgorod. Unless you decide to make a detour via Petropavlovsk in Kazakhstan (Kazakh visa required), the route from the Ural Mountains into Central Siberia is simple: along the main line from Yekaterinburg through cities such as Tyumen, Omsk, Novosibirsk and Krasnoyarsk. After that, lines begin to fan out again.

Budget & Border Alternatives

Border hopping is a good way to cut costs. Don't forget, however, that you will also need to stay overnight in some places, in which case add up to €50 per night for a midrange hotel.

Russia–Mongolia Border

The Russia–Mongolia border on the Trans-Mongolian route is at Naushki on the Russian side and Sükhbaatar on the Mongolian side. There's also a road border at Kyakhta-Altanbulag which is convenient for the Ulan-Ude–Ulaanbaatar bus. Alternatives, with prices are on p254.

Lake Baikal–Ulaanbaatar

Good options are trains (263/264; or 362 on Russian timetables) between Irkutsk and Ulaanbaatar (R4800, 27 hours), and the once- to twice-weekly 5/6 (also on timetables as train 63) between Moscow and Ulaanbaatar which stops in Irkutsk. From Ulan-Ude (Russia) you have bus, train and flight options. See p202 for details.

Mongolia–China Border

The border between Mongolia and China crosses at Zamyn-Üüd (Mongolia) and Èrlián (China). This is often a sleepless leg, as most trains cross at night. See p280 for details.

Russia–China Border

The border between Russia and China on the Trans-Manchurian is at Zabaikalsk (Russia) and Mǎnzhōulǐ (China). There are numerous train and bus options; see p298. Other border crossings are in the Amur and Primorye regions of Russia..

Alternatives: Amur & Primorye Regions

Much of the northeastern border between China and Siberia is an often forgotten region along the Amur River. Here it's possible to roam Siberian forests and visit dwindling settlements of northern minorities, such as the Daur, Evenki, Hezhen and Oroqen.

Khabarovsk (Russia)–Fǔyuǎn (China)

Switch countries on the ferries plying the river between Khabarovsk and Fǔyuǎn (one way is R4000 including one night's lodging, 90 minutes).

Blagoveshchensk (Russia)–Hā'ěrbīn (China)

Blagoveshchensk is off the Trans-Siberian main line. This approach involves crossing the Amur River by frequent boat to/from Hēihé and taking a train to/from Hā'ěrbīn (soft sleeper ¥220, 10½ hours), which has good rail links with Běijīng (¥429, eight to 18 hours).

Hā'ěrbīn (China)–Vladivostok (Russia)

Trains between Vladivostok and Hā'ěrbīn go via Ussuriysk and take over 40 hours. The easiest way is by daily bus from Vladivostok's train station. You can also short-hop to the border on trains from Ussuriysk to Grodekogo (not daily) or by bus. On the China side, there are good connections between Suífēnhé and Hā'ěrbīn.

Vladivostok–Sovetskaya Gavan

A through carriage on the daily train 351 links the Trans-Siberian Railway with the BAM, travelling via Khabarovsk and Komsomolsk-na-Amure between Vladivostok and Sovetskaya Gavan (*kupe* R4369, 40 hours).

Amuro–Yakutskaya Mainline (AYaM)

At the time of research, this new line into Yakutia had been completed between Tynda on the BAM to just beyond Tommot. Currently, most travellers continue to Yakutsk from Neryungri train station by minivan or jeep.

Extending from the Railheads

If you have the time consider taking a train rather than a plane to the railheads. At the Moscow end, the choices lead to many cities of Western and Central Europe, whereas from Běijīng the options include Vietnam and Hong Kong. From Vladivostok you can also connect to South Korea and Japan by ferries.

St Petersburg

It's easy to connect from here to Moscow by either high-speed Sapsan day trains (from R3200) or slower overnight services (*platskart* from R1360). However, there are also several services, some of which bypass Moscow, straight towards the Ural Mountains and beyond, including:

INTO NORTH KOREA

North Korea's Dear Leader Kim Jong-Il famously travelled into Russia and back on a 21-carriage armoured train during his lifetime. What is less known is that it is, in theory, possible for lesser mortals to make a similar train journey between Russia and the infamous 'hermit kingdom'. To be granted a visa to North Korea you must be signed up for an organised tour with a guide, so it's best to first contact agencies such as **Koryo** (www.koryotours.com), **Juche Travel Services** (www.juchetravel-services.com) and **Regent Holidays** (www.regent-holidays.co.uk) for more information. Also read Lonely Planet's *Korea* guide. See www.seat61.com/NorthKorea.htm#.U7_Gg6hFvyd for details of the North Korean and Russian Railways services linking Moscow and Pyongyang, which are currently *not* approved for tourists by the North Korean authorities. However, if you are determined to cross by rail from Russia to North Korea, tourists are permitted to use the trains that shuttle a few times a month between Hasan on the Russian side and Tumangan across the border – it will take time and money to organise, but this route isn't impossible. An alternative is to arrange a flight to Pyongyang from Vladivostok – these go at least once a week.

The established rail route into North Korea for tourists is the Běijīng–Pyongyang service (23½ hours, four per week). However, since this can get booked up at certain times of the year, a Pyongyang–Dāndōng service (6½ hours, daily) is now available. Dāndōng is a four hour train ride east of Shěnyáng on the Trans-Manchurian route.

Train 13/14 Starting/terminating in Novokuznetsk, this service stops at Perm, Yekaterinburg, Tyumen, Omsk and Novosibirsk on the main Trans-Sib route.

Train 39/40 This train with carriages originating from or bound for various destinations in Kazakhstan, including the capital Astana, also pauses in Perm and Yekaterinburg.

Train 59/60 The *Volga* premium service links Nizhny Novgorod with St Petersburg via Vladimir and Moscow.

Train 71/72 The premium *Demidovsky Express* service connecting St Petersburg with Yekaterinburg has *lyuks* (1st-class) carriages and stops in Perm.

Train 145/146 Trains to/from Chelyabinsk run on odd days and go via Moscow, Vladimir, Nizhny Novgorod, Perm and Yekaterinburg.

International
European Russia

Helsinki–St Petersburg Four high-speed Allegro trains (2nd class from R1800, 3½ hours), plus *Lev Tolstoy* (see below). Ferries and buses also.

Helsinki–Moscow via St Petersburg daily train 31/32 (*Lev Tolstoy*; kupe R5880, 14 hours)

Moscow–Tallinn (kupe R8250, 15 hours, daily)

St Petersburg–Vilnius (kupe R6076, 13½ hours) Bypasses Belarus (and Belarus visa formalities) by going via Latvia.

Paris–Berlin–Moscow Three or four services a week (depending on the time of year) connect Paris and Moscow via Germany, Poland and Belarus. There is also the twice weekly **Nice–Moscow** service travelling via Belarus, Vienna, Innsbruck, Verona, Milan and Genoa.

London–Moscow via Brussels, Cologne and Warsaw Take the Eurostar train to Brussels, then a high-speed train to Cologne and change to the train to Warsaw. From here you can connect to Moscow. Using the cheapest tickets this can be done for around a total of €270 one-way.

Běijīng

Běijīng–Hanoi Four-berth rail sleepers, twice-weekly trains, departing Běijīng Thursday and Sunday, departing Hanoi (Vietnam) Tuesday and Friday. The journey takes 40 hours and costs around ¥2081 (US$339) from Běijīng to Hanoi one-way and 7 million dong (US$330) from Hanoi to Běijīng.

Běijīng–Hong Kong (hard sleeper ¥507, 24 hours, every two days). A high-speed train also connects Běijīng with Shēnzhèn (¥976, 10½ hours, twice daily) from where you can take the metro on to Hong Kong, thus completing the journey in under half a day.

Vladivostok (By Sea)

Vladivostok–Donghae (South Korea; from US$205 one way, 20 hours) Continues to Sakaiminato (Japan; from US$265 one way, 43 hours).

Itineraries

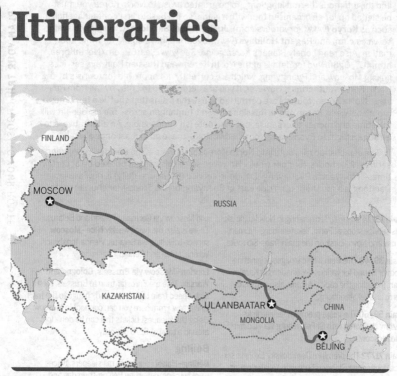

FINLAND

MOSCOW ★

RUSSIA

KAZAKHSTAN

ULAANBAATAR ★

MONGOLIA

CHINA

BĚIJĪNG ★

The Trans-Mongolian Route

This highly popular journey between **Moscow** and **Běijīng** goes via the Mongolian capital of **Ulaanbaatar**, allowing you to compare and contrast the cultures and landscapes of three countries. The train journey in itself takes almost six days, which allows several days in each of the three capital cities for exploration.

In Moscow allow at least three days during which time you should see Red Square and the Kremlin, and take in at least one large gallery. At the other end of the line, the Forbidden City, the Great Wall, the Summer Palace and Tiān'ānmén Square will each take a day. Between these two very different geographic points, taiga, steppe and desert unfold in a mesmerising landscape panorama, with views of iconic Lake Baikal, the Gobi Desert and the Great Wall of China.

A nonstop itinerary is best suited to travellers who want to see Moscow and Běijīng, enjoy the changes of landscape, and experience life on the train as it transitions from Europe to Asia. It can be covered in either direction, but if you wish to spend time in Moscow at the start of the journey, a transit visa will not suffice.

The Trans-Siberian Route

Although this route can be done in either direction, we suggest going against the general flow by starting in **Vladivostok**, at the far eastern end of Russia, so you can finish up with a grand party in either **Moscow** or, better still, **St Petersburg**. The route takes six days without stopovers on the *Rossiya*, the premium train 1/2, which means the absolute minimum required for this itinerary is one week. However, it is best done with stopovers over three to four weeks, and can easily be tailored to your own schedule.

Vladivostok, situated on a stunning natural harbour, merits several days to enjoy Russia's Pacific seaboard and rest from jetlag. It's also worth taking a break of a couple of days at **Khabarovsk**, a lively city on the banks of the Amur River that's an overnight hop from Vladivostok. Save another couple of days for **Ulan-Ude**, a fascinating city where Russian and Buryat cultures mingle, and from where you can venture into the steppes to visit Russia's principal Buddhist monastery, **Ivolginsky Datsan**. Just west of Ulan-Ude the railway hugs the southern shores of magnificent **Lake Baikal**. Allow at least five days to see the lake, visit the equally lovely **Olkhon Island** and spend time in **Irkutsk**, one of the Trans-Siberian's most important rail junctions.

Krasnoyarsk, on the Yenisey River, affords the opportunity for scenic cruises along one of Siberia's most pleasant waterways and can easily be visited on a two-day stopover to see the city itself and the nearby Stolby Nature Reserve. Also well worth stops are the big city **Novosibirsk**, from where you can branch out to the charming Siberian town of **Tomsk**, and **Tyumen**, the access point for **Tobolsk** with its historic kremlin overlooking the Irtysh River.

Crossing the Ural Mountains into European Russia, schedule a stop in **Yekaterinburg**, a city stocked with interesting museums and sites connected to the murder of the last tsar and his family. Further west **Nizhny Novgorod** has some good museums and restaurants plus a thrilling cable car ride. Finally don't miss the tranquil Golden Ring towns of **Vladimir** and/or **Suzdal**, both packed with onion-domed churches, and a million miles away from the manic pace of modern Moscow.

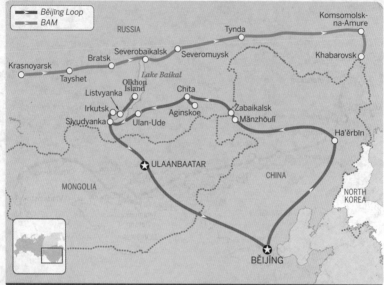

Běijīng Loop
3 WEEKS

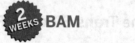

BAM
2 WEEKS

This circular itinerary starts and finishes in Běijīng and can be done in either direction. Allow time in China's capital to see some of the key sights.

An excellent overnight service connects Běijīng with **Hā'ěrbīn (Harbin)**. Russians came here at the end of the 19th century to build the railway, and handsome architectural evidence of their stay remains. The Chinese–Russian border lies an overnight train ride away at **Mǎnzhōulǐ**. If you're not on one of the weekly Trans-Manchurian services that continue across the border and through to Moscow, it's a process of hopping on a bus across to **Zabaikalsk** on the Russian side, where you can reconnect with trains through to **Chita**. Strike out to a couple of beautiful Buddhist monasteries at **Aginskoe**. Detour west from **Ulan-Ude** to **Lake Baikal**, where bases for exploring the lake include **Slyudyanka**, **Irkutsk**, **Listvyanka** and **Olkhon Island**.

Complete the loop by heading to **Ulaanbaatar**, which merits a couple days' stopover. It's a two-night journey back to **Běijīng** through the Gobi Desert.

The 3400km Baikal-Amur Mainline (BAM) travels through some of Siberia's most rugged landscapes. The line officially starts in the drab town of **Tayshet**, but the closest big city, **Krasnoyarsk**, has an airport if you wish to skip all points further west.

At **Bratsk** the train crosses a 1km-long dam. The town also has an excellent open-air ethnographic museum where you can see many traditional Siberian buildings. **Severobaikalsk**, on the northern tip of Lake Baikal, is the best base for exploring this relatively unvisited end of the lake.

En route to Tynda the line climbs over and burrows through mountains, the longest tunnel being 15.3km at **Severomuysk**. Home of the BAM construction company's headquarters, **Tynda** is a must-stop for its BAM museum and good *banya* (bathhouse). Continue working your way east to **Komsomolsk-na-Amure**, the largest and most attractive city on the line and a great place to ponder the sacrifices and achievements made by hardy Soviet pioneers. Finish up your journey in **Khabarovsk**, on the main Trans-Sib line and also with an airport.

Plan Your Trip
Booking Tickets

Online train ticket booking has made securing your dream Trans-Siberian adventure only a few clicks away from reality. However, in some cases it may be necessary to buy tickets at local stations or use an agent to help you secure the seats you want.

Classes of Ticket

Having decided on what route you'd like to follow (see p24), your next couple of choices involve how much comfort you'd like to travel in and when – both decisions will impact the price you'll pay for your tickets. For more about classes of compartments see p46.

Trans-Siberian & Trans-Manchurian

These routes use Russian rolling stock. When booking, you often have the choice of a mixed-sex or women-only *kupe,* although this is not always guaranteed.

➡ **SV (1st class or soft class)** Two-berth compartments.

➡ **Kupe (2nd class)** Four-berth. Berths 33 to 36 are alongside the toilet and can be noisy. The lower the number, the closer you are to the attendant. Note that there may be a discount offered on tickets for the top bunks.

➡ **Platskart (3rd class or hard class)** Carriages sleep 54 passengers in compartments with partitions. Bunks also line the corridors. Not available on the Trans-Manchurian route.

Trans-Mongolian K3/4

This service uses Chinese rolling stock.

➡ **Deluxe two-berth** Showers shared by two compartments.

➡ **Soft class four-berth** Soft sleeper, slightly larger than hard class.

➡ **Hard class four-berth** Similar to the Russian *kupe.*

Classic Trains

Rossiya (train 1/2, westward/eastward) runs between Moscow and Vladivostok. Chinese train K3/4 (Trans-Mongolian) runs between Moscow and Běijīng via Ulaanbaatar. *Vostok* train 19/20 runs between Moscow and Běijīng via Manchuria. Also useful is the 5/6 service connecting Moscow and Ulaanbaatar.

Russian Firmeny Trains

Russian *firmeny* (premium) trains have a higher standard of service and carriages but usually cost more. They provide a fast, useful connection, mostly between regional centres and Moscow.

Advance Bookings

Tickets can't be booked more than 45 days ahead in Russia. In China, bookings for C, D, G and Z express trains begin 10 to 20 days before departure, for others it's five to 10 days. From Ulaanbaatar tickets to Moscow or Běijīng are available a day before departure. Agencies can facilitate earlier bookings in all countries.

Higher-Comfort & Luxury Trains

Trains with more luxurious carriages, offering compartments with their own toilets and showers, and fancy dining cars and bars, are used for package tours. These include:

➡ *Golden Eagle* (www.goldeneagleluxurytrains. com)

➡ *Tsar's Gold* (www.travelallrussia.com/trans-siberian/tsars-gold-train-tour218.html)

➡ *Imperial Russia* (http://rzdtour.com/en/routes/transsib/242)

None are cheap: a 15-day itinerary on the Golden Eagle between Moscow and Vladivostok, for example, starts from around US$23,500 for a Silver Class single. However, the tours do included day trips off the train and all meals.

Apart from the staff, you are unlikely to meet many ordinary Russians, Chinese and Mongolians on these trains, with passengers tending to be well-heeled and older than the average train traveller.

Where to Buy Tickets

While you obviously can buy tickets directly at local stations, this isn't always the most convenient or preferable thing to do – especially when you are trying to secure seats for specific dates.

As long as you are reasonably comfortable with booking tickets online and have a relatively simple itinerary planned out, you can use the website of Russian Railways

PRICES & SERVICES
Price Comparison by Class

ROUTE	SV	KUPE	PLATSKART
Moscow–Vladivostok (train 1/2)	R45,338 (US$1210)	R24,118 (US$644)	R13,650 (US$364)

ROUTE	DELUXE (2-BERTH)	SOFT SLEEPER (4-BERTH)	HARD SLEEPER (4-BERTH)
Běijīng–Ulaanbaatar–Moscow (train K3)	¥5604 (US$912)	¥5114 (US$832)	¥3496 (US$569)
Běijīng–Moscow (train 19)	¥6044 (US$984)	n/a	¥3891 (US$633)
Běijīng–Ulaanbaatar (train K3 & K23)	¥1883 (US$306)	¥1723 (US$281)	¥1222 (US$199)

Prices are for September 2014.

Services

When you book, you will often see a range of prices. The higher ones are with services, usually meaning meals, often a newspaper and cleaner toilets. These are common symbols you will see online.

CLASS	SERVICES
platskart 3 P (3 П)	not air-conditioned
platskart 3 E (3 Э)	air-conditioned
kupe 2 K (2 К)	not air-conditioned, no services
kupe 2 L (2 Л)	air-conditioned, no services
kupe 2 U (2 У)	not air-conditioned, with services
kupe 2 E (2 Э)	air-conditioned, with services
spalny vagon (1st class) 1 L (1 Л)	air-conditioned, no services
spalny vagon (1st class) 1 B (1 Б)	business class, air-conditioned, with services
additional letters МЖ	male-only carriage

(RZD) to secure your Trans-Siberian journey. A small discount for tickets purchased online may also be available.

However, sometimes it will be easier to go through local or international travel agents and booking offices. This will be more expensive (possibly up to 30% pricier than doing it yourself), as you are paying commission on top of the ticket prices; in return, they, rather than you, spend time organising often complicated bookings, and they specialise in stitching together a complete itinerary.

Things to Note

➡ Have your passport and those of fellow travellers handy for all international and distance rail bookings – whether online or at the station.

➡ If you need to have your tickets on the train booked earlier than 45 days in advance, then you will have to use the services of a travel agency or tour company that can guarantee this for you.

➡ In order to book in advance on a westward route on the Trans-Mongolian (train K3) and the Trans-Manchurian (train 19), you will need to use China International Travel Service (CITS) or local or international tour and travel agents, and you usually need to board in Běijīng. Agencies in Hā'ěrbīn (Harbin) and Mǎnzhōulǐ can also arrange tickets on the Trans-Manchurian into Russia.

➡ From Ulaanbaatar, you can't be certain of an advance reservation on the Trans-Mongolian train 3 or train 4 as they won't know how many places are available.

➡ In Russia avoid using the international trains for domestic routes: they are usually more expensive than nonpremium trains and tickets are difficult to come by outside Moscow.

➡ If you can't buy a ticket in advance because the train is full, it may still be possible to negotiate a berth with the attendants on the platform when the train arrives.

➡ Unless otherwise stated, the prices listed in this guide are usually for 2nd-class, four-berth compartments (*kupe*) and don't include meals.

Buying Your Own Tickets Online

Online booking options for Russian trains are very good as you can use **RZD's website** (http://rzd.ru) or the websites of agents to buy an e-ticket. Currently, there are no coordinated online booking systems for the international trains, but many all-purpose websites book these for a fee.

The Russian Railways site allows you to book and pay for Russian domestic train services using a credit or debit card (most foreign ones are accepted), 45 days or less prior to departure.

You will need to set up a user profile in order to purchase the ticket. During the booking process, when asked to fill in 'Document Type' you should pick 'Foreign document' and then enter your passport number.

Electronic Tickets

RZD has two types of electronic tickets:

➡ **e-tickets** These are coupons detailing your your 14-digit order and 14-digit e-ticket numbers. Print them out and exchange for paper tickets at stations in Russia. Some stations have dedicated exchange points and/or self-service terminals, where you can scan the barcode on your printed voucher; at all others you go to the regular booking windows.

➡ **e-registration** Only available for trains where you board at the initial station of the service, these are 'paperless' tickets; you'll still be sent an email confirmation but there's no need to exchange this for a regular ticket. You show the confirmation email and your passport to the *provodnitsa* on boarding the train.

You can also use the self-service terminals at stations to buy tickets directly, or look up train timetables. To do so you will have to insert a credit or debit card and punch in your PIN – you will only be charged if you actually go ahead with the purchase of a ticket.

English-Language Booking Websites

Other online travel sites, which allow you to book tickets and have the ticket delivered to your home or hotel, or pick it up at an agency or at the train station, include:

Express to Russia www.expresstorussia.com

Hostels.ru www.hostels.ru

Real Russia www.realrussia.co.uk

Svezhy Veter www.svezhyveter.ru

Trains Russia www.trainsrussia.com

Visit Russia www.visitrussia.com

HOW TO BUY & READ YOUR TICKET

When buying a ticket in Russia, it's a good idea to arrive at the station or travel agency prepared. If you don't speak Russian, write down the following information in Cyrillic:

➡ How many tickets (билет) you require

➡ Your destination – you'll find the Cyrillic for all destinations in this guide listed in the On The Road chapters.

➡ What class of ticket: св (SV; 1st class), купе (kupe; 2nd class) or плацкарт (platskart; 3rd class)

➡ The preferred date of travel and time of day for departure, using ordinary (Arabic) numerals for the day and Roman numerals for the month.

Also bring your passport; you'll be asked for it so that its number and your name can be printed on your ticket. The ticket and passport will be matched up by the *provodnitsa*

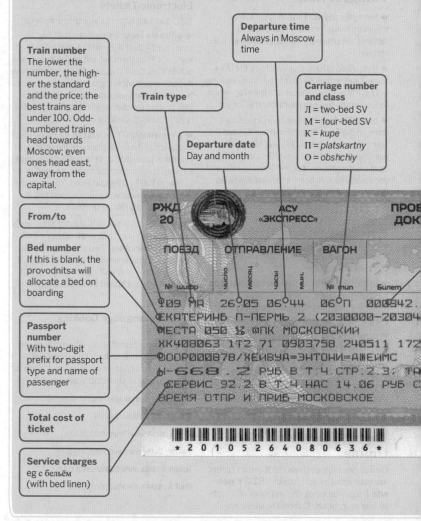

Departure time
Always in Moscow time

Train number
The lower the number, the higher the standard and the price; the best trains are under 100. Odd-numbered trains head towards Moscow; even ones head east, away from the capital.

Train type

Carriage number and class
Л = two-bed SV
M = four-bed SV
К = *kupe*
П = *platskartny*
О = *obshchiy*

Departure date
Day and month

From/to

Bed number
If this is blank, the provodnitsa will allocate a bed on boarding

Passport number
With two-digit prefix for passport type and name of passenger

Total cost of ticket

Service charges
eg с бельём
(with bed linen)

(carriage attendant) before you're allowed on the train – make sure the ticket-seller gets these details correct.

Tickets are printed by computer and come with a duplicate. Shortly after you've boarded the train the *provodnitsa* will come around and collect the tickets. Sometimes they will take both copies and give you one back just before your final destination; often they will leave you with the copy. It will have been ripped slightly to show it's been used. Hang on to this ticket, especially if you're hopping on and off trains. It provides evidence of how long you've been in a particular place if you're stopped by police.

Sometimes tickets are also sold with separate chits for insurance in the event of a fatal accident, or for bed linen and meals, but usually these prices appear on the ticket itself.

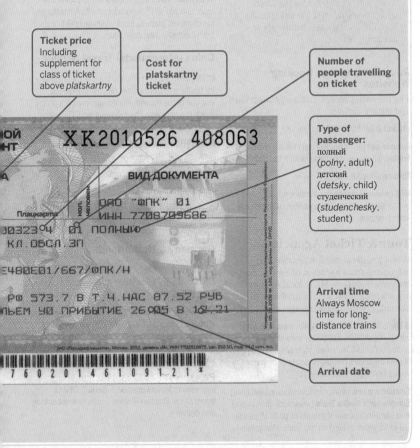

Ticket price
Including supplement for class of ticket above *platskartny*

Cost for platskartny ticket

Number of people travelling on ticket

Type of passenger:
полный (*polny*, adult)
детский (*detsky*, child)
студенческий (*studenchesky*, student)

Arrival time
Always Moscow time for long-distance trains

Arrival date

The choice used to be 'individual or package', but these days tour agencies also create packages for individuals. These range from semi-individual arrangements where you are 'bundled' with several other travellers and a local guide might meet you briefly at a stop, and perhaps even drive you around town for an hour, to fully fledged group tours with a guide to take care of your needs. At the top end of the scale, packages on higher-comfort or luxury trains like the *Tsar's Gold* (higher comfort) and the *Golden Eagle* (luxury) have their own itineraries and stops. These often include extras you can't otherwise get, such as tailor-made stopovers with a program for the whole group or a stretch of the spectacular Circumbaikal route. The price is accordingly higher.

Russian-Language Booking Websites

The following accept Visa and MasterCard and issue e-tickets.

eticket Bilet http://eticket.bilet.ru

Poezda.net (www.poezda.net) Mostly useful for English-language timetable search function.

Tutu.ru www.tutu.ru

UFS (www.ufs-online.ru) A major service used by the Yandex (http://rasp.yandex.ru) timetable search engine.

Tour & Ticket Agencies

While it will be more expensive, buying tickets from agents is often the most convenient option. Many local operators are also equipped to take bookings from abroad. Try the following agencies.

STA USA (☑1-800-781-4040; www.statravel.com) UK (☑0800 819 9339; www.statravel.co.uk) Australia (☑134 782; www.statravel.com.au) Mainly organises packages, some of them for the Vodka Train (see Sundowners).

Sundowners (www.sundownersoverland.com) Sundowner's **Vodka Train** (www.vodkatrain.com) is in semi-independent groups of up to 15 people (18 to 35 years of age) on the Trans-Mongolian

and other routes. A local guide meets the group at stopovers. A St Petersburg–Běijīng route in either direction starts at €2500.

Australasia

Eastern Europe/Russian Travel Centre (☑02 9262 1144; www.eettbtravel.com) In Australia; they also have a New Zealand office. Mostly Russia.

Passport Travel (☑03 9500 0444; www.travelcentre.com.au; Lvl 1, 12-14 Glenferrie Rd, Malvern, Victoria, Australia) Package and individual trips. Strong on China.

Russian Gateway Tours (☑02 9745 3333; www.russian-gateway.com.au) Mostly Russia.

Travel Directors (☑08 9242 4200; www.traveldirectors.com.au) Upmarket Trans-Siberian tour operator.

Travman Tours (☑1800 338 007; www.travman.com.au) CITS representative in Australia and the cheapest place to book westward rail tickets from Australia. Also does tours.

China International Travel Service

CITS (www.cits.net) Usually the cheapest agency for booking a service from Běijīng. Unless you use one of the recommended agencies, it's pretty much the only way. The following are CITS overseas representatives:

International www.chinatraveldesigner.com/trans-siberian-trains

Australia www.travman.com.au

France http://fr.cits.net

Germany www.goldenerdrachen.de

USA www.citsusa.com

Germany & Netherlands

Gleisnost (☑0761-205 5130; www.gleisnost.de; Bertoldstraße 44, Freiburg) Knowledgeable and good value.

Lernidee Reisen (☑030-786 0000; www.lernidee-reisen.de; Eisenacher Straße 11, Berlin) Very knowledgeable, sells tickets in conjunction with transfers and accommodation. Excellent value.

Pulexpress (☑030-887 1470; http://pulexpress.de; Meinekestraße 5, Berlin) Official agent of the Russian Railways, with online booking and delivery.

Trans-Sputnik Nederland ($\boxed{J}$020-797 9800; www.trans-sputnik.nl)

Japan

MO Tourist CIS Russian Centre ($\boxed{J}$03-3432 7232; www.mo-tourist.co.jp) Tours and can help arrange ferries and flights to Russia.

United Kingdom

Go Russia ($\boxed{J}$020-3355 7717; www.justgo-russia.co.uk) Cultural and adventure holiday specialist. Russia, China and Mongolia.

GW Travel Ltd ($\boxed{J}$0161-928 9410; www.gwtravel.co.uk) Luxury Trans-Siberian tours on the *Golden Eagle*.

Imaginative Traveller ($\boxed{J}$0147-366-7337; www.imaginative-traveller.com) Worldwide tours.

Intourist UK ($\boxed{J}$0844-875 4026; www.intouristuk.com) Offices in London and Glasgow.

Regent Holidays ($\boxed{J}$020-7666 1244; www.regent-holidays.co.uk) Specialises in individual and group tours on standard as well as luxury trains.

Russia Experience ($\boxed{J}$0845-521 2910; www.trans-siberian.co.uk) Specialising in packages with accommodation.

Russian National Tourist Office ($\boxed{J}$020-7985 1234; www.visitrussia.org.uk) Offers tours across Russia.

Scott's Tours ($\boxed{J}$020-7383 5353; www.scottstours.co.uk) Russia, China, Central Asia.

Steppes East ($\boxed{J}$0843-634 7901; www.steppeseast.co.uk) Russia, Mongolia and China.

USA & Canada

East Russia Travel Market ($\boxed{J}$206-282-0824; www.traveleastrussia.com) Eco-adventure tour company specialising in Far East Russia and Siberia.

Go To Russia Travel ($\boxed{J}$404-827-0099; www.gotorussia.com) Has offices in Atlanta, San Francisco and Moscow; offers tours and a full range of travel and visa services for Russia.

Mir Corporation ($\boxed{J}$206-624-7289; www.mircorp.com) Books individual and group journeys on regular and luxury private trains.

Trek Escapes ($\boxed{J}$1-800-228-8747; www.trekescapes.com) Handles bookings for other companies as well, such as Sundowners.

Comparative Prices – Asia Trains

Moscow–Běijīng (2nd Class)

In the following tables, the Russian Railways price is the online price without commissions; the CITS price is for tickets bought locally in Běijīng; and the 'Local (Moscow)' price is the walk-in fare at Intourist's Moscow office.

How & Where?	Westbound (Train 3)	Eastbound (Train 4)
CITS (Běijīng)	US$600	n/a
Online or agency	€550-700	€525-650
Local (Moscow)	n/a	€485
Russian Railways	n/a	€440

How & Where?	Westbound (Train 19)	Eastbound (Train 20)
CITS (Běijīng)	US$650	n/a
Online or agency	€550-750	€550-700
Local (Moscow)	n/a	€515
Russian Railways	n/a	€480

Buying Tickets Locally

The international trains, especially the Trans-Mongolian, are popular, so it's often risky to wait and book locally. Generally, it's easier getting tickets if you're going west rather than east, and summer is busier than winter.

Russia

Tickets can be bought at Russian Railways booking offices and many of the private railways booking offices in Russia (ж/д касса). For a list of Russian Railways booking offices, see the English-language homepage http://eng.rzd.ru and look under 'Passengers' then 'Ticket Offices'.

At all major stations there should be working ticket machines that can be used to buy tickets directly or pick up tickets bought online, using your credit or debit card. If these are not available you will have to fall back on the ticket windows manned by humans – a less-appealing prospect as the sellers rarely speak any

ONLINE TIMETABLES

An overview of current timetables for the key Trans-Siberian trains can be found at www.transsib.com/trans-siberian-train-tickets-prices/trans-siberian-timetable.html.

Alternatively, you can use Russian Railways site (http://pass.rzd.ru) to check specific routes and times.

other language than Russian and lines at these windows can be long and tend to move slowly. Before you do this, look around for a **service centre** (сервис центр) where staff may speak some English and can help book your ticket for a small fee (around R250).

If all the above fail, local travel agencies with English speaking staff, such as Real Russia and Ost-West, should be able to assist in securing tickets.

Real Russia (☑499-653 8574; www.realrussia. co.uk; ul Bolshaya Mariinskaya 9, office 313, Moscow) Rail tickets, packages, visa services and visa registration.

Ost-West (☑812-327 3416; www.ostwest.com; Ligovsky pr 10, office 2133, St Petersburg) Offers

rail bookings and full invitation, visa and package-tour services. Also has a Moscow branch.

China

Also see www.chinatripadvisor.com.

China International Travel Service (CITS; ☑010-6522 2991; 1 Dongdan Beidajie Dongcheng District, Běijīng; ◎9am-5pm Mon-Fri; Ⓜ Beijing Train Station) The best place to buy tickets locally.

Monkey Business (Map p310; ☑010-6591 6519; www.monkeyshrine.com; Room 202, Bldg 2, 27 Bei San Li Community, East Courtyard, Chaoyang District, Běijīng; Ⓜ Dongshishitiao) Arranges all kinds of stopovers and homestay programs, and has a lot of experience in booking international trains for independent travellers. In Hong Kong, it goes under the name Moonsky Star Ltd (☑852-2723 1376).

Mongolia

In Ulaanbaatar, you cannot buy tickets in advance for the Běijīng–Moscow or the Moscow–Běijīng trains, because staff in Ulaanbaatar won't know how many people are already on the train. You can only buy a ticket for these trains the day before departure (although you could try asking two days in advance). If you have trouble booking a berth, ask your guesthouse manager or hotel reception desk for assistance.

Plan Your Trip
Arranging Your Visas

You will almost certainly need a visa for Russia and China, and possibly one for Mongolia, too. Arranging these is generally straightforward but can be time consuming, bureaucratic and – depending on how quickly you need the visa – costly. Start the application process at least a month before your trip.

Planning

Costs

Unless noted the following fees are for single entry tourist visas and don't take into account processing costs by agencies.

China
➡ **Australia** AU$60
➡ **Most EU countries** €35
➡ **UK** £30
➡ **USA** $140

Mongolia
➡ **Australia** AU$150
➡ **UK & most EU countries** No need for visa for visits up to 30 days.
➡ **USA** No visa needed for visits up to 90 days.

Russia
➡ **Australia** Both tourist and work visas issued in ten/two working days are A$120/240.
➡ **Most EU countries** Tourist visas issued in ten/four working days are €35/70, work visas €99/136.
➡ **UK** Tourist and work visas issued in five working days/next working day are £50/100 plus a service charge of £32.40/39.60.
➡ **USA** Single or double entry tourist or work visa issued in ten/three working days are $140/250.

General Need to Know

Visas are *not* issued at land borders.

Visas are valid for entry within three months of issue, so don't apply for them too early.

China

A visa is required for all except travellers from Japan, Singapore and Brunei. Visas are most easily obtained from your country of residence.

Mongolia

UK and many European citizens need no visa for visits of up to 30 days (this may change after 2016), US citizens for visits up to 90 days (if they register with immigration within seven days). Others can apply for a 30-day tourist visa for which an invitation is sometimes required if you apply outside your country of residence.

Russia

With few exceptions, you should apply in your country of residence and you will first need an invitation. A tourist visa is valid for up to 30 days, nonextendable. Business visas allow more time – up to three years for US citizens.

Agencies

The following agencies can arrange visas for all three countries and are especially useful for Russian visas.

Action-visas.com www.action-visas.com

CIBT http://cibtvisas.co.uk

Comet Consular Services https://comet-consular.com

IVDS www.visum-ivds.de

Real Russia www.realrussia.co.uk

VisaHQ.com http://russia.visahq.com

Visalink.com.au http://visalink.com.au

ZVS http://zvs.com

Invitations can also be arranged with:

Express to Russia www.expresstorussia.com

Visa Able www.visaable.com

Way to Russia www.waytorussia.net

Embassy Websites

China www.fmprc.gov.cn/mfa_eng/wjb_663304/zwjg_665342 or www.chinese-embassy.info

Mongolia www.mfa.gov.mn, click on Missions.

Russia www.mid.ru/zu_r.nsf/strawebeng

Visas for China

Apart from citizens of Japan, Singapore and Brunei, all visitors to China require a visa. Hong Kong is a Special Administrative Region and is visa-free for most nationalities (see www.immd.gov.hk/ehtml/hkvisas_4.htm).

A standard 30-day single-entry tourist (L) visa can be issued from most Chinese embassies in three to five working days. Express visas cost twice the usual fee, and in some countries (eg the UK and the US), the visa service has been outsourced from the Chinese embassy to a Chinese Visa Application Service Centre, which levies an extra administration fee. This can double the cost.

A standard 30-day visa is activated on the date you enter China, and must be used within three months of the date of issue. Arranging double-entry visas is fairly straightforward, but 60- and 90-day visas can be harder to obtain.

Having a visa mailed to you will take up to three weeks. In the US and Canada, mailed visa applications have to go via a visa agent, at extra cost. In the US, many people use the **China Visa Service Center** (☑800 799 6560; www.mychinavisa.com), taking 10 to 14 days.

From Mongolia & Russia

Getting a Chinese visa in Ulaanbaatar is possible, but takes a week and involves queuing and paperwork. See http://mn.china-embassy.org/eng/lsfw for details. You must provide one passport photo, proof of departure from China (eg an air or train reservation), proof of a booked hotel stay of three nights and a bank statement. In practice, travellers often obtain all this from any travel agency in Ulaanbaatar and simply cancel afterwards.

In Russia, China has consulates in St Petersburg, Moscow and Khabarovsk. At the very least an invitation letter and/or hotel booking, travel itinerary and an onward flight are usually required. In St Petersburg, travellers have successfully organised the invitation and visa through **Milor-Tur** (☑812-982 7489; www.milor-tour.spb.ru; Spassky per 14/35). Seven-day processing costs R3000, three-day processing an extra R1000. You will need to be registered in St Petersburg.

Registration & Extensions

There's no individual registration requirement when you enter China. Remember that if you go to Hong Kong or Macau (which are visa-free for many nationalities) you'll need a new visa or a double-entry visa to return to the mainland.

The Foreign Affairs Branch of the local **Public Security Bureau** (PSB, 公安局, Gōng'ānjú) deals with visa extensions.

Visas for Mongolia

A 30-day tourist visa is easily obtained at any Mongolian embassy, consulate, consulate-general or honorary consul (special exit-permit conditions apply for visas from honorary consuls). Tourist visas can be extended in Ulaanbaatar for stays beyond 30 days.

US citizens can stay in Mongolia for up to 90 days without a visa, but only if they register with immigration within the first seven days of arrival, otherwise they can only stay 30 days. As of the time of research, many other nationalities, including British, Malaysian and Israeli citizens, can stay visa-free for up to 30 days, while Hong Kong and Singaporean citizens can stay visa-free for up to 14 days; this situation could change in 2016 so check first with a Mongolian embassy before leaving home without a visa stamp in your passport.

To get a visa for longer than 30 days, you must be invited or sponsored by a Mongolian citizen, foreign resident (expat) or Mongolian company, or be part of an organised tour. It is therefore possible to get a 90-day visa for most nationalities; you just need to pay the inviting agency a fee of around US$30. Most guesthouses can do this. The **Khongor Guesthouse** (www.khongor-expedition.com) in Ulaanbaatar is very reliable.

If you cannot get to a Mongolian consulate, you can pick up a 30-day tourist visa on arrival at the airport in Ulaanbaatar. There is no guarantee, however. You'll need US$93 and two passport photos and you *must* have an invitation from an organisation or company in Mongolia.

A single-entry transit visa costs between US$25 and US$60, depending on where you apply for it, but cannot be extended. You will need to show your train or plane ticket and a visa for the next country (Russia or China). Transit visas are valid for 72 hours from the date of entry, which will only allow you to get off the Trans-Mongolian train in Ulaanbaatar for a very short time before catching another train to Russia or China.

From China & Russia

For a list of Mongolian embassies and consulates in China and Russia, see p383. Always try to call ahead as hours change frequently. Expect to pay approximately US$40 for normal four-day processing or about US$75 for a same-day rush visa. Invitations are not usually required, but this can be arbitrary and change quickly; it's worth being prepared if you're short of time.

Registration & Extensions

If you stay less than 30 days, you don't need to register. All visitors who plan to stay more than 30 days *must* be registered within seven days of their arrival. This applies to everyone, including US citizens.

You can extend a 30-day tourist visa by another 30 days. For extensions, registration and exit visas, go to the **Office of Immigration, Naturalization & Foreign Citizens** (INFC; ☑11-1882; ⏱9am-1pm & 2-6pm Mon-Fri), 1.8km east of the airport, an inconvenient 15km trek from central Ulaanbaatar. The office is usually busy, so you should expect to spend an hour or two. If you've already registered, you should apply for an extension (US$2 per day; minimum extension seven days) about a week before your visa expires. You'll need a passport-size photo and must pay a T5000 processing fee. The extension will be issued on the same day. Bring cash.

Several guesthouses in Ulaanbaatar will take care of visa extensions (and registration) for a small fee. If you don't have a letter of support you can write your own (handwritten is OK); the letter should state the date of your arrival, the date of extension and the reason for travel.

Getting a visa extension outside the capital is difficult, as your passport would need to be sent back to Ulaanbaatar.

Visas for Russia

Everyone entering Russia needs a visa and should apply before leaving home. From Hong Kong you might try through **Monkey Shrine** (www.monkeyshrine.com). The **Russian consulate in Běijīng** (www.russia.org.cn/eng) has been known to issue transit visas and **Legend Tour** (www.legendtour.ru/eng) in Ulaanbaatar is often successful.

Tourist Visa

For most travellers a tourist visa (single or double entry and valid for a maximum of 30 days, nonextendable, from the date of entry) will be sufficient. Travel agents, Russian hotels and specialised visa agencies can provide the invitation.

Business Visa

If you plan to stay longer than a month, it's advisable to apply for a business visa. These can be issued for three, six or 12 months (or 3 years for US citizens), and are available as single-entry, double-entry or multiple-entry visas. They are valid for up to 90 days of travel within any 180-day period. You don't need to be on business to get one of these visas, but you must have a letter of invitation from a registered Russian company or organisation (arranged via specialist visa agencies).

Transit Visa

For transit by air, this visa is usually good for a maximum of three days. For a non-stop Trans-Siberian Railway journey, it's valid for 10 days, giving westbound passengers a few days in Moscow; those heading east, however, cannot linger in Moscow.

Private Visa

Valid for up to three months and can be issued for single or double entry. To get one you'll need an official invitation certificate from relatives or friends you'll be staying with (this is a big hassle for them to get; applying for a regular tourist or business visa is far simpler).

Application

If the agency is not handling the application as well, you need to lodge it yourself at the consulate. Costs vary depending on the type of visa applied for and how quickly you need it. Check well in advance what these rules might be.

Russian embassies in the UK and US have contracted separate agencies to process the submission of visa applications and check everything is in order; these companies use online interfaces that direct the relevant information into the standard visa application form (available at https://visa.kdmid.ru/PetitionChoice.aspx). In the UK, the agency is **VFS.Global** (http://ru.vfsglobal.co.uk) with offices in London and Edinburgh; in the US **Invisa Logistic Services** (http://ils-usa.com) with offices in Washington DC, New York, San Francisco, Houston and Seattle.

Immigration Form

Immigration forms are produced electronically by passport control at airports. Take care of your half of the completed form as you'll need it for registration and could face problems while travelling – and certainly on leaving – if you can't produce it.

Registration

Visas should be registered within seven days of arrival, excluding weekends and public holidays. The obligation to register is with the accommodating party – your hotel or hostel, or landlord, friend or family if you're staying in a private residence.

If you're staying at a hotel or hostel, the receptionist will register you for free or for a small fee (typically around €10). Once registered, you should receive a slip of paper confirming the dates you'll be staying at that particular accommodation. Keep this safe – that's the document that any police who stop you will request to see.

If staying in a homestay or rental apartment, you'll either need to make arrangements with the landlord or a friend to register you through the post office. See http://waytorussia.net/RussianVisa/Registration.html for how this can be done and for more details on the whole process.

Every time you move city or town and stay for more than seven days, it's necessary to go through the registration process again. There's no need to be overly paranoid about this, but the more thorough your registration record, the less chance you'll have of running into problems. Keep all transport tickets (especially if you spend nights sleeping on trains) to prove to any overzealous police officers exactly when you arrived in a new place.

It's tempting to be lax about registration, and we've met many travellers who were and didn't experience any problems; note, you will not be asked to show registration slips when leaving from Russia's airports.

However, if you're travelling for a while in Russia and particularly if you're visiting off-the-beaten-track places, it's worth making sure you are registered at each destination, since it's not uncommon to encounter fine-hungry cops hoping to catch tourists too hurried or disorganised to be able to explain long gaps in their registration.

Extensions

Extensions are time-consuming and difficult; tourist visas can't be extended at all. Avoid the need for an extension by initially arranging a longer visa than you might need.

Plan Your Trip
Life on the Rails

Whichever route you choose to travel along the Trans-Siberian Railway, you'll have to adjust to an extended period spent living on a train with all its associated quirks and rituals. Come prepared for that experience and your journey will be all the smoother and more enjoyable.

Arriving & Boarding

➡ Russian trains are super punctual, so allow enough time at the station for formalities and buying last-minute supplies before scheduled departures. Check the name of the station closely on your ticket and arrive at least 30 minutes before scheduled departure.

➡ Wait for the platform (платформ) and track (путь) to be displayed on the departure board.

➡ Keep your ticket and passport safe but accessible so you can show them for boarding.

A–Z On The Train
Bedding

Fresh sheets and pillowcases, blankets, and a hand-towel are provided. If the cost isn't included in your ticket (it often is) then you'll pay the *provodnitsa* a small charge for this.

Carriage Layout

Facilities in the carriage will depend on the class of travel, but generally the layout is as follows. On the left as you enter is one bathroom; alongside that is the attendant's compartment. Opposite this compartment is the all-important samovar with hot water for beverages, and directly opposite this, inset on the wall near the attendant's compartment, is (in theory) potable water.

Internet Resources

Circumbaikal Railway (http://kbzd.transsib.ru)

CNVOL.com (www.cnvol.com) About train travel in China.

A Journey on the Trans-Siberian Railway (www.trans-siberian-railway.co.uk) Clive Sampsan's passion for travel, with inspiring photos.

Man in Seat 61 (www.seat61.com) Mark Smith's definitive website.

Trans-Siberian Railway Web Encyclopaedia (www.transsib.ru) Not updated, but still a mine of useful background detail.

Meeting of Frontiers (http://international.loc.gov/intldl/mtfhtml/mfhome.html) Online collection about Russians exploring America and vice versa. Under 'Digital Collections' you'll find an original Trans-Siberian guidebook dating from 1900 and rare books and photos, many relating to Siberian and Far East travel and exploration.

Virtual Tours

Russian Railways (http://eng.rzd.ru/vtour/index.html) A virtual tour inside the *Rossiya*.

Under no circumstances drink the water in the bathrooms; the best and safest water on the train comes from the samovar.

The rest of the carriage is made up of nine closed compartments (1st/SV and 2nd/*kupe* class) or 54 open beds (3rd/*platskart* class). At the other end of the carriage is a second toilet. The rubbish bin is inside a box opposite the second toilet.

Classes & Comforts

In theory, all but the cheapest carriages are air-conditioned in summer and heated in winter – that's why the windows are locked shut (though sometimes you'll be able to open them). In practice, air conditioning can break down or a compartment can be stiflingly overheated.

Some Russian 2nd-class compartments are entirely single-sex these days, although this is not available on all trains.

Deluxe 1st Class & Tourist Trains

Deluxe 1st class is available on train K3/4 (Trans-Mongolian). This entails roomy, two-berth compartments with showers shared between two compartments. Train K23/24 between Běijīng and Ulaanbaatar has a similar deluxe 1st class with showers.

A handful of scheduled trains, including 001Г/002Й *Premium* Moscow–Kazan service and 53/54 (http://grandexpress.ru/en) linking Moscow and St Petersburg, have a luxury *myagky* carriage with compartments sleeping two with their own toilet and shower. Tourist trains such as the *Golden Eagle* have the option of even more luxurious compartments.

1st Class/SV

This class of compartment, called SV (short for *spalny vagon,* or sleeping wagon) or *lyux,* have only two berths, so there's more room and more privacy. They usually also have TVs on which it is possible to watch DVDs. The *provodnitsa* has DVDs for a small fee (there's nothing to stop you from bringing your own, although they'll need to work on a Russian DVD player, compatible with region 5).

Chinese 1st Class – Four Berth

A four-berth compartment is available on the Chinese train K3/4. It's a little more spacious than 2nd class, with wider beds, and the carriages have a newer feel.

2nd Class/Kupe

The compartments in a *kupeyny* carriage (2nd class, also called 'compartmentalised' and often shortened to *kupe*) are standard on long-distance trains. These carriages are divided into nine compartments, each with four reasonably comfortable berths, a fold-down table and enough room between bunks to stand and undress.

In every carriage there's one half-sized compartment with just two berths. This is usually occupied by the *provodnitsa,* or reserved for railway employees, but there is a slim chance that you may end up in it, particularly if you do a deal directly with a *provodnitsa* for a train ticket.

3rd Class/Platskart

You either love them or hate them, and it's worth experiencing this at least once to decide for yourself. A reserved-place *platskartny* carriage, sometimes also called *zhyostky* ('hard class', or 3rd class) and usually abbreviated to *platskart,* is essentially a dorm carriage sleeping 54. The bunks are non-compartmentalised and arranged in blocks of four running down one side of the corridor and in two on the other, with the lower bunk on this side converting to a table and chairs during the day. They're ideal for one-night journeys. In summer the lack of compartment walls means they're not usually as stuffy as a *kupe* can be. Many travellers (women in particular) find *platskart* a better option than being cooped up with three (possibly drunken) Russian men. It's also a great way to meet ordinary Russians.

However, on multiday journeys some *platskart* carriages can begin to resemble a refugee camp, with clothing strung between bunks, a great swapping of bread, fish and jars of tea, and babies sitting on potties while their snot-nosed siblings tear up and down the corridor. Only the hardy would want to do Moscow to Vladivostok or similar nonstop journeys this way.

If you do travel *platskart,* it's worth requesting specific numbered seats when booking your ticket. The ones to avoid are 1 to 4 (next to the attendant and samovar, which means a lot of activity) and 33 to 36 (next to the toilet). Corridor bunks are numbered from 37 (the lower bunk near the toilet and smoking vestibule) to 54 (the upper bunk near the *provodnitsa*). Odd numbers are always lower bunks,

MAN IN SEAT 61 ON THE TRANS-SIBERIAN

'People talk about the Trans-Siberian as if it's just one experience, but I've had completely different experiences on different routes. When I took the Moscow to Beijing Trans-Mongolian train, almost everyone was going the whole route and it was a party all the way. The scenery changes from four days of Siberia to a day in Mongolia with the total contrast of the Gobi Desert, then it changes again on the final day to the mountains of China and, of course, the Great Wall. On the other hand, travelling from Moscow to Vladivostok was seven solid days of Siberia. Russians tend to use the train for various sections of the route, rather than end to end, and there were no other Westerners except for a couple that got on in Irkutsk. Even I was going a bit stir crazy by the time we reached Vladivostok, and the nicest part of that trip was the ferry from Vladivostok to Japan.'

Mark Smith runs the award-winning website www.seat61.com

even numbers upper bunks. The bottom side berth bunks (ie the odd numbers) are shorter than the rest. Anyone over 180cm (6ft) tall will find the 'pedial overhang' untenable, if not downright uncomfortable.

Finally, it's worth experiencing *platskart* while you can as Russian Railways president Vladimir Yakunin announced plans in 2013 to replace these carriages with more comfortable rolling stock in the near future – he sees them as an anachronism in contemporary Russia.

4th Class/Obshchiy

Also called 4th class, *obshchiy* (general) is unreserved. On long-distance trains the *obshchiy* carriage looks the same as a *platskart,* but when it's full, eight people are squeezed into each unenclosed compartment so there's no room to lie down. Suburban trains normally have only *obshchiy* class, which in this case means bench-type seating. On a few daytime-only intercity trains there are higher-grade *obshchiy* carriages with more comfortable, reserved chairs.

Clothing

Loose fitting, comfortable and layered is our advice. Russian train attire often consists of ultra-loud synthetic tracksuit pants, a T-shirt and pullover (or sweatshirt) and thongs (flip-flops) or sandals. In contrast to Russian big-city streetwear, this is not high fashion, but it's highly functional. Variations on this theme – such as loose-fitting jeans and using the tracksuit pants as pyjamas – are a good compromise between style and comfort. In winter a warm jacket or overcoat and a warm hat

and gloves, as well as face and lip cream against cold, should be kept close by for station stops.

Be aware of polite signals or requests by others that you should briefly leave the compartment so that the person can get changed – mostly, this happens just after departure and before arrival.

Electricity

In the age of manifold hand-held devices and digital cameras, power outlets can be a problem in some carriages, especially on older Russian trains. These have a couple of 110-volt outlets for razors, but often a 2nd-class carriage will have only one 220-volt socket, located halfway along the corridor. Ask politely, however, and you can often use a power outlet inside the attendant's carriage. Modern 1st-class and many newer 2nd-class carriages also have power outlets in the compartments.

Essential Items

➡ Pocketknife with corkscrew and openers, plastic or metal mug, plastic or metal cutlery (a metal camping set that fits together is useful).

➡ Lightweight torch (flashlight).

➡ Money belt, neck pouch or ankle stash.

➡ Toilet paper, a small medical kit (the attendant also has one) and whatever hygiene articles you need. Buy some from the attendant, or top up at platform kiosks.

➡ Earplugs or a sleeping mask if white noise or bright light bothers you.

➡ Bottled water.

➡ An electrical plug adaptor if required.

➜ Comfortable clothing suitable for the season, and slip-on footwear.

Comfort Items

Things that are useful or make life more comfortable are a sense of humour, reading material (audio books and e-books are easiest), a camera, a battery charger and a music-capable device loaded with your favourite tunes. Also bring a notepad and pen to plot random thoughts, and don't forget your mobile-phone plug. A large USB stick, a USB cable for transferring to discs in internet cafes, or even a portable hard drive and replacement memory cards for videos and photos can be useful.

Note that if you're doing a lot of travelling in Mongolia, it's useful to bring along sealable ziplock plastic bags to protect your electronics from dust, and a thin silk or cotton sleeping-bag liner to make threadbare bedding more comfortable.

Food

Platform Food

Shopping for supplies on station platforms is part of the fun of the Trans-Siberian Railway (note, however, that in Mongolia and China you will find very little food available on platforms). It's a good idea to have plenty of small change on hand, but you'll rarely have to worry about being overcharged.

The choice of items can be excellent, with bread, fresh dairy products, ice cream, grilled chicken, boiled potatoes, home cooking such as *pelmeni* (dumplings) or *pirozhki* (savoury pies), buckets of forest berries and smoked fish all on offer. Through Siberia you'll always find sellers of fresh pine or cedar nuts. Always check the use-by dates on packaged food.

Compartment Picnics

Instant noodles have made great inroads into Russia's rail system, but serious eating still tends to involve sliced chunks of cucumber and tomato in summer, more often than not cured sausage, perhaps fish, perhaps a cold dish someone prepared at home, all washed down with beer, tea or vodka. A cloth or newspaper is often spread carefully across the compartment table, then the food is unpacked lovingly and eaten with relish. After that – if it's lunch – everyone usually dozes off. If you buy plentifully on the platforms and have the right travel companions, compartment picnics will be a true highlight of your trip.

Strictly speaking, alcohol cannot be carried onto the train; it can only be bought from the restaurant car or the snack seller. In practice, Russians invariably bring their own.

Some train tickets include snacks or small meals which will be distributed by the *provodnitsa*.

SHE WHO MUST BE OBEYED

On any long-distance Russian train journey you'll soon learn who's in charge: the *provodnitsa*. Though sometimes male (*provodnik*), carriage attendants are usually women.

Apart from checking your ticket before boarding the train, doling out linen and shaking you awake in the middle of the night when your train arrives, the *provodnitsa*'s job is to keep her carriage spick and span (most are very diligent about this) and to make sure the samovar is always fired up with hot water. They will have cups, plates and cutlery to borrow, if you need them, and can provide drinks and snacks for a small price.

On long journeys the *provodnitsa* works in a team of two; one will be working while the other is resting.

Initially, a *provodnitsa* can come across as quite fearsome. Very few will speak any other language than Russian. Some sport the most distinctive hairdos you'll come across this side of a drag-queen convention. All look as smart as sergeant majors in their RZD uniforms – and just as ready to knock you into shape if you step out of line! However, if you're polite and respectful to your *provodnitsa*, and bestow on her plenty of friendly smiles, chances are high that she will do her best to make your journey a very pleasant one.

Restaurant Cars & Buffets

The restaurant cars are changed at each country's border, so en route to Běijīng you will get Russian, Chinese and possibly Mongolian menus (although it's unlikely there will be a car attached between the Russian border and Ulaanbaatar).

In restaurant cars, a full meal with accompanying drink typically costs US$20 to US$30, paid in local currency. The cars are open from approximately 9am to 9pm local time, although their hours in Russia are highly unpredictable. With time-zone differences, knowing when to turn up is almost impossible to guess. Generally, Chinese restaurant cars have the best food. On Russian menus, the dishes with prices written alongside them are the ones available that day.

Some trains, especially on the Baikal-Amur Mainline (Baikalo-Amurskaya Magistral; BAM), only have a buffet car with high tables, but these afford good panoramas of the landscape. In the restaurant car there's often a table of pot noodles, chocolate, alcohol, juice and the like.

As well as vendors who go through the carriages with snacks, *provodniki* offer their own drinks and nibbles. Prices are not as cheap as at the kiosks or station halts.

A restaurant or buffet car can be a good place to meet people, or get away from them, depending on the time of day or night and standard of food and service. On some low-grade Russian trains you'll find few signs of edible food or human life, however, except for a few bored staff and the telltale smell of something having been cooked there some time in the distant past. On other trains, the standard isn't too bad.

Interacting With Passengers

Politely greeting fellow travellers when you first enter the compartment, or greeting new arrivals, is a good icebreaker. Let things develop at a natural pace, though. Offering food, even as a token gesture, used to be de rigueur and remains the best way to cultivate a good travelling relationship.

Russians are masters of the art of conversation, so if you're travelling alone it will be easy to meet people. Chinese travellers are also curious and like talking to foreigners. Sometimes the trolley lady selling drinks and snacks will combine business with pleasure by sitting down for a rest and conversation. If you chat for a long time, it's usual to buy a drink or snack in return. Keep small change for this – snack sellers can disappear into the taiga for several hundred kilometres in order to break the high notes. The more skilled deliver the best vodka and conversation on the train.

If you have difficulties with a fellow passenger (a loud DVD player is a possible one), sort it out locally, but if that fails, the *provodnitsa* can swing into action.

Luggage

How much to bring will be a compromise between weight and comfort. The baggage allowance per adult on Chinese international trains is 35kg (20kg on domestic trains). On all Russian trains it's 36kg (50kg in 1st class).

Before boarding, stow things needed for the journey in your day pack; the rest can be locked in your baggage and stored either inside the base of the bottom bunk (you can lift up the bunk) or in the luggage space above the door.

Time Zones

The Trans-Siberian route between Moscow and Vladivostok crosses seven of Russia's 11 time zones. Since November 2014 Moscow has kept its clocks permanently on winter time (GMT/UTC plus three hours), which means that when clocks go forward in spring in Europe and elsewhere, the relevant time differences decrease by one hour. Like Russia, neither China nor Mongolia observe daylight savings time. When it's noon in Moscow it's:

WHERE	TIME	GMT/UTC
Běijīng	5pm (17:00)	+8hr
Ulaanbaatar	5pm (17:00)	+8hr
Yekaterinburg & Tyumen	2pm (14:00)	+5hr
Omsk & Novo-sibirsk	3pm (15:00)	+6hr
Krasnoyarsk	4pm (16:00)	+7hr
Irkutsk & Ulan-Ude	5pm (17:00)	+8hr
Vladivostok	7pm (19:00)	+10hr

Clocks and timetables on trains and at stations show Moscow time *(Moskovskoe vremya)*. Local time is known as *mestnoe vremya*.

The best way to cope with the time zones is to drink plenty of bottled water, avoid overdoing the alcohol and shift your meals and bedtime back or forward according to local time. Travellers who take strong medication will need to exercise caution and seek advice from their doctor before setting out.

Toilets & Showers

The toilets on all major trains are Western type. Unless the train has a closed-system biological toilet (some modern or refitted carriages have these), toilets will be locked before and after arrival at a station. In larger cities, this might be one hour before arrival and one hour after leaving the station, although 10 to 20 minutes on each side of town is more usual. The schedule is attached to the toilet door.

There are no showers in passenger carriages except in 1st class on a few top-quality trains, so a flannel is useful for washing at the basin. Most *firmeny* (premium) trains, however, have a staff carriage with shower and ironing facilities. The *provodnitsa* can organise a visit to this carriage to use the shower for a couple of dollars. Apart from soap and the usual toiletries, pack or buy sufficient toilet paper, although a good attendant will keep the toilets supplied and shipshape. Use the bathroom bin to dispose of sanitary objects. A clothes hook situated in the bathroom is useful for hanging up your day pack or toiletries bag while you go about your ablutions.

Safety & Safekeeping

Russian and Asian trains are generally safe, but be security conscious, especially if you're travelling alone.

➡ Keep your valuables and documents with you at all times in a zipped or buttoned-up pocket. Don't flash large amounts of cash or your credit cards around.

➡ Money belts and ankle stashes are useful, but storing documents and valuables inside your pillowcase while you sleep is the safest stash.

➡ Ask someone you trust to keep an eye on any bag containing valuable equipment while you are away.

➡ If you're alone in a compartment, ask the *provodnitsa* to lock it while you go to the restaurant car or get out at long station stops (never leave luggage completely unattended in an unlocked compartment).

TRAVEL READING ON THE TRAIN

Pack something light, such as a thriller; ploughing through Tolstoy's *War and Peace* is a noble intention, but you will probably be too tired to take it in. If you go for something classic, audio books are a good idea. Some recommended travel books:

➡ **Railway Travel** *The Great Railway Bazaar, Ghost Train to the Eastern Star* and *Riding the Iron Rooster* (Paul Theroux), *Through Siberia by Accident* and *Silverland* (Dervla Murphy), *The Big Red Train Ride* (Eric Newby), *The Trans-Siberian Railway: a Traveller's Anthology* (Deborah Manley), *To the Edge of the World* (Christian Wolmar)

➡ **Russia** *In Siberia* (Colin Thubron), *Travels in Siberia* (Ian Frazier), *Russia: A Journey to the Heart of a Land and its People* (Jonathan Dimbleby), *A History of the Peoples of Siberia* (James Forsyth), *The Shaman's Coat: A Native History of Siberia* (Anna Reid), *Siberia: A Cultural History* (LP author Anthony Haywood), *The Last Man in Russia* (Oliver Bullough)

➡ **Mongolia** *The Lost Country: Mongolia Revealed* (Jasper Becker), *Wild East* (Jill Lawless), *Dateline Mongolia: An American Journalist in Nomad's Land* (LP author Michael Kohn; see also his 2010 book *Lama of the Gobi,* tracing the life of Mongolian mystic Danzan Ravjaa)

➡ **China** *China Road* (Rob Gifford), *River Town: Two Years on the Yangtze* (Peter Hessler)

→ Lock your compartment door from the inside at night and use the additional metal security latch on the door.

→ Generally, the more alcohol in play, the more safety is an issue. In the rare case that you are molested by a fellow passenger, inform the attendant. If you feel unsafe, a move or swap can be organised.

Smoking

Smoking is not allowed anywhere on the train or, officially, on station platforms (even though you may see fellow passengers taking a puff here). If you are caught smoking, you may be liable for a fine.

Wi-fi

On Sapsan trains between Moscow and St Petersburg and Moscow and Nizhny Novgorod, paid wi-fi access and 3G coverage is available. Russian Railways has plans to roll out on-board wi-fi for some other premium train services and routes.

Mobile phone coverage is available all along the main Trans-Siberian lines and 3G is available in places, so if you have internet access on your phone, you may still be able to get online in the midst of Siberia (but no promises!).

Station Stops

Many of the stops along the Trans-Siberian and Asian routes are for two minutes. Halts of 10 to 20 minutes are common at larger towns or junctions, and sometimes extend up to six or seven hours at borders.

From some platforms you have enough time to dash into the station, but let the *provodnitsa* know in advance and don't dilly dally – trains won't wait for you!

→ A timetable of station stops (in Cyrillic) hangs in the carriage, but these times are not set in stone. Check the schedule (or take a photo of it), but also double-check with the *provodnitsa* when you get off.

→ All train clocks show Moscow time. It's useful to be bi-temporal, eg keeping your watch on Moscow time and a mobile device on local time.

→ Take your ticket and passport with you. You might be asked to show them to police on the platform (rare) or to get back on (if you have unremarkable features).

→ If you miss your train, inform station staff immediately. They will try to organise alternatives so you can catch up with your luggage. But don't count on it.

Crossing the Borders

The Trans-Mongolian Railway crosses the Russia–Mongolia border at Naushki-Sükhbaatar, which can take anything from six to 11 hours. Crossing the China–Mongolia border takes about five hours, and the bogies of the carriages are changed to the local gauge here.

The Trans-Manchurian Railway crosses the Russia–China border between Mănzhōulǐ (China) and Zabaikalsk (Russia), which takes about half a day. Again, the bogies must be changed. Remember: toilets are always locked at stops and during bogie changes.

Journey at a Glance

The chapters of this guide cover the major cities in which you may start or finish your journey (Moscow, St Petersburg and Běijīng) and bite-sized chunks of the overall Trans-Siberian route, heading east from European Russia into Siberia and onwards to the Russian Far East and termination in Vladivostok. There are also descriptions of the Trans-Mongolian and Trans-Manchurian routes (both of which terminate in Běijīng) and the Baikal-Amur Mainline (BAM) from the points they diverge from the main Trans-Siberian Railway. Each route has its own appeal but all are united by the experience of being on the train itself. The following will help you plan where best you might want to make a stop along the way.

Moscow

History
Art
Performing Arts

Historical Landmarks

The Kremlin shows off the splendour of Muscovy's grand princes. St Basil's Cathedral recounts the defeat of the Tatars. And on Red Square, Lenin lies embalmed.

Glorious Galleries

The illustrious Tretyakov and Pushkin galleries are only the beginning of the art in Moscow, where contemporary artists and their patrons are taking over former factories and warehouses to display their works.

Theatre & Dance

The city's classical performing arts are still among the best in the world. Nowadays, even the most traditional theatres are experimenting with innovative arrangements and edgy choreography.

p56

St Petersburg

Palaces
History
Art

Imperial Splendour

Grand imperial palaces line the embankments of the Neva River, its tributaries and canals. Restoration over the past two decades has been painstaking; the results are breathtaking.

Revolutionary Road

Everything about St Petersburg is revolutionary: from Peter the Great's determination to forge a new Russia by opening the country to the rest of Europe, to Lenin's leadership of a coup in 1917, which led to the creation of the world's first communist state.

Staggering Collections

The Hermitage collection is unrivalled. The Russian Museum boasts a unique collection of Russian paintings from icons to the avant-garde.

p88

Moscow to Yekaterinburg

Scenery
Culture
Outdoors

Crossing the Ural Mountains

The Ural Mountains are a physical and metaphysical divide between Europe and Asia. The Volga River is a highlight; the scenery is most beautiful east of Kungur.

Multicultural Mashup

Nizhny Novgorod offers an insight into Volga life and has a thriving food-meets-culture scene. Perm has refashioned itself as a 'contemporary art capital', while the less-travelled Kazan and Yaroslavl routes offer insight into Islamic (Kazan) and Orthodox (Yaroslavl) cultures.

Getting Active

Perm is a fine base for hiking, rafting or horseriding; Kungur is good for canoeing, cycling and cross-country skiing.

p113

Yekaterinburg to Krasnoyarsk

Scenery
City Life
Architecture

Into the Taiga

Vistas of dense taiga alternating with farmland unfurls gradually outside your window as you travel deeper into Siberia. On a winter journey, a blanket of snow makes the unchanging look romantic and beautiful.

Big City Lights

They don't call Novosibirsk the capital of Siberia for nothing – enjoy a slew of quirky museums and monuments, a relaxed big-city vibe and pulsating nightlife.

Wooden Lace

Tobolsk and Tomsk, both slight detours off the main Trans-Siberian route, are worth visiting for their attractive wooden buildings with intricately carved facades. Tobolsk also has a handsome, ancient kremlin.

p138

Lake Baikal: Krasnoyarsk to Ulan-Ude

Baikal Views
Outdoors
History

Siberian Pearl

Lake Baikal is the highlight, even viewed through the carriage window. Summer waters lap in shades of blue; winter whiteouts melt the frozen lake into its alpine backdrop.

Make a Splash!

A chilly plunge into Baikal is said to add seven years to your life! Not game? Then give winter dog sledding and ice fishing on Baikal a go.

Exiles and Indegines

The peoples of the Baikal region have lent it a colourful and varied history, especially since the 17th-century Russian Cossacks collided with Mongol Buryats. Later came Tibetan Buddhists, aristocratic Decembrists and revolutionaries. Museums explain all.

p168

Ulan-Ude to Vladivostok

Urban Life
River Life
Religion

End of the Line

Even if Vladivostok wasn't the Trans-Sib terminus it would still be well worth visiting for its remarkable harbour, hilly location and newly upgraded city infrastructure.

Riverside Promenades

The fortunes of Siberian cities are shaped by rivers, especially the Amur. Lively promenades along the banks are part of the appeal in Blagoveshchensk and Khabarovsk, one of the Far East's most happening cities.

Religious Life

Spin prayer wheels at the *datsan* (Buddhist temples) in Aginskoe and Tsugol, both reached from Chita. Learn about Stalin's plan to create a Jewish Zion at Birobidzhan.

p206

The Baikal-Amur Mainline (BAM)

Scenery
Outdoors
Architecture

Taiga & Tunnels

Stare into limitless taiga, strain to view the top of a mountain, then plunge into a long, dark tunnel. The BAM bucks and weaves, skirts 3000m-high peaks, rattles over mountain brooks and burrows into earthquake-prone mountainscape.

Base for Baikal

Severobaikalsk is a superb base from which to explore the surrounding wilds on foot, by bike, on the water or snow. The Great Baikal Trail can be accessed from town.

Soviet Architecture

The Soviet-futuristic BAM stations at Severobaikalsk and Tynda are worth a visit in their own right as are the heroic mosaics in Komsomolsk-na-Amure.

p237

The Trans-Mongolian Route

Scenery
Religion
Outdoors

Steppes & Desert

Taiga gives way to Mongolia's rolling hills, which ease into grassy steppes. Further south the train travels through the Gobi Desert, and once in China it's back to grasslands and spectacular mountain scenery.

Buddhist Art

Some stunning Buddhist monasteries can be visited in Mongolia, including Amarbayasgalant and Gandan. In China, the Yungang caves, crammed with carved Buddhas, are not to be missed.

Saddle Up!

Gorkhi-Terelj National Park is an excellent destination for horseriding, mountain biking or hiking. For wildlife viewing, try Khustain National Park.

p250

The Trans-Manchurian Route

Wildlife
History
Quirkiness

Tiger, Tiger

The Siberian Tiger Park's conservation and breeding programmes are helping save the magnificent feline from extinction.

The Manchus

Make a stop in Shānhǎiguān, where the Great Wall meets the sea, or Chángchūn, home to the Manchu Imperial Palace. Hā'ěrbīn has its own unique history, filled with architectural treasures.

Quirky Sites

Mǎnzhōulǐ is a slightly oddball destination, with its hip-hop statues on the streets and gigantic *matryoshka* doll park. In Hā'ěrbīn you can kick back in Stalin Park, one of the last parks to retain the dictator's name as well as visit an Orthodox church.

p284

Běijīng

Shopping
Architecture
Food

Markets

For a brand-new wardrobe on the cheap, bargain at the Sanlitun Yashou Clothing Market. For more traditional items, browse the ancient shops and stalls of Dashilar silk street or Panjiayuan Market.

Imperial Icons

The Great Wall, Forbidden City, Temple of Heaven and Summer Palace – to name just a few. But don't overlook the best of old Běijīng and relaxing bike rides through its winding alleys and tranquil parks.

Culinary Delights

Gastronomes will be salivating at the capital's amazing selection of Chinese cuisine. Peking duck is the city's signature dish, but head to Wangfujing to try out China's most exotic street snacks.

p301

On the Road

Moscow

Includes

Best Places to Eat

➡ Delicatessen (p78)
➡ Café Pushkin (p79)
➡ Khachapuri (p79)
➡ As Eat Is (p79)
➡ Lavka-Lavka (p79)

Best Places to Stay

➡ Hotel Metropol (p74)
➡ Hotel de Paris (p75)
➡ Kitay-Gorod Hotel (p77)
➡ Blues Hotel (p76)
➡ Godzillas Hostel (p74)

Why Go?

Moscow (Москва) is the start or the end point for your train journey across Mother Russia. If you are travelling east to west, you will be relieved – after days (or weeks) on the train – to reach the cultured, cosmopolitan capital, brimming with opportunities to immerse yourself in history; to indulge in world-class music and art; to feast on fabulous food; and to sample the nightlife in a city that never sleeps. If you are travelling west to east, you may be relieved to depart – to escape the overwhelming urbanity, the bumper-to-bumper traffic, the nonstop noise, the panic-inducing prices. Either way, Moscow is an exhilarating and confounding contrast to the rest of Russia.

Soak it up. Examine the art and move to the music; splurge on a ritzy restaurant; stay out till sunrise; get lost in the crowds. Once you get on that train, you may not get to do it again.

When to Go
Moscow

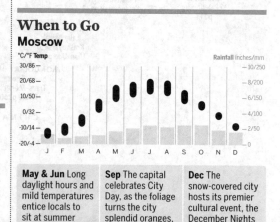

May & Jun Long daylight hours and mild temperatures entice locals to sit at summer terraces.

Sep The capital celebrates City Day, as the foliage turns the city splendid oranges, reds and yellows.

Dec The snow-covered city hosts its premier cultural event, the December Nights Festival.

Arriving by Air

If you arrive by air, you will fly into one of the city's three airports. The majority of international flights go in and out of Domodedovo and Sheremetyevo International Airports; the third airport is Vnukovo. All three airports are accessible by the convenient Aeroexpress train (p87) from the city centre.

If you wish to take a taxi from the airport, go to the taxi desk (or straight to the dispatcher) for an official airport taxi, which will charge between R2000 and R2500 to the centre. Note that driving times vary wildly depending on traffic.

ARRIVING BY RAIL

Rail riders will arrive at one of the central train stations. All trains from St Petersburg arrive at Leningradsky vokzal, while Trans-Siberian trains from the east arrive at Yaroslavsky or Kazansky vokzal. These three railway stations are clustered around Komsomolskaya pl, a bustling square just northeast of the centre. From here, you can hop on the metro (Ⓜ Komsomolskaya) for a quick, easy ride to your destination. Alternatively, most taxi companies offer a fixed rate of R400 to R600 for a train-station transfer.

Guided Tours

Moscow is a big, overwhelming city with a strange alphabet. Letting the locals show you around is a good way to get your bearings and learn something along the way.

Moscow Free Tour (Map p63; ☑ 495-222 3466; http://moscowfreetour.com; Nikolskaya ul 4/5; paid tours R950-1550) Offers a free walking tour, led by knowledgeable and extremely enthusiastic guides. Did we mention it's free?

Moscow 360 (☑ 8-915-205 8360; www.moscow360.org) For unique and informative walking tours (all free!) as well as a bigger-picture tour by air-conditioned minivan (not free).

Moscow Bike Tours (☑ 8-916-970 1419; www.moscowbiketours.com; 3hr tour R1800) Cover more ground and see more sights, while getting fresh air and a bit of exercise.

NEED TO KNOW

Most Moscow museums close on Monday, but the Kremlin and the Armoury close on Thursday instead. Many museums close once a month for 'sanitary day', usually the last week of the month.

Fast Facts

➡ Telephone code: ☑ 495, ☑ 499 or ☑ 498

➡ Population: 12 million

➡ Time zone: GMT/UTC +3 hours

New in Moscow

➡ **Gorky Park** (p72) & Hermitage Gardens (p68)Major green spaces revamped into vibrant centres of sport and culture

➡ **Jewish Museum & Centre of Tolerance** (p69) Groundbreaking museum with interactive multimedia

➡ **Moscow Museum** (p70) The city museum has a new location and a new mission

➡ **Krymskaya Naberezhnaya** (p71) Closed to car traffic and filled with fountains and art

Resources

➡ **Calvert Journal** (www.calvertjournal.com) Articles on Russia's creative culture

➡ **Moscow Times** (www.themoscowtimes.com) Moscow's leading English-language newspaper

➡ **Expat.ru** (www.expat.ru) Run by and for English-speaking expats in Moscow

History

Moscow's recorded history dates to the mid-12th century, when Yury Dolgoruky constructed the first Kremlin on a strategic spot atop the Borovitsky Hill. Moscow soon blossomed into an economic centre.

In the 13th century, the Mongols burned the city to the ground. The Golden Horde was interested in tribute, and Moscow was conveniently situated to monitor the river trade and road traffic. Moscow's Prince Ivan acted as tax collector, earning himself the moniker 'Kalita' (Moneybags), and Moscow developed into a regional capital.

Towards the end of the 15th century, the once diminutive duchy emerged as an expanding state under the reign of Grand Prince Ivan III (the Great). To celebrate his successes, he imported a team of Italian artisans for a complete renovation of the Kremlin. The city developed in concentric rings outward from this centre. Under Ivan IV (the Terrible), the then capital city earned the nickname of 'Gold-Domed Moscow' because of its multitude of monastery fortresses and magnificent churches.

In 1712 Peter the Great startled the country by announcing the relocation of the capital to St Petersburg. In the early 1800s, Moscow suffered further at the hands of Napoleon Bonaparte. But after the Napoleonic Wars, Moscow was feverishly rebuilt and industry prospered.

When the Bolsheviks gained control of Russia in 1917, the capital returned to Moscow. Stalin devised an urban plan for the city: historic cathedrals and monuments were demolished; in their place appeared the marble-bedecked metro and neo-Gothic skyscrapers. In the following decades, Moscow expanded at an exponential rate.

Moscow was the scene of the most dramatic events of the political transition of the early 1990s. Boris Yeltsin led crowds protesting the attempted coup in 1991, and two years later he ordered the army to blast the parliament into submission. Within the Moscow city government, the election of Mayor Yury Luzhkov in 1992 set the stage for the creation of a big-city boss: his interests range from the media to manufacturing. While the rest of Russia struggled to survive the collapse of communism, Moscow emerged as an enclave of affluence.

Early in the new millennium, Moscow was a target for terrorist attacks linked to the ongoing crisis in Chechnya. Over the next decade, suicide bombers in Moscow made strikes in metro stations, at rock concerts, on trains and aeroplanes, and in the international airport, leaving hundreds of people dead and injured and reminding Muscovites that there is no end in sight to the Chechen crisis.

In 2010 long-time mayor Luzhkov lost his job. The new boss was Sergei Sobyanin, hand-picked by the president. His early initiatives included a crackdown on corruption and a slowdown of construction, both of which were welcomed by many Moscow residents.

Meanwhile, the city continues to attract fortune-seekers from around the world. And Moscow – political capital, economic powerhouse and cultural innovator – continues to lead the way as the most fast-dealing, freewheeling city in Russia.

◎ Sights

◉ Kremlin & Kitay Gorod

Red Square and the Kremlin are the historical, geographic and spiritual heart of Moscow, as they have been for nearly 900 years. The mighty fortress, the iconic onion domes of St Basil's Cathedral and the granite mausoleum of Vladimir Lenin are among the city's most important historical sights. The surrounding streets of Kitay Gorod are crammed with churches and old architecture. This is the starting point for any visit to Moscow.

◉ Kremlin

The apex of Russian political power and once the centre of the Orthodox Church, the Kremlin (Кремль; Map p63; www.kreml.ru; adult/student R350/100; ☉10am-5pm Fri-Wed, ticket office 9.30am-4.30pm; Ⓜ Aleksandrovsky Sad) is not only the kernel of Moscow but of the whole country. It's from here that autocratic tsars, communist dictators and modern-day presidents have done their best – and worst – for Russia. These redbrick walls and tent-roof towers enclose some 800 years of artistic accomplishment, religious ceremony and power politics.

Buy your ticket at the Kremlin Ticket Office (Кассы музеев Кремля; Map p63; ☉9.30am-4pm Fri-Wed; Ⓜ Aleksandrovsky Sad) in Alexander Garden, and enter through the Kutafya Tower (Кутафья башня; Map p63). You will pass a series of government

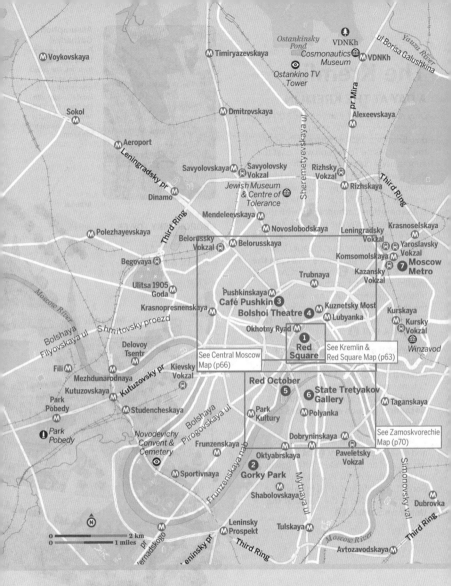

Moscow Highlights

1 Being awestruck by the assemblage of tall towers and onion domes on **Red Square** (p64)

2 Hanging out with Moscow's hipsters in **Gorky Park** (p72) – ride bikes, admire art, play ping-pong or dance under the stars

3 Splurging on a Russian feast amidst 18th-century opulence at **Café Pushkin** (p79)

4 Seeing the dancers slide across *Swan Lake* at the **Bolshoi Theatre** (p82)

5 Exploring the former **Red October** (p71) chocolate factory, now filled with art

galleries, nightclubs and fashion boutiques

6 Ogling the icons, perusing the Peredvizhniki and contemplating the avant-garde at the **State Tretyakov Gallery** (p71)

7 Riding the **Moscow metro** (p87) for a cheap history lesson and art exhibit all in one

The Kremlin

A DAY AT THE KREMLIN

Only at the Kremlin can you see 800 years of Russian history and artistry in one day. Enter the ancient fortress through the Trinity Gate Tower and walk past the impressive Arsenal, ringed with cannons. Past the Patriarch's Palace, you'll find yourself surrounded by white-washed walls and golden domes. Your first stop is **Assumption Cathedral** ❶ with the solemn fresco over the doorway. As the most important church in prerevolutionary Russia, this 15th-century beauty was the burial site of the patriarchs. The **Ivan the Great Bell Tower** ❷ now contains a nifty multimedia exhibit on the architectural history of the Kremlin. The view from the top is worth the price of admission. The tower is flanked by the massive **Tsar Cannon & Bell** ❸.

In the southeast corner, **Archangel Cathedral** ❹ has an elaborate interior, where three centuries of tsars and tsarinas are laid to rest. Your final stop on Sobornaya pl is **Annunciation Cathedral** ❺, rich with frescoes and iconography.

Walk along the Great Kremlin Palace and enter the **Armoury** ❻ at the time designated on your ticket. After gawking at the goods, exit the Kremlin through Borovitsky Gate and stroll through the Alexander Garden to the **Tomb of the Unknown Soldier** ❼.

Assumption Cathedral
Once your eyes adjust to the colourful frescoes, the gilded fixtures and the iconography, try to locate *Saviour with the Angry Eye*, a 14th-century icon that is one of the oldest in the Kremlin.

Arsenal

BOROVITSKY TOWER

Use the entrance at Borovitsky Tower if you intend to skip the churches and visit only the Armoury or Diamond Fund.

Borovitsky Tower

Trinity Gate Tower

Alexander Garden

❻

Great Kremlin Palace

TOP TIPS

» **Lunch** There are no eating options. Plan to eat before you arrive or stash a snack.

» **Lookout** After ogling the sights around Sobornaya pl, take a break in the park across the street, which offers wonderful views of the Moscow River and points south.

Armoury
Take advantage of the free audio guide to direct you to the most intriguing treasures of the Armoury, which is chock-full of precious metalworks and jewellery, armour and weapons, gowns and crowns, carriages and sledges.

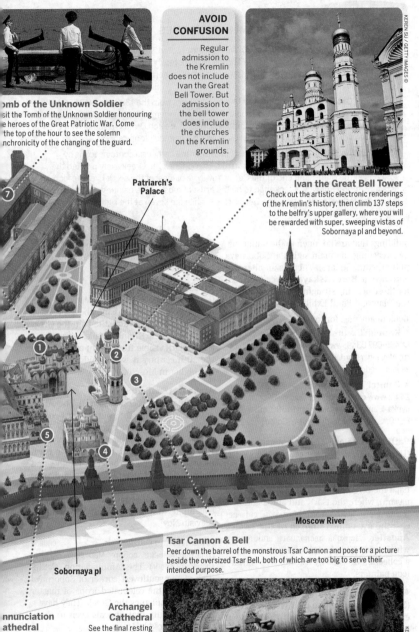

omb of the Unknown Soldier

sit the Tomb of the Unknown Soldier honouring
e heroes of the Great Patriotic War. Come
the top of the hour to see the solemn
nchronicity of the changing of the guard.

AVOID CONFUSION

Regular admission to the Kremlin does not include Ivan the Great Bell Tower. But admission to the bell tower does include the churches on the Kremlin grounds.

KEREN SU / GETTY IMAGES ©

Patriarch's Palace

Ivan the Great Bell Tower
Check out the artistic electronic renderings
of the Kremlin's history, then climb 137 steps
to the belfry's upper gallery, where you will
be rewarded with super, sweeping vistas of
Sobornaya pl and beyond.

Moscow River

Sobornaya pl

Tsar Cannon & Bell
Peer down the barrel of the monstrous Tsar Cannon and pose for a picture
beside the oversized Tsar Bell, both of which are too big to serve their
intended purpose.

nnunciation athedral

dmire the artistic
astery of Russia's
eatest icon painters –
eophanes the Greek
d Andrei Rublyov –
ho are responsible for
any of the icons in the
esis and festival rows
the iconostasis.

Archangel Cathedral
See the final resting
place of princes and
emperors who ruled
Russia for more than
300 years, including
the visionary Ivan the
Great, the tortured
Ivan theTerrible
and the tragic
Tsarevitch Dmitry.

KEN SCICLUNA / GETTY IMAGES ©

HIGHLIGHTS FROM THE KREMLIN CHURCHES

Assumption Cathedral Near the south wall is a tent-roofed, wooden throne made in 1551 for Ivan the Terrible, known as the Throne of Monomakh. One of the oldest Russian icons, the 12th-century red-clothed St George (Svyatoy Georgy) from Novgorod, is positioned by the north wall.

Archangel Cathedral The tombs of all Muscovy's rulers from the 1320s to the 1690s are here, except Boris Godunov. The bodies are buried underground, beneath the 17th-century sarcophagi and 19th-century copper covers. Tsarevich Dmitry, a son of Ivan the Terrible who died mysteriously in 1591, lies beneath a painted stone canopy.

Annunciation Cathedral The iconostasis in the central cathedral contains icons by three of the greatest medieval Russian artists. Theophanes the Greek likely painted the six icons at the right-hand end of the Deesis row (the biggest of the six tiers of the iconostasis). Andrei Rublyov is reckoned to be the artist of most of the paintings at the left end of the festival row – above the Deesis row – while the seven at the right-hand end are attributed to Prokhor of Gorodets.

buildings that are not open to the public, before reaching the main sights at Sobornaya pl (Cathedral Square). There is an alternate entrance at **Borovitskaya Tower** (Map p63) for those heading straight to the Armoury or the Diamond Fund Exhibition.

Book in advance for tours:

➜ **Kremlin Excursion Office** (Map p63; ☑ 495-697 0349; www.kremlin.museum. ru; Alexander Garden; 90-min tour R2500; Ⓜ Aleksandrovsky Sad)

➜ **Capital Tours** (Map p63; ☑ 495-232 2442; www.capitaltours.ru; Gostiny Dvor, ul Ilynka 4, entry 6; Kremlin tours R1600, other tours R900; ⊙10am Fri-Wed; Ⓜ Kitay-Gorod)

Patriarch's Palace　　　　HISTORIC BUILDING
(Патриарший дворец; Map p63) Built for Patriarch Nikon mostly in the mid-17th century, the highlight of the Patriarch's Palace is perhaps the ceremonial **Cross Hall** (Крестовая палата), where the tsar's and ambassadorial feasts were held. From here you can access the five-domed **Church of the Twelve Apostles** (Церковь двенадцати апостолов), which has a gilded, wooden iconostasis and a collection of icons by leading 17th-century icon painters.

Assumption Cathedral　　　　CHURCH
(Успенский собор; Map p63) On the northern side of Sobornaya pl, with five golden helmet domes and four semicircular gables facing the square, the Assumption Cathedral is the focal church of prerevolutionary Russia and the burial place of most of the heads of the Russian Orthodox Church from the 1320s to 1700. A striking 1660s fresco of the Virgin Mary faces Sobornaya pl, above

the door once used for royal processions. If you have limited time in the Kremlin, come straight here.

Ivan The Great Bell Tower　　　　TOWER
(Колокольня Ивана Великого; Map p63) With its two golden domes rising above the eastern side of Sobornaya pl, the Ivan the Great Bell Tower is the Kremlin's tallest structure – a landmark visible from 30km away. Before the 20th century it was forbidden to build any higher in Moscow.

Archangel Cathedral　　　　CHURCH
(Архангельский собор; Map p63) The Archangel Cathedral at the southeastern corner of Sobornaya pl, was for centuries the coronation, wedding and burial church of tsars. It was built by Ivan Kalita in 1333 to commemorate the end of the great famine, and dedicated to Archangel Michael, guardian of the Moscow princes. By the early 16th century it fell into disrepair and was rebuilt between 1505 and 1508 by the Italian architect Alevisio Novi.

Annunciation Cathedral　　　　CHURCH
(Благовещенский собор; Map p63; Blagoveshchensky sobor) The Annunciation Cathedral, at the southwest corner of Sobornaya pl, contains the celebrated icons of master painter Theophanes the Greek. They have a timeless beauty that appeals even to those usually left cold by icons.

★ **Armoury**　　　　MUSEUM
(Оружейная палата; Map p63; adult/student R700/250; ⊙10am, noon, 2.30pm & 4.30pm; Ⓜ Aleksandrovsky Sad) The Armoury dates back to 1511, when it was founded under

Kremlin & Red Square

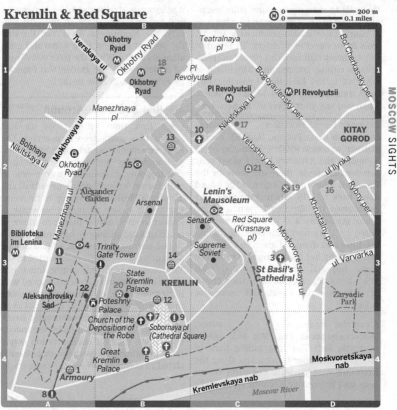

Kremlin & Red Square

◎ Top Sights
1 Armoury	A4
2 Lenin's Mausoleum	C2
3 St Basil's Cathedral	C3

◎ Sights
4 Alexander Garden	A3
5 Annunciation Cathedral	B4
6 Archangel Cathedral	B4
7 Assumption Cathedral	B4
8 Borovitskaya Tower	A4
Diamond Fund Exhibition	(see 1)
9 Ivan The Great Bell Tower	B4
10 Kazan Cathedral	C2
11 Kutafya Tower	A3
12 Patriarch's Palace	B3
13 State History Museum	B2
14 The Kremlin	B3
15 Tomb of the Unknown Soldier	B2

☉ Activities, Courses & Tours
16 Capital Tours	D2
Kremlin Excursion Office	(see 22)
17 Moscow Free Tour	C2

⊜ Sleeping
18 Four Seasons Moscow	B1

⊗ Eating
19 Stolovaya 57	D2

⊕ Entertainment
20 Kremlin Ballet	B3

⊟ Shopping
21 GUM	C2

⊕ Information
22 Kremlin Ticket Office	A3

Vasily III to manufacture and store weapons, imperial arms and regalia for the royal court. Later it also produced jewellery, icon frames and embroidery. To this day, the Armoury still contains plenty of treasures for ogling, and remains a highlight of any visit to the Kremlin. If possible, buy your time-specific ticket to the Armoury when you buy your ticket to the Kremlin.

Diamond Fund Exhibition   MUSEUM
(Алмазный фонд России; Map p63; www.al-mazi.net; admission R500; ☉10am-1pm, 2-5pm Fri-Wed) If the Armoury hasn't sated your lust for diamonds, there are more in the Diamond Fund Exhibition. The fund dates back to 1719, when Peter the Great established the Russian Crown treasury. These gemstones and jewellery were garnered by tsars and empresses, including the 190-carat diamond given to Catherine the Great by her lover Grigory Orlov. The Great Imperial Crown, encrusted with 4936 diamonds, was the coronation crown of Catherine the Great and successive rulers.

Alexander Garden   GARDENS
(Александровский сад; Map p63; Ⓜ Aleksandrovsky Sad) The first public park in Moscow, Alexander Garden sits along the Kremlin's western wall. Colourful flower beds and impressive Kremlin views make it a favourite strolling spot for Muscovites and tourists alike. Back in the 17th century, the Neglinnaya River ran through the present gardens, with dams and mills along its banks. When the river was diverted underground, the garden was founded by architect Osip Bove in 1821.

◉ Red Square & Around

One's first time setting foot on Red Square is a guaranteed awe-striker. The vast rectangular stretch of cobblestones, surrounded by architectural marvels, is jaw-dropping, gasp-inducing gorgeous. In old Russian 'krasny' meant 'beautiful', and 'Krasnaya Ploshchad' lives up to its name. Further, it evokes an incredible sense of import to stroll across the place where so much of Russian history has unfolded.

The narrow streets east of Red Square are known as Kitay Gorod. Settled in the 13th century as a trade centre, this is one of the oldest parts of Moscow, packed with old architecture, charming churches and inviting shops and cafes. Nikolskaya ul is a pleasant pedestrian shopping street, while ul Varvarka contains the neighbourhood's greatest concentration of ancient buildings. The area south of here is slated to become the new Zaryadie Park.

MOSCOW IN...

Two Days

Spend a day seeing what makes Moscow famous: **St Basil's Cathedral**, **Lenin's Mausoleum** and the **Kremlin** (p58). Allow a few hours in the afternoon to gawk at the gold and gems in the **Armoury** (p62). In the evening, attend an opera at the **Bolshoi Theatre** (p82) or dine like a tsar at **Café Pushkin** (p79).

On your second day, admire the art and architecture at **Novodevichy Convent** (p71), then head next door to the eponymous cemetery, where many famous political and cultural figures are laid to rest. In the afternoon, make your way across the river to Kievsky vokzal, where you can hop on board a **river cruise** (p73) along the Moscow River.

Four Days

Art lovers should spend their third day at the **State Tretyakov Gallery** (p71), which houses a world-class collection of Russian art. In the late afternoon, head to whimsical **Art Muzeon** (p71) and fun-filled **Gorky Park** (p72). In the evening, wander around the former **Red October** (p71) factory for dinner, drinks or other entertainment.

Reserve the next morning for shopping at **Izmaylovsky Market** (p84), crammed with souvenir stalls. On your way back into the centre, take a tour around the **Moscow metro** (www.mosmetro.ru), admiring the architectural achievement and the socialist realist artwork in this marvel of urban design. End up on **ul Arbat**, where you can take a seat at a pavement cafe and be entertained by portrait painters, street musicians and other passers-by.

LENIN UNDER GLASS

Red Square is home to the world's most famous mummy, that of Vladimir Lenin. When he died of a massive stroke (on 22 January 1924, aged 53), a long line of mourners patiently gathered in winter's harshness for weeks to glimpse the body as it lay in state. Inspired by the spectacle, Stalin proposed that the father of Soviet communism should continue to serve the cause as a holy relic. So the decision was made to preserve Lenin's corpse for perpetuity, against the vehement protests of his widow, as well as his own expressed desire to be buried next to his mother in St Petersburg.

Boris Zbarsky, a biochemist, and Vladimir Vorobyov, an anatomist, were issued a political order to put a stop to the natural decomposition of the body. The pair worked frantically in a secret laboratory in search of a long-term chemical solution. In the meantime, the body's dark spots were bleached, and the lips and eyes sewn tight. The brain was removed and taken to another secret laboratory, to be sliced and diced by scientists for the next 40 years in the hope of revealing its hidden genius.

In July 1924 the scientists hit upon a formula to successfully arrest the decaying process, but their method was kept secret. This necrotic craft was passed on to Zbarsky's son, who ran the Kremlin's covert embalming lab for decades. After the fall of communism, Zbarsky came clean: the body is wiped down every few days, and then, every 18 months, thoroughly examined and submerged in a tub of chemicals, including paraffin wax. The institute has now gone commercial, offering its services and secrets to wannabe immortals for a mere million dollars.

Every so often, politicians express intentions to heed Lenin's request and bury him in St Petersburg, but it usually sets off a furore from the political left as well as more muted objections from Moscow tour operators. It seems that the mausoleum, the most sacred shrine of Soviet communism, and the mummy, the literal embodiment of the Russian revolution, will remain in place for at least several more years.

⭐ **St Basil's Cathedral** CHURCH
(Покровский собор, Храм Василия Блаженного; Map p63; www.saintbasil.ru; adult/student R250/50, audio guide R200; ⊗ 11am-5pm; Ⓜ Ploshchad Revolyutsii) At the southern end of Red Square stands the icon of Russia: St Basil's Cathedral. This crazy confusion of colours, patterns and shapes is the culmination of a style that is unique to Russian architecture. In 1552 Ivan the Terrible captured the Tatar stronghold of Kazan on the Feast of Intercession. He commissioned this landmark church, officially the Intercession Cathedral, to commemorate the victory. Created from 1555 to 1561, this masterpiece would become the ultimate symbol of Russia.

⭐ **Lenin's Mausoleum** MEMORIAL
(Мавзолей Ленина; Map p63; www.lenin.ru; ⊗ 10am-1pm Tue-Thu, Sat; Ⓜ Ploshchad Revolyutsii) FREE Although Vladimir Ilych requested that he be buried beside his mum in St Petersburg, he still lies in state at the foot of the Kremlin wall, receiving visitors who come to pay their respects. Line up at the western corner of Red Square (near the entrance to Alexander Garden) to see the embalmed leader, who has been here since 1924. Note that photography is not allowed; and stern guards ensure that all visitors remain respectful and silent.

State History Museum MUSEUM
(Государственный исторический музей; Map p63; www.shm.ru; Krasnaya pl 1; adult/student R300/100, audio guide R300; ⊗ 10am-6pm Wed & Fri-Mon, 11am-9pm Thu; Ⓜ Okhotny Ryad) At the northern end of Red Square, the State History Museum has an enormous collection covering the whole Russian Empire from the time of the Stone Age. The building, dating from the late 19th century, is itself an attraction – each room is in the style of a different period or region, some with highly decorated walls echoing old Russian churches.

◉ Tverskoy District

The streets around Tverskaya ul comprise the vibrant Tverskoy District, characterised by old architecture and new commerce. Small lanes such as Kamergersky pereulok and Stoleshnikov pereulok are among Moscow's trendiest places to sip a coffee and watch the big-city bustle.

Central Moscow

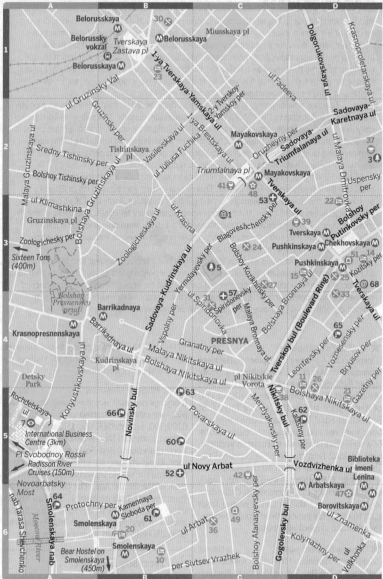

Moscow Museum of Modern Art MUSEUM
(Московский музей современного искусства; MMOMA; Map p66; www.mmoma.ru; ul Petrovka 25; adult/student R250/100; ⊙noon-8pm Tue-Wed & Fri-Sun, 1-9pm Thu; Ⓜ Chekhovskaya) A pet project of the ubiquitous Zurab Tserete-li, this museum is housed in a classical 18th-century merchant's home, originally designed by Matvei Kazakov (architect of the Kremlin Senate). It is the perfect light-filled setting for an impressive collection of 20th-century paintings, sculptures and

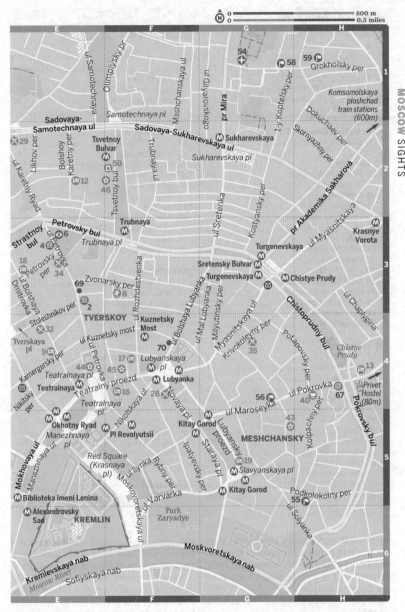

graphics, which include both Russian and foreign artists. The highlight is the collection of avant-garde art, with works by Chagall, Kandinsky and Malevich.

Upper St Peter Monastery   MONASTERY
(Петровский монастырь; Map p66; cnr ul Petrovka & Petrovsky bul; ⊗8am-8pm; MChekhovskaya)
The Upper St Peter Monastery was founded in the 1380s as part of an early defensive ring around Moscow. The main, onion-domed

Central Moscow

Virgin of Bogolyubovo Church dates from the late 17th century. The loveliest structure is the brick Cathedral of Metropolitan Pyotr, restored with a shingle roof. (When Peter the Great ousted the Regent Sofia in 1690, his mother was so pleased she built him this church).

Gulag History Museum   MUSEUM
(Исторический музей ГУЛАГ; Map p66; ☑495-621 7346; www.gmig.ru; ul Petrovka 16; adult/student R150/20; ⊙11am-6pm Tue-Wed & Fri-Sun, noon-8pm Thu; Ⓜ Teatralnaya) Amid all the swanky shops on ul Petrovka, an arch-

way leads to a courtyard that is strung with barbed wire and hung with portraits of political prisoners. This is the entrance to a unique museum dedicated to the Chief Administration of Corrective Labour Camps and Colonies, better known as the Gulag. Guides dressed like guards describe the vast network of labour camps that once existed in the former Soviet Union and recount the horrors of camp life.

Hermitage Gardens   PARK
(Сады Эрмитажа; Map p66; mosgorsad.ru; ul Karetny Ryad 3; ⊙24hr; Ⓜ Pushkinskaya) FREE this

This small, charming garden is full to the brim with all the things that have improved Moscow parks no end in recent years. Today it is possibly the most happening place in Moscow, where art, food and crafts festivals, and concerts occur almost weekly, especially in summer. Apart from welcoming lawns and benches, it boasts a large playground for children, a summer cinema and a cluster of curious food and crafts kiosks. Come here to unwind and mingle with the coolest Muscovites.

Jewish Museum & Centre of Tolerance
MUSEUM

(Еврейский музей и Центр терпимости; www.jewish-museum.ru; ul Obraztsova 11 str 1a; adult/student R400/200; ☺ noon-10pm Sun-Thu; Ⓜ Novoslobodskaya) Occupying a heritage garage, purpose-built to house a fleet of Leyland double-deckers that plied Moscow streets in the 1920s, this vast museum, filled with cutting-edge multimedia technology, tackles the uneasy subject of relations between Jews and the Russian state over centuries. The exhibition tells the stories of pogroms, Jewish revolutionaries, the Holocaust and Soviet anti-Semitism in a calm and balanced manner. The somewhat limited collection of material exhibits is compensated for by the abundance of interactive video displays.

⊚ Presnya

Presnya is Moscow's largest administrative district, encompassing some of the capital's oldest neighbourhoods as well as its newest development at Moscow City. The area around Patriarch's Ponds has become one of the city's best areas for dining.

Patriarch's Ponds
PARK

(Патриаршие пруды; Map p66; Bolshoy Patriarshy per; Ⓜ Mayakovskaya) Patriarch's Ponds harks back to Soviet days, when the parks were populated with children and *babushky*. You'll see grandmothers pushing strollers and lovers kissing on park benches. In summer children romp on the swings, while winter sees them ice skating on the pond. The small park has a huge statue of 19th-century Russian writer Ivan Krylov, known to Russian children for his didactic tales.

Bulgakov House-Museum
MUSEUM

(Дом-музей Булгакова; Map p66; www.dom-bulgakova.ru; Bolshaya Sadovaya ul 10; admission R70; ☺ 1-11pm, to 1am Fri & Sat; Ⓜ Mayakovskaya)

TOMB OF THE UNKNOWN SOLDIER

The **Tomb of the Unknown Soldier** (Могила неизвестного солдата; Map p63) at the north end of Alexander Garden is a kind of national pilgrimage spot, where newlyweds bring flowers and have their pictures taken. The inscription reads: 'Your name is unknown, your deeds immortal.' Every hour on the hour, the guards perform a perfectly synchronized ceremony to change the guards on duty.

Author of *The Master and Margarita* and *Heart of a Dog*, Mikhail Bulgakov was a Soviet-era novelist who was labelled a counter-revolutionary and was censored throughout his life. His most celebrated novels were published posthumously, earning him a sort of cult following in the late Soviet period. Bulgakov lived with his wife Yelena Shilovskaya (the inspiration for Margarita) in a flat in this block, which now houses a small museum and theatre.

White House
NOTABLE BUILDING

(Белый дом; Map p66; Krasnopresnenskaya nab 2; Ⓜ Krasnopresnenskaya) The White House – officially the House of Government of the Russian Federation – fronts a stately bend in the Moscow River, just north of the Novoarbatsky most.

⊚ Arbat & Khamovniki

The side-by-side districts of Arbat and Khamovniki are rich with culture. Moscow's most famous street, **ul Arbat**, is something of an art market, complete with portrait painters and soapbox poets, while the nearby streets are lined with museums and galleries.

Pushkin Museum of Fine Arts
MUSEUM

(Музей изобразительных искусств им. Пушкина; Map p70; www.arts-museum.ru; ul Volkhonka 12; admission each branch R200-300; ☺ 10am-7pm Tue-Sun, to 9pm Thu; Ⓜ Kropotkinskaya) This is Moscow's premier foreign-art museum, showing off a broad selection of European works, including masterpieces from ancient civilisations, Italian Renaissance and Dutch Golden Age.

Zamoskvorechie

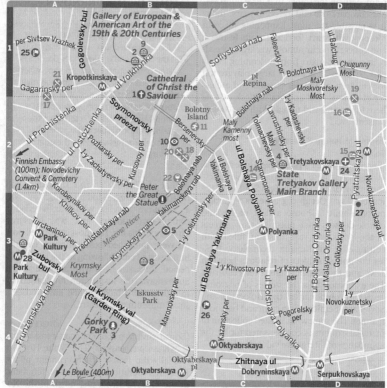

★ **Gallery of European & American Art of the 19th & 20th Centuries** MUSEUM
(Map p70; www.newpaintart.ru; ul Volkhonka 14; adult/child R300/150; MKropotkinskaya) This branch of the Pushkin Museum of Fine Arts contains a famed assemblage of French Impressionist works, based on the collection of two well-known Moscow art patrons, Sergei Shchukin and Ivan Morozov. It includes representative paintings by Degas, Manet, Renoir and Pisarro, with an entire room dedicated to Monet.

★ **Cathedral of Christ the Saviour** CHURCH
(Храм Христа Спасителя; Map p70; ul Volkhonka 15; ☺1-5pm Mon, 10am-5pm Tue-Sun; MKropotkinskaya) **FREE** This gargantuan cathedral was completed in 1997 – just in time to celebrate Moscow's 850th birthday. It is amazingly opulent, garishly grandiose and truly historic. The cathedral's sheer size and splendour guarantee its role as a love-it-or-hate-it landmark. Considering Stalin's plan for this site (a Palace of Soviets topped with a 100m statue of Lenin), Muscovites should at least be grateful they can admire the shiny domes of a church instead of the shiny dome of Ilych's head.

Moscow Museum MUSEUM
(Музей Москвы; Map p70; www.mosmuseum.ru; Zubovsky bul 2; adult/child R300/120; ☺10am-8pm Tue-Wed & Fri-Sun, 11am-9pm Thu; ♿; MPark Kultury) Formerly the Museum of the History of Moscow, this excellent museum has a new name, a new location and a new mission. The permanent history exhibit demonstrates how the city has spread from its starting point at the Kremlin. It is heavy on artefacts from the 13th and 14th centuries, especially household items and weapons. More exciting, the museum has space to launch thought-provoking temporary exhibits, including artists' and other local perspectives on the city.

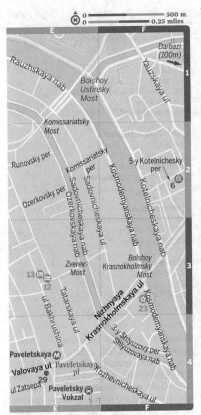

Zamoskvorechie

Zamoskvorechie (meaning 'Beyond the Moscow River') stretches south from opposite the Kremlin, inside a big river loop.

★ State Tretyakov Gallery Main Branch
GALLERY

(Главный отдел Государственной Третьяковской галереи; Map p70; www.tretyakovgallery.ru/en/; Lavrushinsky per 10; adult/student R400/250; ⊗10am-6pm Tue, Wed, Sat & Sun, to 9pm Thu & Fri, ticket office closes 1hr before closing; Ⓜ Tretyakovskaya) The exotic *boyar* castle on a little lane in Zamoskvorechie contains the main branch of the State Tretyakov Gallery, housing the world's best collection of Russian icons and an outstanding collection of other prerevolutionary Russian art. Show up early to beat the queues.

Red October
ART CENTRE

(Завод Красный Октябрь; Map p70; Bersenevskaya nab; Ⓜ Kropotkinskaya) **FREE** This defiant island of Russian modernity and European-ness is a vibrant arts centre filled with cool bars, restaurants and galleries. With an aptly revolutionary name, the former Red October chocolate factory looks straight into Kremlin's eyes – a vivid reminder that Russia is not all about totalitarian control and persecution.

New Tretyakov Gallery
GALLERY

(Новая Третьяковская галерея; Map p70; www.tretyakovgallery.ru/en/; ul Krymsky val 10; adult/student R400/250; ⊗10am-6pm Tue-Wed & Sat & Sun, 10am-9pm Thu & Fri, ticket office closes 1hr before; Ⓜ Park Kultury) The premier venue for 20th-century Russian art is this branch of the State Tretyakov Gallery, better known as the New Tretyakov. This place has much more than the typical socialist realist images of muscle-bound men wielding scythes, and busty women milking cows (although there's that, too). The exhibits showcase avant-garde artists such as Malevich, Kandinsky, Chagall, Goncharova and Popova.

Art Muzeon & Krymskaya Naberezhnaya
SCULPTURE PARK

(Map p70; ul Krymsky val 10; Ⓜ Park Kultury) **FREE** Now fully revamped and merged with the wonderfully reconstructed Krymskaya Naberezhnaya embankment, is this motley collection of (mostly kitschy) sculpture and monuments to Soviet idols (Stalin, Sverdlov, a selection of Lenins and Brezhnevs) that were ripped from their pedestals in the

Novodevichy Convent & Cemetery
CONVENT

(Новодевичий монастырь и кладбище; www.novodev.msk.ru; adult/child R300/100; ⊗8am-8pm, museums 9am-5pm; Ⓜ Sportivnaya) A cluster of sparkling domes behind turreted walls on the Moscow River, Novodevichy Convent is notorious as the place where Peter the Great imprisoned his half-sister Sofia for her part in the Streltsy rebellion. The oldest and most dominant building in the grounds is the white Smolensk Cathedral, its sumptuous interior covered in 16th-century frescoes. Adjacent to the convent, the cemetery (Новодевичье кладбище; ⊗9am-5pm; Ⓜ Sportivnaya) **FREE** is among Moscow's most prestigious resting places – a veritable 'who's who' of Russian politics and culture.

Zamoskvorechie

post-1991 wave of anti-Soviet feeling. All of these stand in a lovely garden with boardwalks and many inviting benches.

★ **Gorky Park**　　　　　　　　　　PARK

(Парк Горького; Map p70; ◎24hr; ▣; Ⓜ Oktyabrskaya) FREE Moscow's main escape from the city within the city is not your conventional expanse of nature preserved deep inside an urban jungle. It is not a fun fair either, though it used to be one. Its official name says it all – Maxim Gorky's Central Park of Culture & Leisure. That's exactly what it provides: culture and leisure in all shapes and forms. Designed by avant-garde architect Konstantin Melnikov as a piece of communist utopia in the 1920s, these days it showcases the enlightened transformation Moscow has undergone in the recent past.

◎ Meshchansky & Basmanny

The Meshchansky and Basmanny districts flank the little Yauza River in the eastern part of the city. The latter is largely comprised of old factories, now taken over by hipsters and housing innovative postmodern galleries and clubs.

Bunker-42 Cold War Museum　　MUSEUM

(Map p70; ☑495-500 0554; www.bunker42.com; 5-ya Kotelnichesky per 11; admission R1300; ◎by appointment; Ⓜ Taganskaya) On a quiet side street near Taganskaya pl, a nondescript neoclassical building is the gateway to the secret Cold War–era communications centre. The facility was meant to serve as the communications headquarters in the event of a nuclear attack. As such, the building was just a shell, serving as an entryway to the 7000-sq-m space 60m underground. Now in private hands, the facility has been converted into a sort of museum dedicated to the Cold War.

Vinzavod　　　　　　　　　　　GALLERY

(Винзавод; www.winzavod.ru; 4 Syromyatnichesky per 1; Ⓜ Chkalovskaya) FREE Formerly a wine-bottling factory, this facility was converted into exhibit and studio space for Moscow artists in 2007. The post-industrial complex is now home to Moscow's most prestigious art galleries, including M&J Guelman, Aidan and XL. The complex also contains several photo galleries, a design studio and furniture showroom, and a concept clothing store, as well as a few funky gift shops and boutiques.

Even if you're not in the market for the next Black Square, you can lounge with the

PARK POBEDY AT POKLONNAYA HILL

Magnificent **Park Pobedy (Victory Park)** (Парк Победы; Kutuzovsky pr; ⊘dawn-dusk; Ⓜ Park Pobedy) **FREE** is a huge memorial complex commemorating the sacrifice and celebrating the triumph of the Great Patriotic War – as WWII is known in Russia. The dominant monument is an enormous obelisk, topped with a sculpture of St George slaying the dragon. Its height is exactly 141.8m, with every 10cm representing one day of the war.

The centrepiece **Museum of the Great Patriotic War** (Центральный музей Великой Отечественной Войны; www.poklonnayagora.ru; ul Bratiev Fonchenko 10; adult/child R250/100; ⊘10am-6pm Tue-Sun Nov-Mar, to 8pm Apr-Oct; Ⓜ Park Pobedy) contains two impressive memorial rooms, as well as an exhibit of dioramas of every major WWII battle involving Soviet troops. Exhibits highlight the many heroes of the Soviet Union, as well as authentic wartime memorabilia.

The unique **Exposition of Military Equipment** (Площадка боевой техники; www. poklonnayagora.ru; adult/child R250/100; ⊘10am-7pm Tue-Sun; Ⓜ Park Pobedy) displays more than 300 examples of weapons and military equipment from the WWII era.

cool cats at the cafe or catch a flick or a lecture at one of the entertainment venues.

🏃 Activities

Sanduny Baths　　　　　　BATHHOUSE
(Map p66; ☎495-628 4633; www.sanduny.ru; Neglinnaya ul 14; male & female 1st class R1500, male 2nd class & female premium R1850, male premium class R2300; ⊘8am-10pm; Ⓜ Kuznetsky Most) Sanduny is the oldest and most luxurious *banya* in the city. The Gothic Room is a work of art with its rich wood carving, while the main shower room has an aristocratic Roman feel to it. There are several classes, as on trains, though regulars say that, here, second male class is actually better than the premium class.

Bersenevskiye Bany　　　　BATHHOUSE
(Берсеневские бани; Map p70; ☎495-281 5086; Bersenevskaya nab 16 str 5; 2 hr R1200, each subsequent hr R600; ⊘8am-11pm, women only Mon-Wed, men only Thu-Sun) Proof that Red October hipsters have no aversion to century-old traditions, this new bathhouse is both elegant and competently run. The vaulted cellars of the former Smirnov distillery (yes, this is the birthplace of Smirnoff vodka) create just the right circulation in the steam room. Unless you are an old Russian *banya* hand, splash some extra money and let them pamper you. If being beaten with twigs qualifies as pampering, that is.

Capital Shipping Co　　　　BOAT TRIPS
(ССК, Столичная Судоходная Компания; ☎495-225 6070; www.cck-ship.ru; 90-min tour adult/child R500/300, 24hr pass R800/400) Ferries ply the Moscow River from May to

September (every 20 minutes); board at any dock along the route. Originally, this was simply a form of transportation, but visitors realised that riding the entire route (1½ hours) was a great way to see the city. Alternatively, buy a full-day pass, which allows you to get on and off at will.

Radisson River Cruises　　　BOAT TRIPS
(www.radisson-cruise.ru; 2.5hr cruise adult/child R900/650, 1.5hr cruise R650/450; ⊘1-9pm; Ⓜ Kievskaya) The Radisson operates big river boats that cart 140 people up and down the Moscow River from the dock in front of the hotel and from the dock in Gorky Park. In summer there are five or six daily departures from each location. Boats are enclosed (and equipped with ice cutters), so the cruises run year-round, albeit less frequently in winter.

🎭 Festivals & Events

Golden Mask Festival　　　　THEATRE
(www.goldenmask.ru) This festival involves two months of performances by Russia's premier drama, opera, dance and musical performers, culminating in a prestigious awards ceremony in April.

Moscow International Film Festival　　FILM
(www.moscowfilmfestival.ru) This 10-day event in June/July attracts filmmakers from the US and Europe, as well as the most promising Russian artists. Films are shown at theatres around the city.

City Day　　　　　　　CULTURAL
City Day, or *den goroda* in Russian, celebrates Moscow's birthday on the first weekend in September. The day kicks off with

a festive parade, followed by live music on Red Square and plenty of food, fireworks and fun.

Moscow Biennale of Contemporary Art ART FESTIVAL
(www.moscowbiennale.ru) This month-long festival, held in odd-numbered years (and sometimes in different months), has the aim of establishing the capital as an international centre for contemporary art. Venues around the city exhibit works by artists from around the world.

December Nights Festival ART, MUSIC
(www.artsmuseum.ru) Perhaps Moscow's most prestigious music event, this annual festival in December is hosted at the Pushkin Museum of Fine Arts (p69), with a month of performances by high-profile musicians and accompanying art exhibits.

🛏 Sleeping

Moscow is flush with international luxury hotels, but more affordable hotels are harder to find. Fortunately, a slew of hostels have opened, offering adequate budget offerings. More midrange accommodations are now also appearing, usually in the form of 'mini-hotels'.

🛏 Kremlin & Kitay Gorod

★ **Hotel Metropol** HISTORIC HOTEL $$$
(Map p66; ☎499-501 7800; www.metropol-moscow.ru; Teatralny proezd 1/4; d R9930-11,400, break-fast R2000; ⊜❄@❄; Ⓜ Teatralnaya) Nothing short of an art nouveau masterpiece, the 1907 Metropol brings an artistic, historic touch to every nook and cranny, from the spectacular exterior to the grand lobby, to the individually decorated (but small) rooms. The breakfast buffet is ridiculously priced, but it's served under the restaurant's gorgeous stained glass ceiling.

🛏 Tverskoy

Godzillas Hostel HOSTEL $
(Map p66; ☎495-699 4223; www.godzillashostel.com; Bolshoy Karetny per 6; dm from R760, s/d R2400/2600; ❄@🛜; Ⓜ Tsvetnoy Bulvar) Tried and true, Godzillas is Moscow's best-known hostel, with dozens of beds spread out over four floors. The rooms come in various sizes, but they are all spacious and light-filled and painted in different colours. To cater to the many guests, there are bathroom facilities on each floor, three kitchens and a big living room with satellite TV.

Anti-Hostel Cosmic HOSTEL $
(Map p66; ☎499-390 8132; http://anti-hostel.ru/; ul Bolshaya Dmitrovka 7/5 str 3; capsules from R1350; 🛜; Ⓜ Teatralnaya) Occupying a converted apartment, this place marries the idea of hostel with that of capsule hotel. The location is hard to beat – Red Square is just a five-minute walk away. Capsules create a tiny, though comfortable universe for guests to enjoy on their own. There is also a nice common area to mingle with fellow capsule-dwellers.

iVAN Hostel HOSTEL $
(Map p66; ☎8-916-407 1178; www.ivanhostel.com; per Petrovsky 1/30 apt 23; dm from R750, d with shared bathroom from R2500; 🛜; Ⓜ Chekhovskaya) iVAN consists of two clean and quiet apartments located in the same tsarist-era residential building, a short walk from Pushkin square. Being a hostel, it naturally has dorms – and very nice ones at that – however its main virtue are several simply-furnished, but tastefully designed private rooms with whitewashed walls and large windows.

★ **Sleepbox Hotel** HOTEL $$
(Map p66; ☎495-989 4104; www.sleepbox-hotel.ru; ul 1st Tverskaya-Yamskaya 27; s without bathroom from R3200, d from R4700, q from R5500; ❄🛜; Ⓜ Belorusskaya) It might draw comparisons with capsule hotels, but it is actually better. Think a comfortable train compartment – it's close to what you get in this

---

SLEEPING PRICE RANGES

➡ **Budget** Budget accommodation is generally less than R3000. Budget accommodation is usually dorm style, although there are a few private rooms in this price range.

➡ **Midrange** Midrange accommodation falls between R3000 and R8000. This wide-ranging category includes privately owned 'minihotels' which usually occupy one or two floors in an apartment building. The rooms have been renovated to comfortably accommodate guests, but the hotel itself (which might have a dozen rooms or less) does not offer other facilities.

➡ **Top End** Top end starts at R8000 and goes all the way up.

immaculately clean and unusual hotel, conveniently located for those arriving by train from Sheremetyevo airport. Shared showers and toilets are very modern and clean; queues are uncommon.

Guest House Amelie GUESTHOUSE $$

(Map p66; ☑ 495-650 1789; www.hotel-amelie.ru; Strastnoy bul 4 str 3 apt 17; s/d without breakfast from R3000/3500; ☎; Ⓜ Chekhovskaya) Amelie benefits from its superb location right by Pushkin Square – it's unlikely you will find a room cheaper than this in the vicinity, and it's a very nicely furnished room, too! On the downside, the hotel is a converted apartment, which means shared bathrooms and an unmarked entrance located on Kozitsky per. Once you find this lane, look out for the entrance number in the building marked as per Kozitsky 3. Dial 17 to be let in.

Pushkin Hotel HOTEL $$

(Отель Пушкин; Map p66; ☑ 495-201 0222; http://otel-pushkin.ru; per Nastasyinsky 5 str 1; s/d from R7000/8000; ✳ ☎; Ⓜ Pushkinskaya) Just off the eponymous square, this hotel strives to fuse 19th-century style with the modern perception of comfort. We'd call it plush, if not for the tiny, B&B-style reception area. There is a restaurant in the premises, but no need to use it since the area is packed with great places to eat and drink.

The entrance was poorly marked when we visited, but it's the only one in the building, so hard to miss. Note huge discounts are available during weekends.

Hotel Savoy BOUTIQUE HOTEL $$$

(Отель Савой; Map p66; ☑ 495-620 8500; www.savoy.ru; ul Rozhdestvenka 3; s/d from R9500/12,600; ☻ ✳ ☎ ☒; Ⓜ Lubyanka) Built in 1912, the Savoy maintains an atmosphere of tsarist-era privilege for its guests, and is more intimate and affordable than other luxury hotels. All rooms are equipped with marble bathrooms and Italian fittings and furnishings. The state-of-the-art health club includes a glass-domed 20m swimming pool, complete with geysers and cascades to refresh tired bodies.

Presnya

Element Hotel HOTEL $$

(Отель Элемент; Map p66; ☑ 495-988 0064; www.hotel-element.ru; Bolshaya Nikitskaya ul 24/1, bldg 5; d R3800-4500; ☻ ✳ ☎; Ⓜ Arbatskaya) This location on trendy Bolshaya Nikitskaya is prime, and prices are unbeatable; so you'll

> ## ONCE & FUTURE HOTEL MOSKVA
>
> The story goes that Stalin was shown two possible designs for the Hotel Moskva on Manezhnaya pl. Not realising they were alternatives, he approved both. The builders did not dare point out his error, and so built half the hotel in constructivist style and half in Stalinist style. The incongruous result became a familiar and beloved feature of the Moscow landscape, even gracing the label of Stolichnaya vodka bottles.
>
> The infamous Hotel Moskva was demolished in 2003, but **Four Seasons** (Map p63; www.fourseasons.com; Okhotny ryad 2; ☻ ✳ ☎ ☒; Ⓜ Okhotny Ryad) has reconstructed the old exterior, complete with architectural quirks. The updated interior, of course, is contemporary and classy, with more than 200 luxurious rooms and suites, as well as a fancy spa and a glass-roofed swimming pool.

forgive the side-street entrance and the fact that rooms can be rented by the hour. It's actually a perfectly respectable place, with spotless rooms, pleasant decor and helpful staff. The cheapest rooms are tiny, so unless you're travelling solo, you'll probably want to upgrade.

★ Hotel de Paris BOUTIQUE HOTEL $$$

(Map p66; ☑ 495-777 0052; www.hotel-deparis. ru; Bolshaya Bronnaya ul 23, bldg 3; s/d from R9000/9450; ☻ ✳ ☎; Ⓜ Pushkinskaya) Steps from the madness of Tverskaya, this is a delightfully stylish hotel tucked into a quiet courtyard off the Boulevard Ring. Situated on the lower floors, the rooms do not get much natural light, but they feature king-size beds, Jacuzzi tubs and elegant design. Service is consistently friendly. Prices drop by 40% on weekends, offering terrific value.

Nikitskaya Hotel BOUTIQUE HOTEL $$$

(Гостиница Никитская; Map p66; ☑ 495-933 5001; www.assambleya-hotels.ru; Bolshaya Nikitskaya ul 12; s/d R9300/11,300, breakfast R500; ☻ ✳ ☎; Ⓜ Okhotny Ryad) If you like small hotels in quaint neighbourhoods you will love the Nikitskaya Hotel. While the building and rooms are perfectly maintained, the hotel preserves an old-fashioned atmosphere of cosiness and comfort. And you can't beat the

SERVICED APARTMENTS

Entrepreneurial Muscovites have begun renting out apartments on a short-term basis. Flats are equipped with kitchens and laundry facilities and they almost always offer wi-fi access. The rental agency usually makes arrangements for the flat to be cleaned every day or every few days. Often, a good-sized flat is available for the price of a hotel room, or less. It is an ideal solution for families or travellers in a small group.

Apartments are around R4300 to R8600 per night. Expect to pay more for fully renovated, Western-style apartments. Although there are usually discounts for longer stays, they are not significant, so these services are not ideal for long-term renters.

Enjoy Moscow (www.enjoymoscow.com; per night from US$155; ☎) This long-standing rental company has a range of apartments – mostly in the Tverskoy district – starting at US$155 per night. The apartments vary in size and decor, but the company provides responsive, reliable service.

HOFA (www.hofa.ru; apts from per night €44; ☎) For a truly authentic (and affordable) experience, stay in a Russian family's apartment (with or without the family). This long-standing agency offers apartments from €44 per night, as well as a variety of home-stay programs.

Intermark Serviced Apartments (www.intermarksa.ru; per night from R6800; ☎) Catering mostly to business travellers, Intermark offers four-star accommodations starting at R6800 per night.

Moscow Suites (www.moscowsuites.ru; studio per night from US$199; ☎) Slick apartments in central locations on Tverskaya or Novy Arbat. Services such as airport pick-up and visa support are included in the price, which starts at US$199 for a studio.

location, in the midst of the excellent restaurants and grand architecture of Bolshaya Nikitskaya. Breakfast is served in the popular attached restaurant, **Ugolyok** (Уголёк; Map p66; ☑495-629 0504; ⊙9am-midnight Sun-Wed, to 1.30am Thu-Sat).

🛏 Arbat & Khamovniki

Bear Hostel on Smolenskaya HOSTEL **$**
(☑495-649 6736; www.bear-hostels.com; Smolensky bul 15; dm R600-950, breakfast R130; ⊖✳@🅐; Ⓜ Smolenskaya) A smart, nononsense hostel with air-conditioned dorms (all co-ed) on the Garden Ring just west of the Arbat. The 50 wide bunk beds have guardrails to protect the young or inebriated. This is the nicest of the reliable Bear hostel chain, which also includes the run-of-the-mill Bear on Mayakovskaya and the larger flagship Bear on Arbatskaya.

Mercure Arbat Hotel BOUTIQUE HOTEL **$$**
(Гостиница Меркурий Арбат; Map p66; ☑495-225 0025; www.mercure.com; Smolenskaya pl 6; d from R7000; ⊖✳🅐; Ⓜ Smolenskaya) We're charmed by this sweet boutique hotel. It's not much to look at on the outside, but the rooms are attractive and rather plush to boot. The most affordable ones have queen-size beds, work space, flat-screen TVs and chic bathrooms with basin sinks. It's surprisingly quiet for its location right on the Garden Ring. Excellent value, especially on weekends. You'll pay extra for the big buffet breakfast.

★**Blues Hotel** BOUTIQUE HOTEL **$$**
(☑495-961 1161; www.blues-hotel.ru; ul Dovatora 8; s/d from R5800/6300; ⊖✳🅐; Ⓜ Sportivnaya) The location is not exactly central, but is not a disadvantage. It is steps from the red-line metro (five stops to Red Square) and a few blocks from Novodevichy, with several worthwhile restaurants in the vicinity. Considering that, this friendly, affordable boutique hotel is a gem, offering stylish, spotless rooms with king-size beds and flat-screen TVs. Further discounts on weekends.

Bulgakov Mini-Hotel HOTEL **$$**
(Map p66; ☑495-229 8018; www.bulgakovhotel.com; ul Arbat 49; d R4000; ⊖@🅐; Ⓜ Smolenskaya) The classy rooms, graced with high ceilings and *Master-and-Margarita*-inspired art, are as good as it gets in Moscow for this price, especially considering the primo location. The bathrooms are tiny but they are private. Enter the courtyard from Plotnikov per and use entrance No 2.

Zamoskvorechie

Three Penguins
HOSTEL $

(Три Пингвина; Map p70; ☑8-910-446 1778; www.3penguins.ru; ul Pyatnitskaya 20 str 2; dm/d R750/R2600; �'; MNovokuznetskaya) It's a very small hostel located in a converted flat with a comfy (we'd even say intimate) common area in the building best identified by Café Illarion, just off ul Pyatnitskaya. Apart from the dorms, it features four doubles – two regular and two with bunk beds.

Weekend Inn Apartments
GUESTHOUSE $$

(Map p70; ☑495-648 4047; www.weekend-inn.ru; ul Pyatnitskaya 10 str 1; d/tr from R3900/4500; MNovokuznetskaya) A short walk from the Kremlin across the river, this modest establishment occupies two upper floors in a 19th-century building. Rooms are spacious, with white-washed walls and minimalist design. Shared bathrooms are immaculately clean and there is a common kitchen area, but there's honestly no reason to bother cooking – the area is packed with cafes.

Park Inn Sadu
HOTEL $$

(Map p70; ☑495-644 4844; www.parkinn.ru; ul Bolshaya Polyanka 17; s/d from R3900/4500; ❄'; MPolyanka) It's a very regular branch of the Park Inn – think slightly impersonal, predictable comforts – which boasts a prime location within walking distance of the Kremlin and the Red October cluster of bars and galleries. Prices fall to a jaw-dropping low in the middle of summer.

IBIS Bakhrushina
HOTEL $$

(Map p70; ☑495-720 5301; www.ibis.com; ul Bakhrushina 11; r from R3990; ❄'; MPaveletskaya) The IBIS's latest incursion into the city centre has improved the hotel scene here in a big way. Yes, it's just another IBIS; but in Moscow knowing exactly what you're getting is a big deal: affordable, comfortable rooms and professional, reliable service. Spa facilities in the adjacent Mercure hotel are available at extra charge.

Mercure Moscow Paveletskaya
HOTEL $$

(Map p70; ☑495-720 5301; www.mercure.com; ul Bakhrushina 11; r from R5900; '; MPaveletskaya) This Mercure branch seems to consist entirely of virtues. Convenient for Domodedovo airport trains and close to Paveletskaya metro station, it is a quality hotel with plush rooms (purple colour prevailing), located in a quiet street of portly 19th-century houses,

offering four-star comforts for a price that's hard to come by in Moscow.

Meshchansky & Basmanny

Privet Hostel
HOSTEL $

(Хостел Привет; ☑495-374 5949; www.privet hostels.ru; per Podsosensky 3, str 2; dm from R800; '; MKurskaya) Declaring itself the largest hostel in the ex USSR, Privet occupies a mansion in the sweet and central Chistye Prudy neighbourhood. All painted in deep purple, four- and six-bed dorms have solid wooden bunk beds with orthopaedic mattresses, and some are equipped with smallish working tables. Showers and toilets look almost luxurious by Russian hostel standards.

Also on the premises is a cafe serving breakfasts (at extra charge), a small communal kitchen, a gym and a small cinema showing films in Russian and English. The entrance is on per Barashevsky.

Kitay-Gorod Hotel
HOTEL $$

(Отель Китай-Город; Map p66; ☑495-991 9971; www.otel-kg.ru; Lubyansky proezd 25; s R3800-5500, d R5200-7500; ◐❄'; MKitay-Gorod) A rare chance for budget-conscious travellers to stay this close to Red Square, not to mention easy access to the metro and many restaurants in the vicinity. Forty-six small but comfortable rooms are situated on two floors of this residential building. The location can be noisy: it's worth requesting air-con as you'll want to keep your windows closed. Prices are lower on weekends.

Godzillas Urban Jungle Lodge
GUESTHOUSE $$

(Map p66; ☑8-925-347 4677; www.godzillas hostel.com/ujl/; ul Pokrovka 21, 3rd fl; s/d with shared bathroom R2450/R3150; '; MChistye Prudy) A branch of Moscow's most popular hostel, this place has about a dozen funky-looking singles and doubles above the popular Coffee Bean cafe in one of the city's loveliest neighbourhoods. Bathrooms are shared, and it's a bit of a walk up a steep and slightly off-putting staircase. But it is about as good as it gets for this price.

Eating

In recent years, Moscow has blossomed into a culinary capital. Many restaurants, especially top-end eateries, accept credit cards, and almost all restaurants have English-language menus. Discounted 'business lunch'

WORTH A TRIP

VDNKH & OSTANKINO

Palaces for workers! There is hardly a better place to see this slogan put into practice than at VDNKh, which stands for Exhibition of Achievements of the National Economy. **VDNKh** (Ⓜ VDNKh) is like a Stalinesque theme park, with palatial pavilions designed each in its own unique style to represent all Soviet republics and various industries, from geology to space exploration.

The highlights are two opulently decorated fountains. Positioned right behind the main gates, People's Friendship Fountain is surrounded by 16 gilded female figures dressed in ethnic costumes representing Soviet republics (the mysterious 16th figure stands for Karelo-Finnish republic disbanded in 1956).

On the approaches to VDNKh from the metro, the soaring 100m titanium obelisk is a monument 'To the Conquerors of Space', built in 1964 to commemorate the launch of Sputnik. In its base is the **Cosmonautics Museum** (kosmo-museum.ru; admission R200; 11am-7pm Tue-Sun, 11am-9pm Thu ; Ⓜ VDNKh) featuring cool space paraphernalia such as the first Soviet rocket engine and the moon-rover Lunokhod.

The looming **Ostankino TV Tower** (Останкинская башня; 8-800-100 5553; tvtower.ru; adult/child R980/490; 10am-8pm Tue-Sun; Ⓜ VDNKh) is located just south of the park. Built in 1967, it was the tallest free-standing structure in the world (surpassing the Empire State Building). At 540m, it is now fourth on the list. At the 337m level, the observation deck is open for visitors. Tours take place hourly and must be booked in advance; bring your passport.

specials are often available weekdays before 4pm. This is a great way to sample some of the pricier restaurants around town. Most upscale places require booking a table in advance.

Kremlin & Kitay Gorod

Stolovaya 57 CAFETERIA $
(Столовая 57; Map p63; 3rd fl, GUM, Krasnaya pl 3; mains R200-300; 10am-10pm; Ⓜ Okhotny Ryad) Newly minted, this old-style cafeteria offers a nostalgic recreation of dining in post-Stalinist Russia. The food is good – and cheap for such a fancy store. Meat cutlets and cold salads come highly recommended. This is a great place to try 'herring in a fur coat' (herring, beets, carrots and potatoes).

Coffee Mania CAFE $$
(Кофе мания; Map p66; www.coffeemania.ru; Mal Cherkassky per 2; breakfast R300-500, mains R500-1100; 8am-midnight Mon-Thu, 8-2am Fri, 10-2am Sat, 10am-midnight Sun; Ⓜ Lubyanka) This place has the same overpriced but appetizing fare as other outlets of the ubiquitous chain, but the fabulous 'grand cafe' interior makes this one a special experience. Marble floors, art-deco chandeliers and elaborate lattice work evoke another era. Efficient service and excellent atmosphere.

Tverskoy

Farmer's Diner BISTRO $
(Новослободский; Map p66; ul Lesnaya 5; R300-450; 11am-11pm; Ⓜ Belorusskaya) This little bistro is run by people obsessed with Williamsburg gastroculture. The burger with caramelized onion is the trademark dish, but the place's main virtue is the two-course set lunch that costs R350 including a drink. It's a convenient pit stop before getting the Aeroexpress to Sheremetyevo airport.

Fresh VEGETARIAN $
(Свежий; Map p66; 965-278 9089; freshrestaurant.ru; ul Bolshaya Dmitrovka 11; mains R450; 11am-11pm; Ⓜ Teatralnaya) Fresh out of Canada, this is the kind of vegetarian restaurant that people pour into not for lifestyle reasons, but because the modern, food and the escapist ambience are actually great. Definitely go for the smoothies. Vegans and rawists will not feel neglected.

★ **Delicatessen** INTERNATIONAL $$
(Деликатесы; Map p66; www.newdeli.ru; Sadovaya-Karetnaya ul 20; mains R450-700; noon-midnight Tue-Sat; Ⓜ Tsvetnoy Bulvar) The affable (and chatty) owners of this place travel the world and experiment with the menu a lot, turning burgers, pizzas and pasta into artfully constructed objects of modern culinary art. The other source of joy is a cabinet filled with bottles of ripening fruity

liquors, which may destroy your budget if consumed uncontrollably (a pointless warning, we know).

Lavka-Lavka INTERNATIONAL $$
(Лавка-Лавка; Map p66; ☑495-724 3532; lavkalavka.com; ul Petrovka 21 str 2; R400-600; ⏰6pm-midnight Mon-Fri, 11am-midnight Sat & Sun; ⓦ; Ⓜ Teatralnaya) 🍴 Welcome to the Russian Portlandia – all the food here is organic and hails from little farms where you may rest assured all the lambs and chickens lived a very happy life before being served to you on a plate. Irony aside, this a great place to sample local food cooked in a funky improvisational style.

🍴 Presnya

Cafe Receptor FUSION $
(Кафе Рецептор; Map p66; www.cafereceptor.ru; Bolshaya Nikitskaya ul 22/2; mains R200-400; ⏰noon-midnight; 🛜🍴ⓦ; Ⓜ Okhotny Ryad) Colourful graffiti, amateur artwork and old photographs adorn the walls of this quirky basement cafe. It creates an arty setting for healthy, veg-heavy meals, fresh juices and fancy teas. There's also free-flowing wine, house cocktails and occasional live music. There is another outlet near **Patriarch's Ponds** (Map p66; Bolshoy Kozikhinsky per 10; Ⓜ Tverskaya).

★ Khachapuri GEORGIAN $$
(Map p66; ☑8-985-764 3118; hacha.ru; Bolshoy Gnezdnikovsky per 10; khachapuri R200-350, mains R400-600; ⓦ🍴; Ⓜ Pushkinskaya) Unassuming, affordable and appetising, this urban cafe exemplifies what people love about Georgian culture: the warm hospitality and the freshly baked *khachapuri* (cheese bread). Aside from seven types of delicious *khachapuri*, there's also an array of soups, *shashlyk* (kebabs), *khinkali* (dumplings) and other Georgian favourites.

★ As Eat Is INTERNATIONAL $$
(Как Есть; Map p66; ☑495-699 5313; www.aseatis.ru; Tryokhprudny per 11/13; mains R500-900; ⏰noon-11pm; 🍴; Ⓜ Mayakovskaya) We love the understated, eclectic interior, with its mismatched textures, appealingly packed bookshelves and vintage detailing. Even more, we love the contemporary seasonal fare, which is delightful to look at and divine to eat. It's the kind of food that would normally cost big bucks, but prices are reasonable. Extra love for the bilingual pun of a name.

★ Favorite AMERICAN $$
(Map p66; ☑495-691 1850; www.favorite-pub.ru; ul Spiridonovka 24; mains R500-800; ⏰8am-last guest; ⓦ; Ⓜ Mayakovskaya) Moscow's Favorite pub is this cool and casual Brooklyn-style hang-out, serving tasty gourmet burgers and grilled steaks. There's micro-brewed beer on tap (Brickstone Beer, made in Moscow) and a football game on the TV.

★ Café Pushkin RUSSIAN $$$
(Кафе Пушкинъ; Map p66; ☑495-739 0033; www.cafe-pushkin.ru; Tverskoy bul 26a; business lunch R750, mains R1000-2200; ⏰24hr; ⓦ🛜; Ⓜ Pushkinskaya) The tsarina of *haute-russe* dining, with an exquisite blend of Russian and French cuisines – service and food are done to perfection. The lovely 19th-century building has a different atmosphere on each floor, including a richly decorated library and a pleasant rooftop cafe.

🍴 Arbat & Khamovniki

Varenichnaya No 1 RUSSIAN $
(Map p66; www.varenichnaya.ru; ul Arbat 29; mains R200-400; ⏰10am-midnight; 🍴ⓦ; Ⓜ Arbatskaya) Retro Soviet is all the rage in Moscow, but this old-style Varenichnaya does it right, with books lining the walls, old movies on the B&W TV, and Cold War–era prices. The menu features tasty, filling *vareniki* and *pelmeni* (different kinds of dumplings), with sweet and savoury fillings. Bonus: an excellent housemade pickled vegie plate to make you pucker.

★ Elardzhi GEORGIAN $$
(Эларджи; Map p70; ☑495-627 7897; www.ginzaproject.ru; Gagarinsky per 15a; mains R600-800; ⓦ; Ⓜ Kropotkinskaya) Moscow's Georgian restaurants are all very tasty, but this one is also tasteful. You'll be charmed from the moment you enter the courtyard, where live rabbits and lambs greet all comers. Sink into a sofa in the romantic dining room or on the light-filled porch; then feast on delicacies, such as the namesake dish, *elarji* (cornmeal with Sulguni cheese).

Zhurfak Cafe RUSSIAN $$
(Кафе Журфак; Map p70; ☑985-212 5050; www.jurfak-cafe.ru; Bolshoy Afanasyevsky per 3; mains R500-800; ⏰9.30am-11pm; 🛜; Ⓜ Kropotkinskaya) One of our favourite secret spots, this smart cafe is named for the MGU Journalism Faculty, which is located nearby. In summer there's a shady outside eating area.

Otherwise, descend into the comfy basement quarters for lively conversation, traditional food, jazz music (Wednesday and Friday) and a hint of Soviet nostalgia.

✕ Zamoskvorechie

Mizandari
GEORGIAN $

(Map p70; ☑8-903-263 9990; nab Bolotnaya 5, str 1; mains R300-400; ☻11am-11pm; Ⓜ️Kropotkinskaya) Georgian restaurants in Moscow tend to be either expensive or tacky. This small family-run place is neither. Come with friends and order a selection of appetisers, such as *pkhali* and *lobio* (both made of walnut paste), *khachapuri* (cheese bread) and *kharcho* (spicy lamb soup). Bless you if can still accommodate a main course after all that!

Ochen Domashneye Kafe
RUSSIAN $

(Очень домашнее кафе; Map p70; ☑495-951 1734; www.dom-cafe.ru; ul Pyatnitskaya 9/28 str 1; R380-550; ☻8am-11pm Mon-Fri, 11am-11pm Sat & Sun; Ⓜ️Novokuznetskaya) The name, which translates as 'a very homey cafe', is also its motto. This is as close as it gets to the kind of food Russians eat at home, which inevitably means borsch (beetroot soup) or mushroom soup for starters, and all kinds of *kotlety* (meat, chicken or fish) as the main course.

★ Produkty
ITALIAN $$

(Продукты; Map p70; ☑8-903-789 3474; facebook.com/productscafe; Bersenevsky per 5, bldg 1; meals R600-1000; ☻noon-midnight Sun-Thu, to 6am Fri & Sat; ☎🖋; Ⓜ️Kropotkinskaya) The success of this Red October highlight is determined by the cool, post-industrial decor, simple Italian food and the proximity to the premises of several editorial offices, including the embattled Dozhd TV. It's not really visible from the street – enter the courtyard on the left of the Burger Brothers window.

✕ Basmanny

★ Darbazi
GEORGIAN $$

(☑495-915 3632; www.darbazirest.ru/; ul Nikoloyamskaya 16; R390-860; ☻noon-midnight; 🖋; Ⓜ️Taganskaya) The vast majority of Georgian restaurants focus on the most popular, tried-and-true fare, such as *shashlyk* and *khinkali*. This classy place goes far beyond these, listing less well-known delicacies with almost encyclopedic meticulousness. Our favourite is *chakapuli* (lamb cooked in white

wine with estragon) and *Megreli kharcho* (duck in walnut sauce).

Odessa-Mama
UKRAINIAN $$

(Map p66; ☑8-964-647 1110; www.cafeodessa.ru; per Krivokolenny 10 str 5; R380-540; ☻noon-midnight; Ⓜ️Chistye Prudy) Come here to celebrate Odessa, affectionately called 'mama' by the residents of this port city. What mama cooks is a wild fusion of Jewish, Ukrainian and Balkan foods, with a strong emphasis on Black Sea fish. It's like island hopping – from *forshmak* (Jewish herring pate) to Ukrainian borsch and eventually to fried Odessa gobies.

🍷 Drinking & Nightlife

Pedestrian streets such as ul Arbat and Kamergersky per are hot spots for strollers and drinkers. Red October in Zamoskvorechie is packed with diverse drinking establishments, while Gorky Park has plenty of summer spots.

🍸 Tverskoy

Noor
BAR

(Map p66; ☑499-130 6030; www.noorbar.com; ul Tverskaya 23; ☻3pm-3am Mon-Wed, noon-6am Thu-Sun; Ⓜ️Pushkinskaya) There is little to say about this misleadingly unassuming bar, apart from the fact that everything in it is close to perfection. It has it all – prime location, convivial atmosphere, eclectic DJ music, friendly bartenders and superb drinks. Though declared 'the best' by various magazines on several occasions, it doesn't feel like they care.

3205
CAFE

(Map p66; ☑905-703 3205; www.veranda3205.ru; ul Karetny Ryad 3; ☻11am-3am; Ⓜ️Pushkinskaya) The biggest drinking/eating establishment in Hermitage Gardens, this verandah positioned at the back of the main building looks a bit like a greenhouse. In summer tables (and patrons) spill out into the park, making it one of the city's best places for outdoor drinking. With its long bar and joyful atmosphere, the place also heaves in winter.

🍸 Presnya

Time-Out Bar
COCKTAIL BAR

(Map p66; www.timeoutbar.ru; 12th fl, Bolshaya Sadovaya ul 5; ☻noon-2am Sun-Thu, noon-6am Fri & Sat; Ⓜ️Mayakovskaya) On the upper floors of the throwback Pekin Hotel, this trendy bar

SERGIEV POSAD

Blue and golden cupolas offset by snow-white walls – this colour scheme lies at the heart of the Russian perception of divinity and the Trinity Monastery of St Sergius (Troitse-Sergieva Lavra; ☑ 496-544 5356; www.stsl.ru; ☺ 5am-9pm) FREE is a textbook example. In Russia it doesn't get any holier than this monastery, for the place was founded in 1340 by the country's most revered saint. St Sergius of Radonezh was credited with providing mystic support to Prince Dmitry Donskoy in his improbable victory over the Tatars in the Battle of Kulikovo Pole (1380). Soon after his death at the age of 78, Sergius was named Russia's patron saint. Since the 14th century, pilgrims have been journeying to this place to pay homage to him.

Note that the monastery is an active religious centre with a visible population of monks in residence. Visitors should refrain from photographing the monks, female visitors should wear headscarves and men are required to remove hats before entering the churches.

Sights

Built in the 1420s, the squat, dark Trinity Cathedral (Троицкий собор) is the heart of the Trinity Monastery. The tomb of St Sergius stands in the southeastern corner, where a memorial service for the saint goes on all day, every day. The icon-festooned interior, lit by oil lamps, is largely the work of the great medieval painter Andrei Rublyov and his students.

The star-spangled Cathedral of the Assumption was modelled on the cathedral of the same name in the Moscow Kremlin. It was finished in 1585 with money left by Ivan the Terrible in a fit of remorse for killing his son. Outside the west door is the grave of Boris Godunov (Могила Бориса Годунова), the only tsar not buried in the Moscow Kremlin or St Petersburg's SS Peter & Paul Cathedral.

Nearby, the resplendent Chapel-at-the-Well (Накладезная часовня) was built over a spring that is said to have appeared during the Polish siege. The five-tier baroque bell tower (Колокольня) took 30 years to build in the 18th century, and once had 42 bells, the largest of which weighed 65 tonnes.

Behind the Trinity Cathedral, the Vestry (☺ 10am-5.30pm Wed-Sun) displays the monastery's extraordinarily rich treasury, bulging with 600 years of donations by the rich and powerful – tapestries, jewel-encrusted vestments, solid-gold chalices and more.

Getting There & Away

The fastest transport option is the express commuter train that departs from Moscow's Yaroslavsky vokzal (R160, one hour, six daily). A couple of long-distance trains call at Sergiev Posad daily on the way to Yaroslavl (platskart R1200, three hours).

---

is nothing but 'now'. That includes the bartenders sporting plaid and their delicious concoctions, especially created for different times of day. The decor is pretty impressive – particularly the spectacular city skyline. Perfect place for sundowners (or sun-ups, if you last that long).

Conversation CAFE
(Разговор; Map p66; www.conversationcafe.ru; Bolshaya Nikitskaya ul 23/14/9; ☎ 🖶; Ⓜ Arbatskaya) Considering its three specialities – coffee, pasta and ice cream – we can't imagine why anybody wouldn't want to stop in at this inviting, contemporary cafe. Soups and sandwiches are also on the menu, but it's the

decadent desserts and wake-me-up coffee drinks that keep the seats filled.

🍷 Arbat & Khamovniki

Gavroche Wine Bar WINE BAR
(Винный бар Гаврош; www.thewinebar.ru; ul Timura Frunze 11; ☺ 9am-midnight Sun-Wed, 9-2am Thu-Sat; ☎; Ⓜ Park Kultury) First came the beer bars, and then the cocktail lounges. It only stands to reason that wine bars would be next. This one is stylish but not pretentious, with exposed brick walls and wines listed on a blackboard behind the bar. You'll find dozens of vintages from around the world, with a menu of Med-style small plates to complement them.

Zhiguli Beer Hall   BREWERY
(Пивной зал Жигули; Map p66; www.zhiguli.
net; ul Novy Arbat 11; ½L beer R210-350; ⏰10-2am
Sun-Thu, 10-4am Fri & Sat; 🔊; Ⓜ Arbatskaya) It's
hard to classify this old-style *stolovaya* (cafeteria) that happens to brew great beer. The
place harks back to the Soviet years, when
a popular *pivnaya* bar by the same name
was a Novy Arbat institution. The minimalist decor and cafeteria-style service recalls
the heyday, although this place has been
updated with big-screen TVs and a separate
table-service dining room.

Zamoskvorechie

Le Boule   BAR
(📱8-926-376 9366; Gorky Park; ⏰noon-midnight;
🔊; Ⓜ Oktyabrskaya) The goatee and mustache
factor is high in this hipster-ridden verandah bar that comes with a dozen petanque
lanes. Grab a pitcher of sangria or a pint of
cider and have a go at what is arguably the
most alcohol-compatible sport. Live bands
often play on the verandah in the early
evening.

★ Gipsy   CLUB, CAFE
(Map p70; www.bargipsy.ru; Bolotnaya nab 3/4;
⏰6pm-1am Sun-Thu, 2pm-6am Fri & Sat) Eu-
phoria reins in this post-modern, nomad
camp of a bar that has a strategic rooftop position on Red October. The decor is
bright-coloured kitsch, which among other
oddities means fake palm trees and toilet
doors covered with artificial fur. The DJ and
live-music repertoire are aptly eclectic. You
don't have to be rich to pass the face control,
but some natural coolness does help.

Meshchansky & Basmanny

★ Sisters Cafe   CAFE
(Map p66; 📱495-623 0932; www.facebook.
com/sistacafe; ul Pokrovka 6; ⏰noon-11pm; 🔊;
Ⓜ Kitay-Gorod) This cosy and quiet cafe-cum-
bar has a distinct feminine touch about
it – as if Chekhov's sisters have finally made
their way to Moscow and started a new life
here. Cheapish smoothies, lemonades and
teas are on offer, but the wine and cocktail
lists are equally impressive. If you're hungry,
they serve lovingly prepared Italian standards. Retro furniture creates a cosy, homely
feeling, but a striking mural with a girl facing a blue abyss suggests that this place is
about dreams and new horizons.

☆ Entertainment

Classical Music

Moscow International House of Music   CLASSICAL MUSIC
(Map p70; 📱495-730 1011; www.mmdm.ru; Ko-
smodamianskaya nab 52/8; tickets R200-2000;
Ⓜ Paveletskaya) This graceful, modern, glass
building has three halls, including Svetlanov
Hall, which holds the largest organ in Russia. Needless to say, organ concerts held here
are impressive. This is the usual venue for
performances by the **National Philharmonic of Russia** (📱495-730 3778; www.nfor.ru), a
privately financed, highly lauded, classical-music organisation. Founded in 1991, the
symphony is directed and conducted by the
esteemed Vladimir Spivakov.

Tchaikovsky Concert Hall   CLASSICAL MUSIC
(Концертный зал имени Чайковского; Map
p66; 📱495-232 0400; www.meloman.ru; Trium-
falnaya pl 4/31; tickets R300-3000; ⏰closed Jul-
Aug; Ⓜ Mayakovskaya) Home to the famous
Moscow State Philharmonic (Moskovskaya
Filharmonia), the capital's oldest symphony orchestra, Tchaikovsky Concert Hall was
established in 1921. It's a huge auditorium,
with seating for 1600 people. This is where
you can expect to hear the Russian classics
such as Stravinsky, Rachmaninov and Shostakovich, as well as other European favourites. Look out for special children's concerts.

Opera & Ballet

★ Bolshoi Theatre   BALLET, OPERA
(Большой театр; Map p66; www.bolshoi.ru; Teatralnaya pl 1; tickets R200-4000; Ⓜ Teatralnaya)
An evening at the Bolshoi is still one of
Moscow's most romantic and entertaining
options for a night on the town. The glittering six-tier auditorium has an electric atmosphere, evoking over 235 years of premier
music and dance. Both the ballet and opera
companies perform a range of Russian and
foreign works here. After the collapse of the
Soviet Union, the Bolshoi was marred by
politics, scandal and frequent turnover. Yet
the show must go on – and it will.

Kremlin Ballet   BALLET
(Кремлевский балет; Map p63; 📱495-628
5232; www.kremlinpalace.org; ul Vozdvizhenka 1;
⏰box office noon-8pm; Ⓜ Aleksandrovsky Sad)
The Bolshoi Theatre doesn't have a monop-
oly on ballet in Moscow. Leading dancers
also appear with the Kremlin Ballet, which
performs in the Kremlin Palace. The Bolshoi
is magical, but seeing a show inside the

Kremlin is something special, too. The repertoire is unapologetically classical. The box office is near the entrance to the metro station.

Circus

Nikulin Circus on Tsvetnoy Bulvar   CIRCUS
(Цирк Никулина на Цветном бульваре; Map p66; ☑495-625 8970; www.circusnikulin. ru; Tsvetnoy bul 13; tickets R400-2500; ⊙box office 11am-2pm & 3-7pm; Ⓜ Tsvetnoy Bulvar) Founded in 1880, this circus is now named after beloved actor and clown Yury Nikulin (1921–97), who performed at the studio here for many years. Nikulin's shows centre on a given theme, which serves to add some cohesion to the productions. There are lots of trapeze artists, tightrope walkers and performing animals.

Live Music

Masterskaya   LIVE MUSIC
(Мастерская; Map p66; www.mstrsk.ru; Teatralny proezd 3 str 3; ⊙noon-6am; ☎; Ⓜ Lubyanka) All the best places in Moscow are tucked into far corners of courtyards, and they often have unmarked doors. Such is the case with this super-funky music venue. The eclectic, arty interior makes a cool place to chill out during the day. Evening hours give way to a diverse array of live-music acts or the occasional dance or theatre performance.

Sixteen Tons   LIVE MUSIC
(Шестнадцать тонн; ☑495-253 1550; www.16tons.ru; ul Presnensky val 6; cover R600-1200; ⊙11-6am, concerts 8pm Sun-Thu, 9pm Thu-Sat, midnight Fri & Sat; ☎; Ⓜ Ulitsa 1905 Goda) Downstairs, the brassy English pub-restaurant has an excellent house-brewed bitter. Upstairs, the club gets some of the best Russian bands that play in Moscow, hosting such names as Mara and Theodor Bastard, among others. Show times are subject to change so check the website for details.

Art Garbage   LIVE MUSIC
(Map p66; www.art-garbage.ru; Starosadsky per 5; ⊙noon-6am; ☎; Ⓜ Kitay-Gorod) Enter this funky club-cafe through the courtyard littered with sculpture. Inside, the walls are crammed with paintings of all genres, and there are DJs spinning or live music playing every night. The restaurant is relatively minimalist in terms of decor, but the menu is creative. Is it art or is it garbage? We'll let you decide.

Rhythm Blues Cafe   LIVE MUSIC
(Блюз Кафе Ритм; Map p66; ☑499-697 6008; www.rhythm-blues-cafe.ru; Starovagankovsky per; ⊙shows 9pm; Ⓜ Aleksandrovsky Sad) If your dog got run over by a pick-up truck, you might find some comfort at the Rhythm Blues Cafe, with down-and-out live music every night, plus cold beer and a whole menu of salty cured meats. Great fun and a friendly vibe, with people actually listening to the music. Book a table if you want to sit down.

🔒 Shopping

GUM   MALL
(ГУМ; Map p63; www.gum.ru; Krasnaya pl 3; ⊙10am-10pm; Ⓜ Ploshchad Revolyutsii) The elaborate 240m facade on the northeastern side of Red Square, GUM is a bright, bustling shopping mall with hundreds of fancy stores and restaurants. With a skylight roof and three-level arcades, the spectacular interior was a revolutionary design when it was built in the 1890s, replacing the Upper Trading Rows that previously occupied this site.

Yeliseev Grocery   FOOD & DRINK
(Елисеевский магазин; Map p66; Tverskaya ul 14; ⊙8am-9pm Mon-Sat, 10am-6pm Sun; Ⓜ Pushkinskaya) Peek in here for a glimpse of pre-revolutionary grandeur, as the store is set in the former mansion of the successful merchant Yeliseev. It now houses an upscale market selling caviar and other delicacies. It's a great place to shop for souvenirs for your foodie friends back home.

Flakon   SHOPPING CENTRE
(www.flacon.ru; ul Bolshaya Novodmitrovskaya 36; ⊙variable; Ⓜ Dmitrovskaya) Like the Bolsheviks a hundred years ago, Moscow hipsters are capturing one factory after another and redeveloping them, according to their hipster tastes. Flakon is arguably the most visually attractive of all the redeveloped industrial areas around town, looking a bit like the far end of Portobello Rd, especially during the weekends. Once a glassware plant, it is now home to dozens of funky shops and other businesses. Shopping for designer clothes and unusual souvenirs is the main reason for coming here. The main shopping area covers two floors of the factory's central building.

Depst   DESIGNER GOODS
(Map p66; www.depst.ru; Tsvetnoy bul 15 (inside Tsvetnoy shopping mall); ⊙10am-10pm) This is

IZMAYLOVSKY MARKET

Never mind the kitschy faux 'tsar's palace' it surrounds, Izmaylovsky Market (www.kremlin-izmailovo.com; Izmaylovskoye shosse 73; ⊙10am-8pm; Ⓜ Partizanskaya) is the ultimate place to shop for *matryoshka* dolls, military uniforms, icons, Soviet badges and some real antiques. Huge and diverse, it is almost a theme park, including shops, cafes and a couple of not terribly exciting museums.

the ultimate place to shop for Russian designer items – from clothes to furniture, and jewellery to cutlery. The shop occupies pretty much the entire underground floor of Tsvetnoy shopping centre, which has a few other trappings, including a nice food court on the top floor.

Association of Artists of the Decorative Arts (AHDI)
SOUVENIRS
(Ассоциация художников декоративно-прикладного искусства; Map p66; www.ahdi.ru; ul Arbat 21; ⊙11am-8pm; Ⓜ Arbatskaya) Look for the ceramic plaque and the small sign indicating the entrance to this 'exposition hall', which is actually a cluster of small shops, each one showcasing arts and crafts by local artists. In addition to paintings and pottery, the most intriguing items are the gorgeous knit sweaters, woolly coats and embroidered dresses – all handmade and unique.

ℹ️ Information

DANGERS & ANNOYANCES
Although street crime is on the rise, Moscow is a mostly safe city with few dangerous areas.
➤ As in any big city, be on your guard against pickpockets and muggers, especially around train stations and in crowded metro cars.
➤ Always be cautious about taking taxis late at night, especially near bars and clubs that are in isolated areas. Never get into a car that already has two or more people in it.
➤ Always carry a photocopy of your passport, visa and registration stamp. If stopped by a member of the police force, do not hand over your passport. It is perfectly acceptable to show a photocopy instead.
➤ Your biggest threat in Moscow is xenophobic or overly friendly drunks.

EMERGENCY
Ambulance (☑ 03)
Fire (☑ 01)
Police (☑ 02)
Universal Emergency Number (☑ 112) Currently functional from mobile phones, this universal number will eventually replace the separate numbers for ambulance, fire and police.

INTERNET ACCESS
➤ Almost all hotels and hostels offer wi-fi, as do many bars, restaurants and cafes. It isn't always free, but it is ubiquitous.
➤ Also popular is shared work space, which offers a comfortable work space, functional wi-fi, and sometimes drinks and snacks, for a per minute or per hour fee.
➤ Most hostels and hotels offer internet access for guests who are not travelling with their own computers. Internet cafes are a thing of the past.
➤ Or try **Ziferblat** (Циферблат; www.ziferblat.net; per min R2) Tverskaya (Map p66; Tverskaya ul 12c1; ⊙11am-midnight; Ⓜ Pushkinskaya); Pokrovka (Map p66; ul Pokrovka 12 c 1; ⊙11am-midnight Sun-Thu, 11am-7pm Fri-Sat; Ⓜ Chistye Prudy).

MEDICAL SERVICES
Hospitals
Both the American Medical Centre and the European Medical Centre accept health insurance from major international providers.
American Medical Centre (Map p66; ☑ 495-933 7700; www.amcenter.ru; Grokholsky per 1; ⊙24hr; Ⓜ pr Mira) Offers 24-hour emergency service, consultations and a full range of medical specialists, including paediatricians and dentists. There is also an on-site pharmacy with English-speaking staff.
Botkin Hospital (☑ 495-945 0045; www.mosgorzdrav.ru; 2-y Botkinsky proezd 5; ⊙24hr; Ⓜ Begovaya) The best Russian facility. From Begovaya metro station, walk 1km northeast on Khoroshevskoe sh and Begovoy pr. Turn left on Begovaya ul and continue to 2-y Botkinsky proezd.
European Medical Centre (Map p66; ☑ 495-933 6655; www.emcmos.ru; Spirodonevsky per 5; ⊙24hr; Ⓜ Mayakovskaya) Includes medical and dental facilities, which are open around the clock for emergencies. The staff speak 10 languages.

Pharmacies
36.6 (Аптека 36.6; ☑ 495-797 6366; www.366.ru) Arbat (Map p66; ul Novy Arbat 15; ⊙9am-10pm; Ⓜ Arbatskaya); Zamoskvorechie (Map p70; Klimentovsky per 12; ⊙8am-10pm; Ⓜ Tretyakovskaya); Tverskaya (Map p66;

Tverskaya ul 25/9; ☺24hr; Ⓜ Mayakovskaya). A chain of pharmacies with many branches all around the city.

MONEY

Banks, exchange counters and ATMs are ubiquitous in Moscow. Credit cards, especially Visa and MasterCard, are widely accepted. You can also use your credit card to get a cash advance at most major banks.

POST

Although international service has improved, mail to Europe and the USA can take two to six weeks to arrive.

Central Telegraph (Map p66; Tverskaya ul 7; ☺post 8am-10pm, telephone 24hr; Ⓜ Okhotny Ryad)

Main Post Office (Map p66; Myasnitskaya ul 26; ☺24hr; Ⓜ Chistye Prudy)

ⓘ Getting There & Away

TRAIN

Stations

Yaroslavsky Vokzal (Yaroslavl Station; Komsomolskaya pl; Ⓜ Komsomolskaya) This train station serves Yaroslavl, Arkhangelsk, Vorkuta, the Russian Far East, Mongolia, China, North Korea; some trains to/from Vladimir, Nizhny Novgorod, Kostroma, Vologda, Perm, Ural Mountains, Siberia; and suburban trains to/from the northeast, including Abramtsevo, Khotkovo, Sergiev Posad and Aleksandrov.

Belorussky Vokzal (Belarus Station; Tverskaya Zastava pl; Ⓜ Belorusskaya) This station serves trains to/from Smolensk, Kaliningrad, Belarus, Lithuania, Poland, Germany; some trains to/from the Czech Republic; and suburban trains to/from the west, including Mozhaysk, Borodino and Zvenigorod. Belorussky is also the starting point for the Aeroexpress train to Sheremetyevo.

Kazansky Vokzal (Kazan Station; Komsomolskaya pl; Ⓜ Komsomolskaya) This station serves trains to/from Kazan, Izhevsk, Ufa, Ryazan, Ulyanovsk, Samara, Novorossiysk, Central Asia; some trains to/from Vladimir, Nizhny Novgorod, the Ural Mountains, Siberia, Saratov, Rostov-on-Don; and suburban trains to/from the southeast, including Bykovo airport, Kolomna, Gzhel and Ryazan.

Kievsky Vokzal (Kyiv Station; Kievskaya pl; Ⓜ Kievskaya) This station serves Bryansk, Kyiv, western Ukraine, Moldova, Slovakia, Hungary, Austria, Prague, Romania, Bulgaria, Croatia, Serbia, Greece, Venice; suburban trains to/from the southwest, including Peredelkino and Kaluga. Kievsky Vokzal is also the starting point for the Aeroexpress train to Vnukovo airport.

TRAINS FROM MOSCOW

Sample Trans-Siberian Trains from Moscow

All prices are for *kupe* (2nd-class) fares unless otherwise stated.

DESTINATION	TRAIN NUMBER	DEPARTURE TIME	STATION	DURATION	FARE
Chita	070	1.05pm	Yaroslavsky	4 days, 11hr	R11,300
Kazan	002 Premium	10.08pm	Kazansky	11½hr	R3045
Krasnoyarsk	056 Yenisey	4.20pm	Yaroslavsky	3 days 15hr	R17,325
Nizhny Novgorod	732 Lastochka	11am	Kursky	4hr	R460 (seat)
Omsk	038 Tomich	10.50pm (even dates)	Yaroslavsky	42hr	R11,700
Novosibirsk	030 Kuzbass	10.50pm (odd dates)	Yaroslavsky	48hr	R10,200
Perm	008	4.50pm	Yaroslavsky	21hr	R5200
Tomsk	038 Tomich	10.50pm (even dates)	Yaroslavsky	56hr	R12,500
Ulaanbaatar	006 Trans Mongolian Express	9.35pm Wed & Thu	Yaroslavsky	4 days, 5hr	R15,200
Vladimir	732 Lastochka	11am	Kursky	1hr 45min	R430 (seat)
Vladivostok	002 Rossiya	1.50pm (odd dates)	Yaroslavsky	6 days, 19hr	R25,000
Yaroslavl	016 Belomorye	10.05am	Yaroslavsky	4hr	R1600
Yekaterinburg	016 Ural	4.50pm	Kazansky	25½hr	R4900

TRAINS FROM MOSCOW

Sample Trains from Moscow to St Petersburg

All trains depart daily from Leningradsky vokzal. Prices are for a *kupe* (2nd-class) ticket unless otherwise stated.

TRAIN	NUMBER	DEPARTURE TIME	DURATION	FARE
Krasnaya Strela	02	11.55pm	8hr	1st/2nd-class R5600/3800
Ekspress	04	11.30pm	8hr	1st/2nd-class R5500/3400
Grand Express	54	11.40pm	9hr	1st/2nd-class R7600/3600
Sapsan	752	6.45am	4hr	R11,800 (seat)
Sapsan	758	1.30pm	4hr	R3400 (seat)
Sapsan	762	4.30pm	4hr	R3200 (seat)
Sapsan	764	7.25pm	4hr	R3200 (seat)

Sample International Trains from Moscow

All trains depart daily. Prices are for a *kupe* ticket.

DESTINATION	TRAIN NUMBER	DEPARTURE TIME	STATION	DURATION	FARE
Helsinki	032 Lev Tolstoi	11pm	Leningradsky	14hr	R9500
Kyiv	001 Stolichny Express	10.54pm (odd dates)	Kievsky	8hr 40min	R4800
Minsk	007 Slavyansky Express	11.03pm	Belorussky	8hr	R4100
Rīga	001 Latvia Express	7pm	Rizhsky	16hr	R6455
Tallinn	034 Tallinn Express	6.05pm	Leningradsky	15½hr	R4700
Vilnius	005 Lietuva	6.55pm	Belorussky	14hr	R7620

Kursky Vokzal (Kursk Station; pl Kurskogo vokzala; Ⓜ Kurskaya) This train station serves Oryol, Kursk, Krasnodar, Adler, the Caucasus, eastern Ukraine, Crimea, Georgia, Azerbaijan. It also has some trains to/from Rostov-on-Don, Vladimir, Nizhny Novgorod, Perm; and suburban trains to/from the east and south, including Petushki, Podolsk, Chekhov, Serpukhov and Tula.

Leningradsky Vokzal (Leningrad Station; Komsomolskaya pl; Ⓜ Komsomolskaya) This train station serves Tver, Novgorod, Pskov, St Petersburg, Vyborg, Murmansk, Estonia, Helsinki; and suburban trains to/from the northwest, including Klin and Tver. Note that sometimes this station is referred to on timetables and tickets by its former name, Oktyabrsky.

Rizhsky Vokzal (Rīga Station; Rizhskaya pl; Ⓜ Rizhskaya) This train station serves Latvia, with suburban trains to/from the northwest, including Istra and Novoierusalimskaya.

Suburban Trains

Most Moscow stations have a separate ticket hall for suburban trains, usually called the Prigorodny Zal and often tucked away beside or behind the station building. These trains are usually listed on separate timetables and may depart from a separate group of platforms.

AIR

Airports

Moscow has three main airports servicing international and domestic flights.

Domodedovo (Домодедово; www.domodedovo.ru) Domodedovo, located about 48km south of the city, has undergone extensive upgrades since 2003, and has become the city's largest and most efficient international airport. The Aeroexpress train leaves Paveletsky vokzal every half hour between 6am and midnight for the 45-minute trip to Domodedovo.

Sheremetyevo (Шереметьево, SVO; ☎ 495-578 6565; www.svo.aero) Sheremetyevo international airport is 30km northwest of the city centre. The Aeroexpress train makes the 35-minute trip between Sheremetyevo (located next to Terminal E) and Belorussky vokzal every half hour from 5.30am to 12.30am.

Vnukovo (Внуково; www.vnukovo.ru) About 30km southwest of the city centre, Vnukovo serves most flights to/from the Caucasus, Moldova and Kaliningrad, as well as domestic flights and a smattering of flights to Europe. The Aeroexpress train makes the 35-minute run from Kievsky vokzal to Vnukovo airport every hour from 6am to 11pm.

Tickets

You can buy domestic airline tickets from most travel agents and at Aeroflot and Transaero offices all over town.

Aeroflot (www.aeroflot.ru) Zamoskvorechie (Map p70; Pyatnitskaya ul 37/19; Ⓜ Tretyakovskaya); Tverskoy (Map p66; ul Petrovka 20/1; Ⓜ Chekhovskaya); Meshchansky (Map p66; ul Kuznetsky most 3; Ⓜ Kuznetsky Most).

Transaero (☑ 495-788 8080; www.transaero. ru/en) Zamoskvorechie (Map p70; Paveletskaya pl 2/3; Ⓜ Paveletskaya); Khamovniki (Map p70; Zubovsky bul 11a; Ⓜ Park Kultury).

BUS

Buses run to a number of towns and cities within 700km of Moscow. In general, bus is not a recommended way to travel, mainly due to the terrible traffic heading out of town. If at all possible, get out of town by train.

Otherwise, the long-distance **Shchyolkovsky Bus Station** (Щёлковский автовокзал; www. busmow.ru; Ⓜ Shchyolkovskaya) is 8km east of the city centre. Buses also depart from outside the various train stations, offering alternative transport to the destinations served by the train.

ⓘ Getting Around

TO/FROM THE AIRPORTS

All three airports are accessible by the convenient **Aeroexpress train** (☑ 8-800-700 3377; www.aeroexpress.ru; R340-400; ⊘ 6am-midnight) from the city centre. If you wish to take a taxi, book an official airport taxi through the dispatcher counter (R2000 to R2500).

BOAT

Capital Shipping Co (p73) ferries ply the Moscow River from May to September (every

20 minutes). Board at any dock along the route. This is more of a tour than a form of transportation, unless you buy the full-day pass, which allows you to get on and off at will.

METRO

The **Moscow metro** (www.mosmetro.ru) is by far the easiest, quickest and cheapest way of getting around Moscow. Also, many of the elegant stations are marble-faced, frescoed, gilded works of art. The 150-plus stations are marked outside by large 'M' signs.

Reliability The trains are generally reliable: you will rarely wait on a platform for more than three minutes. Nonetheless, they do get packed, especially during the city's rush hour.

Tickets Magnetic tickets (R40) are sold at ticket booths. Queues can be long, so it's useful (and slightly cheaper) to buy a multiple-ride ticket (11 rides for R320 or 20 rides for R520). The ticket is actually a contactless smart card, which you must tap on the reader before going through the turnstile.

Maps & Signage Stations have maps of the system at the entrance and signs on each platform showing the destinations. The maps are generally in Cyrillic and Latin script, although the signs are usually only in Cyrillic. The carriages also have maps inside that show the stops for that line in both Roman and Cyrillic letters.

Transfers Interchange stations are linked by underground passages, indicated by *perekhod* signs, usually blue with a stick figure running up the stairs. Be aware that when two or more lines meet, the intersecting stations often (but not always) have different names.

TAXI

The safest and most reliable way to get a taxi is to order one by phone. Normally, the dispatcher will call you back within a few minutes to provide a description and licence number of the car.

Central Taxi Reservation Office (Центральное бюро заказов такси; ☑ 495-627 0000; www.6270000.ru; 30min for R400)

New Yellow Taxi (Новое жёлтое такси; ☑ 495-940 8888; www.nyt.ru; per km R30, min R400)

Taxi Bistro (Такси Бистро; ☑ 495-685 1300; www.taxopark.ru; per 20min R320-420)

St Petersburg

Includes

Best Places to Eat

Best Places to Stay

Why Go?

Beautiful, complex and imperious, with a hedonistic, creative temperament, St Petersburg (Санкт-Петербург) is the ultimate Russian diva. From its early days as an uninhabited swamp, the 300-year-old city has been nurtured by a succession of rulers, enduring practically everything that history and nature's harsh elements could throw at her. Constantly in need of repair but with a carefree party attitude, Petersburg still seduces all who gaze upon her grand facades, glittering spires and gilded domes.

Even if you don't plan to start or end your train journey in St Petersburg, it would be a shame not to visit the city. The long summer days of the White Nights season are particularly special – the fountains flow and parks and gardens burst into colour. The icy depths of winter have their own magic, and are the perfect time for warming body and soul in all those museums and palaces.

When to Go
St Petersburg

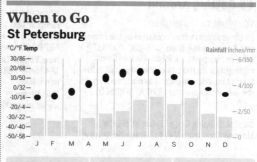

Mid-May–mid-Jul The White Nights, when the sun never sets, is the most popular time to visit.

May & Sep A great time to visit summery St Petersburg without the crowds of the peak months.

Nov–Jan Freezing, dark and blanketed in snow, the winter in St Petersburg is magical.

Arriving in St Petersburg

Most people arrive at St Petersburg's Pulkovo Airport (p111), a brand-new terminal from where an official taxi costs between R800 and R1000 to the city centre. Those on a budget can take a bus (R25) to the nearby Moskovskaya metro station and then connect from there to elsewhere in the city (R28). Arrivals from Helsinki by train come into the Finland Station, next to Ploshchad Lenina metro, while those coming by train from Moscow will arrive at the Moscow Station next to Ploshchad Vosstaniya metro. Boats arrive at one of five ports scattered around the city.

GUIDED TOURS

Those arriving on a cruise ship or by ferry at any of St Petersburg's various ports are able to profit from 72-hour visa-free entry into Russia. The only conditions are that you also leave the city by boat and that you book a guided tour from a licensed operator. These include:

➡ Red October (www.redoctober.ru)

➡ DenRus (www.denrus.ru)

➡ Peter's Walking Tours (www.peterswalk.com)

These operators are used to working with cruise ship and ferry passengers, and tend to offer a far higher standard of tour than the mass-market ones the cruise ships promote. It's important to know that you are still able to use the visa-free entry if you do not book the tour sold by the cruise ship, as long as you privately arrange a tour with one of these companies.

Bridges Up!

From April to November, all bridges across the Neva River rise at around 1.30am nightly to let ships pass through the city and on to the rest of the world, or into Russia's deep interior. Don't find yourself on the wrong side of the river when the bridges go up, or you'll have to wait until they go back down again at around 5am. Alternatively you can take the metro between Sportivnaya and Admiralteyskaya, which shuttles back and forth between 1am and 3am.

NEED TO KNOW

Trains to Irkutsk depart from Ladozhsky vokzal (reached by Ⓜ Ladozhskaya). Trains to Moscow depart from Ⓜ Moskovsky vokzal (reached from Ploshchad Vosstaniya).

Fast Facts

➡ Telephone code: ☎ 812

➡ Population: 4.8m

➡ Number of metro stations: 67

➡ Number of bridges: 342

➡ St Petersburg time: GMT+4

Don't Drink the Water

Tiny traces of *Giardia lamblia*, a nasty parasite that causes stomach cramps, nausea, bloated stomach, diarrhoea and frequent gas, have been found in St Petersburg's water. There's no preventative drug so the best advice is to only drink bottled water during your stay here.

Resources

➡ St Petersburg Tourist Information (http://eng. ispb.info)

➡ St Petersburg Times (www.sptimes.ru)

➡ In Your Pocket St Petersburg (www. inyourpocket.com/russia/ st-petersburg)

History

Starting with the Peter & Paul Fortress, founded on the marshy estuary of the Neva River in 1703, Peter the Great and his successors commissioned a city built to grand design by mainly European architects. By the early 19th century St Petersburg had firmly established itself as Russia's cultural heart. But while writers, artists and musicians – such as Pushkin, Turgenev and, later, Tchaikovsky and Dostoevsky – lived in and were inspired by the city, political and social problems were on the rise.

Industrialisation brought a flood of poor workers and associated urban squalor to St Petersburg. Revolution against the monarchy was first attempted in the short-lived coup of 14 December 1825. The leaders (who included members of the aristocracy and who became known as the Decembrists) were banished to the outer edges of the empire.

The next revolution was in 1905, sparked by the 'Bloody Sunday' of 9 January when more than a hundred people were killed and hundreds more were injured after troops fired on a peaceful crowd petitioning the tsar outside the Winter Palace. The tsar's government limped on, until February 1917, when food shortages and miserable social conditions in the newly renamed Petrograd culminated in popular protests that led to the abdication of Tsar Nicholas II. Lenin and his Bolshevik followers took advantage of the weak Provisional Government that held power for the next six months and staged an audacious coup in the Winter Palace in October 1917.

To protect the city during the ensuing Civil War, the seat of government was moved back to Moscow, and, to break with the tsarist past, Petrograd was renamed Leningrad after Lenin's death in 1924. The city – by virtue of its location, three-million-plus population and industry – remained one of Russia's most important, thus putting it on the frontline during WWII. For 872 days the Germans besieged Leningrad, and one million perished from starvation in horrendous conditions.

During the 1960s and 1970s Leningrad's bohemian spirit burned bright, fostering the likes of dissident poet Joseph Brodsky and underground rock groups such as Akvarium, and later on, Kino. As the Soviet Union came tumbling down, the city renamed itself St Petersburg in 1991. Millions of roubles were spent on restoration for the city's tercentenary celebrations and St Petersburg looks better now than probably at any other time in its history.

◎ Sights

While St Petersburg is a huge and sprawling city spread over many different islands, its main sights are fairly well centred in the Historic Heart of the city, the area broadly surrounding the main avenue, Nevsky pr. Other rich pockets of sights include those on Vasilyevsky Island and the Petrograd Side, just across the Neva River from the Historic Heart, and further down Nevsky pr in the areas around Smolny and pl Vosstaniya.

◎ Historic Heart

★ **State Hermitage Museum**   MUSEUM (Государственный Эрмитаж; Map p94; www. hermitagemuseum.org; Dvortsovaya pl 2; adult/ student R400/free, 1st Thu of month free, camera R200; ⊙10.30am-6pm Tue & Thu-Sun, to 9pm Wed; ⓂAdmiralteyskaya) Mainly set in the magnificent Winter Palace and adjoining buildings, the Hermitage fully lives up to its sterling reputation. You can be absorbed by its treasures for days and still come out wanting more.

The enormous collection (over three million items, only a fraction of which are on display in around 360 rooms) almost amounts to a comprehensive history of Western European art. Viewing it demands a little planning, so choose the areas you'd like to concentrate on before you arrive.

Catherine the Great, one of the greatest art collectors of all time, began the collection. Nicholas I also greatly enriched it and opened the galleries to the public for the first time in 1852.

It was the post-revolutionary period that saw the collection increase threefold, as many valuable private collections were seized by the state, including those of the Stroganovs, Sheremetyevs and Yusupovs. In 1948 it incorporated the renowned collections of post-Impressionist and Impressionist paintings of Moscow industrialists Sergei Shchukin and Ivan Morozov.

The State Hermitage consists of five linked buildings along riverside Dvortsovaya nab. From west to east they are:

➡ **Winter Palace**

This stunning mint-green, white and gold profusion of columns, windows and

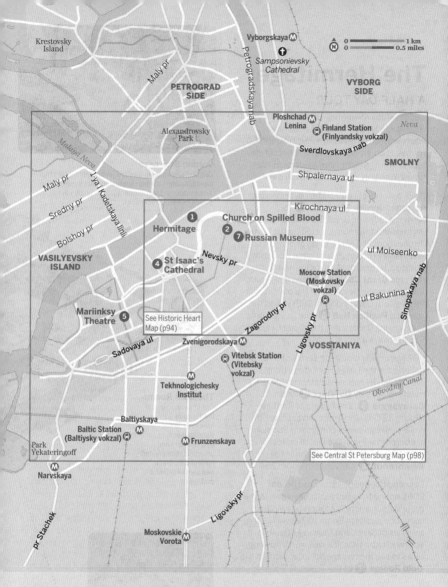

St Petersburg Highlights

1 Spending a day (or more) in the **Hermitage** (p90), one of the world's unrivalled art collections

2 Witnessing the amazing kaleidoscope of colours that is the **Church on Spilled Blood** (p97)

3 Revelling with locals

during the ethereal endless daylight of the **White Nights**

4 Climbing the enormous dome of **St Isaac's Cathedral** (p100) for a bird's-eye view of the imperial city

5 Having the ultimate Russian experience by taking in a ballet at the **Mariinsky Theatre** (p108)

6 Heading out of town to **Tsarskoe Selo** (p102), Catherine the Great's incredible summer palace, to see the magnificent Amber Room

7 Seeing the sublime collection of art, from icons to the avant-garde, at the **Russian Museum** (p100)

The Hermitage

A HALF-DAY TOUR

Successfully navigating the State Hermitage Museum, with its four vast interconnecting buildings and around 360 rooms, is an art form in itself. Our half-day tour of the highlights can be done in four hours, or easily extended to a full day.

Once past ticket control start by ascending the grand **Jordan Staircase** ❶ to Neva Enfilade and Great Enfilade for the impressive staterooms, including the former throne room St George's Hall and the 1812 War Gallery (Room 197), and the Romanovs' private apartments. Admire the newly restored **Great Church** ❷ then make your way back to the Neva side of the building via the Western Gallery (Room 262) to find the splendid **Pavilion Hall** ❸ with its view onto the Hanging Garden and the gilded Peacock Clock, always a crowd pleaser.

Make your way along the series of smaller galleries in the Large Hermitage hung with Italian Renaissance art, including masterpieces by **Da Vinci** ❹ and **Caravaggio** ❺. The Loggia of Raphael (Room 227) is also impressive. Linger a while in the galleries containing Spanish art before taking in the Dutch collection, the highlight of which is the hoard of **Rembrandt** ❻ canvases in Room 254.

Descend the Council Staircase (Room 206), noting the giant malachite vase, to the ground floor where the fantastic Egyptian collection awaits in Room 100 as well as the galleries of Greek and Roman Antiquities. If you have extra time, it's well worth booking tours to see the two special exhibitions in the **Gold Rooms** ❼ of the Treasure Gallery.

TOP TIPS

» **Queues** Reserve tickets online to skip the long lines.

» **Dining** Bring a sandwich and a bottle of water with you: the cafe is dire.

» **Footwear** Wear comfortable shoes.

» **Cloakroom** Bear in mind the only one is before ticket control, so you can't go back and pick up a sweater.

KEVIN OSBORNE / FOX FOTOS / GETTY IMAGES ©

Jordan Staircase
Originally designed by Rastrelli, in the 18th century this incredible white marble construction was known as the Ambassadorial Staircase because it was the way into the palace for official receptions.

The Gold Rooms
One of two sections of the Treasure Gallery, here you can see dazzling pieces of gold jewellery and ornamentation created by Scythian, Greek and ancient Oriental craftsmen.

IMAGE SOURCE / GETTY IMAGES ©

Great Church
This stunningly ornate church was the Romanovs' private place of worship and the venue for the marriage of the last tsar, Nicholas II, to Alexandra Feodorovna in 1895.

Rembrandt
A moving portrait of contrition and forgiveness, *Return of the Prodigal Son* (Room 254) depicts the biblical scene of a wayward son returning to his father.

Da Vinci
Along with the *Benois Madonna*, also here, *Madonna and Child (Madonna Litta;* Room 214) is one of just a handful of paintings known to be the work of Leonardo da Vinci.

St George's Hall

Hermitage Theatre

Pavilion Hall
Apart from the Peacock Clock, the Pavilion Hall also contains beautifully detailed mosaic tables made by Italian and Russian craftsmen in the mid-19th century.

Caravaggio
The Lute Player (Room 237) is the Hermitage's only Caravaggio, and a work that the master of light and shade described as the best piece he'd ever painted.

Historic Heart

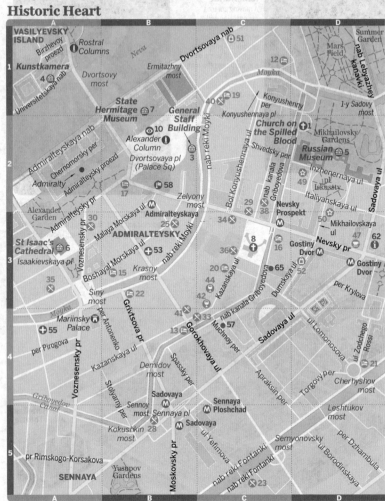

recesses, with its roof topped by rows of classical statues, was commissioned from Bartolomeo Rastrelli in 1754 by Empress Elizabeth. Catherine the Great and her successors had most of the interior remodelled in a classical style by 1837. It remained an imperial home until 1917, though the last two tsars spent more time in other palaces.

➡ **Small Hermitage**

The classical Small Hermitage was built for Catherine the Great as a retreat that would also house the art collection started by Peter the Great, which she significantly expanded.

➡ **Old Hermitage**

At the river end of the Little Hermitage is the Old Hermitage, which also dates from the time of Catherine the Great.

➡ **New Hermitage**

Facing Millionnaya ul on the south end of the Old Hermitage, the New Hermitage was built for Nicholas II, to hold the still-growing art collection. The Old and New Hermitages are sometimes grouped together and labelled the Large Hermitage.

➡ **State Hermitage Theatre**

Built in the 1780s by the classicist Giacomo Quarenghi, who thought it one of his

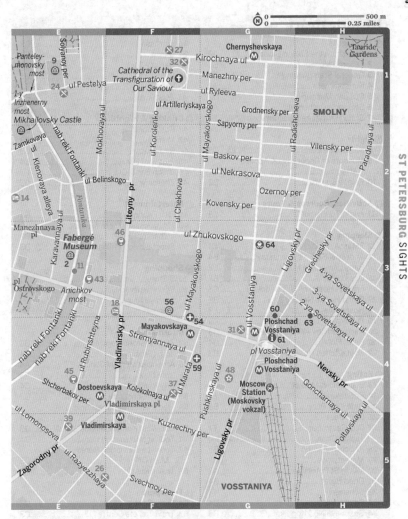

finest works. Concerts and ballets are still performed here. In the same building but accessed from the Neva Embankment are the remains of the Winter Palace of Peter I.

As much as you see in the museum, there's about 20 times more in its vaults, part of which you can visit at the Hermitage Storage Facility. Other branches of the museum include the east wing of the General Staff Building (home to the Hermitage's amazing collection of Impressionist and post-Impressionist works), the Menshikov Palace on Vasilyevsky Island, and the Imperial Porcelain factory in the south of the city.

Palace Square   SQUARE

(Дворцовая пл; Map p94; Ⓜ Admiralteyskaya) This vast expanse is simply one of the most striking squares in the world, still redolent of imperial grandeur almost a century after the end of the Romanov dynasty. For the most amazing first impression, walk from Nevsky pr, up Bolshaya Morskaya ul and under the triumphal arch.

In the centre of the square, the 47.5m Alexander Column was designed in 1834 by Montferrand. Named after Alexander I, it commemorates the 1812 victory over Napoleon.

Historic Heart

◎ Top Sights
1 Church on the Spilled Blood.................D2
2 Fabergé Museum.................................E3
3 General Staff Building.........................B2
4 Kunstkamera.......................................A1
5 Russian Museum.................................D2
6 St Isaac's Cathedral...........................A3
7 State Hermitage Museum...................B1

◎ Sights
8 Kazan Cathedral.................................C3
9 Museum of Decorative & Applied
    Arts...E1
10 Palace Square....................................B2

◎ Activities, Courses & Tours
11 Anglo Tourismo...................................E3

◎ Sleeping
12 3MostA..C1
13 Andrey & Sasha's Homestay..............B4
14 Baby Lemonade Hostel.......................E2
15 Casa Leto..B3
16 Friends Hostel on Griboedov..............C3
17 Guest House Nevsky 3........................B2
18 Hostel Life...F3
19 Pushka Inn...C1
20 Rachmaninov Antique Hotel...............C3
21 Rossi Hotel..D4
22 Soul Kitchen Hostel............................B3

◎ Eating
23 BGL Cafe & Market.............................C5
24 Botanika...E1
25 Café King Pong....................................B3
26 Dom Beat...E5
27 Duo Gastrobar.....................................F1
    Jack & Chan....................................(see 14)
28 Khochu Kharcho..................................B5
29 Marketplace...C2
30 MiX in St Petersburg...........................A3
31 Obed Bufet..G4
32 Schengen...F1
33 Soup Vino..C4
34 Stolovaya No 1 Kopeika......................C3
35 Teplo..A3

36 Terrassa...C3
37 Ukrop..F4
38 Ukrop..C2
39 Vinostudia..E5
40 Yat..C1
41 Zoom Café...B4

◎ Drinking & Nightlife
42 Borodabar..C3
43 Mishka..E3
44 Radiobaby...C3
45 Terminal Bar..E4
46 Union Bar & Grill.................................F3
47 Ziferberg..D3

◎ Entertainment
48 Fish Fabrique.......................................G4
49 Mikhailovsky Opera & Ballet
    Theatre...D2
50 Shostakovich Philharmonia................D3

◎ Shopping
51 8 Store...C1
52 Perinnye Ryady...................................D3
    Staraya Kniga..................................(see 17)
    Taiga...(see 51)

◎ Information
53 36.6 (Historic Centre)........................B3
54 36.6 (Smolny)......................................F4
55 American Medical Clinic.....................A4
56 Cafe Max..F3
57 City Realty...C4
58 French Consulate................................B2
59 Medem International Clinic &
    Hospital..F4
60 Ost-West Kontaktservice....................G3
61 Tourist Information Bureau.................G4
62 Tourist Information Bureau
    Main Office.......................................D3
63 Travel Russia......................................H3

◎ Transport
64 Ferry Centre..G3
65 Train Tickets Centre............................C3

On windy days, contemplate that the pillar is held on its pedestal by gravity alone!

The square's northern end is capped by the Winter Palace (Zimny Dvorets), a rococo profusion of columns, windows and recesses, topped by rows of larger-than-life statues. A residence of tsars from 1762 to 1917, it's now the largest part of the Hermitage (p90).Curving an incredible 580m around the south side of the square is the Carlo Rossi–designed General Staff Building completed in 1829. The east wing now houses a branch of the Hermitage while the west wing is the headquarters of the Western Military District. The two great blocks are joined by a triumphal arch over Bolshaya Morskaya ul, topped by the Chariot of Glory by sculptors Stepan Pimenov and Vasily Demuth-Malinovsky, another monument to the Napoleonic Wars.

★ **General Staff Building**   MUSEUM
(Здание Главного штаба; Map p94; www.hermitagemuseum.org; Dvortsovaya pl 6-8; admis-

sion R100; ⊘10.30am-6pm Tue, Thu-Sun, 10.30am-9pm Wed; Ⓜ Admiralteyskaya) The east wing of this magnificent building, wrapping around the south of Dvortsovaya pl and designed by Carlo Rossi in the 1820s, marries restored interiors with contemporary architecture to create a series of galleries displaying the Hermitage's amazing collection of Impressionist and post-Impressionist works. Contemporary art is here, too, often in temporary exhibitions by major artists.

Entry to the galleries is via a broad new marble staircase, which doubles as an amphitheatre for musical performances held in the glassed-over courtyard. At the time of research, installation of all the artworks was underway and should be completed by the end of 2015.

★ **Church on the Spilled Blood**   CHURCH
(Церковь Спаса на Крови; Map p94; http://cathedral.ru; Konyushennaya pl; adult/student R250/150; ⊘10.30am-6pm Thu-Tue; Ⓜ Nevsky Prospekt) This five-domed dazzler is St Petersburg's most elaborate church with a classic Russian Orthodox exterior and interior decorated with some 7000 sq m of mosaics. Officially called the Church of the Resurrection of Christ, its far more striking colloquial name references the assassination attempt on Tsar Alexander II here in 1881.

The church, which incorporates elements of 18th-century Russian architecture, is so lavish it took 24 years to build and went over budget by 1 million roubles – an enormous sum for the times. Following decades of abuse and neglect during the Soviet era, painstaking restoration began in the 1970s and took 27 years to be completed.

Kazan Cathedral   CHURCH
(Казанский собор; Map p94; http://kazan-sky-spb.ru; Kazanskaya pl 2; ⊘8.30am-7.30pm; Ⓜ Nevsky Prospekt) FREE This neoclassical cathedral, partly modelled on St Peter's in Rome, was commissioned by Tsar Paul shortly before he was murdered in a coup. Its 111m-long colonnaded arms reach out towards Nevsky pr, encircling a garden studded with statues.

Inside, the cathedral is dark and traditionally orthodox, with a daunting 80m-high dome. There is usually a queue of believers waiting to kiss the icon of Our Lady of Kazan, a copy of one of Russia's most important icons.

Look for the victorious Napoleonic War field marshal Mikhail Kutuzov (whose remains are buried inside the cathedral) and his friend and aide Mikhail Barclay de Tolly.

The cathedral's design reflects Paul's eccentric desire to unite Catholicism and Orthodoxy in a kind of 'super-Christianity' as well as his fascination with the Knights of Malta, of which he was a member.

ST PETERSBURG SIGHTS

ST PETERSBURG IN...

Two Days
On day one wander down **Nevsky pr**, dropping in to the **Church on Spilled Blood** (p97) and the **Kazan Cathedral** (p97), **Palace Square** (p95) and **St Isaac's Cathedral** (p100). Then visit the **Yusupov Palace** (p100). In the evening spend some time checking out St Petersburg's drinking scene on Dumskaya ul or ul Zhukovskogo. Devote day two to the wondrous **Hermitage** (p90) and its extraordinary collection, including the modern paintings in the **General Staff Building** (p96) on the other side of Palace Sq (p95). When you leave, relax by taking a sightseeing cruise around the canals. Spend the evening seeing a ballet or opera at the traditional **Mariinsky Theatre** (p108) or the brand-new **Mariinsky II** (p108).

Four Days
On day three start at the **Peter & Paul Fortress** (p101) to see where the city began, and wander past the **Mosque** (p102) and take in the Style Moderne architecture of Kamennoostrovsky pr. Wander across the bridge to Vasilevsky Island and see the fascinating **Kunstkamera** (p101) and then either the **Menshikov Palace** (p101) (for history fans) or the **Erarta Museum of Contemporary Art** (p101) (for art fans). Spend day four outside the city to get a taste of tsarist splendour. Start at **Tsarskoe Selo** (p102) for a visit to the extraordinary **Catherine Palace** (p102), then continue to nearby **Peterhof** (p102) to enjoy its fountains and canals. When you get back to the city in the afternoon, explore the superb **Russian Museum** (p100).

Central St Petersburg

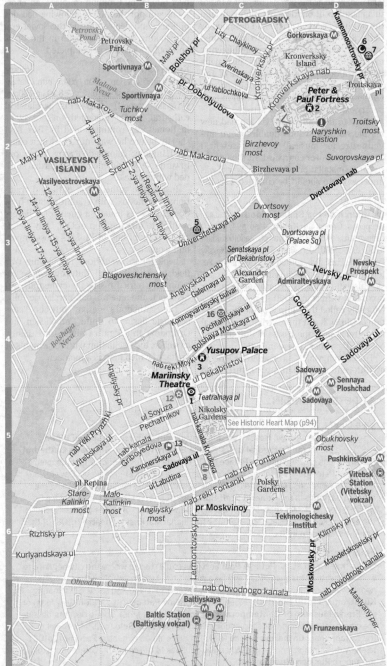

PETROGRADSKY

Petrovsky Pond

Petrovsky Park

Sportivnaya

Sportivnaya

Maly pr

Bolshoy pr

pr Dobrolyubova

Lizy Chaykinoy

Zverinskaya ul

ul Yablochkova

Gorkovskaya

Kronverksky pr

Kronverksky Island

Kronverkskaya nab

6
7

Kamennoostrovsky pr

Peter & Paul Fortress 2

Troitskaya pl

9

Naryshkin Bastion

Troitsky most

Malaya Neva

Tuchkov most

nab Makarova

nab Makarova

Birzhevoy most

Birzhevaya pl

Suvorovskaya pl.

Maly pr

4-ya i 5-ya linii

Sredny pr

1-ya liniya

2-ya liniya

ul Repina

3-ya liniya

VASILYEVSKY ISLAND

Vasileostrovskaya

8-9 linii

12-ya liniya

13-ya liniya

14-ya liniya

15-ya liniya

16-ya liniya

17-ya liniya

Universitetskaya nab

5

Dvortsovy most

Dvortsovaya nab

Dvortsovaya pl (Palace Sq)

Senatskaya pl (pl Dekabristov)

Nevsky pr

Nevsky Prospekt

Blagoveshchensky most

Angliyskaya nab

Galernaya ul

Alexander Garden

Admiralteyskaya

Bolshaya Neva

Konnogvardeysky bulvar

Pochtamtskaya ul

16

Bolshaya Morskaya ul

Gorokhovaya ul

Sadovaya ul

Angliysky pr

nab reki Moyki

3

Yusupov Palace

ul Dekabristov

Mariinsky Theatre

12

1

Teatralnaya pl

Sadovaya

Sadovaya

Sennaya Ploshchad

ul Soyuza Pechatnikov

Nikolsky Gardens

nab kanala Kryukova

See Historic Heart Map (p94)

Obukhovsky most

Pushkinskaya

nab reki Pryazhki

Vitebskaya ul

nab kanala Griboyedova

13

Kanonerskaya ul

Sadovaya ul

8

nab reki Fontanki

nab reki Fontanki

SENNAYA

Vitebsk Station (Vitebsky vokzal)

pl Repina

Staro-Kalinkin most

Malo-Kalinkin most

ul Labutina

Angliysky most

pr Moskvinoy

Lermontovsky pr

Polsky Gardens

Tekhnologichesky Institut

Rizhsky pr

Kurlyandskaya ul

Obwodny Canal

nab Obvodnogo kanala

Moskovsky pr

Klimsky pr

Malodetskoselsky pr

nab Obvodnogo kanala

Maslyany per

Baltiyskaya

Baltic Station (Baltiysky vokzal)

21

Frunzenskaya

N 0 ____ 1 km
0 ____ 0.5 miles

Samsonievsky most
ul Kuybysheva
Petrovskaya nab
Ploshchad Lenina
Finland Station (Finlyandsky vokzal)
Ploshchad Lenina
Arsenalnaya nab
Sverdlovskaya nab
Neva
Liteyny most
nab Kutuzova
nab Robespiera
11 Shpalernaya ul
Zakharevskaya ul
Liteyny pr
Summer Garden
ul Chaikovskogo 14
Tauride Gardens
Tverskaya ul
pl Proletarskoy Diktatury
17
18 15
Chernyshevskaya
SMOLNY
Kirochnaya ul
ul Pestelya
ul Korolenko
Vilensky per
Paradnaya ul
Yaroslavskaya ul
1-y Sadovy most
most Belinskogo
pl Belinskogo
ul Vosstaniya
7-ya Sovetskaya ul
Degtyarny per
ul Moiseenko
Novgorodskaya ul
Inzhenernaya ul
Italiyanskaya ul
Manezhnaya pl
ul Zhukovskogo
Ligovsky pr
Kirillovskaya ul
Gostiny Dvor
Anichkov most
pl Ostrovskogo
Ploshchad Vosstaniya
Sinopskaya nab
Mayakovskaya
pl Vosstaniya
ul Bakunina
nab reki Fontanki
Dostoevskaya
Ploshchad Vosstaniya
Moscow Station (Moskovsky vokzal)
Nevsky pr
Goncharnaya ul
Konnaya ul
Ispolkomskaya ul
Telezhnaya ul
Leshtukov most
Vladimirskaya
Ploshchad Alexandra Nevskogo
most Alexandra Nevskogo
Zagorodny pr
ul Pravdy
pl Alexandra Nevskogo
Zvenigorodskaya
VOSSTANIYA
4
Kremenchugskaya ul
20
ul Marata
ul Pechatnika Grigorieva
10
Ligovsky Prospekt
Romenskaya ul
podyezdny per
Borovaya ul
Voronezhskaya ul
Obvodny Kanal
19
Obvodny Canal
Borovaya ul
Ligovsky pr
Voronezhskaya ul
Kurskaya ul
Prilukskaya ul
Rasstannaya ul

Central St Petersburg

★**Russian Museum** MUSEUM
(Русский музей; Map p94; www.rusmuseum.ru; Inzhenernaya ul 4; adult/student R350/150, 4-palace ticket adult/child R600/300; ☺10am-6pm Wed & Fri-Sun, to 5pm Mon, 1-9pm Thu; MNevsky Prospekt) The handsome Mikhailovsky Palace is home to the country's biggest collection of Russian art. After the Hermitage you may feel you have had your fill of art, but try your utmost to make some time for this gem of a museum. There's also a lovely garden behind the palace.

★**St Isaac's Cathedral** MUSEUM
(Isaakievsky Sobor; Map p94; www.cathedral.ru; Isaakievskaya pl; cathedral adult/student R250/150, colonnade R150; ☺10.30am-6pm Thu-Tue, cathedral closed Wed, colonnade 1st & 3rd Wed; MAdmiralteyskaya) The golden dome of St Isaac's Cathedral dominates the St Petersburg sky-

line. Its obscenely lavish interior is open as a museum, although services are held in the cathedral on major religious holidays. Most people bypass the museum to climb the 262 steps to the *kolonnada* (colonnade) around the drum of the dome, providing superb city views.

French designer Auguste Montferrand began designing the cathedral in 1818, despite the fact that he was no architect. The cathedral took so long to build (until 1858) that Nicholas I was able to insist on an even more grandiose structure than Montferrand had originally planned. More than 100kg of gold leaf was used to cover the 21.8m-high dome alone. Since 1990, after a 62-year gap, services have been held here on major religious holidays even though St Isaac's is officially classed as a museum.

★**Yusupov Palace** PALACE
(Юсуповский дворец; Map p98; ☎812-314 9892; www.yusupov-palace.ru; nab reki Moyki 94; adult/student/child incl audio guide R500/380/280, Rasputin tour adult/student R300/180; ☺11am-5pm; MSadovaya) This spectacular palace on the Moyka River has some of best 19th-century interiors in the city, in addition to a fascinating and gruesome history. The palace's last owner was the eccentric Prince Felix Yusupov, a high-society darling and at one time the richest man in Russia. Most notoriously, the palace is the place where Grigory Rasputin was murdered in 1916, and the basement where this now-infamous plot unravelled can be visited as part of a guided tour.

★**Fabergé Museum** MUSEUM
(Map p94; ☎812-333 2655; www.fsv.ru/en/collection; nab reki Fontanki 21; tour R300; ☺11am-7pm; MGostiny Dvor) Book by email at least five days in advance for one of the hour-long tours of the magnificently restored Shuvalovsky Palace, home to the largest collection of pieces manufactured by the jeweller Peter Carl Fabergé (including nine imperial Easter eggs) and fellow master craftsmen and women of pre-revolutionary Russia.

Museum of Decorative & Applied Arts MUSEUM
(Музей декоративного и прикладного искусства; Map p94; www.spbghpa.ru; Solyanoy per 15; adult/student R100/50 excursion in Russian R200; ☺11am-5pm Tue-Sat; MChernyshevskaya) Also known as the Stieglitz Museum, this fascinating establishment is as beautiful

as you would expect a decorative arts museum to be. An array of gorgeous objects is on display, from medieval furniture to 18th-century Russian tiled stoves and contemporary works by the students of the Applied Arts School, also housed here. This museum is less visited than some of its counterparts in the city, but the quiet atmosphere only adds to its appeal.

Loft Project ETAGI CULTURAL CENTRE

(Лофт проект ЭТАЖИ; Map p98; www.loft-projectetagi.ru; Ligovsky pr 74; ☉ noon-10pm; ⓜ Ligovsky Prospekt) This fantastic conversion of the former Smolninsky Bread Factory has plenty to keep you interested, including many of the original factory fittings seamlessly merged with the thoroughly contemporary design. There are several galleries and exhibition spaces, lots of shops, a hostel, a bar and a cafe with a great summer terrace all spread out over five floors.

◉ Vasilyevsky Island

★ Kunstkamera MUSEUM

(Кунсткамера; Map p94; www.kunstkamera.ru; Tamozhenny per; adult/child R250/50; ☉ 11am-7pm Tue-Sun; ⓜ Admiralteyskaya) Also known as the Museum of Ethnology and Anthropology, the Kunstkamera is the city's first museum and was founded in 1714 by Peter himself. It is famous largely for its ghoulish collection of monstrosities, preserved 'freaks', two-headed mutant foetuses, deformed animals and odd body parts, all collected by Peter with the aim of educating the notoriously superstitious Russian people. While most rush to see these sad specimens, there are also very interesting exhibitions on native peoples from around the world.

Menshikov Palace MUSEUM

(Государственный Эрмитаж-Дворец Меншикова; Map p98; www.hermitagemuseum.org; Universitetskaya nab 15; admission R100; ☉ 10.30am-6pm Tue-Sat, to 5pm Sun; ⓜ Vasileostrovskaya) The first stone building in the city, the Menshikov Palace was built to the grandiose tastes of Prince Alexander Menshikov, Peter the Great's closest friend and the first governor of St Petersburg. It is now a branch of the Hermitage and while only a relatively small part of the palace is open to visitors, it's well worth coming here to see the impressively restored interiors.

★ Erarta Museum of Contemporary Art MUSEUM

(Музей современного искусства Эрарта; www.erarta.com; 29-ya Liniya 2; adult/under 21/family R400/200/650; ☉ 10am-10pm Wed-Mon; ⓜ Vasileostrovskaya then bus 6 or 7, or trolleybus 10 or 11 from the opposite side of the road) This fantastic contemporary art museum has made this far flung and otherwise totally dead area of Vasilyevsky Island a destination in itself. The museum divides neatly into two parts, spread over five floors. On the left-hand side is the permanent collection of some 2000 works of Russian art produced between the 1950s and the present day, while on the right-hand side the same number of floors house temporary exhibits and commercial galleries, where the work on display is also on sale.

◉ Petrograd Side

★ Peter & Paul Fortress FORTRESS

(Петропавловская крепость; Map p98; www.spbmuseum.ru; grounds free, exhibitions adult/student R60-150/40-80; ☉ grounds 8.30am-8pm, exhibitions 11am-6pm Mon, Thu-Sun, 10am-5pm Tue; ⓜ Gorkovskaya) Housing a cathedral where the Romanovs are buried, a former prison

---

HISTORIC RAILWAY STATIONS

St Petersburg's oldest and most elegant station is **Vitebsky vokzal** (Витебский вокзал; Zagorodny pr 52; ⓜ Pushkinskaya), originally built in 1837 to serve the line to Tsarskoe Selo. The current building dates from 1904 and is partly graced with gorgeous Style Moderne (Russian art nouveau) interior decoration.

While at **Moskovsky vokzal** (Московский вокзал; pl Vosstaniya; ⓜ Ploshchad Vosstaniya) look up at the expansive ceiling mural in the main entrance hall. There's a striking giant bust of Peter the Great in the hall leading to the platforms.

Finlyandsky vokzal (Финляндский вокзал; pl Lenina 6; ⓜ Ploshchad Lenina), rebuilt after WWII, is famous as the place where, in April 1917, Lenin arrived from exile and gave his legendary speech atop an armoured car. Lenin's statue, pointing across the Neva towards the old KGB headquarters, stands outside the station.

WORTH A TRIP

PETERHOF & TSARSKOE SELO

Among the several palace estates that the tsars built around St Petersburg as country retreats, the ones not to miss are **Peterhof** (Петергоф; www.peterhofmuseum.ru; ul Razvodnaya 2), 29km west of St Petersburg, and **Tsarskoe Selo** (☑ 812-465 2281; http://eng.tzar. ru; Sadovaya ul 7, Tsar's Village), 25km south of the city in the town of Pushkin.

If time is limited, Peterhof (also known as Petrodvorets) with its breezy Gulf of Finland location is the one to opt for, mainly because of its **Grand Cascade & Water Avenue**, a symphony of more than 140 fountains and canals. To see them you are required to pay to enter the **Lower Park** (Нижний парк; adult/student R500/250, free Nov-Apr; ☺ 9am-8pm). They only work from mid-May to early October, but the gilded ensemble looks marvellous at any time of year.

Tsarskoe Selo (also known as Pushkin) is a wonderful park, and its highlight is the vast baroque **Catherine Palace** (Екатерининский дворец; http://eng.tzar.ru; adult/student R400/200, audio guide R150; ☺ 10am-6pm Wed-Sun, to 9pm Mon), built between 1752 and 1756, but almost destroyed in WWII. The exterior and 20-odd rooms have been expertly restored; the Great Hall and the Amber Room are particularly dazzling.

Getting There & Away

From May to September, the Peterhof Express hydrofoil (one way/return R650/1100, 30 minutes) goes to Peterhof every 30 minutes from 9am until at least 6pm from the jetty in front of St Petersburg's Admiralty.

A far cheaper option is to take a *marshrutka* to Peterhof (R55, 30 minutes). These run frequently from outside the Avtovo (300, 424, 424A) metro station.

Marshrutky 286, 299, 342 and K545 regularly shuttle to Pushkin (R35, 30 minutes) from outside metro Moskovskaya. Infrequent suburban trains run from St Petersburg's Vitebsky vokzal. For Tsarskoe Selo (R55) get off at Detskoe Selo station, from where *marshrutky* (R20) frequently run to the estate.

and various exhibitions, this large defensive fortress on Zayachy Island is the kernel from which St Petersburg grew into the city it is today. History buffs will love it and everyone will swoon at the panoramic views from atop the fortress walls, at the foot of which lies a sandy riverside beach, a prime spot for sunbathing.

Individual tickets are needed for each of the fortress's attractions – the best deal is the combination ticket for the Peter and Paul Cathedral and the Trubetskoy Bastion (adult/child R350/180). The main entrance is across the Ioannovsky Bridge at the island's northeast end; there's also access via the Kronwerk Bridge, which is within walking distance of Sportivnaya metro station.

Mosque MOSQUE
(Соборная мечеть; Map p98; ☑ 821-233 9819; http://dum-spb.ru/kontakty; Kronverksky pr 7; ☺ 7am-9pm; Ⓜ Gorkovskaya) This beautiful working mosque (built 1910–14) was modelled on Samarkand's Gur-e Amir Mausoleum. Its fluted azure dome and minarets are stunning and surprisingly prominent in the city's skyline. Outside of prayer times, if you are respectfully dressed (women should

wear a head covering, men long trousers), you can walk through the gate at the northeast side and ask the guard for entry – the interior is equally lovely.

If you are allowed in, remove your shoes, do not talk and do not take photos.

Museum of Political History MUSEUM
(Музей политической истории России; Map p98; ☑ 812-313 6163; www.polithistory.ru; ul Kuybysheva 4; adult/student R150/60; ☺ 10am-6pm Fri-Tue, 10am-8pm Wed; Ⓜ Gorkovskaya) The elegant Style Moderne Kshesinskaya Palace (1904) is a highly appropriate location for this excellent museum – one of the city's best – covering Russian politics in scrupulous detail up to contemporary times.

The palace, previously the home of Mathilda Kshesinskaya, famous ballet dancer and one-time lover of Nicholas II in his pre-tsar days, was briefly the headquarters of the Bolsheviks, and Lenin often gave speeches from the balcony.

☞ Tours

A number of operators can arrange city tours on foot and Anglo Tourismo can also organise tours by boat. For something more private than Anglo Tourismo's cruises, there are many small boats that can be hired as private water taxis. You'll have to haggle over rates: expect to pay around R2500 an hour for a group of up to six people.

★ Peter's Walking Tours WALKING TOURS
(☑ 812-943 1229; www.peterswalk.com; scheduled tours from R750 per person; ⊙ scheduled tours Apr-Oct) Established in 1996, Peter Kozyrev's innovative and passionately led tours are highly recommended as a way to see the city with knowledgable locals. The daily Original Peterswalk is one of the favourites and leaves daily from Hostel Life (p103) at 10.30am from mid-April to late October.

★ Sputnik Tours WALKING TOURS
(www.sputnik8.com) This online tour agency is one with a difference: it acts as a market place for locals wanting to give their own unique tours of their own city. Browse, select a tour, register and pay a deposit and then you are given the contact number of the guide. A superb way to meet locals you'd never meet otherwise.

Anglo Tourismo BOAT, WALKING TOURS
(Map p94; ☑ 921-989 4722; www.anglotourismo. com; 27 nab reki Fontanki; 1hr tour adult/student R650/550; Ⓜ Gostiny Dvor) There's a huge number of companies offering cruises all over the Historic Heart, all with similar prices and itineraries. However, Anglo Tourismo is the only operator to run tours with commentary in English. Between May and September the schedule runs every 1½ hours between 11am and 6.30pm. From 1 June to 31 August there are also additional night cruises.

VB Excursions WALKING TOURS
(☑ 812-380 4596; www.vb-excursions.com) Offers excellent walking tours with clued-up students on themes including Dostoevsky and Revolutionary St Petersburg. The 'Back in the USSR' tour (R2300 per person) includes a visit to a typical Soviet apartment for tea and bliny.

★☆ Festivals & Events

The city's biggest event is the **Stars of the White Nights Festival**, which includes numerous events ranging from folk to ballet. The official festival dates are the last 10 days of June, but all kinds of arts events and performances take place across the city throughout June and often into July, with the Mariinsky Theatre taking the lead.

🛏 Sleeping

Accommodation is of good standard in St Petersburg and the city has some of the best hostels in Russia. However, it's important to book well ahead for the summer months.

🏠 Nevsky Prospekt & Around

★ Soul Kitchen Hostel HOSTEL $
(Map p94; ☑ 8-965-816 3470; www.soulkitchen-hostel.com; nab reki Moyki 62/2, apt 9, Sennaya; dm/d from R900/3600; ✿@🛜; Ⓜ Admiralteyskaya) Soul Kitchen blends boho hipness and boutique-hotel comfort, scoring perfect 10s in many key categories: private rooms (chic), dorm beds (double-wide with privacy-protecting curtains), common areas (vast), kitchen (vast *and* beautiful) and bathrooms (downright inviting). There is also bike hire, table football, free Macs to use, free international phone calls and stunning Moyka views from a communal balcony.

★ Baby Lemonade Hostel HOSTEL $
(Map p94; ☑ 812-570 7943; www.facebook.com/pages/Baby-Lemonade-Hostel; Inzhernernaya ul 7; dm/d with shared bathroom, incl breakfast from R790/2590, d with bathroom from R3250; @🛜; Ⓜ Gostiny Dvor) The owner of Baby Lemonade is crazy about the 1960s and it shows in the pop-art, psychedelic design of this friendly, fun hostel with two pleasant, large dorms and a great kitchen and living room. It's worth splashing out for the boutique-hotel-worthy private rooms that are in a separate flat with great rooftop views.

Hostel Life HOSTEL $
(Map p94; ☑ 812-318 1808; www.hostel-life. ru; Nevsky pr 47, Vosstaniya; dm from R950, tw/ tr R3325/3515; ✿🛜; Ⓜ Mayakovskaya) From the moment you arrive you're made to feel at home – slippers are provided – and the premises are spacious and bright. The 15 rooms range from doubles to dorms sleeping eight and Room 7 has an amazing corner window on Nevsky pr – surely the best view available for this low price!

★ Friends Hostel on Griboedov HOSTEL $
(Map p94; ☑ 812-571 0151; www.friendsplace.ru; nab kanala Griboyedova 20; dm/d R500/2500; @🛜; Ⓜ Nevsky Prospekt) In a quiet courtyard near Kazan Cathedral, this is our favourite out of the many branches of this truly friendly, very colourful hostel chain. The dorms and rooms are spotless, have lockers and share good bathrooms and a kitchen. Perks

include free international calls, English-speaking staff and organised daily events such as pub crawls and historical walks.

★ Andrey & Sasha's Homestay
APARTMENT $$

(Map p94; ☑ 8-921-409 6701, 812-315 3330; asamatuga@mail.ru; nab kanala Griboyedova 51, Sennaya; s/d R2600/4000; Ⓜ Sadovaya) Energetic Italophiles Andrey and Sasha extend the warmest of welcomes to travellers lucky enough to rent out one of their three apartments (by the room or in their entirety). All are centrally located and eclectically decorated with lots of designer touches and an eye for beautiful furniture, tile work and mirrors. Bathrooms are shared, as are kitchen facilities.

Casa Leto
BOUTIQUE HOTEL $$

(Map p94; ☑ 812-314 6622; http://casaleto.com; Bolshaya Morskaya ul 34; r incl breakfast from R7900; ✳@ 🛜; Ⓜ Admiralteyskaya) A dramatically lit stone stairwell sets the scene for this discreet and stylish boutique hotel with five guest rooms named after famous St Petersburg architects. With king-size beds, heated floors, soft pastel shades and plenty of antiques, the spacious, high-ceilinged quarters are deserving of such namesakes.

★ Rachmaninov Antique Hotel
BOUTIQUE HOTEL $$

(Map p94; ☑ 812-327 7466; www.hotelrachmaninov.com; Kazanskaya ul 5; s/d incl breakfast from R6300/7100; @🛜; Ⓜ Nevsky Prospekt) The long-established Rachmaninov still feels like a secret place for those in the know. Perfectly located and run by friendly staff, it's pleasantly old world with hardwood floors and attractive Russian furnishings, particularly in the breakfast salon which has a grand piano.

Guest House Nevsky 3
HOTEL $$

(Map p94; ☑ 812-710 6776; www.nevsky3.ru; Nevsky pr 3; s/d incl breakfast R4700/5300; 🛜; Ⓜ Admiralteyskaya) The four individually decorated rooms here sport a fridge, TV, safe and a fan, and overlook a surprisingly quiet courtyard just moments from the Hermitage. Guests are able to use the kitchen, making self-catering a doddle – no wonder it gets rave reviews.

3MostA
BOUTIQUE HOTEL $$

(Map p94; ☑ 812-332 3470; www.3mosta.com; nab reki Moyki 3a; s/d from R4500/8000; ✳🛜; Ⓜ Nevsky Prospekt) Near three bridges over the Moyka River, this 26-room property is surprisingly uncramped given its wonderful location. Even the standard rooms are of a good size with tasteful furniture, minibars and TVs. Some rooms have great views across to the Church on the Spilled Blood, and all guests have access to the roof for the panoramic experience.

Pushka Inn
BOUTIQUE HOTEL $$

(Map p94; ☑ 812-312 0913; www.pushkainn. ru; nab reki Moyki 14; s/d incl breakfast from R6000/11,500; ✳🛜; Ⓜ Admiralteyskaya) On a particularly picturesque stretch of the Moyka River, this charming inn is housed in an historic 18th-century building. The rooms are decorated in dusky pinks and caramel tones, with wide floorboards and – if you're willing to pay more – lovely views of the Moyka.

★ Rossi Hotel
BOUTIQUE HOTEL $$$

(Map p94; ☑ 812-635 6333; www.rossihotels. com; nab reki Fontanki 55; s/d/ste incl breakfast from R12,000/12,900/18,000; ✳@🛜; Ⓜ Gostiny Dvor) Occupying a beautifully restored building on one of St Petersburg's prettiest squares, the Rossi's 53 rooms are all designed differently, but their brightness and moulded ceilings are uniform. Antique beds, super-sleek bathrooms, exposed brick walls and lots of cool designer touches create a great blend of old and new.

🛏 Elsewhere in St Petersburg

Location Hostel
HOSTEL $

(Map p98; ☑ 812-329 1274; www.hostel74.ru; Ligovsky pr 74, Vosstaniya; dm/r from R700/1500, design rooms R6000; ⊖🛜; Ⓜ Ligovsky Prospekt) Come and stay in St Petersburg's coolest art gallery and cultural space – the 3rd floor of Loft Project ETAGI is given over to this super-friendly hostel. Some of the dorms here are enormous (one has 20 beds in it!) but the facilities are spotless, and include washing machines and a small kitchen.

★ Alexander House
BOUTIQUE HOTEL $$$

(Map p98; ☑ 812-334 3540; www.a-house.ru; nab kanala Kryukova 27, Kolomna; s/d incl breakfast from R10,625/11,475; ⊖✳🛜; Ⓜ Sadovaya) Owners Alexander and Natalya have converted this historic building opposite the Nikolsky Cathedral, styling each of the 14 spacious rooms after their favourite international cities. While these can vary in success and taste, when they get it right, the effect is great. Lovely common areas include a fireplace-warmed lounge and a vine-laden courtyard containing a guests-only restaurant. Book in advance.

Eating

Restaurants

★Duo Gastrobar FUSION $
(Map p94; ☎812-994 5443; www.duobar.ru; ul Kirochnaya 8a; mains R200-500; ⏱1pm-midnight, until 2am Fri & Sat; Ⓜ Chernyshevskaya) This light-bathed place, done out in wood and gorgeous glass lampshades, has really helped put this otherwise quiet area on the culinary map. Its short fusion menu excels, featuring such unlikely delights as passionfruit and gorgonzola mousse and salmon with quinoa and marscarpone. There are also more conventional choices such as risottos, pastas and salads.

★Marketplace RUSSIAN, INTERNATIONAL $
(Map p94; http://market-place.me; Nevsky pr 24; mains R200-300; ⏱9am-6am; 📶✍; Ⓜ Nevsky Prospekt) The most central branch of this mini-chain that brings a high-class polish to the self-serve canteen concept with many dishes cooked freshly on the spot to order. The hip design of the multi-level space is very appealing, making this a great spot to linger, especially if you indulge in one of the desserts or cocktails served on the 1st floor.

★Jack & Chan INTERNATIONAL $
(Map p94; http://jack-and-chan.com; Inzhenernaya ul 7; mains R350; ⏱10am-midnight; 📶; Ⓜ Gostiny Dvor) The restaurant name, a punning reference to Jackie Chan in Russian, neatly sums up the burger-meets-Asian menu at this fine and stylish casual diner. Try the sweet-and-sour fish and the prawn-and-avocado salad with glass noodles.

Obed Bufet CAFETERIA $
(Обед Буфет; Map p94; 5th fl, Nevsky Centre, Nevsky pr 114; mains R100-200; ⏱10am-11pm; 📶; Ⓜ Mayakovskaya) Just what St Petersburg needs: a well-run, central and inviting cafeteria run by the city's most successful restaurant group. Here you'll find an extraordinary range of salads, soups, sandwiches, pizzas and meat dishes. There is even a 50% discount until noon and after 9pm, making this a superb deal (come at 9pm for the latter though, otherwise there will be no food left).

Stolovaya No 1 Kopeika RUSSIAN $
(Столовая No. 1 Копейка; Map p94; Nevsky pr 25; mains R25-50, set lunch R99; ⏱24hr; Ⓜ Nevsky Prospekt) We doubt there are cheaper places to eat this well on Nevsky – no wonder the lines are long at this self-serve canteen in a cheerfully decorated basement. It's standard Russian dishes but all are freshly prepared and available around the clock.

Botanika VEGETARIAN $
(Ботаника; Map p94; www.cafebotanika.ru; ul Pestelya 7; mains R200-500; ⏱11am-midnight; 📶✍; Ⓜ Chernyshevskaya) Enjoying perhaps the friendliest and most laid-back atmosphere of any restaurant in St Petersburg, this vegetarian charmer wins on all counts. The menu takes in Russian, Indian, Italian and Japanese dishes, all of which are very well realised. Service is friendly, there's no loud TV on, English is spoken and there's even a playroom and menu for the kids.

★Yat RUSSIAN $$
(Ять; Map p94; ☎812-957 0023; http://eatinyat.com; nab reki Moyki 16; mains R500; ⏱11am-11pm; 📶👪; Ⓜ Admiralteyskaya) Perfectly placed for eating near to the Hermitage, this country-cottage-style restaurant has a very appealing menu of traditional dishes, which are presented with aplomb. The *shchi* soup is excellent and they offer a tempting range of flavoured vodkas. There's also a fab kids area with pet rabbits for them to feed. Hand-painted crockery items are available for sale and make excellent souvenirs.

★Teplo MODERN EUROPEAN $$
(Map p94; ☎812-570 1974; www.v-teple.ru; Bolshaya Morskaya ul 45; mains R250-650; ⏱9am-midnight; ❄📶✍; Ⓜ Admiralteyskaya) This much-feted, eclectic and original restaurant has got it all just right. The venue itself is a lot of fun to nose around, with multiple small rooms, nooks and crannies. Service is friendly and fast (when it's not too busy) and the peppy, inventive Italian-leaning menu has something for everyone. Reservations are usually needed.

Dom Beat INTERNATIONAL $$
(Дом Быта; Map p94; www.dombeat.ru; ul Razyezzhaya 12; mains R300-500; 📶✍; Ⓜ Ligovsky Prospekt) As if naming St Petersburg's coolest bar, lounge and restaurant after a Soviet all-purpose store and then dressing the model-gorgeous staff in tailored pastiches of factory uniforms wasn't a solid enough start, the sleek, retro-humorous interior,

sumptuous menu and great atmosphere add up to make this one of the best eating choices in town.

Schengen
INTERNATIONAL **$$**

(Шенген; Map p94; ☑812-922 1197; ul Kirochnaya 5; mains R400-850; ☺11am-midnight; ☎; Ⓜ Chernyshevskaya) A breath of fresh air just off Liteyny pr, Schengen represents local aspirations to the wider world. The menu is truly international, with a Mac & Cheese section, chilli con carne, Thai green curry and Norwegian trout fillet on it, and is served up in a cool and relaxing two-room space where efficient staff glide from table to table. Food is of very high quality and there's a 20% discount until 3.30pm on weekdays.

Vinostudia
ITALIAN **$$**

(Map p94; ☑812-380 7838; www.vinostudia.com; ul Rubinshteyna 38; mains R350-700; ☎☑🍴) Another superb addition to ul Rubinshteyna's impressive eating options, Vinostudia is a serious and passionately run *enoteca*. All wine is available by the glass (R130 to R350) and the staff are knowledgeable and friendly. There's a good Italian-leaning menu, with dishes such as grilled tiger shrimp, calamari and duck breast rounding out more traditional fare.

Khochu Kharcho
GEORGIAN **$$**

(Хочу харчо; Map p94; Sadovaya ul 39/41; mains R500-1200; ☺24hr; ☎☑🍴; Ⓜ Sennaya Ploshchad) This sparkling, friendly and capacious offering right on the Haymarket effortlessly outshines the generally dire offerings to be found elsewhere in this area. A delicious fully photographic menu of comfort food awaits, focused on Mingrelian (West Georgian) cooking, meaning that you can expect calorific *khachapuri* (cheese-stuffed bread), *khinkali* (dumplings), and of course the eponymous *kharcho*, a beef, rice, tomato and walnut soup. This is the best thing that has happened on Sennaya pl for years.

Koryushka
RUSSIAN, GEORGIAN **$$**

(Корюшка; Map p98; ☑812-917 9010; http://ginzaproject.ru/SPB/Restaurants/Korushka/About; Petropavlovskaya krepost 3, Zayachy Island; mains R500; ☺noon-midnight; ☎🍴; Ⓜ Gorkovksaya) Lightly battered and fried smelt (*koryushka*) is a St Petersburg speciality every April, but you can eat the small fish year-round at this relaxed, sophisticated restaurant beside the Peter and Paul Fortress. There are plenty of other very appealing Georgian dishes on

the menu to supplement the stunning views across the Neva.

Café King Pong
ASIAN **$$**

(Map p94; www.kingpong.ru; Bolshaya Morskaya ul 16; mains R500; ☺noon-midnight; ☎☑; Ⓜ Admiralteyskaya) This fun pan-Asian diner, occupying sleek and luminous premises with a retro-glamorous feel just off Nevsky, offers a large menu of very good-quality dishes taking in dim sum, noodles, soups and rice dishes. There are also plenty of vegie options.

Terrassa
EUROPEAN **$$**

(Map p94; ☑812-937 6837; www.terrassa.ru; Kazanskaya ul 3a; mains R600-1000; ☺11am-1am, from noon Sat & Sun; ☎☑; Ⓜ Nevsky Prospekt) Sleek and buzzing, Terrassa is centred on its namesake terrace, which boasts unbelievable views (open only in warmer months). Inside you can watch the chefs, busy in the open kitchen, preparing fresh fusion cuisine that exhibits influences from Italy, Asia and beyond.

MiX in St Petersburg
INTERNATIONAL **$$$**

(Map p94; ☑812-610 6166; www.wstpetersburg.com; Voznesensky pr 6; mains R1000-2200; ☺noon-3pm & 7pm-midnight; ☎; Ⓜ Admiralteyskaya) French cookery star Alain Ducasse is the man behind this slick and creative kitchen attached to the W Hotel. Sublime yet simple dishes tend to be French in essence with an international or Russian edge. A nice touch is the vegetarian set meal, a great deal at R700/1100 for two/three courses. Service and atmosphere are both top-notch.

Cafes & Quick Eats

BGL Cafe & Market
BAGELS **$**

(Map p94; nab reki Fontanki 96; bagels R50-250; ☺11am-11pm; ☎☑) Finally, somewhere decent to enjoy freshly filled bagels! This cool little cafe is popular with a young and worldly crowd, and has a great location overlooking the Fontanka River. Good lunch deals (until 4pm) make this a great lunch stop, with good coffee and cake on offer too. Bagels to go are also available, as are unfilled ones for sale.

Soup Vino
MEDITERRANEAN **$**

(Map p94; ☑812-312 7690; www.supvino.ru; Kazanskaya ul 24; mains R310-410; ☺noon-11pm; ☑; Ⓜ Nevsky Prospekt) This tiny place is a foodie dream. Fresh daily specials such as artichoke salad and gazpacho complement a large range of freshly made soups. There are also several pasta dishes and delicious *panini* that can be taken away or enjoyed in the cute, wood-heavy premises.

Zoom Café
EUROPEAN $

(Map p94; www.cafezoom.ru; Gorokhovaya ul 22; mains R300-450; ⏱9am-midnight Mon-Sat, from 11am Sat, from 1pm Sun; 🛜⏏♿; ⓂNevsky Prospekt) A perennially popular cafe (expect to wait for a table at peak times) with a funky feel and an interesting menu, ranging from Japanese-style chicken in teriyaki sauce to potato pancakes with salmon and cream cheese. Well-stocked bookshelves, a range of board games and adorable cuddly toys encourage lingering.

Ukrop
VEGAN $

(Map p94; www.cafe-ukrop.ru; Malaya Konyushennaya ul 14; mains R200-300; ⏱9am-11pm; 🛜⏏; ⓂNevsky Prospekt) Proving vegie, vegan and raw food can be inventive and tasty as well as wholesome, Ukrop (meaning dill) also makes an effort with its bright and whimsical craft design, which includes swing seats and lots of natural materials.

There's also a branch on **ul Marata** (Укроп; Map p94; ul Marata 23; ⏱9am-11pm; 🛜⏏; ⓂMayakovskaya).

🍸 Drinking & Nightlife

★Borodabar
COCKTAIL BAR

(Map p94; Kazanskaya ul 11; ⏱6pm-6am; 🛜; ⓂNevsky Prospekt) Boroda means beard in Russian, and sure enough you'll see plenty of facial hair and tattoos in this hipster cocktail hang-out. Never mind, as the mixologists really know their stuff – we can particularly recommend their smoked old fashioned, which is infused with tobacco smoke, and their colourful (and potent) range of shots.

★Radiobaby
BAR, CLUB

(Map p94; www.radiobaby.com; Kazanskaya ul 7; ⏱6pm-6am; ⓂNevsky Prospekt) **FREE** Go through the arch at Kazanskaya 5 (not 7 – that's just the street address), turn left through a second arch and you'll find this super-cool barnlike bar on your right. It's divided into several different rooms, there's a 'no techno, no house' music policy, table football, a relaxed crowd and an atmosphere of eternal hedonism. After 10pm each night, the place becomes more a club than a bar.

★Ziferberg
ANTI-CAFE

(Map p94; http://ziferburg.ziferblat.net; 3rd fl, Passage, Nevsky pr 48; 1st/subsequent hr min charge R2/1, max charge R360; ⏱11am-midnight Sun-Thu,

11am-7am Fri & Sat; 🛜; ⓂGostiny Dvor) Occupying much of the 3rd-floor gallery of Passage is this anti-cafe with a range of quirky, boho-hipster decorated spaces, some intimate, others very social. There's an excellent range of activities to enjoy with your coffee or tea, from boardgames and movies to concerts by classical music students, particularly on the weekends.

★Union Bar & Grill
BAR

(Map p94; Liteyny pr 55; ⏱6pm-4am Sun-Thu, until 6am Fri & Sat; 🛜; ⓂMayakovskaya) The Union is a glamorous and fun place, characterised by one enormous long wooden bar, low lighting and a New York feel. It's all rather adult, with a serious cocktail list and designer beers on tap. It's crazy at the weekends, but quiet during the week, and always draws a cool twenty- and thirty-something crowd.

Mishka
BAR

(Мишка; Map p94; www.miskhabar.ru; nab reki Fontanky 40; ⏱6pm-2am Mon-Thu, 2pm-6am Fri-Sun; 🛜; ⓂGostiny Dvor) Hipster ground zero in St Petersburg is this two-room basement place that is massively popular with a cool student crowd. The front room is hectic, smoky and becomes a dance floor later in the evening, while the quiet, non-smoky backroom is a chill-out area. DJs spin nightly and there's a big cocktail list.

Terminal Bar
BAR

(Map p94; ul Rubinshteyna 13a; ⏱4pm-last customer; 🛜; ⓂDostoevskaya) A slice of New York bohemia on one of the city's most happening streets, Terminal is great for a relaxed drink with friends, who can spread out along the length of the enormous bar, while great music (and live piano from anyone who can play) fills the long, arched room under the grey vaulted ceilings. One of our favourites.

Griboyedov
CLUB

(Грибоедов; Map p98; www.griboedovclub.ru; Voronezhskaya ul 2a; cover R200-400; ⏱noon-6am; 🛜; ⓂLigovsky Prospekt) Griboyedov is hands-down the longest-standing and most respected music club in the city. Housed in a repurposed bomb shelter, this one was founded by local ska collective Dva Samolyota. It's a low-key bar in the early evening, gradually morphing into a dance club later in the night.

☆ Entertainment

Check the weekly *St Petersburg Times* for up-to-date listings.

Classical Music, Ballet & Opera

★**Mariinsky Theatre**   THEATRE
(Мариинский театр; Map p98; ☎812-326 4141; www.mariinsky.ru; Teatralnaya pl; ⊙box office 11am-7pm; Ⓜ Sadovaya) The Mariinsky Theatre has played a pivotal role in Russian ballet ever since it was built in 1859 and remains one of Russia's most loved and respected cultural institutions. Its pretty green-and-white main building on aptly named Teatralnaya pl (Theatre Sq) is a must for any visitor wanting to see one of the world's great ballet and opera stages, while its brand-new second stage, the Mariinsky II, is a state-of-the-art opera house for the 21st century.

Mariinsky II   THEATRE
(Мариинский II; Map p98; ☎812-326 4141; www.mariinsky.ru; ul Dekabristov 34; tickets R300-6000; ⊙ticket office 11am-7pm; Ⓜ Sadovaya) Finally opening its doors in 2013 after more than a decade of construction, legal wrangles, scandal and rumour, the Mariinsky II is a showpiece for Petersburg's most famous ballet and opera company. It is one of the most technically advanced music venues in the world, with superb sightlines and acoustics from all of its 2000 seats.

**Mikhailovsky Opera &
Ballet Theatre**   OPERA, BALLET
(Map p94; ☎812-595 4305; www.mikhailovsky.ru; pl Iskusstv 1; Ⓜ Nevsky Prospekt) While not quite as grand as the Mariinsky, this illustrious stage still delivers the Russian ballet or operatic experience, complete with multitiered theatre, frescoed ceiling and elaborate concerts. Pl Iskusstv (Arts Sq) is a lovely setting for this respected venue, which is home to the State Academic Opera & Ballet Company.

Shostakovich Philharmonia   CLASSICAL MUSIC
(Map p94; www.philharmonia.spb.ru; Ⓜ Nevsky Prospekt) Under the artistic direction of world-famous conductor Yury Temirkanov, the Philharmonia represents the finest in orchestral music. The **Bolshoy Zal** on pl Iskusstv is the venue for a full program of symphonic performances, while the nearby **Maly Zal** hosts smaller ensembles. Both venues are used for numerous music festivals, including the superb **Early Music Festival** (www.earlymusic.ru).

Live Music

St Petersburg is a great place to see live bands.

Fish Fabrique   LIVE MUSIC
(Map p94; www.fishfabrique.spb.ru; Ligovsky pr 53; ⊙3pm-6am, concerts from 8pm Thu-Sun, sometimes on other days; 🕾; Ⓜ Ploshchad Vosstaniya) There are St Petersburg institutions and then there's Fish Fabrique, the museum of local boho life that has been going for two decades. Here, in the dark underbelly of Pushkinskaya 10, artists, musicians and counter culturalists of all ages meet to drink beer and listen to music.

JFC Jazz Club   JAZZ
(Map p98; ☎812-272 9850; www.jfc-club.spb.ru; Shpalernaya ul 33; cover R100-500; ⊙7-11pm; Ⓜ Chernyshevskaya) Very small and very New York, this cool club is the best place in the city to hear modern, innovative jazz music, as well as blues, bluegrass and various other styles (see the website for a list of what's on). The space is tiny, so book a table online if you want to sit down.

🛍 Shopping

★**Udelnaya Fair**   FLEA MARKET
(Удельная ярмарка; Skobolvesky pr, Vyborg Side; ⊙8am-5pm Sat & Sun; Ⓜ Udelnaya) This treasure trove of Soviet ephemera, pre-revolutionary antiques, WWII artefacts and bonkers kitsch from all eras is truly worth travelling for. Exit the metro station to the right and follow the crowds across the train tracks. Continue beyond the large permanent market, which is of very little interest, until you come to a huge area of independent stalls, all varying in quality and content.

★**Taiga**   FASHION
(Тайга; Map p94; http://space-taiga.org; Dvortsovaya nab 20; ⊙1-9pm; 🕾; Ⓜ Admiralteyskaya) Like several other of Piter's trendy hang-outs, Taiga keeps a low profile despite its prime location close to the Hermitage. The warren of small rooms in the ancient building are worth exploring to find cool businesses ranging from a barber to guitar workshop. **8 Store** (Map p94; 8-store.ru; Dvortsovaya nab 20; ⊙1pm-9pm; Ⓜ Admiralteyskaya) is one of the best, a stylish boutique stacked with clothes and accessories by local designers.

Perinnye Ryady ARTS & CRAFTS
(Периные ряды, арт-центр; Map p94; ☎812-440 2028; www.artcenter.su; Dumskaya ul 4; ⊙10am-8pm; Ⓜ Nevsky Prospekt) Scores of arts-and-craft stores can be found in this arcade in the midst of Dumskaya ul, among them Collection, with a wide range of painted works, several by members of the Union of Artists of Russia, and Pionersky Magazin, specialising in Soviet-era memorabilia, where you're guaranteed to find a bust of Lenin and colourful propaganda and art posters. There's also a small exhibition space here (adult/student R300/200).

Staraya Kniga BOOKSHOP
(Старая книга; Map p94; Nevsky pr 3; ⊙10am-7pm; Ⓜ Admiralteyskaya) This long-established antique bookseller is a fascinating place to rummage around. The stock ranges from fancy, mint-edition books to secondhand, well-worn Soviet editions, maps and art (in the section next to the art supplies shop). It's a great place to look for an unusual, unique souvenir. Find it in the courtyard off the main road.

ⓘ Information

DANGERS & ANNOYANCES
➡ Watch out for pickpockets, particularly along Nevsky pr and in crowded places such as theatres and cinemas.

➡ From May to September mosquitoes can be nightmarish. The plug-ins that slowly heat repellent-saturated cardboard pads are available everywhere in the city and are very effective. Alternatively bring repellent or cover up and keep the windows closed after rain.

➡ Tiny traces of *Giardia lamblia*, a nasty parasite that causes stomach cramps and diarrhoea, have been found in St Petersburg's water. There's no preventative drug so the best advice is to not drink straight from the tap. To be absolutely safe, drink only bottled water.

EMERGENCY
Most emergency numbers have Russian-speaking operators. If you need to make a police report and don't speak Russian, first contact the Tourist Office.
Ambulance (☎03)
Fire Department (☎01)
Police (☎02)

INTERNET ACCESS
Wireless access is ubiquitous across the city's hotels and restaurants. In nearly all cases it's free, but you'll have to ask for the password. If you don't have a smart phone or a laptop, the following internet cafe is centrally located.
Cafe Max (Map p94; www.cafemax.ru; Nevsky pr 90/92; per hr R120; ⊙24hr; Ⓜ Mayakovskaya) A big fancy place with 150 computers, a game zone and a comfy cafe and beer bar. It's located on the 2nd floor.

MEDICAL SERVICES
Clinics
The American Medical Clinic and the Medem International Clinic are open 24 hours and have English-speaking staff.
American Medical Clinic (Map p94; ☎812-740 2090; www.amclinic.ru; nab reki Moyki 78; ⊙24hr; Ⓜ Admiralteyskaya)
Medem International Clinic & Hospital (Map p94; ☎812-336 3333; www.medem.ru; ul Marata 6; ⊙24hr; Ⓜ Mayakovskaya)

Pharmacies
Look for the sign *apteka*, or the usual green cross to find a pharmacy.
36.6 (Historic Centre) (Map p94; Gorokho-vaya ul 16; ⊙24hr; Ⓜ Sadovaya)
36.6 (Smolny) (Map p94; Nevsky pr 98; ⊙24hr; Ⓜ Mayakovskaya)

MONEY
ATMs are ubiquitous and there are currency-exchange offices all the way along and around Nevsky pr, many of which are open 24 hours a day.

POST
Post office branches are scattered throughout the city. All the major air-courier services are available in St Petersburg.
Main Post Office (Map p98; Pochtamtskaya ul 9; ⊙24hr; Ⓜ Admiralteyskaya)

TELEPHONE
You can buy a local SIM card at any mobile-phone shop for as little as R200, including R100 credit.

TOURIST INFORMATION
The English-speaking staff at the **City Tourist Information Centre** (Map p94; ☎812-310 2822; http://eng.ispb.info; Sadovaya ul 14/52; ⊙10am-7pm Mon-Fri, noon-6pm Sat; Ⓜ Gostiny Dvor) do their best to help with advice and information. There are also kiosks outside the **Hermitage** (Dvortsovaya pl 12; ⊙10am-7pm; Ⓜ Admiralteyskaya), on **Pl Vosstaniya** (Map p94; pl Vosstaniya; ⊙10am-7pm; Ⓜ Ploshchad Vosstaniya) and desks at the airport.

TRAVEL AGENCIES
The following agencies can all organise visa support, hotels, train tickets and transfers.

City Realty (Map p94; ☑ 812-570 6342; www.cityrealtyrussia.com; Muchnoy per 2; ⊙ 9am-7pm Mon-Fri, 9am-5pm Sat; Ⓜ Nevsky Prospekt)

Ost-West Kontaktservice (Map p94; www. ostwest.com; Ligovsky pr 10; ⊙ 9am-6pm Mon-Sat; Ⓜ Ploshchad Vosstaniya)

Travel Russia (Map p94; www.travelrussia. su; Office 408, 4th fl, Senator Business Centre, 2-ya Sovetskaya ul 7; ⊙ 9am-8pm Mon-Fri, 9am-5pm Sat; Ⓜ Ploshchad Vosstaniya)

❶ Getting There & Away

TRAIN

Trans-Siberian Routes

Most travellers continuing to Siberia will travel to and stop over in Moscow, from where they will have a far wider choice of trains continuing east. While the direct St Petersburg to Irkutsk service was discontinued in 2013, it is still possible to head east without going first via Moscow: take train 040Ц or 72 from the Ladozhsky Station to Yekaterinburg (R9000 *kupe*, 35 hours). Both services avoid the capital, and from Yekaterinburg you can connect to all Trans-Siberian services.

Other services that take you from St Petersburg towards Siberia go via Moscow, and include the 145A train from Moscow Station to Chelyabinsk (R7400 *kupe*, 39 hours) and the 74E train from the Ladozhsky Station to Tyumen (R8000 *kupe*, 39 hours).

Long-Distance Trains

There are four major long-distance train stations in St Petersburg. Most commonly used is the **Moscow Station** (Московский вокзал; www. moskovsky-vokzal.ru; Nevsky pr 85; Ⓜ Ploshchad Vosstaniya), which mainly serves Moscow, but also the rest of western Russia, Crimea and the Caucasus.

Other stations include the **Ladozhsky Station** (Ладожский вокзал; www.lvspb.ru; Zanevsky pr 73; Ⓜ Ladoszhskaya), which receives some services to/from Helsinki, the far north of Russia, the Leningrad Oblast and the Ural Mountains; the **Finland Station** (Финляндский вокзал; www.finlyandsky.dzvr.ru; pl Lenina 6; Ⓜ Ploshchad Lenina), for services to/from Helsinki, and the **Vitebsk Station** (Витебский вокзал; Zagorodny pr 52; Ⓜ Pushkinskaya), which has trains for the Baltic states, Eastern Europe, Ukraine and Belarus. Suburban services also run from these stations, as they do from the **Baltic Station** (Балтийский вокзал; Obvodny Kanal 120; Ⓜ Baltiyskaya).

Tickets can be purchased at the train stations and the **Central Train Ticket Office** (Центральные железнодорожные кассы; Map p94; nab kanala Griboyedova 24; ⊙ 8am-8pm Mon-Sat, until 4pm Sun; Ⓜ Gostiny Dvor). Note that all train stations now have fast English-language machines that can sell you tickets on nearly all services, meaning the days of waiting for hours in long lines finally seem to be in the past.

Trains to Moscow

All trains to Moscow from St Petersburg depart from Moscow Station. Take your pick from the overnight sleeper trains or the super-fast Sapsan day trains. All train tickets can be bought online at www.rzd.ru or from the machines at any station in St Petersburg.

Overnight Trains

There are about 10 overnight trains travelling between St Petersburg and Moscow. Most depart between 10pm and 1am, arriving in the capital the following morning between 6am and 8am. On the more comfortable *firmeny* trains, a 1st-class *lyuks* ticket (two-person cabin) runs from R5000 to R6000, while a 2nd-class *kupe* (four-person cabin) is R2000 to R3500. You will often have to pay extra for bed linen,

POPULAR TRAINS FROM ST PETERSBURG TO MOSCOW

NAME & NO	DEPARTURE	DURATION	FARE (KUPE)
1 Krasnaya Strela	11.55pm	8hr	R2900
3 Ekspress	11.59pm	8hr	R2500
53 Grand Express	11.40pm	9hr	R5000-6200
752 Sapsan	6.45am	4hr	1st-/2nd-class R5056/2612
754 Sapsan	1.30pm	4½hr	1st-/2nd-class R4645/2354
161A Sapsan	3.15pm	4hr	1st-/2nd-class R5460/2870
165A Sapsan	7.45pm	4hr	1st-/2nd-class R5530/2870

although with some tickets it – and breakfast – is included.

Sapsan Trains

These high-speed trains travel at speeds of 200km/h to reach Moscow in four to 4½ hours. There are six to eight daily departures. Comfortable 2nd-class seats are R2560 to R3800, while super-spacious 1st-class seats run from R5000 to R6000.

International Destinations

From Helsinki there are four daily Allegro express trains that take you from the Finnish capital to St Petersburg in an impressive 3½ hours; see www.vr.fi for prices and timetables. Services in both directions stop at Vyborg.

St Petersburg is well connected by train to lots of cities throughout Eastern Europe, including Berlin, Budapest, Kaliningrad, Kyiv, Prague and Warsaw, but all trains pass through Belarus, for which you're required to hold a transit visa. The train to Smolensk in Russia also passes through Belarus. Border guards have been known to force people off trains and back to where they came from if they don't have a visa.

AIR

St Petersburg now has a state-of-the-art airport at Pulkovo, following the closure of its two Soviet-era terminals and the opening of the new **Pulkovo Airport** (LED; www.pulkovoairport.ru) nearby. St Petersburg has direct air links with all major European capitals and many larger Russian cities.

BOAT

Between early April and late September, international passenger ferries connect Stockholm, Helsinki and Tallinn with the **Sea Port** (Морской вокзал; ☏ 812-337 2060; www.mvokzal.ru; pl Morskoy Slavy 1). It's a long way from the metro, so either take bus 7 or trolleybus 10 from outside the Hermitage.

In the summer, regular river cruises depart from the **River Passenger Terminal** (☏ 812-262 0239, 812-262 6321; Obukhovskoy Oborony pr 195; Ⓜ Proletarskaya) and float along the Neva to inland Russia, including cruises to Valaam, Kizhi and Moscow. Tours can be booked through most travel agents, or through the **Ferry Centre** (Паромный центр; Map p94; ☏ 812-327 3377; www.paromy.ru; ul Vosstaniya 19; Ⓜ Ploshchad Vosstaniya).

Cruise ships dock at one of five ferry terminals around the city.

BUS

St Petersburg's main bus station, **Avtovokzal** (Автобусный вокзал; Map p98; ☏ 812-766 5777; www.avokzal.ru; nab Obvodnogo kanala 36; Ⓜ Obvodny Kanal) has both international and European Russia services. The website has

current timetables and routes. The single cheapest way to get to Helsinki is to take a *marshrutka* (fixed-route minibus) from pl Vosstaniya (R600); they leave all day when full from the corner of Nevsky pr and Ligovsky pr, opposite the metro station.

Other international buses are offered by a number of companies.

Ecolines (Map p98; ☏ 812-325 2152; www.ccolines.ru; Podezdny per 3; Ⓜ Pushkinskaya) Daily overnight bus from Vitebsk Station to Rīga (R1320, 9 hours). Other buses run to Minsk, Kyiv and Odessa.

Lux Express (Map p98; ☏ 812-441 3757; www.luxexpress.eu; Mitrofanievskoye sh 2, Admiral Business Centre; ⊙ 9am-9pm; Ⓜ Baltiyskaya) Runs five daily buses from the Baltic Station to Tallinn (R1850, seven hours). Daily buses go from the Baltic Station to Rīga (R1095, 11 hours).

ⓘ Getting Around

St Petersburg can be a frustrating place to get around for visitors: the metro, while an excellent system, actually has relatively few stations in the centre of the city, and distances from stations to nearby sights can be long. Many visitors find buses and *marshrutky* a little daunting, as all the signage is in Russian and you need to know where you're going. Many people just walk: bring comfortable shoes!

TO/FROM THE AIRPORT

From Pulkovo Airport, taking a taxi to the city centre has never been easier or safer. Leave the terminal building and outside you'll find an official taxi dispatcher who will ask you for your destination's address, write you a price on a slip of official paper that you can then give to your driver, and who will indicate which taxi to go to. Prices vary, but expect between R800 to R1000 to the centre, depending on where exactly you're headed. Drivers usually won't speak much English, but just hand over the money on arrival – you don't need to tip.

For those on a budget, *marshrutka* K39 shuttles you from outside the terminal building to the nearest metro station, Moskovskaya (R36, every 5 minutes, from 7am to 11.30pm). The bus terminates at the Moskovskaya metro station, so you don't need to worry about where to get off, and you can connect to the rest of the city from there. There's also bus 39 (R25, every 15 minutes, from 5.30am to 1.30am) that runs the same route over longer hours, but trundles along somewhat more slowly.

BUS, MARSHRUTKA, TROLLEYBUS & TRAM

Tickets (R21 to R25 depending on the service) are bought inside the vehicle. Bus stops are marked by roadside 'A' signs (for *avtobus*),

RAISING THE BRIDGES

From the end of April to November, all major bridges rise at the following times nightly to let seagoing ships through. The schedule (which changes every year by five minutes here or there) governs the lives of the city's motorists and nighthawks trying to get from one area to another.

- Most Alexandra Nevskogo 2.20am to 5.10am
- Birzhevoy most 2am to 4.55am
- Blagoveshchensky most 1.25am to 2.45am and 3.10am to 5am
- Bolsheokhtinsky most 2am to 5am
- Dvortsovy most 1.25am to 2.50am and 3.10am to 4.55am
- Liteyny most 1.40am to 4.45am
- Troitsky most 1.35am to 4.50am
- Tuchkov most 2am to 2.55am and 3.35am to 4.55am

trolleybus stops by 'm' (representing a handwritten Russian 'T'), tram stops by a 'T'; all usually indicate the line numbers, too. Stops may also have roadside signs with little pictures of a bus, trolleybus or tram. *Marshrutky* stop anywhere

you hail them (except on Nevsky pr, where they're banned from operating). Most transport runs from 6am to 1am.

The following are some useful routes across the city:

➡ Along Nevsky pr between Admiralty and Moskovsky vokzal. Buses 7 and 22; trolleybuses 1, 5, 7, 10 and 22. Trolleybuses 1 and 22 continue out to pl Alexandra Nevskogo. Trolleybuses 5 and 7 continue to Smolny.

➡ From Ligovsky pr via Troitsky most to Peter & Paul Fortress and Petrograd Side take *Marshrutka* K76.

➡ From the Hermitage to the far side of Vasilyevsky Island take bus 7; trolleybus 10.

METRO

The St Petersburg **metro** (www.metro.spb.ru; ☺ 6am-12.45am) is a very efficient five-lined system. The network of some 67 stations is best used for travelling long distances, especially connecting the suburbs to the city centre.

Zhetony (tokens), valid for one ride, can be bought from the booths in the stations. You're supposed to buy an extra ticket if you're carrying a large amount of luggage. If you are staying more than a day or two, however, it's worth buying a smart card (R55), which is good for loading multiple journeys over a fixed time period. The more trips you buy, the more you save – though note, you can't share a card with a friend.

Moscow to Yekaterinburg

Route Info

➡ Distance: 1814km

➡ Duration: 26 hours

➡ Time zones: Moscow, Moscow +5

Best Places to Stay & Eat

➡ Smile (p130)

➡ Jouk-Jacques hotel (p131)

➡ Hotel Giuseppe (p121)

➡ Grill Taverna Montenegro (p135)

➡ Perekrestok Dzhaza (p121)

Why Go?

For travellers, this section of the journey across European Russia will often be accompanied by the excitement of the journey ahead. It is a relatively densely populated section with three main routes. One veers northeast via Yaroslavl and a second (used by Yekaterinburg's flagship Ural train 16) goes southeast via multicultural Kazan. The more usual route, however, passes through the ancient town of Vladimir. Then at Nizhny Novgorod it crosses the Volga – a geographic highlight of this leg – before continuing to Perm, which has several good cultural sights and access to the Perm-36 former prison camp. Kungur, set in rolling hills, has a spectacular ice cave, and finally the train rattles sublimely across the Europe–Asia border and into Yekaterinburg. Note that if you're planning to stop at Golden Ring towns, it's only worth booking a *kupe* (2nd-class compartment) from Nizhny Novgorod onwards.

When to Go
Nizhny Novgorod

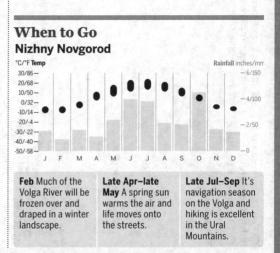

Feb Much of the Volga River will be frozen over and draped in a winter landscape.

Late Apr–late May A spring sun warms the air and life moves onto the streets.

Late Jul–Sep It's navigation season on the Volga and hiking is excellent in the Ural Mountains.

Moscow to Yekaterinburg Highlights

1 Exploring the museums of **Nizhny Novgorod** (p127)

2 Taking in one of the Golden Ring towns such as exquisite **Suzdal** (p120)

3 Strolling through the ice cave of **Kungur** (p137) and enjoying a moment of pitch darkness

4 Sailing the **Volga** on a short excursion in Nizhny Novgorod (p127) or Kazan (p120)

5 Wandering through multicultural **Kazan** (p120), Tatarstan's dynamic capital

6 Checking out the shock of the new at **PERMM** (p132), Perm's museum of modern and contemporary art

7 Taking a tour through **Perm-36** (p136), the haunting Gulag camp memorial

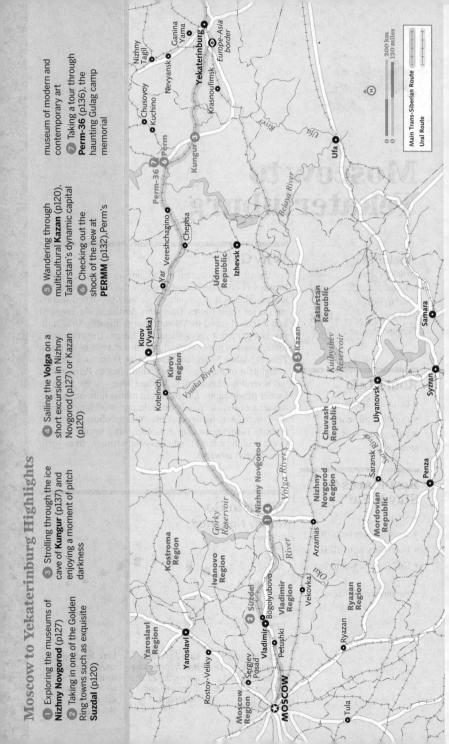

Main Trans-Siberian Route

Ural Route

0   300 km
0   120 miles

ⓘ The Route

MOSCOW TO NIZHNY NOVGOROD

0km from Moscow

For travellers leaving from Moscow and taking the train eastwards, departure will mean finding the right station (check your ticket carefully) and leaving plenty of time (about an hour is good) to pass through security, stocking up on last-minute snacks and waiting for the platform and track to be shown on the departure board. Once the doors have closed and the train slowly crawls away from the railhead, the *provodnitsa* (carriage attendant) will walk around the carriage to tear the silver seal on the tickets and give you bedding if this is not already in the compartment.

Gradually the train slips away from the platforms and station and sets a course between the streets, backyards and apartment buildings of the capital towards provincial Russia. Most likely you will see comic signs warning Muscovites against taking shortcuts across the tracks. Everywhere, Muscovites will be taking shortcuts across the tracks, some of them carrying plastic shopping bags or rushing to work.

13km

A short distance beyond Los the train crosses the Moscow Ring Road. This stretch of track through outer Moscow has been immortalised by the Soviet underground writer Venedikt Yerofeyev in his novel *Moscow to the End of the Line*. The main character travels to Petushki on a whistle-stop *elektrichka* (suburban train) at the time of Gorbachev's liquor ban, philosophising on the virtues of alcohol and the evils of the Soviet lifestyle while toasting every station. He consumes mind-boggling cocktails, such as the 'Tear of a Young Communist League Girl', which consists of three brands of cheap Soviet eau de toilette, mouth rinse, nail polish and lemonade. Don't try to repeat this fictional experience, or you'll never get anywhere, let alone to Siberia.

190km (210km)

About three hours after departing, the train reaches Vladimir, where most trains pause for about 20 minutes. Approaching the city, look for the golden spires and domes of the Assumption Cathedral high on the embankment to the north. Vladimir has some of the oldest churches in Russia and it was here that in 1157 Prince Andrei Bogolyubsky established his capital and shaped the town with architecture based on Kyivan and Western traditions. Almost 20 years later a plot was hatched to get rid of him and on one fateful night his flunkies burst into the chamber while he slept and finished him off with an axe.

200km (220km)

Just beyond Vladimir you pass the small town of Bogolyubovo, another of the historic highlights of the region and the place where Prince Andrei built his palace. Today it is largely a monastery complex dating from the 18th century. You can glimpse this if you look north as the train approaches, and east of it is the Church of the Intercession – the paragon of Russian church architecture, sitting in splendid isolation at the confluence of the Nerl and Klyazma Rivers.

254km (274km)

Tracing the valleys of the Klyazma and Oka Rivers, the train passes several other ancient towns. One of these is Kovrov, mostly known as the centre of the peculiar sport of motoball – football on motorcycles. This is followed by the pretty Gorokhovets at 363km (382km), home of the popular ski resort of Puzhalova Gora (www.puzhalova.ru).

441km (460km)

The train slows and arrives at Nizhny Novgorod, one of the most interesting and attractive cities in the region. Most trains stop for about 10 minutes, which is another chance to step onto the platform and engage in some serious hunting and gathering of supplies.

NIZHNY NOVGOROD TO PERM

442km (461km)

If you have done the Moscow to Nizhny stretch of the route overnight, one of the first things you will see on waking is the Volga River – a fine way to start a day at any time of year. In spring, however, it's impressive because the river is coated with a crust of ice broken by bluish waters. The

---

MOSCOW TO YEKATERINBURG ROUTE PLANNER

The following is a suggested itinerary for covering the main sights of the area:

Day 1 Leave Moscow; 2½-hour train to Vladimir; stay Suzdal.

Day 2 Tour Suzdal; return to Vladimir; train to Nizhny Novgorod.

Day 3 Explore Nizhny Novgorod.

Day 4 Continue exploring Nizhny Novgorod or excursion to Gorodets; night train (14½ hours) from Nizhny Novgorod to Perm.

Day 5 Look around Perm.

Day 6 Visit Perm-36 Gulag camp or do a day trip to Kungur.

Day 7 Train (six hours) to Yekaterinburg.

Moscow to Yekaterinburg

★ MOSCOW
0km

2hr,
45min

3hr,
5min

3hr,
15min

● Vladimir
190km

● Vekovka
207km

● Rostov-Veliky
224km

50min

2hr,
45min

● Yaroslavl
282km

2hr

● Nizhny Novgorod
441km

9hr,
5min

● Kostroma
376km

5hr,
13min

9hr,
34min

● Kotelnich
869km

● Kazan
820km

1hr,
30min

● Kirov (Vyatka)
956km

4hr,
40min

3hr,
10min

● Argyz
1107km

● Balezino
1192km

4hr,
31min

3hr,
40min

● Perm
1434km

● Krasnoufimsk
1456km

5hr,
15min

3hr,
41min

● Yekaterinburg (Sverdlovsk-Pass)
1814km

East to Vladivostok

Volga flows roughly north–south for 3530km – that's the equivalent of the distance by rail from Moscow to the city of Tayga in Siberia – and culminates in a beautiful wetland at its delta on the Caspian Sea.

In the 13th century, the entire Volga region was conquered by the heirs of Chinggis (Genghis) Khaan, the Mongol-led Golden Horde. Challenged by the marauder armies of Timur (Tamerlane) in the south and upstart Muscovite princes in the north, the Golden Horde eventually fragmented into separate khanates: Kazan, Astrakhan, Crimea and Sibir. In the 1550s Ivan the Terrible razed Kazan and Astrakhan, and claimed the Middle and Lower Volga for Muscovy (modern-day Moscow), the capital of the new Russian state. This was a critical juncture in Russian history as the collapse of Kazan allowed Slavic Russians to move into the Ural Mountains region around Perm, a stepping stone into Siberia.

The landscape after Nizhny Novgorod is a typical blend of farmland, forest clearings and forest itself that is not yet the true taiga of conifer we associate with Russia.

510km to 956km (530km to 956km)

After passing Semenov (510km), which is home of the *khokhloma* folk-art style, the train reaches Kotelnich (869km), the junction with the old Trans-Siberian route from Yaroslavl. Kotelnich is famous as a dinosaurs' playground – numerous Permian-period giant-lizard fossils have been discovered here. Just outside Kotelnich the train crosses the Vyatka River, a meandering 1367km waterway that accompanies the railway route to Kirov (956km), which is better known by its old name: Vyatka, same as the river. Most trains stop here for about 15 minutes. Not a lot of meaningful activity can be fit into the stopover at Vyatka, but you can celebrate having reached the northernmost point of your whole Trans-Siberian journey.

1126km

Yar is the first town you'll pass through in the Udmurt Republic, home to the Udmurts, one of Russia's four major groups of Finno-Ugric people. In contrast to Tatarstan further south, Udmurtia is a poor region which, unlike Tatarstan, never seriously considered independence when the Soviet Union collapsed, and has therefore received less money from Moscow than its Tatar neighbour. Around here the countryside becomes picturesque, with plenty of pretty painted log cabins.

1192km

At Balezino there's a change of locomotive during the roughly 20-minute halt.

1221km to 1314km

After crossing the Cheptsa River, the train enters the town of the same name. Cheptsa (1223km) is the junction with the line that runs between Perm and Kazan. About 40km further east, you'll cross into Perm Region and reach the foothills of the Ural Mountains, which stretch about 2000km from Kazakhstan to the Arctic Kara Sea. However, the Ural Mountains rarely break 500m above sea level in these parts, prompting the Russian academician Peter Pallas to drily note in 1770 on one of his journeys that the middle section of the Ural Mountains were particularly inconspicuous. Nevertheless, as the landscape unfolds you will have glimpses of verdant rolling hills and pine and birch forests, and this is one of the more attractive sections of the route before Kungur. In Perm Region (by the time you reach Vereshchagino; 1314km), local time is two hours ahead of Moscow time.

PERM TO YEKATERINBURG

1434km

The train rolls across the wide Kama River into the industrial city of Perm, where most trains stop for 20 minutes. On the northern side of the train is a steam locomotive, and the station itself has a small railway museum on the 2nd floor.

1535km

The railway turns southeast after Perm and reaches Kungur, the centre of the Stroganov patrimony. This industrial family virtually ruled the Ural Mountains from the time of Ivan the Terrible to the reign of Peter the Great, and with the implicit agreement of Ivan the Terrible it also financed Yermak's campaign across the Ural Mountains into Siberia. From Kungur, the railway follows the meandering course of the Sylva River, which on a fine day is dotted with anglers casting lines into the shallows, behind them a picturesque backdrop of low mountains. This stretch, in fact, offers the entertaining contrast of scenery and anglers beyond the window, the creaking of fittings inside the train as it struggles around the curves, and – if you are in *platskart* (3rd class) – the likely interior scenario of weary travellers huddling over crosswords on their bunks, mentally ticking off the kilometres. The best scenery is on the left, which in this direction you will have to admire from the corridor in *kupe*.

1777km

The landscape recedes to unremarkable upland once the train leaves the valley of the Sylva River, and the next major point is the one-dog station of Vershina (6km after Pervouralsk) at the border between Europe and Asia, marked by a white monument. You will need to have your wits about you to catch it, located on the south (right-hand, heading east) side of the line.

1814km

The train travels along the Chusovaya River as it approaches Yekaterinburg, through a valley that was long the heart of the mining industry in the Ural Mountains. The first major station in Asian Russia – but still 260km short of the official beginning of Siberia – is Yekaterinburg, where you can expect a 15- to 20-minute stop.

Vladimir   Владимир

🎵 4922 / POP 340,000 / TIME MOSCOW

Vladimir may look like another Soviet Gotham City, until you pass the medieval Golden Gate and stop by the cluster of exquisite churches and cathedrals, some of the oldest in Russia. Hiding behind them is an abrupt bluff with spectacular views of the Oka Valley. Prince Andrei Bogolyubsky chose Vladimir as his capital in 1157 after a stint in the Holy Land where he befriended European crusader kings, such as Friedrich Barbarossa. They sent him their best architects, who designed the town's landmarks, fusing Western and Kyivan traditions. Vladimir flourished for less than a century under Andrei's successor Vsevolod III, until a series of devastating Tatar-Mongol raids led to its decline and dependence on Moscow. The last, a 1408 siege, is vividly if gruesomely reenacted in Andrei Tarkovsky's film *Andrei Rublyov*.

ⓘ KILOMETRE POSTS

Use kilometre markings as approximations, as variances are inevitable. Over the years, the route of the Trans-Siberian has changed, making many of the kilometre markings inaccurate. For example, several different lines lead out of Moscow, each with their own markers from the railhead. Two join to form one line near Fryazevo, whereafter markers show the distance from Kursk Station. Further down the track, at the junction of this line and a former mainline route via the town of Yaroslavl, the distances are measured from Moscow via the old Yaroslavl route. On this first leg, the figures in bold brackets are the actual distance you've travelled from Moscow's Yaroslavl Station via Vladimir up to Kotelnich.

◉ Sights

Assumption Cathedral   CHURCH

(Успенский собор; ☑ 4922-325 201; pl Sobornaya; adult/child R80/30; ☉ services 7am-8pm Tue-Sun, visitors 1pm-4.45pm) Set dramatically on a high bluff above the Oka River, this finest piece of pre-Mongol architecture is the legacy of Prince Andrei Bogolyubsky – the man who started the shift of power from Kyiv to Northeastern Rus, which eventually evolved into Muscovy. Construction of this white-stone version of Kyiv's brick Byzantine churches began in 1158 – its simple but majestic form was adorned with fine carving, innovative for the time.

Inside the working church, a few restored 12th-century murals of peacocks and prophets can be deciphered about halfway up the inner wall of the outer north aisle; this was originally an outside wall. The real treasures, though, are the Last Judgment frescoes by Andrei Rublyov and Daniil Chyorny, painted in 1408 in the central nave and inner south aisle, under the choir gallery towards the west end.

Comply with the standard church dress code (no shorts for men; covered hat, long skirts for women) at all times and be especially mindful of people's sensitivities outside the designated 'tourist time'.

Cathedral of St Dmitry   CHURCH

(Дмитриевский собор; Bolshaya Moskovskaya ul 60; adult/child R50/30; ☉ 10am-5pm Wed-Mon summer, to 4pm winter) Never before or after this beauty was built between 1193 and 1197 have Russian stone carvers achieved such artistic heights. The attraction here is the cathedral's exterior walls, covered in an amazing profusion of images. The top centre of the north, south and west walls all show King David bewitching the birds and beasts with music.

Vladimir prince Vsevolod III (Vsevolod the Big Nest) had this church built as part of his palace. He appears at the top left of the north wall, with a baby son on his knee and other sons kneeling on each side. Above the right-hand window of the south wall, Alexander the Great ascends into heaven, a symbol of princely might; on the west wall appear the labours of Hercules.

Chambers   MUSEUM

(Палаты; Bolshaya Moskovskaya ul 58; adult/child R180/100; ☉ 10am-5pm Tue-Sun) The grand 18th-century court building between the two cathedrals is known as Palaty – the Chambers. It contains a children's museum, art gallery and historical exhibition. The former is a welcome diversion for little ones, who may well be suffering from old-church fatigue. The art gallery features art since the 18th century, with wonderful depictions of the Golden Ring towns.

History Museum   MUSEUM

(Исторический музей; ☑ 4922-322 284; Bolshaya Moskovskaya ul 64; adult/child R50/30; ☉ 10am-5pm Wed-Mon) This museum displays many remains and reproductions of the ornamentation from Vladimir's two cathedrals. It is part of an extensive exhibition that covers the history of Vladimir from Kyivan princes to the 1917 revolution. Reminiscent of Moscow's History Museum, the red-brick edifice was purpose-built in 1902.

Golden Gate   HISTORIC BUILDING

(Золотые ворота; www.vladmuseum.ru; Zolotye Vorota; adult/child R50/30; ☉ 10am-6pm Fri-Wed) Vladimir's Golden Gate, part defensive tower, part triumphal arch, was modelled on a very similar structure in Kyiv. Originally built by Andrei Bogolyubsky to guard the western entrance to his city, it was later restored under Catherine the Great. You can climb the narrow stone staircase to check out the **Military Museum** (☑ 4922-322 559; adult/child R40/20; ☉ 10am-6pm Fri-Wed) inside. It's a small exhibit, the centrepiece of which is a diorama of old Vladimir being ravaged by nomadic raiders in 1238 and 1293.

⌨ Sleeping

Given the proximity of the much more idyllic Suzdal, there is no big reason for overnighting in Vladimir, unless you need to catch an early morning train to Moscow or Nizhny Novgorod.

Samovar   HOSTEL $

(Самовар; ☑ 8-900 586 0151; www.samovarhostel.ru; ul Kozlov tupik 3; dm from R400, d R1400; ☎ ⊛) For starters, they do have a real samovar, inviting for a tea party (not in the Boston sense, though). More importantly, it's a brand-new purpose-built hostel with English-speaking personnel, many amenities and great atmosphere. The surroundings are admittedly slightly dingy, but the stairs leading to the garden by Assumption Cathedral are right in front of the entrance.

Rus   HOTEL $$

(Русь; ☑ 4922-322 736; www.rushotel33.ru; ul Gagarina 14; s/d with breakfast from R2900/3400;

DON'T MISS

THE CHURCH OF PERFECTION

Tourists and pilgrims all flock to Bogolyubovo, just 12km northeast of Vladimir – the reason being a small 12th-century church standing amid a flower-covered floodplain.

The **Church of the Intercession on the Nerl** (Церковь Покрова на Нерли; ⊙10am-6pm Tue-Sun) is the golden standard of Russian architecture. Apart from ideal proportions, its beauty lies in a brilliantly chosen waterside location (floods aside) and the sparing use of delicate carving.

Legend has it that Prince Andrei Bogolyubsky had the church built in memory of his favourite son, Izyaslav, who was killed in battle against the Bulgars. As with the Cathedral of St Dmitry in Vladimir, King David sits at the top of three facades, the birds and beasts entranced by his music. The interior has more carvings, including 20 pairs of lions. If the church is closed (from October to April the opening hours are more sporadic), try asking at the house behind.

To reach this famous church, get bus 152 from the Golden Gate or Sobornaya pl in Vladimir and get off by the hard-to-miss **Bogolyubsky Monastery**, which contains remnants of Prince Andrei's palace. Walk down Vokzalnaya ul, immediately east of the monastery. At the end of the street, cross the railroad tracks and follow the cobblestone path across the field. You can catch a ride in the horse-drawn carriage for R250 per person, two people minimum.

⊗⊚) Occupying an old mansion-house in a quieter street not far from the main drag, this new hotel offers nice and comfortable, if slightly faceless rooms. Reception staff is superfriendly.

★**Voznesenskaya Sloboda**　HOTEL **$$$**
(Вознесенская слобода; ☑4922-325 494; www.vsloboda.ru; ul Voznesenskaya 14b; d with breakfast R4800; P⊗⊚) Perched on a bluff with tremendous views of the valley, this hotel might have the most scenic location in the whole of the Golden Ring area. Outside is a quiet neighbourhood of old wooden cottages and villas dominated by the elegant Ascension church. The interior of the new building is tastefully designed to resemble art nouveau style c 1900.

The popular restaurant Krucha is on the premises.

✗ Eating & Drinking

The main drag ul Bolshaya Moskovskaya is lined with cafes. You will not stay hungry, but you'll be pressed to find any outstanding culinary delights in Vladimir.

Piteyny Dom Kuptsa Andreyeva　RUSSIAN **$$**
(☑4922-232 6545; www.andreevbeer.com/dom; Bolshaya Moskovskaya ul 16; mains R250-400; ⊙11am-midnight; ⊚) Merchant Andreyev's Liquor House, as the name translates, makes a half-hearted attempt to pass off as an old-world Russian *kabak* (pub), but its main virtue is a dozen of home-brewed beers on tap

and hearty Russian meals, including all the classics – from *shchi* (cabbage soup) to bliny.

Salmon & Coffee　INTERNATIONAL **$$**
(Лосось и кофе; www.losos-coffee.ru; Bolshaya Moskovskaya ul 19a; mains R300-600; ⊚) Salmon is yet to be found in the Oka, while coffee is not exactly what medieval princes had for breakfast. But instead of hinting at the city's past, this DJ cafe serving Asian as well as European dishes is here to give a cosmopolitan touch to the ancient town. Lots of dark wood, dim lights and magenta-coloured metal railings create a cool, intriguing atmosphere.

ⓘ Information

Post & Telephone Office (Почтамт и переговорный пункт; ul Podbelskogo; ⊙8am-10pm)

ⓘ Getting There & Away

Vladimir is on the main Trans-Siberian line between Moscow and Nizhny Novgorod and on a major highway leading to Kazan.

TRAIN

There are frequent services from Moscow, with the old-school Lastochka (R300, three daily) and the modern Sapsan (R900, two daily) being the fastest – they cover the distance in 1¾ hours. Both of these continue to Nizhny Novgorod (2 hours; Lastochka R300, Sapsan R1050). All long-distance trains heading towards Tatarstan and Siberia also call at Vladimir.

ALTERNATIVE ROUTE TO YEKATERINBURG VIA KAZAN

The route across European Russia to Yekaterinburg via Kazan is the least travelled of the three major lines on this leg, but it is a fascinating one because it allows you to stop over in Kazan (Казань), an attractive city situated on the Volga River. Kazan is the capital of the Tatarstan Republic – the land of the Volga Tatars, a Turkic people commonly associated with Chinggis Khaan's hordes, although they prefer to identify themselves with the ancient state of Volga Bulgaria, which was devastated by the Mongols. The independent Kazan khanate was created in 1438. It was ravaged in 1552 by Ivan the Terrible's troops and Tatar allies, and the collapse of Kazan caused such unease further east in the surviving khanate of Sibir (in Western Siberia) that Sibir nominally began paying tribute to Ivan. Kazan's collapse also cleared the way for Slavic Russian farmers to pour into the Ural Mountains region around Perm.

As well as time spent taking in Kazan's highlight, the kremlin, allow time to walk around and soak up the multicultural atmosphere of the city. Tatar autonomy is strong here and not just about bilingual street signs. It also ensures that Tatarstan benefits greatly from vast oil reserves in this booming republic. The post-Soviet cultural revival, manifested by the popularity of modern Muslim fashions and Tatar-language literature, characterises its self-confidence.

Football fans might be familiar with the city because of its popular club **Rubin Kazan** (www.rubin-kazan.ru). A highlight in the more traditional sense is the **kremlin** (кремль).

Kul Sharif Mosque (Мечеть Кул Шариф; kremlin; museum admission R100; ⊘noon-9pm Fri, 10am-6pm Sat-Thu) After you enter the main gate, an alley leads past this enormous mosque, completed in 2005, which is named after the imam who died defending the city against the troops of Ivan the Terrible in 1552.

Hermitage Kazan (Эрмитаж-Казань; kremlin; admission R150; ⊘10am-5.30pm Tue-Thu, Sat & Sun, noon-8.30pm Fri) Located inside the former cadet school building, the Hermitage Kazan has top-flight rotating exhibitions; many are from the collection of St Petersburg's Hermitage.

National Museum of the Republic of Tatarstan (Национальный музей Республики Татарстан; Kremlyovskaya ul 2; admission R150; ⊘10am-6pm Tue-Sun) Located opposite the kremlin's main entrance, this museum occupies an ornate 1770 building. It has a large archaeology collection as well as jewellery, weapons and exhibits on the history of the Tatar people and its literary figures.

BUS

Bus is a poor option for Moscow or Nizhny Novgorod – train is much faster and more reliable. Conveniently for those heading to Suzdal (R65, one hour, half hourly), the bus station is right in front of the train station. Buses also go to Yaroslavl (R560, five hours, two daily).

TAXI

Taxi drivers charge R700 for a one-way trip to Suzdal.

ⓘ Getting Around

The train station is located about 500m southeast of the centre. Trolleybus 5 from the train and bus stations runs up and along Bolshaya Moskovskaya ul, passing the main sights and hotels.

Suzdal   Суздаль

☑ 49231 / POP 12,000 / TIME MOSCOW

The Golden Ring comes with a diamond and that's Suzdal. If you have only one place to visit near Moscow, come here – even though everyone else will do the same. In 1864, local merchants failed to coerce the government into building the Trans-Siberian Railway through their town. Instead it went through Vladimir, 35km away. As a result Suzdal was bypassed not only by trains, but by the 20th century altogether. This is why the place remains largely the same as ages ago – its cute wooden cottages mingling with golden cupolas that reflect in the river, which meanders sleepily through gentle hills and flower-filled meadows.

As it happens, Suzdal served as a royal capital when Moscow was a mere cluster of

Hotel Volga (☎843-231 6349; www.volga-hotel.ru; ul Said-Galieva 1; with breakfast s R1500-2500, d R1700-5800; ❄❋@☎) Plan a couple of nights in Kazan; the Hotel Volga is an affordable choice 10 minutes by foot from Kazan-1 train station.

Hotel Giuseppe (Гостиница Джузеппе; ☎843-292 6934; www.giuseppe.ru; Kremlyovskaya ul 15/25; with breakfast s R2900-5300, d R3900-7000, ste R6600-14,000; ❋☎) This excellent hotel has hints of a Venetian villa (and a good upmarket restaurant).

Perekrestok Dzhaza (Перекресток Джаза; ☎843-264 2550; www.tatinter.ru/perekrestok-dzhaza; ul Karla Marksa 55; mains R600; ⊙restaurant 11am-midnight Sun-Thu, to 2am Fri & Sat; cafe 8am-11pm daily; ☎) The 'Jazz Crossing' has a contemporary European feel and excellent Russian and international dishes. It's ideal for drinks or dinner.

Kazan Askhane-Chai Yorty (Дом чая, кафе 'Казанская ашхане'; ul Baumana 64; mains R80, pastry R40; ⊙9am-8pm Mon-Fri, to 7pm Sat, to 6pm Sun) If you're on a tight budget and feel like trying some Tatar food, check out this eatery in the centre.

Kazan Tourist Information Centre (Казанский туристско-информационный центр; ☎843-292 3010; www.gokazan.com; Kremlyovskaya ul 15/25; ⊙9.30am-6.30pm Mon-Fri, to 3.30pm Sat) The excellent city tourist office has a good sheet map of town (also available in many hotels).

Kazan is the unchallenged highlight of this route, and after it you can doze for about five hours until the Kama River crossing at around 1150km (after Agryz). Kazan has two railway stations. The old station is on ul Said-Galieva in the centre and is variously known as Kazan-1, 'Stary Vokzal' or Kazan-Pass (passenger). The historic building is now a waiting room. Long-distance tickets are sold in the building alongside the large suburban station. Queues are shorter at ticket counters on the 2nd floor, where the service centre is also located. Kazan-2 (also known as Vosstanie-Pass on timetables) is located north of the centre and has a convenient metro station. Many of the Siberian trains go through this but there is little infrastructure for travellers around the station; check your ticket carefully.

Almost every second day the overnight *Ural* (16) departs Moscow's Kazansky station late afternoon and arrives at 4.35am, before the night is over (*platskart/kupe* R2312/2865, 11½ hours). Better in all senses is the premium 002Й from Moscow (not to be confused with train 2, the *Rossiya*), towing carriages ranging from *platskart* (R2217) through *kupe* (R3116) and *lyuks* (R5955) to *myagky* (soft class; R14,200).

cowsheds. It transformed into a major monastic centre in the times of Ivan the Terrible and an important commercial hub later on. But nowadays, it seems perfectly content in its retirement from both business and politics.

Sights

★ Kremlin FORTRESS
(Кремль; exhibits each R30-70, joint ticket adult/child R250/100; ⊙10am-6pm Wed-Mon) This kremlin is the grandfather of the one in Moscow. In the 12th century, it was the base of prince Yury Dolgoruky, who ruled the vast northeastern part of Kyivan Rus and, among many other things, founded an outpost, which is now the Russian capital. The 1.4km-long earth rampart of Suzdal's kremlin encloses a few streets of houses and a handful of churches, as well as the main cathedral group on Kremlyovskaya ul.

The **Nativity of the Virgin Cathedral**, its blue domes spangled with gold, was founded in the 1220s. Only its richly carved lower section is original white stone, though, the rest being 16th-century brick. The inside is sumptuous, with 13th- and 17th-century frescoes and 13th-century damascene (gold on copper) west and south doors.

Within the kremlin, the **Archbishop's Chambers** (Архиерейские палаты; Kremlyovskaya ul; admission R70; ⊙10am-5pm Wed-Mon) houses the **Suzdal History Exhibition** (10am-5pm Wed-Mon; admission R70), which includes the original 13th-century door from the cathedral, photos of its interior and a visit to the 18th-century Cross Hall which was used for receptions. The tent-roofed 1635

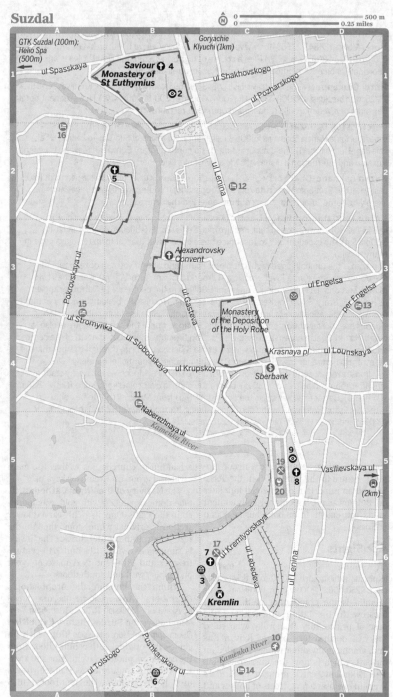

Suzdal

GTK Suzdal (100m);
Helio Spa
(500m)

Goryachie
Klyuchi (1km)

ul Spasskaya

ul Shakhovskogo

ul Pozharskogo

Saviour
Monastery of
St Euthymius

16

5

ul Lenina

12

Alexandrovsky
Convent

Pokrovskaya ul

ul Gasteva

ul Engelsa

per Engelsa

15

Monastery
of the Deposition
of the Holy Robe

13

ul Stromynka

ul Slobodskaya

ul Krupskoy

Krasnaya pl

ul Lounskaya

Sberbank

11

Naberezhnaya ul

Kamenka River

9

19

Vasilievskaya ul

8

20

(2km)

18

17

7

ul Kremlyovskaya

ul Lebedeva

3

1

ul Lenina

Kremlin

ul Tolstogo

Pushtkarskaya ul

10

Kamenka River

6

14

Suzdal

kremlin **bell tower** (звоница) on the east side of the yard contains additional exhibits.

Torgovaya Ploshchad   SQUARE
Suzdal's Torgovaya pl (Market Sq) is dominated by the pillared **Trading Arcades** (Торговые ряды; 1806–11) along its western side. There are four churches in the immediate vicinity, including the **Resurrection Church** (admission R50). Make the precarious climb to the top of the bell tower and be rewarded with wonderful views of Suzdal's gold-domed skyline. The five-domed 1707 **Emperor Constantine Church** (Цареконстантиновская церковь) in the square's northeastern corner is a working church with an ornate interior.

Saviour Monastery of St Euthymius   MONASTERY
(Спасо-Евфимиев мужской монастырь; ☏ 49231 20 746; grounds & individual exhibitions each adult/student R70/30, all-inclusive ticket adult/student R350/150; ⊙ 10am-6pm Tue-Sun) Founded in the 14th century to protect the town's northern entrance, Suzdal's biggest monastery grew mighty in the 16th and 17th centuries after Vasily III, Ivan the Terrible and the noble Pozharsky family funded impressive new stone buildings, and big land and property acquisitions. It was girded with its great brick walls and towers in the 17th century.

Right at the entrance, the **Annunciation Gate-Church** (Благовещенская надвратная церковь) houses an interesting exhibit on Dmitry Pozharsky (1578–1642), leader of the Russian army that drove the Polish invaders from Moscow in 1612.

A tall 16th- to 17th-century cathedral **bell tower** (Звонница) stands before the seven-domed **Cathedral of the Transfiguration of the Saviour** (Спасо-Преображенский собор). Every hour on the hour from 11am to 5pm a short concert of chimes is given on the bell tower's bells. The cathedral was built in the 1590s in 12th- to 13th-century Vladimir-Suzdal style. Inside, restoration has uncovered some bright 1689 frescoes by the school of Gury Nikitin from Kostroma. The tomb of Prince Dmitry Pozharsky is by the cathedral's east wall.

The 1525 **Assumption Refectory Church** (Успенская церковь), facing the bell tower, adjoins the old **Father Superior's chambers** (Палаты отца-игумена), which house a display of Russian icons and the excellent naïve art exhibition showcasing works by local Soviet-era amateur painters.

The old **Monastery Dungeon** (Монастырская тюрьма), set up in 1764 for religious dissidents, is at the north end of the complex. It now houses a fascinating exhibit on the monastery's prison history, including displays of some of the better-known prisoners who stayed here. The Bolsheviks used the monastery as a concentration camp after the 1917 revolution. During WWII, German and Italian officers captured in the battle of Stalingrad were kept here.

The combined **Hospital Chambers & St Nicholas Church** feature a rich collection of church gold treasures.

WORTH A TRIP

VOLGA-URAL MOUNTAINS SIDE TRIP

The Volga, one of Europe's great rivers, winds for some 3530km through Russia's heartland and has been a part of the continent's longest 'highway' for time immemorial. Travelling along or alongside the Volga you encounter spectacular hilltop kremlins in Nizhny Novgorod, Kazan and Astrakhan, bombastic architecture in Volgograd, numerous lively provincial capitals, as well as picturesque stretches such as the Samara Bend.

Trains cross the Volga at Yaroslavl (the northern route in European Russia), Nizhny Novgorod (the major route) and Kazan (a southern route through Tatarstan). Each of these is worth a stopover, but for longer Volga trips Nizhny Novgorod and Kazan are the best starting points. From Nizhny Novgorod it's possible to take day trips on hydrofoils to the artists' town of Gorodets.

Each price and time listed for the following Volga-Ural Mountains side trip are from the previous stop in the route:

South to the Volga delta Leave the Trans-Sib at **Nizhny Novgorod** and head south by train to **Kazan** (R1717, nine hours, daily), continuing on to **Ulyanovsk** (R759, six hours, two daily). From Ulyanovsk the easiest way to **Samara** (R500, five hours, several daily) is by bus. From there, get back on the rails again to continue to **Volgograd** (R1580, 17 hours, frequent), **Astrakhan** (R982, eight to 11 hours, two daily) and the **Volga Delta**.

Northeast return leg The simplest and best way to rejoin the Trans-Sib is to return from the lower Volga by rail via Volgograd, **Ufa** (Bashkortostan; R2215, 25 hours) and **Chelyabinsk** (R1122, 9½ hours), then head north to rejoin the Trans-Siberian route at **Yekaterinburg** (R843, five hours).

How long and how much? Plan a minimum of two weeks and about €100 per day in all-up costs, including transport, for this side trip with a couple of stopovers. Add time in the delta (an extra R8000 for a day trip) and on one of the Ural Mountains lakes.

Intercession Convent CONVENT
(Покровский монастырь; Pokrovskaya ul) FREE It's one of the classic Suzdal pictures – the whitewashed beauty surrounded by green meadows on the banks of the lazily meandering river. Inside it's all flowers. The nuns, who live in wooden cottages left over from a rustic hotel that existed on the premises, seem to be quite obsessed with floriculture. This convent was founded in 1364, originally as a place of exile for the unwanted wives of tsars.

Museum of Wooden Architecture & Peasant Life MUSEUM
(Музей деревянного зодчества и крестьянского быта; www.vladmuseum.ru; ul Pushkarskaya; adult/student R200/80; ☉9am-7pm Thu-Tue May-Oct, to 4pm Nov-Apr) This open-air museum, illustrating old peasant life in this region of Russia, is a short walk across the river, south of the Kremlin. Besides log houses, windmills, a barn, and lots of tools and handicrafts, its highlights are the 1756 Transfiguration Church and the simpler 1776 Resurrection Church.

☂ Activities

The rolling hills and attractive countryside around Suzdal are ideal for cycling, with bicycles available for rent at many hotels.

Helio Spa BANYA
(Горячие ключи; ☎49231 24 000; www.parilka.com; ul Korovniki 14; ☉11am-1am) Rural Suzdal is a great place to cleanse body and soul in a Russian *banya* (hot bath). Beautiful, lakeside *bani* are available at Helio Park Hotel (former Goryachie Klyuchi) starting at R1200 per hour for up to four people. Each is an individually designed wooden cottage with different types of steam.

Boat Cruise CRUISE
(R250) Four times a day, a small tented boat takes tourists on a 40-minute cruise on the Kamenka River, leaving from the bridge by the kremlin. It's a good chance to watch and take pictures of Suzdal's many monasteries and churches from a different perspective.

🛏 Sleeping

Suzdal is experiencing a tourist boom, which means there is plenty of choice in the mid-range and high-end bracket – from quaint two- or three-room guesthouses to vast holiday resorts. You may save up to R1000 per night if you avoid coming to Suzdal during weekends or holidays.

Godzillas Suzdal HOSTEL $

(☑ in Moscow 495 699 4223; www.godzillashostel. com; Naberezhnaya ul 32; dm with breakfast from R700; 🛜) An affiliate of the namesake hostel in Moscow, this big log-cabin facility overlooking the river opened just a few years ago, but has already undergone a thorough renovation. Each dorm room has its own bathroom and balcony. Guests can also enjoy the blooming garden and Russian *banya*, as well as the chill-out lounge and the bar in the basement.

★ Surikov Guest House GUESTHOUSE $$

(Гостевой дом Суриковых; ☑ 49231 21 568; www.surikovs.ru; ul Krasnoarmeyskaya 53; with breakfast, weekdays d/tr/q R2000/2500/3000, weekends d/tr/q R2500/3000/3500; 🛜) Drifting into the boutique hotel category, this guesthouse is positioned at a picturesque bend of the Kamenka River under the walls of St Euthymius monastery. It has modestly sized, but comfortable rooms equipped with antique-styled furniture made by the owner, and a Russian restaurant catering for guests only on the first floor. Visitors rave about this place.

Pushkarskaya Sloboda RESORT $$

(Пушкарская слобода; ☑ 49231 23 303; www. sloboda-gk.ru; ul Lenina 45; with breakfast, hotel d R2900, village d from R4300; ✳✲) This holiday village has everything you might want from your Disney vacation including accommodation in the log-cabin 'Russian inn' or the re-production 19th-century 'Gunner's Village'. It also has three restaurants, ranging from the rustic country tavern to a formal dining room; a spa centre with a pool; and every service you might dream up. It's attractive, family-friendly and good value.

Stromynka 2 HOTEL $$

(Стромынка 2; ☑ 49231 25 155; www.stromynka2. ru; ul Stromynka 2; s/d from R2600/3000; P🛜) A cross between a Russian gingerbread cottage and a Swiss chalet, this medium-sized hotel prides itself on having used only natural materials in the construction. Large and airy rooms are well equipped, smell like untreated wood and offer nice views of the Kamenka River valley. Bikes are available for hire.

Petrov Dom GUESTHOUSE $$

(Петров дом; ☑ 49231-23 326, 8-919-025 8884, 8-910-188 3108; www.petrovdom.ru; per Engelsa 18; r weekdays R1500, weekends R2000, holidays R2500; 🛜) Vlad and Lena offer three nicely furnished and strictly nonsmoking rooms in their wooden dacha-style house with a lovely garden on a quiet street (not to be confused with ul Engelsa). This is a great option for travellers with children, with a sumptuous breakfast included. Self-caterers are welcome to use the kitchen and garden grill. It's not signposted – look out for a house with a geometrically perfect triangular roof and a sun symbol on the gates.

Nikolayevsky Posad RESORT $$$

(Николаевский посад; ☑ 49231 23 585; www. nposad.ru; ul Lenina 138; with breakfast, dm R1050, weekdays s/d/tr from R3650/4300/4950, weekends & holidays s/d/tr from R4750/5600/6950; P✳🛜✲) This large, manicured resort is located right by St Euthymius monastery. It has modern and comfortable, if slightly faceless rooms as well as four- to eight-bed dorms in two-storey buildings styled as merchants' mansion houses. There is a nice restaurant, a 'hangover' cafe on site and a 25m pool (in case the hangover lingers). Bicycles are available for rent.

Although created by Russians, Nikolayevsky Posad has been recently taken over by the Best Western chain.

✖ Eating & Drinking

★ Chaynaya RUSSIAN $

(Чайная; www.restoran-suzdal.ru/chaynaya; ul Kremlyovskaya 10g; R120-350; ⊙ 10am-9pm) It is hidden inside a kitschy crafts market, but the place is a gem. Russian standards – bliny, *shchi* (cabbage soup), mushroom dishes and pickles – are prominently represented, but it is all the unusual (and rather experimental) items on the menu that make the place so special. Red buckwheat pancakes anyone? Pickled apple stuffed with herring?

Or the ultimate treat – fried, salted cucumber with pickled ashberry served on a toast with sour cream and horseradish paste? If you are in a group, definitely order a samovar of tea, which will be served with cream sugar and *baranki* (doughnut-shaped cookies).

Kvasnaya Izba RUSSIAN $

(☑ 8-915 779 0577; www.kvasnaya-izba.ru; ul Pushkarskaya 51; R200-400; ⊙ 10am-9pm; 🛜) It is

AROUND BEAR'S CORNER

In Soviet times most Trans-Siberian trains went via Yaroslavl, northeast of Moscow, rather than via Vladimir and Nizhny Novgorod, as they do today. This is still a viable alternative that reunites you with the main route shortly before the Ural Mountains. The most practical train to use on this route is the Moscow–Yaroslavl high-speed *elektrichka* (R760, 3¾ hours, twice daily), which leaves the capital around 8am and calls at Rostov-Veliky (R430, three hours, twice daily) en route.

Rostov-Veliky   Ростов-Великий

Rostov is ideal for recovering from Moscow's chaos.

Kremlin (www.rostmuseum.ru; grounds R50, joint ticket to exhibitions adult/student R450/550, individual exhibitions R40-80; ⊙10am-5pm) The sunset-pink impregnable walls and perfectly proportioned towers of the kremlin rise magnificently above shimmering Lake Nero. Rostov (first chronicled in 862) was the original capital of Kyivan princes who moved into the land later known as Muscovy and Russia. Today it is a sleepy village-like town which wakes with the sound of cockerels and gets eerily quiet when darkness falls, especially in winter. Rostov is about 220km northeast of Moscow. The train and bus stations are in the drab modern part of the town, 1.5km north of the kremlin.

Russkoye Podvorye (Русское подворье; ☎48536-64 255; ul Marshala Alexeyeva 9; s without bathroom weekdays/weekends/holidays R800/1000/1200, d weekdays/weekends/holidays R1700/2200/2500; ❀❄) This newish hotel in Rostov-Veliky occupies the arcaded house of 18th-century merchant Ivan Khlebnikov. Inside, it is quite modern, with floral ornaments and comfy beds. Breakfast is served in perhaps the best restaurant in town. You can splash an extra R2000 on a suite with a Jacuzzi.

Yaroslavl   Ярославль

Yaroslavl is one hour further down the line. It was founded by its namesake Kyivan prince, who – as legend goes – came to the place then known as Bear's Corner and axed the local tribe's totem bear, which now appears on the city's coat of arms.

---

slightly out of the way, but it's worth an extra walk if you'd like to sample all kinds of *kvas*, Russia's traditional drink made of fermented rye bread. Flavours on offer include apple, thyme and blackcurrant. You may have it as a refreshment, but it goes equally well with the hearty Russian meals here.

Kvas is so synonymous with the traditional lifestyle in Russia that there is even an ironic term – '*kvas* patriot'.

Graf Suvorov & Mead-Tasting Hall   RUSSIAN $
(Граф Суворов и зал дегустаций; Trading Arcades, ul Lenina 63a; tasting menu R130-350) This place has vaulted ceilings and kitschy wall paintings depicting Russian military hero Count Suvorov's exploits in the Alps. It serves standard Russian food and a few dozen varieties of locally produced *medovukha*, a mildly alcoholic honey ale that was drunk by princes of old. Go for tasting sets, which include 10 samples each. Apart from the regular one, there are separate sets of berry- and herb-flavoured *medovukha*.

Salmon & Coffee   INTERNATIONAL $$
(Лосось и кофе; www.losos-coffee.ru; Trading Arcades, ul Lenina 63a; mains R340-590; ⊙10am-11pm) Like its sister in Vladimir, Suzdal's S&C is about the best place for an unhurried lunch or a cup of coffee. It is, however, much quainter, with lots of whitewashed wood interior aged to evoke the 'Cherry Orchard' dacha ambience. Despite the name, salmon is not really prominent on the menu, which includes inventive fusion European dishes and sushi.

❶ Information

Post & Telephone Office (Почтамт и переговорный пункт; Krasnaya pl; ⊙8am-8pm) Open 24 hours for phone calls.

Sberbank (Сбербанк; ul Lenina 73a; ⊙8am-4.30pm Mon-Fri) Exchange office and ATM.

❶ Getting There & Away

A train/bus combination via Vladimir is by far the best way of getting from Moscow. Buses run every 45 minutes to/from Vladimir (R115, one hour). The bus station is 2km east of the centre

Church of John the Baptist at Tolchkovo (Церковь Иоанна Крестителя в Толчково; 2-уа Zakotoroslnaya nab 69; adult/student R60/30; ☺10am-4.30pm Wed-Sun) Embraced by the mighty Volga and the smaller Kotorosl rivers, Yaroslavl's centre is dotted with onion domes like no other place in Russia, such as this record-breaking 15-dome beauty.

Church of Elijah the Prophet (Церковь Ильи Пророка; Sovetskaya pl; adult/student R80/40; ☺9.30am-7pm) This exquisite church dominates Sovetskaya pl. It has some of the Golden Ring's brightest frescoes – by the ubiquitous Gury Nikitin of Kostroma and his school – and detailed exterior tiles. The church is closed during wet spells.

Music & Time (Музыка и время; ☎4852-328 637; Volzhskaya nab 33a; adult/student/child R180/100/70, joint ticket for all exhibits adult/student/child R300/100/100; ☺10am-7pm) The city's best attraction is the riverside promenade passing most churches and museums of note, such as this unique museum, which contains ex-conjuror John Mostoslavsky's impressive collection of clocks, musical instruments, bells and old vinyl records. Guides, including the owner himself, turn each tour into a bit of a concert.

Alyosha Popovich Dvor (Алеша Попович Двор; ☎4852-643 101; www.ap-dvor.ru; ul Pervomayskaya 55; s/d from R2600/3400; P 🕾) Themed on Russian fairytales and slightly kitschy in the post-Soviet theme park way, Alyosha occupies what looks like an old Russian *terem* (wooden palace). Inside it has small but comfortable rooms with bathrooms.

City Hostel (☎4852-304 192, 8-910-973 5263; ul Sverdlova 18; dm from R450, s/q R1500/3000) Modern and arguably stylish, this hostel boasts a quiet but central location. Doubles are available, but avoid the two noisy ones near the entrance.

Dudki Bar (☎4852-330 933; ul Sobinova 33) No Yaroslavl visit is complete without a bash at this bar – a two-storey affair which is good for eating during the day and partying all night.

The main station is Yaroslavl Glavny, on ul Svobody, 3km west of the centre. There are several eastbound trains daily that will get you back on the main Trans-Siberian line at Perm (R1500 to R3500, 20 hours, four daily).

on Vasilievskaya ul. Some long-distance buses pass the central square on the way.

Nizhny Novgorod
Нижний Новгород

📞 831 / POP 1.25 MILLION / TIME MOSCOW

A glorious setting is not something most Russian cities can boast, but Nizhny (as it is usually called) is a lucky exception. The mighty clifftop kremlin overlooking the confluence of two wide rivers – the Volga and the Oka – is the place where merchant Kuzma Minin and Count Dmitry Pozharsky (men commemorated in a monument in front of St Basil's Cathedral, Moscow) rallied a popular army to repel the Polish intervention in 1612.

Nizhny has been a major trading centre since its foundation in 1221. In the 19th century when the lower bank of the Oka housed the country's main fair – *yarmarka* – it was said that 'St Petersburg is Russia's head; Moscow its heart; and Nizhny Novgorod its wallet'. During Soviet times the city was named Gorky, after the writer Maxim Gorky, born here in 1868. Closed to foreigners by the Soviets, Gorky was chosen as a place of exile for the dissident physicist Andrei Sakharov.

Nizhny is often called Russia's 'third capital', but it is the fifth-largest Russian city and markedly quieter than Moscow and St Petersburg, with a laid-back ambience characteristic of the Volga cities downstream.

◉ Sights

★**Kremlin**   HISTORICAL SITE
(Нижегородский Кремль; www.ngiamz.ru) **FREE** Built upon remnants of an earlier settlement, Nizhny Novgorod's magnificent kremlin dates back to 1500–15 when the Italian architect Pyotr Fryazin began work on its 13 towers and 12m-high walls. Inside, most of the buildings are government offices. The small 17th-century **Cathedral of the Archangel Michael** (Собор Михаила Архангела) is a functioning church. Behind it, an eternal flame burns near a striking **Monument to Heroes of WWII**.

Nizhny Novgorod

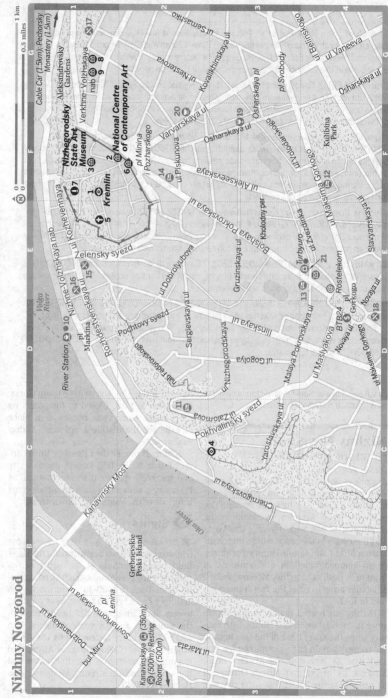

Nizhegorodsky State Art Museum

National Centre of Contemporary Art

Kremlin

Volga River

Oka River

Grebnevskie Peski Island

Kulibina Park

Cable Car (1.5km); Pechorsky Monastery (1.5km)

Aleksandrovsky Gardens

Verkhne-Volzhskaya nab

Kanavinskaya (350m); (500m); Resting Rooms (500m)

River Station

Nizhny Novgorod

Dmitry Tower   MUSEUM
(Дмитриевская башня; museum R60, kremlin wall walk incl other towers Russian/foreigner R180/240; ⊙10am-5pm Tue-Sun, kremlin wall walk May-Oct) The Dmitry Tower, the main entrance to the kremlin, has changing exhibitions on local history. This is a good place to start a 1.2km walk around the kremlin walls.

Cable Car   CABLE CAR
(Kazanskaya naberezhe; one way R75; ⊙6.45am-10pm Mon-Sat, from 9am Sun, closed 11am-1pm Mon & Thu) Connecting Nizhny Novgorod with the unattractive settlement of Bor across the Volga, this cable car offers a spectacular 13-minute ride. In winter there are views of dot-sized figures fishing on Volga ice below, and in summer there's swamp, lush greens and gentle blues. Take any bus

to Sennaya bus station and walk back for a few minutes towards the mosque. The ride peaks at over 80m and is a nerve-shattering 3.6km long.

Pechorsky Monastery   MONASTERY
(Privolzhskaya sloboda 108) This 17th-century monastery, overlooking the Volga, is perfect for a tranquil stroll in small but picturesque grounds. Take any *marshrutka* or bus from pl Minina i Pozharskogo to pl Sennaya.

Museum of the Nizhny Novgorod Diocese   MUSEUM
(Церковно-археологический музей Нижегородской епархии; admission R100; ⊙9am-5pm) Located inside the Pechorsky Monastery, this small museum has a moving exhibition on Bolshevik repressions against the church and a floor with changing exhibitions on religious themes.

Annunciation Monastery   MONASTERY
(Благовещенский монастырь; ul Garshina; ⊙7am-8pm) FREE Set at the foot of attractive parkland, the 13th-century Annunciation Monastery, above Chernigovskaya ul, is one of Nizhny Novgorod's oldest buildings. Most of the churches themselves are from the 17th century and are well worth visiting for their interiors.

Museum of Volga People's Architecture & Culture   MUSEUM
(Музей архитектуры и быта народов Нижегородского Поволжья; ☎831-422 40 54; Gorbatovskaya ul 41; admission R60; ⊙10am-5pm Tue-Sun) The open-air Museum of Volga People's Architecture & Culture has a pleasant woodland setting and a collection of traditional wooden buildings from Russian and Mordva (a Finno-Ugric people) villages. The museum is located in the remote Shchelokovsky Khutor Park, which is the final stop of bus 28 (30 minutes, every hour), passing ul Belinskogo in the centre. *Marshrutka* 62 also stops close by.

Sakharov Museum   MUSEUM
(Музей Сахарова; pr Gagarina 214; admission R70; ⊙9am-5pm Sat-Thu) The Sakharov Museum is in the flat where dissident scientist Andrei Sakharov spent six years in exile. The Nobel laureate was held incommunicado until 1986 when a KGB officer came to install a telephone – when it rang, Mikhail Gorbachev was calling to inform Sakharov of his release. The phone is a highlight of the exhibition. To get there, take bus 1 from

NIZHNY NOVGOROD'S STATE MUSEUMS

Nizhny Novgorod has an excellent ensemble of museums inside and around the kremlin.

Nizhegorodsky State Art Museum (Нижегородский государственный художественный музей; www.ngiamz.ru; admission R100; ⏲11am-6pm Wed-Mon) The former governor's house inside the kremlin is now the Nizhegorodsky State Art Museum. Exhibits range from 14th-century icons to 20th-century paintings by artists such as Nikolai Rerikh and Vasily Surikov.

The museum begins (on the left after you enter) with 14th-century icons. The entire collection is chronological, so you can see by room 6 how rudimentary landscape perspectives creep into 17th-century icons. After the icons comes the large collection of mostly oil-on-canvas paintings by Russian masters, culminating in Soviet art. The English descriptions are excellent.

National Centre of Contemporary Art (Государственный центр современного исктуства; www.ncca.ru; admission R100; ⏲noon-8pm Tue-Sun) Situated in the former arsenal on the right after you enter the main gate of the kremlin, this top-ranking gallery has changing exhibitions of international and Russian contemporary artists. From early 2015 the complete arsenal will have been restored and the centre will also have a concert venue, expanded exhibition space and a restaurant.

Western European Art Collection (Собрание Западноевропейское искусство; www.ngiamz.ru; Verkhne-Volzhskaya nab 3; admission R120; ⏲11am-6pm Wed & Fri-Mon, noon-8pm Thu) This fine gallery is just a short walk from the kremlin along Verkhne-Volzhskaya nab, an attractive street lined with restored 19th-century buildings. Inside the art gallery you find a collection of mostly anonymous or lesser-known European painters who, despite their modest credentials, produced some remarkable works.

Rukavishnikov Mansion (Усадьба Рукавишникова; www.ngiamz.ru; Verkhne-Volzhskaya nab 7; Russian/foreigner R80/200, tours R200/300; ⏲10am-5pm Tue-Thu, noon-7pm Fri-Sun) This exhibition space is located inside a 19th-century mansion once belonging to the Rukavishnikov merchant family. You can wander through the rooms on your own or join one of the hourly 40-minute excursions in Russian and English. Furniture and the illustrious interior of the unusual mansion are the threads running through the tours or a visit, and these are complemented by changing exhibitions – often with a focus on household furnishing and objects.

pl Minina i Pozharskogo or *marshrutka* 3 or 19 from pl Gorkogo to the Muzey Akademika Sakharova stop.

Tours

Team Gorky TOUR COMPANY
(☎831-278 9404; www.teamgorky.ru; ul 40 let Oktyabrya 1a; ⏲8.30am-7.30pm Mon-Fri) Gorky takes visitors on summer canoe and rafting tours, and winter ski treks in the Nizhny Novgorod region and beyond. Weekend cross-country ski tours cost R7300. Be flexible about dates as individuals join groups.

Sleeping

★Smile HOSTEL $
(☎831-216 0222; www.smilehostel.net; Bolshaya Pokrovskaya ul 4; dm/d R590/1690; ⊜@☜) Bright, friendly and efficient, this centrally located hostel has two doubles with twin beds that can be booked as a single, and five- six- and eight-bed dorms. There's free tea and coffee, separate male and female bathroom facilities and a nice communal area.

Resting Rooms HOSTEL $
(Комнаты отдыха; ☎831-248 2107; train station; 12/24hr from R400/690, registration R300) Located in a separate building on your right as you exit the train station.

AZIMUT Hotel Nizhny Novgorod HOTEL $$
(☎831-461 9242; www.azimut-nn.ru; ul Zalomova 2; with breakfast s R3500, d R3700-5000, ste R7400; ⊜☜) This ugly concrete eyesore has good refurbished rooms, some with fabulous river views. Steps just to the left as you exit lead directly to the Rozhdestvenskaya bus stop, where bus 45 picks up for pl Minina i Pozharskogo and buses 43, 26 and 5 go to

the train station. Ploshchad Gorkogo is 1km by foot.

Ibis Hotel
HOTEL **$$**

(Ибис Отель; ☑831-233 1100; www.ibishotel.com; ul Maksima Gorkogo 115; r from R3100; ☯@☎) Nizhny's Ibis offers a high standard of rooms and comforts, with the advantage that it's large enough to cope with busy periods.

★Jouk-Jacques
BOUTIQUE HOTEL **$$$**

(Жук-Жак; ☑831-433 0462; www.jak-hotel.ru; Bolshaya Pokrovskaya ul 57; with breakfast s R3750-6825, d/ste R6825/9375; ✳☎) This cosy boutique hotel is one of the best in town. Rooms are modern and decorated in soft tones, some facing the yard. The cheapest are a bit cramped but they're neat, and breakfasts are superb.

✗ Eating & Drinking

Biblioteka
ITALIAN **$**

(Библиотека; Bolshaya Pokrovskaya ul 46; mains R250; ☯11am-10pm; ☑) Upstairs from the Dirizhabl bookshop with generic but tasty Italian dishes in an informal, quirky atmosphere.

★Restoratsia Pyatkin
RUSSIAN **$$**

(Ресторация Пяткин; ☑831-430 9183; Rozhdestvenskaya ul 23; mains R400; ☯noon-midnight; ☛) Pyatkin makes you feel like a merchant back in his mansion after a great trading day at the fair. The menu is full of Volga fish specialities; it brews the unusual apple *kvas* for R65 and has a children's menu.

Bezukhov
RUSSIAN, INTERNATIONAL **$$**

(Безухов; www.bezuhov.ru; Rozhdestvenskaya ul 6; mains R400; ☯24hr; ☎☑) This literary cafe with antique furnishings, stucco ceiling and the feel of a living room is part of a Nizhny Novgorod project called 'Eda i Kultura' (Food and Culture), which brings food and culture together into a delicious whole. The menu is overflowing with salads, pastas and fish, poultry and red-meat dishes, and augmented by good breakfasts.

Vesyolaya Kuma
UKRAINIAN **$$**

(ul Kostina 3; mains R400; ☯noon-midnight Sun-Wed, to 2am Thu-Sat) Set among a row of lesser restaurants, the 'Happy Godmother' merrily serves hearty borsch and other Ukrainian fare.

Tiffani
INTERNATIONAL **$$**

(Тиффани; ☑831-419 4101; Verkhne-Volzhskaya nab 8; mains R600; ☯11am-2am; ☎☑) This upmarket all-rounder is a restaurant during the day and evening, a cafe at any time and has well-known DJs on some nights. The views across the Volga to the forest are spectacular.

★Art-Cafe Bufet
BAR

(Арт-Кафе Буфет; Osharskaya ul 14; ☯noon-2am; ☎) Descending the steps of this excellent art bar is to step into a bohemian world of monkey-motif wallpaper. The ambience is relaxed and alternative, and it stages lots of events as part of the Eda i Kultura movement.

Tsiferblat
ANTI-CAFE

(Циферблат; http://nino.ziferblat.net; Kovalikhinskaya ul 4a; 1st 30min R60, R1 per min subsequently; ☯11am-midnight Sun-Thu, to 2am Fri & Sat; ☎) This anti-cafe, located upstairs in the building with the 'Photohouse' sign, has cosy rooms for reading, playing the piano, balalaika and guitar, indulging in a board game or simply enjoying the coffee and tea.

🛍 Shopping

Dirizhabl
BOOKSTORE

(Bolshaya Pokrovskaya ul 46; ☯10am-9pm Mon-Sat, 11am-8pm Sun) A good selection of maps and local guidebooks, and some books in foreign languages.

ℹ Information

BTB24 (БТБ24; pl Maksima Gorkogo 4/2) ATM, accepts major cards.

Central Post Office (Центральный почтамт; pl Gorkogo; ☯8am-8pm Mon-Fri, 10am-5pm Sat & Sun) Has a railway and airline booking office.

Rostelekom (pl Gorkogo; per 30min R50; ☯9am-9pm)

ℹ Getting There & Away

TRAIN

Nizhny Novgorod train station is still sometimes known as Gorky-Moskovsky vokzal, so 'Gorky' appears on some timetables. It is on the western bank of the Oka River, at pl Revolyutsii. The service centre at the train station is helpful for buying rail tickets and also has internet. It also has convenient resting rooms for overnight stays.

Westbound

Two high-speed trains link Nizhny Novgorod with Moscow's Kursky vokzal, via Vladimir. The Sapsan (seat R1325, four hours, two daily) and the much cheaper Lastochka (seat R790, four hours, three daily), run to Moscow's Kursky vokzal. The Volga (059) runs to/from St Petersburg (R2800, 14½ hours, daily). Over a dozen other trains also serve Moscow (R1100, seven hours) via Vladimir (R700, three hours). Prices vary throughout the year according to season and demand.

Eastbound

Trans-Siberian flagships run to Perm (R2495, 14½ hours, daily) and beyond, but lesser trains do the trip for R1650. For Kazan (R1717, nine hours, daily) the No 41 is a top-flight (and the only) choice. Other trains go to Yekaterinburg (R3227, 21 hours, five to eight daily) and beyond.

AIR

The Nizhny Novgorod International Airport is 15km southwest of the city centre. **S7** (www.s7.ru) flies at least daily to/from Moscow and **Lufthansa** (www.lufthansa.com) flies directly to/from Frankfurt six times a week. Airline tickets are available at agencies around the city, including **Turbyuro** (Турбюро; ☎ 381-437 0101; www.tourburo.nnov.ru; ul Zvezdinka 10b; ⊙ 8am-8pm Mon-Sat).

BOAT

The **river station** (Речной вокзал) is on Nizhne-Volzhskaya nab, below the kremlin. A **Vodokhod Tour Office** (Водоходъ; ☎ 831-461 8030; www.vftour.ru; ⊙ 10am-9pm Mon-Fri, to 7pm Sat & Sun) inside the station building and the cash office on the embankment sell mostly weekend day trips departing early morning to the ancient Makaryev Monastery (R1500) at the village of Makaryevo, 60km to the east. Book ahead. Food and an excursion are included. Hydrofoils to Gorodets leave from their own pier.

BUS

Buses to Vladimir (R540, four hours, eight daily), Kostroma (R900, nine hours, daily) and Gorodets (R170, two hours, almost every half hour) depart from the small **Kanavinskaya bus station** (Автостанция Канавинская; ☎ 831-246 2021; www.nnov.org/transport/busm/kanavinskaya; ul Sovetskaya 20a). Private operators run minibuses to Moscow (R700, six hours, at least six daily), which depart across the road from the train station; others start from the bus station.

❶ Getting Around

The train station (Московский вокзал) is located across the river from the kremlin and is connected to the centre by buses, minibuses and the metro.

The three major hubs for public transport are the train station (Московский вокзал), pl Minina i Pozharskogo (пл Минина и Пожарского) near the kremlin, and pl Gorkogo (пл Горкого) south of this. Buses and *marshrutky* from the train station serve both and you can change for one or the other at the stop on the city side of the bridge, Kanavinsky most. At pl Minina i Pozharskogo, transport heading back to the train station picks up from the kremlin side of the road.

The city's metro has a useful link between pl Gorkogo and the train station.

Perm   Пермь

☑ 342 / POP 991,000 / TIME MOSCOW +2HR

The word 'Perm' once meant a mysterious Finno-Ugric land encompassing most of the northwestern Ural Mountains that was slowly colonised by Russians since the early medieval ages. But the city is relatively new, founded by the lieutenants of Peter I in 1723.

It is believed that Chekhov used Perm as the inspiration for the town his Three Sisters were so desperate to leave, and Boris Pasternak sent his Doctor Zhivago to a city clearly resembling Perm.

Today the city has some interesting museums and cultural attractions, and is also the base from which to visit one of the best wooden architecture museums in Russia, located in Khokhlovka; the famous ice cave in Kungur; and a grim reminder of Soviet-era political persecution – the Perm-36 labour camp.

◉ Sights

A green line runs through the centre connecting the major sights, with descriptions at each location in Russian and English. Permturist (p134) has a free, multilingual *Green Line* booklet for self-guided city walks. This is complemented by a red line through the centre, focusing on local love stories.

★ Museum of Contemporary Art PERMM
ART GALLERY

(Музей современного искусства PERMM; ☎ 342-254-35-73; www.permm.ru; ul Monastyrskaya 2; admission R100; ⊙ noon-9pm Tue-Sun) The brainchild and legacy of its former curator Marat Guelman, who was -sacked amid fallout over an exhibition satirising the Sochi Winter Olympics of 2014, the Museum of Contemporary Art PERMM is housed inside the former river station hall on the banks of

Perm

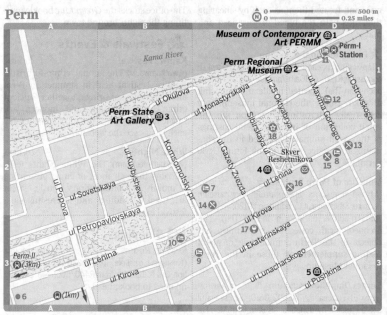

0 — 500 m
0 — 0.25 miles

the Kama River and has changing exhibitions. Trolleybus 1 and bus 3 take you there.

★ **Perm State Art Gallery**   ART GALLERY
(Художественная галерея; ☎342-212 9524; www.sculpture.permonline.ru; Komsomolsky pr 4; admission R120; ⊙11am-6pm Tue-Sun) Housed in the grand Cathedral of Christ Transfiguration on the banks of the Kama, the Perm State Art Gallery is renowned for its collec-

tion of Permian wooden sculpture. Take trolleybus 1 to the stop Galereya or trams 3, 4, 7, 12 and 13 to the stop Tsum.

The brightly coloured figures are a product of an uneasy compromise between Christian missionaries and the native Finno-Ugric population. The Finno-Ugric population closely identified the Christian saints these sculptures depict with their ancient gods and treated them as such by smearing their lips with the blood of sacrificed animals.

★ Perm Regional Museum
MUSEUM

(Пермский краевой музей; ul Monastyrskaya 11; admission R120; ⊙10am-7pm Tue, Wed & Fri-Sun, noon-9pm Thu) Located inside the imposing Meshkov House, the regional museum only gets really interesting when you see the small collection of intricate metal castings of the 'Perm animal style' used in the shamanistic practices of ancient Finno-Ugric Permians.

Museum of Perm Prehistory
MUSEUM

(Музей пермских древностей; www.museum perm.ru; Sibirskaya ul 15; admission R120; ⊙10am-7pm Fri-Sun & Tue-Wed, noon-9pm Thu) The archaeological collection sometimes has objects in the 'Perm animal style' of metal casting supplementing those in the Perm Regional Museum.

Sergei Diaghilev Museum
MUSEUM

(Дом Дягилева; ☑342-212 0610; Sibirskaya ul 33; admission by donation; ⊙9am-6pm Mon-Fri, call ahead 31 May-1 Sep) The Sergei Diaghilev Museum is a small, lovingly curated school museum dedicated to the impresario (1872–1929) who turned Russian ballet into a world-famous brand. Children speaking foreign languages, including English, serve as guides on interesting general tours as well as themed ones, such as the history of the house.

☞ Tours

Krasnov
ADVENTURE TOURS

(Краснов; ☑342-238 3520; www.uraltourism.ru; ul Borchaninova 4; ⊙10am-6.30pm Mon-Fri, 11am-5pm Sat) Offers active and adventure tourism such as rafting or cross-country skiing in the Ural Mountains, beginner Russian courses, river cruises and many more activities. The Russian version of the website has a wider and sometimes less expensive choice.

Permturist
ADVENTURE TOURS

(Пермтурист; ☑excursions 342-218 6999; www. hotel-ural.com/tourist; office 219, ul Lenina 58; ⊙10am-7pm Mon-Fri, Sat by arrangement) Located inside the Hotel Ural, Permturist organises excursions in Russian and English such as to the Kungur ice cave (from R7000, plus admission), as well as city tours in Perm and Kama river cruises. It can also help with information about, and whether, tours are running to the Perm-36 former Gulag camp.

The office stocks the *Green Line* booklet outlining the sights around town.

★☆ Festivals & Events

Kamwa Festival
CULTURAL

(www.kamwa.ru) The annual 'ethno-futuristic' Kamwa Festival held in summer in Perm and Khokhlovka brings together ancient ethno-Ugric traditions and modern art, music and fashion. Dates vary considerably each year – see the website.

White Nights
CULTURAL

(www.permfest.com) The White Nights festival runs through most of June, presenting a month of contemporary music, street art, theatre, readings and interesting side-festival events.

🛏 Sleeping

Resting Rooms
RESTING ROOMS $

(Комнаты отдыха; ☑342-230 21 76; Main Station, 3rd fl; 12/24hr from R440/660; ☜) Usually no need to book ahead.

★ Hotel Edem
HOTEL $$

(☑342-255 37 87; ul Maxima Gorkogo 21b; r R2200-2800; 🕾) The five large rooms with double beds in this excellent minihotel are named by their colour scheme – the 'Pink Room', and so on. As with some minihotels, service is friendly but patchy; here you get a kettle, coffee, plates and cutlery, as well as a fridge in some to make good use of the 24-hour supermarket across the road.

Travel Otel
MINIHOTEL $$

(☑342-222 1818; hotel.travel@bk.ru; ul Maxima Gorkogo 14b; s incl breakfast R4100-5200, d per person incl breakfast R2900-3700; ☜🕾) This quiet, modern minihotel has 10 large and stylish doubles which are excellent value, as well as five higher category singles.

Hotel Ural
HOTEL $$

(Гостиница Урал; ☑342-218 6262; www.hotel-ural.com; ul Lenina 58; s incl breakfast R3100-3900, d incl breakfast R4000-4800, ste incl breakfast R5500-12,000; ☜@🕾) This one-time Soviet monolith rising up in the heart of the city has adapted to the age and boasts a shimmering, high-tech lobby and modern, reasonably sized rooms.

Hotel Astor
HOTEL $$

(Гостиница Астор; ☑342-212 2212; www. astorhotel.ru; ul Petropavlovskaya 40; s incl breakfast R3800-4300, d incl breakfast R4600-5600; ☜❄🕾) ✒ Spotless white dominates this hotel's colour scheme. It's a favourite among business travellers, and rooms are low-allergy.

Hotel Prikamye
HOTEL $$

(Гостиница Прикамье; ☑342-219 8353; www.prikamie-hotel.ru; Komsomolsky pr 27; s incl breakfast R3200-4500, d incl breakfast R3700-5200, ste incl breakfast R5500; ☏) Nicely spruced-up rooms in this former Soviet eyesore make Prikamye a very decent option. Deals are better if you book well ahead on the web.

✖ Eating

Vkus Stranstvy
CAFETERIA $

(Вкус странствий; Sibirskaya ul 8; meals R300; ☉11am-9pm Mon-Sat; ☏) With the feel of a midpriced restaurant, the cheerful 'Taste for Travel' neo-*stolovaya* (canteen) serves some of the best cafeteria food in the Ural Mountains.

Sakartvelo
GEORGIAN $$

(Сакартвело; ☑342-254 3045; http://sakartvelo-perm.ru; ul Lenina 24; mains R350; ☉11am-midnight Sun-Fri, to 2am Sat; ☏✐) This excellent Georgian restaurant makes good use of chilli in its dishes, including the excellent Tbilisi salad, a borsch with a chilli edge, and a good variety of shashlyk (meat kebab), served in a lavish but homely interior.

Pasternak
RUSSIAN $$

(Пастернак; ☑342-235 1716; ul Lenina 37; Pasternak: mains R450; ☉9am-2am Mon-Fri, 11am-2am Sat & Sun; ☏) This restaurant for the well heeled and the literary inclined is actually two in one. Pasternak downstairs has a lounge-like, postmodernist cafe feel, while Zhivago upstairs is a fully fledged upmarket restaurant.

★ Grill Taverna Montenegro
BALKAN $$$

(Гриль-Таверна Монтенегро; ul Maxima Gorkogo 28; meals R1000; ☉noon-midnight Mon-Sat, to midnight Sun; ☏) The trompe l'œil village fresco downstairs, upstairs pseudo-portico and outdoor terrace lend nice touches to this excellent restaurant. The Kalmyk lamb kebab is superbly grilled.

☖ Drinking & Nightlife

Kama
BREWERY

(Кама; www.pivzavodkama.ru; Sibirskaya ul 25; mains R400; ☉noon-2am; ☏) This microbrewery does several tasty varieties of own-brew. The food, including its vegetarian borsch, is reasonably priced by Russian microbrewery standards. Sometimes good bands perform live here; other times it's a guitar soloist with canned backing.

☆ Entertainment

Tchaikovsky Theatre of Opera & Ballet
THEATRE

(Театр оперы и балета Чайковского; ☑ticket office 342-212 3087; www.arabesque.permonline.ru/; ul Petropavlovskaya 25; ☉ticket office 10am-2pm & 3-7pm) One of Russia's top ballet schools. Prices are from about R100 to R1000, depending on seat, venue and performance.

❶ Information

Main Post Office (ul Lenina 29; per hr R42; ☉8am-10pm Mon-Fri, 9am-6pm Sat & Sun) Also offers internet access.

❶ Getting There & Away

Inside the Hotel Ural you will find a **railways booking office** (☑342-233 0203; ☉8am-7pm Mon-Fri, to 6pm Sat & Sun) and an **Aviakassa** (☑342-233 2509; ☉8.30am-8pm Mon-Fri, 10am-5pm Sat & Sun).

TRAIN

Perm-II, the city's major train station, is on the Trans-Siberian route. Many trains travel the route to/from Moscow, including all of the Trans-Siberian *firmeny* (premium, long-distance trains). If you're on a tighter budget, many cheaper trains do the route from R2190. Heading east, the next major stop on the Trans-Siberian route is Yekaterinburg (*platskart/kupe* R1000/1444, six hours); bear in mind that Yekaterinburg's flagship Ural train runs via Kazan, *not* Perm. For Kazan (R1800, 19 hours) the most direct route is with an inconvenient change in Izhevsk. Getting a bus can be better. Note that some trains depart from the *gorny trakt* (mountain track) on the north side of Perm-II, as opposed to the *glavny trakt* (main track).

AIR

Several airlines fly to Moscow (from R7000, two hours, frequent).

BOAT

The river station (Речной вокзал) is at the eastern end of ul Monastyrskaya, in front of Perm-I station. Boats do short tours of the Kama in the navigation season. Permturist (p134) offers a wide range of boats and tours at competitive prices, such as one-way from St Petersburg from €503 and Perm–Astrakhan return from €370. Krasnov (p134) also sells tours but the prices it gives are higher.

BUS

From the **bus station** (Автовокзал; http://avperm.ru; ul Revolyutsii 68) numerous buses go to Kungur (R208, 1¼ hours); there are frequent buses to Khokhlovka (R90, 1½ hours) and two daily buses to Ufa (R1100, 11½ hours). Buses to Kazan depart every two days, with some additional services Friday and Saturday (R1370, 12 hours).

ℹ Getting Around

Perm-II train station is 3km southwest of the centre. Trolleybus 5 connects Perm-II with Hotel Ural, tram 7 connects Perm-II with the corner of ul Lenina and ul Maksima Gorkogo via ul Petropavlovskaya, and tram 11 connects ul Maxima Gorkogo with the central market (about 400m from the bus station) via ul Petropavlovskaya and ul Borchaninova. Bus 42 and *marshrutka* (fixed-route minibus) 1t travel between the bus station and the airport.

Around Perm

Khokhlovka   Хохловка

Architecture-Ethnography Museum   MUSEUM

(☑ 342-299 7181; www.museum.perm.ru; admission R120; ☉ 10am-6pm, closed last Mon in month) This museum is located near Khokhlovka, about 45km north of Perm. Its impressive collection of wooden buildings includes two churches dating from the turn of the 18th century. Most of the structures are from the 19th or early 20th centuries, including an old firehouse, a salt-production facility and a Khanty *izba* (traditional wooden cottage). A few buses a day serve Khokhlovka from Perm (R90, 1½ hours), the best ones departing Perm at 9.55am and returning from Khokhlovka at 4.30pm.

PERM-36: RUSSIA'S ONLY SURVIVING GULAG CAMP

The gulag system of forced labour was an abhorrent aspect of life in the former Soviet Union. Throughout most of its history from 1946 to 1987, Perm-36, located some 125km east of Perm, was a labour camp for dissidents. It is a haunting site, isolated and set deep in a landscape which in summer is verdant and filled with birdsong. Countless artists, scientists and intellectuals spent years in the cold, damp cells here, many in solitary confinement. They worked at mundane tasks like assembling fasteners and survived on measly portions of bread and gruel.

Soviet Gulag camps were invariably built of wood, and most of them have simply rotted back into the taiga and tundra. Perm-36 is the exception: a former Gulag camp which has survived intact. In 1994, it became a museum complex run by the international human rights organisation, Memorial, which was founded by the dissident Andrei Sakharov.

All this made it an important focal point in Perm's 'culture-led recovery' under Perm Territory's former governor, Oleg Chirkunov. The highlight was its annual Pilorama festival of culture, which included concerts and political forums. However, when Chirkunov's successor, Viktor Basargin, took office in 2012, funding cuts stalled Perm's reinvention of itself as a cultural centre, and when Memorial's directors of Perm-36 were replaced by a ministerial appointee in mid-2014, the human rights organisation decided to pull out of the former Gulag camp altogether. Sadly, in late August 2014 the museum closed.

Future plans are for a new state-funded exhibition on the gulag system (with one section about the Romanovs, according to reports), but whether this will retain the bite it had under Memorial's tutelage remains to be seen. Some even fear it will tread softly on political repression and the gulag system.

Regardless of when a new museum opens – or museum politics – it's worth visiting this unique site to get a feeling for what a Gulag campwas like. The Gulag camp is located in the village of Kuchino, about 25km from the town of Chusovoy, which itself is 100km from Perm. To reach it, take a bus bound for Chusovoy or Lysva, get off at Tyomnaya (R200, two hours) station, walk back to the main road and backtrack to the Kuchino turn-off (also leading to Makhnutino), then walk another 2.5km to the village. Permturist in Perm can help with the latest information on the Gulag camp and available tours.

Kungur Кунгур

☑ 34271 / POP 66,000 / TIME MOSCOW +2HR

Kungur's run-down appearance belies a skyline graced by a multitude of pretty church cupolas, including the 18th-century Tikhvinskaya Church in the centre and the Transfiguration Church on the other bank of the Sylva. The frozen magic of its ice cave, however, is the main attraction, drawing a stream of curious visitors.

The beautiful countryside surrounding Kungur is great for outdoor sports, and bicycles as well as rafts, canoes and cross-country skis can be hired inexpensively at Stalagmit.

◉ Sights

Kungur Ice Cave CAVE
(guided tour R500-600; ⊙10am-4pm, laser show 11am, 1pm & 3pm) The Kungur Ice Cave is about 5km out of town. The network of caves stretches for more than 5km, although only about 1.5km are open to explore. The ancient Finno-Ugric inhabitants of the Perm region believed the cave to be the home of a fiery underground creature, and the grottoes are adorned with unique ice formations, frozen waterfalls and underground lakes. You can enter only on guided tours which depart every two hours. Bring warm clothes for the first grottoes. The cost of the excursion includes admission to a small museum on the site with displays of rocks and fossils.

Regional Museum MUSEUM
(ul Gogolya 36; admission R70; ⊙10am-5pm Wed-Sun) Founded in 1663 on the banks of the meandering river, Kungur was a copper-smelting centre during the 17th and 18th centuries, which is a key focus of the Regional Museum.

🛏 Sleeping & Eating

Stalagmit Tourist Complex HOTEL $
(☑34271-62 602; http://hotel.kungurcave.ru; Kunger Cave; s incl breakfast R800-2000, d incl breakfast R1400-3000; ❂🛜🌐) This popular complex is close to the cave entrance and offers excellent rooms with their own bathroom (the cheaper ones don't have fridges and TV). Take bus 9 from the train station to the last stop.

Hotel Iren HOTEL $
(☑34271-32 270; ul Lenina 30; without bathroom s R800, d R1300, with bathroom s incl breakfast R1300-1800, d incl breakfast R2200-2500; ❂🛜) In the centre of town, Hotel Iren is good value, but it doesn't have a lift. Even the rooms without bathrooms are pleasant enough, and the shared toilets and showers are very clean.

Tri Medvedya RUSSIAN $
(ul Vorovskaya 5; mains R175; ⊙noon-2am Sun-Thu, to 3am Sat & Sun; 🛜) Across the bridge in the centre of town, the riverside cafe-disco Tri Medvedya has very decent food. Helpful staff can order a taxi for you back to the bus and train stations.

❶ Getting There & Around

In Kungur, the bus and train stations are located alongside each other. Bus 9 (every one to two hours) plies the route between Hotel Iren, the train and bus stations, and the Stalagmit complex.

Located on the Trans-Siberian route, Kungur is served from Perm by frequent intercity trains (R670, 1½ hours), suburban trains (R138, 2¼ hours, four daily) and trains to/from Yekaterinburg (R463 to R1258, four hours). Bus is the best option from Perm, however, with departures every one to two hours; the most convenient leaves Perm at 8.25am or 9.25am and returns from Kungur at 6.40pm or 7.55pm (R181, 2½ hours).

Yekaterinburg to Krasnoyarsk

Route Info

➡ Distance: 2287km

➡ Duration: 35 hours

➡ Time zones: Moscow +5, Moscow +6, Moscow +7

Best Places to Stay

➡ Red Star Hostel (p146)

➡ Hotel Yamskaya (p155)

➡ Avenue Hotel (p160)

➡ Gogol Hotel (p165)

Best Places to Eat

➡ Nigora (p147)

➡ Yermolaev (p152)

➡ La Maison (p161)

➡ Slavyansky Bazar (p165)

Why Go?

This leg of the journey isn't the most visually exciting, with little more to see than endless miles of semitaiga and farmland. Perhaps the best way to make the journey, then, is on a series of night trains – you won't miss much in the way of scenery and you'll save on hotels. If you do take day trains, there is admittedly a certain pleasure to be gained from the unchanging countryside and the opportunity it provides to reflect on Russia, life or whatever takes your fancy. After the historically important city of Yekaterinburg, your journey takes you into Siberia and eventually on to its buzzing capital, Novosibirsk. But the main attractions on this leg both require detours off the Trans-Siberian route. From oil-rich Tyumen, consider a trip to picturesque Tobolsk. Further on, branch lines will take you to the friendly student town of Tomsk.

When to Go

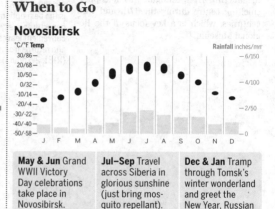

Novosibirsk

May & Jun Grand WWII Victory Day celebrations take place in Novosibirsk.

Jul–Sep Travel across Siberia in glorious sunshine (just bring mosquito repellant).

Dec & Jan Tramp through Tomsk's winter wonderland and greet the New Year, Russian style.

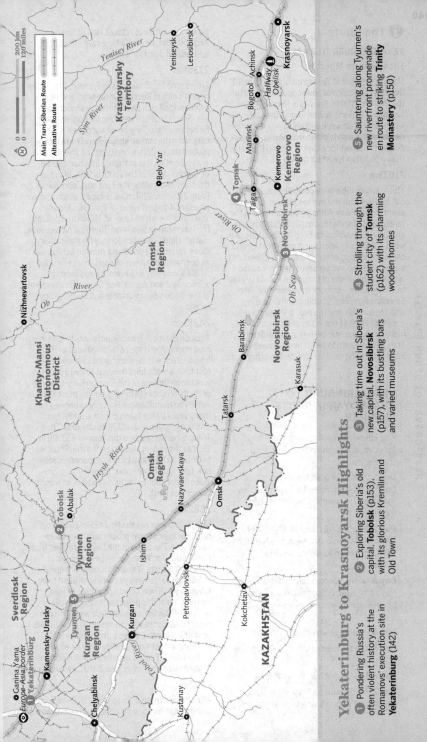

Yekaterinburg to Krasnoyarsk Highlights

1 Pondering Russia's often violent history at the Romanovs' execution site in **Yekaterinburg** (142)

2 Exploring Siberia's old capital, **Tobolsk** (p153), with its glorious Kremlin and Old Town

3 Taking time out in Siberia's new capital, **Novosibirsk** (p157), with its bustling bars and varied museums

4 Strolling through the student city of **Tomsk** (p162) with its charming wooden homes

5 Sauntering along Tyumen's new riverfront promenade en route to striking **Trinity Monastery** (p150)

ℹ The Route

YEKATERINBURG TO OMSK

1814km from Moscow

Major trains halt at Yekaterinburg for 15 to 30 minutes. The cultural and economic capital of the Ural Mountains, the city is famous as the birthplace of Boris Yeltsin and as the place where Tsar Nicholas II and his family met their deaths at the hands of the Bolsheviks. Wander across the street for a look at the old train station, which now houses a railway museum.

2102km

This is where Siberia officially begins. Look out for the kilometre marker and celebrate the event in some way. After all, you are now in the famed land of snowstorms, Gulag camps and enthusiastic hospitality. Even for Russians, the word 'Sibir' – or 'Siberia' – is an evocative one, conjuring images of hardy Sibiryaki (Siberians), endless steppe and perpetual taiga. It's also where the influence of European Russia begins to visibly wane – in more ways than one. 'We Siberians have real trouble communicating with Muscovites and the like,' a fellow traveller admitted to LP as our train rolled through yet more taiga. 'Our mentalities are so different. They always seem to be rushing somewhere after something or other. We, on the other hand,

YEKATERINBURG TO KRASNOYARSK ROUTE PLANNER

The following is a suggested itinerary for covering the main Trans-Sib stops in the area.

Day 1 Overnight train from Yekaterinburg to Tobolsk. Spend a day in Tobolsk then sleep in the train-station resting rooms.

Day 2 Take the morning *elektrichka* to Tyumen (3½ hours). Check out Tyumen, then night train to Novosibirsk (16 hours).

Day 3 Arrive Novosibirsk midafternoon. Have a shower. Do some laundry. Catch up on email. Have a well-deserved night out.

Day 4 Explore Novosibirsk.

Day 5 Bus to Tomsk (4½ hours). Explore Tomsk.

Day 6 Spend another day in Tomsk.

Day 7 Head south to Taiga via *elektrichka* for train connections to Krasnoyarsk.

prefer a much more relaxed kind of lifestyle.' And with that, he took a long swig on his beer and settled down for a nap.

2138km

Trains stop for 15 minutes in Tyumen, the region's oldest Russian settlement, and now a dynamic oil-rich city. There's not much to see directly outside the train station, so you'd be better off stocking up on supplies if necessary from the station shop. From Tyumen our route detours 221km northeast off the official Trans-Siberian line to the old Siberian capital of Tobolsk. Most of the route is fairly bland as the train slinks along the Tura and Tobol Rivers. From 210km to 216km, east-facing windows have pleasant if distant views of Tobolsk's kremlin. You cross the Irtysh River at 216km and pull into the train station 5km later. There's a picturesque market right on the platform, with stalls selling many varieties of dried and smoked fish, as well as beer and ubiquitous cheap Chinese noodles. As it's a long way into town, a good strategy – especially if you are arriving late – is to make use of the station's comfortable and clean resting rooms.

2428km

Back on the main Trans-Siberian route east, the next major stop is for 12 to 15 minutes at tiny Ishim, which was famous for its 19th-century Nikolskaya trade fairs (revived since 1991). This was the birthplace of the Russian fairy-tale writer Pyotr Yershov (1815–69), whose most famous work, *The Humpbacked-Horse,* was banned for many years by the tsar's censors. Ishim has a striking, whitewashed 1793 cathedral. The Trans-Siberian reached this town of 65,000 in 1913 as the railway was extended from Tyumen to Omsk. At 2497km, local time becomes Moscow time plus three hours. Swampy land provides opportunities for birdwatchers, in warmer seasons at least.

2562km

Most trains (but not the No 1/2 Rossiya) stop briefly at agricultural-processing town Nazyvaevskaya. The name of the town is derived from the Russian for 'to name' and while tough to directly translate, it sounds most unimaginative to Russian ears. If you're coming straight from Moscow you'll now be into day three of your journey. It's at this point that many travellers on Trans-Siberian trips lasting a week or more report that disorientation sets in. If you feel like something to read, papers and magazines (in Russian) are continually offered by salespeople on the trains. There's usually a fair selection of sudoku puzzle books as well, if that's your thing.

2711km

After the impressive six-span Irtysh River bridge, trains pause for 15 to 40 minutes in Omsk, where

Fyodor Dostoevsky was exiled in 1849. That leaves plenty of time to nip out and have a look at the fine Lenin statue right outside the station. You may even have time to send an email from the internet cafe on the ground level of the station. It's to the left of the entrance.

OMSK TO KRASNOYARSK

If you notice an increase in passing trains after Omsk, blame it on coal from the Kuzbas Basin east of Novosibirsk going to the smelting works of the Ural Mountains. In freight terms this is the world's busiest section of railway.

3035km

Barabinsk was once a place of exile for Polish Jews. The surrounding Barabinsk Steppe is a boggy expanse of grassland and lakes that was formerly the homeland of the Kirghiz people. Many train engines and carriages that service the Trans-Siberian put in here for repairs at some point or other. The shop on the platform has been full of drunken local teens dancing to disco music on LPs around plastic tables the last few visits. If you're in the mood to join in, you'll have time to down a beer and strut your stuff to a couple of tracks in the 30-minute stop here.

3330km

Get ready for the seven-span, 870m-long bridge across the Ob, one of the world's longest rivers. It's also extremely busy, with all manner of barges and cargo ships going about their business.

3336km

Some trains stop for up to 50 minutes in Novosibirsk (the Rossiya stops for 19 minutes). Jump out and inspect the grand station interior, a real temple of the Trans-Siberian. Also try to have a quick look at the two WWII memorial statues on platform 1 depicting a family waving off soldiers to the front. The Nazis never got this far, but lots of Siberians left for the war from this station.

3565km

The 15-minute halt at the intriguingly named but entirely unspectacular town of Taiga provides plenty of time to wish you were heading 79km north up the branch line to Tomsk. This is not a Womble (as Brits of a certain age may expect, from the kids' TV program) but a charming old Siberian city that lost much of its regional importance when it was bypassed by the Trans-Siberian Railway. Myth says that the city fathers, fearing the dirt and pollution it would bring, declined the offer to have the town connected to the railway. However, the truth is rather more prosaic – swampland made the construction of a bridge over the river Ob problematic, and a decision was taken not to lay lines to the city. Its beautiful wooden buildings and lively cafe scene are well worth the short detour.

Yekaterinburg to Krasnoyarsk

West to Moscow ↑

1814km ● Yekaterinburg (Sverdlovsk Pass)

4hr, 15min

2138km ● Tyumen

3hr, 45min

2428km ● Ishim

1hr, 30min ● Tobolsk (221km)

2562km ● Nazyvaevskaya

1hr, 45min

2716km ● Omsk

To Nizhnevartovsk, Purpe & Novy Urengoy ↓

3hr, 30min

3035km ● Barabinsk

3hr, 45min

3343km ● Novosibirsk

3hr, 15min

3565km ● Taiga

2hr

2hr

3713km ● Mariinsk

1hr, 50min ● Tomsk (79km)

3846km ● Bogotol

1hr

3914km ● Achinsk-1

2hr, 45min

4098km ● Krasnoyarsk

East to Vladivostok ↓

3713km

Spot another engine-repair yard to the south as you approach the station at Mariinsk, a 25-minute stop along the banks of the Kiya River. Originally named Kiysk, the town grew wealthy as the focus of a Siberian gold rush. It was renamed in 1857 to honour Tsar Alexander II's wife, Maria. Fifty years later, the town finally got round to unveiling a statue in her honour. Many of the furniture and metal factories that operated here in Soviet times are closed now, leaving few employment opportunities. Do your bit to help the local economy by buying a beer or *kvas* (fermented rye-bread water) and some dried fish from the women who meet the trains and offer all manner of goods. We were tempted by a large fluffy toy, but common sense eventually prevailed.

3820km

The line enters vast Krasnoyarsky Territory, with enormous mineral and forest wealth. It covers 2.5 million sq km, stretching all the way to the Arctic coast. A journey through this stretch of the Trans-Siberian is particularly memorable around sunset, with sunlight flickering hypnotically through the branches of endless rows of trees. Time, perhaps, to get out that dried fish and reflect once more on Russia and its colossal territory.

3846km

The train makes a very brief stop at Bogotol, another example of a town being formed around the Trans-Siberian. A train station was opened here in 1893, but it was another 18 years before the subsequent settlement was awarded town status. Bogotol is today home to a locomotive-production factory, hence the tiny model train perched on top of the welcome-to-town sign.

3914km

Next up is Achinsk. This small town, built around an alumina refinery, has its origins in the founding of a fortress in the area in 1683. In the 19th century, soap made in Achinsk was famous all over Russia. The train stops here for just a minute or two before twisting through woodlands and over hills with yet more cinematic landscapes to enjoy.

3932km

A small, easily missed white obelisk south of the train line marks the halfway point between Moscow and Běijīng (via Ulaanbaatar).

4098km

Major services stop for 20 minutes at Krasnoyarsk. That's just long enough to nip out and see a fine communist-era mural in red mosaics decorating a wall on the station square outside before heading on.

Yekaterinburg
Екатеринбург

☑ 343 / POP 1.35 MILLION / TIME MOSCOW + 5HR

Gem rush, miners' mythology, the execution of the Romanovs, the rise of Russia's first president, Boris Yeltsin, and legendary gangster feuds of the 1990s – Yekaterinburg is not only Russia's fourth-largest city, it is like a piece of conceptual art with a fascinating historical subtext.

Bustling but less than startling on the outside, the political capital of the Ural Mountains is overflowing with history and culture, while its economic growth is manifested in a thriving restaurant scene and, as in many other regional capitals, atrocious traffic.

With one of the best international airports in Russia and a couple of agencies experienced in dealing with foreign travellers, Yekaterinburg is a good base camp for exploring the Ural Mountains.

History

Yekaterinburg was founded as a factory-fort in 1723 as part of Peter the Great's push to exploit the Ural region's mineral riches. The city was named after two Catherines: Peter's wife (later Empress Catherine I) and the Russian patron saint of mining.

The city is notorious, however, for being the place where the Bolsheviks murdered Tsar Nicholas II and his family in July 1918. Six years later, the town was renamed Sverdlovsk, after Yakov Sverdlov, a leading Bolshevik who was Vladimir Lenin's right-hand man until his death in the flu epidemic of 1919. The region still bears Sverdlov's name.

WWII turned Sverdlovsk into a major industrial centre, as hundreds of factories were transferred here from vulnerable areas west of the Ural Mountains. The city was closed to foreigners until 1990 because of its many defence plants.

During the late 1970s a civil engineering graduate of the local university, Boris Yeltsin, began to make his political mark, rising to become regional Communist Party boss before being promoted to Moscow in 1985. Several years later he was standing on a tank in Moscow as the leading figure in defending the country against a putsch by old-guard communists. He became the Russian Federation's first president in June 1991.

That year Yekaterinburg took back its original name. After suffering economic depression and Mafia lawlessness in the early 1990s, the city has boomed in recent years. Yekaterinburg is one of the very few cities in Russia governed by a mayor, Yevgeny Roizman, not from a party loyal to the kremlin.

◉ Sights

Each summer from May after the snow has cleared, Yekaterinburg paints a red line on the footpath to guide visitors past major sights. It's marked on the tourist office (p148) city map.

★ Romanov Death Site   CHURCH, MEMORIAL
(Место убийства Романовых; ul Karla Libknekhta & ul Tolmachyova 34; ⊘dawn-dusk) The massive Byzantine-style **Church upon the Blood** (☑343-371 6168; ul Tolmachyova 34) (Храм на Крови) dominates this site where Tsar Nicholas II, his wife and children were murdered by Bolsheviks on the night of 16 July 1918. Nearby, the pretty wooden **Chapel of the Revered Martyr Grand Princess Yelizaveta Fyodorovna** (⊘10am-6pm Mon-Fri) honours the imperial family's great-aunt and faithful friend.

The executions took place in the basement of a local engineer's house, known as Dom Ipatyeva (named for its owner, Nikolai Ipatyev). During the Soviet period, the building housed a local museum of atheism, but it was demolished in 1977 by then governor Boris Yeltsin, who feared it would attract monarchist sympathisers, and for many years the site was a vacant block marked by a small cross and the wooden chapel to Grand Princess Yelizaveta Fyodorovna. Yelizaveta Fyodorovna was a pious nun who met an even worse end than the other Romanovs when she was thrown down a mineshaft, poisoned with gas and buried.

Rastorguev-Kharitonov Mansion   HISTORIC BUILDING
(Усадьба Расторгуев-Харитонова; ul Karla Libknekhta 44) Situated across the road from the site where the Romanov family were executed, this mansion dates from the late 18th and early 19th centuries and has a pretty park behind it.

Ascension Church   CHURCH
(Вознесенская церковь; ul Klary Tsetkin 11; ⊘dawn-dusk) The restored late-18th-century Ascension Church is the oldest in Yekaterinburg and rises up moodily alongside parkland perfect for a stroll.

Istorichesky Skver   PARK
The prettiest and most lively part of Yekaterinburg in summer is the landscaped parkland alongside the City Pond (Gorodskoy prud), where pr Lenina crosses a small dam. This was where Yekaterinburg began back in 1723.

The **Monument to the Founders of Yekaterinburg** (Памятник основателям Екатеринбурга) standing on one side of the square depicts founders Vasily Tatishchev and George Wilhelm de Gennin. The old **water tower** (Водонапорная башня) here is one of the city's oldest structures.

Yekaterinburg Museum of Fine Arts   ART GALLERY
(Екатеринбургский музей изобразительных искусств; ☑343-371 0626; www.emii.ru; ul Voevodina 5; admission R150; ⊘11am-7pm Tue & Fri-Sun, to 8pm Wed & Thu) The star exhibit of the Museum of Fine Arts is its elaborate Kasli Iron Pavilion, which won prizes in the 1900 Paris Expo. The museum has a good collection of icons, paintings and decorative art, whereas the Vaynera **branch** (☑343-371 0626; www.emii.ru; ul Vaynera 11; admission R150; ⊘11am-7pm Tue & Fri-Sun, to 8pm Wed & Thu) has a small collection of 20th-century Russian avant-garde works and mostly low-key changing exhibitions.

Vysotsky Viewing Platform   NOTABLE BUILDING
(ul Malysheva 51; viewing platform R250-300, museum free; ⊘viewing platform 1-11pm, museum 10am-7pm Wed-Sat, 11am-6pm Sun) Take the lift up 54 floors and 180m to the viewing platform for one of Russia's best urban panoramas. Children under 15 must be accompanied by an adult. The name of the tower is a pun on the Russian word for 'high' and the name of the singer Vladimir Vysotsky. A small museum is dedicated to 'Russia's raspy Dylan' here, with his original Mercedes.

Architecture and Design History Museum   INDUSTRIAL MUSEUM
(Музей истории архитектуры и дизайна; ☑343-371 33 69; ul Gorkogo 4a; closed for restoration in mid-2014; ⊘11am-6pm Tue-Sat) Situated on Istorichesky skver (Historical Sq), this museum is where the first ironworks was established in Yekaterinburg in 1723. Today the 19th-century factory and mint building here house machinery and industrial technology used in the mining industry from the 18th and 19th centuries to WWII. Note that the museum was closed for restoration

Yekaterinburg

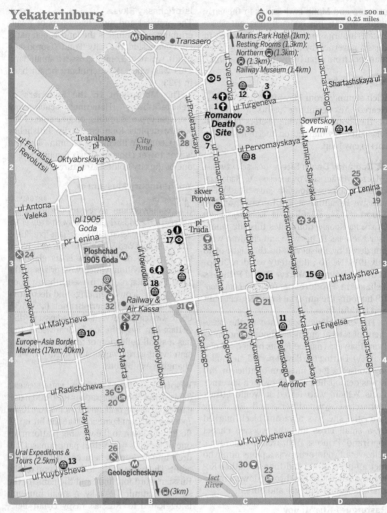

during our visit, but is expected to reopen in 2015.

Literary Quarter NEIGHBOURHOOD
(www.ompu.ur.ru) Located north of skver Popova, the Literary Quarter features restored wooden houses, some of them now museums about celebrated local writers such as Dmitry Mamina-Sibiryak and Pavel Bazhov; a full list of museums is on the website.

Urals Mineralogical Museum MUSEUM
(Уральский минералогический музей; 343-219 03 88; ul Krasnoarmeyskaya 1a; admission R100; 11am-7pm Mon-Fri, to 5pm Sat & Sun) A private collection offering a stunning introduction to the region's semiprecious stones, located in the Bolshoy Ural Hotel.

Ural Geological Museum MUSEUM
(Уральский геологический музей; 343-257 4938; http://ugm.ursmu.ru; ul Khokhryakova 85; admission R120; 11am-5.30pm Tue-Sat) Over 500 minerals from the Ural Mountains region and a collection of meteorites. It's inside the Urals State Mining University.

Military Technology Museum MUSEUM
(Музей Военной Техники; www.ugmk.com/ ru/value/mvt; ul Lenina 1, in Verkhnyaya Pyshma;

Yekaterinburg

admission exhibition hall R100, outdoor exhibition free) This vast indoor and open-air collection of tanks and armoured vehicles is the best of the bunch of military museums in and around Yekaterinburg, located on the northern outskirts in Verkhnyaya Pyshma. Take bus 111 or *marshrutky* 111 or 111a from stop 'Kinotsentr Zarya' (at 'Uralmash' metro station) to 'Zavodskaya'.

Urals Military History Museum MUSEUM
(Военно-исторический музей Урала; ☑343-350 1742; http://ugvim.ru; ul Pervomayskaya 27; admission R50; ☉ 9am-4pm Thu-Sun, to 8pm Wed) Worthwhile for buffs, this military museum has two halls, one dedicated to the Urals Volunteer Tank Corp. In the yard is a collection of tanks and planes.

Metenkov House-Museum of Photography MUSEUM
(Фотографический музей "Дом Метенкова"; ☑343-371 0637; ul Karla Libknekhta 36; admission R150; ☉10am-6pm Mon-Fri, from 11am Sat & Sun) Features several evocative photos of old Yekaterinburg and changing exhibitions.

Nevyansk Icon Museum MUSEUM
(Музей Невянская икона; ☑343-220 66 50; ul Engelsa 15; ☉noon-8pm Wed-Sun) **FREE** Excellent icons from the 17th to the 20th century, from the local Nevyansk school.

Railway Museum MUSEUM
(Железнодорожный музей; ul Chelyuskintsev; ☑343-358 4222; ul Chelyuskintsev; admission R100; ☉10am-6pm Tue-Sat) Railway buffs will enjoy the good collection here, housed in and around the old train station, dating from 1881. Exhibits highlight the history of the railroad in the Ural Mountains, including a re-creation of the office of the Soviet-era railway director.

☞ Tours

Ekaterinburg Guide Centre ADVENTURE TOURS
(Екатеринбургский центр гидов; ☑343-384 00 48; www.ekaterinburgguide.com; office 12, pr Lenina 52/1) Organises English-language tours of the city and trips into the countryside, including Nevyansk, Tobolsk and Nizhnyaya Sinyachikha, as well as winter activities and summer hiking and rafting expeditions. Day trips cost anything between

R1500 and R8800, depending on destination and numbers. It also books hotel and hostel accommodation, often at discount rates. The centre can also take you to the historic but hard-to-reach Verkhoturye. If taking the seven-hour tour to Nevyansk and the nearby old potters' village of Tavolgi, ask to stop on the way at the village of Kunary, where a local blacksmith has turned his wooden *izba* (log house) into a masterpiece of naive art.

Yekaterinburg For You　　TOUR GUIDE
(📞 8-912 28 00 870; www.yekaterinburg4u.ru) Experienced guide and journalist Luba Suslyakova offers a range of city and regional tours, including Nevyansk and the pottery town of Tavolgi, winter dog sledding, and the eclectic Mafia Tour, which takes visitors into the graveyards where Yekaterinburg's rival 'Uralmash' and 'Central' gangsters of the 1990s rest in peace.

Ural Expeditions & Tours　　ADVENTURE TOURS
(📞 343-382 53 66; http://welcome-ural.ru; office 4, ul Baumana 6; ⊙ 11am-5pm Mon-Fri) This group of geologists who graduated from the Sverdlovsk Mining Institute leads trekking, rafting and horse-riding trips to all parts of the Ural Mountains, including Taganay and Zyuratkul National Parks. English-speaking guides.

🛏 Sleeping

Contact **Ekaterinburg Guide Centre** (Екатеринбургский центр гидов; 📞 343-359 3708; www.ekaterinburgguide.com; office 12, ul Lenina 52/1) for accommodation in its centrally located hostel rooms, which are upstairs from the office, as well as other budget alternatives.

★ **Red Star Hostel**　　HOSTEL $
(📞 343-383 5684; www.redstarhostel.ru; ul Narodnoy Voli 69, off ul Rozy Lyuksemburg; 6-12-bed dm R550-650, d R1600) This excellent hostel opened in 2014 and has quickly established itself as a comfortable, very professionally run place, with 44 beds divided among male, female and mixed dorms, and a double with a large bed. The six-bed male dorm has no windows but good ceiling ventilation. It can do registration. Take trolleybus 1 or 9 from the train station to stop Kuybsheva.

Resting Rooms　　RESTING ROOMS $
(Комнаты отдыха; 📞 343-358 5783; 4th fl; 12/24hr from R750/1200; ⊜ 🕾) Book ahead as these fill fast.

★ **Hotel Tsentralny**　　HOTEL $$
(Отель Центральный; 📞 343-350 0505; www.hotelcentr.ru; ul Malysheva 74; s incl breakfast R3600-4680, d incl breakfast R4650-6120; ⊜ 🕾) This historical hotel is housed in a grand art nouveau building in the heart of town, with excellent business-class and standard rooms. Eating and nightlife are never far away from here. Trolleybuses 1 and 9 are among the many going there from the train station.

★ **Hotel Chekhov**　　HOTEL $$
(Гостиница Чехов; 📞 343-282 9737; http://chekhov-hotel.ru; ul 8 Marta 32; s incl breakfast R4500-5500, d incl breakfast R5000-6000; 🕾) Hotel Chekhov is a newcomer to Yekaterinburg's hotel scene and offers modern, stylishly furnished rooms which make good use of exposed brick in an historic building. Take bus 23 from the train station to TRTs Grinvich.

SIBERIA – THE GRAPHIC NOVEL

Graphic novels have never taken off in Russia, with even the genre's best works largely dismissed as being fit purely for children. This lack of a comic-book tradition makes Nikolai Maslov's *Siberia*, released by the US-based Soft Skull Press, all the more astonishing. Drawn entirely in pencil on paper, Maslov's tale of a Soviet youth (the book's original title) spent in Siberia is bleak, bitter and beautiful.

Portraying with almost unbearable honesty the faces of the drunks and bullies he grew up with, Maslov had reportedly never actually read a graphic novel before he approached the French publisher of *Asterix* in Russia with the first pages of the book and asked him to finance the rest. The publisher agreed, allowing Maslov to quit his job as a night watchman and devote himself to his work. Maslov tells the story of his often brutal life with a complete lack of sentimentality, using matter-of-fact, almost crude frames to portray characters and everyday scenes in Western Siberian villages and towns. One of the few works of art to portray everyday life in Soviet Siberia, as opposed to Solzhenitsyn-type Gulag camp tales, Maslov's book has yet to find a publisher in his native Russia.

Marins Park Hotel
HOTEL **$$**

(Маринс Парк Отель; ☑343-228 0000; www. sv-hotel.ru; ul Chelyuskintsev 106; s incl breakfast R2320-3200, d incl breakfast R3120-4000; ✸🛜) Formerly known as the Sverdlovsk, Marins Park is quite successfully reinventing itself as a modern congress hotel; all rooms are small, and renovation in the cheaper ones is simply a coat of pastel paint, but others are modern and it has two enormous advantages: it's right across the road from the train station, and it does your laundry same-day for free.

HHotel Apartments
APARTMENT **$$**

(HHotel Апартаменты; ☑343-219 5488; www. hhotel.ru; apt from R2300) Very centrally located apartments in new buildings for short stays of a couple of days or more.

Novotel Yekaterinburg Centre
HOTEL **$$$**

(☑343-253 5383; http://novotel-ekaterinburg.ru; ul Engelsa 7; s incl breakfast R5900-7700, d incl breakfast R6900-8100, ste incl breakfast R9000; ☺✸🛜) This excellent four-star chain hotel in the centre has variable rates and good deals online. The easiest way from the station is trolleybus 1 or 9 to ul Rozy Lyuksemburg stop.

✖ Eating

Ul 8 Marta between pr Lenina and ul Malysheva has lots of eating and drinking options, and ul Vaynera has a moderate choice of eateries.

★ Nigora
UZBEK **$**

(Нигора; ☑343-295 1417; http://nigora.ru; ul Kuybysheva 56; mains R200; ☺noon-midnight) Yekaterinburg has several of these inexpensive Uzbek restaurants, all with young staff attired in Uzbek caps serving delicious Uzbek specialities. *Manti* (steamed, palm-sized dumplings), soups, sausages and shashlyk feature on the menu, including a very worthy lamb shashlyk.

Stolle
CAFE, RUSSIAN **$**

(Штолле, Shtolle; ul Maxima Gorkogo 7a; pirogi from R100; ☺10am-10pm Sun-Thu, to midnight Fri & Sat; 🛜🍴) Stolle specialises in sweet and savoury Russian *pirozhki* (pies), which you can buy by weight at the counter for takeaway or enjoy here in a relaxed atmosphere to the gentle twinkling of jazz music.

Khmeli Suneli
GEORGIAN **$$**

(Хмели Сунели; ☑343-350 6318; www.hmeli.ru; pr Lenina 69/10; mains R450; ☺10am-midnight Mon-Thu, to 2am Fri, noon-2am Sat, noon-midnight Sun; 🛜) This large Georgian restaurant has a relaxed feel and is currently the best of its ilk in Yekaterinburg, serving a large range of soups, salads, fish and red-meat dishes and delicious shashlyk.

Thank God It's Friday
INTERNATIONAL, BAR **$$**

(ul 8 Marta 8; burgers R325-535, steaks R650-1000; ☺9am-2am Mon-Wed, to 4am Thu, to 8am Fri & Sat, 11am-2am Sun; 🛜) 'TGIF' is loud and boisterous, has staff who introduce themselves by name before they take your order, and kitsch decoration many will know from other branches. The food's capably prepared but it's the atmosphere that draws people here for drinks and meals.

Pozharka
PUB FOOD **$$**

(ul Malysheva 44; mains R450; ☺noon-midnight Sun-Thu, to 2am Fri & Sat) Pozharka is popular for its range of 15 beers and vast menu of pub food, including seafood, red meats and poultry and lots of sausage dishes.

Dacha
INTERNATIONAL, RUSSIAN **$$$**

(Дача; ☑343-379 3569; pr Lenina 20a, enter from ul Khokhryakova; mains R500-800, business lunches R300; ☺noon-midnight) Each room in this elegant restaurant is decorated like a Russian country house, from the casual garden to the more formal dining room.

Vertikal
INTERNATIONAL **$$$**

(Вертикаль; ☑343-200 5151; www.vertical51. ru; ul Malysheva 51, fl 51; mains R850-2100; ☺noon-midnight Sun-Thu, to 2am Fri & Sat) Located on the 51st floor of the Vysotsky tower, Vertikal offers a formal, upmarket experience of pan-European dishes and some steaks, and its trump card: sensational views over town. Reserve ahead.

🍺 Drinking & Nightlife

★ Rosy Jane
PUB

(pr Lenina 34; mains R600-1500; ☺6am-4am; 🛜) This English-style pub aims at the New Russian drinking and eating crowd, who grace the bar and perch at polished wood tables gourmandising on steak and other very well-prepared Russian and international dishes. Steaks are top of the range.

★ New Bar
BAR

(ul 8 Marta 8; ☺10am-2am Mon-Thu & Sun, to 6am Fri & Sat; 🛜) Relaxed art-scene cafe and cocktail bar on the top floor of Mytny Dvor mall.

Dr Scotch
PUB

(ul Malysheva 56a; ☉noon-2am) Doc Scotch is one of the liveliest pubs in town and has the advantage of being very central. Expect lots of wood in the interior and even more beer.

Ben Hall
PUB

(☑343-251 6368; ul Narodnoy Voli 65; mains R450; ☉noon-2am Sun-Thu, to 4am Fri & Sat) This popular pub hosts local rock bands at weekends, its owner being a well-known musician. Trams 15 and 27 from Operny Teatr or along pr Lenina to Tsirk (Цирк) drop you close by.

☆ Entertainment

Philharmonic
CLASSICAL MUSIC

(Филармония; ☑tickets 343-371 4682; http:// filarmonia.e-burg.ru; ul Karla Libknekhta 38; tickets from R100) Yekaterinburg's top venue for the classical performing arts often hosts visiting directors and soloists, as well as the regular performances of the acclaimed Ural Mountains academic orchestra.

Opera & Ballet Theatre
OPERA, BALLET

(Театр оперы и балета; ☑343-350 8101; www. uralopera.ru; pr Lenina 45a; tickets from R100) This ornate baroque theatre is a lovely place to see the Russian classics of a high standard.

🛍 Shopping

Grinvich
SHOPPING MALL

(www.grinvich.com; ul 8 Marta 46; ☉10am-10pm) This enormous shopping complex near the ul Vaynera pedestrian zone is an oasis away from the traffic.

ℹ Information

Main Post Office (Почтамт; pr Lenina 39; per MB R2.50; ☉8am-10pm Mon-Fri, 9am-6pm Sat & Sun) With internet.

Tourist Information Service (TIS; ☑343-222 2445; http://its.ekburg.ru; ul 8 Marta 21; ☉10am-7pm Mon-Fri) Helpful official city tourist office, with free maps of town showing the Red Line walking trail to major sights.

Tourist Information Service (☑343-222 2445; http://its.ekburg.ru; Koltsovo Airport, International terminal, fl 2; ☉10am-7pm Mon-Fri) Airport branch of the city tourist office.

Traveller's Coffee (ul 8 Marta 8; ☉8am-midnight; 🛜) Free internet with an order.

ℹ Getting There & Away

TRAIN

Yekaterinburg – sometimes still called 'Sverdlovsk' on timetables – is a major rail junction with connections to all stops on the Trans-Siberian route. The station has resting rooms (p146), and the closest toilets to the platforms are on the right as you exit the tunnel.

All trains to Moscow stop at either Perm (R1000, 5½ hours) or Kazan (R1580, 14½ hours). Frequent trains to/from Moscow include the Ural (R3777, 26 hours, every couple of days) via Kazan (R2312, 13½ hours), but many other trains are cheaper. Heading east, the next major stops are Tyumen (R975, five hours), Omsk (R1580, 14 hours) and Novosibirsk (R2434, 22 hours). If you want to travel direct to Tobolsk (R1200, 10 hours) without stopping in Tyumen, the Novy Urengoy and Nizhnevartovsk services do this. You can buy tickets at outlets throughout the city, including the convenient **Railway & Air Kassa** (ЖД и Авиа кассы; ☑343-371 0400; www.bilet-vsegda.ru; ul Malysheva 31d; ☉24hr).

AIR

The main airport is **Koltsovo** (☑343-226 8582; www.koltsovo.ru), 15km southeast of the city centre. Frequent services include Moscow, Novosibirsk, Krasnoyarsk, Irkutsk, St Petersburg and Samara. International services include Frankfurt, Běijīng, Prague and Astana. **Transaero** (Трансаэро; ☑343-287 0873; http://transaero.ru; ul Nikolaya Nikonova 6; ☉9am-8pm) and **Aeroflot** (☑343-356 5570; www.aeroflot.ru; ☉9am-6pm Mon-Fri) have offices here.

BUS

The **main bus station** Yuzhny avtovokzal (Южный автовокзал; ☑343-257 1260; ul 8 Marta 145) is 3km south of the city centre, but most buses pass the northern bus station (Северный автовокзал; Severny avtovokzal), conveniently located by the train station. Here you can catch frequent buses to Alapaevsk (R297, three hours, five daily) for Nizhnyaya Sinyachikha.

ℹ Getting Around

The Sverdlovsk-Passazhirskaya train station is located 2km from the centre at the top of ul Sverdlova/Karla Libknekhta. Many trolleybuses such as 1, 3 and 9 and marshrutky (pay on board) run along ul Sverdlova/ul Karla Libknekhta between the train station and pr Lenina. Marshrutka 55 connects the train station with pl 1905 Goda, continuing along ul 8 Marta to the Grinvich shopping centre. Bus 24 runs along ul 8 Marta to the northern bus station alongside the train station. Trams 13, 15 and 18 cover long stretches of pr Lenina.

Bus 1 links the train station and Koltsovo airport (one hour) from 6.30am to 11.30pm. Marshrutka 26 goes from the airport to metro pl

1905 Goda. *Marshrutka* 39 goes to metro Geologicheskaya.

A single metro line runs between the north-eastern suburbs and the city centre, with stops at the train station (Uralskaya), pl 1905 Goda and ul Kuybysheva near the synagogue (Geologicheskaya).

Around Yekaterinburg

Ganina Yama   Ганина Яма

Monastery of the Holy Martyrs   MONASTERY
(☑ 343-217 9146) After the Romanov family was shot in the cellar of Dom Ipatyeva, their bodies were discarded in the depths of the forests of Ganina Yama, 16km northeast of Yekaterinburg. In their honour, the Ortho-dox Church has built the exquisite Monas-tery of the Holy Martyrs at this pilgrimage site. Expect to pay around R3600 to R4200 as an individual (less in groups) on tours conducted by Ekaterinburg Guide Centre or Luba Syuslakova.

The nearest train station to Ganina Yama is Shuvakish, served by *elektrichka* (subur-ban train; R46, 30 minutes, every one to two hours) from the central station. Buses from the northern bus station (Severny) run out here at 3.30pm on Saturday and 10am on Sunday (platform 11), returning at 8pm on Saturday and 11.30am on Sunday.

Nevyansk & Around

The small town of Nevyansk is in the heart of the former patrimony of the Demidovs, a family of industrialists who effectively con-trolled much of the Ural Mountains and who received Peter I's blessing to develop the region. At their most decadent stage, they bought the Italian feudal title of Count San-Donato.

Nevyansk History and Architecture Museum   MUSEUM
(☑ excursion booking 343-562 2056; http://museum-nev.ru; pl Revolyutsii 2; museum R70, Nevyansk tower excursion per group of 1-5 people R1500; ☉ museum 9am-6pm Tue & Thu-Sun, 9am-8pm Wed, excursions 9am-7pm Apr-Sep) The main highlight in Nevyansk is the Nevyansk Leaning Tower, an impressive structure flanked by an equally impressive Saviour-Transfiguration Cathedral. The worthwhile excursions (in Russian) into the tower are the only way to climb up for the fantastic views unless you can latch onto a group. *El-ektrichka* (R115, 2½ hours, 9 daily) – some of them express trains (1½ hours) – run to Nevyansk, most bound for Nizhny Tagil.

Byngi   HOMESTAY $$
(☑ 8-922 158 2183, in Germany Oct-Mar +49 (0)421-40 89 66 60; www.semken.eu; ul Frunse 25, in Byngi; s/d €48/63, with full board €70/107; ☉ May-Sep) Seven kilometres from Nevyansk, the love-ly Byngi is the perfect place to experience Russian life in an Old Believers' village. Here an entrepreneurial German and his Russian wife have converted an *izba* into a guesthouse in the main building and erected four summer yurts in the yard. Excursions are available, and on a visit you will be very much integrated eclectically into local life in

STRADDLING THE CONTINENTS

The Ural Mountains have numerous monuments marking the border between Europe and Asia. Interestingly, the border was thought to be the Don River by the Ancient Greeks, but Yekaterinburg's founder Vasily Tatishchev drew it at the Ural Mountains in the mid-18th century, based on ideas of the day.

One of the more historic monuments is located 40km west of Yekaterinburg near Pervouralsk. It was erected in 1837 to commemorate a visit by Tsar Alexander II, who drank wine there and inadvertently began a favourite pastime of locals – drinking a glass in Europe and another glass in Asia (as if you needed an excuse!). To reach the monu-ment, take a taxi (about R1000 return if you order in advance) to Pervouralsk. Expect to pay another R200 per hour for the driver to wait. Very frequent bus 150 leaves from the Severny bus station to Pervouralsk (R87; platform 9).

The city has erected a new border marker, more conveniently located just 17km out of Yekaterinburg and looking a little like a mini Eiffel Tower. This one is more kitsch, but a taxi will take you out there for about R600 return, with an hour at the monument.

Expect to pay R3600 to R4000 as an individual (less in groups) with reliable outfits like Ekaterinburg Guide Centre (p145) or Yekateringburg For You (p146).

and around the village. *Elektrichka* (R115, 1½ to 2½ hours, 9 daily) serve Nevyansk.

Nizhnyaya Sinyachikha & Around
Нижняя Синячиха

Architecture Museum   MUSEUM
(☑ 343-467 5118; admission R100/160; ☉ 10am-5pm) The pretty village of Nizhnyaya Sinyachikha, about 150km northeast of Yekaterinburg and 12km north of the town of Alapaevsk, is home to an excellent open-air Architecture Museum. Here you will find 15 traditional Siberian log buildings, featuring displays of period furniture, tools and domestic articles. Five buses a day go to Alapaevsk (R297, three hours) from Yekaterinburg (Yuzhny avtovokzal). A **taxi** (☑ 343-463 0703; one way from Alapevsk R250-300) can take you to the museum.

While in town, visit the stone cathedral, which houses a good collection of regional folk art. This impressive ensemble of art and architecture was gathered from around the Ural Mountains and recompiled by the single-handed efforts of Ivan Samoylov, an enthusiastic local historian.

Tyumen   Тюмень

☑ 3452 / POP 507,000 / TIME MOSCOW + 5HR

Founded in 1586, Tyumen was the first Russian settlement in Siberia. These days the city is the youthful, business-oriented capital of a vast, oil-rich *oblast* (region) stretching all the way to the Yamal and Gydansk peninsula on the Arctic Kara Sea. There's enough here to keep you (mildly) entertained for a day or so, but if you have limited time you'd be much better off seeing nearby Tobolsk instead.

◉ Sights

If the weather is good, the best way to experience the city is by taking a stroll in central **City Park** (Городской Парк), or by walking along the riverside promenade.

★**Trinity Monastery**   MONASTERY
(Троицкий монастырь; ul Kommunisticheskaya 10) Riverside Trinity Monastery is undoubtedly Tyumen's most appealing architectural complex. Its kremlin-style crenellated outer wall is pierced by a single gate tower. Behind, gold domes top the striking **Troitsky Church** in the centre of the courtyard and, next to the black-turreted main gate, the

Tyumen

⊚ **Top Sights**
1 Riverside Promenade.........................A2
2 Trinity Monastery A1

⊚ **Sights**
3 Archangel Mikhail Church B3
4 City Park..C4
5 Fine Arts Museum.............................. D4
6 House-Museum of 19th- &
   20th-Century History......................B3
7 Lovers Bridge A2
8 Selskhoz Academy B3
9 Voznesensko Georgievskiy
   Church..B2
10 Znamensky Cathedral........................B3

🛏 **Sleeping**
11 Business Hotel Eurasia C3
12 Vsye Prosto B4

🍴 **Eating**
13 Berlusconi... C4
14 Don Julio B4
15 In Da USA..C3
    Malina Bar...................................(see 13)
16 Schaste..D5
17 Yermolaev..B3

1727 **Peter & Paul Church**. The monastery is a pleasant 30-minute walk northwest from the city centre.

★**Riverside Promenade**   PROMENADE
(Набережная) Tyumen's sleek new riverside promenade runs northwest from the centre almost all the way to Trinity Monastery. The promenade offers great views of the **Voznesensko Georgievskiy Church** (Вознесенско-Георгиевский храм; Beregovaya ul) reflected in the Tura River from the opposite (east) bank. **Lovers Bridge** (Мост влюблённых; ul Kommunisticheskaya) leads over to the east bank, where you can explore curiously twisted old wooden houses along tree-lined **Beregovaya ul** (notably numbers 73 and 53).

Fine Arts Museum   MUSEUM
(Музей изобразительного искусства; ul Ordzhonikidze 47; admission per exhibition R100-150; ☉ 10am-6pm Tue-Sun) The Fine Arts Museum has several rotating and permanent exhibits ranging from ornate window frames saved from the city's old wooden houses to tiny, intricately carved bone figures produced by Siberian artists. It gets expensive if you want to see all of the exhibits, however.

Tyumen

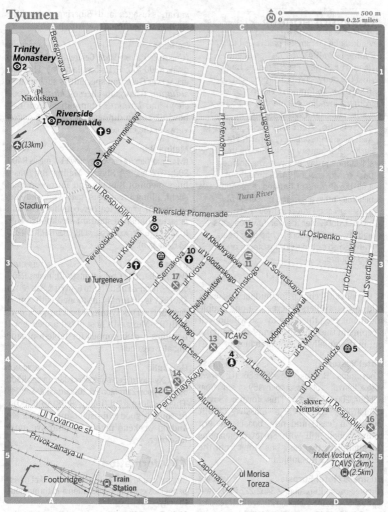

House-Museum of 19th- & 20th-Century History

MUSEUM

(Музей истории дома XIX-XX вв; ul Respubliki 18; admission R160; ⏱10am-6pm Wed-Sun) This museum contains artefacts from Tyumen's past and is housed in the city's finest carved cottage.

Znamensky Cathedral

CHURCH

(Знаменский собор; ul Semakova 13) With its voluptuously curved baroque towers, the 1786 Znamensky Cathedral is the most memorable of a dozen 'old' churches that have recently come back to life following years of neglect.

Archangel Mikhail Church

CHURCH

(Храм Михаила Архангела; ul Turgeneva) The attractive Archangel Mikhail Church sits at the top of a hill just off ul Lenina. Follow ul Turgeneva southwest behind the church to a network of back streets full of old wooden houses.

📖 Sleeping

★ Vse Prosto

HOSTEL $

(Всё Просто!; ☎3452-441 072; www.hostelvse-prosto.ru; ul Pervomayskaya 40/1; dm R590-750, s/d R990/1490; @ 🛜) This marvellous hostel just a 7-minute walk from the train station

CORPSE OF HONOUR

Vladimir Lenin himself paid a visit to Tyumen – in 1941. Yes, he was already dead. The Soviets evacuated his body (just the body – his brain remained in Moscow) to Tyumen to keep it safe from the invading Germans. The body was kept under a veil of secrecy in the **Selskhoz Academy** (Сельсхоз Академия; ul Respubliki 7), an attractive early-20th-century brick building that still stands today, before being shipped back to Moscow in 1945. Throughout it all, the citizens of Tyumen remained blissfully unaware of the presence of a distinguished guest in their midst. Indeed, until after the war, few Russians had any idea the corpse had ever been transferred out of its mausoleum on Red Square!

is the obvious choice for budget and even midrange travellers. There's just one double room, but even the dorm-averse will do well sleeping in the spacious dorms and hanging out in the equally spacious kitchen.

Hotel Vostok HOTEL $$
(Гостиница Восток; ☑ 3452-686 111; www.vostok-tmn.ru; ul Respubliki 159; s/d from R2500/3200; ☻@☎) This former Soviet monstrosity has seen a massive facelift (inside, at least) and now boasts modern rooms, albeit still with Soviet dimensions (ie small). It's two easy bus stops from the centre along ul Respubliki.

Business Hotel Eurasia HOTEL $$$
(Бизнес-отель Евразия; ☑ 3452-222 000; www.eurasiahotel.ru; ul Sovetskaya 20; s/d incl breakfast from R4900/6900; ☻✳@☎) While not overloaded with character, it covers business travellers' needs with well-appointed rooms, a decent restaurant and a fitness centre. But the best part is that everything in the minibar is free of charge!

✗ Eating & Drinking

★ **Yermolaev** RUSSIAN $$
(Ермолаев; ul Lenina 37; mains R250-550; ☾noon-1am; ☎) This spacious place is a bit like a Soviet-themed beer hall. There are eight types of mostly unfiltered homebrew (from R135) and an extensive picture menu that includes traditional Russian fare, Ba-

varian sausages and Siberian specialities such as *stroganina* (raw frozen fish).

Schaste GEORGIAN $$
(Счастье; Kalinka Trade Centre, ul Respubliki 65; mains R300-700; ☾11.45am-1am; ☎) This eatery serves Georgian specialities such as fried *suluguni* (Georgian cheese), *kharcho* (beef stew) and *khinkali* (dumplings) in a fishbowl-like main dining hall with 270-degree views of the city centre.

Malina Bar CAFE $$
(Малина Бар; ul Pervomayskaya 18; meals R400-800; ☾24hr; ☎) Stylish Malina Bar has a huge menu of Russian and European food, sushi, filling breakfasts, fast wi-fi and cosy seating in grand leather couches. Upstairs is sister Italian restaurant-steakhouse **Berlusconi** (ul Pervomayskaya 18; mains R300-1200; ☾11am-3am).

In Da USA AMERICAN $$
(Ин Да Юса; ul Chelyuskintsev 10; mains R300-500; ☾noon-2am Su-Thu, to 6am Fri & Sat; ☎) In Da USA is, naturally, festooned with Americana and serves Tyumen's best burgers along with Tex-Mex and a host of bar appetisers. It becomes a club famous for table-top dancing at weekends.

Don Julio MEXICAN $$
(Дон Хулио; ul Pervomayskaya 38a; mains R300-500; ☾noon-2am Mon-Fri, to 4am Fri & Sat; ☎) This Mexican food (mains R300 to R500) is reasonably good (this isn't Cancun, after all), and on weekend nights DJs and live music take over.

ℹ Information

City maps and bus-route plans are sold at newspaper kiosks in the train station and throughout the city.

Main Post Office (Почтамт; ul Respubliki 56; ☾8am-10pm Mon-Fri, 9am-6pm Sat & Sun)

ℹ Getting There & Away

Rail tickets are sold by **TCAVS** (ul Lenina 61) (also on **ul Respubliki** (ul Respubliki 156; ☾8am-8pm).

TRAIN
Several day and overnight trains go to Omsk (*platskart/kupe* R880/1824, 8½ hours) and points east along the Trans-Siberian mainline, including Novosibirsk (*platskart/kupe* R2500/4500). Dozens of westbound trains serve Yekaterinburg and beyond.

There are many daily trains to Tobolsk (*platskart* R550 to R800, 3½ hours), plus a rather ill-timed nightly *elektrichka* (suburban train; R254, four hours, 11.54pm). There's also a train to Tomsk (R3500/6200, 23 hours, even-numbered days at 9.17am).

BUS

From the **bus station** (ul Permyakova), 3km east of the centre, buses to Tobolsk (R550, four hours, seven daily) travel via Rasputin's home town of Pokrovskoe (R200, 1½ hours).

ⓘ Getting Around

From the train station, bus 27 serves Hotel Vostok and passes near the bus station – hop off at the Krosno stop, and cross ul Respubliki. Taxis around town cost R150.

Tobolsk   Тобольск

✆ 3456 / POP 101,000 / TIME MOSCOW + 5HR

Once Siberia's capital, Tobolsk is one of the region's most historic cities, sporting a magnificent kremlin and a charmingly decrepit old town. Tobolsk is off the Trans-Siberian main line but is easily reached from Tyumen.

The centre of the Russian colonisation of Siberia, Tobolsk was founded in 1587. Its strategic importance started to wane in the 1760s, when the new Great Siberian Trakt (post road) took a more southerly route. However, until the early 20th century it remained significant as a centre for both learning and exile. Involuntary guests included Fyodor Dostoevsky en route to exile in Omsk, and deposed Tsar Nicholas II and his family, who spent several months here in 1917 before being taken to Yekaterinburg and executed.

Buses from the inconvenient train station (some 10km north) give visitors a dismal first impression. Concrete drabness reaches a glum centre around Hotel Slavyanskaya, but don't be put off. Tobolsk's glories begin 3km further south around the splendid kremlin. Immediately beyond and below the kremlin, the old town sinks into the Irtysh's boggy floodplain.

⊙ Sights

★**Kremlin**   HISTORIC BUILDING

(⊙grounds 8am-8pm) The centrepiece of the tower-studded 18th-century kremlin is the glorious 1686 St Sofia Cathedral (Софийский собор; Krasnaya pl 2). Less eye-catching from the outside, but with splendid arched ceiling murals, is the 1746 Intercession Cathedral (Покровский собор). Between the two is a 1799 **bell tower**, built for the Uglich bell, which famously signalled a revolt against Tsar Boris Godunov. The revolt failed; in a mad fury, Godunov ordered the bell to be publicly flogged, detongued and banished to Tobolsk for its treacherous tolling.

A tatty copy of the bell is displayed in the Deputy's Palace Museum. Built in 1855, the kremlin prison is now the **Castle Prison Museum** (Тюремный замок; Krasnaya pl 1; admission R300; ⊙10am-6pm Tue-Sun), where you can get a sense of the grim life behind bars in both Tsarist and Soviet times. The elegant **Arkhiereysky Mansion** (Архиерейский Дом) was closed for renovations when we visited and will eventually be reopened as an Orthodox history museum; the intriguing **Trading Arches** (Гостиный двор) were being converted into yet another museum.

Wooden stairs lead beneath the kremlin's **Pryamskoy Vzvoz** (Прямской Взвоз; gatehouse) to the wonderfully dilapidated old town full of weather-beaten churches and angled wooden homes sinking between muddy lanes.

★**Deputy's Palace Museum**   MUSEUM

(Дворец наместника; www.tiamz.ru; Krasnaya pl 1; admission R300; ⊙10am-6pm Tue-Sun) Tobolsk's best museum occupies a beautiful 18th-century former administration on the southwestern edge of the kremlin. The Romanovs called in here during their brief stint in Tobolsk in 1917, and a section of this remarkably modern museum is devoted to their time in Tobolsk. Tactile multimedia exhibits profile the characters who shaped Siberia before the Bolshevik revolution, and hometown heroes such Dmitry Mendeleyev, who created the first periodic table. There's an impressive collection of local art up on the third floor.

Most exhibits have English placards. The space-age multimedia displays are in Russian only but are fun to play with regardless. Visitors really emerge from here with a sense of Tobolsk's importance in the 18th and 19th centuries, when it was the capital of all Siberia.

★**Minsalim Folk Art**   ART GALLERY

(Мастерская Минсалим; www.minsalim.ru; ul Oktyabrskaya 2; ⊙9am-6pm) **FREE** Minsalim is a master bone-carver who turns mammoth tusks and antler fragments into detailed figurines related to myths and legends of

Tobolsk

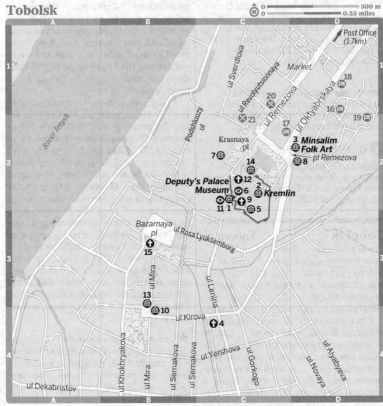

the local brand of shamanism. With a long moustache and flowing mane, eccentric Minsalim is something of a shaman himself, and will gladly lead you on a tour of his workshop behind the gallery. His son and some members of staff speak English.

Gubernsky Museum   MUSEUM
(Губернский музей; ul Oktyabrskaya 1; admission R200; ☉10am-6pm Tue-Sun) Built in 1887 for the 300th anniversary of the founding of Tobolsk, the Gubernsky Museum has displays on the history of Tobolsk, a mammoth skeleton and a display of bone carvings.

Kornilov Mansion   MUSEUM
(Дом Корнилова; ul Mira 9) The grand Kornilov mansion, named after a 19th-century statesman and philanthropist, is closed while being converted into a museum dedicated to the Romanovs, but is still worth a look for its lavish exterior.

Tobolsk Rayon
Administration Building   HISTORIC BUILDING
(ul Mira 10) Less eye-catching than the Kornilov Mansion opposite, the Tobolsk Rayon Administration Building was the home-in-exile of the last tsar, before his fateful journey to execution in Yekaterinburg. It's now a museum of legal studies (admission free).

Archangel Mikhail Church   CHURCH
(Церковь Архангела Михаила; ul Lenina 24) The attractive Archangel Mikhail Church has a colourfully restored interior. The character of Tatiana Larina in Pushkin's epic *Eugene Onegin* is said to have been modelled on Natalya Fonvizina, a Decembrist wife who prayed here.

Zachary & Elisabeth Church   CHURCH
(Церковь Захария и Елизаветы; Bazarnaya pl 8) The 1759 Zachary & Elisabeth Church, with its soaring black-tipped spires, is extremely photogenic.

Tobolsk

⌂ Sleeping & Eating

While Tobolsk has seen a modest tourist boom in recent years, there is still no restaurant scene to speak of.

Resting Rooms
HOSTEL $

(Комнаты отдыха; komnaty otdykha; ☑ 3456-62 522; train station; dm 12-/24-hr from R500/600, s/d from 1200/1800) Clean and friendly. The location is utterly impractical for visiting the city, but ideal if you're arriving late or waiting for an early morning connection.

★ Hotel Yamskaya
HOTEL $$

(Гостиница Ямская; ☑ 3456-226 177; yamskaya-tobolsk@mail.ru; ul Bolshaya Sibirskaya 40; s/d/tw incl breakfast R2100/2600/3000; ☎) With cosy rooms, friendly service, a perfect location near the kremlin and a warm and inviting overall atmosphere, this 12-room hotel borders on boutique. The prices are extremely reasonable for what you get.

Hotel Sibir
HOTEL $$

(Гостиница Сибирь; ☑ 3456-222 390; pl Remezova 1; s/d incl breakfast from R2200/3900; ☎) Sibir's rooms are comfortable, spacious and festooned with classy old photos, giving it a

historical vibe. It's the closest to the kremlin of all Tobolsk's hotels. The breakfast is tasty and filling and the 24-hour restaurant (meals R150 to R600, beer from R100, no English menu) does a mean fish soup (*pokhlebnaya ribnaya;* R170).

Hotel Georgievskaya
HOTEL $$

(Гостиница Георгиевская; ☑ 3456-220 909; www.hotel-georgievskaya.ru; ul Lenekaya 35; s R2380-2960, d R3330-4040; ❀☎) Right behind a Dostoevsky statue, this large hotel has spacious rooms that are a tad overdone with velvet curtains, satin bedspreads and the like. The bathrooms are quite nice and there's a sumptuous restaurant.

Hotel Tobol
HOTEL $$

(Гостиница Тобол; ☑ 3456-246 614; ul Oktyabrskaya 20; s/d/tw incl breakfast from R2200/2800/3300; ☎) The Tobol is a renovated Soviet hotel, which means rooms on the small side and generic furniture, but at least it's clean, well-located and relatively affordable. There's a bowling alley and a disco on the ground level if you get bored.

Ladeyny
RUSSIAN $

(Ладейный; ul Revolutsionnaya 2; mains R200-400; ⊙11am-2am; ☎) This place is a revolution as far as Tobolsk is concerned – an extra-large Siberian *izba* (wood house) that specialises in Siberian fish and homemade *pelmeni* (ravioli) and *vareniki* (dumplings). Nights sometimes bring live music. The English menu is extremely rare for these parts.

Kofeynya u Ershova
CAFE $

(Кофейня у Ершова; ul Remezova 7; mains R120-300; ⊙10am-11pm) An easy stop near the kremlin for relatively quick and cheap Russian eats – think lunch standards such as *bishteks* (Russian-style hamburger), *solyanka* (pickled vegetables and potato soup) and stuffed *bliny* (pancakes).

❶ Information

Post Office (Почта; Komsomolsky pr 42; ⊙8am-6pm)

❶ Getting There & Away

There are many day and overnight options to/from Yekaterinburg (*platskart/kupe* R1200/2300, 10 hours) and points west via Tyumen (*platskart* R550 to R800, 3½ hours). A better way to Tyumen is on the daily 8.40am *elektrichka* (R254, four hours).

 The No 125 train trundles to Novosibirsk on odd-numbered days at 9.21am (R1400/3750,

ABALAK MONASTERY

From Tobolsk, a quiet road skirts the border of the ancient Tatar kingdom of Isker, continuing 25km to Abalak. Here the region's holiest monastery was built on the site of a miraculous materialising icon, which was last spotted in Australia long after the Soviets had turned the church into a tractor barn. There are charming views over the bend in the Irtysh River, with 249 steps leading down to the riverbank. Today the monastery is working again, with a copy of the icon over the door.

Set in the pristine countryside a short walk from the Abalak monastery, the charming Abalak Holiday Centre has a few cosy rooms and a restaurant serving traditional Russian food.

24 hours) via Omsk, while the No 115 is a late-night option to Omsk on odd-numbered days (R2200/4500, 13¼ hours, 1.26am).

Buses are another option to Tyumen (R550, four hours) via Pokrovskoe (R300, 2½ hours). Eight buses per day to various destinations pass through nearby Abalak, site of an interesting monastery.

In the warm months ferries cruise the Irtysh north to Salekhard (1st-, 2nd-, 3rd-class R3000/1200/900, five days, about six monthly) via Khanty-Mansisk (two days), and south to Omsk (R2200/1000/850, three days, about three monthly).

ⓘ Getting Around

Bus 4 and *marshrutka* 20 link the train station, new town and kremlin. Taxis to/from the station cost around R250.

Omsk   Омск

☑ 3812 / POP 1.145 MILLION / TIME MOSCOW + 6HR

With its modest sights hidden behind busy roads, this big industrial city is not worth a special detour. You may find it a convenient stopover to break up long journeys.

If you're looking to kill some time, the **Fine Arts Museum** (Музей изобразительных искусств; ul Lenina 23; admission R100; ☺10am-6pm Tue-Sun) displays a lot of fussy decorative arts. The rectilinear 1862 building, a historical curiosity in itself, was built as the Siberian governor's mansion and hosted passing tsars. In 1918–19, however, the building was home to Admiral Kolchak's counter-revolutionary government.

Cross the the bridge at ul Lenina and continue north and you'll pass several parks and more notable buildings, including the ornate **Drama Theatre** (Омский театр драмы; www.omskdrama.ru; ul Lenina 8a); a 1905 building housing another branch of the **Fine Arts Museum** (ul Lenina 3); and the massive,

turquoise-and-gold-domed **Assumption Cathedral** (Успенский собор; Sobornaya pl), rebuilt after the collapse of the USSR. Check out the great catalogue in the Ibis Sibir hotel for more walking tours and sightseeing ideas.

🛏 Sleeping & Eating

Resting Rooms   HOSTEL $

(Комнаты отдыха; komnaty otdykha; ☑3812-442 347; train station; 12-/24-hr from R700/1200) Spacious and with en suites, these are some of the best train station rooms we've seen in Siberia.

Hotel Turist   HOTEL $$

(Отель Турист; ☑3812-316 414; www.tourist-omsk.ru; ul Broz Tito 2; s/d incl breakfast from R3000/3600; ☺@🖐🛜) A fairly central renovated Soviet high-rise with bright rooms and fine views of the river from upper floors. There's a 25% discount on weekends, 40% discount if you check in after 10pm, and the minibar is free of charge.

Ibis Sibir   HOTEL $$$

(☑3812-311 551; www.ibishotel.com; ul Lenina 22; s/d incl breakfast from R4000/4600; ❄️@🛜) Bright and cheery, the always-reliable Ibis shuns Soviet dimensions and is by far the nicest hotel in Omsk. Beds are lavish, the breakfast excellent and there's a catalogue in English outlining sightseeing opportunities in and around Omsk. No minibar.

★ **Gollandskaya Chashka**   INTERNATIONAL $$

(Голландская Чашка; www.hollcup.ru; 3rd fl, Pyat Zvyozd shopping mall, ul Karla Libknekhta; mains R250-450; ☺10am-midnight; 🛜) Excellent northern European and Russian comfort food, elaborate salads, mulled wine, inviting decor, reasonable prices, fine city views – there's plenty to like about Chashka. Follow pr Marksa over the bridge and take the second left.

Kolchak ITALIAN **$$**

(Ресторан-клуб Колчакъ; ul Broz Tito 2; mains R300-500; 🖝) Conveniently located near the River Station, Kolchok combines an Irish Pub and an Italian restaurant under one roof. There's an excellent beer selection including Leffe on tap, and a business lunch of Russian faves.

ℹ Information

K2 Adventures (📞 3812-693-075; www. adventuretravel.ru) Igor Fedyaev is the guru of adventure travel in Western Siberia. English-speaking, affable and responsive, he specialises in mountaineering expeditions in Altai and elsewhere, but can arrange just about any tour around Omsk or elsewhere in the region.

Post Office (Почтамт; ul Gertsena 1; ⏰8am-10pm Mon-Fri, 9am-6pm Sat & Sun)

ℹ Getting There & Away

There are numerous train connections both east towards Novosibirsk (*platskart/kupe* from R1300/3000, about 8½ hours) and west towards Yekaterinburg. Destinations off the main line served from Omsk include Tomsk (R2400/4250, 14 hours, even-numbered days) and Tobolsk (R2200/4500, 12 hours, odd-numbered days at 8.30pm, even-numbered days at 10.16am).

An *elektrichka* serves Novosibirsk Tuesdays, Thursdays and Sundays at 2.55pm (1st/2nd/3rd-class R1600/1250/840, 6¾ hours).

Various pleasure cruises depart from a jetty near the Yubileyny Bridge at ul Lenina, notably for Achairsky Monastery (R400 return, 4½ hours return, five times daily mid-May to early September).

In the warm months ferries cruise the Irtysh River to Salekhard on the Arctic Circle (1st/2nd/3rd class R4500/2000/1500, eight days) via Tobolsk (R2200/1000/850, three days) and Khanty-Mansisk (R2800/1500/1200, five days), departing roughly three times monthly.

ℹ Getting Around

From the train station, trolleybus 4 and bus 69 are among many options that go to the centre along pr Marksa.

Novosibirsk Новосибирск

📞 383 / POP 1.5 MILLION / TIME MOSCOW + 6HR

Once crusty and impersonal, Russia's third-largest city has embraced its status as capital of Siberia and opened its doors to the world. A slew of quirky museums and monuments, a relaxed big-city vibe, a pulsating nightlife and a wealth of great accommodation at both the high and low ends make Novosibirsk a logical and worthwhile Trans-Siberian pit stop. You can also jump off from here to architecturally splendid Tomsk, some 4½ hours away by bus.

Novosibirsk grew up in the 1890s around the Ob River bridge built for the Trans-Siberian Railway, and the city is festooned with original examples of the wood-lace architecture that prevailed at the time before the Soviets took over and started chucking concrete everywhere. Named Novo-Nikolaevsk until 1925 for the last tsar, it grew rapidly into Siberia's biggest metropolis, a key industrial and transport centre exploiting coalfields to the east and mineral deposits in the Ural Mountains.

Despite its daunting scale, Novosibirsk has a manageable centre focused on pl Lenina. The city's main axis, Krasny pr, runs through this square linking most points of interest.

◎ Sights

⭐**N.K. Rerikh Museum** MUSEUM

(Музей Н.К. Рериха; www.sibro.ru; ul Kommunisticheskaya 38; admission R100, free every 2nd Sat; ⏰10am-6pm) This museum is dedicated to the works and life of the painter Nikolai Rerikh (Nicholas Roerick), beloved in these parts because of his life-long passion for Altai. While the many paintings on display are reproductions, they provide a thorough synopsis of his life's work, and you can buy affordable prints in the excellent gift shop.

Rerikh was also a writer, philosopher, scientist, archaeologist, statesman and traveller. An epic five-year expedition around Central Asia (including Altai) and the Himalayas in the 1920s provided fodder for many of his paintings and philosophies. That journey is explored in depth here, making the museum an inspiring spot for modern-day vagabonds. Incredibly, the expedition traversed 35 mountain passes of more than 4,000 metres! There is a 15-minute movie in English on the artist's life, and rooms dedicated to the works of his wife and two sons – talented artists, writers and/or thinkers in their own right. The second Saturday of every month sees free classical music concerts at 3pm.

Novosibirsk

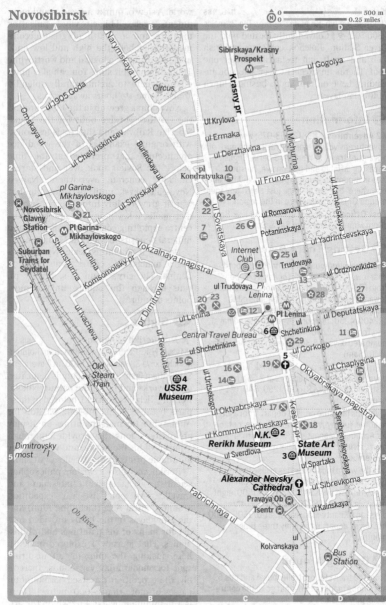

★ **State Art Museum** MUSEUM
(Художественный музей; Krasny pr 5; admission R100; ⏰ 11am-7pm Tue-Fri, 1-7pm Sat & Sun) The highlight is the museum's collection of 65 original paintings by Nikolai Rerikh on the second floor, mostly mountainscapes from the celebrated drifter's time in the Himalayas. The second floor also has a room of 17th-century European (mostly Dutch) masters, a collection of icons and several rooms dedicated to 18th- to 19th-century Russian

Novosibirsk

art. The third floor has some wonderful pieces from the Soviet era.

★**USSR Museum**   MUSEUM
(Музей СССР; ul Gorkogo 16; admission R150; ◷ noon-6pm Tue-Sat) While the collection of '70s Soviet bric-a-brac in this basement museum isn't particularly original, you get free rein over the place, which means photo ops galore. Dress yourself up (don't worry, it's allowed!) as a Soviet apparatchik, country *dyevushka* (girl) or Great Patriotic War soldier and snap away. We killed an afternoon here taking goofy selfies.

★**Alexander Nevsky Cathedral**   CHURCH
(Собор Александра Невского; Krasny pr 1a) The 1898 Alexander Nevsky Cathedral is a red-brick Byzantine-style building with gilded domes and colourful murals.

Regional Museum   MUSEUM
(Краеведческий музей; Krasny pr 23; admission R250; ◷ 10am-5.30pm Tue-Sun) In an elegant mansion, the Regional Museum was closed for renovations when we last visited. It has Altai shaman coats, cutaway pioneer houses and some splendid religious artefacts.

Chapel of St Nicholas   CHURCH
(Часовня Святителя Николая; Krasny pr) The pretty little Chapel of St Nicholas was said to mark the geographical centre of Russia

when it was built in 1915. Demolished in the 1930s, it was rebuilt in 1993 for Novosibirsk's centenary. Today it is an oasis of calm in the bustling city centre.

🛏 Sleeping

The best Novosibirsk hostels book out fast, especially from May to October, so booking ahead isn't a bad idea, and can usually be done informally by email. At the top end, a new **Marriott** (ul Ordzhonikidze) was going up opposite the Drama Theatre.

Zokol Hostel   HOSTEL $
(☏ 383-223 3611; www.zokolhostel.ru; ul Shchetinkina 34; dm R500-650, d R1600-1800; ✉ 🛜) With down-to-earth English-speaking staff, a superb sightseeing map and an ideal location within walking distance of the train station, the Zokol is the most user-friendly of Novosibirsk's many hostels. It's an intimate basement space with 19 beds in mostly windowless triples and quads, plus two cosy kitchen/common areas. The R100 breakfast is a bargain.

Provence Hostel   HOSTEL $
(Хостел Прованс; www.provence-hostel.ru; ul Chaplygina 45; dm R650-700, d R2200; @ 🛜) Occupying the third floor of an attractive century-old brick building, 42-bed Provence is the biggest hostel in Novosibirsk and one of the best. The location is absolutely prime,

WORTH A TRIP

DETOUR: SEYATEL – RAILWAY LOCOMOTIVE MUSEUM

A worthy 30-minute foray out of Novosibirsk is the **Seyatel – Railway Locomotive Museum** (Музей железнодорожной техники; www.parovoz.com; admission R80; ⊙11am-5pm Sat-Thu), with more than 100 exhibits ranging from Soviet steam engines to pre-Revolution carriages. Take *marshrutka* 1015 (R30) from Novosibirsk Glavny train station to Seyatel train station. You can return to central Novosibirsk the same way or jump on an hourly *elektrichka* (suburban train; R50).

the beds lovely, the English-speaking staff capable, the ambience bright and cheery. The kitchen/common area could be larger.

FunKey Hostel   HOSTEL $
(☑383-263 6503; www.funhostel.ru; ul Frunze 5/2; dm R600-700, d R1600; ☺��) Funky indeed. They back up their quirky name with one of Siberia's most creative hostel spaces. Bright paint and murals enliven walls, extra-tall bunk beds penetrate soaring ceilings and guests kick back in a delightfully wide-open kitchen/common area. Not as English-savvy or informative as some other hostels.

Hostel Dostoevsky   HOSTEL $
(☑8-983-510 7583; www.hosteldostoevsky.com; ul Gorkogo 85, 3rd fl; ⊙dm R450-650; ☺🖥) Climb the dodgy stairs to the oasis that is the Dostoevsky, Novosibirsk's original hostel, newly relocated to the city centre. It's an arty, bustling space with predominantly large (8- to 12-bed) dorms and an airy, open common area.

⭐**Avenue Hotel**   MINIHOTEL $$
(Авеню Отель; ☑383-227 0534; www.avenu.vipngs.ru; ul Sovetskaya 57; s incl breakfast R2400-3400, d R2800-3800; 🖥) The five rooms in the main wing of this quiet minihotel are huge and exceptionally well appointed – a welcome change from the standard renovated Soviet fare. And staff are friendly to boot! Cheaper rooms are in a neighbouring annexe. Both buildings are in a quiet residential courtyard behind ul Sovetskaya 55.

Hotel Tsentralnaya   HOTEL $$
(Гостиница Центральная; ☑383-222 7294; www.hotel-1.ru; ul Lenina 3; s/tw/tr from

R1500/1800/1800; 🖥) The cheapest private rooms in the centre are the simple 'economy' rooms, with shared bathrooms, found here. With peeling wallpaper and saggy beds, they retain every morsel of their Soviet, um, charm. That said, they are clean and the location can't be beat.

DoubleTree by Hilton   HOTEL $$$
(☑383-223 0100; www.novosibirsk.doubletreebyhilton.com; ul Kamenskaya 7/1; s/d incl breakfast weekday from R7000/8100, weekend from R4000/5100; ☺❄@🖥🏊) Has all the amenities you would expect, highlighted by luscious beds, mood lighting, ginormous plasma TVs, rain showers and (separate) extra-long bathtubs. The weekend rates are ripe for occasional splurgers, although we'd like to see a bit more space in the standard rooms.

Congress-Hotel Novosibirsk   HOTEL $$$
(Конгресс-Гостиница Новосибирск; ☑383-364 0101; www.hotel-novosibirsk.ru; Vokzalnaya magistral 1; s/d incl breakfast from R4300/4600; ☺❄@🖥) Boasting awesome views of the city centre from its upper floors, this formerly glum Soviet-era tower has been transformed into a plush modern hotel with fantastic service. It's possible to get two nights for the price of one if you arrive after midnight for the first night, and weekend rates are at least 30% less.

✗ Eating

⭐**Vilka-Lozhka**   CAFE $
(ul Frunze 2; meals R100-180; ⊙9am-10pm; 🖥) This upmarket *stolovaya* (canteen) is popular for a reason – hip and cool with groovy tunes and piping hot Russian staples like *bliny* (pancakes) and borsht at dirt-cheap prices. They even have beer on tap (from R80).

Nikolaevskaya Pelmennaya   RUSSIAN $
(Николаевская Пельменная; Krasny pr 13; mains R130-180; ⊙10am-10.30pm) Cheap and simple *pelmeni* with meat and fish fillings in an equally modest cafe located beneath a sex shop.

Universam Avangard   SUPERMARKET $
(Универсам Авангард; ul Lenina 10; ⊙24hr) Centrally located and well stocked – a godsend for self-caterers.

Shashlikoff   RUSSIAN $$
(Шашлыкофф; ul Lenina 12; mains R200-300; ⊙9am-1am; 🖥) This popular chain is fan-

tastic value. The signature shashlyk (meat kebabs) come in meat and fish varieties, accompanied by a full complement of Russian soups and salads and washed down with home-brewed beer (from R85). Additional branches opposite the **train station** (Vokzalnaya magistral 1; 🕾) and on **Krasny pr** (Krasny pr 17; 🕾).

Tiflis GEORGIAN $$
(Тифлис; www.tiflisnsk.ru; ul Sovetskaya 65; mains R350-600; ⊙11am-11pm; 🖉) This atmospheric tavern-cavern offers the most authentic Georgian cuisine in town. The filling and delicious *khachapuri po-adzharski* (Georgian cheese bread with a raw egg swimming in the middle) is well worth a try.

⭐ **La Maison** EUROPEAN $$$
(ul Sovetskaya 25; mains R600-1500; ⊙noon-midnight) In a beautiful former theatre dating to 1908, this is Novosibirsk's most sumptuous restaurant. The French- and Russian-leaning menu features quail, rabbit, rack of lamb and octopus along with upmarket versions of *solyanka* and other Russian country faves. Extensive wine list and rich desserts such as *mille-feuille*.

🍷 Drinking & Nightlife

⭐ **Friends Cocktail Bar** BAR
(Krasny pr 22; ⊙6pm-6am) With bearded bartenders whipping up some of Siberia's best (and strongest) cocktails and a convivial crowd, this is unquestionably Novosibirsk's best spot to warm up for a night out. Indeed you may elect to not go anywhere else. Reliably action-packed on weekdays as well as weekends, and you can eat at equally trendy **People's Bar & Grill** (Krasny pr 22; mains R350-800; ⊙24hr) in the same building.

Truba BAR
(Труба; http://jazzclubtruba.ru in Russian; ul Frunze 2; ⊙7pm-late; 🕾) It bills itself as a jazz bar but the lineup rums the gamut from jazz and blues to trash rock and grunge. Whatever is playing, this underground institution is well worth checking out. On Wednesdays beer and wine are R50.

Lebowsky CLUB
(Krasny pr 42a; admission R500; ⊙10pm-6am Thu-Sat, 6-11pm Sun) Novosibirsk's best club at the time of research, Lebowsky is a fairly intimate affair that often draws top Moscow DJs.

NOVOSIBIRSK'S WOODEN HOUSES

While it can't quite match the wood-lace architecture of nearby Tomsk, Novosibirsk has some fine Tsar-era houses hidden among the hulking Soviet structures of the centre. Photogenic streets include **ul Kommunisticheskaya** (check out Nos 3, 13, 19, 21, 23, 25 and 36), **ul Oktyabrskaya** (Nos 5, 9, 15 and 47), **ul Chaplygina** (Nos 25, 27 and 29) and **ul Gorkogo** (Nos 18, 20, 40, 81 and the brick No 26a).

Rock City CLUB
(Рок Сити; 🖉383-227 0108; www.rockcity.ru; Krasny pr 37; admission R150-350) Everything from Latin dancing to DJs to heavy-rock concerts. Thursday is ladies' night and Tuesdays feature two-for-one cocktails.

☆ Entertainment

⭐ **Opera & Ballet Theatre** THEATRE
(Театр оперы и балета; 🖉383-347 8484; www.opera-novosibirsk.ru; Krasny pr 36; admission R200-4000; ⊙Oct-Jun, most shows at 6.30pm) For classical culture don't miss an evening at this gigantic silver-domed theatre. Built in 1945, it's the largest theatre in Russia – bigger even than Moscow's Bolshoi. The grand interior alone makes performances here one of the city's highlights. Ticket prices depend on seats and performances.

Brodyachaya Sobaka LIVE MUSIC
(Бродячая Собака; http://sabaka.su in Russian; Kamenskaya ul 32; ⊙noon-midnight, til 6am Fri & Sat; 🕾) Weekends usually see live music performing at this grungy cabaret bar, while weekdays bring all manner of performing arts – check the website for the schedule.

Philharmonia CLASSICAL MUSIC
(Филармония; www.philharmonia-nsk.ru; Krasny pr 32; tickets R200-1500; ⊙Oct-Jun, most shows 7pm) Classical music concerts.

Spartak Stadium SPORTS
(Стадион Спартак; 🖉383-224 0488; http://fc-sibir.ru; ul Frunze 15) This 12,500-capacity venue is the home of local football team, Sibir. Games are usually played on Saturday or Sunday, and tickets cost from R200 to R700.

TRAINS FROM NOVOSIBIRSK

DESTINATION	MAIN TRAINS & FREQUENCY	PRICE PLATSKART/ KUPE	DURATION
Almaty	301 (odd-numbered days, 4.48pm)	R3569/5120	41hr
Severobaikalsk	92 (even-numbered days, 6.04pm)	R3090/6350	40hr
Tashkent	369 (7 per month, 1.51pm)	R8270/10,310	63hr
Tobolsk	116 (odd-numbered days, 1.04am)	R3300/6400	21¾hr
Tomsk	38 (odd-numbered days, 3.36am), 392 (odd-numbered days, 12.37am)	from R838/1555	5½hr

🛍 Shopping

Book Look BOOKSHOP
(2nd fl, Pyramid Shopping Centre, Krasny pr 29/1; ⊘9am-9pm) Has the best selection of maps in town, including maps of all Western Siberia *oblasti* (regions).

ℹ Information

Internet Club (ul Trudovaya 1; per hr R50; ⊘24hr)
Main Post Office (Главпочтамт; ul Sovetskaya 33; ⊘8am-10pm Mon-Fri, 9am-6pm Sat & Sun)

ℹ Getting There & Away

The well-located **Central Travel Bureau** (Центральное Бюро путешествий; Krasny pr 25; ⊘9am-8pm) is one of dozens of places to buy rail and air tickets, and also sells bus tickets (commission R100 to R200).

TRAIN

The city's huge main train station, **Novosibirsk Glavny** (ul Shamshurina 43), sits right on the Trans-Siberian main line and there are plenty of trains west to Moscow (48 to 55 hours) via Omsk, Tyumen and Yekaterinburg, and east to Irkutsk and beyond via Krasnoyarsk. The destinations listed in the table are off the Trans-Siberian main line. For Tobolsk you might be better off transferring in Tyumen. For Tomsk the bus is a better option.

AIR

Novosibirsk's **Tolmachyovo Airport** (http://en.tolmachevo.ru), 30km west of the city, is well connected to Moscow (four hours) and various other domestic destinations. International destinations served by direct flights from Novosibirsk include Běijīng, Prague and several cities in Central Asia, plus seasonal flights to Bangkok.

BUS

From the **bus station** (Автовокзал; Krasny pr 4) buses depart every hour or so to Tomsk (R544, 4½ hours). For roughly double the price, shared taxis shave an hour or more off that time but can take a while to fill up.

ℹ Getting Around

Buses 8, 21 and 37 link the train station with the river station via pl Lenina, Krasny pr and the bus station.

The metro has a major north–south line running beneath Krasny pr and across the river to ul Studencheskaya and pl Karla Marksa. For the main train station you'll need metro stop Ploshchad Garina-Mikhaylovskogo, which is on a second three-stop line that intersects with the major line at Sibirskaya/Krasny pr. Generally, buses are handier than the metro within the centre.

From the bus station, bus 111z (111з) goes to Tolmachyovo airport every 30 minutes from 6am to 12.30am, stopping by the train station on the way. Allow an hour to get there (more during Novosibirsk's infamous rush hour). A **taxi** (✆383-212 212) to the airport ordered by phone costs R350 (30 minutes, or one hour during rush hour).

Tomsk   Томск

✆3822 / POP 524,000 / TIME MOSCOW + 6HR
One of Siberia's oldest cities, Tomsk was founded in 1604 and was a major trade outpost before the founding of Novosibirsk (then Novo-Nikolaevsk) and the subsequent relocation of the Trans-Siberian railway line.

It's a university city where around one in every five residents is a student – hence the youthful, intellectual atmosphere.

Magnificent in snow, but pleasant at any time of the year, Tomsk also boasts endless examples of fine wooden buildings and an animated cafe and art scene. The city has enjoyed a reputation as the 'cultural capital of Siberia' since the 1960s, when artists, writers, and theatre and film directors were invited to take up residence here.

◉ Sights

★ Resurrection Hill HISTORICAL SITE
This was the location of Tomsk's original fortress, and the replica of its central wooden *spasskaya bashnya* (saviour's tower) that stands on it today was built in 2004 for the city's 400th anniversary celebrations. Next to the tower, the **History of Tomsk Museum** (Исторический музей Томска; admission R125; ☉10am-7pm Tue-Sun) has spouted its own wooden observation tower (admission R43); try to spot the seven historic churches from the top. The museum's moderately interesting collection of old artefacts and clothing is well presented, with placards in English.

For R100 you can rent historical costumes for silly photo ops. The stone just outside the museum entrance marks the founding of the city. Also up on Resurrection Hill is a pretty **Catholic Church** (ul Bakunina 4) dating to 1883.

★ Oppression Museum MUSEUM
(Музей НКВД; pr Lenina 44; admission R50, camera R100, tours in Russian/English R200/400; ☉10am-6pm) The gloomy basement of this former NKVD (proto-KGB) building is now a memorable Oppression Museum. Tours are recommended, but should be ordered in advance. Look out for the stunning Gulag map, the system of Soviet labour camps depicted as an uncountable mass of red dots across the territory of the former USSR.

Prisoners who passed through here included gulag chronicler Eufrosinia Kersnovskaya and the family of the purged Kazakh writer Akhmet Baytursınuly. Outside the museum are two monuments to victims of Stalinist repression – the larger to local victims, the second to Poles slaughtered by Uncle Joe and his cronies.

★ Ploshchad Lenina HISTORIC SITE
Central pl Lenina isn't really a square so much as a jumbled collection of beautifully restored historic buildings interspersed with banal Soviet concrete lumps. The frustrated **Lenin statue** (pl Lenina), now relegated to a traffic circle, points at the ugly concrete of the **Drama Theatre** (Драматический театр; ☑3822-512 223; www.dramatomsk.ru; pl Lenina 4; ☉Oct-Jun), apparently demanding 'build more like that one'. Fortunately, nobody's listening. Topped with a golden angel, in a second circle beside Lenin, is the **Iverskaya Chapel** (Иверская часовня; ☉10am-6pm), whose celebrated icon is dubbed 'Tomsk's Spiritual Gateway'.

The drama theatre is flanked by the splendid 1784 **Epiphany Cathedral** (Богоявленский собор; pl Lenina 7), the former **trading arches** (Гостиный Двор), and the elegant 1802 Hotel Magistrat.

Tomsk Art Museum ART MUSEUM
(Художественный музей; www.artmuseum.tomsk.ru; per Nakhanovicha 3; admission per exhibit R100; ☉10am-6pm Tue-Sun) Well worth popping into for its wide range of permanent and temporary exhibits. The highlight is the collection of 19th- and early-20th-century Russian art, and there's a small exhibit of 12th- to 13th-century religious icons.

University HISTORIC BUILDING
(Томский Государственный Университет) The classically colonnaded main buildings of the university lie in resplendently leafy grounds, giving Tomsk the sobriquet 'Oxford of Siberia'. There's not much open to the public, but there's nothing to stop you taking a walk around the grounds.

Regional Museum MUSEUM
(Краеведческий музей; pr Lenina 75; admission R200; ☉10am-6pm Tue-Sun) Housed in the splendid Atashev Palace, this modest museum has a 2500-year-old bear amulet and an interesting exhibit on the Great Tea Trail. But it's the building, commissioned in 1842 by the gold-mining entrepreneur Ivan Atashev, that's the main attraction. It was once used as a church, hence the incongruous steeple tower and wonderful organ hall.

Voznesenskaya Church CHURCH
(Вознесенская церковь; ul Oktyabrsky Vzvoz 10) This Gothic edifice with five gold-tipped black spires has great potential as a Dracula movie set. A truly massive bell hangs in its lurid-pink belfry.

YEKATERINBURG TO KRASNOYARSK TOMSK

WWII Memorial MONUMENT

(Памятник Второй Отечественной войны (Лагерный сад) A Tomsk landmark, this moving mother-and-son monument is at the very southern end of pr Lenina. The beautiful birch tree park (Лагерный сад) here is a local favourite for strolls, not least for its fine views across the Tom River.

Tours

Tomskturist WALKING TOURS

(Томсктурист; ☎ 3822-528 179; www.tomsk-turist.ru; pr Lenina 59; ☺ 9am-7pm Mon-Fri, 11am-4pm Sat) Tomskturist can arrange two-hour walking tours of the city, with English-, French- and German-speaking guides, although the price (R4500) makes this more of a group option. Can also help sort out Altai border-zone permits, arrange regional excursions and sell plane and train tickets. Darya speaks English.

Sleeping

Lucomoria Hostel HOSTEL $

(☎ 3822-504 218; www.lucomoria.ru; ul Sovetskaya 75; ☺@⎙) An excellent all-around hostel within walking distance of the centre, with comfortable beds, a nice kitchen, double rooms with queen beds, and a six-bed women's dorm. Door code: 19.

Dom Okhotnika Hostel HOSTEL $

(Хостел Дом Охотника; ☎ 3812-258 646; www-hunter-hostel.ru; ul Gagarina 42; dm R400-600, d R1200; ☺⎙) Rich with potential because of its location in the lovely 19th-century 'Hunter's House', the spartan interior unfortunately lacks the charm of the glorious exterior. Still, the location is the best of Tomsk's hostels and the private rooms are fantastic value. However, the large dorm rooms are geared more towards locals than tourists. No English spoken.

8th Floor Hostel HOSTEL $

(☎ 3822-565 522; www.8hostel.com; ul Dzherzhinskogo 56; dm R450-550, d R1200; ☺@⎙) This 20-bed hostel is – wouldn't you know it – on the 8th floor of a Soviet high-rise. It checks out nicely on all fronts, especially the cocoon-like bunk beds, but finding it is tricky. It's in the 10-storey building behind ul Kirova 39; take the southernmost entrance and dial 55.

Hotel Sputnik HOTEL $$

(Гостиница Спутник; ☎ 3812-526 660; www.sputnik.tomskturist.ru; ul Belinskogo 15; s/d without

bathroom R1050/2300, with bathroom incl breakfast from R3500/4200; ☺@⎙) The winner of Tomsk's first hotel competition in the 1990s, the Sputnik remains one of the few decent midrange places to stay, especially after a recent makeover. The rooms, however, retain

Tomsk

their small Soviet dimensions and narrow beds. The breakfast is hardly worth getting up for.

★ **Gogol Hotel** HOTEL $$$
(☑ 3822-909 709; http://gogolhotel.ru; s/d incl breakfast R3900/4500, ste R5900-8000; ❂ ❊ ❒) Bordering on boutique, this classy 19-room property has quickly become Tomsk's most sought-after address. Rooms are spacious with muted grey tones and walls emblazoned with photos of old Tomsk. You can swim in the king-sized beds and the breakfast is fantastic.

Hotel Magistrat HOTEL $$$
(Гостиница Магистрат; ☑ 3822-511 111; www.magistrathotel.com; pl Lenina 15; d/tw incl breakfast from R5800/6600; ❊ ❒) Behind the palatial 1802 facade, the rooms and restaurant are done up in the ultra-luxurious style that Russians seem to love but foreigners find overdone. You can't beat the location, however. No lift.

✖ Eating

Obzhorni Ryad RUSSIAN $
(Обжорный ряд; ul Gertsena 1; mains R100-200; ◷ 11am-11pm; ❒) For penny-pinchers in search of good-value Russian fare, look no further than this *stolovaya*, whose name translates as Guzzler's Row.

Pelmeni Project RUSSIAN $
(pr Lenina 81; mains R150-250; ◷ 24hr; ❒) Besides the best *pelmeni* in town, this buzzing, centrally located eatery serves Russian staples, burgers and even some Italian fare. The outdoor terrace is ripe for people-watching in the warm months.

People's Bar & Grill INTERNATIONAL $$
(pr Lenina 54; mains R250-450; ◷ noon-2am; ❒) This trendy bar-and-grill embraces pop culture with movie-star photos, music videos and Hollywood-inspired dishes – Big Lebowski (beef steak with potatoes) and Pulp Fishion (salmon steak). Another branch just off **pr Frunze** (ul Krasnoarmeyskaya 31; mains R250-450; ◷ noon-2am; ❒).

Vechny Zov RUSSIAN $$
(Вечный Зов; ul Sovetskaya 47; mains R200-800; ◷ noon-2am; ❒) Named after a popular Soviet TV serial, this the place to sample Siberian specialities like *stroganina, muksun* (an Ob River whitefish) and bear meat. Try the four-meat (bear, deer, pork, beef) *pelmeni*. It boasts a mock Siberian ranch outside and a cosy antique-filled home feel inside.

★ **Slavyansky Bazar** RUSSIAN $$$
(Славянский Базар; ☑ 3812-515 553; pl Lenina 10; mains R500-1200; ◷ noon-midnight; ❒) On the bank of the Tom River, Slavyansky Bazar

is Tomsk's fanciest restaurant, housed in a 19th-century building. Penny-pinchers can order from the *pelmeni/vareniki* menu or stop in for the business lunch. Chekhov ate at an earlier incarnation of the present-day establishment in 1890. The food was one of the few things he liked about the city.

🍷 Drinking & Nightlife

★Bulanzhe CAFE
(Буланже; pr Lenina 80; mains R200-350; ⏱10am-11pm; 📶) Fantastic cafe – bright and cheery with an exciting menu of international food, fresh salads, great coffee and a wide tea selection. The Belgian waffles are highly recommended. It's a place to chat and chew rather than work on a laptop.

★Underground Jazz Café BAR
(www.jazzcafe.tomsk.ru; pr Lenina 46; cover charge weekends R250 to R400; ⏱noon-midnight Sun-Thu, noon-2am Fri & Sat; 📶) A hip and literally underground basement with live jazz, including frequent US guests, most weekends. Also has an extensive drinks and food menu. We liked the vegetarian borsch and the screenings of old black-and-white films.

Sibirsky Pub PUB
(Сибирский Паб; pl Novosobornaya 2; Guinness per pint R340; ⏱1pm-1am; 📶) Siberia's first British pub was founded over a century ago by a certain Mr Crawley, an Anglo-Egyptian

albino who'd got stuck in Tomsk after touring with a circus freak show. Today's pub is no relation. Bands play live at weekends.

☆ Entertainment

★Tom Tomsk FC SPORTS
(Томь Томск ФК; tickets from R300) **Trud Stadium** (ul Belinskogo 15/1) is the home of Siberia's top football club. Since 2004 Tom Tomsk has spent most years in the Russian Premier League, making it Europe's most easterly top-flight football club. Unfortunately the team was relegated to the second flight in 2014. At the stadium there's a shop selling Tomsk scarves and T-shirts. It's open 11am to 7pm Monday to Friday, and on weekends on home match days.

Human Puppets Theatre 2+ku PUPPET THEATRE
(Театр живых кукол 2+ку; www.2ky.tomsk.ru; Yuzhny per 29; admission R200-500) Housed in a quaint log cabin near the WWII memorial (take ul Savinikh all the way down until you can't go any further), this one-man, homey 'robotic puppet' theatre is a real experience, and one you don't need to understand Russian to appreciate.

Aelita Theatre THEATRE
(Театр Аэлита; ☑3822-514 436; www.aelita.tom. ru in Russian; pr Lenina 78) Eclectic offerings

---

WOODEN ARCHITECTURE

Much of Tomsk's appeal lies in its well-preserved late 19th- and early-20th-century 'wooden-lace' architecture – carved windows and tracery on old log and timber houses. There are a few streets to hone in on if touring the city on foot.

Ul Tatarskaya has perhaps the richest concentration of such houses. It's reached via the steps beside a lovely old house at **prospekt Lenina 56** (пр Ленина 56). The best examples are on the block north of ul Trifonova, where you'll also find the modest **Red Mosque,** (Красная Мечеть; ul Tatarskaya 22) which dates from 1904. It was used as a vodka factory by the atheist Soviets, but was reopened to worshippers in 1997. Over on the east side of pr Lenina, **ul Gagarina** is similarly endowed with graceful heritage houses.

A few blocks east of ul Belinskogo, near the corner of ul Krasnoarmeyskaya and ul Gertsena look out for the spired, bright-turquoise **Russian-German House** (Российско-Немецкий Дом; ul Krasnoarmeyskaya 71) (1904); the **Dragon House** (Дом Дракона; ul Krasnoarmeyskaya 68) (late 19th century) which is home to a clinic; and the fan-gabled **Peacock House** (Дом Павлина; ul Krasnoarmeyskaya 67a) (early 20th century). **Ul Dzerzhinskogo,** one block east of ul Krasnoarmeyskaya, is worth a wander too, for wood houses as well as the colourful outdoor **Dzherzhinskogo Market** (Дзержинского рынка; ul Dzherzhinskogo), which sprawls for a full block south of ul Kartashova, providing photo ops as well as fuel in the form of local fruits and nuts.

Other streets worth strolling are **per Kononova** (look for **No 2** (per Kononova 2), where the doomed communist mastermind Sergei Kirov lodged in 1905); and nearby **ul Shishkova**.

from rock concerts to Indian dance to experimental plays.

Philharmonia · CONCERT HALL
(Филармония; ☑ 3822-515 956; http://bkz.
tomsk.ru; pl Lenina 1) Classical music and great big-band jazz. Hosts the Tomsk International Jazz Festival in the first week in June.

Organ Hall · CLASSICAL MUSIC
(pr Lenina 75; tickets R200-500; ☉ concerts at 7pm, noon on Sun) Beautiful organ concerts are held several times a month upstairs in the Atashev Palace. The acoustics are brilliant.

ℹ Information

Afisha (www.afisha.westsib.ru) Has concert and cinema details.
Main Post Office (Почтамт; pr Lenina 95; ☉ 8am-10pm Mon-Fri, 9am-6pm Sat & Sun) Stamps, but no postcards of Tomsk (find postcards in most museums).
Netcafe (Неткафе; pr Lenina 44; per hr R47; ☉ 9am-11pm) Another branch (pr Lenina 41; per hr R47; ☉ 9am-11pm) south of the university.
Sent to Siberia (http://senttosiberia.wordpress.com) A now-departed American Fulbright scholar's humorous and affectionate account of life in Tomsk.

ℹ Getting There & Away

TRAIN
From Tomsk I (main) train station, the Barnaul-bound train goes via Novosibirsk (*platskart/ kupe* R700/1250, eight hours, 9.20pm on even-numbered days). There is a train on odd-numbered days to Moscow (R7350/11,060, 56 hours) via Novosibirsk and Yekaterinburg, and a train every fourth day to Vladivostok via Irkutsk and Khabarovsk.

For more frequent connections east (towards Irkutsk) and west (towards Novosibirsk), take an *elektrichka* to Taiga (R112, two hours, 9.06am and 4.15pm) or a bus to Yurga (R210, two hours, four daily); most mainline Trans-Siberian trains stop at both stations. *Elektrichki* from Taiga to Tomsk depart at 7.07am and 4.15pm.

BUS
For Novosibirsk, buses (R544, 4½ hours, every hour) are handier and quicker than trains. The

central **bus station** (Автовокзал; ☑ 3822-540 730) is right next to the main train station.

ℹ Getting Around

The Tomsk 1 (main) train station is about 2km southeast of the centre. Buses 4, 12 and 12a run from the train station to the centre via pr Kirova and pr Lenina, while tram 2 trundles to the centre via pr Kirova and ul Sovetskaya.

Within the centre, trolleybuses 1 and 3, or bus 17, run along pr Lenina.

Tomsk's antiquated and atmospheric trams are a great way to take a cheap (R15) city tour. Tram 1 trundles all the way to the city's northern outskirts via ul Sovetskaya and ul Bolshaya Podgornaya, while tram 2 runs the length of ul Sovetskaya.

Good maps are available in the train station and at street kiosks.

CHEKHOV ON TOMSK – 'BORING CITY, DULL PEOPLE'

Not everyone falls in love with Tomsk. Playwright Anton Chekhov – who visited the city on his way to Russia's Far East – certainly didn't. 'Tomsk isn't worth a damn,' he wrote in his diary. 'A boring city...with dull people.' He also described it as 'a drunken city' where there were 'no beautiful women at all'. He also complained that a waitress had wiped a spoon 'against her backside' before handing it to him. But then, as legend has it, he did almost drown while crossing the Tom River, so maybe he was feeling grumpy. The city had its revenge though. In 2004, on Tomsk's 400th anniversary, a caricature of the famous writer was unveiled, in the form of a bronze statue entitled 'Anton Pavlovich [the writer's patronymic] through the eyes of a drunk lying in a ditch'. The statue is on the riverbank opposite Slavyansky Bazar restaurant. Rubbing its well-polished nose is said to bring good luck.

Lake Baikal: Krasnoyarsk to Ulan-Ude

Includes

Route Info

➜ Distance: 1544km

➜ Duration: 24 hours

➜ Time zones: Moscow +7,
Moscow +8

Best Places to Stay & Eat

➜ Belka Hostel (p190)

➜ Iris (p176)

➜ Mergen Bator (p200)

➜ Nikita's Homestead (p194)

➜ Kochevnik restaurant
(p185)

➜ Rassolnik (p186)

Why Go?

If you've made it this far from Moscow or Běijīng, this 1500km ribbon of rail and sleeper is where things get interesting. Arguably the most varied stretch of the line, bid farewell to your *provodnitsa* (carriage attendant) along its length for some of the most memorable experiences Siberia has to offer.

Most travellers making only a single stop on their Trans-Sib odyssey do so in Irkutsk, surely Siberia's most engaging city. Only a smidgen over 350 years old, this grand city packs in heaps of history. When you tire of ornate facades, stuccoed palaces and streets of traditional timber dwellings, glorious Lake Baikal, the unrivalled highlight of any rail trip across Russia, is just a short bus ride away.

When the tracks finally peel away from Baikal's mind-boggling vistas, Trans-Sibbers find themselves in the Republic of Buryatiya, an exotically Asian retreat of Buddhist temples and shamanist traditions, increasingly coming under the gravitational pull of southern neighbour Mongolia.

When to Go

Irkutsk

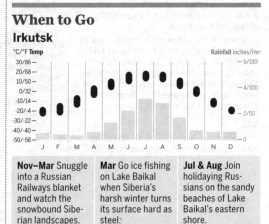

Nov–Mar Snuggle into a Russian Railways blanket and watch the snowbound Siberian landscapes.

Mar Go ice fishing on Lake Baikal when Siberia's harsh winter turns its surface hard as steel.

Jul & Aug Join holidaying Russians on the sandy beaches of Lake Baikal's eastern shore.

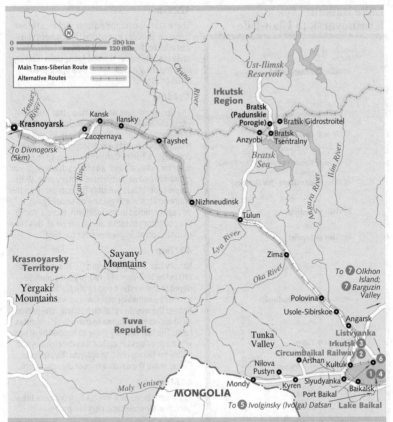

Krasnoyarsk to Ulan-Ude Highlights

1 Gazing out across the **southern shores of Lake Baikal** from a slow train between Irkutsk and Ulan-Ude, possibly the most attractive section of the entire Trans-Sib line

2 Taking the ultimate Trans-Sib branch line trip on the **Circumbaikal Railway** (192) for some stunning Baikal vistas

3 Admiring the ostentatious 19th-century architecture of **Irkutsk** (p179), once known as the 'Paris of Siberia'

4 Walking, cycling or hitching a lift across frozen **Lake Baikal**

5 Mooching with the monks at Buddhist temple **Ivolginsky (Ivolga) Datsan** (p203)

6 Navigating a section of the **Great Baikal Trail** (p191) between Listvyanka and Bolshie Koty

7 Enjoying a couple of meditative days on wonderful **Olkhon Island** (p193) or getting away from it all in the often overlooked **Barguzin Valley** (p205)

ℹ The Route

KRASNOYARSK TO TAYSHET

4098km from Moscow

Heading east out of Krasnoyarsk your fellow travellers will not have even fathomed there's a foreigner in their midst before the train crosses

the 1km-long Yenisey River bridge, whose 1898 original won a gold medal at the 1900 Paris Expo (along with the Eiffel Tower). The Yenisey traditionally marks the unofficial border between Eastern and Western Siberia.

Lake Baikal:
Krasnoyarsk to Ulan-Ude

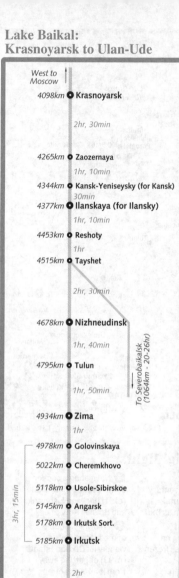

West to
Moscow

4098km ● **Krasnoyarsk**

2hr, 30min

4265km ● Zaozernaya

1hr, 10min

4344km ● **Kansk-Yeniseysky (for Kansk)**

30min

4377km ● **Ilanskaya (for Ilansky)**

1hr, 10min

4453km ● Reshoty

1hr

4515km ● Tayshet

2hr, 30min

4678km ● **Nizhneudinsk**

1hr, 40min

4795km ● Tulun

1hr, 50min

4934km ● Zima

1hr

4978km ● Golovinskaya

5022km ● Cheremkhovo

5118km ● Usole-Sibirskoe

5145km ● Angarsk

5178km ● Irkutsk Sort.

5185km ● Irkutsk

3hr, 15min

To Severobaikalsk
(1064km – 20–26hr)

2hr

5311km ● Slyudyanka

2hr, 20min

5477km ● Babushkin

2hr, 10min

5640km ● Ulan-Ude

East to
Vladivostok

4229km

There's no stop for the Rossiya, but most other trains do shudder to a halt at Uyar, where you can admire the cream-and-green art nouveau–style station. Understandably the town is rarely referred to by its full name, Uyarspasopreo-brazhenskoye.

4344km

The Rossiya makes its first stop after Krasno-yarsk at Kansk-Yeniseysky, which serves the settlement of Kansk. Founded in 1636, this historic town boasts a scattering of century-old buildings, a Trinity Cathedral whose spire can be seen for miles around, an impressive bronze war memorial and an illuminated victory arch. With ample time, this is possibly the only place on this entire stretch worth getting off to see (just). If you are confined to the platform, there's always the obligatory steam train to marvel at, this time mounted on an impressive marble plinth.

4377km

Ilansky has a small museum (⊙10am-5pm Mon-Fri) in the 100-year-old, red-brick locomotive depot at the western end of the station, and a freshly painted locomotive and water tower behind the wooden station building. The *provod-nitsa* allows passengers to roam for 20 minutes here. The last exciting thing to happen here was when a previous LP author was detained by the police for taking photographs on the platform. Better leave the camera in your compartment.

4474km

The train passes into Irkutsk Region; local time becomes Moscow time plus five hours.

4501km

If you're heading from Moscow to Běijīng via Chita, you're halfway there.

4515km

The Rossiya stops for just two minutes at Tay-shet; other trains can loiter here for 20 minutes, giving you time to photograph yet another beached steam loco, a large, newly renovated station building and an incongruously attractive, Italian-built water tower behind. This is the Trans-Siberian's westernmost junction with the BAM (the Baikal-Amur Mainline or Baikalo-Amurskaya Magistral), and many travellers and locals find themselves waiting here for connec-tions to Severobaikalsk and Tynda. Tayshet was once an infamous transit point for Gulag camp prisoners. The town even gets a less-than-complimentary mention in Aleksandr Solzhenit-syn's *The Gulag Archipelago* (not recommended reading on a trip to Russia, believe us). Surpris-ingly English-speaking help is available here, making the town worth an overnight stay.

TAYSHET TO IRKUTSK

4515km to 4600km

If riding straight through from Moscow, you're now on day three but only halfway to the Pacific. As the railway skirts the foothills of the Sayany Mountains, endless taiga and a real sense of wilderness set in.

4644km

Now you can crack open a celebratory tub of instant porridge or sachet of three-in-one coffee – you've made it halfway from Moscow to Vladivostok.

4649km

Welcome to UK, no not Blighty but the station of Ук which may just have the shortest name of any Trans-Sib station. No stop for the Rossiya though.

4678km

There's a 13-minute stop at mildly historical Nizhneudinsk. Cossacks first built a small fortress here in 1649 and for more than two centuries the town served as an important centre for gold and fur traders. The St Nicholas Church and the regional museum (ul Lenina 27; ◷8am-5pm) entice few off the rails, but an 18km hike along the Uda River to the 20m-high Ukovsky waterfalls could make for an adventurous side trip. Further east the landscape flattens out and the forests have been extensively logged.

4795km

The next stop is timber Tulun, where you'll have just two minutes to contemplate the merits of the architecturally confident station building. From here a road heads 225km north to Bratsk on the BAM. The town has a far-flung Decembrist Museum but very few visitors.

4934km

There's an overgenerous 30-minute break in proceedings at the former exile town of Zima, which translates ominously as 'winter'.

5087km

More translation is required at Polovina, whose name means roughly 'halfway' (between Moscow and Vladivostok), which it was in the early 20th century before the line was rerouted in many places. No stop for the Rossiya.

5118km

From Polovina the train heads southeast and is joined by the Angara River around Usole-Sibirskoe, where a shuddering stop may jolt you from your slumber but hopefully not from your bunk altogether. The town supplies much of Russia's salt and many of its matches.

5145km

By the time you reach oil-rich Angarsk, where there's a clock museum and a couple of good restaurants if you really want to get off, it's probably time to start collecting your belongings if you're alighting at Irkutsk.

5178km

Heading west on some services originating in Irkutsk, you may rejoice at having a compartment all to yourself – that is until hordes of locals board at Irkutsk Sortirovka, a marshalling yard on the city's western outskirts.

5185km

The train crosses the Irkut River 3km before Irkutsk station. Once nicknamed the 'Paris of Siberia', Irkutsk is the most popular Siberian stop for most transcontinental travellers, notably as a launching point to reach Lake Baikal, 70km further southeast.

IRKUTSK TO ULAN-UDE

5185km to 5321km

Moving on from Irkutsk, the line takes a sharp right where the tracks once continued along the Angara River to Port Baikal, a stretch flooded by the Angara Dam project. The early 1950s rerouting includes the tightest twists and the steepest descent on the entire line (providing great opportunities for photos of the train) just before Kultuk, where passengers get their first tantalising glimpse of Lake Baikal.

5311km

The first stop after Irkutsk for the Rossiya is at Slyudyanka where Baikal is so close it's tempting to dash down for a quick dip. However, the scheduled stop here – usually no longer than two minutes – means that you could run the very real risk of being stranded in Siberia as

KRASNOYARSK TO ULAN-UDE ROUTE PLANNER

Here's a suggested itinerary for continuing from Krasnoyarsk to Ulan-Ude:

Day 1 Take an overnight train from Krasnoyarsk to Irkutsk (18 hours).

Day 2 Arrive Irkutsk, then head out for a tour of the city.

Day 3 Bus to Taltsy Museum of Wooden Architecture then on to lakeside Listvyanka for one night.

Day 4 Return to Irkutsk; catch train for short hop to Slyudyanka for more lake views and perhaps a ride on the Circumbaikal Railway to Port Baikal.

Day 5 Skirt around the picturesque southern shore of Lake Baikal on a day train to Ulan-Ude.

the train chugs off without you. If that prospect doesn't appeal, stay on the platform and snap up a snack of smoked *omul* (a fish native to Lake Baikal) from the countless hawkers instead. If the *provodnitsa* won't let you off, perform the transaction through a window (if one will open). For the next 200km or so the stuffy carriages fill with a fishy aroma, especially on hot days. If you've not bought any *omul*, fellow travellers are certain to offer you some.

5352km

There's no stop for the Rossiya between Sly-udyanka and Ulan-Ude as it rattles around the southern shores of Lake Baikal. However the Rossiya is not the best service to take on this stretch of the line as it does the journey either side of midnight.

5352km

The town of Baikalsk was once home to a cellulose plant, the biggest polluter of Lake Baikal. Thankfully it was closed down in 2013. Many come to ski at a big resort just above the town.

5352km to 5561km

Bag a left-facing window for this stretch (right-facing if you're travelling west), considered by most seasoned Trans-Sibbers as the most scenic on the entire line. The tracks run just metres from the lake at some points, at others delving into thick forest. The views across Baikal are superb at any time of year, but especially on crisp sunny days in late winter when the entire lake freezes into one mammoth block of white ice. If you're stuck on the 'wrong' side of the train, don't despair – the views of the Khamar Daban Mountains are equally impressive. Imagine the 18th- and 19th-century tea caravans from China emerging over the ridges to catch their first glimpse of Lake Baikal below.

5391km

Some trains make a two-minute halt at the lakeside fishing village of Vydrino. You've now entered the fascinating Republic of Buryatiya, which is in the same time zone as Irkutsk Region. This stretch of the Trans-Siberian is possibly the most worthwhile place to leave the comfort of your compartment. Some 5km to the south lie the Teplye Lakes, wonderful bodies of water cupped by steep wooded hills. The name 'Teplye' means warm as the water is kept above freezing year round by thermal springs. There's a cheap *turbaza* (holiday camp) nearby.

5420km

Just after another Baikal fishing settlement called Tankhoi, the train rumbles over a bridge spanning the fast-flowing Pereyomnaya River, one of 300 rivers feeding Lake Baikal. The village is home to the headquarters of the Baikal Biosphere Reserve in which you now find yourself.

5477km

The village of Babushkin (for Mysovaya) is a blur from the Rossiya, but in the early 20th century, before the line around the south of Lake Baikal was built (and occasionally afterwards), this was where the icebreakers *Angara* and *Baikal* – carrying wagons and passengers from Port Baikal – would dock. Both of the ships were built in Newcastle-upon-Tyne and the *Angara* survives as a museum in Irkutsk. The *Baikal* went to the bottom of Lake Baikal during the Russian Civil War, though no one is sure exactly where it lies.

5530km

The Trans-Sib waves farewell to Lake Baikal's bluer-than-blue waters just before the village of Posolskaya. A road from here heads to Lake Baikal and the village of Posolskoe, where a recently renovated and very picturesque monastery looks out across the water.

5561km

Around half an hour after Posolskaya, the Rossiya zips through Selenga (for Selenginsk), the nearest stop on other trains to the incredible Selenga Delta.

5561km to 5641km

At Selenga the Trans-Sib joins up with the Selenga River carrying its load of silt (and Mongolian pollution) to Lake Baikal. The line hugs the left riverbank as far as Tataurovo, after which it crosses to the right bank, just in time to arrive at Ulan-Ude.

Krasnoyarsk   Красноярск

☑ 391 / POP 1 MILLION / TIME MOSCOW +7HR

More orderly and affluent than the average Siberian city, million-strong Krasnoyarsk enjoys an appealing setting amid low hills punctuated by jagged rock formations. While its architecture isn't particularly inspiring, scattered throughout the predominantly unaesthetic concrete of post-WWII industrialisation are a few outstandingly well-embellished timber mansions and a sprinkling of unexpected art nouveau curves. Pleasant river trips, the nearby Stolby Nature Reserve and an outstanding regional museum make Krasnoyarsk an agreeable place to break the long journey between Tomsk (612km west) and Lake Baikal.

◉ Sights & Activities

★ **Stolby Nature Reserve**   NATURE RESERVE
(www.stolby.ru) Krasnoyarsk's biggest draw are the fingers and towers of volcanic rock called **stolby**. These poke above the woods

in the 17,000-hectare Stolby Nature Reserve (Zapovednik Stolby). To reach the main concentration of rock formations, follow the track (7km long) near Hotel Snezhnaya Dolina (bus 50), or take the year-round **chairlift** (Фуникулёр; R250) belonging to the ski resort. From the top, walk for two minutes to a great viewpoint or around 40 minutes to reach the impressive **Takmak Stolby**.

New paths and steps mean going it alone is not the daredevil experience it once was, but English-language tours with SibTour-Guide (p178) are a much more pleasant and entertaining affair. Be aware that infected ticks are dangerous between May and July and tick protection or predeparture encephalitis jabs are essential at this time.

Regional Museum   MUSEUM

(Краеведческий музей; www.kkkm.ru; ul Dubrovinskogo 84; admission R150; ⊙10am-6pm Tue-Wed & Fri-Sun, 1-9pm Thu) Housed in an incongruously attractive 1912 art nouveau Egyptian temple, this is one of Siberia's better museums. Arranged around a Cossack explorer's ship, surprisingly well-presented exhibitions across the two floors examine every facet of the region's past, from Cossacks and gentlemen explorers to the Tunguska explosion and local fauna, prerevolution institutions to religious art.

Highlights include the 20th-century 'nostalgia' section on the upper level and the 4m-tall mammoth skeleton looking like something straight off a Hollywood museum movie set. There are touch-screen games for kids throughout and a decent cafe to look forward to at the end.

Surikov Museum-Estate   MUSEUM

(Музей-усадьба Сурикова; www.surikov-dom. com; ul Lenina 98; admission R100; ⊙10am-6pm Wed-Sun) The Surikov Museum-Estate preserves the house, sheds and vegetable patch of 19th-century painter Vasily Surikov (1848–1916). The heavy-gated garden forms a refreshing oasis of rural Siberia right in the city centre. More of Surikov's work is on show at the old-school **Surikov Art Museum** (Художественный музей Сурикова; ul Parizhskoy Kommuny 20; admission R100; ⊙10am-6pm Tue-Wed & Fri-Sun, 1-9pm Thu).

Resurrection Church   CHURCH

(Благовещенская церковь; ul 9 Yanvarya) The top-heavy but elegant Resurrection Church (1804–22) was decapitated in the 1930s but given a new tower in 1998–99. Its icon-filled interior billows with incense.

Literature Museum   MUSEUM

(Литературный музей; ul Lenina 66; admission R50; ⊙10am-6pm Tue-Sat) This quaint museum within a glorious 1911 merchant's mansion occasionally hosts classical music performances.

Chasovnya Chapel   NOTABLE BUILDING

(Часовня Параскевы Пятницы; top of Karaulnaya Hill) For some spectacular city views climb Karaulnaya Hill (there's no bus) to the little chapel featured on the Russian 10-rouble banknote (now slowly being replaced

---

WESTERN LAKE BAIKAL

Lake Baikal (Озеро Байкал), the 'Pearl of Siberia', is a crystal-clear body of the bluest water. It's drinkably pure, surrounded by rocky, tree-covered cliffs and so vast that you can sail for hours without the mountain backdrops becoming appreciably closer.

Shaped like a banana, Lake Baikal – 636km from north to south, but only 60km wide – was formed by rifting tectonic plates. Though nearly 8km of the rift is filled with sediment, it is gradually getting deeper as the plates separate. It will eventually become the earth's fifth ocean, splitting the Asian continent. In the meantime it's the world's deepest lake: 1637m near the western shore. As such, it contains nearly one-fifth of the world's fresh, unfrozen water – more than North America's five Great Lakes combined. Swimmers brave enough to face Baikal's icy waters (never warmer than about 15°C) risk vertigo, as it is possible to see down as far as 40m. In February and March you can drive right across on the 1m-thick ice, though this is safest in the north and most practical between Severobaikalsk and Ust-Barguzin.

The lake itself is a living museum of flora and fauna, 80% of which is found nowhere else on the planet, most famously the loveable black-eyed *nerpa* (freshwater seals) and salmonlike *omul* fish, which are delicious smoked. Don't worry if you're not getting off the train around Baikal as they're sold on the station platforms, most notably in Slyudyanka.

Krasnoyarsk

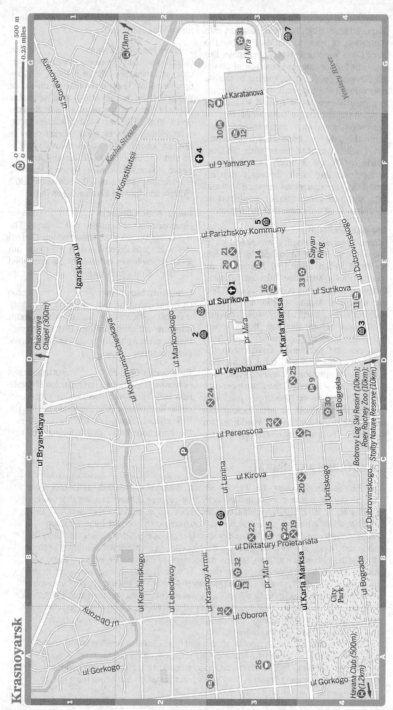

Krasnoyarsk

with a coin). It was designed in 1855 by Konstantin Thon, the architect behind Moscow's Christ the Saviour Cathedral. At midday a deafening one-gun salute is fired from just below the chapel.

SV Nikolai MUSEUM

(Пароход-музей Святитель Николай; admission R50; ⊙10am-8pm Tue-Sun) Permanently docked below an ugly brown-concrete exhibition centre (formerly the Lenin Museum) is the SV *Nikolai,* the ship that transported future Soviet leader Vladimir Ilyich to exile in Shushenskoe and the future Tsar Nikolai II across the Yenisey in 1891.

Intercession Cathedral CHURCH

(Покровский собор; ul Surikova) This pleasingly small old church dating from 1795 has an interior of unusually glossed and intricately moulded stucco framing haloed saints.

Roev Ruchey Zoo ZOO

(Зоопарк Роев ручей; www.roev.ru; admission R200; ⊙9am-9pm) Take bus 50 or 50A to this humane zoo near the Bobrovy Log Ski Resort to see numerous Siberian species.

Bobrovy Log Ski Resort SKI RESORT

(Лыжный курорт Бобровый Лог; www.bobrovylog.ru; ul Sibirskaya 92) Below the Stolby the slap and swish of skis and snowboards can be heard at the Bobrovy Log ski resort. Snow cannons keep the slopes going well into May, and in the summer months the Roedelbahn (a kind of downhill forest roller coaster), a pool and regular sports events keep the fun level high. Bus 37 runs from the train station direct to the resort.

🛏 Sleeping

Krasnoyarsk has the full range of post-Soviet accommodation options, from unrenovated Soviet dumps to boutique design hotels, and vibe-rich hostels to five-star residences.

City Centre

★**SibTourGuide Hostel** HOSTEL $

(☑8-950 985 8608; www.sibtourguide.com; pr Mira 85, apt 72; dm/d R700/900; @🛜) Krasnoyarsk's best backpacker halt and one of Eastern Siberia's finest hostels has a great central location with fish-tank views of the bustle on pr Mira. Facilities are spotless, rooms are light and airy and there's a washing machine (R200) and full-service kitchen, plus the full range of SibTourGuide trips can be arranged directly with staff.

Rates include a R100 breakfast/meal voucher for the nearby Gastropub Tolsty Kray. Only eight beds, so book well ahead.

Hotel Sever HOTEL $

(Гостиница Север; ☑391-266 2266; www.hotel-sever.net; ul Lenina 121; s/d from R500/570; 🛜) Take a trip back to the good 'ole USS of R at this Soviet armpit of a hotel, a last resort for budget Trans-Sibbers. Most of the rooms are high-ceilinged, overheating, never-renovated affairs with the standard monster fridge in the corner, imaginative plumbing solutions and ancient nailed-down lino. On the upside there's cheap visa registration (R100) and a decent cafe serving breakfast fare, plus you get to leave at the end of your stay.

★ Iris
BOUTIQUE HOTEL **$$**

(Ирис; ☑ 391-227 2292; www.iris-apart-hotel.ru; pr Mira 37; s/d R3600/4000; ☞) Housed in a 19th-century former religious school for girls, the romantic French theme and impeccable personal service sets the Iris apart from most Siberian hotels. The 10 rooms are done out in soothing beiges and light browns but the pièce de résistance here are the two romantic design suites, all period wallpaper, belle époque furniture and mock chateau elements. Set in a quiet courtyard, well away from the thundering thoroughfares. Breakfast and cheery welcomes included.

Hotel Ogni Yeniseyya
HOTEL **$**

(Гостиница Огни Енисея; ☑ 391-227 5262; www.oe-hotel.ru; ul Dubrovinskogo 80; s/tw from R1275/2200; ☞) One of the last budget options left; there's a vast selection of rooms here, but whatever you plump for, make sure it has Yenisey views.

Dom Hotel
HOTEL **$$$**

(☑ 391-290 6666; www.dom-hotel24.ru; ul Krasnoy Armii 16a; r R4400-7600; @☞) Centred around a rather characterless courtyard, the 81 light-filled rooms at Krasnoyarsk's top business hotel are immaculately maintained and have become a firm favourite among foreigners looking for Western comforts. Staff are courteous and there is an inexpensive on-site restaurant. Breakfast costs extra.

Soft Hotel
HOTEL **$$$**

(☑ 391-228 2700; www.softhotel.ru; ul Surikova 16; s/d from R5900/6800; ❊☞) With its European business standard facilities, waxy antique-style furniture, 21st-century bathrooms (with bidets!) and high-flying ceilings, taking the soft option might be the way to go now in Krasnoyarsk. More roubles equals more space though the five *ekonom*-class rooms have lower-standard furniture. Efficient service and good value for money – only the views and the non-buffet breakfast disappoint slightly.

Hotel Krasnoyarsk
HOTEL **$$$**

(Гостиница Красноярск; ☑ 391-274 9400; www.hotelkrs.ru; ul Uritskogo 94; s/tw from R4300/5780; ❊☞) Every Soviet metropolis has one: a concrete lumpen hotel celebrating the city's name in metre-high lettering. But unlike many of these stale relics, the sprawling eight-storey Krasnoyarsk is well kept with bright corridors, totally rebuilt full-service rooms and English-speaking receptionists. Rates are also decidedly 'post-Soviet' but at least breakfast is included.

Hotel Metelitsa
HOTEL **$$$**

(☑ 391-227 6060; www.hotel-metelica.ru; pr Mira 14; s/d from R4300/R6000; ❊☞❊) Exclusive minihotel of the type favoured by Russia's oil-stained business elite and the ugliest gallery of pop stars you're ever likely to see. Every room is done out differently, some with design-mag flair, and bathrooms are far from bog standard. Staff speak reluctant English and there's a pool where you can pretend you are by an alpine lake. Breakfast included.

Hotel Oktyabrskaya
HOTEL **$$$**

(Гостиница Октябрьская; ☑ 391-227 3780; www.hoteloctober.ru; pr Mira 15; s R4200-6300, d R5600-6300; ☞) Comfortable and professionally run with rooms approximating Western standards, albeit without air-conditioning. Satellite TV includes Western channels and some English is spoken. The trendy lobby area has a stylish juice bar. Rates include breakfast.

🛏 Stolby Area

Snezhnaya Dolina
HOTEL **$$**

(Гостиница Снежная Долина; ☑ 391-269 8110; www.sneg-dolina.ru; per cottage from R5300, s R700-3200, d R1400-3700; ☞❊) This accommodation complex has a hotel, a minimotel and rows of cosy cottages meaning lots to choose from. There's a swimming pool, a tennis court and a decent restaurant, but the main draw here is the clean air and the proximity to the *stolby* and ski slopes.

✗ Eating

Rada
VEGETARIAN **$**

(Рада; ul Lenina 74; mains R100-200; ⊘ 10am-10pm; ❊❊☑) Krasnoyarsk's sole vegetarian food halt is a cheerfully hip, colourful cafe serving a menu of buckwheat burgers, fish-free paella, vegie *pelmeni* and lots of juice and tea (no coffee: Rada is a completely caffeine-free zone.). The English-speaking owner tweaks the menu a couple of times a year.

Buddha Bar & Lounge ASIAN, EUROPEAN $
(ul Karla Marksa 127; mains R150-250; ⊗noon-midnight; 🕸🍴) This low-lit, incense-infused vegetarian cellar lounge is a calming place to escape the city-centre blare. Order a plate of exotic Tibetan food from the English-speaking waitress, then give the bar-top prayer wheel a spin before retreating to the cushioned lounge where nightly DJs drift chill-out music to a chilled crowd. As if Siberia wasn't chilly enough.

Miks Patio FAST FOOD $
(Микс-Патио; ul Perensona 20; mains R30-100; ⊗10am-10pm Mon-Sat, from 11am Sun) With budget-airline decor, a menu heavy with Slavic and Italian comfort food and prompt service, this is the *stolovaya* dragged into the 21st century.

Kalinka-Malinka Stolovaya No 2 CANTEEN $
(pr Mira 100; mains R40-80; ⊗10am-10pm) Celebrating the varied cuisines of former Soviet republics this self-service canteen has a loud, plasticky interior scattered with the odd Soviet nostalgia knick-knack kept well out of punters' reach. The range of dishes extends across a vast swath of the planet, from unpronounceable Georgian fare to peasanty Ukrainian dishes and Siberian stodge. Some dishes charged per 100g.

Sem Slona CANTEEN $
(ul Karla Marksa 95; mains R30-80; ⊗24hr) Got a sudden craving for buckwheat at 3am? Then brave the darkened streets and make your way to this all-hours, no-nonsense canteen plating up solid Russian favourites with a growl. The name translates as 'I could eat an elephant' – this being Siberia, a horse just won't do.

Krasny Yar Supermarket SUPERMARKET $
(Гастроном Красный яр; ul Karla Marksa 133; ⊗24hr) Best supermarket in the city centre with a whole row of ATMs on the right as you enter. Branches across the city.

★**Gastropub Tolsty Kray** CAFE $$
(Гастропаб Толстый Край; www.esc24.ru; ul Lenina 116; mains R200-400; ⊗10am-11pm; 🕸) While its English-teacher, expat and traveller clientele, wired castle-themed cellar setting and suitably international menu provide good enough reason to drop in at this Anglophone sanctuary, this great cafe also gives guests a five-minute free (yes free!) call to any number in the world from their table, plus there's free wi-fi and a computer hooked up to the web. Add to this a globalised beer menu, inventive coffees, real porridge, top-notch cooking and regular live music and you might be looking for ul Lenina 116 sooner rather than later. Used to be known as the English School Cafe.

Mike & Molly ITALIAN $$
(www.mikeandmollycafe.ru; ul D Proletariata 32a; mains R200-500; ⊗11am-midnight) The stylishly unassuming interior of this Italian job suggests the focus is firmly on the food and that assumption would be right. Possibly Krasnoyarsk's best lasagnes, pastas, salads and proper starters land promptly on your table as you kick back on the black-cloth wall sofas with a glass of Chianti. Sadly, the sullen service oh-so Siberioso.

Mama Roma ITALIAN $$
(☎391-266 1072; pr Mira 50a; pizzas R200-470, pasta R180-490; ⊗9am-1am; 🕸) Herb-infused air wafts temptingly out of this long-established Italian eatery, where chequered tablecloths and admirable attempts at pasta, risotto and pizza may make you feel you're in Rome or Naples – but only if you've never been there.

🍸 **Drinking & Nightlife**

★**Shanti Bar** BAR
(ul D Proletariata 28; ⊗noon-midnight Sun-Thu, to 2am Fri & Sat) Descend the street steps into a cool, low-lit world of Indian food, hookah pipes and herb infusions all enjoyed to a subcontinental soundtrack. Hindu gods wave multi-armed at guests as they enter a transient state on cushion-strewn couches, chilling out with a cocktail or a glass of wine. Located in Krasnoyarsk's safest street – it's bang opposite the regional FSB headquarters.

Traveller's Coffee CAFE
(pr Mira 54; ⊗8am-midnight; 🕸) The tempting aroma of newly milled beans lures passers-by into this trendy coffee house where the circular brown-cream leather tub-seats give the impression you're sitting in a cuppa. Friendly service and sensibly priced milkshakes, muffins and pancakes.

Krem CAFE
(☎391-258 1538; pr Mira 10; ⊗24hr; 🕸) Krasnoyarsk's classiest coffee house has black-and-white photography, dark-wood furniture, a

YENISEYSK ЕНИСЕЙСК

Easily reachable by bus, historic Yeniseysk makes an engaging excursion off the Trans-Sib from Krasnoyarsk, 340km away. Founded in 1619, this was once Russia's great fur-trading capital, with world-famous 18th-century August trade fairs (recently revived for tourists), and 10 grand churches punctuating its skyline. Eclipsed by Krasnoyarsk despite a burst of gold-rush prosperity in the 1860s, the town is now a drowsy backwater with an unexpectedly good **Regional Museum** (ul Lenina 106; admission R100; ⊘ 9am-5pm Mon-Sat), some faded commercial grandeur along ul Lenina and many old houses; over 70 are considered architectural monuments. Most appealing of the surviving churches are the walled 1731 **Spaso-Preobrazhensky Monastery** (ul Raboche-Krestyanskaya 105) and the **Assumption Church** (Uspenskaya tserkov; ul Raboche-Krestyanskaya 116)with its unusual metal floor and splendid antique icons.

To reach Yeniseysk, take a bus (R620, seven hours, 10 daily) from Krasnoyarsk's bus station. The journey time makes a day trip impossible so organise accommodation beforehand through SibTourGuide (see below) in Krasnoyarsk.

Further North Along the Yenisey

From mid-June to early October, passenger ships slip along the Yenisey River from Krasnoyarsk to Dudinka in the Arctic Circle (4½ days) via Yeniseysk (17 hours) and Igarka (74-79 hours). There are three to four sailings per week, most departing early morning. Returning upstream, journeys take 50% longer so most independent travellers choose to fly back to Krasnoyarsk. Foreigners are not allowed beyond Igarka as Dudinka and nearby Norilsk are 'closed' towns. Contact SibTourGuide in Krasnoyarsk for timetables, tickets and round-trip tours.

belt-stretching dessert menu and reasonably priced lattes and espressos.

Kofemolka
CAFE

(Кофемолка; pr Mira 114; ⊘ 10am-midnight; 🛜) Sip roasts from every corner of the bean-growing world amid faux mahogany as dark as the roasts and geometrically patterned screens that divide things up into intimate gossip booths. Long dessert menu.

☆ Entertainment

Havana Club
CLUB

(Гавана Клуб; www.havanakrk.narod.ru; ul Bograda 134; ⊘ Mon-Thu 9pm-1am, to 3am Fri & Sat) Big nightclub with three dance floors and local DJs.

Opera-Ballet Theatre
THEATRE

(Театр оперы и балета; ☑ 391-227 8697; www.opera.krasnoyarsk.ru; ul Perensona 2) The architecturally nondescript Opera-Ballet Theatre has daily performances of productions such as *Carmen, Swan Lake* and *Romeo and Juliet* starting in the early evening, October to June.

Philharmonia
LIVE MUSIC

(Филармония; ☑ 391-227 4930; www.krasfil.ru; pl Mira 2b) The Philharmonia has three con-

cert halls showcasing folk, jazz and classical music.

Puppet Theatre
PUPPET THEATRE

(☑ 391-211 3000; www.puppet24.ru; ul Lenina 119) Classic Russian puppet shows such as *Chuk i Gek, Doktor Aybolit* and *Goldilocks* for kiddies and adults alike.

Rock-Jazz Kafe
LIVE MUSIC

(Рок-Джазз Кафе; ☑ 391 252 3305; ul Surikova 12; ⊘ 4pm-6am Tue-Sun) This dark venue showcases live bands around an upturned motorcycle from 10pm most days.

ℹ Orientation

The city centre's grid layout is easy to navigate, but there's no central square. The zoo, ski resort and Stolby Reserve are more than 10km west along the Yenisey's south bank.

ℹ Information

Post Office (ul Lenina 62; ⊘ 8am-8pm Mon-Fri, 9am-6pm Sat)

Sayan Ring (☑ 391-245 4646; www.sayanring.com; ul Uritskogo 41; ⊘ 10am-7pm Mon-Fri) Agency specialising in Tuva and Khakassia tours.

SibTourGuide (☑ 391-251 654, 8-950 985 8608; www.sibtourguide.com) Experienced tour guide Anatoly Brewhanov offers personalised hiking trips into the Stolby, imaginative tours around Krasnoyarsk and general travel assistance. He also runs the city's best hostel, provides authentic 'rural experiences' at his dacha, organises cruises along the Yenisey and leads trips to the site of the Tunguska Event, all while maintaining an info-packed website.

❶ Getting There & Away

TRAIN

TSAVS is the most central booking office, though the station itself is relatively central and often queue-free. Krasnoyarsk has the following rail connections:

Irkutsk *platskart/kupe* R1800/3300; 18 hours; up to nine daily

Moscow *platskart* R5000, *kupe* R10,000 to R15,000; two days, 16 hours; up to seven daily

Novosibirsk *platskart* R1400 to R2000, *kupe* R2600 to R3600; 12 hours; up to 11 daily

Severobaikalsk *platskart* R2000 to R2200, *kupe* R3900 to R4300; from one day, four hours to one day, 11½ hours; three daily

Tomsk *platskart* R1250; 18 hours; every other day

BOAT

Every few days in summer, passenger boats from Krasnoyarsk's spired river station (Речной вокзал) ply the Yenisey to Dudinka (1989km, 4½ to five days) but foreigners may not proceed beyond Igarka. SibTourGuide (p178) can arrange tickets.

Summer hydrofoils to Divnogorsk depart up to five times a day, returning an hour later. Buy tickets on board.

❶ Getting Around

Krasnoyarsk's train station is located at the western end of the city centre, around 2km from the main action. The easiest way to get into the very centre of town is to take regular, if slow, trolleybus 7.

Within the city centre, almost all public transport runs eastbound along ul Karla Marksa or pr Mira, returning westbound on ul Lenina. Useful bus 50 starts beyond the zoo, passes the Turbaza Yenisey and comes through the centre of town.

From June to September, cycle hire is available near the Rezanov Statue (per hour R200).

Divnogorsk   Дивногорск

📞 39144 / POP 28,300 / TIME MOSCOW +7HR

From Krasnoyarsk, a popular day trip by bus or summer hydrofoil follows the Yenisey River 27km to Divnogorsk town through a wide, wooded canyon. Some 5km beyond

Divnogorsk's jetty is a vast 90m-high **dam**. Turbine-room visits are not permitted, but if you're lucky you might see ships being lifted by a technologically impressive inclined plane to the huge Krasnoyarsk Sea behind. A few kilometres beyond you can observe ice fishing from December to March or, in the summer, boats and yachts can be hired.

The Krasnoyarsk–Divnogorsk road has a panoramic overlook point at km23 and passes quaint **Ovsyanka** village. From the main road you can walk 100m (crossing the train tracks) to Ovsyanka's cute wooden **St Inokent Chapel** (ul Shchetinkina) then 50m right to find the **house-museum** (ul Shchetinkina 26; admission R100; ⊙10am-6pm Tue-Sun) of famous local writer Victor Astafiev, who died in 2001. Directly opposite in Astafiev's grandma's cottage-compound is the more interesting **Last Bow Museum** (ul Shchetinkina 35; admission R100; ⊙10am-6pm Tue-Sun) giving a taste of rural Siberian life.

Hydrofoils (45 minutes, up to five daily) depart from Krasnoyarsk's river station and regular *marshrutky* (R70) leave from Krasnoyarsk's bus station. Taxis meet boats on arrival in Divnogorsk and want at least R1000 return to shuttle you to a point overlooking the dam. However, it's potentially cheaper, safer and more fun to hire a mountain bike from a stand 200m downstream from the quay. SibTourGuide (p178) in Krasnoyarsk offers various tailored excursions in English or will include the Divnogorsk loop as part of its 'Ten-Rouble Tour'.

Irkutsk   Иркутск

📞 3952 / POP 587,900 / TIME MOSCOW +8HR

The de facto capital of Eastern Siberia, pleasantly historic Irkutsk is by far the most popular stop on the Trans-Siberian Railway between Moscow and all points east. With Lake Baikal a mere 70km away, the city is the best base from which to strike out for the western shoreline. Amid the 19th-century architecture, revived churches, classy eateries and numerous apartment hostels, plentiful English-speaking agencies can help you plan anything from a winter trek across the lake's ice to a short walking tour through the city.

In recent years Irkutsk has seen something of a tourist boom, spawning a municipally funded information centre, detailed city maps planted at strategic points and a handful of freshly conceived museums,

Irkutsk

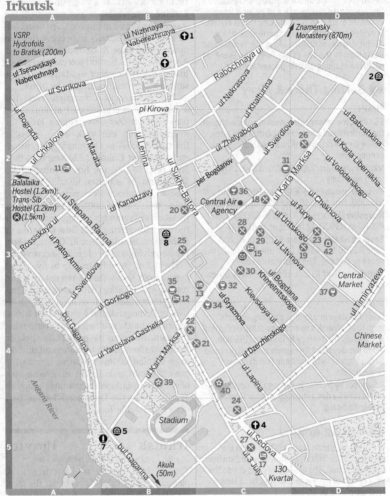

as well as the blockbuster 130 Kvartal project, an entire neighbourhood given over to typical Siberian timber buildings housing new restaurants, bars, cafes and the odd museum.

History

Founded in 1661 as a Cossack garrison to extract the fur tax from the indigenous Buryats, Irkutsk was the springboard for 18th-century expeditions to the far north and east, including Alaska – then known as 'Irkutsk's American district'.

As Eastern Siberia's trading and administrative centre, Irkutsk dispatched Siberian furs and ivory to Mongolia, Tibet and China in exchange for silk and tea. Constructed mostly of local timber, three quarters of the city burnt down in the disastrous blaze of 1879. However, profits from the 1880s Lena Basin gold rush swiftly rebuilt the city's most important edifices in brick and stone.

Known as the 'Paris of Siberia', Irkutsk did not welcome news of the October Revolution. The city's well-to-do merchants only succumbed to the Red tide in 1920, with the capture and execution of White Army com-

Volkonsky House-Museum · MUSEUM

(Дом-музей Волконского; ☑ 3952-207 532; per Volkonskogo 10; admission R200, with Trubetskoy House-Museum R300; ⊘ 10am-6pm Tue-Sun) The duck-egg-blue and white home of Decembrist Count Sergei Volkonsky, whose wife Maria Volkonskaya cuts the main figure in Christine Sutherland's unputdownable book *The Princess of Siberia,* is a small mansion set in a scruffy courtyard with stables, a barn and servant quarters. Renovated in the late 1980s, the house is now a museum telling the story of the family's exile in Irkutsk.

In the decade leading up to the Volkonskys return to St Petersburg in 1856, the house was the epicentre of Irkutsk cultural life, with balls, musical soirées and parties attended by wealthy merchants and high-ranking local officials. A tour of the building with its big ceramic stoves and orginal staircases takes visitors from the family dining room, where governor Muriev-Amursky once feasted on fruit and veg grown by Volkonsky himself in the garden out back, to the upstairs photo exhibition including portraits of Maria and other women who romantically followed their husbands and lovers into exile.

Emotionally charged items on show include Maria's pyramidal piano, a browsable book of images collected by fellow Decembrist wife, Ekaterina Trubetskaya, of the various places the Decembrists were imprisoned, and Maria's music box sent from Italy by her sister-in-law.

Znamensky Monastery · MONASTERY

(ul Rabochego Shtaba) `FREE` Stranded on the wrong side of a thundering roundabout, the 1762 Znamensky Monastery is 1.9km northeast of Skver Kirova. Echoing with mellifluous plainsong, the wonderful interior has muralled vaulting, a towering iconostasis and a gold sarcophagus holding the miraculous relics of Siberian missionary St Inokent. Celebrity graves outside include the nautically themed tomb of Grigory Shelekhov, the man who claimed Alaska for Russia, and a much humbler headstone belonging to Decembrist wife Ekaterina Trubetskaya (directly in front of you as you enter).

White Russian commander Admiral Kolchak was executed by Bolsheviks near the spot where his statue was controversially erected in November 2004 at the entrance to the monastery grounds; the plinth is exaggeratedly high enough to prevent die-hard mander Admiral Kolchak, whose controversial statue was re-erected in 2004. Soviet-era planning saw Irkutsk develop as the sprawling industrial and scientific centre that it remains today.

◉ Sights

Irkutsk's centre can be easily explored on foot – you'll only need to hop aboard a bus or *marshrutka* to see the Angara Dam and the Znamensky Monastery.

Irkutsk

communists from committing acts of vandalism. Trolleybus 3 trundles this way.

130 Kvartal   NEIGHBOURHOOD
(130th Block; www.130kvartal.irk.ru; btwn uls Sedova & 3 Iyulya; ⊙24hr) FREE What does a city boasting some of Siberia's most impressive original timber architecture do to improve the visitor experience? Yes, that's right, recreate an entire quarter of yet more wooden buildings, some transported here from other locations, some fake. The unromantically named 130 Kvartal south of the Raising of the Cross Church is nonetheless a pleasant place to stroll, packed with restaurants, cafes and commercial museums, and culminating in Eastern Siberia's only real 21st-century (and quite impressive) shopping mall.

Guarding the entrance to this timber theme park is a monster bronze *babr,* the mythical beast that features on the Irkutsk municipal coat of arms. The spot has become a popular place to have that 'I've been to Irkutsk' photo taken.

Trubetskoy House-Museum   MUSEUM
(Дом-музей Трубецкого; ul Dzerzhinskogo 64; admission R200, with Volkonsky House-Museum R300; ⊙10am-6pm Wed-Mon) Carted off for renovation in 2007, Irkutsk's second Decembrist house-museum made a comeback in 2012 with English-language information, touchscreens and tinkling background music. This pleasingly symmetrical mini-mansion was actually built for the daughter of Decembrist Sergei Trubetskoy – the original Trubetskoy house near the Znamensky Monastery burnt down in 1908. The lower level tells the Decembrists' story, from failed coup to arrival in Irkutsk, while the upper floor displays personal items belonging to Ekaterina Trubetskaya, Trubetskoy's French wife who died in Irkutsk.

Regional Museum   MUSEUM
(Краеведческий музей; ☎3952-333 449; www.museum.irkutsk.ru; ul Karla Marksa 2; admission R200; ⊙10am-7pm Tue-Sun) Irkutsk's rapidly ageing Regional Museum occupies a fancy 1880s brick building that formerly housed the Siberian Geographical Society, a club of Victorian-style gentlemen explorers. The highlights here are the downstairs ethnographical exhibitions and the nostalgic display of 20th-century junk upstairs, as well as the small gift shop selling birch-bark boxes, jewellery made from Baikal minerals and other interesting souvenirs.

City History Museum
MUSEUM

(www.history.irk.ru; ul Frank-Kamenetskogo 16a; admission R120; ⊙10am-6pm Thu-Tue) Despite its palatial 19th-century home (built by wealthy merchant Sibiryakov in 1884) what should be Irkutsk's main repository of the past is in fact a rather limited exhibition on the city's history with absolutely nothing in English. Highlights include some interesting pre-Russian wooden yurts and tepees, a model of the Kazansky Cathedral, some fascinating blown-up photos of 19th-century Irkutsk and a 20th-century section with bric-a-brac from the Revolution up to the late 1990s.

Museum of City Life
MUSEUM

(ul Dekabrskikh Sobyty 77; admission R120; ⊙10am-6pm Thu-Tue) This small museum filling six rooms of a former merchant's house illustrates just why 19th-century Irkutsk was nicknamed the 'Paris of Siberia'. Changing exhibitions of everyday and decorative items such as lamps, dolls, tableware and porcelain are donated free of charge by the people of Irkutsk and are displayed against a background of period wallpaper, elegant double doors and high ceilings. The ticket is also valid for the tiny **Tea Museum** above the tourist office opposite.

Sukachev Regional Art Museum
ART GALLERY

(Иркутский областной художественный музей имени В. П. Сукачёва; ul Lenina 5; admission R100; ⊙10am-6pm Wed-Mon) The grand old art gallery has a valuable though poorly lit collection ranging from Mongolian *thangkas* (Tibetan Buddhist religious paintings) to Russian Impressionist canvases. However, the main reason for coming here may be to see a top-notch temporary show (extra charge).

Raising of the Cross Church
CHURCH

(Krestovozdvizhenskaya tserkov; ul Sedova 1) The 1758 baroque Raising of the Cross Church has a fine interior of gilt-edged icons and examples of intricate brickwork in a rounded style that's unique to Irkutsk and the Selenga Delta village of Posolskoe.

Kazansky Church
CHURCH

(ul Barrikad) The gigantic Kazansky Church is a theme-park-esque confection of salmon-pink walls and fluoro turquoise domes topped with gold baubled crosses. Get off tram 4 two stops northeast of the bus station.

Angara Dam
LANDMARK

Some 6km southeast of the centre, the 1956 Angara Dam is 2km long. Its construction raised Lake Baikal by up to 1m and caused environmental problems, most notably the silencing of the so-called singing sands on Baikal's eastern shore. The dam itself is hardly an attraction but moored nearby is the **Angara icebreaker** (admission R150; ⊙10am-8pm).

Originally imported in kit form from Newcastle-upon-Tyne to carry Trans-Siberian Railway passengers across Lake Baikal (the trains went on her bigger sister ship *Baikal*, sunk during the Russian Civil War), it's now a less-than-inspiring museum reached by a permanent gangway. Trolleybuses 3, 5, 7 and 8 head this way.

Statue of Tsar Alexander III
MONUMENT

(Памятник Александру III) Adorning the Angara embankment a recast statue of Alexander III (a copy of the 1904 original) has the only tsar ever to visit Siberia looking as though he's holding an invisible balloon on a string.

Saviour's Church
CHURCH

(Спасская церковь; Spasskaya tserkov) Constructed in 1706 this is the oldest stone-built church in Eastern Siberia and has remnants of the original murals on its facade. Until the late 1990s it housed a museum, hence the rather bare interior.

Bogoyavlensky Cathedral
CHURCH

(Богоявленский собор; ul Nizhnaya Naberezhnaya) This fairy-tale ensemble of mini onion domes atop restored salmon, white and green towers first appeared on the Irkutsk skyline in 1718, but during the Soviet decades served as a dormitory and a bakery. The interior is a fragrant riot of aureoled Byzantine saints with no surface left plain.

☞ Tours

Local tour companies are useful not only for organising excursions but also for booking hotels and most kinds of tickets. All of Irkutsk's hostels can arrange Baikal tours.

Baikaler
TOUR COMPANY

(☏3952-336 240; www.baikaler.com) Imaginative Jack Sheremetoff speaks very good English and is well tuned to budget-traveller needs. Original personalised tours, two great hostels and a friendly welcome.

Baikal Adventure
TOUR COMPANY

(www.baikal-adventure.com) Energetic agency specialising in adventurous trekking, biking, climbing and caving trips and full-blown expeditions.

BaikalComplex
TOUR COMPANY

(☑3952-461 557; www.baikalcomplex.com) Well-organised operation offering Lake Baikal accommodation and trips tailored for international travellers.

Baikalinfo
TOUR COMPANY

(☑3952-707 012; www.baikalinfo.ru) Baikal tours as well as transfers, hikes and fishing trips.

Green Express
TOUR COMPANY

(☑3952-734 400; www.greenexpress.ru) Professional outfit specialising in outdoor activities.

BaikalExplorer
TOUR COMPANY

(☑8-902-560 2440; www.baikalex.com) Runs Baikal cruises, fishing and diving trips.

🛏 Sleeping

Irkutsk's accommodation options have been expanding for years, but it's still a good idea to book ahead in the summer months. A handful of hostels have become permanent fixtures but many small apartment hostels still pop up for the hot months only. Despite new arrivals, there's still a noticeable lack of midrange options available.

★ Baikaler Hostel
HOSTEL $

(☑3952-336 240; www.baikaler.com; apt 11, ul Lenina 9; dm R600; ❋@🖥) Experienced tour guide Jack Sheremetoff had a super-central apartment hostel in Irkutsk long before the word even entered the Russian language. Despite competition, the city's original backpacker haven is still *the* place to meet travellers and organise trips. The spotless, air-conditioned dorms are spacious, but beds are limited so book ahead. The entrance is at the rear of the building.

Admiral Hostel
HOSTEL $

(☑8-902 560 2440; apt 1, ul Cheremkhovsky 6; dm R500-700; @🖥) With its Kolchak-inspired name, this cosy 13-bed apartment hostel has become well-established digs for Trans-Siberian wanderers. The lower bunks sport privacy curtains, staff sell bus tickets to Olkhon Island, there's a free (light) breakfast and you can even get your washing done. Enter from the rear of the building.

Trans-Sib Hostel
HOSTEL $

(☑8-904 118 0652; www.irkutsk-hostel.com; per Sportivniy 9a, apt 8; dm/d R600/1600; @🖥) Well-established, cosy backpacker hostel around a 10-minute walk from the train station offering a kitchen, washing machine, a high bathroom-to-bed ratio and one of the best ranges of owner-led tours in town. Rates include a light breakfast.

Balalaika Hostel
HOSTEL $

(☑8-950 132 0262; www.baikaler.com; per Sportivniy 5a, apt 1; dm R600; 🖥) Brand-new hostel run by Baikaler for a mixed crowd of Russians and foreign backpackers with lots of communal space. Good location a 10-minute walk from the train station plus the full range of Baikaler tours and transfers available.

Hotel Uzory
HOTEL $

(☑3952-209 239; ul Oktyabrskoy Revolyutsii 17; s/tw R800/1200) Clean, unpretentious rooms (23) with leopard-skin-patterned blankets but communal bathrooms and toilets. It's popular with independent travellers but maintains a tradition of employing Irkutsk's sourest receptionists.

Hotel Viktoria
HOTEL $$

(☑3952-986 808; www.victoryhotel.ru; ul Bogdana Khmelnitskogo 1; s R3600-4000, d R4200-4600; ❋@🖥) Just a few steps off ul Karla Marksa, the 30 rooms at this purpose-built tower hotel remain stylish and unfrumpy despite the antique-style furniture and flowery wall coverings. If you've been in Russia a while, the courteous staff, baths in every room and online booking could feel almost eccentric. Lower rates from September to May.

Hotel Yevropa
HOTEL $$

(Гостиница Европа; ☑3952-291 515; www.europehotel.ru; ul Baikalskaya 69; s/d from R3190/3960; ❋🖥) Behind nine Doric columns immaculate rooms are realistically priced at this gleaming four-star favourite. Reception staff speak English and the Western-style breakfast is reportedly the best in town.

Hotel Sayen
HOTEL $$$

(☑3952-500 000; www.sayen.ru; ul Karla Marksa 13b; r R9700-15,500; ❋🖥) Described by some as the finest luxury sleep east of the Ural Mountains, this very central Japanese hotel gets rave reviews and justifiably so. The 24 rooms enjoy design-mag decor, big baths and gadgets galore, going beyond the standards of many Western hotels. The 24-hour room service, two pricey restaurants and a celebrated Japanese spa provide additional ways to lighten your wallet of roubles.

Kupechesky Dvor HOTEL $$$
(☑ 3952-797 000; www.kupecheskyhotel.ru; ul Sedova 10; d & tw R4600; ☎) Rising high above the 130 Kvartal this professionally run, freshly minted timber hotel mixes traditional wooden architecture with boldly contemporary design features. The 14 rooms come with big colour-swirl carpets, retro light switches, revolving TV towers and some of the best bathrooms in the city. English-speaking service is top-draw and breakfast in the tiny reception area is included.

Marussia BOUTIQUE HOTEL $$$
(☑ 3952-500 252; www.marussiahotel.ru; ul Sedova 12; s/d R4200/4500; ☎) This spanking new, timber-built 14-room boutique hotel in the 130 Kvartal has an unpretentious feel with a brown-beige colour scheme, stripped wooden floors sporting rustic rugs but 21st-century bathrooms. Breakfast is taken in the hotel's first-rate cafe and receptionists speak your lingo.

Baikal Business Centre HOTEL $$$
(☑ 3952-259 120; www.bbc.ru; ul Baikalskaya 279; s R4100-6600, tw R4900-6600; ❋☎) If you're in Irkutsk on business, this white and blue-glass tower is where you'll want to unsheathe the company credit card. Rooms are just about international standard, there's a business centre and rates are slashed at weekends.

Hotel Zvezda HOTEL $$$
(☑ 3952-540 000; www.zvezdahotel.ru; ul Yadrintseva 1ж; r from R4400; ❋☎) Within a Swiss chalet–style building, the 64 rooms here are modern and comfortable, service is pleasant and English is spoken, though you'd expect little less for these room rates. Its atmospheric restaurant specialises in game and exotic meats.

✕ Eating

Mamochka CAFE $
(Мамочка; ul Karla Marksa 41; mains R80-100; ⏱10am-9pm) With its menu of imaginative salads, filling soups and (almost) healthy mains, this is no ordinary point-and-eat canteen. Swab the decks with a Slovak lager then sit back and admire the interior, a mishmash of old newspapers and Soviet bric-a-brac.

Govinda VEGETARIAN $
(2nd fl, ul Furye 4; mains R50-100; ⏱11am-8pm; ❋✐) Irkutsk's only meat-free restaurant is a small self-service affair with a half-hearted Indian theme and a menu of soya sausages, basmati rice, spicy soups, mild curries, quorn chilli con carne, imaginative desserts and whole plantations of tea.

Syty Shmel CANTEEN $
(Сытый шмель; ul Kievskaya 1; ⏱10am-8pm; mains R60-120; ☎) Take your hunger to the 'full-bellied bumble bee' for some tasty Russian dining to a gentle soundtrack. This is the *stolovaya* taken to classier level with only natural ingredients going into the pizzas, cakes, *plov* and pancakes. There's free coffee at breakfast time, but limited seat numbers mean things get packed out come the lunching hour.

Appetite CANTEEN $
(cnr uls Sukhe-Batora & Karla Marksa; mains R60-120; ⏱8am-9pm) When it's midday feeding time in the city centre, this gaudy self-service canteen with red leatherette seating divided into cubicles and a menu of meatballs, pasta, pancakes and the odd healthy option is the one of the cheapest places to seek out. The Buryat serving staff speak no English so just point at what you want.

Domino FAST FOOD $
(Домино; ul Lenina 13a; pizzas & pancakes R40-100; ⏱24hr) Domino may tout itself as a pizza joint but has saved many an early morning breakfast hunter with its bliny and strong coffee.

Blinnaya Giraffe RUSSIAN $
(ul Sukhe-Batora 8; pancakes R50-105; ⏱9am-10pm Mon-Fri, from 10am Sat & Sun) Revamped pancake joint with zany giraffe theme and life-jacket-orange seating. The menu also features pizzas, soups and salads.

Slata SUPERMARKET $
(Слата; ul Karla Marksa 21; ⏱24hr) Supermarkets are surprisingly rare in Irkutsk so this centrally located, open-all-hours store is a godsend. Stocks a lot of ready-to-eat meals (meatballs, steaks, salads), ideal for long train journeys.

★ Kochevnik MONGOLIAN $$
(Кочевник; ☑3952-200 459; ul Gorkogo 19; mains R300-1200; ⏱11.30am-midnight) Take your taste buds to the Mongolian steppe for some yurt-size portions of mutton, lamb and steak as well as filling soups and *buuzy*

(dumplings), sluiced down with a bottle from the decent foreign wine list. Smiley service, a picture menu, low prices and an exotically curtained summer terrace make this one of the most agreeable places to dine in town.

★Rassolnik   RUSSIAN $$
(130 Kvartal, ul 3 Iyulya 3; mains R300-500; ⊙10am-midnight) Arguably the best eating addition in the 130 Kvartal, this retro restaurant serves up a 100% Soviet-era menu (think upmarket *pelmeni, okroshka, shchi, kvas* and grandmother's pickles) in a plush Stalinist banqueting hall bedecked in nostalgia-inducing knick-knackery. Classic Soviet-era films are projected onto one wall, the menu is designed like a 1960s scrapbook and waiting staff are dressed for the ocassion.

★Figaro   ITALIAN $$
(www.figaro-resto.com; ul Karla Marksa 22; mains R300-700; ⊙10.30am-midnight) It's pretty obvious from the outside that Figaro is no ordinary Siberian eatery. The glass fronted dining space peppered with works of art and graced with unpretentiously stylish laid tables fills daily with diners downing award-winning pastas, seafood platters and meat dishes including lamb, wild boar and duck prepared by real Western European chefs. All bread and pastry is made fresh every day and a friendly, inclusively European ambience dominates.

Snezhinka   CAFE $$
(Снежинка; ☑3952-344 862; Litvinova 2; mains R200-500; ⊙10am-midnight) This cosy belle époque-style cafe has attentive English-speaking service and regularly wins local awards for its food. It's been around since 1961, making it the city's longest-serving eatery.

Kafe Elen   CAFE $$
(ul Timiryazeva; meals R180-350; ⊙9am-10pm Mon-Fri, from 10am Sat & Sun; ❀) Bubbling aquariums, rattan furniture and lots of potted plants make this a tranquil breakfast and lunch spot as you watch the trams trundle past the church opposite.

Arbatski Dvorik   RUSSIAN $$$
(Арбатский дворик; ☑3952-200 633; ul Uritskogo; mains R350-1500; ⊙noon–last customer; ❡) This upmarket restaurant is all inside-out, the walls lined with imitation facades, doorways and street lamps. However there's

nothing topsy-turvy about the impeccable service and well-crafted menu. Oddly, it's accessed via the gaudy Fiesta fast-food place below.

🍷 Drinking & Nightlife

★Belaya Vorona   CAFE
(Белая ворона; ul Karla Marksa 37; ⊙9am-10pm Mon-Fri, 10am-11pm Sat & Sun; ❡) Disciples of the bean should definitely head to the 'White Raven', a relaxing cellar-based coffee hang-out on the main drag. A funky soundtrack provides background for caffeine and cakes or a late breakfast as you catch up on emails or wish you could read the Cyrillic paperbacks in the small book exchange. Overheats slightly in winter.

★Liverpool   PUB
(Паб Ливерпуль; ul Sverdlova 28; ⊙noon-3am; ❡) You'll never walk (or drink) alone at Irkutsk's most popular theme pub. Enter through a mocked-up red telephone box to find an interior tiled in Beatles photos and old vinyl LPs and strewn with reminders of northwest England's erstwhile musical prowess. The beer menu is global, the service laid-back and mimicky local bands regularly strum for drinkers.

Bierhaus   PUB
(☑3952-550 555; www.bier-haus.ru; ul Gryaznova 1; ⊙noon-2am Mon-Thu, until 4am Fri & Sat, until midnight Sun; ❡) Upmarket Bavarian-style *bierstube* (beer hall with heavy wooden furniture) serving Newcastle Brown and Guinness as well as German beers and sausages. Enter from ul Karla Marksa.

Cheshskaya Pivovarnya   PUB
(Чешская пивоварня; ul Krasnogvardeyskaya 29; ⊙5pm-2am Tue-Thu, from 4pm Fri & Sat, to midnight Sun & Mon) You'll smell this place before you see it as Irkutsk's unpretentious microbrewery-pub creates its own Pilsner Urquell lager, pumping out a pungent hop aroma in the process.

Chili   BAR
(Чили; ☑3952-332 190; ul Karla Marksa 26; cocktails from R200; ⊙24hr) Aztec-themed nightspot and all-day bar where you can join Irkutsk's moneyed youth on beige couches bathed in flamingo neon for a flashy cocktail or overpriced meals (R250 to R600).

Ryumochnaya BAR

(Рюмочная; ul Litvinova 16; ⊙24hr) If low-cost inebriation is your quest, this no-frills bar is your place.

Lenin Street Coffee CAFE

(ul Lenina 9; ⊙8.30am-9pm; 🖥) Simple, no-nonsense coffee place with a Western feel and pricey drinks. Good central place to hang out and surf the web.

Panorama Club CLUB

(www.clubpanorama.ru; ul Dekabrskikh Sobyty 102) Four dance floors pounding to different music styles and an international DJ guest list.

Akula CLUB

(www.akula-club.ru; bul Gagarina 9; ⊙from 10pm Fri & Sat) Nothing subtle about this place – expect top DJs, litres of ethanol-based beverages and public nudity at some point.

☆ Entertainment

Okhlopkov Drama Theatre THEATRE

(Иркутский академический драматический театр имени Н. П. Охлопкова; ☎3952-200 477; www.dramteatr.ru; ul Karla Marksa 14) Shakespeare, Russian classics and local playwright Vampilov staged regularly (in Russian) from September to June.

Aystyonok Puppet Theatre PUPPET THEATRE

(Театр кукол Аистёнок; ☎3952-205 825; www.aistenok-irkutsk.ru; ul Baikalskaya 32) Marionette shows for the kiddies.

Philharmonic Hall LIVE MUSIC

(Филармония; ☎3952-242 968; www.filarmoniya.irk.ru; ul Dzerzhinskogo 2) Historic building staging regular children's shows and musical programs from jazz to classical.

🛍 Shopping

Prodalit BOOKSHOP

(Продалить; ul Furye; ⊙10am-7pm Mon-Fri, to 6pm Sat & Sun) This large bookstore on the 2nd floor of a small shopping centre sells regional and city maps, Baikal- and Irkutsk-themed coffee table books and Lonely Planet guides in Russian.

Karibu CLOTHING

(ul Timiryazeva 34; ⊙10am-7pm Mon-Sat, noon-5pm Sun) Tiny shop selling beautifully furry *unty* (traditional deerskin cowboy boots) made on-site and typically costing around R10,000. Some English spoken.

❶ Information

Irk.ru (www.irk.ru) Local city info.

Post Office (ul Karla Marksa 28; ⊙8am-8pm Mon-Fri, 9am-6pm Sat & Sun)

Tourist Office (☎3952-205 018; www.irkvisit.info; ul Dekabrskikh Sobyty 77; ⊙9am-6pm Sep-May, to 8pm Jun-Aug; 🖥) Municipally funded tourist office with English-speaking staff, free wi-fi, free city maps and lots of well-produced brochures and booklets on Irkutsk and Lake Baikal. Between June and August staff are posted at strategic points around the city handing out info.

WWW Irkutsk (www.irkutsk.org) Bags of information on every aspect of the city.

❶ Getting There & Away

TRAIN

Unlike many other large cities along the Trans-Sib, the station is the best place in Irkutsk to buy tickets, despite its slightly awkward location.

Irkutsk has the following rail connections:

Běijīng *kupe* R14,000; two days, 22 hours; twice weekly

Chita *platskart/kupe* R1750/3300; 16 hours to 20 hours; up to six daily

Khabarovsk *platskart/kupe* R4500/8900; two days, 14 hours; three daily

Krasnoyarsk *platskart/kupe* R1750/3300; 18 hours; up to nine daily

Moscow *platskart/kupe* R5900/11,800; three days, three hours to five days, 18 hours; up to seven daily

Severobaikalsk *platskart/kupe* R2550/5000; one day, ten hours; daily

Slyudyanka *elektrichka* R100; four hours; four daily

Ulaanbaatar *kupe* R4800; 27 hours; daily

Ulan-Ude *platskart* R1100, *kupe* R2000 to R2700; 6½ hours to 8½ hours; up to nine daily

Vladivostok *platskart/kupe* R5350/10,700; three days; three daily

---

❶ THE EASY WAY TO OLKHON ISLAND

To Khuzhir on Olkhon Island, convenient door-to-door transfers (R800) can be arranged through any of Irkutsk's hostels. Minibuses pick up from any hostel in the morning and drop off passengers at any guesthouse in Khuzhir midafternoon. Hostels sell tickets even to nonguests.

WORTH A TRIP

TALTSY ТАЛЬЦЫ

About 47km southeast of Irkutsk, 23km before Listvyanka, **Taltsy Museum of Architecture & Ethnography** (Архитектурно-этнографический музей Тальцы; www.talci.ru; 47km from Irkutsk on the Baikalsky trakt; admission R200; ⏱10am-5pm) is an impressive outdoor collection of old Siberian buildings set in a delightful riverside forest. Amid the renovated farmsteads are two chapels, a church, a watermill, some Evenki graves and the eye-catching 17th-century Iliminsk Ostrog watchtower. Listvyanka–Irkutsk buses and *marshrutky* stop on request at Taltsy's entrance (look out for the roadside 'Музей' sign), and the ticket booth is a minute's walk through the forest.

AIR

Irkutsk's antiquated little 'international' **airport** (www.iktport.ru) is handily placed near the city centre. Foreign destinations include Bangkok, Běijīng, Seoul and Ulaanbaatar. Direct flights to Germany were scrapped in 2011 but might restart in the coming years.

For Moscow Domodedovo there are direct flights with **S7 Airlines** (from R10,500, three daily). Irkutsk also enjoys direct air links to many other domestic destinations, with tickets for all services sold through the convenient **Central Air Agency** (Центральная авиакасса; ☎3952-500 703; http://ikt.moyreys.ru; ul Gorkogo 29; ⏱8am-7pm).

BOAT

In summer hydrofoils buzz along the Angara River to Listvyanka and up Lake Baikal to Bolshie Koty, Olkhon Island, Ust-Barguzin and Nizhneangarsk. Departures are from the Raketa hydrofoil station (Речной Вокзал) beyond the Angara Dam in Solnechny Mikro-Rayon, two minutes' walk from bus 16 stop 'Raketa'. Timetables are posted by the quay. Services in the other direction to Bratsk leave from a separate jetty in the city centre.

All services are operated by VSRP (www.vsrp.ru; ☎3952-287 115). Check the English-language website for all times and prices.

BUS

From the partially renovated **bus station** (ul Oktyabrskoy Revolyutsii; ⏱5.30am-8pm) book tickets at least a day ahead in summer for Arshan (R400, four to five hours, daily), Listvyanka (R100, 1¼ hours, hourly) via Taltsy (R80), Bratsk (R867, 11 hours) and Ust-Kut (on the

BAM railway; R1570, 12 hours). The station has a left-luggage office.

Minibuses to Ulan-Ude (R800, seven hours) and Slyudyanka (R160, two hours) depart throughout the day from the train-station forecourt.

ⓘ Getting Around

Irkutsk's Trans-Sib station is located on the opposite side of the River Angara to the city centre, but is well linked by public transport. With luggage, the simplest way to get to the city centre is to hop aboard tram 1, 2 or 4A which stop frequently outside the station building. Buses 16 and 20 run to Skver Kirova.

Within the central area, walking is usually the best idea as one-way systems make bus routes confusing.

Listvyanka Листвянка

☏ 3952 / POP 1880 / TIME MOSCOW +8HR

As the closest lakeside village to Irkutsk, Listvyanka – aka the 'Baikal Riviera' – is the touristy spot to which most travellers are funnelled to dunk their toes in Baikal's pure waters. Having picked at *omul*, admired the hazy views of the Khamar Daban mountains on the opposite shore and huffed their way from one end of the village to the other, most are on a *marshrutka* back to Irkutsk late afternoon. But there's more to Listvyanka than this; others stay longer to hike the Great Baikal Trail, discover more about the lake at the Baikal Museum and chill out at one of Siberia's most ecofriendly sleeps.

If you're looking for beach fun, you're at the wrong address – the eastern shore (Buryatiya) is the place to build sandcastles. However, what the Buryat shore doesn't have is Listvyanka's range of activities: anything from short boat trips to diving and jet-skiing in the summer, and ice-mountain biking to lake treks and ice sculpting in the winter.

⊙ Sights & Activities

Sourcing a map at Irkutsk's tourist office before you set off will save a lot of hunting.

Baikal Museum MUSEUM
(ul Akademicheskaya 1, Rogatka; admission R300; ⏱9am-7pm) One of only three museums in the world dedicated solely to a lake, this sometimes overly scientific institution examines the science of Baikal from all angles. Pass quickly by the gruesomely discoloured fish samples and seal embryos in formalde-

Baikal

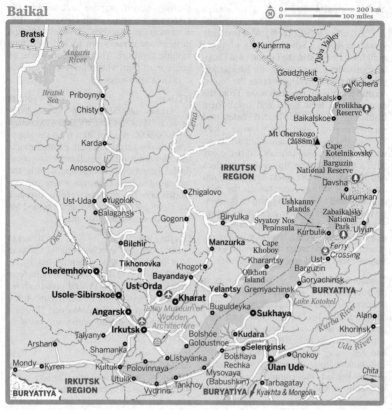

hyde to the tanks containing two frolicsome nerpa seals and the various Baikal fish that you may later encounter on restaurant menus. A new attraction is a minisub simulator which takes you deep down into Baikal's nippy waters.

Adjoining the building is a park containing over 400 species of plants, some rare or endangered.

St Nicholas Church
CHURCH

(Krestovka) Listvyanka's small mid-19th-century timber church is dedicated to St Nicholas, who supposedly saved its merchant sponsor from a Baikal shipwreck.

Retro Park
ART GALLERY

(Krestovka) This garden near the St Nicholas Church is full of wacky sculpture pieces fashioned from old Soviet-era cars and motorbikes.

Nerpinarium
AQUARIUM

(www.baikalnerpa.ru; ul Gorkogo 101A; admission R300; ⊙11am-5pm Tue-Fri, to 6pm Sat & Sun) Thirty-minute seal shows in a silver building resembling an upturned ship next to the Priboy Hotel.

Baikal Dog Sledding Centre
DOG SLEDDING

(☎8-908 660 5098; ul Kulikova 136a) From December to March the centre offers thrilling dog sledding on forest tracks. All kinds of tours are available, from 5km tasters to multiday trans-Baikal ice expeditions costing tens of thousands of roubles. Some English spoken. Book through Baikaler.

🛏 Sleeping

Many Irkutsk tour agents and even some hostels and hotels have their own guesthouse or homestay in Listvyanka. For turn-up-and-hope homestays the best street to try first is ul Chapaeva.

★ Belka Hostel
HOSTEL $

(☑ 8-952 626 1251; www.baikaler.com; ul Chapaeva 77a; dm/tw R600/1500; @) ⚲ Previously known as Baikaler Eco-Hostel, this purpose-built hostel located at the far end of ul Chapaeva provides top-notch digs for backpacker prices, leaving Listvyanka's other flat-footed accommodation in its green wake. From the energy-saving light bulbs and basalt-foam insulation to the solar-heated water and solar-generated electricity, owner Jack Sheremetoff has crafted a low-impact haven with lots of personal touches. Start the day with a bit of sun worship on the yoga deck and breakfast on the forest-facing chill-out area; end it with a scramble up the mini climbing wall and a scrub-down in the *banya* before snuggling up in a hand-made timber bed (no bunks) in an en suite dorm. Two guest kitchens, 24-hour reception and many other features you won't find anywhere else. Booking well ahead is essential. No wi-fi.

Derevenka
HOTEL $$

(☑ 8-914 877 5599; www.baikal-derevenka.ru; ul Gornaya 1; s/d R2000/3000, camping pitch R180; 🔊) On a ridge behind the shore road, cute little wooden huts (named after Baikal's winds) with stove-heaters, private toilets and hot water (but shared showers) offer Listvyanka's most appealing semi-budget choice. Behind the complex is Listvyanka's only official campsite. Rates include breakfast.

Dream of Baikal Hotel
HOTEL $$

(☑ 395 249 6888; www.dreamofbaikal.ru; ul Gorkogo 105; s R2000-2700, d R2400-3100; 🔊) Set just an endemic species' throw from Baikal's lulling waves/crumbly ice, this brand-new, clumsily named, purpose-built hotel by the market is a step up from Listvyanka's usual timber guesthouses. Rooms bedecked in generous drapery are packed with faux antique furniture. The reception works 24 hours apart from when the receptionist dozes off just after lunch.

U Ozera
HOTEL $$

(У Озера; ☑ 3952-496 777; www.listvyanka-baikal.ru; Irkutsk Hwy km3; d R3300-4300, cottages R4000-5000; 🔊) Just 10m from the shoreline, it's not surprising that all nine rooms (doubles only) at this small hotel have wonderful lake views. Rooms are a little too intimate but have balconies where you can stretch out. The cottages sleeping two lack the views but offer more space. Located between Krestovka and Rogatka.

Devyaty Val
GUESTHOUSE $$

(☑ 3952-496 814; www.9val.irk.ru; ul Chapaeva 24; d R1800-2200; @ ✉) Friendly, family-run guesthouse where the huge, good-value *lyux* rooms with big beds, TV and private shower and toilet in a long timber extension are a big step up from the *polo-lyux*. There's a small indoor pool and sauna, and rates include breakfast.

Priboy
HOTEL $$

(☑ 3952-496 725; upper fl, ul Gorkogo 101; r from R2500) Spitting distance from the lake in the port area, this glass-and-steel hunk of incongruity has seen renovation in recent years, rendering the four lake-view rooms some of the best deals in town. The other 15 chambers are less spectacular but rates include breakfast taken in the downstairs cafe.

SOMETHING FISHY

No trip to Baikal is complete without tasting **omul**, a distant relative of salmon that's delicious when freshly hot-smoked. There are over 50 other varieties of Baikal fish, including perch, black grayling, ugly frilly-nosed bullheads and tasty *sig* (lake herring). While the lake isn't Russia's greatest place for anglers, from February to April it offers the unusual spectacle of **ice fishing**. There are two forms: individuals with immense patience dangle miniature hooked lines through Inuit-style ice holes; elsewhere, especially in shallow waters, whole teams of villagers string long, thin nets beneath the ice and pull out *omul* by the hundred.

You can get beneath the ice yourself with two professional Irkutsk-based scuba-diving outfits: **Three Dimensions** (☑ 3952-587 575; www.dive-baikal.ru) and **SVAL** (☑ 3952-295 051; www.svaldiving.ru). But the lake's greatest divers are the unique **nerpa seals**. Indigenous to Lake Baikal, they are the only seal in the world to spend its entire existence in a freshwater environment and thrive in many locations on the lake's shore, but usually (and wisely) away from human populations.

THE GREAT BAIKAL TRAIL

Inspired largely by the Tahoe Rim Trail (a hiking path encircling Lake Tahoe in California and Nevada), in summer 2003 a small band of enthusiasts began work on the first section of what was grandly named the Great Baikal Trail (GBT; in Russian, Bolshaya Baikalskaya Tropa, BBT). Every summer since has seen hundreds of volunteers flock to Lake Baikal's pebbly shores to bring the GBT organisation's stated aim – the creation of a 2000km-long network of trails encircling the whole of Lake Baikal – closer to fruition. This lofty ambition may still be a far-off dream, but the GBT is nonetheless the first such trail system in all Russia.

These rudimentary bits of infrastructure, the GBT organisation hopes, will attract more low-impact tourists to the region, thus encouraging ecofriendly businesses to flourish and providing an alternative to industrial and mass tourism development. Volunteers and local activists are also involved in raising awareness of environmental issues among local people, visiting schools and fundraising. Nomination as a finalist in National Geographic's 2008 Geotourism Challenge is arguably the GBT's greatest achievement to date and greatly raised its profile in the world of ecotourism.

Many Baikal explorers simply enjoy trekking the 540km of trails created thus far, but every year young and old from around the world join work crews for a few enjoyable weeks of clearing pathways, cutting steps, creating markers and cobbling together footbridges. Those eager to volunteer should visit the **GBT website** (www.greatbaikaltrail.org) for more details.

Baikal Chalet GUESTHOUSE $$
(☑ 3952-461 557; www.baikalcomplex.com; ul Gudina 75; tw R2000) The 13 comfortable twin rooms in this timber guesthouse around 800m back from the lake are a good deal. Its sister guesthouse in Bolshie Koty offers similar rates and standards. Breakfast included.

Krestovaya pad HOTEL $$$
(☑ 3952-496 863; www.krestovayapad.ru; ul Gornaya 14a; tw & d R4000-7500; ☎) This stylishly upmarket complex with very comfortable international-standard pine-clad rooms dominates the hillside above Krestovka.

Hotel Mayak HOTEL $$$
(Отель Маяк; ☑ 3952-496 925; www.mayakhotel. ru; ul Gorkogo 85a; s/tw R4800/5100; ☎) There were once (now mothballed) plans to transform Listvyanka and other villages on the shores of Lake Baikal into purpose-built resorts with plasticky upmarket hotels like the 'Lighthouse'. The village's most in-your-face hotel has Western-standard rooms, a good restaurant and an unbeatable location near the hydrofoil quay.

 Eating

Near the port, the large fish and souvenir market is the best place to buy smoked *omul* and is surrounded by greasy spoons offering cheap *plov* (meat and rice, Uzbek pilaflike dish) and shashlyk.

Berg House RUSSIAN $
(ul Gorkogo 59; mains R250-370; ☺ 11am-2am; ☎) Between the Mayak Hotel and the post office, this Anglophone-friendly cafe has understatedly laid picnic tables, pleasant service, large portions of fish and meat and Ukrainian Obolon beer on tap.

Café Podlemore CAFE $
(ul Gorkogo 31; mains R120-160; ☺ 9am-midnight) The Podlemore has porridge and oven-fresh pastries, but rather flummoxed serving staff. Early opening makes it a popular breakfast halt.

Proshly Vek RUSSIAN $$
(Прошлый век; ul Lazlo 1; meals R200-450; ☺ noon-midnight) Listvyanka's most characterful eatery has a nautical theme, a fish-heavy menu and Baikal views. The upper floor is filled with fascinating old junk which you can admire while tucking into *omul* done any which way you please.

ℹ Orientation

The village extends 4.5km from Rogatka at the mouth of the Angara to the market area. A single road skirts the shore with three valleys running inland where most of Listvyanka's characterful timber dwellings and accommodation options are located. There's no public transport which can mean some very long walks.

CIRCUMBAIKAL RAILWAY КРУГОБАЙКАЛЬСКАЯ ЖЕЛЕЗНАЯ ДОРОГА

Excruciatingly slow train ride or a great social event? Opinions are mixed, but taking one of the four-per-week Slyudyanka–Port Baikal trains along this scenic, lake-hugging branch line remains a very popular tourist activity. The most picturesque sections of the route are the valley, pebble beach and headland at Polovinnaya (around halfway), and the bridge area at km149. Note that most trains *from* Port Baikal travel by night and so are useless for sightseeing.

The old stone tunnels, cliff cuttings and bridges are an attraction even for non-train-buffs who might drive alongside sections of the route on winter ice roads from Kultuk. Hiking the entire route or just sections of the peaceful track is also popular and walking a couple of kilometres from Port Baikal leads to some pleasant, if litter-marred, beaches. Or get off an Irkutsk–Slyudyanka *elektrichka* at Temnaya Pad three hours into the journey and hike down the stream valley for about an hour. You should emerge at km149 on the Circumbaikal track, from where you can continue by train to Port Baikal if you time things well.

At the time of research, Matanya trains departed from a side platform at Slyudyanka I station at 1.20pm on Monday, Thursday, Friday and Sunday – check timetables carefully. An additional but more expensive tourist train direct from Irkutsk departs at 8.20am on Wednesday and Saturday, reaching Slyudyanka at 10.30am. Matanya trains arrive in Port Baikal in the evening after the last ferry for Listvyanka has departed, so organising accommodation in advance is advisable.

The wonderfully detailed but now woefully out-of-date website Circumbaikal Railway (http://kbzd.irk.ru/Eng/) has photographs of virtually every inch of the route.

Agencies such as Krugobaikalsky Ekspress (☑ 3952-202 973; www.krugobaikalka.ru) run organised Circumbaikal tours from Irkutsk (R2300) with transfers back to the city at the end of the day.

❶ Information

ATMs can be found in the Mayak and Priboy hotels.

Post office (ul Gorkogo 49; ⊘ 8am-1pm & 2-8pm Mon-Fri, 9am-6pm Sat)

Tourist Office (☑ 3952-656 099; hydrofoil quay; ⊘ 10am-6pm) Located at the *marshrutka* terminus (there are several imposters) this surprisingly useful office hands out free maps as well as providing bus, ferry and hydrofoil timetables and offering imaginative Baikal boat trips. Bike rental available.

❶ Getting There & Away

Hourly *marshrutky* (R100, 1¼ hours) leave for Irkutsk from outside the tourist office (where tickets are bought). The last service departs at 9pm.

From mid-May to late September, hydrofoils stop at Listvyanka between Irkutsk and Bolshie Koty three times a day.

A tiny, battered car ferry lumbers across the never-frozen Angara River mouth to Port Baikal from Rogatka four times a day mid-May to mid-October; just twice a day in the winter months. See VSRP (p188) for details of all boat services.

Port Baikal   Порт Байкал

☑ 3952 / POP 425 / TIME MOSCOW +8HR

You'd be excused for dismissing Port Baikal as a rusty semi-industrial eyesore when seen from Listvyanka across the unbridged mouth of the Angara River. But the view is misleading. A kilometre southwest of Stanitsa (the port area), Baranchiki is a ramshackle 'real' village with lots of unkempt but authentic Siberian cottages and a couple of handy accommodation options. Awkward ferry connections mean that Port Baikal remains largely uncommercialised, lacking Listvyanka's attractions but also its crowds. It's thus popular with more meditative visitors, but the main draw is that it's both the beginning and terminus of the Circumbaikal Railway.

From 1900 to 1904 the Trans-Siberian Railway tracks from Irkutsk came to an abrupt halt at Port Baikal. They continued on Lake Baikal's far eastern shore at Mysovaya (Babushkin), and the watery gap was plugged by ice-breaking steamships, including the *Angara,* now restored and on view in Irkutsk. Later, the tracks were pushed south and around the lake. This Circumbaikal line required so many impressive tunnels and bridges that it earned the nickname 'The Tsar's Jewelled Buckle'. With the damming of the Angara River in the 1950s, the original Irkutsk–Port Baikal section was submerged and replaced with an Irkutsk–Kultuk shortcut (today's Trans-Siberian). That left poor little Port Baikal to wither away at the dead end of a rarely used but incredibly scenic branch line.

🛏 Sleeping & Eating

If the last ferry back to Listvyanka has just left, the Paradis is full and the Yakhont seems too expensive, it's always possible to fall back on several basic homestays in Baranchiki. Ask around or look out for 'сдаются комнаты' signs. If all else fails, the train station has rest rooms and food. Apart from the Yakhont restaurant, a couple of poorly stocked grocery kiosks are the only other sources of sustenance.

Gostevoy Dom Paradis   GUESTHOUSE $
(📞3952-607 450; www.baikal.tk; ul Baikalskaya 12; full board R1500) This timber guesthouse is set 400m back from the lakeside. Various pine-clad but rather spartan rooms share two Western-style toilets and a shower.

Yakhont   HOTEL $$
(📞3952-250 496; www.baikalrest.ru; ul Naberezhnaya 3; s/tw R3200/3500) Port Baikal's top digs can be found in a traditionally designed log house decorated with eclectic good taste by the well-travelled English-speaking owners. There's a communal kitchen-dining room, above which rooms have perfect Western bathrooms. The large restaurant below the hotel is the village's sole eatery. Advance bookings are essential.

❶ Getting There & Away

The ferry to Rogatka near Listvyanka's Baikal Museum runs four times daily between mid-May and mid-October at 8.15am, 11.15am, 4.15pm and 6.15pm (departures at 6.40am, 10.45am, 3.50pm and 5.15pm from Rogatka) but only twice in winter. Check the schedule beforehand. From mid-June to August there are direct hydrofoils to/from Irkutsk. All services are operated by VSRP (p188).

One or two trains per day come via the slow Circumbaikal route from Slyudyanka.

Bolshie Koty Большие Коты

POP 50 / TIME MOSCOW +8HR

Tiny and roadless, this serene Baikal village is what the great Siberian escape is all about. But things weren't always this quiet; in the 19th century Koty experienced a mini gold rush and boasted soap and candle factories, a glassworks, churches and a school. Today all that's long since over, leaving Irkutsk's nouveau riche to assemble their lakeside dachas in peace.

A section of the Great Baikal Trail runs between Koty and Listvyanka, a fabulous full- or half-day hike (around 20km). Take plenty of food (drink from the lake) as there's none en route.

Three minutes' walk from the hydrofoil quay, the **Lesnaya 7 Hostel** (📞8-904 118 7275; www.lesnaya7.com; ul Lesnaya 7; dm R700; @) fills a traditional timber house where showers run hot and the 12 beds are all in double rooms. Booking ahead is essential.

The only way to reach Bolshie Koty (unless you hike from Listvyanka) is aboard one of the three hydrofoils a day from Irkutsk (via Listvyanka). Check VSRP (p188) for times and ticket prices. Winter ice roads briefly unite the village with the outside world.

Olkhon Island
Остров Ольхон

POP 1500 / TIME MOSCOW +5HR

Halfway up Lake Baikal's western shore and reached by a short ferry journey from Sakhyurta (aka MRS), the serenely beautiful Olkhon Island is a wonderful place from which to view the lake and relax during a tour of Siberia. Considered one of five global poles of shamanic energy by the Buryat people, the 72km-long island's 'capital' is the unlovely village of Khuzhir (Хужир), which has seen something of an unlikely tourist boom over the last decade, mainly thanks to the efforts of Nikita's Homestead (p194).

Escaping Khuzhir's dusty, dung-splattered streets is the key to enjoying Olkhon. Every morning tours leave from Khuzhir's guesthouses to the north and south of the island, the most popular a seven-hour bounce in a UAZ minivan to dramatic Cape Khoboy at Olkhon's very northern tip, where Baikal seals sometimes bask. Driver-guides cook fish soup for lunch over an open fire, but few speak any English. See the Nikita's

Homestead website (www.olkhon.info) for details of this and other excursions. Otherwise, rent a bike and strike out on your own. Maps are available from Nikita's but take all food and water with you as there's none outside Khuzhir.

Some of Olkhon Island falls within the boundaries of the Pribaikalsky National Park. As of summer 2014 there was no charge to enter the park but this might not always be the case (an admission charge of R60 was levied for a couple of years).

◉ Sights & Activities

The museum and Shaman Rocks provide minor distraction in Khuzhir.

Museum   MUSEUM
(ul Pervomayskaya 24; admission R100; ⊘2-8pm Sun-Fri) Khuzhir's small museum displays a random mix of stuffed animals, Soviet-era junk, local art and the personal possessions of its founder, Nikolai Revyakin, a teacher for five decades at the school next door.

Shaman Rocks   LANDMARK
A short walk north of Nikita's, the unmistakable Shaman Rocks are neither huge nor spectacular, but they have become the archetypal Baikal vista found on postcards and travel-guide covers. A long strip of sandy beach lines the Maloe More (Little Sea) east of the rocks.

⌷ Sleeping & Eating

Khuzhir has an ever-growing range of places to stay, though the vast majority of independent travellers bunk down at Nikita's Homestead. If all 50 rooms at Nikita's are full, staff can arrange homestays costing around R850 with meals taken at the Homestead canteen. Booking ahead anywhere in Khuzhir is only necessary during July and August. There's no ATM on the island, so you'll need to bring enough cash to cover your stay.

★ Nikita's Homestead   GUESTHOUSE $
(☑8-914 895 7865; www.olkhon.info; ul Kirpichnaya 8; full board per person R1000-1500; ⊘reception 8am-11pm) Occupying a sizeable chunk of Khuzhir, this intricately carved timber complex has grown (and continues to grow) into one of Siberia's top traveller hang-outs. The basic rooms in myriad shapes and sizes are attractively decorated

with petroglyphs and other ethnic finery and heated by wood-burning stoves – but only a select few have showers (put your name down for the *banya*).

The organic meals are served three times a day in the large canteen near reception and two other (paid) eateries stand behind. There's a small cycle-hire centre and a packed schedule of excursions and activities. Note there is no alcohol for sale at Nikita's and consumption on the premises is frowned upon.

U Olgi   GUESTHOUSE $
(☑8-908 661 9015; ul Lesnaya 3-1; full board per person R1000) This well-liked option has nine rooms, three in a typical village house and six in a purpose-built, pine-fragrant building opposite. New showers and flushing toilets plus scrumptious Siberian fare cooked by Olga herself make this a winner every time. Book through Baikaler (p183) in Irkutsk.

Solnechnaya   GUESTHOUSE $
(Солнечная; ☑3952-683 216; www.olkhon.com; ul Solnechnaya 14; full board per person R1100-1450; @) No happening scene like at Nikita's, but it's still a pleasant place to stay offering a good range of activities. Accommodation is in two-storey cabins and tiny single-room shacks with verandahs. Enter from ul Solnechnaya or from near the relay station at the top of the hill.

ⓘ Getting There & Away

The simplest way to reach Olkhon is aboard the morning *marshrutka* that leaves Irkutsk's hostels around 8.30am. Many other services run in July and August but can be impossible to track down in Irkutsk.

With a little warning, agencies or hostels can usually find you a ride in a private car to/from Irkutsk (5½ hours) for R1500 per seat, R6000 for the whole car. Prices include the short ferry ride to/from MRS; from mid-January to March an ice road replaces the ferry. When ice is partly formed or partly melted, the island is completely cut off for motor vehicles, though an ad hoc minihovercraft service is sometimes operated by locals.

In summer a hydrofoil service operates from Irkutsk to Olkhon, dropping passengers near the ferry terminal, from where it's possible to hitch a paid lift into Khuzhir. See VSRP (p188) for times and prices.

South Baikal & the Tunka Valley

The windows of Trans-Siberian trains passing between Irkutsk and Ulan-Ude frame attractive lake vistas along much of Baikal's south coast. Few Westerners are actually tempted off the train along this stretch but if they are, it's usually at Slyudyanka, the starting point for the Circumbaikal train rides and a launch pad into the remotely scenic Tunka Valley.

Slyudyanka   Слюдянка

📞 39544 / POP 18,600 / TIME MOSCOW +8HR

The lakeside railway town of Slyudyanka provides a grittier alternative to Listvyanka for those eager to get up close to Lake Baikal's waves/groaning ice and the Trans-Siberian Railway, which hugs the lake's pebbly shore either side of town. Most alight from a train at the glittering, solid-marble **train station**, which is a mere five-minute walk from Lake Baikal. Amid the nearby railway repair sheds and admin buildings you'll also find a fascinating little **museum** (ul Zheleznodorozhnaya 22; admission R100; ⊙8am-noon & 1-5pm Wed-Sun) housed in an ornate wooden building set back from ul Zheleznodorozhnaya. There are exhibitions on the Circumbaikal Railway, the history of Slyudyanka and Lake Baikal, plus heaps of railway paraphernalia. Geology buffs should consider heading to the privately run **Baikal Mineral Museum** (ul Slyudyanaya 36; admission R150; ⊙10am-7pm), which claims to exhibit every mineral known to man.

A popular picnic excursion is to **Cape Shaman**, an easy 4km stroll north towards Kultuk along Baikal's gravelly shore. A more strenuous trail heads up **Pik Cherskogo** (aka Mt Chersky) along the former post road to Mongolia. Owners of the Slyudyanka Hostel run guided trips there and to the former marble and mica (*slyud* in Russian, hence the town's name) mines southeast of the town.

🛏 Sleeping & Eating

Slyudyanka Hostel   HOSTEL $
(📞39544-53 198, 8-902 576 7344; www.hostel-s.com; ul Shkolnaya 10, apt 7; dm R500; @) Six-bed hostel-homestay at the southern end of town providing a great opportunity to experience small-town Siberian family life. A fully equipped kitchen, heaps of outdoorsy tours

and hikes and evenings of authentic Baikal hospitality await those who make the effort to find the place. It's a 20-minute walk, five-minute *marshrutka* ride (No 1) or R120 taxi journey along ul Parizhskoy Komuny. Booking ahead is pretty much essential.

Vsyo budet OK   SUPERMARKET $
(Всё будет ОК; ul Lenina 118; ⊙9am-10pm) The 'Everything's Gonna Be OK' supermarket opposite the bus station is the place to stock up on enough noodles, cheese, bread and instant porridge to keep you going all the way to the Ural Mountains.

ℹ Getting There & Away

Elektrichki (R100, four daily) from Irkutsk take four hours to arrive at Slyudyanka 1 station; ordinary passenger trains (*platskart* R670, up to eight daily) take just two to 2½ hours. Slyudyanka is also the usual starting point for the Circumbaikal Railway trip. From the bus station *marshrutky* run to Arshan (two hours, two daily) and Irkutsk (R158, two hours, at least hourly).

Arshan   Аршан

📞 30156 / POP 2460 / TIME MOSCOW +8HR

Backed by the dramatic, cloud-wreathed peaks of the Eastern Sayan Mountains, the once drowsy Buryat spa village of Arshan has been rudely awoken from its slumber in recent years. The fast-flowing Kyngarga River still murmurs with ice-cold water from elevated valleys above the village, the prayer wheels still twirl at the tranquil little Buddhist temples and cows still blunder through the streets, but Russian-style tourism has intruded into the idyllic scene, bringing 24-hour *banya,* cut-price vodka, pounding stereos and grisly service in its wake. But despite this Arshan is still the best base in the Tunka Valley from which to strike out into the mountains, with some superb hikes accessible on foot from the village.

Arshan in Buryat means 'natural spring' and it's the pleasantly sweet, health-giving mineral water that most Russians come for. The huge **Sayany Spa** stands at the entrance to the village on the main street (ul Traktovaya), which then fires itself 2km straight towards the mountains.

Opposite the spa grounds, the **Dechen Ravzhalin Datsan** has two sparkling new prayer wheels, a miniature stupa and a dazzlingly colourful interior. From here ul Traktovaya then climbs in a parade of shops, derelict Soviet architecture and plasticky cafes and guesthouses towards the bus station, after which it swerves west to the sprawling **Kurort Arshan** resort where you can sample the water for free (pass through the turnstile near the souvenir kiosks). Head up the stream from here to access the mountain footpaths or cross the river and walk 20 minutes through the forest to the diminutive **Bodkhi Dkharma Datsan**, set in an idyllic mountain-backed glade.

🛏 Sleeping

Even late at night locals line the bottom end of ul Traktovaya like hitchhikers, brandishing their 'Жильё' (rooms) signs in hope. These sometimes turn out to be unacceptably basic homestays from R300 per bed – check standards before committing. Even if you turn up unannounced you'll have few problems getting a room, even at busy times (July and August). This is probably the way to go in Arshan. Otherwise, try to book ahead at a guesthouse.

Yasnaya Polyana   GUESTHOUSE $
(Ясная Поляна; ☑8-904 114 7808; ul Traktovaya 109; s/d R400/800; ☉ Jun-Sep) A friendly local English teacher runs this compound of 10 pine cottages, each containing two beds, a table, a stove ring and sometimes a kettle. Otherwise, things are pretty basic with a sun-heated shower (best in the evenings) and outdoor washing facilities. To find it, take the second left on entering the village (at ul Traktovaya 99) and keep going until you see a large unmarked green gate on your left.

Pensionat Vershina   GUESTHOUSE $
(☑8-950 388 7590; ul Mikrorayon 22/1; s/d R400/800) Located near the Sayany Spa, this purpose-built two-storey guesthouse has cosy timber rooms with shared showers, free *banya* and a small cafe.

Arshansky Bor   GUESTHOUSE $
(☑8-950 050 6481; ul Bratev Domshevikh 44; dm R350-450) This unmarked pink building is the best budget place to overnight until the Priyut Alpinista is rebuilt. Rooms are dim and spartan, and facilities display the pressures of mass occupation, but there's a large kitchen, a common room and a barbecue area.

Monetny Dvor   GUESTHOUSE $$
(☑8-904 115 6390; ul Traktovaya 89; d from R2000) Timber-built 24-bed guesthouse with

rooms in a main building and three two-storey cottages. Cycle hire available.

Priyut Alpinista   GUESTHOUSE
(www.iwf.ru; ul Bratev Domshevikh 8) Long a favourite with backpackers, trekkers and climbers, the 'Mountaineer's Refuge' sadly burnt down in 2008. However, there are plans to rebuild it on the same site, three minutes' walk along ul Pavlova from the bus station. In the meantime, contact the owners of the Arshansky Bor for details of the trips into the mountains that used to run from the Priyut Alpinista.

🍴 Eating

Eateries are thin on the ground as most Russians prebook full board at the spas. Some of the cafes at the top of ul Traktovaya are truly dire.

Zakusochnaya Khamar Daban   CANTEEN $
(Закусочная Хамар Дабан; ul Traktovaya; mains R40-100; ☉10am-1am; ❅) Located opposite the Sayan Sanatorium, this basic but pleasant canteen serves up a large menu of Buryat and Russian comfort food and cheap beers. The handwritten menu can be a challenge.

Novy Vek   RUSSIAN $$
(Новый век; ul Traktovaya 4; ☉10am-2am) For a proper sit-down meal try this restaurant near the Arshan Spa that has also sprouted a nightclub, entertainment centre and *stolovaya*.

ℹ Getting There & Away

The miniature bus station near the top of ul Traktovaya has the village's only ATM, plus left-luggage lockers. Arshan has the following bus and *marshrutka* connections:

Irkutsk R400, daily

Slyudyanka R200, two hours, one or two daily

Ulan-Ude R710, 11 hours, three daily

Beyond Arshan

From the turn-off for Arshan it's just 9km along the Tunka Valley road to the village of **Zhemchug** (Жемчуг) where, for around R100, you can wallow in a series of hot pools that leave a chalky-green residue on skin and clothes.

Around 25km further along the road, the valley's unkempt, low-rise little 'capital' **Kyren** (Кырен) is home to the **Tunka National Park HQ** (www.tunkapark.ru; ul Lenina 69). Its small onion-topped **church** (ul

Kooperativenaya) adds foreground to the photogenic alpine backdrop.

The valley road ends at Mondy (Монды) near Munku-Sardyk (3491m), the highest mountain in Eastern Siberia and scene of an annual mass ascent (May) marking the beginning of the climbing season. From the nearby Mongolian border post a road runs 21km to appealing Khövsgöl Lake, Baikal's little sister.

Some 190km west beyond Mondy, the dumbfoundingly far-flung Oka Region has been dubbed 'Tibet in miniature'. The 'capital' Orlik (Орлик) is the obvious place to arrange treks and horse-riding trips into some seriously isolated backcountry.

Ulan-Ude   Улан - Удэ

☑ 3012 / POP 404,000 / TIME MOSCOW +8HR

With its smiley Asian features, cosy city centre and fascinating Mongol-Buddhist culture, the Buryat capital is one of Eastern Siberia's most likeable cities. Quietly busy, welcoming and, after Siberia's Russian cities, refreshingly exotic, it's a pleasant place to base yourself for day trips to Buddhist temples and flits to eastern Lake Baikal's gently shelving beaches, easily reachable by bus. For some travellers UU is also a taster for what's to come in Mongolia.

Founded as a Cossack *ostrog* (fort) called Udinsk (later Verkhneudinsk) in 1666, the city prospered as a major stop on the tea-caravan route from China via Troitskosavsk (now Kyakhta). Renamed Ulan-Ude in 1934, it was a closed city until the 1980s due to its secret military plants (there are still mysterious blank spaces on city maps).

⊙ Sights

Lenin Head   MONUMENT
(pl Sovetov) Ulan-Ude's main square is entirely dominated by the world's largest Lenin head (where are all the others with which it competes?), which some maintain looks comically cross-eyed. The 7.7m-high bronze bonce was installed in 1970 to celebrate Lenin's 100th birthday. Oddly, UU's bird population never seems to streak Lenin's bald scalp with their offerings – out of respect for the great man's achievements say diehard communists (but perhaps due to the barely visible antibird spikes, say the rest).

Khangalov Museum of Buryat History   MUSEUM
(Музей истории Бурятии имени М. Н. Хангалова; Profsoyuznaya ul 29; admission per fl R80-120; ⊙10am-6pm Tue-Sun) Housed in a badly ageing Soviet-era structure, the historical museum charges per single-room floor; the best of these is Buddiyskoe Iskustvo (3rd floor), displaying *thangkas*, Buddhas and icons salvaged from Buryatiya's monasteries before their Soviet destruction. Other exhibits include fascinating, gaudy papier mâché models of deities and bodhisattvas rescued from Buryatiya's many prewar *datsany* (temples), home shrine tables and often gory Tibetan medical charts. The less interesting Buryat history floor (2nd) can be spied for free from the balcony above.

Rinpoche Bagsha Datsan   BUDDHIST TEMPLE
(ul Dzerzhinskogo) Roosting high above the city's far north, the inside of this new and unexpectedly modern Tibetan temple looks like a kind of Buddhist-themed bus terminal, though the 6m-high gilt Buddha is pretty impressive and if you catch the monks doing their thing with drums, cymbals and chanting the atmosphere can be electric. However the real show-stealer here is the panoramic view, with the smog-hazed city ringed by rumpled dust-bare peaks.

A new feature is the circular walk around the temple featuring pavilions with grotesque, man-size representations of the Chinese signs of the zodiac. Take *marshrutka* 97 from outside the Hotel Baikal Plaza on pl Sovetov to the last stop (right by the temple entrance).

Ethnographic Museum   MUSEUM
(Verkhnyaya Berezovka; admission R150; ⊙9am-5pm Wed-Fri & Sun, 10am-6pm Sat) In a forest clearing 6km from central Ulan-Ude, this outdoor collection of local architecture plus some reconstructed burial mounds and the odd stone totem is worth the trip. It's divided into seven areas, each devoted to a different nationality, tribe or ethnic group. There are Hun-era standing stones, Evenki *chumy*, traditional Buryat yurts, timber European townhouses and a whole strip of Old Believers' homesteads, all brimming with period furniture and inhabited by costumed 'locals' giving craft demonstrations.

Marshrutka 37 from outside the Hotel Baikal Plaza on pl Sovetov passes within 1km and drivers are used to detouring to drop off tourists.

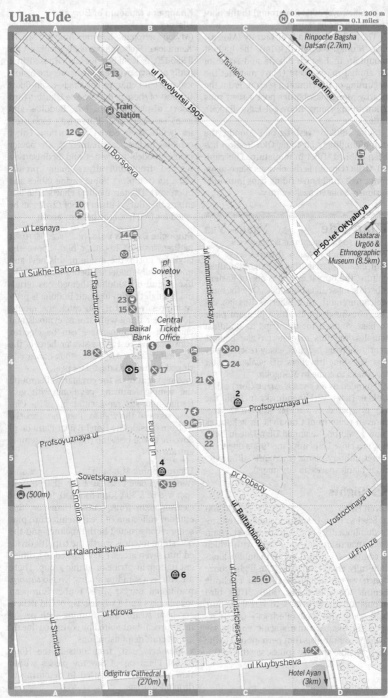

Ulan-Ude

Ulan-Ude

Opera & Ballet Theatre THEATRE
(Бурятский государственный академический театра оперы и балета; ☑ 3012-213 600; www.uuopera.ru; ul Lenina 51) UU's striking Stalinist-era theatre reopened after lengthy renovation in June 2011 (the first performance was for a group of foreign tourists from the luxury Golden Eagle train). Visitors cannot fail to be impressed by the level of craftsmanship inside, though some might be slightly surprised at the new lick of paint and rub of polish given to all the Soviet symbols, including a couple of smirking Stalins.

Ulan-Ude City Museum MUSEUM
(ul Lenina 26; admission R60; ☉ 10am-6pm) Occupying the merchant's house where imperial heir Nicholas II stayed in 1891, this small museum has exhibits examining Verkhneudinsk's role in the tea and fur trades, the huge fairs that took place at the trading arches and several other aspects of the city's past.

Odigitria Cathedral CHURCH
(ul Lenina 2) Built between 1741 and 1785, UU's largest church was also the first stone structure to appear in the city. Used as a museum store from 1929 until the fall of communism, its exterior has been renovated in a chalky white and the domes once again tipped with gold, but the interiors are plain whitewash, awaiting their Byzantine decoration.

Nature Museum MUSEUM
(Музей природы Бурятии; ☑ 3012-214 149; ul Lenina 46; admission R100; ☉ 10am-6pm Tue-Sun) The Nature Museum has taxidermically stuffed animals and a scale model of Lake Baikal showing just how deep it is.

Geological Museum MUSEUM
(Геологический музей Бурятии; ul Lenina 59; ☉ 11am-5pm Mon-Fri) **FREE** This museum displays rocks, crystals and ores from the shores of Lake Baikal as well as art (for sale) made using multihued grit, sand and pebbles.

Tours

Ulan-Ude has several agencies happy to sell you Buryatiya and Baikal tours. Recommended companies and individuals all speak English and are tuned in to the needs of Western travellers.

★ **Baikal Naran Tour** TOUR COMPANY
(☑ 3012-215 097; info@baikalnaran.com; Office 105, Hotel Buryatiya, ul Kommunisticheskaya 47a) There's nothing director Sesegma (aka Svetlana) can't arrange for travellers in Buryatiya. An award-winning tour company and by far the best folks to approach if you want to see the republic's more remote corners, Old Believer villages, the Selenga Delta, the Barguzin Valley and the region's Buddhist and shamanist heritage.

Denis Sobnakov
TOUR GUIDE

(☑8-950 391 6325; www.burtour.com; ul Lenina 63) English-speaking Denis runs the city's best hostel as well as fun-packed walking tours of UU and many other Buryatiya-wide trips.

MorinTur
TOUR COMPANY

(☑3012-443 647; www.morintour.com; Hotel Sagaan Morin, ul Gagarina 25) Focuses on east Baikal, offering various ice and fishing adventures, a horse-sledge trip, seal watching, rafting in the Barguzin Valley and climbing on Svyatoy Nos (Holy Nose) Peninsula.

Buryat-Intour
TOUR COMPANY

(☑3012-216 954; www.buryatintour.ru; ul Erbanova 12) Can arrange birdwatching in the Selenga Delta, river rafting excursions, visits to Novoseleginsk and city tours. Also sells Ulan Ude–Ulaanbaatar bus tickets.

🛏 Sleeping

UU now has hostels and luxury hotels but little else in between. The city doesn't suffer from very high occupancy, except in the summer months when booking ahead is advisable.

★ Ulan-Ude Travellers House
HOSTEL $

(☑8-950 391 6325; www.uuhostel.com; ul Lenina 63, apt 18; dm R500-650; 🛜) So central is this high-ceilinged apartment hostel, you might even catch a glimpse of Lenin's conk from one of the windows. The 14 beds are divided between two spacious, ethnically themed dorms (Russian and Buryat), there's a small kitchen where a free light breakfast is laid out daily, heaps of UU information is pasted on the walls and there's a washing machine for guests to use.

Exceptionally friendly owner Denis is a professional tour guide, fluent English-speaker and guitar demon – bring your six-string for a common-room jam session. He is also planning to open a second branch in the village of Turka on the shores of Baikal itself. A percentage of the hostel's profits go to a local orphanage.

GBT Hostel
HOSTEL $

(☑3012-553 470; per Nakhimova 9-2; dm R600, d R1300; @🛜) An entirely different scene from the Travellers House, this homestay-hostel occupies a suburban house built by Japanese prisoners of war, 2.5km northeast of the city centre. Two dorms sleep 10 and there's one double as well as a fully equipped kitchen. Book ahead and arrange a free station pick-up as it's almost impossible to find on your own. As the name suggests, the owners are heavily involved in the Great Baikal Trail project and this is one of the best places to get trekking info.

Resting Rooms
HOSTEL $

(Комнаты отдыха; ☑3012-282 696; komnaty otdykha, Ulan-Ude train station; 12/24-hr R660/1320) Basic train station dorms good for a couple of hours sleep if arriving in the small hours, but no more.

Hotel Ayan
HOTEL $$

(Отель Аян; ☑301 241 5141; www.ayanhotel.ru; ul Babushkina 164; s/d from R1000/1600; ❄🛜) The inconvenient location 2km south of the city centre is more than recompensed by pristine international-standard rooms, some with air-conditioning. The cheapest singles are a good deal and every room has its own water heater. There's also a tiny cafe should you get peckish from all the stair climbing you'll do here – incredibly, this six-storey new-build has no lift. A taxi from the train station costs around R170 or arrange a R300 private transfer with the hotel.

Hotel Buryatiya
HOTEL $$

(Гостиница Бурятия; ☑3012-21 4888; www.buryatiahotel.com; ul Kommunisticheskaya 47a; s/d from R1950/2700; 🛜) The mammoth Buryatiya, the former Intourist hotel, has 220 rooms of wildly differing sizes and standards: from Soviet-era broom cupboards with dodgy plumbing to almost palatial European-standard quarters. One advantage to staying here is the convenience of extra services (internet room, tour companies, souvenir kiosks, ATMs) on the 1st floor.

Hotel Geser
HOTEL $$

(Отель Гэсэр; ☑3012-216 151; www.geser-hotel.ru; ul Ranzhurova 11; s/tw from R3100/4300) Fully modernised, the former Party hang-out is a popular if slightly overpriced option. Most of the 70-plus rooms are of a decent standard – the only Soviet features remaining are clacking parquet floors and the odd clunky fridge. Rates include breakfast and some staff members speak English.

Mergen Bator
HOTEL $$$

(Отель Мэргэн Батор; ☑3012-200 002; www.mergen-bator.ru; ul Borsoyeva 19b; tw/d R5000/7000; ❄🛜) UU's only 21st-century hotel is a swish pad indeed and completely on a par with any Western four-star establishment. From the trendy retro-veneered corridors to the commendably equipped fitness centre (R500 for non-guests), the modern-as-tomorrow bathrooms to the impeccable service, this place is worth splashing out on. Breakfast is included and can be served in your room free of charge.

Hotel Sagaan Morin   HOTEL $$$

(Отель Сагаан Морин; ☎ 3012-444 019; www.sagaan-morin.ru; ul Gagarina 25; s/tw R3500/4/00; ☎) The gleaming 17-storey, 89-room 'White Horse' offers spacious, crisply designed, almost understated rooms, lots of amenities and a 14th-floor restaurant (Panorama) with look-while-you-eat city vistas.

Hotel Baikal Plaza   HOTEL $$$

(Отель «Байкал Плаза»; ☎ 3012-210 070; www.baikalplaza.com; ul Erbanova 12; s/tw R3500/4200) The 68 modern, if slightly cramped, rooms were arguably UU's finest offering when first renovated a few years ago, and the central location overlooking the Lenin Head is unrivalled. Overtaken by slicker outfits, the Plaza has lowered its prices in recent years.

✗ Eating

Ul Kommunisticheskaya and the surrounding streets are packed with (sometimes very) basic dumpling canteens.

For a fascinating insight into traditional Buryat life, Baikal Naran Tour (p199) can arrange dinner in a yurt with a local family out in the suburbs of Ulan-Ude.

Eco Café   INTERNATIONAL $

(ul Tereshkovoy 26a; mains R40-80; ⊙9am-11pm; ✐) Fancifully claiming the city has 'tired of heavy food', the folks behind this subterranean, but bright cafe opposite the UU's drama theatre go against the Buryat grain with light vegetarian and meat dishes, all made using organic ingredients from local suppliers. Take tram 1 or 2 to the Sayany stop.

Shene Buuza   BURYAT $

(Шэнэ бууза; ul Lenina 44; mains R30-60; ⊙9am-9pm) Squeaky-clean, 21st-century version of the traditional Buryat buuznaya (dumpling canteen). The decor might be shiny and plastic but the menu of Buryat comfort food is as traditional and cheap as every other buuznaya in town.

Appetite   CANTEEN $

(ul Lenina 55; mains R30-70; ⊙9am-10pm) Join the local office worker lunch crush at this self-service canteen and buuzy-free zone where the Russian comfort food is piled high by gruff Buryat servers. Put together a three-course meal for less than R200 and consume in the austere privacy of your white MDF booth while admiring the Lenin Head opposite.

Golden Bird   FAST FOOD $

(ul Lenina 52; mains R40-110; ⊙9am-10pm) Lurid, loud self-service canteen with precisely weighed rations of standard Russian comfort food served on plastic plates and swilled down with Slovak lager.

Sputnik Supermarket   SUPERMARKET $

(Супермаркет Спутник; ul Kommunisticheskaya 48; ⊙24hr) A convenient but pricey supermarket stocking foreign groceries.

Chay Khana   UZBEK $$

(Чай Хана; Evropa Business Centre, ul Baltakhinova; mains R300-400; ⊙11am-midnight Mon-Thu, to 2am Fri, 1pm-2am Sat, to midnight Sun) This high-perched Uzbek restaurant has a triangular cushion-scattered dining space, trendy oriental fabrics and a menu of exotic plov, grilled meats and imaginative salads. But it's the spectacular views of UU and the Selenga valley that are the real showstopper here, best enjoyed from the summer terrace. Take the lift to the 9th floor, then the stairs. The business centre building is nicknamed 'the toilet' – you'll soon see why.

Baatarai Urgöö   BURYAT $$

(Barguzinsky Trakt, Verkhnyaya Berezovka; mains R200-400; ⊙11am-11pm; ☎) This yurt complex in the Verkhnyaya Berezovka suburb is a great lunch spot after a visit to the Ethnographical Museum. Take a seat in the main tent and give your taste buds the Buryat treatment in the form of buuzy (meat-filled dumplings), bukhuler (meat broth), arbin (raw cow's liver in horse stomach fat) and a glass of airag (fermented mare's milk).

The dining space is decorated with suits of Mongol armour, traditional buryat furniture and folk costumes, and the serving staff are also dressed for the part. Take marshrutka 37 from pl Sovetov to the yurt stop.

Modern Nomads   MONGOLIAN $$

(ul Ranzhurova 1; mains R200-1000; ⊙11am-11pm) Clean-cut and very popular Mongolian place, good for a quick snack and a beer or for a full-blown dinner splurge costing thousands. Meat features heavily on the menu, but there are many vegie-friendly salads and other dishes with a contemporary twist to choose from, too.

Viva Italia   ITALIAN $$
(ul Kommunisticheskaya 43; pizzas R300-400; ◎11am-1am Sun-Thu, to 2am Fri & Sat; ✿) A 1980s Italian pop soundtrack, a long, ambitious and slightly overpriced menu of Appenine fare (stick to the pizzas), a European-style lounge and almost every tipple known to Homo-alcoholus – if you must go Italian in Buryatiya, this is the place to go.

🍷 Drinking

Churchill   PUB
(Черчилль; www.pubchurchill.ru; ul Lenina 55; ◎noon-2am) A bekilted Scottish piper (well a bagpiping dummy at least) greets you at the door of this relatively upmarket British-themed pub. The Brit paraphernalia extends throughout the two stylishly finished halls, the food is tasty and there's an international draught beer menu at central London prices.

Bar 12   BAR
(12th fl, Mergen Bator Hotel, Ul Borsoyeva 19b; ◎24hr) Capping off the Mergen Bator hotel, this bar probably offers the best views of any in Russia, with the entire Buryat capital and the surrounding mountainscape laid out dramatically below you. The bar's party piece is to rotate through 360 degrees every 30 minutes meaning you see the entire panorama without leaving your seat. Drinks and food are pretty pricey.

Bochka   BEER HALL
(ul Kommunisticheskaya 52; ◎11am-1am Sun-Thu, to 2am Fri & Sat) Large timber beer hall

---

> ### 🛈 ULAN-UDE TO ULAANBAATAR
>
> With flights between the two capitals once again grounded, there are just two ways to travel from the Buryat capital to Ulaanbaatar. The least comfortable way is by Trans-Mongolian **train**, which takes 23 hours to complete the 657km trip and waits a minumum of five hours on the border at Naushki. A much cheaper and convenient way to go is to hop aboard the daily **coach** (R1300, 10 hours), which leaves from the main bus station. Tickets can be bought from Baikal Naran Tour and the Ulan-Ude Travellers House hostel.

---

serving a range of Russian and international brews to rinse down the succulently smoky shashlyk. The covered terrace is *the* place to do some elbow bending on sultry summer evenings.

Kofeynya Marco Polo   CAFE
(Кофейня Marco Polo; ul Kommunisticheskaya 46; ◎8am-11pm; ☎) This cosy coffee house has a touch of Central European character, great desserts and wi-fi.

🛍 Shopping

Baikal Naran Tour Souvenir Kiosk   SOUVENIRS
(room 105, Hotel Buryatiya, ul Kommunisticheskaya 47a) This tiny kiosk in the Baikal Naran Tour office sells authentic Buryat souvenirs such as oriental costumed dolls, shaman drums and colourful felt hats.

Central Market   MARKET
(ul Baltakhinova) Tidy, Soviet-era market selling unusual local produce such as pine nuts, reindeer meat, buckthorn juice, *salo* (raw pig fat) and seasonal fruit and veg. At the back of the building are several stores offering *unty,* beautifully decorated reindeer skin boots. Prices start from around R9000 a pair.

🛈 Orientation

UU's small city centre is easily explored on foot. Divided into two districts, the communist-era upper city is centred around pl Sovetov and the Lenin Head; descend ul Lenina to the partially pedestrianised lower city, the former merchant quarter, half of which still serves as the commercial hub extending from the 19th-century trading rows (pl Revolyutsii). Dusty streets of crooked timber dwellings make up the other half. The recently renovated embankment bends round from the new bus station to the Odigitria Cathedral.

🛈 Information

Handy ATMs can be found in the Buryatiya hotel and at the train station.

Andriy Suknyov (☎8-902 564 2678; suknev@gmail.com) Owner of the GBT Hostel, energetic Andriy is the best person to contact for volunteer activities in the region, including work with disabled children in Talovka and trail construction on the GBT.

Baikal Bank (Байкал Банк; pl Sovetov 1; ◎9am-8pm Mon-Fri, 9am-7pm Sat) Most central place for changing dollars and euros.

Post Office (ul Lenina 61; ◎8am-10pm Mon-Fri, 9am-6pm Sat & Sun; ☎)

Tourism Portal (www.uutravel.ru) Official tourism website with a smattering of interesting information in English.

Visit Buryatiya (☑3012-210 332; www.visit buryatia.ru) Official tourist board which runs a summertime-only yurt-based information office on pl Sovetov.

ℹ Getting There & Away

TRAIN

There's no need to traipse out to the station to buy tickets – most hotels and hostels can arrange them for you or you can head for the **Central Ticket Office** (ul Erbanova 14; ⊗9am-7pm) opposite the Lenin Head.

When travelling to Irkutsk, take a day train for superb views of Lake Baikal.

Ulan-Ude has the following rail connections:

Běijīng *kupe* R6000; two days to two days, 15 hours; two weekly

Chita *platskart/kupe* R1300/2400; 10 hours to 12 hours; up to six daily

Irkutsk *platskart/kupe* R1200/1600; seven hours to nine hours; up to nine daily

Ulaanbaatar *kupe* R3000; 23 hours; daily

BUS

Ulan-Ude's main bus station is a tiny but user-friendly affair located to the west of pl Sovetov. Buy all tickets at least a day in advance. The city has the following connections:

Arshan R710, 11 hours, three daily

Barguzin R550, seven hours, three daily

Ivolga R40, 40 minutes, many daily (*marshrutka* 130)

Kurumkan R660, nine hours, daily

Kyakhta R350, three hours, hourly

Ust-Barguzin R435, six hours, twice daily

Additional official/unofficial *marshrutky* to Arshan (R700, six hours), Irkutsk (R800, eight hours) and Chita (R1150, seven hours) run from the train station forecourt, departing throughout the day when full.

ℹ Getting Around

As the crow flies, the train station is located only around 600m north of pl Sovetov, but the walk is twice the distance. If you don't fancy stretching your legs, the best option is to take a taxi which should not cost more than R150.

From pl Sovetov *marshrutky* 28, 55 and 77 run a few times hourly to the airport while *marshrutka* 37 passes the hippodrome, Ethnographic Museum and Baatarai Urgöö restaurant. Marshrutka 97 climbs to the Rinpoche Bagsha Datsan.

Around Ulan-Ude

Ivolginsk (Ivolga) Datsan

Possibly the last person you might expect to have backed the building of a Buddhist temple was Stalin, but in 1946 permission came from the Kremlin to erect a *datsan* in Buryatiya, in gratitude to the locals for their sacrifices during WWII it's often claimed. But instead of reviving the erstwhile centre of Buryat Buddhism at Gusinoe Ozero, the authorities granted a plot of marshy land near the village of Ivolga, 35km from central Ulan-Ude, on which the temple was to be built. The first temple was a modest affair, but today the *datsan* has grown large and is expanding fast. The confident epicentre of Russian Buddhism attracts large numbers of the devout as well as tourists on half-day trips from the Buryat capital.

The Ivolginsky *datsan* was one of only two working Buddhist temples in Soviet days (the other was at Aginskoe); most of what you see today has been built in the last two decades. A clockwise walk around the complex takes in countless monastery faculties, administrative buildings, monks' quarters and temples, but the most elaborate of all is the Itygel Khambin Temple honouring the 12th Khambo Lama, whose body was exhumed in 2002. To general astonishment, seven decades after his death his flesh had still not decomposed. Some 'experts' have even attested that the corpse's hair is still growing, albeit extraordinarily slowly. The body is displayed six times a year, attracting pilgrims from across the Buddhist world.

To reach the monastery, first take *marshrutka* 130 (R40, 40 minutes, four hourly) from Ulan-Ude's bus station to the last stop in uninteresting Ivolga. There another *marshrutka* (R20, no number, just a picture of the monastery or the word Дацан pasted to the front windscreen), waits to shuttle visitors the last few kilometres to the monastery compound. Otherwise contact agencies in Ulan-Ude, which offer private transfers and tours with well-informed guides.

Eastern Baikal

Sparsely scattered beach villages of old-fashioned log cottages dot the pretty east Baikal coast. Further north is the dramatic Barguzin Valley, from which Chinggis

(Genghis) Khaan's mother, Oilun-Ehe, is said to have originated. Some of the area has been slated for mass-tourism development but little has appeared in the intervening years, save for a mirror-smooth shore-hugging road which has cut journey times significantly. Ulan-Ude agencies can book basic accommodation along the east coast where summer *turbazy* (holiday camps) are popular among sand-seeking Russians.

Access to the coast is across a forested pass from Ulan-Ude via tiny **Baturino** village with its elegantly renovated Sretenskaya Church.

After around 2½ hours' drive, the newly paved road first meets Lake Baikal at pretty little **Gremyachinsk** (Гремячинск), a popular trip out of Ulan-Ude for hurried Trans-Siberian travellers with a day to spare. Buses stop at a roadside cafe from which Gremyachinsk's sandy but litter-strewn beach is a 15-minute walk up ul Komsomolskaya. *Marshrutky* back to Ulan-Ude are often full so consider prebooking your return.

Approximately 5km from Gremyachinsk, at least 10 large tourist camps are strung around **Lake Kotokel**, whose thermal springs keep it warm year-round. At the northern end of the lake rises **Monastyrsky Island**, once home to an isolated hermitage and a church.

The main road offers surprisingly few Baikal views until the fishing port of **Turka**, from where there are pleasant walks to several secluded bays in either direction.

LAKE BAIKAL: KRASNOYARSK TO ULAN-UDE EASTERN BAIKAL

SELENGA DELTA

Some 300 waterways feed Lake Baikal, but none compare in size and volume to the Selenga River. One of only 80 rivers around the world to form a delta, the Selenga dumps its load of sand (and pollution from Mongolia) on Baikal's eastern shore in a huge fan of islands, reed beds and shallow channels measuring 35km across. Over 200 bird species draw spotters from all over the world; motorboat trips can be arranged through Ulan-Ude agencies. Between birdwatching sessions many bed down in the village of Posolskoe where the Western-standard **Sofiya Hotel** (☑8-914 638 9521) shares a lakeside location right beside a beautifully renovated monastery.

Bigger **Goryachinsk** (Горячинск), around 3km from the lake, is centred on a typically institutional hot-springs *kurort* (spa) with cheap cottage homestays in the surrounding village.

Further north through the uninhabited taiga lies the quaint little fishing hamlet of **Maksimikha** (Максимиха) where picturesque Baikal beaches stretch northwest. From here the blacktop bends before zipping through the forest to Ust-Barguzin.

Ust-Barguzin　　Усть - Баргузин

☑30131 / POP 7170 / TIME MOSCOW +8HR

Low-rise Ust-Barguzin has sandy streets of traditional log homes with blue-and-white carved window frames. These are most attractive towards the northern end of the main street, ul Lenina, where it reaches the Barguzin River **ferry**. From here, views are magical towards the high-ridged peaks of the Svyatoy Nos Peninsula. Other than watching the rusting car ferry being towed by a fume-belching motorboat across the fast-flowing Barguzin River, the only attraction here is the **Banya Museum** (☑30131-91 574; per Bolnichny 9; ⊙by appointment only), displaying four traditional timber *bani* lovingly fashioned by national-park ranger and guide, Alexander Beketov, who also runs a very comfortable **homestay** (☑30131-91 574; full board per person R1550, tent pitch R100) at the same address. The Beketovs provide a superb base and run tours to the Barguzin Valley and the national park. Their welcome and home-cooked meals make Ust-Barguzin a preferable base to Barguzin.

Daily *marshrutky* to Ulan-Ude (R435, five hours) run twice a day and will pick you up from your accommodation if you book ahead. In July and August a daily hydrofoil links Ust-Barguzin with Irkutsk and Khuzhir on Olkhon Island; check out VSRP (p188) for details. In February and March the ice drive across Lake Baikal to Severobaikalsk takes around five hours.

Svyatoy Nos (Holy Nose) Peninsula Полуостров Святой Нос

Rising almost vertically out of shimmering waters, dramatic Svyatoy Nos is one of Lake Baikal's most impressive features. It's within the mostly impenetrable **Zabaikalsky National Park** and joined to Ust-Barguzin by a muddy 20km sandbar that's possible but painful to drive along (there's also a toll). Guides can be hired at the **national park offices** (per Bolnichny 9) in Ust-Barguzin for all-day trek-climbs to the top of the peninsula, more than 1800m above Lake Baikal. The views from the summit are truly awe-inspiring.

Nerpa seals are particularly abundant off the peninsula's west coast around the **Ushkanny Islands,** accessible by charter boat from Ust-Barguzin. Contact Alexander Beketov at the national-park headquarters. Prices begin at around R6000.

Barguzin & the Barguzin Valley
Баргузин И Баргузинская Долина
📞 30131 / POP 5700 / TIME MOSCOW +8HR

The road north from Ust-Barguzin emerges from thick forests at Barguzin, a low-rise town of wooden cottages that dates back to 1648. Walking from the bus station you can see its handful of dilapidated historic buildings in about 20 minutes by heading along ul Krasnoarmeyskaya past the cursorily renovated old **church** to pl Lenina. Opposite the quaint little post office, the wooden-colonnaded **former Uezdnogo Bank** (ul Krasnoarmeyskaya 54) was once the grand home of Decembrist Mikhail Kyukhelbeker. Other exiles to make a home in Barguzin were Jews from Poland and European Russia who arrived here in the 1830s and 1860s. The last signs of the Jewish community can be seen in the crumbling old **cemetery** (a block northeast of the church) where crooked Hebrew-inscribed graves stand to the left and Orthodox headstones, including that of Kyukhelbeker himself, to the right.

Hidden in the village school and difficult to access, the small **museum** (📞8-924 391 3126; www.barguzinmuseum.ru; ul Kalinina 51a; admission R100) has some interesting Decembrist-related exhibits as well as the usual dusty rocks and mammoth bones.

Barguzin's real interest is as a launch pad for visiting the stunningly beautiful **Barguzin Valley** as it opens out into wide lake-dotted grassland, gloriously edged by a vast Toblerone of mountain peaks. These are most accessibly viewed across the meandering river plain from **Uro** village. Similarly inspiring panoramas continue for miles towards the idyllic village of **Suvo**, overshadowed by rock towers of the **Suvo Saxony** (Suvinskaya Saksoniya), so-called for its similarity to rock formations on the Czech–Saxony border. A few kilometres beyond Suvo the roadside **Bukhe Shulun** (Byk), a huge boulder resembling a bull's hoof, is considered to have miraculous powers. Heading north you'll pass through widely scattered, old-fashioned villages where horse carts and sleighs outnumber cars. Way up on the valley's mountainous west side, **Kurumkan** (411km northeast of Ulan-Ude) has a small but photogenic peak-backed *datsan*. The valley tapers to a point 50km north of Kurumkan at **Alla** where a tiny *kurort* (spa) can accommodate guests in the summer months.

Buy tickets ahead for Ulan-Ude–Barguzin *marshrutky* (R550, seven hours, three daily) and services to Kurumkan (R660, nine hours, two daily). From Barguzin public transport to Ust-Barguzin, Uro and Kurumkan is rare, though there's usually at least one service early morning and in the afternoon. Hitchhike or arrange a tour through the Beketovs in Ust-Barguzin.

Ulan-Ude to Vladivostok

Route Info

➜ Distance: 3648km

➜ Duration: Two days, 13½ hours

➜ Time zones: Moscow +8 to Moscow +10

Best Places to Stay & Eat

➜ Boutique Hotel (p224)

➜ Optimum Hostel (p231)

➜ Gatsby (p225)

➜ Paulaner Bräuhaus (p233)

➜ Pyongyang restaurant (p233)

Why Go?

The Trans-Siberian's last leg covers a staggering 3648km as it rolls into Russia's 'wild east'. This region has always lived by its own rules. 'Moscow is far' runs the local mantra. The people, like the countryside, are a bit wilder and more rugged than their Western brethren. Travelling this way before the Trans-Siberian was built, Anton Chekhov wrote that it 'seethes with life in a way that you can have no conception of in Europe'. And that's still apt.

Out the window, the taiga and Stalin-era housing blocks may seem similar to back west, but off the tracks lurk surprises such as Blagoveshchensk, a border town of tsar-era buildings on the Amur River; Birobidzhan, Stalin's failed 'Zion'; and the charming riverside city of Khabarovsk. The railway ends at the stunning mountains-meet-ocean setting of Vladivostok, a once-closed navy port that today is Asia's uniquely Russian rising powerhouse.

When to Go

Vladivostok

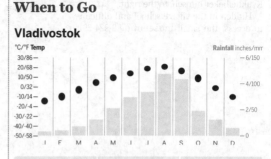

| Feb–Mar Still the season for snowy delights, yet not too dark or too slushy. | Jun Essentially midspring, with all the beauty and climatic uncertainty that entails. | Sep–Oct Better weather, more square hectares of autumn foliage than anywhere on earth. |

ℹ The Route

ULAN-UDE TO CHITA
5655km from Moscow

Trans-Mongolian trains bid farewell to the main Trans-Sib route at Zaudinsky, virtually a suburb of Ulan-Ude. The main line then follows the wide Uda Valley with bare rolling hills visible across the plains. At an unmarked station about half an hour out of Ulan-Ude (before Onokhoi), a marshalling yard serves as a steam-loco graveyard. The scenery here is pretty, as the wide, flood-prone valleys continue, their rolling meadows backed distantly by trees on the north-facing slopes.

5771km

Quaint log-cabin settlements are scattered with patches of attractive woodland. You enter Zabaikalsky Territory 20km beyond Novoilyinsky. Local time becomes Moscow time plus six hours.

5784km

Petrovsky-Zavod is the station for the mildly historic town of Petrovsk-Zabaikalsky. The station name (and the old name of the town) means 'Peter's Factory', so called for the huge ironworks you may spot from the train. Decembrists jailed here from 1830 to 1839 are commemorated in a large mural on the station building; it's worth getting off to take a snap if there's time (although the Rossiya makes only a two-minute stop here). There's also a good Decembrist Museum not far from the station, and if you're on the Decembrist trail through Siberia the town could make a good off-the-beaten-track day trip from Ulan-Ude. A few minutes out of Petrovsk-Zabaikalsky look out for a cemetery to the right of the tracks where some Decembrists are buried.

5800km to 6300km

The tracks now head northeast following the Khilok Valley, with the Yablonovy Mountains forming blue shadows in the distance.

5884km

At the small airbase town of Bada, look up from your instant noodles to admire a MiG-fighter monument.

5925km

The train slows as it leaves the valley and climbs into the mountains, affording inspiring views of the winding river and fields filled with wildflowers.

5932km

Khilok is the next major stop, and the station has some art-deco features. Some trains pause here for up to 20 minutes. There is a machine shop for repairing train engines here but little else, as the town is a product of the railway and even

has a yellow Trans-Sib train hurtling across its coat of arms.

6130km

Soon after Mogzon you will reach the highest point (1040m) on the world's longest rail journey at Yablonovaya, where trains pass through a slender gap in the rock.

6198km

Most trains loiter for 25 minutes at Chita, long enough to explore the cathedral in the station forecourt. At the station, fans of the *Long Way Round* TV show will recognise the freight platform where Ewan McGregor et al struggled to heave their bikes aboard a Tynda-bound goods wagon.

CHITA TO MOGOCHA
6198km to 6450km

For the next 250km or so east the Trans-Siberian route follows the Ingoda and Shilka Rivers. Stay awake, as it's the most scenic part of this entire route. The best views are to the south, so if heading east grab an aisle seat in *platskart* for this part of the journey. But don't ignore the north side of the train with its rolling, colourful hills. Unfortunately, the 1/2 Rossiya (and the identically timed 7/8 train) trundles this way by night, so consider other options such as train 133/134, or (when the days are long) 392 from Chita to Blagoveshchensk.

6264km

River views open up around Darasun.

6295km

You'll have 18 minutes at the platform in the industrial city of Karymskaya – enough time to quickly check out the brand-new Orthodox church on the north side of the tracks.

6312km

The picturesque village of Tarskaya is where the Trans-Manchurian peels off and heads south to the Chinese border.

6312km to 6412km

For the next 100km or so the train rumbles along the Ingoda past a series of quaint villages strewn with classic Siberian *izby* (wooden houses) adorned with colourful, intricately carved shutters. Just east of Tarskaya station, spot the weather-beaten Orthodox church on the far (south) side of the Ingoda. Come spring you'll see plenty of fishermen in the river.

6417km

East of Onon the Ingoda merges with the Onon River to become the Shilka River.

Main Trans-Siberian Route	
Trans-Mongolian & Trans-Manchurian Routes	
Alternative Routes	
Other Railway Lines	

0 — 500 km
0 — 300 miles

Ulan-Ude to Vladivostok Highlights

1 Poking around for the best views of the bays, bridges and islands of mountain-spiked **Vladivostok** (227).

2 Spinning prayer wheels around Buddhist temples at **Tsugol** (p218) and **Aginskoe** (p217)

3 Taking a sunny cruise on the Amur River before a night of clubbing in hip **Khabarovsk** (p221)

4 Strolling past exquisite tsarist-era buildings along the Amur River in **Blagoveshchensk** (p218)

6445km

Look south to see piles of train wheels east of the station in Shilka, where some trains stop. The hills are pretty, as the route follows the Shilka River, marred by the derelict factories of Kholbon (6465km).

6489km

On most trains (but not the Rossiya), the brakes squeal again at Priiskovaya, from where a 10km branch line heads north to the old silver-mining town of Nerchinsk. This is where the Treaty of Nerchinsk was signed in 1689, carving up Russian and Chinese spheres of influence in the Far East.

Around 6510km

Keep an eye out for the picturesque church in the Byankino Valley, as well as a few other buildings on the floodplain across the Shilka River.

6526km

Another renovated cube of a station meets the eye at Kuenga, after which the Trans-Sib route turns sharply north, while a 52km branch line heads to Sretensk, the eastern terminus of the Trans-Baikal Railway. Until the Amur Railway was completed in 1916, Trans-Sib passengers used to disembark from the train here to board Khabarovsk-bound steamers.

ULAN-UDE TO VLADIVOSTOK ROUTE PLANNER

Here's a suggested itinerary for finishing up the Trans-Siberian from Ulan-Ude to Vladivostok:

Day 1 Take overnight train to Chita (10 hours); take shared taxi to Aginskoe for night.

Day 2 Share taxi back to Chita; night train to Blagoveshchensk (36 hours).

Day 3 On train to Blagoveshchensk.

Day 4 Tour Blagoveshchensk and spend the night.

Day 5 Take night train 35 to Birobidzhan. Spend the morning taking in the synagogue and riverfront, and continue on later that day (by *marshrutka* or afternoon commuter train) to Khabarovsk.

Day 6 Tour Khabarovsk and spend the night.

Day 7 Take an overnight train to Vladivostok (13 hours).

Day 8 Arrive in Vladivostok.

6587km

Most train services take a lengthy breather at Chernyshevsk-Zabaikalsky, giving you time to stock up from the food and drink sellers (unless it's 3am). It's named after the 19th-century exile Nikolai Chernyshevsky, whose silver-painted statue is on the platform.

Around 6660km

There are sweeping views to the north of the train across the Siberian plains.

6906km

Some trains stop for 15 minutes at Mogocha, a railway and gold-mining town of 12,000 souls who endure one of the harshest climates on earth. Winter temperatures in this permafrost zone can plunge to a rail-splitting -62ºC.

MOGOCHA TO MAGDAGACHI

7000km to 7600km

The tracks on this stretch of the line run only about 50km north of the Amur River, the border with China. At one time, strategic sensitivity meant that carriages containing foreigners had their window blinds fastened down during this stretch – so don't complain about the monotony of the scenery!

7004km

At the station in Amazar, you have an 18-minute stop; there's a nearby graveyard of steam locomotives to see.

7079km

About two hours east of Amazar the train arrives at the border between Zabaikalsky Territory and Amurskaya Region, marking the end of Siberia and the beginning of the Russian Far East – you'll notice no difference whatsoever (geographically, most of the Far East is considered part of Siberia).

7111km

Settled in low-lying hills, Yerofey Pavlovich is named after the Siberian explorer Yerofey Pavlovich Khabarov (the remainder of his name went to the big city further down the line). The station building here must be one of the oddest on the line, with its curving steps up from the platform flanked by what look like two Lego dragons.

7273km

You'll be well into day six of your journey from Moscow by Bamovskaya, the southern terminus of the 'Little BAM', which runs north to connect with the BAM proper (the Baikal-Amur Mainline or Baikalo-Amurskaya Magistral) in Tynda. The Little BAM was built long before the BAM with slave labour in the 1930s (although much of it was dismantled in WWII and rebuilt in the 1970s). It constitutes the southern arm of the AYaM

Ulan-Ude to Vladivostok

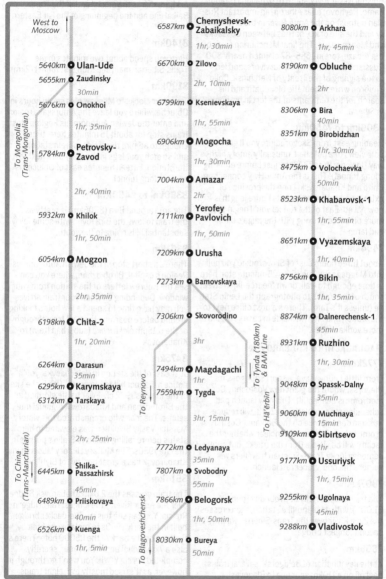

West to Moscow →

5640km ● **Ulan-Ude**
5655km ● Zaudinsky
    30min
5676km ● Onokhoi
    1hr, 35min
5784km ● **Petrovsky-Zavod**

To Mongolia (Trans-Mongolian)

    2hr, 40min
5932km ● Khilok
    1hr, 50min
6054km ● **Mogzon**
    2hr, 35min
6198km ● **Chita-2**
    1hr, 20min
6264km ● Darasun
    35min
6295km ● **Karymskaya**
6312km ● Tarskaya
    2hr, 25min

To China (Trans-Manchurian)

6445km ● **Shilka-Passazhirsk**
    45min
6489km ● Priiskovaya
    40min
6526km ● Kuenga
    1hr, 5min

6587km ● **Chernyshevsk-Zabaikalsky**
    1hr, 30min
6670km ● **Zilovo**
    2hr, 10min
6799km ● Ksenievskaya
    1hr, 55min
6906km ● **Mogocha**
    1hr, 30min
7004km ● **Amazar**
    2hr
7111km ● **Yerofey Pavlovich**
    1hr, 50min
7209km ● **Urusha**

7273km ● **Bamovskaya**

7306km ● Skovorodino

To Reynovo

    3hr
7494km ● **Magdagachi**
    1hr
7559km ● Tygda
    3hr, 15min
7772km ● Ledyanaya
    35min
7807km ● Svobodny
    55min
7866km ● **Belogorsk**
    1hr, 50min

To Blagoveshchensk

8030km ● **Bureya**
    50min

8080km ● Arkhara
    1hr, 45min
8190km ● **Obluche**
    2hr
8306km ● Bira
    40min
8351km ● Birobidzhan
    1hr, 30min
8475km ● Volochaevka
    50min
8523km ● **Khabarovsk-1**
    1hr, 55min
8651km ● **Vyazemskaya**
    1hr, 40min
8756km ● **Bikin**
    1hr, 35min
8874km ● Dalnerechensk-1
    45min
8931km ● **Ruzhino**
    1hr, 30min
9048km ● Spassk-Dalny
    35min
9060km ● Muchnaya
    15min
9109km ● Sibirtsevo
    1hr
9177km ● **Ussuriysk**
    1hr, 15min
9255km ● Ugolnaya
    45min
9288km ● **Vladivostok**

To Tynda (180km) & BAM Line

To Ha'erbin

(Amur-Yakutsk Mainline, or Amuro-Yakutskaya Magistral), which extends to Yakutsk in the Sakha Republic (although passenger services only reach Tommot).

7306km

If you plan to head north on the Little BAM, do not get off in Bamovskaya, as few Tynda-bound trains stop there. Instead, connect in Skovorodino, where an impressive Soviet steam locomotive holds court in front of a pretty pink station.

From Skovorodino, a spur line follows the Bolshoi Never River south to Dzhalinda (station name: Reynovo) near Albazin, an important Russian outpost on the Amur River in the 17th century and the site of key battles between Cossacks and Manchurians. The final Manchurian siege of the Albazin fort in 1686–87 claimed nearly 800 Russian lives, with only 66 survivors, and led to the signing of the Treaty of Nerchinsk. Colin Thubron writes about the bloodbath and his search for the remnants of the fort in his book *In Siberia*.

7306km to 7450km

Heading east from Skovorodino, you'll get periodic views of a polished, unusually empty highway (look north at 7342km, just before entering a long tunnel). This is the Amur Hwy connecting Chita and Khabarovsk. Long the province of extreme adventurers only, its entire length is now paved. East of the tunnel you'll begin to see more pine trees mixing with the taiga's birch and larch.

7494km

About three hours east of Skovorodino you pull into Magdagachi. The 15- to 25-minute stop here is time enough to walk down the tree-lined street south of the tracks to photograph the Lenin Statue (unless it's 1am). There's a post office next to the station and an ATM inside in case you need more vodka money.

MAGDAGACHI TO KHABAROVSK

7772km

From little Lednyanaya, a short spur goes to Ulegorsk, where the giant new Vostochny Cosmodrome is being built. This new launch pad, scheduled for completion in 2018, will reduce Russian dependence on the Baikanur Cosmodrome in Kazakhstan. It's unclear whether the facility will be visible from the tracks, but surely someday lucky Trans-Siberian travellers will witness the odd spacecraft launch.

7807km

The train stops briefly at Svobodny (pop 61,000), with its piano-like station, then crosses the Zeya River over the Trans-Siberian Railway's second-longest bridge.

7866km

At the key junction of Belogorsk, several trains peel off on a 110km spur line to Blagoveshchensk, the administrative capital of Amurskaya Region with a ferry service to Hēihé, China. More than 150 years after the Russians were driven out of the Amur region at Albazin, Count Nikolay Muravyov-Amursky broke the treaty of Nerchinsk and regained the Left Bank of the Amur under a treaty signed in Argun (modern-day Àihuī, China), 30km south of Hēihé.

8080km

Arkhara marks the official end of the Trans-Baikal line and the beginning of the Far Eastern Line.

8140km

Here you spend about two minutes in the Trans-Siberian main line's longest tunnel (2km).

8190km

Turn your clocks to Moscow plus seven hours in Obluche, where you leave the Amurskaya region and enter the Jewish Autonomous Region. Most trains stop for about 15 minutes here, time enough to admire the art-deco train station and stretch your legs in the leafy park next to the station. Fifteen minutes east of Obluche is another long tunnel.

8350km to 8450KM

The area around Bira (8306km) is pretty as the train follows the Bira River, with some fairly substantial hills rising to the south.

8351km

There's a short stop in the Jewish Autonomous Region's capital, Birobidzhan, where you can see the Hebrew letters of the station from your window. Depending on when your train arrives you may have time to spend a few hours looking around before boarding the next train through or the 6.15pm *elektrichka* (suburban train) to Khabarovsk.

8475km

Just east of the station in Volochaevka, you'll notice a distinct hill to the north. This is the site of the famous 1922 civil-war battle glorified in the Birobidzhan and Khabarovsk regional museums. The man who orchestrated this victory, Marshal Vasily Blyukher, was elevated to hero status before falling victim to Stalin's purges in the late 1930s. The Military History Museum in Khabarovsk has a great portrait of Blyukher.

8514km

The train crosses the 2.6km Khabarovsk Bridge over the Amur River – the longest rail bridge in Russia. You can see this double-decker bridge, built in the early 1990s to replace one built by the tsar, on the back of the R5000 note. There's also a 7km tunnel under the Amur, secretly completed during WWII. You won't go through it, however, as it's used mostly by freight trains.

8523km

If you're not overnighting in pleasant Khabarovsk, you have a 30-minute stop on most trains – enough time to admire the Khabarov statue out front and the train station, which resembles the old *duma* (parliament) building on central ul Muravyova-Amurskogo. You can also switch for a train to connect with the BAM at Komsomolsk-na-Amure.

8523km to 9200km

All trains from Khabarovsk to Vladivostok depart during the evening, leaving you mostly in the dark for the final 13 hours of your Trans-Siberian odyssey. One reason for the cover of darkness is that the line, in places, comes within 10km of the sensitive Chinese border.

8606km

Here you cross the Khor River, which flows into the Ussuri River on the border of China. The train shadows the Ussuri all the way to Lesozavodsk (8938km).

8651km

Most trains stop for 15 minutes at Vyazemskaya, where there will be plenty of people selling bread, salmon caviar, dried fish and pickles. From here the forests are dominated by deciduous trees, such as maple and elm, which briefly blaze in a riot of autumn colours during September.

8756km

You'll probably be settling down for some sleep by the time the train makes a brief stop in Bikin. The line crosses the Bikin River here and follows it south to the border between Khabarovsky and Primorsky Territories (8780km). The southern forests of the 165,900-sq-km Primorsky Territory are the world's most northerly monsoon forests and home to black and brown bears, the rare Amur (Siberian) tiger and the virtually extinct Amur leopard.

8931km

There's a 15-minute stop in the dead of night at Ruzhino.

9010km to 9080km

About 30km either side of Spassk-Dalny (9048km), you may be able to make out Lake Khanka, a 4000-sq-km, lotus-covered lake that straddles the China–Russia border.

9177km

At Ussuriysk, you can contemplate changing to the branch line west to Hā'ěrbīn (Harbin) in China; the train goes only twice a week and is monotonously slow. Ussuriysk, formerly named Nikolskoe in honour of the tsarevich's 1891 visit, and home to a smattering of historic buildings, was once of greater size and importance than nearby Vladivostok.

9249km

After a week of travel from Moscow, you finally meet the Pacific Ocean – in the form of the Amursky Gulf – just south of the town of Prokhlodnaya. It should be dawn by now as the train travels south along the hilly peninsula that forms the eastern side of Amursky Gulf, passing a series of beach towns such as Okeanskaya (9266km), Sanatornaya (9269km) and Sedanka (9271km). Further south, Vladivostok rises in a series of concrete tower blocks on the hillsides.

9288km

Your epic journey ends (or begins) on the platform at the station in Vladivostok. Before leaving, take a moment to admire the old locomotive on the platform beside the monument commemorating the completion of the great railroad you've just travelled along.

Chita   Чита

☑ 3022 / POP 324,000 / TIME MOSCOW +9HR

Of all Eastern Siberia's major cities, Chita is the least prepared for visitors. Literally put on the map by the noble-blooded Decembrists, one of whom designed its street-grid layout, today there's nothing aristocratic about this regional capital where Soviet symbols still embellish Stalinist facades, shaven-headed conscripts guard pillared military headquarters and Chinese cross-border peddlers lug monster bales past a well-tended Lenin statue. Non-Chinese foreigners are still a rarity here, tourism being a thing that happens elsewhere.

Echoes of the Decembrist chapter in Chita's history make the city just worth visiting, and a number of attractive old timber merchants' houses grace its arrow-straight streets. It's also the jumping-off point for two of Russia's best Buddhist temples at Aginskoe and Tsugol.

History

Founded in 1653, Chita developed as a rough-and-tumble silver-mining centre until it was force-fed a dose of urban culture in 1827 by the arrival of more than 80 exiled Decembrist gentlemen-rebels – or more precisely, by the arrival of their wives and lovers who followed, setting up homes on what became known as ul Damskaya (Women's St). That's now the southern end of ul Stolyarova, where sadly only a handful of rotting wooden cottages remains amid soulless concrete apartment towers.

As gateway to the new East Chinese Railway, Chita boomed in the early 20th century, despite flirting with socialism. Following the excitement of 1905, socialists set up a 'Chita Republic' which was brutally crushed within

Chita

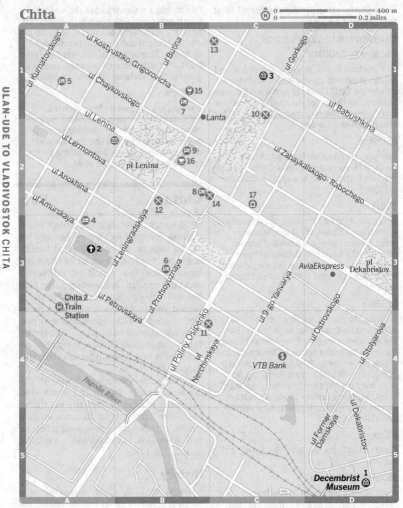

a year. After the 'real' revolutions of 1917, history gets even more exciting and complex. Bolsheviks took over, then lost control to Japanese forces who possibly intercepted part of Admiral Kolchak's famous 'gold train' before retreating east. By 1920 Chita was the capital of the short-lived Far Eastern Republic, a nominally independent, pro-Lenin buffer state whose parliament stood at ul Anokhina 63. The republic was absorbed into Soviet Russia in December 1922 once the Japanese had withdrawn from Russia's east coast. Closed and secretive for much of the Soviet era, today Chita is still very much a military city and once again flooded with Chinese traders.

◎ Sights

★ Decembrist Museum
MUSEUM
(Музей Декабристов; ul Selenginskaya; admission R130; ◎10am-6pm Tue-Sun) If you're on the Decembrist trail through Siberia, this small but comprehensive museum is one of the best, though there's not a word of English anywhere. It's housed in the 18th-century Archangel Michael log church, an unexpected sight amid the neighbourhood's shambolic apartment blocks. Inextricably

Chita

linked to the Decembrist story, this was where they came to pray, where Annenkov married his French mistress Pauline and where the Volkonskys buried their daughter Sofia.

The ground-level exhibition begins with the names of all the Decembrists picked out in gold on a green background, followed by interesting items such as the original imperial order sentencing the noble rebels to banishment in Siberia and oils showing their leaders' executions.

The 2nd floor looks at the wives who followed their menfolk into the Nerchinsk silver mines and the fates of all the Decembrists once they were allowed to settle where they pleased.

At the time of research the museum building was under threat of confiscation by the Russian Orthodox Church.

Kuznetzov Regional Museum   MUSEUM
(Краеведческий музей имени А.К. Кузнецова; ☑3022-260 315; ul Babushkina 113; admission R140; ⊙10am-5.45pm Tue-Sun) The unexpectedly lively Kuznetzov Regional Museum is housed in an early-20th-century mansion. Here you'll find some pretty in-

teresting local exhibits, including a very thorough examination of the heritage and architectural renaissance of the city and region. There's a decent cafe on the premises.

Datsan   BUDDHIST TEMPLE
(ul Bogomyagkova; ⊙24hr) Chita's main Buddhist temple lies just outside the centre, a 15-minute walk or R150 taxi ride along Bogomyagkova from where it meets ul Babushkina. It's a recently built affair, but well kept and with all its prayer wheels, butter lamps and yin-yang drums firmly in place. The tranquil grounds are home to a tiny *buuzy* joint.

Cathedral   CHURCH
(Кафедральный собор; train station forecourt) The train station reflected in its gilt onion domes, Chita's bright turquoise cathedral is the city's most impressive building, though inside it's lamentably plain. The original pre-Stalin cathedral stood on the main square, right on the spot where Lenin now fingers his lapels.

🛏 Sleeping

Chita has little budget accommodation and homestays are nonexistent. Hotels are often full, meaning many travellers who fail to book ahead often have no choice but to check into top-end hotels.

Hotel Arkadia   HOTEL $$
(Гостиница Аркадия; ☑3022-352 636; www.arkadiyachita.ru; ul Lenina 120; s R1800-2800, tw R2500-3800; 🛜) Chita's best deal has well-kept rooms, clean bathrooms, on-line booking, efficient staff and no-fuss visa registration. Often offers very good rates on popular booking websites.

Hotel Zabaikale   HOTEL $$
(Гостиница Забайкалье; ☑3022-359 819; www.zabhotel.ru; ul Leningradskaya 36; s from R2500, tw from R3200; 🛜) Unbeatably located overlooking the main square, the cheaper renovated rooms at this huge complex are a fairly good deal. The hotel has a huge range of facilities including an air and rail ticket office, a spa, a children's playroom and a gym.

Grand City Hotel   HOTEL $$
(☑3022-212 233; www.hotel-grandcity.ru; ul Amurskaya 96a; dm/s/tw from R800/1900/2400; 🛜) Chita's newest hotel is situated right opposite the railway station making it a convenient place to zip open the rucksack if arriving by train. That's just about where

THE DECEMBRIST WOMEN

Having patently failed to topple tsarist autocracy in December 1825, many prominent 'Decembrist' gentlemen revolutionaries were exiled to Siberia. They're popularly credited with bringing civilisation to the rough-edged local pioneer-convict population. Yet the real heroes were their womenfolk, who cobbled together the vast sleigh/carriage fares to get themselves to Siberia.

And that was just the start. Pauline Annenkova, the French mistress of one aristocratic prisoner, spent so long awaiting permission to see her lover in Chita that she had time to set up a fashionable dressmakers' shop in Irkutsk. By constantly surveying the prisoners' conditions, the women eventually shamed guards into reducing the brutality of the jail regimes, while their food parcels meant that Decembrists had more hope of surviving the minimal rations of their imprisonment. The Decembrist women came to form a core of civil society and introduced 'European standards of behaviour'. As conditions eventually eased, this formed the basis for a liberal Siberian aristocracy, especially in Chita and Irkutsk where some Decembrists stayed on even after their formal banishment came to an end.

the positives end as except for the two-level *lyux* rooms with corner window views of the cathedral, the 64 bedrooms are spartan and cheaply furnished. Breakfast and diabolical service included.

Hotel Vizit
HOTEL $$$

(Гостиница Визит; ☏ 3022-356 945; www.chita-hotelvizit.ru; ul Lenina 93; s/tw R3400/6400; ❄️ 🛜) Occupying the 5th floor of an ultramodern smoked-glass tower at the busy intersection of ul Lenina and ul Profsoyuznaya, this is Chita's best luxury offering with relaxing en suite rooms, English-speaking receptionists and sparkling bathrooms. Some doubles have baths and the air-con provides relief from Chita's superheated summers.

Hotel Montblanc
HOTEL $$$

(☏ 3022-357 272; www.eldonet.ru; ul Kostyushko-Grigorovicha 5; s R3450-4000, tw R4250-4800; ❄️ 🛜) A block away from the main square, this purpose-built business hotel has immaculately snazzy rooms, though at these prices the plumbing could be a touch more professional. The buffet breakfast is served in the Ukraine-themed restaurant and check-out time at reception provides an opportunity to witness just how badly Russian and Chinese businessmen can behave.

Hotel Dauria
HOTEL $$$

(Гостиница Даурия; ☏ 3022-262 350; ul Profsoyuznaya 17; s from R2000, d from R4000; 🛜) Renovated over a decade ago, the ageing but still comfortable rooms here are a last resort. That said, it is possibly Chita's most charcterful choice, housed in a historical

building. A poor breakfast is included. Reservations are essential.

🍴 Eating & Drinking

Eating out isn't high on the list of things to enjoy in Chita, but despite the lack of choice and unimaginative menus, you won't go hungry.

Mama Roma
ITALIAN $

(www.mamaroma.ru; ul Lermontova 9; pizzas R195-350, other mains around R300; ⏱11am-10pm) Chequered tablecloths, glass divides, an English menu (!) and pleasant staff make this pizzeria an unexpectedly welcoming experience near the train station, probably as it's part of a chain.

Privoz
CANTEEN $

(Привозъ; ul Lenina 93; canteen mains R20-80; ⏱10am-midnight Sun-Wed, to 1am Thu-Sat) Nautically themed self-service canteen plating up Eurasian staples for prices so low they'll shiver your timbers. There's a fancier restaurant upstairs and look out for the country's first 'monument to the New Russian' in front of the building.

Poznaya Altargana
BURYAT $

(Позная Алтаргана; ul Leningradskaya 5; pozi R35; ⏱10am-10pm) If *pozi* are your thing, pink-and-flowery Poznaya Altargana is your place, but the tasty *plov* and meatballs are an equally filling alternative. There's a larger branch at ul Babushkina 121.

Khmelnaya Korchma
UKRAINIAN $$

(Хмельная корчма; ☏ 3022-352 134; ul Amur-skaya 69; mains R150-400; ⏱noon-midnight

Mon-Thu & Sun, noon-3am Fri & Sat; ⊛) Plastic sunflowers, dangling onion strings, folksy embroidered tea towels and a menu of borsch, *salo* (pork fat), *vareniki* (sweet dumplings) and *holubtsi* (cabbage rolls stuffed with rice) teleport you to rural Ukraine. Live music, liberal helpings and a low-priced lunch menu (R150) possibly make this Chita's best option.

Kafe Traktyr　　　　　RUSSIAN **$$**
(Кафе Трактир; ☑ 3022-352 229; ul Chkalova 93; mains R230-500; ⊙noon-2am) Russian home-style cooking is served at heavy wooden tables in this rebuilt wooden-lace cottage, with a quietly upmarket Siberian-retro atmosphere. The summer beer-and-shashlyk tent is a popular drinking spot.

Harat's Pub　　　　　PUB
(ul Leningradskaya 15a; ⊙noon-2am) Savour the slightly surreal experience of sipping a pint of Newcastle Brown in an Irish pub in Chita, while pondering just where the owners got all those Celtic flags, old US number plates and imitation Tiffany lamps. Friendly service.

Shokoladnitsa　　　　　CAFE
(ul Leningradskaya 36; ⊙9am-midnight; 🛜) This Europeanly stylish peaceful oasis of a cafe is good for people-watching from the big windows while sipping a beer or coffee and making full use of the free wi-fi.

🛍 Shopping

Zabaikalsky Khudozhestvenny Salon　　　　　SOUVENIRS
(Забайкальский художественный салон; ul Lenina 56; ⊙10am-7pm Mon-Fri, to 6pm Sat, 11am-6pm Sun) This huge shop stocks every perceivable souvenir from across the entire Russian Federation, from Buryat dolls to Kostroma linen, Dzhgel plates to Chita fridge magnets. Local artists' work and the owner's photography also available.

❶ Information

Lanta (Ланта; ☑ 3022-353 639; www.lanta-chita.ru; ul Leningradskaya 56; ⊙9am-7pm Mon-Fri) Runs limited tours of Chita and Zabaikalsky Region. No English spoken.

Main Post Office (ul Butina 37; ⊙8am-10pm Mon-Fri, 9am-6pm Sat & Sun) Quaintly spired wooden building on pl Lenina.

VTB Bank (ВТБ Банк; ul Amurskaya 41; ⊙9am-6pm Mon-Fri) Has ATMs and currency exchange window.

❶ Getting There & Away

TRAIN
Chita has the following rail connections:
Běijīng *kupe* R7000; two days, five hours; weekly
Blagoveshchensk *platskart/kupe* R2600/3700; one day, 14 hours; two daily
Khabarovsk *platskart/kupe* R3600/6700; one day, 15½ to 17½ hours; up to three daily
Tynda *platskart/kupe* R2300/3300; 27 hours; every other day
Ulan-Ude *platskart/kupe* R1300/2400; 10 hours to 12 hours; up to six daily
Zabaikalsk *platskart/kupe* R1100/1500; 12 hours; daily

AIR
Kadala Airport (www.aerochita.ru) is 15km west of central Chita. Take bus 40 or *marshrutka* 12 or 14. **AviaEkspress** (АвиаЭкспресс; ☑ 3022-450 505; www.aviaexpress.ru; ul Lenina 55; ⊙8am-10pm) sells tickets for all flights, including the twice daily service to Moscow (R12,500).

BUS
The only two services you're likely to need are the *marshrutky* to Aginskoe (R300, two hours, hourly) and the long-distance minivans to Ulan-Ude (R800, seven hours). Both leave from a stop on the train-station forecourt.

Around Chita

Aginskoe　　　　　Агинское
☑ 30239 / POP 16,700 / TIME MOSCOW +9HR
For an intriguing day trip from Chita, take a *marshrutka* (R300, two hours, hourly) to the spruced-up Buryat town of Aginskoe. Scenery en route transforms from patchily forested hills via river valleys into rolling grassy steppe.

Once in Aginskoe, hop straight into a taxi (R100) to visit the beautiful old Buddhist **datsan** (6km west of the centre), a large complex of brightly decorated temples and monastery faculties. Back on the central square, the admirably well-curated **Tsybikov Museum** (ul Komsomolskaya 11; admission R100; ⊙10am-1pm & 2-5.30pm Mon-Fri) takes an in-depth look at the local Buryat culture. Opposite stands the custard-yellow 1905 **St Nicholas Church** whose reconstruction was bankrolled by former Moscow mayor Yury Luzhkov.

For food, try the greasy spoons around the market where there's also a supermarket and an ATM.

WORTH A TRIP

NERCHINSK НЕРЧИНСК

Anyone with a knowledge of Russian history will be familiar with the name Nerchinsk. The 1689 Treaty of Nerchinsk recognising Russia's claims to the trans-Baikal region was signed here and 130 years later the Decembrists were sent to work the silver mines around the village. Once one of Eastern Siberia's foremost towns but inexplicably by-passed by the Trans-Siberian Railway just 10km to the south, Nerchinsk leads a forgotten existence with just a few fading reminders of its rich past. If you're looking to break up the long 2200km trip from Chita to Blagoveshchensk, hop off here. Most don't.

The only visitable attraction is the **Butin Palace Museum** (ul Sovetskaya 83; admission R100; ⊙ 10am-1pm & 2-5.30pm Tue-Sat). Mikhail Butin, the local silver baron, built himself this impressive crenellated palace, furnished with what were then claimed to be the world's largest mirrors. He'd bought the mirrors at the 1878 World Fair in Paris and miraculously managed to ship them unscathed all the way to Nerchinsk via the China Sea and up the Amur River. These four mammoth mirrors form the centrepiece of the collection, along with a delightful pair of hobbit-style chairs crafted from polished tangles of birch roots. Three-quarters of the palace, including the grand, triple-arched gateway (demolished in 1970), still stands in ruins.

A block from the museum, the active 1825 **Voskresensky Cathedral** (ul Pogodaeva 85) looks like an opera house from the outside; its interior is plain and whitewashed. Head around the sports pitch with its little silver Lenin to the imposing though now crumbling 1840 **Trading Arches**, desperately in need of renovation. Nearby is a fine colonnaded pharmacy and the very grand facade of the pink former **Kolobovnikov Store** (ul Shilova 3), now a barnlike Torgovy Tsentr filled with some desultory stalls and kiosks.

About 1km south of the museum, just before the post office and bank, a little pink column-fronted building was once the **Dauriya Hotel** (ul Sovetskaya 32). As locals will proudly tell you, Chekhov stayed here in June 1890. Diagonally across the same junction a minuscule bus station is the departure point for services to Priiskovaya.

To reach Nerchinsk, take any train from Chita to Priiskovaya (*platskart/kupe* R900/1200, six hours) on the trans-Siberian main line, 10km from Nerchinsk. Change there onto local *marshrutky*.

Tsugol Цугол

Set just 2km from the 'holy' Onon River, Tsugol village is not particularly pretty but the perfectly proportioned **Tsugol Datsan** is surely the most memorable Buddhist temple in Russia. Built in 1820, it is just four years younger than Aginskoe Datsan and even more photogenic, with gilded Mongolian script-panels, wooden upper facades and tip-tilted roofs on each of its three storeys. The interior is less colourful than the Ivolginsk temple, but clinging to the front is a unique, colourfully painted, wrought-iron staircase.

Getting to/from Tsugol is a pain – it lies 13km from Olovyannaya, reachable by a single morning bus from Chita. From Olovyannaya take a taxi (at least R500, more if asked to wait) or hike along the river. On the return journey, you could ask around in Olovyannaya for an unofficial *marshrutka* back to Chita (or Aginskoe) – otherwise it's a long, lonely wait for the overnight train (it leaves at 2am so this may be an opportunity to test your hitchhiking skills). Alternatively, ask around at hotels in Chita for excursions to Tsugol.

Blagoveshchensk
Благовещенск

☑ 4162 / POP 210,000 / TIME MOSCOW +9HR

It's sometimes easy to forget where you are out here – in deepest Asia – until you find a place like this modest border town, 110km south of the Trans-Siberian and across the Amur River from China. The mix of scattered tsarist-era buildings and Chinese tourists walking past Lenin statues is fascinating. On hot days, locals share the river, jumping in from beaches on opposite shores.

☉ Sights & Activities

A good starting point for a wander around is on the riverfront at pl Lenina, where teen skaters take over the Lenin statue steps and tots take over the fountains. From here a short walk west along the pleasant riverside promenade, or along parallel ul Lenina, takes you to yawning pl Pobedy.

Tsarist-Era Buildings   HISTORIC BUILDING

At the regional museum, pick up the darling *Stary Blagoveshchensk* (Old Blagoveshchensk) map (R10, in Russian) to plot your own walking tour of the dozens of glorious tsarist-era buildings on shady backstreets around the centre. The most impressive buildings are on ul Lenina within a few blocks of the museum and on and around nearby pl Pobedy. Anton Chekhov came through Blagoveshchensk during his epic trip through the Far East in 1890 (and headed straight to a Japanese prostitute, as recounted luridly in his later-published letters). A bust commemorating Chekhov's visit is on the facade of the lovely Institute of Geology and Wildlife Management building on pl Pobedy.

Amur Regional Museum   MUSEUM

(Амурский областной краеведческий музей; ul Lenina 165; admission R120; ☉10am-6pm Tue-Thu, to 9pm Fri, 11am-7pm Sat & Sun) A short walk northwest of pl Pobedy, this museum is housed in a former tsarist-era trading house and Soviet-era HQ for the Communist Youth League (Komsomol). Inside are 26 halls, with plenty of interesting photos, 1940s record players and a meteor that fell in 1991 near Tynda. Russian-history buffs will enjoy the model of the 17th-century Cossack fortress in nearby Albazin and a painting depicting the Manchurian invasion of the fort in 1685. This battle swung control of the upper Amur to the Chinese for the next two centuries.

River Cruises   BOAT TRIPS

(per person R150) One-hour daytime and evening river cruises leave from a pier at the east end of ul Amurskaya from mid-May through September.

🛏 Sleeping & Eating

Green Hostel   HOSTEL $

(☑8-924-841 9008; ul Ostrovskaya 65; dm R500-700; 🛜) This basic not terribly friendly place has three dorm rooms with lino floors and a shared kitchen. Hard to find, the hostel is near the corner of ul Ostrovskaya, one block east of the bus station.

Hotel Armeniya   HOTEL $$

(☑4162-230 799; www.armeniablag.ru; ul Krasnoflotskaya 147; s/d incl breakfast from R2900/3800; ✳🛜) In an ideal location on the riverfront walkway, Armeniya has modern carpeted rooms done up in earthy hues, with flatscreen TVs and flashy, capsule like showers. The best rooms have river views. There are several restaurants on-site, including a patio pizza spot and an overdecorated dining room serving Armenian fare.

Yubileynaya   HOTEL $$

(Гостиница Юбилейная ☑4162-370 073; www.blghotel.ru; ul Lenina 108; s/d from R1800/2600; ✳@🛜) This 150-room beast overlooking the river won't win any beauty contests, but the location near pl Lenina is ideal. Rooms are simple spruced-up Soviet fare, while the international restaurant (mains R200 to R500), festooned with old beer posters, is more 21st century.

Zeya Hotel   HOTEL $$

(Гостиница Зея; ☑4162-539 996; www.hotelzeya.ru; ul Kalinina 8; s/d from R2040/2520; ✳@🛜) Zeya makes a valiant attempt to make Soviet rooms look cheery, but goes a bit over the top with the extra-frilly curtains and bedspreads. Twelve-hour rates available. It's near the river just west of pl Pobedy.

Mega   INTERNATIONAL $

(Торгово-развлекательный центр Мега; ul 50 Let Oktyabrya; mains R120-350; 🛜) Across from the bus station, Mega has a top-floor food court (with free wi-fi).

Kofinya na Bolshoi   CAFE $$

(Кофейня на Большой; ul Lenina 159; mains R350-700; ☉8am-1am; 🛜) Pleasant cafe with decent cappuccinos and a wide range of fare including eggs and bliny for breakfast, and risotto and pizzas later on. In the same building is a sprawling multilevel eatery and pub serving microbrews and traditional Russian fare.

SharLot Cafe   EUROPEAN $$

(ul Lenina 113; mains R250-600; ☉9am-midnight; 🛜) One of the best options in the centre for a meal, SharLot has tasty salads, grilled fish and meat dishes, risottos and other eclectic fare. Abstract artwork, young hip waitstaff and groovy tunes draw a stylish crowd.

❶ Getting There & Around

Blagoveshchensk is 110km off the Trans-Siberian, reached via the branch line from Belogorsk. The train station is 4km north of the river on ul 50 Let Oktyabrya, the main north–south artery. Take bus 30 (unless it's heading to 'mikro-rayon') to reach the centre.

Trains heading east backtrack to Belogorsk on their way to Khabarovsk (*kupe/platskart* from R4000/2400, 13 hours, daily). Heading west, trains serve Chita (*kupe/platskart* R5200/2700; one day, 13 hours; odd-numbered days) and Tynda (*kupe/platskart* R4700/2600, 16¼ hours, odd-numbered days).

Additional options are available from Belogorsk to the north or Bureya to the east. *Marshrutky* (fixed-route minibuses) connect Blagoveshchensk's **bus station** (cnr ul 50 let Oktyabrya & ul Krasnoarmeyska) with the train stations in Belogorsk (R340, two hours, at least hourly from 7.15am to 7.20pm) and Bureya (R572, 3½ hours, three daily). Don't miss the awesome mosaic of Soviet *sportsmeny* (athletes) opposite the bus station.

The **River Terminal** (Речной вокзал; ul Chaykovskogo 1), 500m east of the Druzhba Hotel, sends eight daily boats to Hēihé, China (one-way/return R1125/1550, 15 minutes), where there's an evening train to Harbin. You'll need a Chinese visa and a multiple-entry Russian visa to return.

Birobidzhan Биробиджан

☑ 42622 / POP 80,000 / TIME MOSCOW +10HR

Quiet and shady, Birobidzhan is the capital of the 36,000-sq-km Jewish Autonomous Region and is a couple of hours shy of Khabarovsk on the Trans-Siberian line (if you're heading east). Its concept has always been a bit more interesting than its reality (as evidenced by the quick influx of Jews coming to 'Stalin's Zion' in the 1930s, then leaving the undeveloped swamp just as quickly). Still, its sleepy provincial feel and riverside setting make it worth a half-day visit – more if the weather's good or if you want to explore the city's Jewish heritage.

The town is quite walkable. The main streets ul Lenina and partially pedestrian ul Sholom-Aleykhema parallel the tracks just a five-minute walk south on ul Gorkogo from the train station. The Bira River is another five minutes along, where you'll find a pleasant sculpture-lined walkway with piped-in music and peaceful views.

History

The Soviet authorities conceived the idea of a homeland for Jews in the Amur region in the late 1920s and founded the Jewish Autonomous Region in 1934 with its capital at Birobidzhan (named for the meeting place of the Bira and Bidzhan Rivers). Most of the Jews came from Belarus and Ukraine, but also from the US, Argentina and even Palestine. The Jewish population never rose above 32,000, and dropped to 17,500 by the end of the 1930s, when growing anti-Semitism led to the ban of Yiddish and synagogues. The Jewish population rose gradually to about 22,000 by 1991, when Russia's Jews began emigrating en masse to Israel. The Jewish population has now levelled off at 3000 to 4000.

◉ Sights & Activities

Jewish Birobidzhan CULTURAL HERITAGE
A few vestiges of Birobidzhan's Jewish heritage remain. Note the Hebrew signs on the **train station**, the lively **farmers market** (ul Sholom-Aleykhema) and the **post office** on the riverfront at the southern terminus of ul Gorkogo. On the square in front of the train station a **statue** commemorates Birobidzhan's original Jewish settlers, and on the pedestrian stretch of ul Sholom-Aleykhema is a quirky **statue of Sholem Aleichem** (Памятник Шолом-Алейхему); *Fiddler on the Roof* was based on Aleichem's stories.

Regional Museum MUSEUM
(Областной краеведческий музей; ul Lenina 25; admission R100; ⊙10am-6pm Wed-Fri, 9am-5pm Sat) Next door to Freid, this museum has an excellent exhibit on the arrival of Jewish settlers to Birobidzhan in the 1930s, plus boars and bears and a minidiorama of the Volochaevka civil war battle.

🛏 Sleeping & Eating

Resting Rooms HOSTEL **$**
(Комнаты отдыха; ☑42622-91 605; Train Station; dm per 12-/24-hr from R550/1100, lyux R2000) The simple train-station rooms are probably the best option for a quick visit. It's an easy walk from the centre.

Hotel Vostok HOTEL **$$**
(Гостиница Восток; ☑42622-65 330; ul Sholom-Aleykhema 1; s/d R2500/3300; ❋ 🛜) Birobidzhan's central hotel has bright rooms (but saggy beds) in a good location on a pedestrianised street near the market.

✕ Eating & Drinking

Felicita   CAFE **$$**
(ul Gorkogo 10; mains R250-780; ⊘10am-midnight;
☎) A short stroll from the train station, Fe-
licita is attractive, Italian-themed cafe,
with coffee, salads, light meals and rather
mediocre pizzas.

Teatralny   SHASHLYK **$**
(Театральный; pr 60 let SSSR 14; mains
R200-300; ✵) An average indoor Chinese
restaurant in winter, in the warm months
its outdoor patio near the river is *the* place
to eat shashlyk (meat kebabs) and guzzle
draught beer. It's behind Birobidzhan's gar-
gantuan Philharmonic Hall.

David Trade Centre   RUSSIAN **$$**
(Торговый центр Давид; cnr pr 60 let SSSR
& ul Gorkogo; mains R250-750; ☎) Inside this
small shopping gallery, you'll find a street-
side patio for kebabs and casual dining, plus
fast-food stalls inside. It's located diagonally
across from the Philharmonic.

ℹ Information

Sign up for free internet access at the **library** (ul
Lenina 25; ⊘9am-7pm Mon-Thu, to 6pm Fri &
Sat), next door to the museum (but no wi-fi).

ℹ Getting There & Away

Coming from the west on the Trans-Siberian, you
can easily stop off, have a look and grab a late
train or bus for Khabarovsk.

All Trans-Siberian trains stop here, but if
you're heading to Khabarovsk, it's cheaper on
the *elektrichka* (suburban train; R315, three
hours, three daily); a *platskartny* seat on other
trains starts at R530.

You can also catch *marshrutky* to Khabarovsk
(R280, three hours, hourly until 6pm) from
beside the train station.

Khabarovsk   Хабаровск

📞 4212 / POP 590,000 / TIME MOSCOW +10HR

The Far East's most pleasant surprise – and
a welcome break after days of relentless
taiga on the train – Khabarovsk boasts a
dreamy riverside setting, vibrant nightlife
and broad boulevards lined with pretty
tsarist-era buildings. Unlike so many places,
the city has developed its riverside in the
public interest. It has a great strolling area
with multicoloured tiles, parks, monuments
and walkways. A one-day stop is easily filled
looking around.

It's hot in summer, but winter temperatures give it the unglamorous title of 'world's
coldest city of over half a million people'.
A dazzling display of ice sculptures occupy central pl Lenina from January until
the spring thaw. Khabarovsk's City Day is a
good time to visit – it's 31 May, or the closest
Saturday.

History

Khabarovsk was founded in 1858 as a military post by Eastern Siberia's governor-
general, Count Nikolay Muravyov (later
Muravyov-Amursky), during his campaign
to take the Amur back from the Manchus. It
was named after the man who got the Russians into trouble with the Manchus in the
first place, 17th-century Russian explorer Yerofey Khabarov.

The Trans-Siberian Railway arrived from
Vladivostok in 1897. During the Russian Civil War (1920), the town was occupied by Japanese troops. The final Bolshevik victory in
the Far East was at Volochaevka, 45km west.

In 1969, Soviet and Chinese soldiers
fought a bloody hand-to-hand battle over
little Damansky Island in the Ussuri River.
Since 1984, tensions have eased. Damansky
and several other islands have been handed
back to the Chinese.

◉ Sights & Activities

Walking is the main activity in Khabarovsk.
Three good spots are the riverfront, Dina-
mo Park and ul Muravyova-Amurskogo
with its impressive turn-of-the-20th-centu-
ry architecture. Some buildings to look out
for on the latter are the striking red-and-
black-brick Far Eastern State Research
Library (Дальневосточная государственная
научная библиотека; ul Muravyova-Amurskogo
1), built from 1900 to 1902; the mint-green
Style Moderne (Russian take on art nouveau) Tsentralny Gastronom (ul Muravyova-Amurskogo 9), built in 1895 and topped by
a statue of Mercury; and the former House
of Pioneers (Дом пионеров; ul Muravyova-Amurskogo 17).

Khabarovsk Territorial Museum   MUSEUM
(ul Shevchenko 11; admission R350; ⊘10am-6pm,
closed Mon & last Fri of month) Located in an
evocative 1894 red-brick building, this museum contains an excellent overview of Russian and Soviet history. Galleries take you
decade by decade through the past with fascinating propaganda posters, old film clips,

Khabarovsk

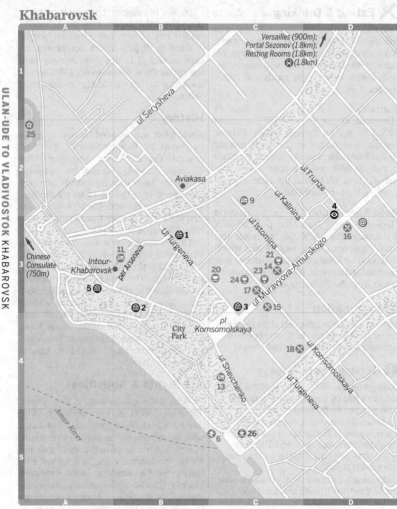

audio snippets, black and white photos (like the sad crowds gathered at the announcement of Stalin's demise) and rooms with period furnishings and accoutrements that give a taste of what life was like.

There's even a small section devoted to the Gulag (fitting, since the nearby prison population was bigger than the city's in the '30s). Another section has garments, sleds and carvings of native peoples. The less intriguing new building has a wing dedicated to the Amur River, with live fish in tanks and more stuffed animals.

Archaeology Museum MUSEUM
(Музей Археологии; ☎ 4212-24 177; ul Turgeneva 86; admission R220; ☉ 10am-6pm Tue-Sun) This small five-room gallery displays tools and living essentials from early peoples. Pottery, animal skin huts, dugout canoes, a tiny model settlement and many early hand tools are here. Don't miss replicas of small 'Paleolithic Madonnas', early carvings (in mammoth tusks) of the female form.

There's also an atmospheric log-lined hut on the main floor, with furs, dried fish, a wolf's head and stuffed birds. In front of the museum, check out the reproductions of the

petroglyphs found at the ancient Sikachi-Alyan site.

Far Eastern Art Museum ART GALLERY

(Дальневосточный художественный музей; ul Shevchenko 7; admission R200; ⊙ 10am-6pm Tue-Sun) Lots of religious icons, Japanese porcelain and 19th-century Russian paintings are on display here.

☞ Tours

The most popular area tour offered by travel agents is to the interesting Nanai village of **Sikachi-Alyan**, where you can view the

Sikachi-Alyan petroglyphs – stone carvings supposedly dating back 12,000 years. Hunting and fishing opportunities abound in the wild and woolly Khabarovsky *kray* (territory).

Amur River Cruise BOAT TRIPS

(River boat landing; admission from R450) Vital to Khabarovsk's rise, the Amur River can be seen on (at times rollicking) party boats. Cruises on the *Moskva-81* depart every two hours from 12.30pm to 12.30am, provided enough customers show up.

Portal Sezonov TOURS

(Портал Сезонов; ☑ 4212-398 288; www.dvtravel.ru; ul Leningradskaya 58) Located in the train station, the respected Portal Sezonov runs a wide range of tours, including hiking and fishing trips, as well as city tours. English-speaking guides available.

Sergey Outfitter TOURS

(Туристическая компания "Вэлком"; ☑ 4212-735 990; www.sergoutfitter.com; ul Dzerzhinskogo 24; ⊙ 9am-7pm Mon-Sat) Burly Sergey Khromykh is your man if you are looking to do some hunting or fishing in the vast wilderness of Khabarovsk Territory or elsewhere in the Far East.

🛏 Sleeping

Resting Rooms HOSTEL $

(Комнаты отдыха; ☑ 4212-383 710; train station 3rd fl; 4-bed dm 12/24hr R800/1200, s 12/24hr R1100/1600; 🛜) The train station's nice resting rooms are a fine option if you're just passing through. Free wi-fi in 15-minute increments.

Kakadu Hostel HOSTEL $

(☑ 8-914 772 8783; www.kakaduhostel.ru; ul Sheronova 10, entrance 1, 7th fl; dm R650-750; ✳🛜) This friendly hostel has pleasant 4- to 8-bed bunk rooms, and draws a handful of young Russian travellers. There's a kitchen, a tiny verandah in each room and free laundry, but no English is spoken. Get directions before setting out.

★ Hostel Valencia GUESTHOUSE $$

(☑ 8-914 172 7262; www.hostelvlc.com; ul Dzerzhinskogo 21a, 3rd fl; r with shared bathroom from R1600) Named after the city where the owners lived for many years, this friendly 8-room guesthouse has bright, attractively designed rooms that are kept sparklingly clean. The owners run two other locations offering similarly good values (on **ul Lenina 33** and **ul**

Khabarovsk

Dikopoltseva 10). Spanish spoken. Hard to find, the hotel is tucked 75m back from the road (behind a multistorey hair salon).

Versailles HOTEL $$
(Версаль; ☎4212-659 222; versal-hotel. net; Amursky bul 46a; s/d incl breakfast from R3200/3500; ❄@☎) This cheerful hotel, an easy walk from the train station, has pleasant red-carpeted rooms with fridge and small sitting area. It's set back from the street, fronted with seal lamp posts – just like back in France.

Hotel Tsentralnaya HOTEL $$
(Гостиница Центральная; ☎4212-303 300; ul Pushkina 52; s/d from R1700/1880; ❄☎) It's been years since the staff would let us see a room (maybe they were burned by Paul Theroux when he stayed here while researching *The Great Railway Bazaar*), but you can expect the standard diet of lightly renovated Soviet fare. Half the 200 rooms look over pl Lenina. A booking fee of 25% applies.

Hotel Intourist HOTEL $$
(Гостиница Интурист; ☎4212-312 313; http:// intour-khabarovsk.ru; Amursky bul 2; s/d from R3200/3600; ❄@☎) Teeming with tour groups, this big Bolshevik still breathes as if it's 1975. Service is so-so and the cheaply renovated rooms have thick floral bedspreads and worn carpets (but do have remarkable

river views on upper floors). The entrance is on per Arseneva.

★Boutique Hotel BOUTIQUE HOTEL $$$
(☎4212-767 676; www.boutique-hotel.ru; ul Istomina 64; s/d incl breakfast from R4600/5500; ❄@☎) Khabarovsk's most foreigner-friendly hotel has large, attractive rooms adorned with black-and-white photos from a bygone era. Throw in gorgeous bathrooms, luxurious white bedspreads and the full complement of mod cons, plus a great location.

Amur Hotel HOTEL $$$
(Гостиница Амур; ☎4212-221 223; www. amurhotel.ru; ul Lenina 29; s/d from R3500/4500; ☺❄@☎) A solid option, the Amur serves up bright, comfortably furnished rooms that range from small to spacious, and there's a sauna (though it's pricey). It's a long stroll to the riverfront action, but there's a good restaurant on-site (the scallops with black rice is excellent), plus several decent eating and drinking options nearby.

Parus HISTORIC HOTEL $$$
(Гостиница Парус; ☎4212-335 555; www.ho-tel-parus.com; ul Shevchenko 5; r incl breakfast from R5700; ❄@☎) Part of a century-old brick building near the water, the 80-room Parus sure makes a grand entrance – with chandeliers, iron staircase and reading room. Rooms

are also overdone, but sizeable and with expensive Italian furniture and flat-screen TVs. Friendly, English-speaking service.

✖ Eating

LaVita CAFE $
(ul Muravyova-Amurskogo 26; light dishes R130-250; ⏲8.30am-midnight; 🛜) A well-situated cafe with comfy chairs, sweet desserts and savoury snacks including quiche (R130) and pay-by-weight pies filled with meat and cabbage, mushrooms and other ingredients. Decent coffee too.

Stolovaya Lozhka & Tempo Pizza RUSSIAN $
(Столовая Ложка и Темпо Пицца; ul Dikopoltseva 29; meals R250-450; ⏲stolovaya 9am-9pm, pizzeria 10am-midnight; 🛜) One of a host of upmarket *stolovye* (canteens) that have been cropping up all over Russia, this one boasts an outdoor beer patio and is twinned with a pizzeria selling by the slice.

Blin FAST FOOD $
(Блин; Lotus Shopping Centre basement, ul Muravyova-Amurskogo 5; bliny R40-100; ⏲10am-11pm) Locals queue up for the bliny here.

Maxim SUPERMARKET $
(Максим; ul Muravyova-Amurskogo 3; ⏲24hr) Good centrally located supermarket.

Trattoria Semplice ITALIAN $$
(☑4212-206 051; ul Pushkina, facing Pl Lenina; pizza small/large around R350/520; ⏲11am-11.30pm; ✑) White-painted plank walls, linen curtains and fresh-cut flowers brighten up this downstairs space near pl Lenina. The piping-hot thin-crust pizzas are among the city's best and a small pie can feed two (unless you're famished). One minus: the pounding four-to-the-floor disco beats.

Demokratiya CAFE $$
(Демократия; ul Muravyova-Amurskogo 12; mains R350-700; ⏲noon-1am; 🛜) Join hipsters drinking home brew in this low-lit space. It has good salads and business lunches from R180.

Russky Restaurant RUSSIAN $$$
(Ресторан "Русский"; ☑4212-306 587; Ussuriysky bul 9; mains R650-1450; ⏲noon-1am) The kitsch factor at this Russian folk themed restaurant is high but the food is tasty. Feast on Siberian borsch, smoked halibut with pan-seared potatoes or grilled pork loin in one of two dining rooms – one decked out

like a wood-lined rustic dwelling, the other evoking imperial pomp.

🍷 Drinking & Nightlife

Khabarovsk is most definitely a party town, with arguably the best nightlife east of the Volga.

Gatsby LOUNGE BAR
(☑4212-604 333; ul Istomina 49; ⏲noon-4am Mon-Thu, to 8am Fri & Sat, 5pm-4am Sun; 🛜) Handsomely designed Gatsby has a main-level restaurant and lounge (with good food from R300 to R700). Downstairs is a swanky bar in one room (with big comfy seats around a horseshoe-shaped bar), and a small dance floor with DJ in another room. It draws a young stylish crowd, but the vibe overall is remarkably welcoming. The after parties are legendary here.

Harat's BAR
(ul Muravyova-Amurskogo 44; ⏲5pm-6am) This traditionally decorated Irish-style pub has a good beer selection (with 17 or so on tap) and feels less gloomy than other Khabarovsk drinking spots owing to its upstairs location (with windows!). Live bands play frequently, with occasional cover charges (up to R300).

Harley Davidson Bar BAR
(ul Komsomolskaya 88; ⏲24hr) Features nightly shows (rock or country bands, cabaret, 10 brews on tap, tattooed bartenders and a looooong wooden bar. Upstairs is a verandah

---

ⓘ GETTING CHINESE VISAS IN THE FAR EAST

It's best to arrange Chinese visas in your home country, although foreigners with verve can attempt to obtain a Chinese visa on the road. In the Far East, only the consulate in Khabarovsk (p383) provides this service.

A one-month tourist visa for Europeans costs from R1200 for five-day processing (expedited visas sometimes possible with a higher fee). Americans pay R4800 (10-day processing only). You'll need a letter of invitation, application form and copies of your immigration card, latest hotel registration and Russian visa. All forms are in Russian. Travel agencies in Khabarovsk may be able to assist.

bar with street views. Cover charge runs R300 on weekends.

Chocolate
CAFE, LOUNGE BAR

(ul Turgeneva 74; mains R500-1200; ⊙24hr; ☎) A cafe with a pricey menu of slick international dishes (fajitas, sauteed squid, smoked duck breast) by day, it becomes a prime party spot after hours.

Hospital
CLUB

(Клуб Госпиталь; http://hospitalclub.ru; ul Komsomolskaya 79; cover R300-1000; ⊙Fri & Sat) One of Russia's top clubs, with several packed dance chambers and a consistent line-up of top DJ talent from Russia and abroad. YouTube has highlights.

☆ Entertainment

Platinum Arena
ICE HOCKEY

(Платинум Арена; ☑4212-316 140; ul Dikopoltseva 12) This is the home arena for Khabarovsk's ice hockey team, the Amur Tigers, a hot ticket from October to March.

Lenin Stadium
FOOTBALL

(Стадион Ленина; Riverfront Sports Complex; tickets R150) Home to Khabarovsk's first-division football team, SKA-Energiya.

Theatre of Musical Comedy
THEATRE

(Театр музыкальной комедии; ☑4212-211 196; ul Karla Marksa 64; tickets R100-1000) Funny operettas run from November to April; big musical acts run from May to October. There's also the occasional ballet.

TRANSPORT CONNECTIONS FROM KHABAROVSK

DESTINATION	MAIN TRAINS SERVING DESTINATION* & FREQUENCY	RAIL PRICE (PLAT-SKART/KUPE)	RAIL DURATION	AIRLINES SERVING DESTINATION	AIR PRICE (FROM R)	AIR DURATION & FREQUENCY
Běijīng	N/A	N/A	N/A	Aeroflot, Aurora	10,300	3hr, 2 weekly
Blagoveshchensk	35 (daily)	R2300/3800	16hr	Yakutia	4700	2hr, 5 weekly
Irkutsk	1 (even dates), 7 (odd dates), **43 (even dates)**, 99 (odd dates), 133 (odd dates), 207 (even dates)	from R5200/9500	58hr	Aeroflot, Ir-Aero	5800	3¾hr, almost daily
Komsomolsk	351 (daily), **667 (daily)**	from R1100/2000	10hr	N/A	N/A	N/A
Moscow	1 (even dates), **43 (even dates)**, 99 (odd dates)	from R9100/16,100	5½ days	Aeroflot, Transaero, VIM Airlines	14,800	8½hr, several daily
Neryungri (via Tynda)	325 (daily)	R2700/4800	36hr	N/A	N/A	N/A
Seoul	N/A	N/A	N/A	Asiana	17,000	3hr, almost daily
Vladivostok	2 (odd dates), **6 (daily)**, 8 (even dates), 100 (even dates), 134 (odd dates), 351 (daily)	from R1700/3000	11-15hr	Aeroflot, Ir-Aero	2200	1¼hr, daily

*Trains originating in Khabarovsk in bold.

🛍 Shopping

Tainy Remesla   SOUVENIRS
(Тайны ремесла; ul Muravyova-Amurskogo 17; ⊘10am-7pm) This is the best souvenir shop in town, located in the old House of Pioneers building.

ℹ Information

Stock up on Far East maps at **Knizhny Mir** (Книжный мир; ul Karla Marksa 37; ⊘9am-8pm). Get online at the **Post Office** (Почта; ul Muravyova-Amurskogo 28; per hr R150; ⊘internet 8am-8pm Mon-Fri, 9am-6pm Sat & Sun). The **Intour-Khabarovsk** (Интур-Хабаровск; ☑4212-312 313; www.intour-khabarovsk.com; Hotel Intourist, Amursky bul 2; ⊘9am-6pm) travel agency gives out a free city map.

ℹ Getting There & Away

Most travel agents book train or air tickets for a modest commission. The best booking agent is **Aviakasa** (Авиакасса; Amursky bul 5; ⊘8.30am-8pm Mon-Sat, 9am-6pm Sun) because of its generous opening hours.

TRAIN

The full-service train station is lovely, with a handy supermarket nearby (to left of station when exiting). Note that almost all trains to Vladivostok are overnight.

Note that the westbound/eastbound 1/2 Rossiya train between Moscow and Vladivostok (*platskart* from R14,200) is significantly more expensive than all other trains (*platskart* from R9100), and only slightly faster (six days versus six days and 18 hours). The 7/8 train between Novosibirsk and Vladivostok is also relatively expensive.

For Birobidzhan, take any westbound train or a cheaper *elektrichka* (R320, three hours, three daily).

AIR

The airport is 7km east of the train station.

BOAT

Many companies at the **river terminal** (Речной вокзал; Ussuriysky bul; ⊘8am-7pm) offer morning and evening departures to Fŭyuǎn, China (90 minutes), which cost R4000 including tour and overnight lodging. A good company is **Tor** (☑4212-584 666). The hydrofoil service to Komsomolsk-na-Amure no longer operates.

BUS

The bus station (Автовокзал; ul Voronezhskaya 19), 500m north of the train station (go by tram or bus 4), sends nine buses daily to Komsomolsk (R500, 6½ hours) and hourly *marshrutky* to Birobidzhan (2¾ hours) until 6pm.

ℹ Getting Around

From Khabarovsk's train station, about 3.5km northeast of the waterfront, bus 4 goes to pl Komsomolskaya (board opposite the station and head southeast) and trams 1 and 2 go near pl Lenina.

From the airport, 9km east of the centre, trolleybus 1 goes to pl Komsomolskaya along ul Muravyova-Amurskogo and bus 35 goes to the train station (25 minutes) and bus station. A taxi to the centre from the airport is R500; usually R300 or R400 the other way.

Trolleybuses and trams cost R18.

Vladivostok   Владивосток

☑4232 / POP 610,000 / TIME MOSCOW + 10HR

At first look, Vladivostok is something like 'Russia's San Francisco' – a real stunner, with pointed mountains springing up above a network of bays, most strikingly the crooked dock-lined Golden Horn Bay (named for its likeness to Istanbul's). Closer up, it can be a little grey, with Soviet housing blocks squeezed between new condos and century-old mansions. But it's a great place to kick off or finish a Trans-Siberian trip – however, be warned: leg muscles not used to the ups and downs of hilly streets will get extremely sore.

Timing wise, June can often be grey and wet, while September and October are the nicest, sunniest months (another thing Vladivostok has in common with San Francisco). Vladivostok's City Day is 2 July, or the closest Saturday to it.

History

Founded in 1860, Vladivostok (meaning 'To Rule the East') became a naval base in 1872. *Tsarevitch* Nicholas II turned up in 1891 to inaugurate the new Trans-Siberian rail line. By the early 20th century, Vladivostok teemed with merchants, speculators and sailors of every nation in a manner more akin to Shànghǎi or Hong Kong than to Moscow. Koreans and Chinese, many of whom had built the city, accounted for four out of every five of its citizens.

After the fall of Port Arthur in the Russo-Japanese War of 1904–05, Vladivostok took on an even more crucial strategic role, and when the Bolsheviks seized power in European Russia, Japanese, Americans, French and English poured ashore here to support the tsarist counterattack. Vladivostok held out until 25 October 1922, when Soviet

Vladivostok

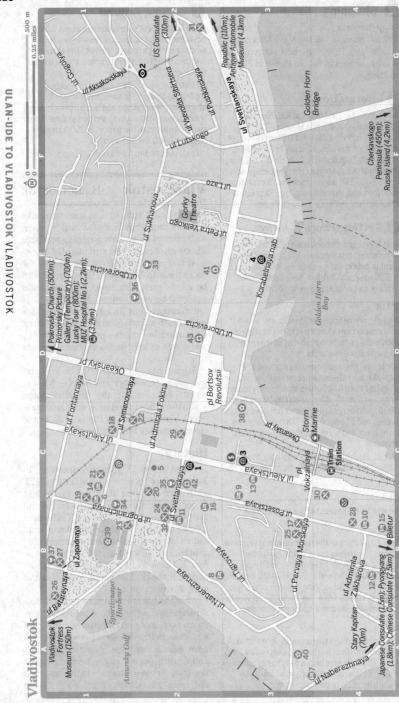

Vladivostok

forces finally marched in and took control – it was the last city to fall.

In the years to follow, Stalin deported or shot most of the city's foreign population. Closed from 1958 to 1992, Vladivostok opened up with a bang – literally (Mafia shoot-outs were a part of early business deals) – in the '90s, and is only starting to settle down in recent years.

Billions were spent on infrastructure thanks to the 2012 Asian Pacific Economic Conference (APEC). Vladivostok's infrastructure was torn asunder and rebuilt for the APEC summit on Russky Island. The most eye-catching developments include two giant suspension bridges: one across Golden Horn Bay to the previously difficult-to-access Cherkavskogo Peninsula, the other spanning more than 4km to Russky Island across the Eastern Bosphorus Strait. A brand-new university campus opened there in 2012, and officials hope to turn the area into a high-tech research hub in the future – something of a 'Silicon Valley of the East'.

◉ Sights & Activities

◉ Central Vladivostok

On tree-lined streets around the city centre you'll find plenty of tsarist-era buildings from Vladivostok's first crazy incarnation a century past. The main areas for locals to mill about is **pl Bortsov Revolutsii** (on ul Svetlanskaya at the southern end of Okean-sky pr) and ul Fokina (aka 'the Arbat'), which is partially pedestrianised and dotted with cafes and shops.

Nearby **Sportivnaya Harbour** has a popular beach, and beer and shashlyk stands. You can hire paddle boats and rowboats here, and there's an amusement park just off the waterfront.

Arsenev Regional Museum   MUSEUM
(Приморский Государственный Объединенный музей имени В. К. Арсеньева; ☑ 4232-413 977; ul Svetlanskaya 20; admission R200; ⊙ 10am-7pm Tue-Sun) One of the city's most fascinating museums, the Arsenev Regional Museum, which dates from 1890

received a recent makeover adding interactive displays to its three floors of galleries.

Exhibits delve into local history, covering early explorers to the region, Vlad's vibrant Chinatown from the early 1900s, and civil war (with a short silent film playing across a broken screen). In the 'Vremya Dela' room, you can touch and smell the exhibits (the fragrant jar of sea cucumbers is quite powerful). Docents are eager to help, but generally speak Russian only, though occasional English-speaking guides are available for free tours.

Primorsky Picture Gallery ART GALLERY

(Приморская государственная картинная галерея; ☑ 4232-427 748, 4232-411 162; pr Partizanski 12; admission varies; ☺ 11am-7pm Tue-Sun) Vladivostok's bipolar art museum's original locale (ul Aleutskaya 12) has long been under renovation, but may be open by the time you read this. While most of the impressive collection is in storage, bits and pieces rotate through the annexe east of Park Provotsky.

S-56 Submarine MUSEUM

(Подводная лодка С-56; ☑ 4232-216 757; Korabelnaya nab; admission R100; ☺ 9am-8pm) Perched near the waterfront, the S-56 submarine is worth a look. The first half is a ho-hum exhibit of badges and photos of men with badges (all in Russian). Keep going: towards the back you walk through an officers' lounge with a framed portrait of Stalin and then onto a bunk room with Christmas-coloured torpedoes. Outside note the '14', marking the WWII sub's 'kills'.

Vladivostok Fortress Museum MUSEUM

(Музей Владивостокская Крепость; ☑ 4232-400 896; ul Batareynaya 4a; admission R200; ☺ 10am-6pm) On the site of an old artillery battery overlooking Sportivnaya Harbour, this museum has cannons outside and a six-room indoor exhibit of photos and many, many guns inside. English explanations.

Funicular FUNICULAR

(Фуникулёр; ul Pushkinskaya; tickets R9; ☺ 7am-8pm) Vladivostok's well-oiled funicular railway makes a fun 60-second ride up a 100m hill every few minutes. At the top, cross ul Sukhanova via the underpass to a great lookout over the bay. It's next to a statue of Saints Cyril and Methodius (inventors of the Cyrillic alphabet) on the campus of DVGTU.

The base of the funicular is about a 15-minute walk from the centre.

⊙ Outer Vladivostok

Much of the water facing Vladivostok is quite polluted but it gets cleaner as you go north. Sunbathers can get on a northbound *elektrichka* and hop off at any beach that looks good – try Sedanka, where there are a few resorts with services. You'll find better swimming on Popov or Russky Islands.

Russky Island ISLAND

A fully militarised island for most of the past 150 years, this big island just offshore, which only opened to foreigners in the early 2000s, has been reinvented as a business and academic zone (as home to the sprawling – and off limits to visitors – Far Eastern Federal University (www.dvfu.ru) campus). There's great tourism potential here, but at the moment Russky Island is very much a DIY attraction.

Access to the island is by bus over the suspension bridge. Take a northbound bus 29 or bus 15 from Okeansky pr. The more-frequent bus 15 takes you to the DVFU campus, from where you can transfer to a minibus 29, which makes a loop, stopping in Rynda and other spots on the island. Rynda has a couple of resorts and the best beaches (just hop out when you see one you like). There are many forts on the island, including the Voroshilov Battery (Музей Ворошиловская батарея; admission R100; ☺ 9am-5pm Wed-Sun), where three massive cannons aim roughly at Hokkaido. The battery, now a military museum, was built in 1933–34 and housed 75 soldiers at its peak. Underground you can explore the guts of the battery, while above ground there are great views of the Pacific.

Under construction at research time, the massive Primorsky Aquarium (www.russian-aquarium.ru) will house an array of sea life exhibits, plus shows of marine mammals.

Antique Automobile Museum MUSEUM

(Музей автомотостарины; http://automoto museum.vl.ru; ul Sakhalinskaya 2a; admission R100; ☺ 10am-6pm Tue-Sun) If you're a bit of a car (or Soviet) nerd, the Antique Automobile Museum is an absolute classic. A room full of Sovietmobiles (motorcycles too) from the 1930s to 1970s includes a 1948 M&M-green GAZ-20 'Pobeda' (Victory). Take bus 31 along ul Svetlanskaya and exit after it reaches ul Borisenko's end.

Fort No 7
FORTRESS

(Форт No 7; admission R250; ⏱10am-6pm Tue-Sun) Attention fort fans: Vladivostok teems with sprawling, rather unique subterranean forts built between the late 19th and early 20th century to ward off potential Japanese (or American) attacks. Sixteen protective forts (including four on Russky Island) and hundreds of artillery batteries and other military objects encircle Vladivostok. Many buses pass here (like No 107 from the train station); get off at 'Akademicheskaya' stop (one after 'Zarya'), and walk 20 minutes east on the road leading up the hill (you may have to ask directions).

Popov Island
ISLAND

Just beyond Russky Island, Popov Island is better regarded for its beaches and filled with many guesthouses and dachas. You'll probably need to stay overnight if you head out here, as there is usually only one boat per day (R100, 1½ hours), departing in the early evening from Vladivostok's first wharf. Ask at a travel agent if they can help with accommodation.

⏰ Tours

Vladivostok travel agents run a variety of city and regional tours, but they can get pricey.

Heading outside of Vladivostok into Primorsky Territory, the most interesting tour is probably to Sikhote-Alin Nature Reserve, home to the Russian-American Siberian (Amur) Tiger project. It's a short flight or an 11-hour drive to Terney, where the 3440-sq-km forested reserve is head-quartered. Chances of seeing a tiger are basically nonexistent, but the reserve is thick with birds, seals and other wildlife, and the scenery is incredible. Dalintourist and Lucky Tour run six-day trips here from about €1300 per person (including guide, transport, accommodation and meals) and can be combined with a stay at Lazovsky Nature Reserve east of Nakhodka, home to a population of about 20 tigers.

The Far East is all about its Amur tigers, and at Gaivoron, 235km north of Vladivostok, you can see a couple at the Russian Academy of Sciences biological research reserve, run by Dr Victor Yudin and his daughter. Tours by Vladivostok agents include about 90 minutes of tiger time, lunch and a four-hour ride each way. It's not possible to go independently.

Dalintourist
TOURS

(☑4232-228 055; www.dalintourist.ru; ul Admirala Fokina 8a; ⏱9am-7pm Mon-Fri, 10am-3pm Sat) Runs area tours and can arrange English-speaking guides.

Lotos Co
TOURS

(☑4232-414 130; www.lotosco.ru; ul Dalzavodskaya 1, office 303; ⏱10am-6pm Mon-Fri) Offers a comprehensive assortment of tours, including visits to Russky Island, Popov Island and nature trips to the Primorsky Territory (waterfall visits, river rafting).

Lucky Tour
TOURS

(☑4232-449 944; www.luckytour.com; ul Moskovskaya 1; ⏱9.30am-6pm Mon-Fri) Interesting tour to Khasan on the North Korea border; requires several weeks' notice.

Vladivostok Digger Club
TOURS

(Владивостокский диггер-клуб (ВДК); ☑4232-552 086; www.vladdig.org) This outfit leads hour-long to full-day tours of Fort No 7 and other forts, batteries and the tunnels (some 3.5km long) that link them.

✨ Festivals & Events

Vladivostok's big rock festival, V-Rox (www.vrox.vladivostok3000.ru/en), launched in 2013 to much acclaim. Held in mid-August, the four-day fest features some 70 different concerts and DJ sessions around town (including in open-air venues), with performers from Russia, China, Japan, the USA and other corners of the globe.

🛏 Sleeping

★Optimum Hostel
HOSTEL $

(☑4232-729 111; ul Aleutskaya 17; dm/d R750/2100; ❋🛜) In a great central location, Optimum Hostel is the pick of the bunch for value. Clean wood-floored dorm rooms sleep three to six, and there's free laundry and a guest kitchen. Bonus: there's usually someone on hand who speaks a bit of English. It's set in a grand 8-storey 1930s building topped with statues. Head up the steps from street level and look for the 'Optimum' buzzer.

Antilopa
HOSTEL $

(☑4232-727 115; 4th fl, ul Pogranichnaya 6; dm R450; ❋🛜) This tiny three-room hostel is a friendly, well-priced option in the centre. Noise from the bar next door can be an issue for light sleepers. Russian only spoken. Free laundry.

Teplo
HOSTEL $$

(☑ 4232-909 555; www.teplo-hotel.ru; ul Posetskaya 16; dm/d R650/2000; ✱ 🖵 🕾) New in 2014, Teplo brings a dash of style to Vlad's lodging options with a lounge-like lobby (with sofas and table football), and a white-brick corridor leading back to the small but appealing rooms. Each is equipped with TV, fridge and half bath (shower and sink only). There's free laundry and a guest kitchen, and the location on a quiet but central street is excellent.

Vlad Marine Inn
HOSTEL $$

(☑ 4232-2080 280; www.vlad-marine.ru; ul Posetskaya 53; dm R500, d with/without private bathroom R2100/1600; ✱ 🕾) In a green clapboard building, this appealing new hostel has just five rooms, each with polished wood floors and ample natural light. Dorm beds have small individual flat-screen TVs, and the three doubles are quite nice for the price. The downside: it's hard to find. Look for the tiny shrub-lined lane leading uphill off Posetskaya.

Sakura Hostel
GUESTHOUSE $$

(☑ 4232-773 011; 3rd fl, ul Semenovskaya 5; dm/d/tr R810/1620/2300; 🕾) A pleasant but simple six-room guesthouse with a great location, Sakura has twittering caged birds, and quirkily furnished rooms full of toy stuffed animals and books. Run by a friendly old soul (who speaks Russian only). Guest kitchen.

Hotel Moryak
HOTEL $$

(Гостиница Моряк; ☑ 4232-499 499; www.hotelm.ru; ul Posetskaya 38; s/d from R2100/2600; 🖵 ✱ 🕾) This grey-brick yet cheerful place has an endearing lobby with a stuffed version of the hotel namesake – a sea man. The rooms are compact with thin walls (and mattresses) and *tiny* bathrooms. Threadbare econo rooms are quite worn. Laundry is a reasonable R250 per bag. No lift.

Equator Hotel
HOTEL $$

(Гостиница Экватор; ☑ 4232-300 110; www.hotelequator.ru; ul Naberezhnaya 20; s/d from R3500/3800; @ 🕾) This old-school Soviet hotel has basic midrange rooms that are fairly spacious but minimally equipped. Book an upper-floor even-numbered room for a sea view.

Azimut
HOTEL $$

(☑ 4232-412 808; www.azimuthotels.com; ul Naberezhnaya 9; s/d from R2970/3330; 🕾)

Under renovation at the time of research, this place has fairly dumpy rooms; their best feature is the excellent sea view. It's in a peaceful location, but a long (uphill) walk to the centre. Check-in is on the 7th floor, where there's also a small terrace bar with fine views.

Hotel Zhemchuzhina
HOTEL $$

(Гостиница Жемчужина; ☑ 4232-414 387; www.gemhotel.ru; ul Bestuzheva 29; s/d from R3500/3800; 🕾) Formerly the Chayka, this is a well-located but charmless cheapie. Registration costs R100. Pay extra for wi-fi.

Hotel Versailles
HOTEL $$$

(Гостиница Версаль; ☑ 4232-264 201; www.hotel-versailles.ru; ul Svetlanskaya 10; s/d incl breakfast R5800/6300; ✱ @ 🕾) The Versailles does a decent job of recapturing the pre-USSR grace of the century-old hotel that reopened in the '90s, despite enigmatic pairings in the lobby ('70s lounge seats, tsarist-style chandeliers). Quarters are plenty roomy with exquisite furniture and lovely bathrooms.

Hotel Primorye
HOTEL $$$

(Гостиница Приморье; ☑ 4232-411 422; www.hotelprimorye.ru; ul Posetskaya 20; s/d incl breakfast from R4000/4200; @ 🕾) In a good location, Primorye has decent rooms with playful details such as funny artwork and a clock, though the design is rather dated and the beds are rock-hard. The best rooms are two-room suites with views of the warships in Golden Horn Bay. An enticing bakery adjoins the lobby.

✖ Eating

Eating options coat the town, offering more class and types of cuisine than pretty much anywhere between here and Moscow. For provisions, stop in the open-air **market** (off ul Semenovskaya & ul Aleutskaya) across from Clover House.

Some restaurants offer 'business lunches' from noon to 4pm for R200 to R350. In good weather, **open-air stands** sell beer (R150) and cook up sizzling shashlyk (R250) and *shawarma* (doner kebab; R150) on the waterfront north of Sportivnaya Harbour.

Stolovaya No 1
CAFETERIA $

(Столовая №1; ul Svetlanskaya 1; meals R180-250; ⊘ 7am-1am; 🕾 🍴) A mix of old-timers and students line up for above-average *stolovaya* fare and appealing ambience – complete with Anglo rock on the stereo, vintage posters (note the giant USSR wall map) and a bar serving espresso drinks and booze. Great central location.

Five O'Clock
CAFE $

(ul Admirala Folkina 6; snacks R40-100; ⊙8am-9pm Mon-Fri, 9am-9pm Sat, 11am-9pm Sun; 🖉) This much-loved local haunt on pedestrianised ul Admirala Folkina serves coffee, muffins, cakes and quiche, all made daily and sold for less than an espresso costs at most other cafes.

Republic
CAFETERIA $

(Республика; meals R180-320; ⊙9am-11pm Mon-Fri, 10am-11pm Sat & Sun; 🖉) These perfectly respectable twin *stolovye*, one located on ul Aleutskaya, the other on ul Svetlanskaya, draw more than a couple of cheap dates with their tasty Russian dishes, home brew (from R70) and funky interiors. Both have bars on-site.

Clover House
FAST FOOD, SUPERMARKET $

(ul Semenovskaya 15; ⊙10am-9pm; 🔊🖉) A convenient mall housing a supermarket with a deli, and a top-floor food court with incredible views (and free wi-fi).

★Pyongyang
KOREAN $$

(Кафе Пхеньян; ul Verkhneportovaya 68b; mains R350-750; ⊙noon-midnight; 🖉) Staffed by female newcomers from North Korea who periodically break out in karaoke, this DPRK-sponsored establishment is just strange enough to be considered a must-visit. You can pick from a photo menu of excellent food such as *bibimbap* (rice mixed with fried egg and sliced meat) and spicy fried pork with kimchi.

★Mauro Gianvanni
PIZZA $$

(Мауро Джанванни; 🖉4232-220 782; ul Fokina 16; mains R300-700; ⊙noon-midnight; 🖉) This slick little brick-oven pizzeria – run by an Italian – has a modern interior, though most sit out on the deck when weather behaves. The dozen-plus pizzas are crispy and tasty, probably the best east of the Urals.

Belle Bazaar
CAFE $$

(ul Pervaya Morskaya 6/25; mains R350-800; ⊙10am-midnight) A pleasant cafe with comfy armchairs amid living-room-like decor (lamps, wallpaper, shelves of knick-knacks). A fine place to linger over decadent desserts, salads or pastas.

Oceanarium
INTERNATIONAL $$

(Океанариум; ul Batereynaya 4; mains R400-900; ⊙noon-midnight) Above the oceanarium, this welcoming and handsomely sited eating and drinking spot has fine views over the harbour and serves up salads, grilled meats and fish (plus hookahs) to a trendy crowd. Decent beers are on hand (including Guinness and Paulaner on tap).

Nostalgiya
RUSSIAN $$

(Ностальгия; 🖉4232-410 513; ul Pervaya Morskaya 6/25; mains R300-700; ⊙9am-10pm) This compact, long-running restaurant offers hearty and tasty Russian meals with a little for-the-tsars pomp. Most visitors come for the souvenir shop or a snack at the cafe.

Korea House
KOREAN $$

(Semenovskaya 7b; mains R400-800; ⊙noon-midnight; 🔊) A first-rate place for barbecue meat, sushi and the classic *bibimbap*. It's tucked down a lane, barely visible from Semenovskaya.

Dva Gruzina
GEORGIAN $$

(Два Грузина; ul Pogranichnaya 12; mains R180-360; ⊙11am-1am) Sample trademark Georgian *khachapuri* (cheese bread) and juicy plates of *chanakhi* (lamb, eggplant and tomato stew) and barbecued beef.

Presto
CAFE $$

(ul Svetlanskaya 15; mains R280-720; ⊙9am-11pm; 🔊🖉) A good pit stop for coffee, desserts and bistro fare (quiche, mussels, risotto, crepes) with a jazzy soundtrack and small cafe tables.

Pizza M
PIZZA $$

(Пицца M; 🖉4232-413 430; ul Posetskaya 20; pizzas R270-520; ⊙11am-11pm) Classier than its name might suggest, the M (next to Hotel Primorye) is one of Vlad's coolest hang-outs, with two unique rooms setting their style sights higher than the humble slice. The pizzas are quite good.

Paulaner Bräuhaus
GERMAN $$

(ul Fontannaya 2; mains R350-700; ⊙11am-1am) Step into this spacious new beer hall for excellent Paulaner brews made on-site, which go nicely with the roast duck, oven-baked spare ribs, crackling roast pork and other meaty dishes. Waitstaff in lederhosen and Bavarian plaid up the charm factor.

München
GERMAN $$

(Мюнхен; ul Svetlanskaya 5; mains R400-700; ⊙noon-2am) More meaty meals and towers of home brew in a basement beer-hall setting.

🍷 Drinking & Nightlife

★ Zuma
LOUNGE BAR

(☑4232-222 666; ul Fontannaya 2; ⊙11am-2am Sun-Thu, 24hr Fri & Sat; 🛜) A stylish but welcoming place, this restaurant-lounge is decked out in an elaborate but classy Angkor Wat–themed interior, replete with design surprises (check out the massive black granite bar). Cocktails are pricey (around R400), but there's Leffe on tap and mouthwatering pan-Asian cooking (sushi, dumplings, stir-fries), plus creative salads, rack of lamb and more (mains R400 to R1000).

Stary Kapitan
PUB

(Старый Капитан; ☑4232-771 077; www.old-captainpub.ru; Leitenanta Shmidta 17A; ⊙noon-1am Sun-Thu, to 3am Fri & Sat) Facing the marina, the Old Captain has an excellent selection of draught beers, such as German Weihenstephan (pints around R300). Lots of great seafood dishes (pan-seared tiger prawns and scallops) and appetisers (salt-ed herring with black bread toast) go nicely with the brews (mains R435 to R900). Reserve on weekends, when there's live music. In the same complex are two other restaurants, including Parus with outdoor waterfront views.

Mumiy Troll
BAR

(Мумий Тролль; ul Pogranichnaya 6; ⊙24hr) A fun and lively bar that draws a mix of locals and expats, rock-loving Mumiy Troll has live bands most nights (from 10pm). There's rarely a cover.

Rock's Cocktail Bar
BAR

(ul Svetlanskaya) If you prefer a grungier crowd, this basement dive is for you. Cool kids get dancing – and things often get sloppy – late night, as the DJ pays homage to Kurt, Layne, Zack and other '90s icons.

Moloko & Myod
LOUNGE BAR

(Молоко и Мёд; ul Sukhanova 6a; mains R400-700; ⊙noon-midnight Sun-Thu, to 2am Fri & Sat; 🛜) A trendy spot with a street-side terrace, 'Milk & Honey' has a daily brunch plus coffee, pricey cocktails and upscale dishes such as seafood risotto. Blankets warm terrace dwellers on chilly evenings.

Sky Bar
LOUNGE BAR

(12th fl, Hotel Hyundai, ul Semenovskaya 29; ⊙6pm-2am) Offers great views.

Yellow Submarine
CLUB

(ul Naberezhnaya 9a; cover R100-500) Right next to Zabriskie Point, this thumping club draws a younger crowd to hear a mix of live music and techno-spinning DJs.

Cukoo
CLUB

(Ку-Ку; Okeansky pr 1a; cover R500; ⊙10pm-2am Mon-Thu, to 6am Fri & Sat) One of Vladivostok's poshest clubs, the dance floor here seethes at weekends. Dress to impress to hurdle *face control*.

☆ Entertainment

Stadium Dinamo
SPORTS

(Стадион Динамо; ul Pogranichnaya; tickets R180-300) The popular local football team, Luch-Energiya, plays games at this bayside stadium from April to November.

Zabriskie Point
LIVE MUSIC

(Забриски Поинт; ☑4232-215 715; ul Naberezhnaya 9a; cover R500-800; ⊙9pm-5am Tue-Sun) Zabriskie is Vladivostok's main rock and jazz club, drawing an older crowd to view live music acts such as Blues Line. Pricey, but not without character.

Philharmonic Hall
CLASSICAL MUSIC

(Филармония; ☑4232-223 075; ul Svetlanskaya 15) Hosts classical music and jazz performances.

🛍 Shopping

Flotsky Univermag
OUTDOOR GEAR

(Флотский универмаг; ul Svetlanskaya 11; ⊙10am-7pm Mon-Fri, to 6pm Sat & Sun) For unusual souvenir turf, follow the navy – this outfitter has those cute blue-and-white-striped navy undershirts (R270) and other navy gear, as well as useful travel gear such as flashlights, knives, maps and toothpaste. Also has an OK map selection.

Nostalgiya
SOUVENIRS

(Ностальгия; ul Pervaya Morskaya 6/25; ⊙10am-8pm) Nostalgiya keeps a good range of pricey handicrafts (wood boats from R250 and way up) and many art pieces.

GUM
SOUVENIRS

(ГУМ; ul Svetlanskaya 35; ⊙10am-8pm Mon-Sat, to 7pm Sun) This Soviet-style department store is the Far East's most elegant art deco building. Some traditional souvenirs on the 1st floor.

ℹ Information

Dom Knigi (Дом Книги; ul Svetlanskaya 43; ⏱10am-7pm Mon-Sat, 11am-5pm Sun) is the best spot for city and regional maps.

INTERNET ACCESS, POST & TELEPHONE

Interface (Интерфейс; ul Semenovskaya 8; per hr R70; ⏱9am-2am)

Post Office (Почта; ul Aleutskaya; per MB R5.30; ⏱8am-10pm Mon-Fri, 9am-6pm Sat & Sun) Post, telephone and internet opposite the train station.

MEDIA

Vladivostok City (www.vladivostok-city.com) Though not entirely up-to-date, this official website is useful for pre-trip planning. Loads of restaurant and entertainment listings.

MEDICAL SERVICES

MUZ Hospital No 1 (МУЗ-Больница №1; ☎4232-453 275; ul Sadovaya 22)

MONEY

There are currency-exchange desks and ATMs all over town.

Sberbank (Сбербанк; ul Aleutskaya 12; ⏱8.45am-8pm Mon-Sat, 10am-5pm Sun) Accepts travellers cheques (2% commission).

ℹ Getting There & Away

Ticket agents all over town sell plane and train tickets, including **Biletur** (Билетур; ☎4232-407 700; ul Posetskaya 17; ⏱8am-7pm Mon-Sat, 9am-6pm Sun).

TRAIN

Save money by avoiding the No 1 Rossiya train to Moscow.

The Hāˈěrbīn train is a headache, with many stops and a long border check. Departures are early evening on Mondays and Thursdays, but the first night you only go as far as Ussurinsk, where they detach your car from the 351. You stay overnight in Ussurinsk and depart the next day for the border and Hāˈěrbīn. It's much quicker and easier to take a bus to Hāˈěrbīn. If you're headed to Běijīng by train, you'll need to go to Hāˈěrbīn first and transfer there.

TRANSPORT CONNECTIONS FROM VLADIVOSTOK

DESTINATION	MAIN TRAINS SERVING DESTINATION & FREQUENCY	RAIL PRICE (R)	RAIL DURATION	AIRLINES SERVING DESTINATION	AIR PRICE (FROM R)	AIR DURATION & FREQUENCY
Běijīng	351 to Ussurinsk (Mon & Thu)	*kupe* 5400 (to Harbin)	40hr (transfer in Harbin)	Aeroflot, China Southern, S7	9500	2½hr, almost daily
Hāˈěrbīn (Harbin)	351 to Ussurinsk (Mon & Thu)	*kupe* 5400	40hr	Aeroflot	6600	1¼hr, 2 weekly
Irkutsk	1 (even dates), 7 (odd dates), 99 (even dates), 133 (even dates)	from 6000/11,900	70hr	S7, Ural Airlines	13,500	4hr, daily
Khabarovsk	1 (even dates), 5 (daily), 7 (odd dates), 133 (even dates), 351 (daily)	from 1700/3000	11-15hr	Aeroflot, Ir-Aero	2200	1¼hr, daily
Moscow	1 (even dates), 99 (even dates)	from 9600/16,600	6 days	Aeroflot, S7, Transaero	9900	10hr, frequent
Seoul	N/A	N/A	N/A	Aeroflot, Korean Air	11,500	2½hr, daily

WORTH A TRIP

AROUND VLADIVOSTOK

The broad, mountainous Primorsky Territory is beloved by locals with cars, who visit the beaches and mountains. You might consider renting a car and doing the same, but note that some areas near the Chinese border require permits. Those without their own wheels lean on pricey tours to get further away. One easy trip to do by public transport is to Nakhodka, where Primorsky's best beaches are a short bus or taxi ride away. Ten daily express buses travel to Nakhodka from Vladivostok's bus station (R385, 3 hours); the first is at 8.20am. Less frequent *elektrichkas* make the trip in around 5 hours (R258).

AIR

Vladivostok has a newly renovated airport (www.vvo.aero), located in Artyom (50km from the centre), with convenient rail access to the centre.

BOAT

Storm Marine (☑ 4232-302 704; www.parom. su; office 124, Marine Terminal; ☺ 9am-1pm & 2-6pm Mon-Fri) Sends a passenger-only ferry to Donghae, South Korea (from US$205 one way, 20 hours), continuing on to Sakaiminato, Japan (from US$265 one way, 43 hours), every Wednesday at 2pm.

BUS

Buses to Harbin, China, depart daily (except Sunday) around 6.30am (R2900, eight hours) from the **bus station** (ul Russkaya), 3km north of the centre. There are also frequent departures for Nakhodka (four hours) and other destinations in the Primorsky Territory. Some southbound destinations may be off limits to foreigners without a permit.

ℹ Getting Around

The centrally located train station is easy walking distance from most hotels listed. From in front of the train station, buses 23, 31 and 49 run north on ul Aleutskaya then swing east onto ul Svetlanskaya to the head of the bay. For trips of more than 5km, you'll save money ordering a taxi by phone. Try **PrimTaxi** (☑ 4232-555 255) or the curiously named **Cherepakha** (Turtle; ☑ 4232-489 948).

TO/FROM THE AIRPORT

A speedy rail link (the plush Aeroexpress) connects the train station with the airport (43km north in Artyom). There are 10 trains daily, departing every one or two hours between 8am and 8pm (50 minutes, R200).

Bus number 107 (R100) also connects the train station and airport, departing every one to two hours from 8.25am to 8pm.

A taxi booth in the arrivals area charges R1500 for trips to the centre (45 minutes to one hour).

The Baikal-Amur Mainline (BAM)

Route Info

➡ Distance: 4287km

➡ Duration: Four days, one hour

➡ Time zones: Moscow +5 to Moscow +7

Best Places to Stay

➡ Baikal Trail Hostel (p243)

➡ Biznestsentr (p249)

➡ Zolotaya Rybka (p243)

➡ Hotel Taiga (p242)

➡ Hotel Olymp (p243)

Why Go?

Most people know the Trans-Siberian Railway, but how many can say they've heard of the 'other' Trans-Sib, its poor country cousin, the BAM (Baikal-Amur Mainline or Baikalo-Amurskaya Magistral)? The branch line to end all branch lines, the BAM begins as a set of points at Tayshet and ends more than 4200 lonely kilometres further east at Sovetskaya Gavan, passing through some jaw-slackeningly off-the-map places en route. As great railway journeys go, this is a Soviet epic, a rail-clanging odyssey you'll never forget.

But it's a miracle the BAM was ever built at all. Costing billions of dollars and declared a 'Hero Project of the Century', construction was fraught with seemingly insurmountable difficulties. The line opened fully in 1991, just as the USSR collapsed. Today, only a handful of trains ply the route.

Riding the BAM's snail-paced trains takes you to some very out-of-the-way places. Only Severobaikalsk on Lake Baikal is geared for visitors.

When to Go

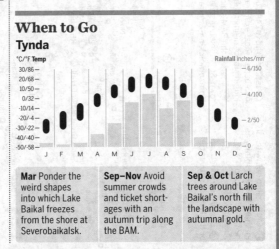

Tynda

Mar Ponder the weird shapes into which Lake Baikal freezes from the shore at Severobaikalsk.

Sep–Nov Avoid summer crowds and ticket shortages with an autumn trip along the BAM.

Sep & Oct Larch trees around Lake Baikal's north fill the landscape with autumnal gold.

BAM Highlights

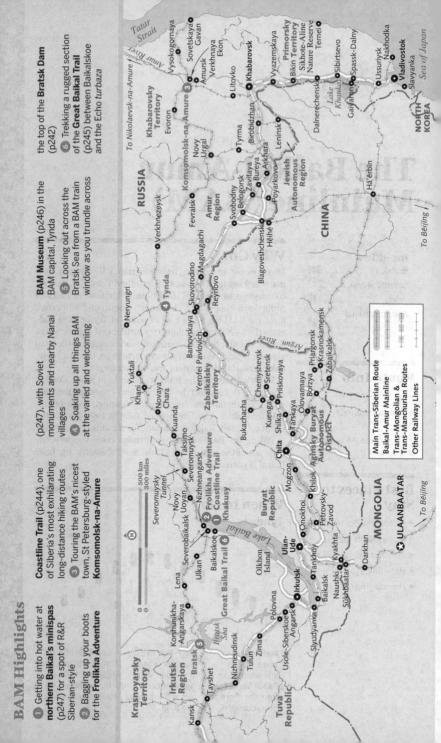

1 Getting into hot water at **northern Baikal's minispas** (p247) for a spot of R&R Siberian-style

2 Bagging up your boots for the **Frolikha Adventure Coastline Trail** (p244), one of Siberia's most exhilarating long-distance hiking routes

3 Touring the BAM's nicest town, St Petersburg-styled **Komsomolsk-na-Amure**

(p247), with Soviet monuments and nearby Nanai villages

4 Soaking up all things BAM at the varied and welcoming **BAM Museum** (p246) in the BAM capital, Tynda

5 Looking out across the Bratsk Sea from a BAM train window as you trundle across the top of the **Bratsk Dam** (p242)

6 Trekking a rugged section of the **Great Baikal Trail** (p245) between Baikalskoe and the Echo turbaza

ℹ The Route

TAYSHET TO SEVEROBAIKALSK

0km from Tayshet

The junction with the Trans-Sib at Tayshet is the official start of the BAM (there's finally a new monument recognising the fact). If you're a BAM purist you can start from here, but most connect through on daily services from Krasnoyarsk.

293km to 339km

The first major stops along the BAM are for Bratsk, a sprawling city of almost 250,000 people on the edge of the Bratsk 'Sea', an artificial lake created in the 1960s by the building of the Bratsk Hydroelectric Station. The railway line actually crosses the top of the gigantic 1km-long dam at the 330km mark, presenting wide views on both sides. If you get off you must choose between three Bratsk stations: Anzyobi (293km from Tayshet) for the crushingly dreary central (Tsentralny) area, Padunskiye Porogiye (326km) for Energetik, or Gidrostroitel (339km) for the dam. Bratsk's biggest attraction is the Angara Village open-air ethnographical museum.

552km

The taiga closes in on the line as you travel the next 600km towards the jagged mountains hemming in the northern end of Lake Baikal. Korshunikha-Angarskaya is the train station for the claustrophobic 1960s iron-ore processing town of Zheleznogorsk-Ilimsky. A 2km walk diagonally uphill to your right as you leave the station brings you to the town's one modest attraction, the **Yangel Museum** (☉9am-4pm Mon-Fri), which not only celebrates a local astroscientist friend of cosmonaut Yury Gagarin, but also has a well-arranged exhibition on local wildlife, an art gallery and a section on ZI's twin town in Japan.

573km

One of the few branch lines off the BAM veers north from Khrebtovaya to Ust-Ilimsk, a town of almost 100,000 people on the Angara River 215km away. The historic town of Ilimsk lies drowned at the bottom of the reservoir created by the Ust-Ilimsk Dam. Ust-Ilimsk is connected by overnight coach to Irkutsk.

720km

A few kilometres after Lena the line swings across the Lena River on a single-track bridge with views down onto a large timber port to the north.

930km

At Ulkan station, a small but eye-catching metallic Lenin relief stands against a bright red 'flag' on the east end of the platform, but you'll only have three minutes to admire it.

982km

After Kunerma the track performs a full 180-degree loop. Hurry for the camera before you disappear into the 6km-long Daban tunnel.

1028km

Around half an hour before reaching Lake Baikal, some trains make a brief stop at picturesque minispa Goudzhekit.

1063km

Though architecturally dull, Severobaikalsk is by far the most interesting stop on the entire route. The surrounding area, which takes in the northern part of Lake Baikal, is beautiful and offers lots of opportunities for outdoor adventure. Outside there's a steam train and a statue commemorating the workers from across the USSR who toiled on the BAM.

SEVEROBAIKALSK TO TYNDA

1090km

This is where the BAM gets serious. From Severobaikalsk to the fishing village of Nizhneangarsk, 30km north, the line skirts Lake Baikal, though views are often better from the road (unencumbered by tunnels). At Nizhneangarsk 2 station, look out for the small airport, from where there are flights to Ulan-Ude and Irkutsk.

BAM ROUTE PLANNER

Here's a suggested itinerary for the BAM:

Day 1 Take an overnight train from Krasnoyarsk to Bratsk to see the dam holding back the Bratsk 'Sea'.

Day 2 Overnight hop to Severobaikalsk.

Day 3 Take a dip in Lake Baikal or a boat trip; chill out at the Baikal Trail Hostel.

Day 4 Excursion from Severobaikalsk to Baikalskoe, Nizhneangarsk or one of the minispas at Dzelinda or Goudzhekit. Catch the night-day train to Tynda.

Day 5 After spending most of the day on the train, wash off in the town's *banya* (bathhouse).

Day 6 Explore Tynda's BAM Museum before catching a sleeper to Komsomolsk-na-Amure.

Day 7 Arrive in Komsomolsk-na-Amure; spend the day exploring this surprisingly attractive city. Overnight train to Sovetskaya Gavan.

Day 8 Arrive at BAM's end on the Tatar Strait.

Baikal-Amur Mainline (BAM)

West to Moscow

0km	**Tayshet**
	7hr
293km	**Bratsk (Anzyobi)**
	5hr
552km	**Korshunikha-Angarskaya**
	3hr, 40min
720km	**Lena**
	2hr, 40min
930km	**Ulkan**
	2hr, 20min
1063km	**Severobaikalsk**
	35min
1090km	**Nizhneangarsk**
	4hr
1385km	**Severomuysky Tunnel**
	2hr, 30min
1469km	**Taksimo**
	5hr
1719km	**Novaya Chara**
	3hr
1864km	**Khani**
	2hr, 45min
2013km	**Yuktali**
	4hr
2216km	**Larba**
	2hr, 35min
2348km	**Tynda**
	7hr, 40min

To Bamovskaya (Trans-Siberian)

2690km	**Verkhnezeysk**
	3hr
2846km	**Tungala**
	3hr, 40min
3014km	**Fevralsk**
	3hr, 10min
3162km	**Etryken**
	3hr, 45min
3298km	**Novy Urgal**
	7hr, 40min

To Khabarovsk (Trans-Siberian)

3615km	**Postyshevo**
	1hr, 25min
3679km	**Evoron**
	3hr, 20min
3819km	**Komsomolsk-na-Amure**
	7hr, 25min
4039km	**Vyskogornaya**
	6hr, 15min
4253km	**Vanino**
	20min
4287km	**Sovetskaya Gavan-Sortirovochny**

1105km

Only local *elektrichki* (suburban trains) stop at the Evenki village of Kholodnaya by the Verkhnyaya Angara River delta.

1142km

The tiny hot-springs spa at Dzelinda is also served by local slow trains.

1150km to 2500km

The next 1300km or so give you ample time to appreciate the truly massive engineering achievement of the BAM. Many consider this the most interesting section of the line, as it climbs over densely forested, mountainous terrain along switchbacks and through several tunnels. The train stops at least once an hour at communities established by BAM construction workers and their families in the 1970s and 1980s.

1242km

The first major halt on this section is the low-rise ferroconcrete station belonging to Novy Uoyan, though there's no reason to get off here save to stretch your legs. Trains snake across the flood plain of the Verkhnyaya Angara River until the line slams into the mountains again.

1385km

The 15.3km-long Severomuysky tunnel is the longest in Russia and was only completed in 2004 after years of severe technical difficulties with the permafrost. The tunnel replaced more than 50km of track, which had steep gradients and was prone to avalanches.

1469km

The born-of-the-BAM town of Taksimo provides the next opportunity to escape the muggy air of *platskart* and take on a few provisions at the station kiosks. Get some much-needed exercise during the long stop (up to 50 minutes) by running to see the BAM Pioneer Monument. There are wilderness hiking possibilities in the surrounding mountains and along the Muya River, and flights operate south to Ulan-Ude from the tiny airport.

1535km

Local time becomes Moscow time plus six hours.

1561km

At Kuanda look out for the Golden Link Monument commemorating the uniting of the two sections of the BAM in 1984.

1850km to 1950km

Shortly before Khani (1864km) you enter the Sakha Republic and continue along its border with the Zabaikalsky Territory and the Amur Region. Shortly beyond Olyokma (1918km) the train veers southeast and follows the Olyokma River into Tynda Region.

2000km to 2210km

The train leaves the Olyokma River, veers due east and rumbles into Yuktali (2013km), where there's a 35-minute stop. The next four hours are very scenic as you follow the Nyukzha River southeast until just before Larba (2216km).

2348km

Finally you roll into Tynda, the unofficial BAM 'capital', with a '70s train station that looks like a science-fiction film set. If you're coming straight from Moscow, you've been travelling for almost five days. The main BAM trains all terminate in Tynda, so you'll have a layover if you are continuing east to Komsomolsk or west to Severobaikalsk or Moscow.

In the TV series *Long Way Round*, Ewan McGregor went north by motorcycle from here on the AYaM (Amuro-Yakutskaya Mainline or Amuro-Yakutskaya Magistral) highway, bound for Yakutsk in the Sakha Republic. There's also an AYaM train line that goes north into Sakha and south to Bamovskaya on the Trans-Siberian.

TYNDA TO SOVETSKAYA GAVAN

2348km to 2690km

Heading east on the BAM, the 364 train to Komsomolsk pulls out at 5.26pm and crosses the mighty Gulyuy River twice (at 2364km and 2409km). Night falls as you cross several more rivers and enter the swamps leading into Verkhnezeysk (2690km) on the Zeysk Reservoir.

2779km to 2894km

The stretch from Ogoron to Dugda is about the prettiest the eastern BAM has to offer, with a range of snow-capped mountains to the northeast and patches of thick taiga near the tracks, but eastbound travellers will need to get up early. The best stretch is 10km either side of Tungala (2846km).

3015km

In Fevralsk (3014km) on the Byssa River, you get 35 minutes to contemplate the permafrost below, or gold mines and pulp mills outside town. It's a two-minute walk south to the little town centre, with food shops and a post office with internet access. The train station has an ATM.

3155km

You leave Amurskaya Region and enter Khabarovsky Territory between the station stops of Ulma (3149km) and Etryken (3162km).

3298km

After crossing the Bureya River (3292km), the train stops for 35 minutes in Novy Urgal, a coal-mining town near green hills and the white waters of the Akisma River. If you are having one of those rare macabre instincts for an authentic, fading pocket of '70s Sovietlandia, stop. Otherwise, move on. You can switch to the 663 here for a short cut to the Trans-Siberian line and Khabarovsk.

3382km

A couple of hours later, the train passes through the 2km Dusse-Alin Tunnel. Gulag camp labourers toiled over this during Stalin's watch, but it was only completed and put into use in 1982.

3615km

In Postyshevo, locals sell the town's famous red *ikra* (caviar) on the platform in late summer and autumn. The interesting station has socialist-realist bas-reliefs over both entrances, and a psychedelic, copper-toned, honeycombed ceiling.

3819km

Five hours east of Postyshevo, the 364 terminates in the BAM's loveliest city, Komsomolsk-na-Amure, with direct links to Khabarovsk on the Trans-Siberian, by bus or boat.

3819km to 4253km

While most people get off in Komsomolsk, the BAM still has another 468km to go. Two night trains tackle this final 12-hour stretch. Some train mates may joke you're on an 'international route' as the train clanks through a couple of ho-hum villages passed on the way – Kenada (4080km) and Toki (4243km); they liken them phonetically with 'Canada' and 'Tokyo' (it's OK to fake a chuckle).

The BAM then pulls into view of a snaking Pacific bay lined with shipyards at Vanino (4253km; population 18,500), where boats leave for Sakhalin Island. Vanino's often foggy bay, looked over by two lighthouses, sees some 20 million tonnes of goods shipped in and out each year (including coal, lumber and gas).

4287km

The BAM terminates at Sovetskaya Gavan-Sortirovochny ('SovGavan' on train timetables; not to be confused with the city of Sovetskaya Gavan, about 25km further south).

Bratsk   Братск

☑ 3953 / POP 246,300 / TIME MOSCOW +5HR

Unless you're a fan of BAM or dam, Bratsk is perhaps not worth leaving the 'comfort' of your carriage bunk, though it does neatly break up the journey from both Irkutsk and Krasnoyarsk to Severobaikalsk. The city's raison d'être is a gigantic dam (GES), which drowned the original historic town in the 1960s. New Bratsk is an unnavigable necklace of concrete 'subcities' and belching industrial zones, with the spirit-crushingly dull Tsentralny area at its heart.

WORKING THE BAM

As you gaze from your carriage window at the wall of pine and birch passing slowly by, spare a thought for the poor BAM workers whose orange Russian Railways jackets occasionally punctuate the green. Dispatched for a month at a time to impossibly remote locations and armed with only rudimentary tools, this army of workers somehow keep the tracks straight and level in the harshest of conditions. Their accommodation and food are basic, and bear attacks are not unknown.

◉ Sights & Activities

Bratsk Dam   LANDMARK

(Братская ГЭС; www.irkutskenergo.ru) A ferro-concrete symbol of the USSR's efforts to harness the might of Siberia's natural assets, between 1967 and 1971 the Bratsk hydro-electric power station was the world's largest single electricity producer. Slung between high cliffs and somehow holding back the mammoth Bratsk Sea – no one can deny it's a striking spectacle, especially as the BAM trains pass right across the top.

Angara Village   MUSEUM

(ul Komsomolskaya; admission R100; ⊙10am-5pm Wed-Sun) Some 12km from Tsentralny, this impressive open-air ethnographic museum contains a rare 17th-century wooden watchtower and buildings rescued from submerged old Bratsk. A series of shaman sites and Evenki *chumy* (tepee-shaped conical dwellings) lie in the woods behind. Take a taxi or arrange a visit through Taiga Tours.

🛏 Sleeping

Hotel Shvedka   HOTEL $

(Гостиница Шведка; 8-902 179 0580; www.hotel-shvedka.ru; ul Mira 25; s from R1050, d from R1400; 🛜) Rooms here range from battered and cheap to almost design standard. Ask to see which you're getting before you commit. Breakfast is extra.

Hotel Taiga   HOTEL $$

(Гостиница Тайга; ☑3953-414 710; www.hotel-taiga.ru; ul Mira 35; s R2500, d from R2800; 🛜) The flashiest show in town is this renovated Soviet hulk where cramped rooms are packed with tasteless furniture but have clean 21st-century bathrooms. Some staff speak English, guest visas are registered and there's a decent hotel restaurant. Breakfast is extra.

ℹ Information

Taiga Tours (☑3953-416 513; www.taiga-tours.ru; 2nd fl, Hotel Taiga) Permits and guides to visit the dam's turbine rooms.

ℹ Getting There & Away

For Tsentralny, get off BAM trains at the Anzyobi (Анзеби) station and transfer by bus or *elektrichka*. Tickets are best bought at the station.

Bratsk has the following rail connections:

Irkutsk *platskart/kupe* R1650/3100; 17 hours to 19½ hours; one or two daily

Krasnoyarsk *platskart/kupe* R1400/2600; 13 hours; up to four daily

Moscow *platskart/kupe* R5700/11,400; three days, four hours; one or two daily

Severobaikalsk *platskart/kupe* R1400/2600; 14 hours to 16 hours; up to four daily

Irkutsk can also be reached by Western-standard coach (R870, 11 hours) from the Tsentralny **bus station** (ul Yuzhnaya) and summer hydrofoil from a river station in southeast Tsentralny. Check VSRP (☑3952-287 115; www.vsrp.ru) for details of the latter.

Severobaikalsk
Северобайкальск

☑30130/30139 / POP 24,900 / TIME MOSCOW +5HR

Founded as a shack camp for railway workers in the mid-1970s, Severobaikalsk has grown into the most engaging halt on the BAM, where travellers vacate stuffy railway compartments to stretch legs in the taiga or cool off in Lake Baikal. The town itself is a grid of soulless, earthquake-proof apartment blocks with little in between, but the mountainscape and nameless wilderness backing the lake quickly lure hikers and adventurers away from the concrete. They discover a land more remote, less peopled and generally more spectacular than Baikal's south, a place where lazy bears and reindeer-herding Evenki still rule.

◉ Sights

BAM Museum   MUSEUM

(Музей истории строительства БАМа; ul Mira 2; admission R50; ⊙10am-1pm & 2-6pm Tue-Sat) The town's friendly little museum has exhibits on BAM railway history (workers' medals, grainy black-and-white photos, 'old' BAM tickets), some Buryat artefacts and a few mammoth bones. Around the corner is a small art gallery where local artists display their works.

HERO PROJECT OF THE CENTURY

The BAM is an astonishing victory of belief over adversity. This 'other' trans-Siberian line runs from Tayshet (417km east of Krasnoyarsk) around the top of Lake Baikal to Sovetskaya Gavan on the Pacific coast. It was begun in the 1930s to access the timber and minerals of the Lena Basin, and work stopped during WWII. Indeed, the tracks were stripped altogether and reused to lay a relief line to the besieged city of Stalingrad (now Volgograd).

Work effectively started all over again in 1974 when the existing Trans-Siberian Railway was felt to be vulnerable to attack by a potentially hostile China. The route, cut through nameless landscapes of virgin taiga (mountain pine) and blasted through anonymous mountains, was built by patriotic volunteers and the BAM was labelled 'Hero Project of the Century' to encourage young people from across the Soviet Union to come and do their bit. Despite this source of free labour, building on permafrost pushed the cost of the project to US$25 billion, some 50 times more than the original Trans-Siberian Railway.

New 'BAM towns' grew with the railway, often populated by builders who decided to stay on. However, the line's opening in 1991 coincided with the collapse of the centrally planned USSR and the region's bright Soviet future never materialised. While Bratsk and Severobaikalsk survived, many other smaller, lonely settlements became virtual ghost towns. Today, only a handful of passenger trains a day use the line.

Railway Station   NOTABLE BUILDING
(pr 60 let SSSR; ☺5am-midnight) The epicentre of town is a striking construction with a nostalgically stranded steam locomotive standing guard to the right. The sweeping architecture of the brave-new-world station resembles a ski jump – thanks to a previous mayor's love of the sport, it's claimed.

Orthodox Church   CHURCH
(Leningradsky pr) SB's newest Orthodox church sports two impressive onion domes in gleaming gold and a monster chandelier inside. It stands just beyond the town's grey-concrete war memorial.

☞ Tours

Severobaikalsk has a surprising number of agencies and individuals to arrange accommodation and backcountry excursions.

Ecoland   TOUR COMPANY
(☑30130-36 191; www.ecoland-tour.ru) This award-winning tour agency specialises in horse-riding trips, Baikal boat excursions and trekking.

Maryasov Family   TOUR GUIDE
(☑8-924 391 4514; baikalinfo@gmail.com) The English-speaking Maryasov family run Severobaikalsk's hostel, information centre and tourism association as well as organising guided treks to Baikalskoe and Lake Frolikha, seal-spotting trips to Ayaya Bay and Evenki-themed excursions to the village of Kholodnoe.

Rashit Yakhin/BAM Tour   TOUR GUIDE
(☑30139-21 560; www.gobaikal.com; ul Oktyabrya 16/2) This experienced full-time travel-fixer, guide and ex-BAM worker suffered an immobilising stroke in the mid-1990s rendering his spoken English somewhat hard to follow. Nonetheless, Rashit is quick to reply to emails and is always keen to please.

🛏 Sleeping

⭐**Baikal Trail Hostel**   HOSTEL $
(☑30130-23 860, 8-914 834 6802; www.baikaltrailhostel.com; ul Studencheskaya 12, apt 16; dm R600; @🛜) Initially set up to house Great Baikal Trail volunteers this small but spacious apartment-hostel is well equipped with essential backpacker facilities such as kitchen and washing machine. It's one of the best places in town to arrange backcountry treks and trips to the northern end of Lake Baikal.

Zolotaya Rybka   GUESTHOUSE $$
(Золотая Рыбка; ☑30130-21 134; www.baikalgoldenfish.ru; ul Sibirskaya 14; d R1200-2500) Well signposted from ul Olkhonskaya, SB's best guesthouse maintains immaculate and imaginatively designed rooms in three buildings providing glimpses of Lake Baikal through the trees. There are spotless toilets and showers, guests have access to kitchens and a cook prepares a restaurant-standard breakfast on request (R300 extra).

Hotel Olymp   HOTEL $$
(Гостиница Олимп; ☑30130-23 980; www.hotelolymp.ru; ul Poligrafistov 2b; s & d

FROLIKHA ADVENTURE COASTLINE TRAIL

A part of the Great Baikal Trail, this incredible, relatively demanding 100km adventure trekking route runs between the delta of the Verkhnyaya Angara River and the spa hamlet of Khakusy on Baikal's eastern shore. You'll need a boat to find the start of the trail at the mouth of the river, from where it takes eight days to reach Khakusy via countless lonely capes and bays, wild camping by the lake all the way. Exhilarating river crossings (including a biggie – the Frolikha River), deserted beaches and show-stopping Baikal vistas punctuate the trail, and from Ayaya Bay a there-and-back hike to remote Lake Frolikha beckons. For more information and trail maps, contact Severobaikalsk tour agencies, the Baikal Trail Hostel (p243) or Dresden-based Baikalplan (www.baikalplan.de).

R1600-2500; 🛜) Severobaikalsk's smartest sleep option has sparkling, cool, airy rooms though the plumbing could be more professionally screwed down. For this price you might expect breakfast and free wi-fi – you get neither.

✗ Eating

For quick eats – *pozi* (dumplings), shashlyk, *plov* (meat and rice, Uzbek pilaf-like dish) and beer – try the fast food row east of the station on pr 60 let SSSR or the greasy spoons around the Torgovy Tsentr. Otherwise, pickings are meagre indeed.

TiTs
CAFE $

(ТиЦ; Railway Culture Centre, Tsentralny pl; mains R40-70; ⊘11am-5pm & 6pm-1am) Climb the gloss-painted stairs for a return to Soviet-style 1980s dining. The food is basic and cheap, the dinner ladies belligerently un-smiling, the alcohol plentiful and the hand-scrawled menu a challenge even to Russian speakers.

Anyuta
CAFE $

(Анюта; ul Poligrafistov 3a; mains R80-200; ⊘6pm-2am Tue-Sun) Evening dinner nook housed in a red-brick building amid high-rise blocks at the northern end of town.

VIST Supermarket
SUPERMARKET

(ВИСТ) Branches of the town's VIST supermarkets, at Leningradsky pr 5 (⊘8.30am-9pm) and ul Studencheskaya (⊘8.30am-8pm), stock a limited range of groceries.

ℹ Information

There are ATMs at the railway station, in the Zheleznodorozhnik Culture Centre and at the Leningradsky pr branch of the VIST Supermarket.

Post Office (Почта; Leningradsky pr 6; ⊘9am-2pm & 3-7pm Mon-Fri, 9am-2pm Sat)

Tourist Office (train station forecourt; ⊘9am-6pm Jun-Aug) Tiny kiosk on the train station forecourt providing information on the North Baikal area.

Warm North of Baikal (www.privet-baikal.ru) English-language website belonging to the local tourism association with tons of information and listings.

ℹ Getting There & Away

TRAIN

Severobaikalsk's BAM station is located just 500m from the central square, heading up Leningradsky pr. Tickets are best bought direct from the station where queues are rare.

Severobaikalsk has the following rail connections:

Bratsk *platskart/kupe* R1400/2600; 14 hours to 16 hours; up to four daily

Irkutsk *platskart/kupe* R2600/5000; one day, 14 hours; daily

Krasnoyarsk *platskart/kupe* R2200/4300; one day, four hours; up to four daily

Moscow *platskart* R6200, *kupe* R8300 to R12,500; three days, 18 hours; one or two daily

Tynda *platskart/kupe* R2000/3800; 26 hours; daily

BOAT

From late June to late August a hydrofoil service runs the length of Lake Baikal between Nizhne-angarsk, Severobaikalsk and Irkutsk via Olkhon Island. Check VSRP (p242) for times and ticket prices.

BUS

Marshrutky cluster outside Severobaikalsk's train station and run to the following destinations:

Baikalskoe R70, 45 minutes, two daily

Goudzhekit R120, 45 minutes, three daily

Nizhneangarsk Airport R50, 50 minutes, half-hourly

NORTHERN BAIKAL'S MINISPAS

Seismic activity in the northern Baikal area shakes free lots of thermal springs around which tiny spas have sprouted. These are great places to soothe aching muscles after days of contortion in your BAM carriage bunk, though facilities are pretty basic. Costs are low for accommodation, food and bathing.

Goudzhekit   Гоуджекит

Some 39km northwest of Severobaikalsk, Goudzhekit's lonely BAM station is beautifully situated between bald, high peaks that stay dusted with snow until early June. Five minutes' walk to the right, the tiny timber spa has two pools fed by thermal springs whose waters gurgle at a soothing 40°C.

There are two basic hotels at the spa, but most visitors just come for the day. Take the *marshrutka* which leaves from in front of Severobaikalsk train station at 9am, noon and 3pm, returning around an hour later.

Dzelinda   Дзелинда

Tiny timber Dzelinda 90km east of Severobaikalsk is another hot-springs spa on the BAM railway but with a much more appealing forest location than Goudzhekit. Thermal springs keep the outdoor pools at a toasty 44°C even in winter, and when the surrounding hills are thick with snow and the temperature plunges to -35°C, a warm swim can be exhilarating. Guests stay in timber houses, one of which has an intricately carved gable. All meals are provided. Book transport and accommodation through Severobaikalsk helpers and tour companies.

Khakusy   Хакусы

To land at this idyllically isolated hot-spring **turbaza** (holiday camp; www.hakusy.com) requires permits in summer (available through Severobaikalsk tour companies and hotels), but these are waived in February and March, when it takes about an hour to drive across the ice from Severobaikalsk. Bathing is fun in the snow and frozen steam creates curious ice patterns on the wooden spa buildings. In summer make sure you book the ferry well in advance as it's a popular trip among Russian holidaymakers. An alternative way to reach Khakusy is along the 100km Frolikha Adventure Coastline Trail.

Around Severobaikalsk

Nizhneangarsk   Нижнеангарск

☑ 30130 / POP 5000 / TIME MOSCOW +5HR

Until the BAM clunked into town, Nizhneangarsk had led an isolated existence for more than 300 years, cobbling together its long streets of wooden houses and harvesting Baikal's rich *omul* (a type of fish) stocks. If truth be told, not much changed when the railway arrived, but despite the appearance of larger Severobaikalsk 30km away, the 5km-long village remains the administrative centre of northern Baikal.

The **Regional Museum** (ul Pobedy 37; admission R100; ⊙10am-6pm Mon-Fri) chases the history of the region back to the 17th century and includes several Evenki exhibits.

To the east of the town a long spit of land known as **Yarki Island** caps the most northerly point of Lake Baikal and keeps powerful currents and waves out of the frag-

ile habitat of the Verkhnyaya Angara delta. Scenic low-altitude flights cross Lake Baikal to Ulan-Ude (six per week) when weather conditions allow. *Marshrutky* (R50, 50 minutes) from Severobaikalsk run every 30 minutes along ul Pobedy then continue along the coast road (ul Rabochaya) to the airport.

Baikalskoe   Байкальское

This timeless little fishing village of log-built houses 45km south of Severobaikalsk has a jaw-droppingly picturesque lakeside location backed by wooded hills and snow-dusted peaks. Your first stop should be the small, informal **school museum** (admission R100; ⊙10am-4pm) where hands-on exhibits tell the story of the village from the Stone Age to the seal hunts of the 20th century. The only other sight is the wooden **Church of St Inokent**, which strikes a scenic lakeside pose.

Most come to Baikalskoe on a day trip from Severobaikalsk, but if you do want to stay the night, arrange a homestay through tour agencies and fixers in Severobaikalsk. There's no cafe, just a couple of shops selling basic foodstuffs. *Marshrutky* (R90, 45 minutes) leave from outside Severobaikalsk train station early in the morning and in the early evening each day, returning an hour or so later.

A section of the Great Baikal Trail heads north from the fishing port for 20 minutes up a cliff-side path towards the radio mast. From here there are superb views looking back towards the village. Beyond that, Baikalskoe's shamanic **petroglyphs** hide in awkward-to-reach cliff-side locations and can only be found with the help of a knowledgeable local. The well-maintained trail continues another 18 scenic kilometres through beautiful cedar and spruce forests and past photogenic **Boguchan Island** to chilly **Lake Slyudyanskoe**. Next to the lake stands **Echo**, a small *turbaza* (holiday camp) – book through the Maryasov family in Severobaikalsk (p243).

The hike makes for a rewarding day trip and, with the path hugging the lake most of the way, there's little chance of getting lost. From the Echo *turbaza* head along a dirt track through the forest to the Severobaikalsk–Baikalskoe road to hitch a lift, or pre-arrange transport back to Severobaikalsk. Alternatively, some hikers tackle the day the other way round, catching the morning *marshrutka* to Echo *turbaza* then timing the hike to make the evening *marshrutka* back to Severobaikalsk.

Tynda Тында

📞 41656 / POP 35,500 / TIME MOSCOW +9HR

The king of the BAM, Tynda is a non-descript BAM HQ flanked by low-lying pine-covered hills. Many stop here, as it's a hub for trains between Severobaikalsk, Komsomolsk-na-Amure and, on the Little BAM (p210), Blagoveshchensk to the south, or, on the in-progress AYaM (Amuro-Yakutskaya Magistral, or Amuro-Yakutskaya Mainline), Neryungri and Tommot to the north.

Don't expect quaint. Tynda is fully Soviet – there was nothing but a few shacks before BAM centralised its efforts here in 1974. Liven up your visit by arriving during a festival. The **Bakaldin Festival** rotates between several nearby Evenki villages in late May or early June, with traditional song, dance, reindeer rides and plenty of reindeer shash-lyk and other native delicacies. March sees the **Reindeer Hunter and Herder Festival**.

⊙ Sights & Activities

Besides the BAM Museum, about the only other thing worth checking out in Tynda is the dramatic sledgehammer-wielding **BAM worker statue** (on ul Mokhortova 10, just south of central ul Krasnaya Presnaya, near its eastern end). **Zarya** is a native Evenki village nearby. Bus 105 from the train station goes eight times daily (30 minutes).

Contact adventurer **Alexey Podprugin** (📞 8-914-552 1455; bamland@mail.ru) for kayaking, hiking and cross-country skiing trips.

BAM Museum MUSEUM
(Музей истории БАМа; ul Sportivnaya 22; admission with/without guide R35/25; ⊙ 10am-2pm & 3-6pm Tue-Fri, to 7pm Sat) Tynda's pride and joy has four rooms of BAM relics and photos (no English), but also covers native Evenki culture, WWII, local art and regional wildlife. One section covers the Little BAM and the Gulag prisoners who built it in the 1930s. They lived (and died) in 24 BAM lagery ('bamlag', or labour camps) between Tynda and Bamovskaya. Photos chronicle the extreme hardships these prisoners endured. Two rooms are dedicated to the big BAM, sections of which were built from the 1930s to 1950s before Stalin died and the project was mothballed. Displays cover the period between its relaunch in 1974 and completion in 1984 (although it wasn't fully operational until 1991). The museum is hard to find: After crossing the pedestrian bridge from the train station, take the first left, continue 200m and turn right up Sportivnaya, where you'll soon see it on your left.

🛏 Sleeping & Eating

Resting Rooms HOSTEL $
(Комнаты отдыха; 📞 41656-73 297; bed per 6/12/24hr from R640/980/1650) Comfy and clean dorm rooms in the train station. Shower available for non-guests (R150).

Hotel Yunost HOTEL $$
(Гостиница Юность; 📞 41656-43 534; ul Krasnaya Presnaya 49; s/d from R2000/3700, s/d with shared bathroom R1000/2400) Faded but fine option in centre; Dervla Murphy recuperated here as related in her book *Through Siberia by Accident*.

OVERLAND FROM TYNDA TO YAKUTSK

Travellers in Tynda often have their sights on Yakutsk in the Sakha Republic. To get to Yakutsk you must first take a train to Neryungri, 5½ hours north. From there you can either fly with Yakutia Airlines (R10,500, 1¾ hours, daily except Sunday), or embark on one of the Far East's classic overland journeys: 15 to 20 bumpy hours in a Russian UAZ jeep or van to cover 810km on the AYaM (Amuro-Yakutskaya Magistral) highway.

Daily departures from the Neryungri train station are timed for the 6.22am arrival of the train from Khabarovsk. Most trips are in 11-passenger vans, but if passengers are lacking you may end up in a four-passenger jeep. The price varies with the season, but typically costs around R3500 per person. It's a pretty trip that cuts over a mountain pass and through tracts of virgin taiga (mountain pine) before traversing the Lena River by *parom* (car ferry) an hour south of Yakutsk. However, it's extremely rough in patches and quite dusty in the warmer months.

Passenger services on the AYaM train line run further north to Aldan (six hours) and Tommot (eight hours), but you'll keep well ahead of the train (and avoid a possible overnight stay in either Aldan or Tommot) by getting a head start from Neryungri. The AYaM train line actually extends a couple of hundred kilometres beyond Tommot, although passenger services terminate there. The line is being extended to Nizhny Bestyakh (opposite Yakutsk on the Lena River), and plans are to open the entire route to passenger services. This may happen within the next couple of years, but we're not taking bets.

Piv Bar Teremok
PIZZA $

(Пив Бар Теремок; ul Krasnaya Presnaya; mains around R380; ⊙noon-midnight; 🛜) Serves up palatable pizzas, Drakon draught beer (from Khabarovsk) and free wi-fi, with seating on an open-sided veranda. To find it, turn left at the eastern end of ul Krasnaya Presnaya, and walk up 50m.

❶ Information

The train station has an ATM and left-luggage office (R120).

❶ Getting There & Away

The **train station** – the city's most striking landmark – is across the Tynda River. A pedestrian bridge leads 1km north to ul Krasnaya Presnaya.

Train 75 heads via BAM to Moscow (*kupe/platskart* R14,700/8000; five days) on even-numbered days, stopping in Severobaikalsk (*kupe/platskart* R4200/2400; 27 hours), while train 77 to Novosibirsk (*kupe/platskart* R11,300/6200; two days, 19 hours) takes the Little BAM south on odd-numbered days to connect with the Trans-Siberian line at Skovorodino.

There are several daily departures to Neryungri, including the 325 (from R620, 5½ hours), which departs around 1am. Train 364 trundles to Komsomolsk daily at 5.20pm (*kupe/platskart* R4300/2400; one day, 12 hours), and 325 heads daily to Khabarovsk at 2am via Skovorodino (*kupe/platskart* R4300/2400; 28 hours; daily).

Komsomolsk-na-Amure
Комсомольск - на - Амуре

📱 4217 / POP 280,000 / TIME MOSCOW +7HR

After days of taiga and grey Soviet towns, Komsomolsk-na-Amure hits the BAM adventurer like a mini St Petersburg. Set along a few grand boulevards, the city is worth a night or more if you are getting on or off the BAM. Komsomolsk was built virtually from scratch by Stalin in the 1930s as a vital cog in the Soviet Union's military industrial complex. The location was no accident: the city was far removed from potential prying eyes along the Pacific Coast and Chinese border, yet its position along the Amur allowed for relatively easy transport of goods. Imitating the tsars, Stalin erected elaborate neo-Renaissance and neoclassical buildings in the city centre, only festooned with stars, crescents and statues of model Soviet citizens instead of the usual angels and goblins. To build the city he enlisted Communist Youth League (Komsomol – hence the city's name) volunteers as well as Gulag labourers. Around town, factories sprouted up to produce ships, weapons, electricity and, most famously, Sukhoi (Su) fighter jets in a factory that still works today.

◉ Sights

Soviet Mosaics
STREET ART

Komsomolsk has a wealth of wonderful murals adorning the sides of apartment blocks

Komsomolsk-na-Amure

THE BAIKAL-AMUR MAINLINE (BAM) KOMSOMOLSK-NA-AMURE

some old fish-skin jackets and other Nanai artefacts, plus a space suit not unlike Yury Gagarin wore.

Memorials   MONUMENT

Just northwest of the river terminal is the impressive **WWII memorial**, which features stoic faces chipped from stone, with nearby pillars marking the years of WWII. Other memorials include a garbage-strewn sculpture park dedicated to **Gulag victims** (near pr Lenina 1).

☞ Tours

River Cruises   BOAT TOURS

(River Terminal; admission R250) On summer weekends you can hop aboard 90-minute cruises along the Amur River. Boats depart at 3pm Saturday and Sunday as well as 7pm Thursday and Saturday. Buy tickets onboard.

Nata Tour   TOURS

(Hara-Typ; ☎4217-201 067; www.komsomolsk-nata.ru; office 110, ul Vasyanina 12; ◎10am-6pm Mon-Fri) This travel service arranges three- to five-hour 'Stalin tours' of city communist sites (including a Gulag camp; from R1200 per person); adventure tours involving fishing, rafting or skiing; and day trips and/or homestays at Verkhnyaya Ekon. White-water rafting trips involve a train ride to Novy Urgal on the BAM. Slower one- to several-day floats can be done closer to Komsomolsk. Tours of the **Yury Gagarin Aircraft Factory**, where the Su jets are built, can also be arranged.

and factories. Most were the creation of Khabarovsk-based artist Nikolai Dolbilkin, who lived here in the 1950s and '60s. Among the best are the double triptych **WWII mosaic** (2nd fl, cnr pr Mira & ul Truba) in the central grey *dom kultura* building near Sudostroitel Park (now inside a children's play space); the **nauka (science) mosaic** (pr Lenina) at the Polytechnical Institute, a block east of Hotel Voskhod; and the stunning **electric worker mosaic** (alleya Truda) on the side of the TETs electric station (be mindful of the belligerent security guards at this last one).

Municipal Museum of Regional
Studies   MUSEUM

(cnr alleya Truda & ul Kirova; admission R220; ◎9.30am-5pm Tue-Fri, 10am-5pm Sat & Sun) In a newly inaugurated building near Sudostroitel Park, several rooms of photos and knick-knacks show how Komsomolsk rose from the tent camps of original pioneers in 1932 to an industrial Soviet city. It also contains

🛏 Sleeping

Nata Tour can arrange homestays (R1000 per person including breakfast).

Resting Rooms
HOSTEL **$**

(Комнаты отдыха; ☑ 4217-284 193; train station; 12/24hr dm from R640/1100, s 12/24hr without bathroom R935/1650) A fine option if you need a break from sleeping on trains.

★ Biznestsentr
HOTEL **$$**

(Бизнесцентр; ☑ 4217-521 522; bc@etc.kna. ru; ul Dzerzhinskogo 3; s/d incl breakfast from R2800/3500; ❄@🛜) Komsomolsk's most modern hotel has bright, comfortably furnished rooms with modern bathrooms (including space-shuttle-like shower capsules). English-speaking receptionists are on hand.

Dacha Krushcheva
GUESTHOUSE **$$**

(Дача Хрущёва; ☑ 4217-540 659; ul Khabarovska 47; r R2100-3400; ❄🛜) Built for Nikita Khrushchev, this backstreet dacha is a step back in time. The suites could fit a Young Pioneers troupe and all six rooms have 1970s furnishings, but big new windows. There's a 25% booking charge.

Hotel Voskhod
HOTEL **$$**

(Гостиница Восход; ☑ 4217-535 131; pr Pervostroiteley 31; s/d from R2850/3300; ⊜@🛜) A 10-minute walk from the train station, this eight-storey beast has decent recently renovated rooms.

🍴 Eating

In the summer you can feast on shashlyk (R200) and cold drinks along the riverfront.

Market
MARKET

(Рынок; cnr pr Lenina & pr Mira) Load up on essentials at this small outdoor market.

Kofeynya
CAFE **$**

(Кофейня; ul Oktyabrsky 48; snacks R60-130; ⊙24hr; 🛜) A fine spot for eggs, bliny or *kasha* (porridge) in the morning, set meals at lunchtime (R170 to R250) and light snacks at other times, plus diverse coffees.

Bistro
STOLOVAYA **$**

(ul Lenina 19; meals R180-300; ⊙9am-10pm) Beside pl Lenina, this clean modern *stolovaya* serves tasty, affordable staples: baked dishes, roast meats, and the usual beet or potato salads are all on offer.

Shinok Pervach
UKRAINIAN **$$$**

(Шинок Первач; ul Dzerzhinskogo 34/5; ul Internatsionalny; mains R450-850; ⊙noon-1am; 🛜)

BAM ENDS, SAKHALIN BECKONS

BAM completists will end up in the grey Soviet port town of Vanino (actually the BAM ends 15 minutes beyond Vanino, in Sovetskaya Gavan-Sortirovka). From Vanino, there is theoretically a daily 4pm boat (in reality, it leaves when full when the weather allows) to Kholmsk on Sakhalin Island (tickets R1670 to R3025, 18 hours). The Russian-only information numbers are ☑ 42137-74 088 in Vanino and ☑ 42433-66 098 in Kholmsk. Call the day before to reserve a seat – they should have a reasonable idea of whether the next day's ship will sail. But no guarantees.

☑ Among the best restaurants in town, Shinok Pervach serves up tasty grilled fish, roast meats and zingy salads. The chunky wooden tables and circular dining room festooned with ribbons bestow a certain peasant chic. It's pricey, and watch out for hidden charges. Located off ul Internatsionalny, a 15-minute walk northwest of the waterfront.

ℹ Getting There & Around

From Komsomolsk's pink **train station** (pr Pervostroiteley) the excruciatingly slow 351 leaves daily for Vladivostok (*kupe/platskart* R3700/2100, 24½ hours). There are also services to Khabarovsk (*kupe/platskart* from R2000/1100, 10 hours).

On the BAM, 363 heads west to Tynda (*kupe/platskart* R4300/2400; one day, 13 hours; daily); to reach Severobaikalsk; change in Tynda. The daily train 351 heads east to Vanino (*kupe/platskart* R2200/1200, 11 hours). The BAM's first/last stop, Sovetskaya Gavan-Sortirovka, 15 minutes east of Vanino, is not to be confused with the city of Sovetskaya Gavan, an hour away from Vanino by bus.

Local and long-distance buses leave from the **bus station** (☑ 4217-542 554; ⊙6am-10.30pm) near the river. Buses bound for Khabarovsk (from R640, six hours) leave every 90 minutes or so from 7am.

For a DIY adventure, head down the Amur River by hydrofoil to its terminus in Nikolaevsk-na-Amure (from R4085, 11 hours). The boat departs three days a week from the **river terminal** (currently 7am on Monday, Thursday and Friday).

Within the city, handy tram 2 runs from the train station along ul Lenina and pr Mira to the river terminal (R15).

The Trans-Mongolian Route

Route Info

➡ Distance: 2217km

➡ Duration: Two days, six hours

➡ Time zones: Moscow +5

Best Places to Stay & Eat

➡ LG Guesthouse (p268)

➡ Zaya's Hostel (p268)

➡ Hotel Örgöö (p267)

➡ Garden Hotel (p282)

➡ Namaste (p270)

➡ Mongolians (p269)

Why Go?

The Trans-Mongolian route is the most diverse leg of the cross-continental journey, cutting across three distinct cultures, landscapes and languages. It includes some of the most awe-inspiring sights of the long journey, not the least of which is the Gobi Desert, but also the vast Mongolian steppes and the stunning gorges outside Běijīng. The major jumping-off point is Ulaanbaatar, where many travellers head for the colourful Naadam Festival, but any time of year reveals a surprisingly fast-paced city with great cultural attractions and heady nightlife. For the full Mongolia experience, venture outside the capital, where nomads pitch their gers on the open prairie alongside their huge herds of livestock. Before leaving Russia, pause to explore Ulan-Ude, where you could take in the historic towns of Novoselenginsk and Kyakhta. The China leg is a relatively short hop but has its own unique character, highlighted by the beguiling Yungang Caves near Dàtóng.

When to Go
Ulaanbaatar

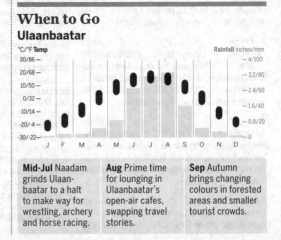

Mid-Jul Naadam grinds Ulaanbaatar to a halt to make way for wrestling, archery and horse racing.

Aug Prime time for lounging in Ulaanbaatar's open-air cafes, swapping travel stories.

Sep Autumn brings changing colours in forested areas and smaller tourist crowds.

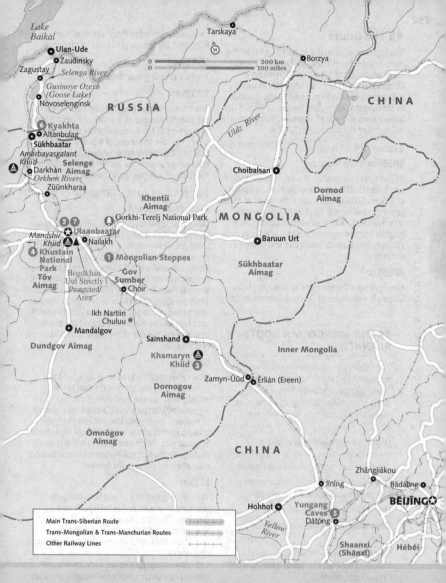

Trans-Mongolian Route Highlights

① Enjoying a meal of boiled mutton and fermented mare's milk in a ger (yurt) on the vast **Mongolian steppes** (p277)

② Attending a mystical ceremony at the country's largest monastery, Ulaanbaatar's **Gandan Khiid** (p262)

③ Absorbing some of the earth's energy at **Shambhala** (p279), near Khamaryn Khiid

④ Spotting rare wild horses at **Khustain National Park** (p277)

⑤ Staring in wonder at the 51,000 Buddhist statues inside the **Yungang Caves** (p283) near Dàtóng

⑥ Exploring the antiquated border town of **Kyakhta** (p255), once a thriving trading post on the ancient tea route

⑦ Celebrating the midsummer **Naadam** (p266) festival, featuring Mongolia's best wrestlers, archers and race horses

ⓘ The Route

The Trans-Mongolian line branches off from the main Trans-Siberian route at Zaudinsky, about 13km southeast of Ulan-Ude. Mongolia and China each have their own kilometre markers. In Mongolia the markers measure the distance to the Russian–Mongolian border, so 0km is the border town of Naushki. Once in China the markers measure the distance to Běijīng.

ZAUDINSKY TO NAUSHKI

5655km from Moscow

At Zaudinsky the branch line turns south and continues to follow the Selenge River, crossing at around 5701km. Here you'll see herds of cattle grazing across low green hills beside a wide, lazy river, and villages of wooden houses with brightly painted window shutters and flourishing gardens that explode with fruits and flowers in summer.

5769km

After you pass the town of Zagustay, the train follows the shoreline of Gusinoe Ozero (Goose Lake), surrounded by thick woods of pine and birch that are usually prevalent further north.

5885km

Another crossing over the Selenge River.

5902km

The train arrives at Naushki (5902km in Russia but 0km for Mongolia), a small, uneventful town that serves as the Russian border post. If you haven't gotten to the end of *War and Peace* by now you'll certainly have the chance here as the train hangs around the border for several hours for customs and passport checks.

SÜKHBAATAR TO ULAANBAATAR

21km from Naushki

Mongolia's chief border town, Sükhbaatar (population 19,700) is set at the junction of the Selenge and Orkhon Rivers. Founded in the 1940s, it's named after the revolutionary hero Damdin Sükhbaatar, who in 1921 famously rode his horse to Russia to enlist the aid of the Bolsheviks after Mongolia was invaded by White Russian troops. The train stops for an hour or two (depending on which train you're on), giving you time to stretch your legs and perhaps head across the street to grab a meal in one of the small Mongolian restaurants.

63km

When you cross the Eröö River look out for cranes, herons and other waterfowl in the marshy areas on the west side of the train. Having entered Mongolia you'll also sense a change of scenery: the forests thin out into the lush green pastures of the fertile Selenge River basin. You may also notice new scents (in the form of mutton) as the Mongolian dining car is attached after the train crosses the border.

123km

The rolling green hills of northern Mongolia break momentarily as the train pulls into Darkhan. The train stops for about 20 minutes. You can buy some *buuz* (mutton-filled dumplings) from the ladies who sell them out of plastic containers.

Should you venture off the rails, the most interesting sight in the area is Amarbayasgalant Khiid, the best-preserved Buddhist monastery in Mongolia, a two-hour drive from Darkhan over rough roads.

274-290km

This is the most scenic stretch of the Trans-Mongolian route, a 15km ride through a pretty valley and alongside the Kharaa River.

355-365km

The train passes the area of Hui Doloon Khutag, where the Naadam horse races are held from 10 to 12 July. In the days before Naadam locals

---

TRANS-MONGOLIAN ROUTE PLANNER

The following is a suggested itinerary for covering the main sites along the Trans-Mongolian route. This is a quick pace, so consider adding a few days to make the journey at a more leisurely pace:

Day 1 Leave Ulan-Ude and take a 3½ hour *marshrutka* (minibus) to Kyakhta, cross border, overnight in Sükhbaatar.

Day 2 Travel to Darkhan and arrange a taxi to Amarbayasgalant Monastery.

Day 3 Continue to Ulaanbaatar.

Days 4 & 5 Tour Ulaanbaatar and around.

Day 6 Travel to Dalanjargalan by local train and continue by jeep to Ikh Nartiin Chuluu, overnight.

Day 7 Tour Ikh Nartiin Chuluu.

Day 8 Return to Dalanjargalan and travel to Sainshand by road or train.

Day 9 Visit Khamaryn Khiid, continue on night train to Zamyn-Üüd.

Day 10 Cross border, continue by bus to Dàtóng.

Day 11 Tour Dàtóng and Yungang Caves.

Day 12 Train to Běijīng (seven hours).

move out here en masse, creating a city of scattered gers. After another 20km the train curves around a valley towards Ulaanbaatar, where you'll get your first glimpse of the smokestacks and urban sprawl of the Mongolian capital.

404km

After a long march through the industrial outskirts the train pulls into Ulaanbaatar for 30 minutes. If stopping off here, expect throngs of people on the platform offering tours, taxi rides or a bunk in a local guesthouse.

ULAANBAATAR TO ZAMYN-ÜÜD

415–440km

South of Ulaanbaatar, the railway winds through the gently swelling hills of the Bogdkhan Uul mountain range. Trees eventually disappear and the landscape becomes a 180-degree panorama of steppe, the only interruptions being grazing horses and the occasional ger.

649km

There's a 15-minute stop at Choir, where a statue of the first Mongolian cosmonaut stands in front of the station. During the Soviet era this neglected town of 13,000 people was home to Mongolia's biggest air base.

From Choir, it's possible to detour south for one hour to Ikh Nartiin Chuluu, an area of rocky outcrops that provide shelter for endangered argali sheep.

Continuing south, the train enters the flat, arid and sparsely populated Gobi Desert. Occasional stops at small outposts in the desert provides glimpses of dilapidated shacks and villagers hauling water or galloping alongside the train on horseback. Any small bodies of water attract livestock, and you'll probably spot horses, camels, sheep and goats (sorry, no yaks in this part of the country).

876km

The train stops for around 20 minutes at Sainshand (Good Pond). The vendors on the platform selling *buuz* run out of product quickly, so you'll need to act fast. About 40km south of Sainshand is Khamaryn Khiid, one of the most important Buddhist monasteries in the Gobi.

1113km

The bleak, dusty landscape continues to the border town of Zamyn-Üüd. Travel writer Paul Theroux visited the town in the mid-1980s and commented that Zamyn-Üüd was 'a wreck of a town set on glaring sands and so lacking in events that when a camel went by everyone watched it'. Sadly, not much has changed since then. From here you can cross by road or rail over the border to China. If you're coming from China you'll have to wait around for the next local train heading north, or ask around for a share taxi.

Ulan-Ude to Běijīng

West to Moscow

5640km	Ulan-Ude
5655km	Zaudinsky
	4hr, 45min
5902km	Naushki

RUSSIA
MONGOLIA

21km	Sükhbaatar
	1hr, 50min
123km	Darkhan
	2hr
235km	Züünkharaa
	3hr
404km	Ulaanbaatar
	4hr, 15min
649km	Choir
	3hr, 45min
876km	Sainshand
	3hr, 20min
1113km	Zamyn-Üüd

MONGOLIA
CHINA

842km to Běijīng	Èrlián (Erenhot)
	4hr, 15min
498km	Jíníng
	1hr, 50min
371km	Dàtóng
	3hr, 10min
193km	Zhāngjiākou
	2hr, 30min
73km	Bādálǐng
	1hr, 30min
0km	BĚIJĪNG

To Vladivostok (Trans-Siberian) & Běijīng (Trans-Manchurian)

RUSSIA–MONGOLIA BORDER CROSSINGS

Naushki–Sükhbaatar

Russia and Mongolia use the same rail gauge, so no bogie-changing is required. However, the time saved is eaten up in customs procedures and general hanging around – it can last six to 11 hours!

Southbound travellers fill out customs forms in duplicate, then Russian border guards collect their passports. When you get your passport back, you can get off the train. There usually are no moneychangers here, but you can change roubles to tögrög when you arrive in Sükhbaatar (or Ulaanbaatar).

Train 4 from Moscow arrives at night, so most travellers stay on or near the train. Train 362 from Irkutsk arrives in the daytime and hangs around the station for 3½ hours, so there's plenty of time to get off and wander around Naushki. The station also has a shower block where you can get a hot shower for R100. There's a farmers market just outside the station (walk to the southern end of the platform and cross the street). There's also a small park and a little hill to climb for the view. Just make sure to ask the *provodnitsa* (carriage attendant) about departure times so you know when to return.

The customs and immigration process is repeated by Mongolian officials in Sükhbaatar where, if you need it, there should be no problem buying a ticket for the 8.55pm train to Ulaanbaatar. The trip takes nine hours and costs T7200 *obshchiy* (hard seat), T16,000 *platskart* (hard sleeper) or T23,500 *kupe* (soft sleeper). *Marshrutky* (fixed-route minibuses; T25,000, six hours) to Ulaanbaatar depart when full from a lot outside the station; these are a good bet in daylight hours.

There are some cafes near Sükhbaatar station, plus some ATMs and moneychangers at the station itself.

Northbound travellers can expect to spend a few hours at Sükhbaatar station. Train 3 from Běijīng arrives at 8.50pm, but train 361 (Ulaanbaatar–Irkutsk) goes through during the day. The daily Sükhbaatar–Ulan-Ude train leaves at 10.45am and, if you can score a ticket, costs T63,630.

At Naushki station a couple of ATMs dispense roubles. The local Naushki–Ulan-Ude train ride, for R320 *platskart* (3rd class, open carriage), is an attractive but excruciatingly

ZAMYN-ÜÜD TO BĚIJĪNG
842km (from Běijīng)

Compared to Zamyn-Üüd, the Chinese side of the border, Èrlián, is a veritable megalopolis. From here it takes about 13 hours to get to Běijīng by direct train.

For the first several hours the train continues through the Gobi, now in the ostensibly autonomous region of Inner Mongolia. Mongolians make up only about 15% of the population here, and since 1949 China has done its best to assimilate them, eradicating their nomadic lifestyle, even though they have been permitted to keep their written and spoken language. Further south, the desert slowly gives way to grasslands and you'll spot Mongol shepherds tending their flocks.

It's a long journey between Ulaanbaatar and Běijīng, so if you're getting a little antsy, go to the dining car, where most of the train's socialising takes place. The Chinese dining car is arguably the best on the entire trans-continental route – but we'll let you be the judge of that.

498km

There is a stop at the main rail junction of Jíníng, where vendors sell drinks, snacks and colourful balloons on the platform. This is where the Ulaanbaatar–Hohhot train breaks off the main line and heads west.

371km

The train creaks into Dàtóng, where it halts for 25 minutes. Dàtóng is the centre of China's coal industry but the region remains an important centre of Chinese history and was the powerbase for the Tang dynasty (618–907). Slip off the train here for a trip to nearby Yungang Caves.

300km

From Dàtóng the line turns east, entering Héběi province. Héběi is characterised by its mountainous tableland where the Great Wall runs. There are good views of the Wall on the northern side of the tracks between 295km and 275km. In addition, keep your eyes peeled for the occasional walled villages, typically composed of thick rammed-earth walls with traditional homes stuffed into their small interior. One example can slow ride (six hours). The more frequent *marshrutky* from Kyakhta are faster (three hours, R250).

Kyakhta–Altanbulag

You can avoid the extreme tedium of the direct train crossing by taking this alternative road route into or out of Mongolia. There's a daily bus (R1300, 12 hours) to Ulaanbaatar departing at 7.30am from a stop near the Opera House roundabout in Ulan-Ude. Contact Buryat-Intour (p200) in Ulan-Ude for tickets. From Ulaanbaatar, buses leave from the parking lot in front of the train station. Tickets cost T47,000 and can be purchased in the domestic railway office on the 2nd floor. You can buy a ticket one week in advance.

More interesting, though, is to take a minibus to the Mongolian border at Kyakhta. Going the other way, shared taxis for Sükhbaatar leave from a parking lot next to the Ulaanbaatar train station. In Sükhbaatar there are shared taxis to the border town Altanbulag.

The Russia–Mongolia border (9am to 8pm Russian side, 8am to 7pm Mongolian side) is open to bicycles and vehicles, and some officials speak English. You can't walk across, so pedestrians need to negotiate passage with private drivers. Start as close as possible to the front of the chaotic queue: processing takes about two hours, with only a handful of vehicles allowed through at any one time. The going rate is R150 (or T6000) per passenger across no-man's-land. The Mongolian side has a small bank where you can change money and there are also private moneychangers in Altanbulag (they hang out near the border). There are no moneychangers on the Russian side, so if you're coming from Mongolia it's a good idea to have a few roubles on hand to get you into Kyakhta, where you can change more.

From Altanbulag it's another 26km to Sükhbaatar train station. Rides here in a shared vehicle should cost R50 or T2500.

Going from Mongolia to Russia, your driver will probably drop you in Kyakhta's Sloboda district, near the Voskresenskaya Church. From here you can take a *marshrutka* (R10) into the town centre and the bus stand.

be seen between the 264km and 263km markers on the south side of the tracks.

193km

The train stops for 10 minutes in the industrial city of Zhāngjiākou. Formerly known as Khaal-ga, which means 'door' or 'gate' in Mongolian, this town was where the ancient tea caravans crossed the Great Wall. From here the terrain becomes increasingly hilly and the scenery is quite dramatic as the train travels across a plateau punctuated by cropland and tree-filled gullies.

85km

From here the train begins its final approach to Běijīng, swiftly entering a mountainous zone that separates the Chinese capital from the northern plains. There are some 60 tunnels to pass through and while it can be difficult to spot the kilometre markers you can easily count down (or count up if you're heading north) the tunnel numbers, painted at the entrance of the tunnels (on the right side). The first number is the tunnel number, the second is the kilometre marker and the third is the length of the tunnel. Each time the train emerges from a tunnel there are stunning scenes of canyons, rivers and soaring rock towers.

0km

Make a toast with any leftover Russian vodka; you've reached Běijīng, the end of the line. If you're starting your journey in Běijīng, take a moment to wipe down the windows with a dust cloth; the photo opportunities are excellent outside Běijīng and you'll want a clear shot (heading north the best views are out the left side of the train).

Kyakhta, Russia   Кяхта

☏ 30142 / POP 20,000 / TIME MOSCOW +5HR

Formerly called Troitskosavsk, the Kyakhta of two centuries ago was a town of tea-trade millionaires whose grandiose cathedral was reputed to have had solid silver doors embedded with diamonds. By the mid-19th century as many as 5000 cases of tea a day were arriving via Mongolia on a stream of horse or camel caravans, which returned loaded with furs.

This gloriously profitable tea trade was brought to a shuddering end with the completion of the Suez Canal and the Trans-Siberian Railway, leaving Kyakhta to wither away into a dust-blown border settlement. Wonderfully preserved by 70 years of communist neglect, the town is dotted with remnants of a wealthier past, which make Kyakhta well worth the trip from Ulan-Ude.

Travellers should be aware that Kyakhta lies well within the Russian border zone and is officially off limits to foreigners without a permit. Ask Ulan-Ude agencies and helpers for the latest situation (travellers do still visit without permits).

◉ Sights

Kyakhta Museum   MUSEUM
(ul Lenina 49; admission R200; ⊙10am-6pm Tue-Sun) Kyakhta's star attraction is its delightfully eccentric museum, perhaps rather comically dubbed the 'Hermitage of the East' by some overzealous locals. It's certainly one of Siberia's fullest museums with room after musty room of exhibits relating to the tea trade, local plants and animals, Buryat traditions, Asian art and Kyakhta's bit part in WWII. Many of the older exhibits were hauled back to Troitskosavsk by 19th-century Russian gentlemen explorers who launched trans-Asian expeditions from the town. No English signage or information.

Uspenskaya Church   CHURCH
(ul Krupskaya) For years Kyakhta's only working church, this beautiful, late-19th-century building was closed twice during the communist decades (1938 and 1962). Leave a donation for its upkeep.

Voskresenskaya Church   CHURCH
(Sloboda) Reopened in 2011 following painstaking restoration, the brilliant-white Resurrection Church is the last outpost of European Christianity before Mongolian Buddhism takes over. Take *marshrutka* 1 from ul Lenina.

Trinity Cathedral   CHURCH
(ul Lenina) The impressive shell of the 1817 cathedral lies at the heart of the overgrown central park at the end of ul Lenina.

✖ Eating

Letnee Kafe   CAFE $
(Летнее кафе; ul Lenina, opposite Hotel Turist; ⊙11am-midnight) No-frills Central Asian shashlyk, *plov* and beer stop on the main drag.

Café Sloboda   CAFE $
(Кафе Слобода; Sloboda; ⊙11am-11pm) Simple, cheap and clean cafe located 400m along the road from the Voskresenskaya Church, where the road peels off towards the border crossing.

❶ Orientation

Modern Kyakhta is effectively two towns. The main one is centred around ul Lenina, where the bus terminus sits next to the 1853 trading rows *(ryady gostinya)*. The smaller Sloboda district, 4km to the south, is where the border post is.

❶ Getting There & Away

Hourly *marshrutky* (R350, three hours) leave from Ulan-Ude's main bus station. There are a couple of options for crossing to/from Mongolia (p254).

Darkhan, Mongolia Дархан

☑ 01372 / POP 74,740 / TIME MOSCOW + 5HR

Darkhan (which means Blacksmith), was founded in the early 1960s by the Soviets as an industrial hub for coal production and wheat farming. Today it's a peaceful town of wide streets and big parks, without any of the congestion and crowds seen in Ulaanbaatar. While there are few attractions, it's a decent place to break up a road journey or as a jumping off point to see Amarbayasgalant Monastery.

Darkhan is divided into an 'old town' near the train station and a 'new town' to the south, with most hotels, restaurants and amenities located in the latter.

In the new town is the appealing little **Museum of Darkhan-Uul** (admission T2500; ⊙9am-1pm & 2-6pm Mon-Fri), which contains a well-presented collection of archaeological finds, traditional clothing, religious artefacts and stuffed wildlife.

You can find midrange accommodation about 10 minutes' walk from the bus station at the **Kharaa Hotel** (☑7037 0069, 9137 0069; kharaa_hotel@yahoo.com; r with breakfast from T40,000; @ ⓢ), which has clean rooms and a lively bar downstairs. Decent Western and better Mongolian cuisine can be found at

Texas Pub (meals T7500-14,000; ⏱11am-midnight; 🛜) in the heart of the new town.

There are hourly bus connections between Darkhan and Ulaanbaatar (T8000, 3½ hours) from the main **bus station** (Авто Вокзал). For Sükhbaatar (T8000, two hours), vans leave from outside the market in the new town. For Amarbayasgalant Khiid, hire a taxi from the taxi stand; a round trip should cost about T130,000.

The train is far slower than the bus, but if you are determined to stay on steel wheels, daytime train 272 leaves Darkhan at 8.48am and arrives in Ulaanbaatar 7½ hours later. Going north, the daily Ulaanbaatar–Sükhbaatar train (271) leaves Darkhan for Sükhbaatar at 5.55pm (about three hours).

Amarbayasgalant Khiid
Амарбаясгалант Хийд

Tucked up a remote valley 35km from any main road, Amarbayasgalant Monastery is one of the finest examples of Buddhist architecture in Mongolia. While not the easiest place to reach, it's worth considering if you have a particular interest in Buddhism or off-the-beaten-path sites.

The monastery was built between 1727 and 1737 by the Manchu emperor Yongzheng, and dedicated to the great Mongolian Buddhist and sculptor Zanabazar, whose mummified body was moved here in 1779. It is in the Manchu style, down to the inscriptions, symmetrical layout and imperial colour scheme.

At its height, Amarbayasgalant was home to more than 2000 monks; most were executed or shipped to labour camps during the Stalinist purge of 1937. The monastery was re-opened in 1990 and today there are around 30 monks.

The richly decorated main temple, **Tsogchin Dugan**, has a life-size **statue of Rinpoche Gurdava**, a lama from Inner Mongolia who lived in Tibet and Nepal before returning to Mongolia in 1992 and raising much of the money for the temple's restoration.

Ceremonies are usually held at 10am, so arrive early or stay overnight to see them.

A couple of new monuments – a golden **Buddhist statue** and a **stupa** – are situated on the hills behind the monastery. You could continue hiking up the mountains for even better views of the valley.

IF Tour Ger Camp (📞9918 9981, 9119 0808; iftour@yahoo.com; ger/r/cabin T50,000/50,000/60,000; ⏱May-Oct), about 1km northwest of the monastery, offers clean and cosy accommodation in gers or in a cabin. Flush toilets are available as well as hot showers (although water pressure is weak). Meals available.

No regular public transport goes to the monastery, so you'll need to organise a taxi from Darkhan (T130,000; 2 hours each way), get a price in writing to avoid confusion later. Alternatively, organise a tour from Ulaanbaatar, spending a night at the monastery and then getting dropped off at Darkhan where you can rejoin the Trans-Mongolia Railway. Expect to pay $300 to $400 for this itinerary.

Ulaanbaatar Улаанбаатар
📶 011 / POP 1,286,300 / TIME MOSCOW + 5HR

After several days of travelling across the Eurasian landmass, approaching Ulaanbaatar by train can be a jolting experience. Rolling green hills covered in pine trees harbour the occasional ger, and horsemen can be seen galloping alongside the train tracks. Then as the train bends into the Tuul River valley, the stunning urban sprawl of the Mongolian capital unfolds before your eyes.

Ulaanbaatar is a bizarre cocktail of ancient temples, crumbling Soviet-era apartment blocks, newer glass towers and derelict suburbs of gers and brick houses. Where roads exists, tiny Hyundais and giant Hummers jostle for position, scattering the crowds of jaywalkers. But don't allow the city's harsh appearance to put you off. The chaotic capital bursts with activity and will delight you with its friendly locals, quirky sights and live-for-the-moment buzz.

UB, as it's colloquially known, has several excellent museums and a lively Buddhist monastery in Gandan Khiid. International cuisine is surprisingly varied and brew pubs overflow onto bright patios. If the crowds and dust become too much, go for a hike up Bogdkhan Uul, the forested holy mountain to the south of the city. Beautiful countryside, national parks and nomadic culture can be found within a one- or two-hour drive in any direction.

Most of the city spreads east–west along the main road, Enkh Taivny Örgön Chölöö (Peace Ave). At the centre is Chinggis Khaan Square.

Central Ulaanbaatar

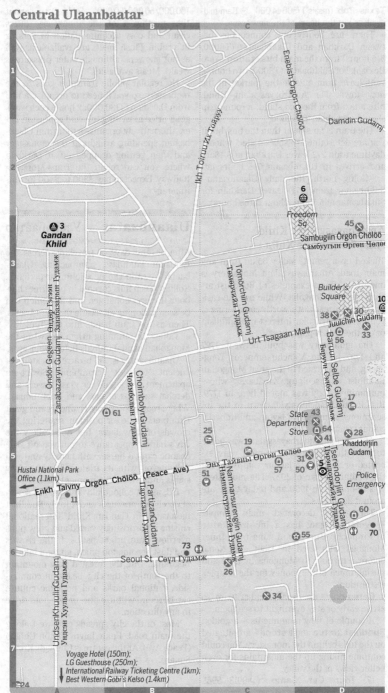

Enebish Örgön Chölöö

Damdin Gudamj

Ikh Toiruu Ikh Toiruu

6

Freedom Sq

45

Sambuugiin Örgön Chölöö
Самбуугийн Өргөн Чөлөө

3
Gandan Khiid

Ondor Gegeen Öndör Гэгээн
Zanabazaryn Gudamj Занабазарын Гудамж

Tömörchin Gudamj
Төмөрчийн Гудамж

Builder's Square

38 **30** **10**

Juulchin Gudamj

56

Urt Tsagaan Mall

33

ChoimbolynGudamj Чойболын Гудамж

Baruun Selbe Gudamj Баруун Сэлбэ Гудамж

17

61

State Department Store

43
64
41

28

Khaddorjiin Gudamj

25

19

57

31
50

5

Tserendorjiin Gudamj Цэрэндоржийн Гудамж

Police Emergency

Hustai National Park Office (1.1km)

Enkh Taivny Örgön Chölöö (Peace Ave)
Парижаа Гудамж

51

Enkh Taivny Örgön Chölöö
Намнансүрэнгийн Гудамж

Namnansurengiin Gudamj

60

11

PartizanGudamj Паризаа Гудамж

73

55

70

Seoul St Сөүл Гудамж

26

UndsenKhuuliinGudamj Үндсэн Хуулийн Гудамж

34

Voyage Hotel (150m);
LG Guesthouse (250m);
International Railway Ticketing Centre (1km);
Best Western Gobi's Kelso (1.4km)

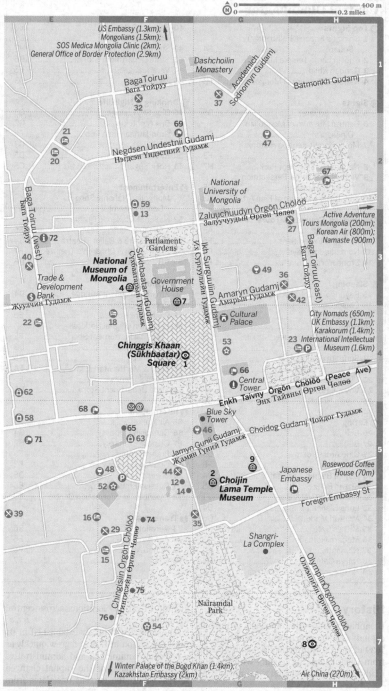

0 _____ 400 m
0 _____ 0.2 miles

US Embassy (1.3km);
Mongolians (1.5km);
SOS Medica Mongolia Clinic (2km);
General Office of Border Protection (2.9km)

Dashchoilin
Monastery

Batmonkh Gudamj

Baga Toiruu
Бага Тойруу

32

37

Academich
Sodnomyn Gudamj

69

47

Negdsen Undestnii Gudamj
Нэгдсэн Үндэстний Гудамж

20

21

67

59
13

National
University of
Mongolia

Zaluuchuudyn Örgön Chölöö
Залуучуудын Өргөн Чөлөө

Active Adventure
Tours Mongolia (200m);
Korean Air (800m);
Namaste (900m)

72

27

Parliament
Gardens

Baga Toiruul (east)
Бага Тойруул

National
Museum of
Mongolia

40

Trade &
Development
Bank

4

Sükhbaataryn Gudamj
Сүхбаатарын Гудамж

Government
House

Ikh Surguuliin Gudamj
Их Сургуулийн Гудамж

49

36

Amaryn Gudamj
Амарын Гудамж

City Nomads (650m);
UK Embassy (1.1km);
Karakorum (1.4km);
International Intellectual
Museum (1.6km)

Жуулчин Гудамж

7

42

22

18

Cultural
Palace

53

23

Chinggis Khaan
(Sükhbaatar)
Square   1

66

Central
Tower

Enkh Taivny Örgön Chölöö (Peace Ave)
Энх Тайвны Өргөн Чөлөө

62

68

Blue Sky
Tower

58

65

46

Choidog Gudamj Чойдог Гудамж

71

63

Jamyn Gunii Gudamj
Жамян Гүний Гудамж

Rosewood Coffee
House (70m)

48

52

44

12

14

2   Choijin
Lama Temple
Museum

9

Japanese
Embassy

Foreign Embassy St

39

16

29

15

74

35

Shangri-
La Complex

75

54

Nairamdal
Park

76

Chingisiin Örgön Chölöö
Чингисийн Өргөн Чөлөө

Olympiin Örgön Chölöö
Олимпийн Өргөн Чөлөө

8

Winter Palace of the Bogd Khan (1.4km);
Kazakhstan Embassy (2km)

Air China (270m)

Central Ulaanbaatar

History

Ulaanbaatar traces its roots back to the old capital, Örgöö, which was established in 1639 at the Da Khuree Khiid, about 420km from Ulaanbaatar. In keeping with the nomadic lifestyle, the capital was moved frequently to various locations across central Mongolia.

The capital was finally established in its present location in 1778 and grew quickly as a religious, commercial and administrative centre. The name of the capital changed several times; the current one dates from

1924 when the communists formalised Ulaanbaatar (Red Hero) in honour of the communist triumph.

From the 1930s the Soviets built the city in typical Russian style: lots of uniform apartment blocks, large brightly coloured theatres and cavernous government buildings. Tragically, the Soviets also destroyed almost all of the monasteries and temples.

A large influx of rural migrants in the early 2000s put tremendous strain on the city's basic infrastructure. Housing is inadequate, roads are jammed and the city's power grid is stretched to the limit. But private investment has also poured in, causing a mini-boom in glass towers, shopping malls and the like.

◉ Sights

Chinggis Khaan (Sükhbaatar) Square

SQUARE

(Чингис Хааны Талбай) In July 1921 in the centre of Ulaanbaatar, the 'hero of the revolution', Damdin Sükhbaatar, declared Mongolia's final independence from the Chinese. The square now features a bronze statue of Sükhbaatar astride his horse. In 2013 the city authorities changed the name from Sükhbaatar Square to Chinggis Khaan Square, although many citizens still refer to it by the old name.

Peaceful anti-communism protests were held here in 1990, which eventually ushered in the era of democracy. Today, the square (talbai) is occasionally used for rallies, ceremonies and rock concerts and festivals, but is generally a relaxed place where kiddies drive toy cars and teens whiz around on bikes. Near the centre of the square, look for the large plaque that lists the former names of the city – Örgöö, Nomiin Khuree, Ikh Khuree and Niislel Khuree.

The enormous marble construction at the north end was completed in 2006 in time for the 800th anniversary of Chinggis Khaan's coronation. At its centre is a seated bronze Chinggis Khaan statue, lording it over his nation. He is flanked by Ögedei (on the west) and Kublai (east). Two famed Mongol soldiers (Boruchu and Mukhlai) guard the entrance to the monument.

Behind the Chinggis monument stands Parliament House, which is commonly known as Government House. An inner courtyard of the building holds a large ceremonial ger used for hosting visiting dignitaries.

To the east of the square is the 1970s Soviet-style Cultural Palace, a useful landmark containing the Mongolian National Modern Art Gallery and several other cultural institutions. At the southeast corner of the square, the salmon-pinkish building is the State Opera & Ballet Theatre. Just south of the Opera House is the symbol of the country's new wealth, Central Tower, which houses luxury shops including Louis Vuitton and Armani.

The bullet-grey building to the southwest is the Mongolian Stock Exchange, which was opened in 1992 in the former Children's Cinema. Across from the Central Post Office

ULAANBAATAR IN...

Two Days

Ulaanbaatar's main sights can be seen in a couple of days. On your first morning in town pay a visit to the **National Museum of Mongolia** (p263) then take a turn around **Chinggis Khaan (Sükhbaatar) Square** and see the **Mongolian Statehood History Museum** (p262). Grab lunch at **Millie's Cafe** (p270) and then visit the nearby **Choijin Lama Temple Museum** (p263). Watch a Mongolian cultural show in the evening. The following day get up early and head up to **Gandan Khiid** (p262) in time to catch the monks chanting. Next visit the **Central Museum of Mongolian Dinosaurs** (p264) and later in the day head south to the **Winter Palace of the Bogd Khan** (p262). Finally, climb the steps to the **Zaisan Memorial** (p265) to watch the sun set.

Four Days

On day three visit the **Zanabazar Museum of Fine Arts** (p264) and then head out of town to the **Chinggis Khaan statue** (p277). In the evening down a pint or two on the deck of the **Grand Khaan Irish Pub** (p271) and then hit **iLoft** (p271) nightclub after midnight. On day four take a day trip either to **Terelj** (p277) or **Mandshir Khiid** (p276). Have dinner at **Mongolians** (p269) then go for drinks and get great views at **Blue Sky Lounge** (p271).

is a **statue of S Zorig**, who at the age of 27 helped to lead the protests that brought down communism in 1990 (and was tragically assassinated in 1998).

Mongolian Statehood History Museum

MUSEUM

(Монголын Төрийн Түүхийн Музей; Chinggis Khaan Sq; ◷10am-1pm & 2-5pm Tue-Sun) FREE Located inside the Government House, this free museum showcases Mongolia's diplomatic relations stretching back to the time of the great khaans.

The highlight is the upstairs hall where visiting heads of state gather in front of the nine horsetail banners (the same ones on display in the stadium during Naadam). On the main level you can see seals used by Mongolian royalty and gifts given by foreign leaders to Mongolia's presidents.

The museum also has an interesting gift shop where you can buy government-sanctioned souvenirs, such as commemorative coins and Chinggis Khaan replica statues.

★ Gandan Khiid

BUDDHIST MONASTERY

(Гандан Хийд, Gandantegchinlen Khiid; Öndör Gegeen Zanabazaryn Gudamj; admission T4000; ◷8.30am-7pm) Around the start of the 19th century, more than 100 *süm* (temples) and *khiid* (monasteries) served a population of about 50,000 in Urga (the former name of Ulaanbaatar). Only a handful of these buildings survived the religious purges of 1937. It wasn't until the early 1990s that the people of Mongolia started to openly practise Buddhism again. This monastery is one of Mongolia's most important, and also one of its biggest tourist attractions. The full name, Gandantegchinlen, translates roughly as 'the great place of complete joy'.

Building was started in 1838 by the fourth Bogd Gegeen, but as with most monasteries in Mongolia, the purges of 1937 fell heavily on Gandan. When the US vice president Henry Wallace asked to see a monastery during his visit to Mongolia in 1944, prime minister Choibalsan guiltily scrambled to open this one to cover up the fact that he had recently laid waste to Mongolia's religious heritage. Gandan remained a 'show monastery' for other foreign visitors until 1990 when full religious ceremonies recommenced. Today more than 600 monks belong to the monastery.

As you enter the main entrance from the south, a path leads towards the right to a courtyard containing two temples. The northeast building is **Ochidara Temple** (sometimes called Gandan Süm), where the most significant ceremonies are held. As you follow the *kora* (pilgrim) path clockwise around this building, you see a large statue behind glass of Tsongkhapa, the founder of the Gelugpa sect. The two-storey **Didan-Lavran Temple** in the courtyard was home to the 13th Dalai Lama during his stay here in 1904 (when he fled Lhasa ahead of a British invasion of Tibet).

At the end of the main path as you enter is the magnificent white **Migjid Janraisig Süm**, the monastery's main attraction. Lining the walls of the temple are hundreds of images of Ayush, the Buddha of Longevity, which stare through the gloom to the magnificent Migjid Janraisig statue.

The original statue was commissioned by the eighth Bogd Khan in 1911, in hopes that it might restore his eyesight – syphilis had blinded him; however, it was carted away by Russia in 1937 (it was allegedly melted down to make bullets). The new statue was dedicated in 1996 and built with donations from Japan and Nepal. It is 26m high and made of copper with a gilt gold covering. The hollow statue contains 27 tonnes of medicinal herbs, 334 Sutras, two million bundles of mantras, plus an entire ger with furniture!

To the east of the temple are four **colleges of Buddhist philosophy**, including the yellow building dedicated to Kalachakra, a wrathful Buddhist deity.

To the west of the temple is the **Öndör Gegeen Zanabazar Buddhist University**, which was established in 1970. It is usually closed to foreigners.

You can take photos (camera T5000, video T10,000) around the monastery and in Migjid Janraisig Süm, but not inside the other temples. Try to be there for the captivating ceremonies – they generally start at around 9am, though you may be lucky and see one at another time. Most chapels are closed in the afternoon.

★ Winter Palace of the Bogd Khan

MUSEUM

(Богд Хааны Өвлийн Ордон; ⏚11-342 195; Chingisiin Örgön Chölöö; adult/student T5000/2000; ◷9am-5.30pm mid-May–mid-Sep, 9.30am-4.30pm Fri-Tue mid-Sep–mid-May) Built between 1893 and 1903, this palace is where Mongolia's eighth Living Buddha, and last king, Jebtzun Damba Hutagt VIII (often called the Bogd Khan), lived for 20 years.

For reasons that are unclear, the palace was spared destruction by the Russians and turned into a museum. The summer palace, on the banks of Tuul Gol, was completely destroyed.

There are six **temples** in the grounds; each now contains Buddhist artwork, including sculpture and *thangka*. The white building to the right as you enter is the **Winter Palace** itself. It contains a collection of gifts received from foreign dignitaries, such as a pair of golden boots from a Russian tsar, a robe made from 80 unfortunate foxes and a ger lined with the skins of 150 snow leopards. Mongolia's Declaration of Independence (from China in 1911) is among the exhibits. The Bogd Khan's penchant for unusual wildlife explains the extraordinary array of stuffed animals in the palace. Some of them had been part of his personal zoo – look out for the photo of the Bogd's elephant, purchased from Russia for 22,000 roubles. The Winter Palace is a few kilometres south of Chinggis Khaan Sq. It is a bit too far to walk, so take a taxi or catch bus 7 or 19. There is a fee of T50,000/70,000 to use a camera/video.

National Museum of Mongolia   MUSEUM
(Монголын Үндэсний Музей; ☑ 7011 0913; cnr Juulchin Gudamj & Sükhbaataryn Gudamj; adult/student T5000/2500; ☉ 9.30am-5.30pm, closed Sun & Mon mid-Sep–mid-May) Mongolia's National Museum sweeps visitors from the Neolithic era right to the present day.

The 1st floor has some interesting exhibits on Stone Age sites in Mongolia, as well as petroglyphs, deer stones (stone sculptures of reindeer and other animals) and burial sites from the Hun and Uighur eras. Look for the remarkable **gold treasure** (including a golden tiara), found in 2001 by archaeologists digging near the Kul-Teginii Monument in Övörkhangai.

The 2nd floor houses an outstanding collection of costumes, hats and jewellery, representing most of Mongolia's ethnic groups. Take a gander at some of the elaborate silverwork of the Dariganga minority or the outrageous headgear worn by Khalkh Mongols. Some of the outfits contain 20–25kg of silver ornamentation!

The 3rd floor is a must-see for fans of the Mongol horde. The collection includes real examples of 12th-century Mongol armour, and correspondence between Pope Innocent IV and Guyuk Khaan. Written in Latin and Persian and dated 13 November

1246, it bears the seal of the khaan. There is also a display of traditional Mongolian culture with, among other things, a furnished ger, traditional herding and domestic implements, saddles and musical instruments. In the 20th-century-history section, look out for Damdib Sükhbaatar's famous hollow horsewhip, inside which he hid a secret letter written in 1920 by the Bogd Khan enlisting the aid of the Russian Red Army.

The final hall contains a self-congratulatory display of Mongolia's recent history and the 1990 democratic revolution, with no mention of the breadlines of the early 1990s or other hardships of the transition from communism to democracy.

★ Choijin Lama Temple Museum   MUSEUM
(Чойжин Ламын Хийд-Музей; ☑ 11-324 788; off Jamyn Gunii Gudamj; adult/student/child T5000/1500/500, audio guide free; ☉ 9am-5.30pm Tue-Sat) This temple museum is a hidden gem of architecture and history, smack in the middle of downtown Ulaanbaatar. It was the home of Luvsan Haidav Choijin Lama ('Choijin' is an honorary title given to some monks), the state oracle and brother of the Bogd Khan. Construction of the monastery commenced in 1904 and was completed four years later. It was closed in 1938 and probably would have been demolished had it not been saved in 1942 to serve as a museum demonstrating the 'feudal' ways of the past. Although religious freedom in Mongolia recommenced in 1990, this monastery is no longer an active place of worship.

There are five temples within the grounds. As you enter, the first temple you see is the **Maharaja Süm**. The **main temple** features statues of Sakyamuni (the historical Buddha), Choijin Lama and Baltung Choimba (the teacher of the Bogd Khan), whose mummified remains are inside the statue. There are also some fine *thangka*s and some of the best *tsam* masks in the country. The *gongkhang* (protector chapel) behind the main hall contains the oracle's throne and a magnificent statue of *yab-yum* (mystic sexual union).

The other temples are **Zuu Süm**, dedicated to Sakyamuni; **Yadam Süm**, which contains wooden and bronze statues of various gods, some created by the famous Mongolian sculptor Zanabazar; and **Amgalan Süm**, containing a self-portrait of Zanabazar himself and a small stupa apparently brought to Ulaanbaatar by Zanabazar from Tibet.

The complex is located off Jamyn Gunii Gudamj, with the entrance on the south side.

Zanabazar Museum of Fine Arts   MUSEUM

(Занабазарын Уран Зургийн Музей; ☑11-326 060; Juulchin Gudamj; adult/student/child T5000/2000/600, audio guide T1600; ☺9am-5.30pm) This fine-arts museum has a superb collection of paintings, carvings and sculptures, including many by the revered sculptor and artist Zanabazar. It also contains other rare, and sometimes old, religious exhibits such as scroll *thangka* (paintings) and Buddhist statues, representing the best display of its kind in Mongolia. A bonus is that most of the exhibit captions in the museum are in English.

The second room contains some fine examples of the sculptor's work, including five Dhyani, or Contemplation, Buddhas (cast in 1683) and Tara in her 21 manifestations.

Also worth checking out are the wonderful *tsam* masks (worn by monks during religious ceremonies) and the intricate paintings, *One Day in Mongolia* and the *Airag Feast*, by the renowned artist B Sharav. These paintings depict almost every aspect of nomadic life.

As you enter the building on the left, a room displays ancient art, including deer stones that date to the Bronze Age. To the right is a shop selling souvenirs and contemporary art.

The building itself carries some historical value. It was built in 1905, making it one of the oldest Manchu-era commercial buildings in the city. It was first used as a Chinese Bank, Soviet troops stayed here in the 1920s and it later served as Ulaanbaatar's first State Department Store. It has been an art museum since 1966.

Central Museum of Mongolian Dinosaurs   MUSEUM

(☑9918 5165; www.dinosaurmuseum.mn; Sambuugiin Örgön Chölöö, Freedom Sq; adult/child T2000/500; ☺10am-10pm) Mongolia has plenty of fossils and dinosaur eggs and skeletons to show off - the country is second only to the United States in terms of the number of fossils located. This museum serves to show them off. The centrepiece of the museum is a 3m-tall, 5-tonne, flesh eating Tyrannosaurs Bataar, a cousin of T-Rex. This particular specimen made international headlines in 2012 when it sold for over US$1 million at an auction in Texas. The Mongolian government protested that the fossil had been illegally smuggled out of Mongolia and demanded its return. The legal battle ended when a US judge ruled in favor of Mongolia. The museum also includes examples of velociraptors, protoceratops and a nest of oviraptor eggs.

The museum is housed inside the former Lenin Museum, constructed in 1974. At the time of writing the museum was under renovation and just one room was open to the public. The entrance is on the eastern side of the building.

International Intellectual Museum   MUSEUM

(Оюун Ухааны Олон Улсын Музей, Mongolian Toy Museum; ☑11-461 470; www.iqmuseum.mn; Peace Ave 10; admission T3000; ☺10am-6pm Mon-Sat; ☑) This museum has a collection of puzzles and games made by local artists. One puzzle requires 56,831 movements to complete, says curator Zandraa Tumen-Ulzii. There are dozens of handmade chess sets and traditional Mongolian puzzles that are distant cousins to Rubik's cube. An enthusiastic guide will show you how the puzzles operate and will even perform magic tricks. A fascinating place for both kids and adults. The museum is located in eastern UB, in a hard-to-spot building hidden behind an abandoned circular building which appears to have suffered a fire at some point.

Victims of Political Persecution Memorial Museum   MUSEUM

(Улс Төрийн Хилс Хэрэгт Хэлмэгдэгсдийн Дурсгалын Музей; ☑7011 0915; cnr Gendenin Gudamj & Olympiin Örgön Chölöö; adult/child T3000/1000; ☺10am-5pm, closed Sat & Sun Nov-Feb) This little-known museum houses a series of haunting displays that chronicle the communist purges of the 1930s – an aggressive campaign to eliminate 'counter-revolutionaries'. During the campaign, intellectuals were arrested and put on trial, sent to Siberian labour camps or shot. Mongolia lost its top writers, scientists and thinkers.

The neglected building that houses the museum is one of the oldest in Ulaanbaatar. It was once the home of former prime minister P Genden, who was executed in Moscow by the KGB in 1937 for refusing Stalin's orders to carry out the purge. Stalin found a more willing puppet in Marshal Choibalsan, whose purge ended in the deaths of more than 27,000 Mongolians, mostly lamas. On the ground floor of the museum is a replica of Genden's office, with his desk and other personal effects.

The descriptions are only in Mongolian so it's a good idea to bring a guide who can make sense of it all. The guard who keeps the key to the place sometimes disappears for several days so you may find it closed during normal hours.

Zaisan Memorial & Buddha Park MONUMENT
`FREE` This memorial is the tall, thin landmark on top of Zaisan hill, south of the city. Built by the Russians to commemorate 'unknown soldiers and heroes' from various wars, this masterpiece of socialist realism offers sweeping views of the city and surrounding hills, as well as a workout on the climb up. Next to the hill is a small park containing a 16m-tall standing image of Sakyamuni (historical Buddha). Below the statue is a small room containing *thangkas*, sutras (religious books) and images of the Buddha and his disciples. Bus 7 from Bayangol Hotel will get you here.

Beatles Square SQUARE
(Tserendorjiin Gudamj) The plaza located between the State Department Store and the Circus has an unofficial name – Beatles Square; so named after a new monument to the Fab Four located close to its northern end. The monument features bronze images of John, Paul, George and Ringo on one side and on the other, a sculpture of a young man sitting in a stairwell strumming a guitar. The sculpture recalls the 1970s era in Ulaanbaatar when groups of teenagers would gather in apartment stairwells and sing Beatles songs, which they learned from contraband records smuggled here from Eastern Europe. The plaza – surrounded by cafes, restaurants and cashmere shops – is a popular meeting place and hub of activity in summer when locals relax by the fountains.

National Amusement Park AMUSEMENT PARK
(Үндэсний Соёл Амралтын Хүрээлэн, Children's Park; adult/student T1000/700; 🎢) Known to almost everyone as the 'Children's Park', this small amusement park features rides, games and paddleboats. The target audience is the 12-and-under set, so it's perfect if you are travelling with small kids. The park entrance is on the southeast corner. For the rides you buy individual tickets, around T3000 to T5000 a pop. It's open year round; in winter there's ice skating for T2000 per 90 minutes.

🎫 Tours

Most guesthouses offer their own range of tours, which tend to be unimaginative jeep trips that follow a standard route. Dedicated tour operators typically charge more than the guesthouses, but you'll likely get better service, guides and food, as well as a more interesting itinerary.

Active Adventure Tours Mongolia CYCLING, HORSE RIDING
(🖊 11-354 662; www.tourmongolia.com; Erkhuugiin Gudamj) 🍃 Good for bike and horse trips, this eco-conscious Mongolian-run outfit also runs traditional homestays (per night, full board $15) and employs sustainable tourism practices by hiring local guides rather than shipping them out from Ulaanbaatar.

Goyo Travel TOUR
(🖊 11-313 050; www.goyotravel.com; Peace Ave, Golomt Town, Tower A, Door 1a) An experienced and reliable British-Mongolian outfit, Goyo has a variety of countrywide trips and some unique tours that can include hot air ballooning and kayaking on the Tuul Gol. Particularly good with film and media groups or high-end travel. Well-regarded for personal service and tailored trips.

Mongolia Canoeing CANOEING
(🖊 11-685 503, 9982 6883; www.mongoliacanoeing.com) A German-run outfit that offers canoe trips on the Tuul River. Day or overnight trips are possible from Ulaanbaatar.

Mongolia Expeditions ADVENTURE TOUR
(🖊 11-329 279, 9909 6911; www.mongoliaexpeditions.com; Jamyn Gunii Gudamj 5-2) Specialises in adventure travel, including cycle touring, mountaineering, caving and rafting trips, as well as less vigorous options such as bird-watching tours. This is a good option if you are planning a climbing trip to Tavan Bogd or if you want to do a tour by bike. Sponsors the Mongolia Bike Challenge.

★ Nomadic Journeys ADVENTURE TOUR
(🖊 11-328 737; www.nomadicjourneys.com; Sükhbaataryn Gudamj 1) 🍃 A joint Swedish-Mongolian venture, this business concentrates on low-impact tourism, environmental protection and community development. It runs fixed-departure yak, camel and horse treks and can also arrange rafting trips on the Tuul Gol. Its trip in Terelj is unique – you walk while yaks haul your own portable ger on a cart. Also good for taimen fishing trips. If you are looking for a standard jeep

THE TRANS-MONGOLIAN ROUTE ULAANBAATAR

tour this operator may not suit your needs as it caters to travellers seeking unique experiences.

Stepperiders
HORSE RIDING

(☑9911 4245; www.stepperiders.mn) A leader in horse-riding trips near Ulaanbaatar. Runs its own camp with horses near Bogd Khan Uul.

Stone Horse
HORSE RIDING

(☑9592 1167; www.stonehorsemongolia.com) ✐ Offers horse treks in the Khan Khentii Mountains (trips start from just one hour out of Ulaanbaatar). Professional outfit with quality horses and eco-conscious policies. Also offers reasonably priced homestay opportunities with herders near Ulaanbaatar.

✿ Festivals & Events

Tsagaan Sar
LUNAR NEW YEAR FESTIVAL

Held sometime between late January and early March depending on the lunar calendar.

Ulaanbaatar Marathon
SPORTS

(◷1st Sat in Jun) This event closes all the streets in downtown UB as thousands of runners race around the city. Runners can participate in 5k, 10k, 21k or 42k races.

Naadam
CULTURAL

(◷11 & 12 Jul) The biggest event in Ulaanbaatar is undoubtedly the Naadam (Festival). Some visitors may not find the festival itself terribly exciting, but the associated activities during the Naadam week and the general festive mood make it a great time to visit.

Playtime
MUSIC

(◷Jul or Aug) The annual two-day music festival Playtime features the country's top rock bands and hip-hop artists. It's held at a venue outside the city, usually in August. Check the **Hi-Fi CD Shop** (Seoul St), or any CD shop, for location and tickets.

🛏 Sleeping

Most room rates include breakfast, although at the budget places this may just be tea, coffee and some bread and jam. Expect 15% value-added tax (VAT) to be tacked onto your bill at top-end places.

Around Chinggis Khaan Square

★Chuka Guesthouse
GUESTHOUSE $

(☑9999 5672, 9856 1999; chuka927@gmail.com; Bldg 33, entrance V; dm/r US$15/25; ☎) This new guesthouse enjoys a central location in a quiet courtyard set behind the National Academy Drama Theatre. It's pricier than some of its competitors but the quality of the rooms stands out. It's well-kept, furnishings are modern and the bunk beds are soft and warm. It has a fully equipped kitchen and a cosy lounge. Look for the red awning over the outside windows.

★Lotus Guesthouse
GUESTHOUSE $

(☑11-325 967, 9909 4943; www.lotuschild.org; Baga Toiruu West; dm US$8-15, r US$30; @☎) This homey place feels more like a boutique hotel than a guesthouse. Rooms are individually styled, some with traditional Mongolian furniture. It has a cosy atmosphere but some parts can be a little dim. Location is central and quiet. It's run by the Lotus Children's Centre, an NGO that helps orphaned children, and it employs young Mongolians who used to live in the orphanage. An annex, in an apartment away from the centre, takes overflow if the main block is full.

Sunpath Guesthouse
GUESTHOUSE $

(☑9914 3722, 11-326 323; www.sunpath-mongolia.com; Baga Toiruu West, Bldg 37, door 56; dm/d US$6/20; @☎) This bright, family-run guesthouse offers spacious dorms and private rooms across a couple of stairwells. The facilities are very clean and well-maintained and it occupies a cute downtown location. There's the usual guesthouse services including wi-fi, a jam-and-toast breakfast and countryside tours. On the downside, there is just one bathroom, which means waiting in line in the morning. Travellers also report pressure to book a tour through the guesthouse.

UB Guesthouse
GUESTHOUSE $

(☑11-311 037, 9119 9859; www.ubguest.com; Baga Toiruu, Bldg 41, entrance 2, door 21; dm/s/tw/d US$8/20/22/25; @☎) This well-established and central guesthouse has several rooms stretching around a Soviet-era apartment block. It's clean and there are plenty of bathrooms but the common room is a bit small and the place does get very busy in summer. Owner Bobbi has plenty of experience in helping backpackers with logistics and trip planning. Midnight curfew and 10am checkout are minuses, free early morning pick-up from the train station a plus. Skip the meagre breakfast and try one of the nearby cafes. Enter from the back of the building, behind Golomt Bank.

★**Hotel Örgöö**　　　BOUTIQUE HOTEL $$$
(☏7011 6044; www.urgoohotel.com; M100 Bldg, Juulchin Gudamj; d/ste incl breakfast T185,000/225,000; ❄☎) This boutique hotel has just 10 rooms, each one decked out in

THE NAADAM FESTIVAL

The high point of the Mongolian year is the Naadam Festival, held on 11 and 12 July. Part family reunion, part fair and part nomad Olympics, Naadam (meaning 'games') has its roots in the nomad assemblies and hunting extravaganzas of the Mongol armies.

Smaller Naadams are held throughout the country and are well worth attending if you want to get close to the action and have a more authentic experience. For locations and dates, check the government website **Mongolia Travel** (www.mongolia.travel) and search under Calendar of Events/July.

The Naadam in Ulaanbaatar does have all the traditional events, but it's typically crowded and somewhat exhausting as you end up having to do a lot of driving and walking about. Perhaps the best part of the Ulaanbaatar Naadam is the extravagant opening ceremony, which features some great costumes and performances.

To find out what's going on during the festival, look for the events program in the two English-language newspapers; there are often sports matches and other events in the lead-up to the main two days.

The Tournament

The wrestling starts at the stadium immediately after the opening ceremony. The final rounds on day two, just before the closing ceremony, are the most exciting matches. Mongolian wrestling has no time limits; a match ends only when a wrestler falls (or any body part other than feet or hands touches the ground).

Archery is held in an open stadium next to the main stadium. Archers use a bent composite bow made of layered horn, bark and wood. Arrows are usually made from willow branches and vulture feathers.

Horse racing is held about 28km west of the capital at Hui Doloon Khutag. Buses and minivans travel there from the road to the north of the stadium (T2000). It is also possible to take the 'Railbus' (T3500) from the main train station. Tour operators can organise vehicles or you could take a taxi (about T25,000). The racing, which takes place not on a track but on the open steppe, has six categories, based on the age of the horse and the distance of the race (between 15km to 30km). Jockeys are children aged six to 12. Note that traffic to/from the race track is one way, depending on whether a race is starting or ending. To avoid getting caught in a back-up it's best to go very early in the morning (before 8am). Alternatively, go in the early evening and camp out.

The smallest event, anklebone shooting, is held in a large tent next to the archery stadium. This entails flicking a small, wedge-shaped piece (made from reindeer horn) at a small target (made from sheep anklebones) about 3m away. Apart from providing some shade, the tent has an electric atmosphere as competitors are spurred on by the yodelling of spectators.

Tickets

Admission to the archery and horse racing is free, but you'll need a ticket to enter the stadium for the opening/closing ceremonies and wrestling matches. Ticket costs vary per section; the north side of the stadium (which is protected from the sun and rain by an overhang and has the best view of the opening event) is more expensive, with tickets going for around T25,000. Tickets are distributed via the tour operators and hotels. It's also possible to buy tickets at the Naadam stadium (located 2km south of Chinggis Khaan Sq) or from a window on the north side of the Cultural Palace. Small batches of tickets are sold each day and lines to buy them are long, so the best way to get a ticket is through your hotel or guesthouse. If you're desperate, some locals try to sell their extra tickets at the stadium, but you'll need to pay more than face value.

brown and beige furnishings, with flat-panel TVs and modern, but small, bathrooms. The prime selling point here is the location, overlooking a little park near the National Museum. The breakfast is a bit disappointing for the price. Note that the air-con units in the back can be noisy at night and service is generally spotty. Overall a nice place to stay if you are looking for something quaint but keep expectations in check.

Ulaanbaatar Hotel HOTEL $$$

(☑11-320 620; www.ubhotel.mn; Baga Toiruu; s T150,000-180,000, d T240,000, lux T280,000; ❋@☎) The Ulaanbaatar Hotel is the grand old dame of Mongolia. Opened in 1961, this was where Soviet dignitaries stayed during their visits to the 'Red Hero'. It still carries an air of the Khrushchev era with its high ceilings, chandeliers, a marble staircase and a lavish ballroom. Rooms are well-appointed but some are a bit small. Despite being considered a top-end hotel you might experience some imperfections here – fickle air-con, poor service, spotty hot water, unreliable wifi, and other minor inconveniences – consider it part of the adventure. The hotel also contains two restaurants, a coffee shop, a travel agency, business centre and sauna.

Bayangol Hotel HOTEL $$$

(☑11-328 869; www.bayangolhotel.mn; Chingisiin Örgön Chölöö 5; s/d T182,000/224,000; @☎) One of Ulaanbaatar's biggest and most reliable hotels, the Bayangol consists of two 12-storey towers a five-minute walk south of Chinggis Khan Sq (along a very busy road). It was built in 1964 to accommodate overseas tour groups and the structures are now dated, with small elevators and shabby decor. The standard rooms are badly in need of renovation but the business rooms have been tastefully updated. Only basic English is spoken. Prices include breakfast.

State Department Store Area

★ Zaya's Hostel GUESTHOUSE $

(☑11-331 575, 9918 5013; www.zayahostel.com; Peace Ave; s US$30-35, d/tr US$40/45; @☎) While most guesthouses in town are located in crumbling old Russian flats, this one is in a modern building with hardwood floors, sparkling bathrooms, a comfortable lounge, fresh paint and new furnishings. Owner Zaya speaks English, enjoys a good conversation and is happy to help travellers looking for volunteer opportunities. A simple

breakfast is included. Zaya is not too keen on groups of noisy backpackers, however, so if you are looking for a party guesthouse, skip this one. The hostel is on the 3rd floor of an orange building, about 100m north of Peace Ave (behind the glass-fronted Peace Tower, and then a bit past the Seoul Hotel).

★ Khongor Guest House GUESTHOUSE $

(☑9925 2599, 11-316 415; www.khongor-expedition. com; Peace Ave 15, apt 6; dm/s/d US$8/15/18; @☎) This popular guesthouse is run by a friendly couple, Toroo and Degi, who work hard to help guests with logistical matters, tours, visa issues and airport or train station runs. Their countryside tours get positive reports from travellers and business is casual – tours are usually paid for when you get back. The guesthouse is a simple affair with small private rooms and slightly larger dorms. There's a cosy lounge with three computers and a kitchen. The entrance of the guesthouse is around the back of the third building west of the State Department Store. Credit cards are accepted.

Golden Gobi GUESTHOUSE $

(☑9665 4496, 11-322 632; www.goldengobi.com; dm US$7, d with/without bathroom US$23/19; @☎) This family-run place has a fun, youthful vibe, with colourful walls, two lounges and lots of soft sofas. Dorms and private rooms are clean and comfortable and the bathrooms are kept tidy. On the downside, it can get very crowded in summer and just trying to get some face time with the manager could require getting in a long line. This has led to some mixed reviews by guests. It's inside a courtyard about 100m east of the State Department Store.

Train Station Area

LG Guesthouse GUESTHOUSE $

(☑7011 8243, 9985 8419; www.lghostel.com; Narny Gudamj; dm US$8, s/d US$25/30; @☎) With 34 rooms, this is the largest guesthouse in the city. It has dorms and private rooms with attached bathroom, a common area, a kitchen where you can cook your own meals and a restaurant on the ground floor with dishes for T5000-8500. Bathrooms are clean and have hot-water boilers – important in summer when other places only have cold water. It's a little out of the centre, on the road towards the train station. They also have a small annex close to the State Department Store.

Voyage Hotel
HOTEL $$

(☎11-327 213; www.voyagehotel.mn; Narny Gudamj; s/d/lux T150,000/105,000/140,000; @☎) Representing good value, the 30-room Voyage has attentive staff and pleasant rooms. Facilities include two restaurants (European and Korean), free internet and sauna. The low price is a reflection of its less-than-perfect location, on the busy road to the train station.

Best Western Gobi's Kelso
HOTEL $$$

(☎7736 3636; www.bestwesternmongolia.com; Jansrai Gudamj 27/1; r T229,000; ☎) A ten-minute walk from the train station, this Best Western is a smart choice for weary travellers stumbling off the Trans-Siberia looking for quality digs. Rooms are spacious, there's a substantial breakfast included and management bends over backwards to ensure a pleasant stay. While convenient for the station, it's a good 30 to 40 minute hike to downtown, or a short cab ride.

✗ Eating

If you've had your fill of *buuz*, Ulaanbaatar's restaurants offer a decent variety of cuisines from which to get your fix of burgers, curry, ramen or croissant.

Some of the best Mongolian food is found at hotel restaurants including the **Chairman** (Corporate Hotel, 2nd fl Chingisiin Örgon Chölöö; ⊙11am-11pm) restaurant on the 2nd floor of the Corporate Hotel and the **Karakorum** (Kempinski Hotel Khan Palace; ⊙11am-11pm) restaurant in the Kempinski Hotel. **Rock Sugar** (☎7611 7777; Namnansurengiin Gudamj; ⊙11am-midnight; ☎) has good *khuushuur* (fried mutton pancakes). The Modern No-

mads chain of restaurants (there are five branches in UB) get good business from the tour operators, although the food is often underwhelming.

Of course, the best Mongolian food is home cooking. Some tour operators can arrange meals with local families. Try contacting **EcoVoyage Mongolie** (☎9556 0270; www.ecovoyagemongolie.com).

Shashlik Stands
SHASHLIK $

(State Department Store; shashlik T7500; ⊙noon-11pm Jun-Aug) In summer you can get shashlik (meat kebab), usually served with onions and cucumber, prepared by Uzbek and Mongolian street vendors and served in tents outside the State Department Store. A true taste of Central Asia not to be missed!

Shilmel Buuz
MONGOLIAN $

(☎8881 0518; Amaryn Gudamj; buuz T600, salads T1500; ⊙10am-6pm Mon-Fri) This small *guanz*, with plastic tablecloths and bare walls, may not have much atmosphere but it's well known for serving some of the best *buuz* in the city (nearly homemade quality). Unlike most other cafes, the dumplings here are not overly fatty and come piping hot from a special steamer. Try a few with *suutei tsai* (Mongolian milk tea). It's the westernmost in a string of five, small restaurants. Look for the picture of the two kids gorging on a big plate of *buuz*.

★ Mongolians
MONGOLIAN $$

(☎9909 7716; Ikh Toiruu 93, Barilga Mega Store; mains T7000-12,000; ⊙11am-midnight; ⊞) Part museum, part restaurant, this place sports great atmosphere, with walls lined with

---

CAFE & BAKERY BONANZA

Coffee has come to Ulaanbaatar in a big way and cafes can be found on every downtown street, some of them also serving freshly baked bread, meals or desserts. The following are all recommended.

Narya (☎11-317 098; Builder's Sq, Juulchin Gudamj; dishes T6000-10,000; ⊙8.30am-8pm Mon-Fri, 9am-7pm Sat & Sun; ☎) Funky little cafe with local art and cheery vibe, serving baked goods and Western meals.

Café Amsterdam (☎11-321 979; Peace Ave; items T6000-9000; ⊙7am-10pm; ☎⊞) A Dutch-influenced backpacker hub serving Illy coffee and light meals.

Sachers (☎11-324 734; Baga Toiruu west; snacks T800-2500, light meals T8000-10,000; ⊙9am-9pm; ☎) German-run bakery/cafe with oven-fresh bread loaves and soups.

Coffee Bean & Tea Leaf (☎9999 7833; Juulchin Gudamj; drinks 4300-7900; ⊙8am-9.30pm Mon-Fri & 9am-9.30pm Sat-Sun) Chain cafe with several branches in UB. Good for coffee and cold drinks but the food is disappointing.

Mongolian antiques and old photos. The menu is contemporary Mongolian, with stir-fried meats, dumplings and boiled mutton with some Russian and European influence. If you want to go all out, order the *khorkhog* (meat chunks cooked in a metal steamer with scalding hot rocks added to the pot to aid cooking), enough for six to eight people (you must call and order six hours in advance). Two nights a week a traditional Mongolian band plays here at 8pm (usually Monday and Tuesday). Mongolians is 600m east of the US embassy.

Luna Blanca VEGAN $$
(Juulchiin Gudamj; dishes T7000-10,000; ⊘10am-9pm; ✍🖶) ✿ Famous for being the first vegan restaurant in Mongolia, this place remains very popular for its consistently tasty and healthy food. The kitchen whips up classic Mongolian dishes such as the Flour Power (*tsuivan*), and Mongol Combo Plate (with *buuz* and *khuushuur*), as well as European fare like spaghetti and goulash. We're particularly fond of the 'Power Lunch', with soy meat, mashed potatoes and gravy. The atmosphere is refreshingly clean, alcohol-free, kid-friendly and (best of all) great value for money. There is also some excellent local art on the walls created by the well-known painter Tugs-Oyun.

Millie's Café AMERICAN $$
(✍11-330 338; Marco Polo Bldg; mains T10,000-18,000; ⊘8am-8pm Mon-Sat; 🛜✍🖶) Since it first opened its doors in 1998, Millie's has been a favourite among expats seeking Western comfort food. The owners – Daniel and Densmaa – warmly greet patrons to their sun-lit restaurant, and promptly serve up tasty burgers, sandwiches and soups. Special treats include smoothies, lemon pie and a delicious chocolate cake (which sells out early). Don't miss Daniel's famous Cuban sandwich, only available on Tuesdays.

Modern Nomads 2 MONGOLIAN $$
(✍7012 0808; Amaryn Gudamj; meals T7500-22,000; ⊘10am-midnight Mon-Fri, 11am-11pm Sat & Sun) The menu is actually mostly European but there are a few classic Mongolian dishes, so this is a decent place to try *khuushuur*, *buuz*, a Mongolian soup or even sheep head. It's part of a chain of restaurants but this branch seems to get slightly better reviews than the others. A picture menu makes ordering easy.

★**Veranda** WESTERN $$$
(✍11-330 818; Jamyn Gunii Gudamj 5/1; mains T12,400-23,000; ⊘7am-midnight Mon-Fri, noon-midnight Sat & Sun; ✍) While it's not particularly old, this fine-dining restaurant has an almost colonial air to it, with couch seating inside and a big porch overlooking the Choijin Lama Temple Museum. The food is surprisingly good, with starters that include smoked-salmon rolls and spinach salad with feta, and an array of delectable main dishes that fuse Italian and French recipes, such as lamb ratatouille, grilled duck and peppercorn steak. Breakfast is available on weekdays.

★**Namaste** INDIAN $$$
(✍9927 0957; Baga Toiruu North; dishes T12,000-18,000; ⊘11.30am-10pm; 🛜✍) Treat your taste buds to some gourmet Indian cuisine prepared by three chefs from Uttaranchal. Try the delicious *saag gosht* (beef in spinach sauce) or *murg makhni* (butter chicken), both will melt in your mouth. Order a side of garlic naan and rice and if you are still hungry there are kebabs and juicy chicken meatballs. Vegetarian options are available, as well as classic street food like *gol-gappa*

DINING GUANZ-STYLE

There are dozens of Mongolian budget restaurants (*guanz*) and they can be found on every block in the city. Some are chain restaurants and you'll start to recognise prominent eateries, including Zochin Buuz (Зочин Бууз), Khaan Buuz (Хаан Бууз) and Zochin Cafe (Зочин Кафэ). They serve up *buuz* (steamed mutton-filled dumplings), *tsuivan* (fried noodles) plus soups and *bifshteks on-dogtei* (beefsteak with egg). They are often quite dire – think globs of mashed potatoes, chunks of fatty mutton, and rice topped with ketchup – so keep your expectations low. Some of the chains operate 24 hours. Meals cost T5000 to T9000.

Look for them at these locations:

➡ **Khaan Buuz** (Хаан Бууз; Peace Ave) Opposite the State Department Store. English language and picture menu available.

➡ **Zochin Cafe** (Sambuugiin Örgön Chölöö) This place is 80m east of the fire station, one of the better cheapies.

(pastry with chickpeas). The main branch is on the northeast bend of Baga Toiruu, 270m north of the Zaluuchuud Hotel, and there is another restaurant in the **Flower Hotel**.

★**Bull** HOT POT $$$
(Seoul St; meal per person T15,000; ⊙ 11.30am-midnight; ◢) A local favourite, this hot-pot place gets a steady stream of patrons at its three locations – two on Seoul St and another **branch** (Blue Mon Bldg, Baga Toiruu East; meal per person T15,000; ⊙ 11.30am-10pm) diagonally opposite the Chinese embassy. Order an array of raw vegetables, sauces and thinly sliced meats, which are brought to your table on platters, then cook the ingredients in your personal cauldron of boiling broth. It's a great alternative to the meat-heavy menus you'll experience at most other restaurants in town and service is top-notch.

Rosewood Kitchen + Enoteca ITALIAN $$$
(Seoul St, Mandal Bldg; mains T9500-38,000; ⊙ 7.30am-9.30pm Mon-Sat; ◢◢) Run by a jovial Bostonian named Cliffe, this new place serves gourmet pastas, pizzas, sandwiches and salads. It's all made with high-quality local and imported ingredients and many items are made in-house, including the tasty breads. The grilled asparagus is a favourite appetiser. There's also a bakery and deli with delicious muffins, bagels, cookies and salads that make for good takeaway snacks. The atmosphere is smart and businesslike. It's tucked off the street in the ground floor of a five-storey grey building next to a large ger. A **second location** (◢ 7731 0561; Elchingiin Gudamj; ⊙ 7.30am-9pm Mon-Sat) is just north of the Korean embassy.

Self-Catering

Stock up for your train ride or a trip to the countryside by visiting the 1st floor of the **State Department Store** (◢ 11-319 292; Peace Ave 44), or for a better selection try **Merkuri Market** (Мэркури; ⊙ 10am-7pm Mon-Sat, 10am-6pm Sun).

🍷 Drinking & Nightlife

Locally brewed beers have taken off in UB. Most bars are open 11am to midnight daily and all serve food of the meat-and-potatoes variety.

★**iLoft** CLUB
(◢ 9909 0528; Amaryn Gudamj; admission T20,000, drinks from T5000; ⊙ 10am-3am; ◢) This multi-use venue operates as a restaurant and cafe during the day and transforms into a pulsing nightclub after dark. There's leather seating, a large dance floor, techno beats and a mature crowd. iLoft hosts salsa dancing on Thursdays (starting at 8pm) and an exciting line up of DJs or themed parties on other days. It's located behind the Best Western Hotel.

Grand Khaan Irish Pub PUB
(◢ 11-336 666; Seoul St; ⊙ 11am-midnight; ◢) In summertime it seems like half of Ulaanbaatar is crowded onto the deck of this old stand-by. Order a pint and join them. The pub-grub menu (meal with beer T18,000–45,000) includes an array of salads.

Revolution PUB
(Beatles Sq; beer T3000-7000; ⊙ 8am-midnight Mon-Fri, noon-midnight Sat & Sun; ◢) Revolution is like your neighborhood pub back home, everyone seems to know each other. A friendly and welcoming place for a beer or cocktail. Tasty Western-style meals (mains T7000–13,000) available, too.

Brix Nightclub CLUB
(Baga Toiruu East; admission T10,000-20,000; ⊙ 10-3pm) One of the top clubs in town, Brix is always busy and caters to a mostly 20s crowd of young professionals letting their hair down. Professional DJs spin club music and top-40 dance music while bartenders serve up potent, and sometimes flammable drinks. There are theme parties a couple of times a month, frequent dance acts on stage and unexpected surprises – confetti, foam or other nonlethal objects may be shot in your direction.

Blue Sky Lounge LOUNGE
(◢ 7010 9779; Blue Sky Tower, 23rd fl, Peace Ave 17; ⊙ noon-midnight) Stylish place for a drink at the top of the iconic Blue Sky Tower.

☆ Entertainment

Check the English-language weeklies for info on coming events. The Arts Council of Mongolia (www.artscouncil.mn) produces a monthly cultural-events calendar that covers most theatres, galleries and museums.

★**Mongolian National Song & Dance Ensemble** TRADITIONAL MUSIC, DANCE
(◢ 11-323 954; admission T7000) The Mongolian National Song & Dance Ensemble puts on performances for tourists throughout the summer in the National Academic Drama Theatre. Shows are less frequently staged at

the Cultural Palace (p261) on the northeast corner of Chinggis Khaan Sq.

You can also see traditional song and dance at the Choijin Lama Temple Museum (p263) in summer at 5pm.

★ **National Academic Drama Theatre**   DRAMA

(☑ 7012 8999, 7011 8187; cnr Seoul St & Chingisiin Örgön Chölöö; admission T15,000-30,000; ⊙ ticket sales 10am-7pm) During most of the year, this large, red-hued theatre shows one of a dozen or so Mongolian-language productions by various playwrights from Mongolia, Russia and beyond. *Don Quixote* was playing when we last visited. Schedules are sporadic. You can buy tickets in advance at the booking office, which is inside the small concrete guardhouse on the right-hand side of the theatre.

On the left-hand side of the theatre, as you approach it from the road, is a door that leads to a **puppet theatre** (☑ 11-321 669; admission T1500-2500; ⊙ noon, 2pm, 4pm Sat & Sun; ⋒), which is great if you are travelling with children.

Altain Orgil   FOLK MUSIC

Well-known folklore ensemble that plays traditional Mongolian music, including long songs and throat singing. Their stage outfits are influenced by the robes worn by shaman. In summer they play 30-minute concerts every night in one of the restaurants owned by the Modern Nomads chain, usually either **City Nomads** (☑ 11-454 484; Peace Ave) or **Khaan Ger Grill & Bar** (☑ 7711 5544; www. modernnomads.mn; ⊙ 11am-midnight). The concert, which begins at 7.30pm, is free to watch if you order something from the restaurant. You'll need to call ahead to these restaurants to find where the band will be playing.

State Youth & Children's Theatre   TRADITIONAL MUSIC, DANCE

(☑ 9665 0711; www.tumenekh.wordpress.com; Nairamdal Park; admission T15,000; ⊙ 6pm May-Oct; ⋒) The Tumen Ekh Song & Dance Ensemble at the State Youth & Children's Theatre is the most popular cultural show in town, featuring traditional singers, dancers and contortionists. It's a great chance to hear *khöömei* (throat singing) and see some fabulous costumes. You can buy folk music CDs (T22,000) or a DVD (T30,000) of the show. There is a cafe and gallery in the traditional-style hall. Enter the western gate of the

National Amusement Park (Children's Park) (p265) and make the first left.

State Opera & Ballet Theatre   OPERA, BALLET

(☑ 7011 0389; Chinggis Khaan Sq; admission T8000-15,000; ⊙ closed Aug, box office 10am-1pm & 2-6pm Wed-Sun) Built by the Russians in 1932, the State Opera & Ballet Theatre is the salmon-pinkish building on the southeast corner of Chinggis Khaan Sq. On Saturday and Sunday evenings throughout the year, and sometimes also on weekend afternoons in the summer, the theatre holds stirring opera (in Mongolian) and ballet shows.

Mongolian original operas include *Three Fateful Hills* by famous playwright D Natsagdorj, and the more recent *Chinggis Khaan*, by B Sharav. Other productions include an exhilarating (but long) rendition of *Carmen*, plus plenty of Puccini and Tchaikovsky.

A board outside the theatre lists the shows for the current month in English. Advance purchase is worthwhile for popular shows because tickets are numbered, so it's possible to score a good seat if you book early.

UB Jazz Club   JAZZ

(☑ 9969 8146; Seoul St; ⊙ 10am-midnight) FREE As the name suggests, this is a dedicated jazz club, the only one in Ulaanbaatar.

🛍 Shopping

UB abounds with shops selling tacky tourist souvenirs as well as locally produced cashmere clothing and blankets. A few of the better places for that special Mongolian keepsake are below.

★ **Mary & Martha Mongolia**   SOUVENIRS

(www.mmmongolia.com) 🖉 Fair-trade shop selling handicrafts, felt products and modern Kazakh wall hangings. Has some innovative little products like computer bags and mobile-phone cases made with traditional designs.

Amarbayasgalant Antique   ANTIQUES

(☑ 11-310 000; Juulchin Gudamj 37/31) A quality shop for the serious buyer, it sells enormous sutras, traditional headdresses, Buddhist statues and other rare items. Some of the items are creations of Zanabazar and not for sale. Great for browsing.

Egshiglen Magnai National Musical Instrument Shop MUSICAL INSTRUMENTS
(☏ 11-328 419; Sükhbaataryn Gudamj) At this shop on the east side of the Museum of Natural History, *morin khuur* range from T200,000 to T950,000. There are also *yattag* (zithers) and two-stringed Chinese fiddles.

Cashmere House CASHMERE
(Peace Ave; ⏰ 11am-7pm Mon-Sat) Excellent cashmere garments can be purchased here. It's opposite the Russian embassy.

State Department Store SHOPPING CENTRE
(Их Дэлгүүр; ☏ 11-313 232; www.nomin.mn; Peace Ave 44) Known as *ikh delguur* (big shop), this is virtually a tourist attraction in itself, with the best products from around the city squeezed into one building.

The 1st floor has a foreign-exchange counter and a supermarket. The 2nd and 3rd floors have outlets for clothing, cashmere and leather goods. The 4th floor has a children's section. The 5th floor has electronics. The 6th floor has a food court, bookstore and a large room containing souvenirs, traditional clothing, maps and books about Mongolia.

Books in English BOOKS
(☏ 9920 3360; Peace Ave) Sells used books, including guidebooks. It's tough to spot, located in the basement of an apartment block. Keep your eyes peeled for the yellow-and-blue sign.

Map Shop MAPS
(Ikh Toiruu; ⏰ 9am-1pm & 2-6pm Mon-Fri, 10am-4pm Sat) Near the Elba Electronics shop. Has a good selection of maps for parts of Mongolia beyond the capital.

Seven Summits OUTDOOR GEAR
(☏ 11-329 456; www.activemongolia.com/seven_summits; btwn Peace Ave & Seoul St) Stocks German-made Vaude gear, GPS units, maps, stoves and gas, travel books and accessories. It also hires out gear, including tents, sleeping bags, gas stoves, mountain bikes and inflatable kayaks. It's opposite the CPO.

ℹ Information

DANGERS & ANNOYANCES

Pickpockets have been a long-time problem in Ulaanbaatar, especially on Peace Ave between Chinggis Khaan Sq and the State Department Store. Leave valuables in your hotel and clip zippers together on backpacks to deter probing hands. Be careful when walking out of upscale restaurants and nightclubs at night. Don't become paranoid, but don't let your guard down either. The recent appearance of Tourist Police seems to have reduced robberies.

When taking a taxi from the train station into town, don't leave your bags in the trunk of the car as the driver may hold them for ransom (use official cabs to avoid this problem). There are also increasing reports of random acts of violence against foreigners in Ulaanbaatar. The problem mostly occurs in or near bars, typically fuelled by excess alcohol. When moving about at night, stick to well-lit streets and do so with a group of friends – there is safety in numbers.

EMERGENCY

Tourist Police in fluorescent vests prowl the main downtown areas in summer, assisting visitors in distress.

You can also call the police in an emergency on the following numbers.
Emergency Aid/Ambulance (☏ 103)
Police Emergency (☏ 102)

INTERNET ACCESS

There's a growing number of wireless hotspots in Ulaanbaatar. Your hotel may offer free wi-fi, or you can easily get online at cafes including Café Amsterdam or Narya.

Internet Cafe (☏ 7010 2486; Peace Ave; per 10min T100; ⏰ 9am-8pm Mon-Fri, 11am-5pm Sat & Sun) Located inside the Central Post Office.

MAPS

The 1:10,000 *Ulaanbaatar City Map* is updated yearly. It's available at hotels, souvenir shops and the central post office.

MEDIA

Pick up English-language newspapers the *Mongol Messenger* (www.mongolmessenger.mn; T500) and the *UB Post* (http://ubpost.mongolnews.mn; T600) for local news and entertainment information.

MEDICAL SERVICES

The best place for most of your health-care needs is the SOS clinic, but life-or-death emergencies are evacuated to Seoul or Běijīng.

SOS Medica Mongolia Clinic (☏ 11-464 325, after hours 9911 0335; Bldg 4a, Big Ring Rd; ⏰ 9am-6pm Mon-Fri) This clinic has a staff of Western doctors on call 24 hours (after hours call 9911 0335). Its services don't come cheap (examinations start from around US$195), but it's the best place to go in an emergency.

Intermed (☏ 7000 0203; www.intermed.mn; Chinggis Ave 41, Khan-Uul District; ⏰ 8am-5pm Mon-Fri, 8am-1pm Sat) High quality private hospital with Mongolian and Korean doctors.

MONEY

Banks, ATMs and moneychangers are widespread. ATMs (you'll find them in department stores, hotel lobbies and the central post office) dispense tögrögs. You can get dollars from a bank teller with your debit card and passport (fees from your home bank will apply). There's a handy moneychanger on the 1st floor of the State Department Store.

Trade & Development Bank (T&D Bank; ✆11-327 095; ☉9am-4pm Mon-Fri) Will change travellers cheques into tögrög for a 1% fee or into US dollars for a 2% fee. Will also replace lost Amex travellers cheques.

Valiut Arjiljaa (Moneychangers; Baga Toiruu West, btwn Peace Ave & Juulchin Gudamj; ☉8.30am-9pm) The square next to the Ard bus stop has several private moneychangers with the best rates in town.

POST

Central Post Office (CPO, Töv Shuudangiin Salbar; ✆11-313 421; cnr Peace Ave & Sükhbaataryn Gudamj; ☉7.30am-9pm Mon-Fri, 9am-8pm Sat & Sun) Located near the southwest corner of Chinggis Khaan Sq. The Postal Counter Hall is the place to post mail, packages and check poste restante (counter No 9; you'll need to show your passport). EMS express (priority) mail can also be sent from here. There is also a good range of postcards, small booklets about Mongolia in English and local newspapers for sale. On Sunday, although it's open, most services are nonexistent. Express services such as FedEx are more reliable if sending important documents.

TOURIST INFORMATION

Ulaanbaatar Information Centre (✆7010-8687; www.tourism.ub.gov.mn; Baga Toiruu West 15; ☉9am-6pm) Located in the Ulaanbaatar Bank building (door is on the north side). This office (run by the city) has a rack of brochures but the staff here seem pretty indifferent to visitors.

TRAVEL AGENCIES

Ulaanbaatar has no shortage of travel agents and tour operators who can help organise ger visits and other excursions or obtain train tickets.

Air Market (✆11-305 050; www.airmarket.mn; cnr Peace Ave & Chingisiin Örgön Chölöö; ☉9am-8pm)

Legend Tour (✆9919 3843, 11-315 158; www.legendtour.ru; Seoul St, Chonon Burt Center Bldg, 3rd fl) The Russian embassy usually refers travellers to Legend Tour for visa help. Some travellers have given some negative feedback about this operation, but it may be your only choice if you want that elusive Russian visa. Make sure you are clear on the full itinerary and any additional costs.

❶ Getting There & Away

TRAIN

Ulaanbaatar's train station is in the city's southwestern corner around 2km from the centre. It has an ATM, a small cafe and some basic shops. The domestic ticketing office is in a separate building to the left of the entrance to the platform. Give yourself plenty of time because traffic to the station can be bad during much of the day.

The yellow **International Railway Ticketing Centre** (Narny Gudamj; ☉8am-7.20pm) is 200m northwest of the train station, hidden behind some old buildings. Inside the office, specific rooms sell tickets for direct trains heading to destinations in Russia and China. A receptionist at an information desk in the lobby can point out the correct room to buy tickets. Tickets for international trains can be booked up to one month in advance. However, the trains that originate in Moscow or Běijīng don't go on sale until the day before departure because they need to wait for seat availability from their counterparts in either China or Russia.

For China, most travellers book an international train ticket all the way to Běijīng. If you want to save some money (and don't mind an adventure), take a local train to the border, cross into China by jeep, and then continue to Běijīng or Dàtóng by local train.

For Russia, most travellers take the daily bus to Ulan-Ude as it's faster than the local train (12 hours versus 31 hours). The express Moscow–Ulaanbaatar or Moscow–Běijīng trains are little better, completing the journey in about 18 hours.

AIR

Chinggis Khaan International Airport is 18km southwest of the city. The airport has ATMs and banking services. There's also a post office and internet access for T50 per minute. A tourist booth opens when planes arrive. A new airport 52km south of Ulaanbaatar was under construction at the time of writing and is expected to open in late 2016.

The domestic routes are covered by AeroMongolia and Hunnu Air. On domestic routes AeroMongolia and Hunnu allow you 15kg for luggage (combined carry-on and check-in). You'll pay around T3000 per kilogram over the limit. Flight days always change so check updated schedules.

AeroMongolia (✆11-330 373; www.aeromongolia.mn; Monnis Bldg, ground fl, Chingisiin Örgön Chölöö)

Hunnu Air (✆7000 2222; www.hunnuair.com; 10-1 Chingisiin Örgön Chölöö)

MIAT (Mongolian Airlines; ☎11-333 999; www. miat.com; Chingisiin Örgön Chölöö; ☺9am–6pm Mon-Sat, 9am-3pm Sun) It only offers international flights.

Foreign airline offices include the following:

Aeroflot (☎11-320 720; www.aeroflot.ru; Seoul St 15; ☺9am-6pm Mon-Fri, 10am-3pm Sat)

Air China (☎7575 8800; www.airchina.com; Narny Gudamj 87; ☺9am-1pm & 2-5pm Mon-Fri, 10am-4pm Sat, 9am-noon Sun) Located on Narny Gudamj in the southeast of town.

Korean Air (☎11-317 100; www.koreanair.com; 3rd fl, Chinggis Khaan Hotel; ☺9am-6pm Mon-Fri)

INTERNATIONAL TRAINS DEPARTING ULAANBAATAR

DESTINATION	TRAIN NUMBER	DEPARTURE DAY	DEPARTURE TIME	DURATION
Běijīng	24	Mon or Thu (plus extra summer train)*	7.15am	30hr
Běijīng (originates in Moscow)	4	Sun	6.35am	30hr
Hohhot	34	Mon, Fri	8.50pm	25hr
Irkutsk	263	daily	9.15pm	30hr
Moscow	5	Tue, Fri	1.50pm	70hr
Moscow (originates in Běijīng)	3	Thu	3.25pm	70hr

*Train 24 changes its departure day each year (depending on whether it's run by China or Mongolia railway). The Chinese train typically leaves Ulaanbaatar on Thursday, while the Mongolian typically leaves Ulaanbaatar on Monday. The Chinese and Mongolians swap operating duties in May.

An extra train 24 is put on for the summer holiday season (it usually runs June to September). When operated by Mongolia it will most likely depart Ulaanbaatar on Wednesday, when run by China it will most likely run on Monday.

Ulaanbaatar–China Train Fares
The costs (in tögrög) for destinations in China from Ulaanbaatar:

DESTINATION	HARD SLEEPER	SOFT SLEEPER	DELUXE
Běijīng	130,050	217,750	184,550
Dàtóng	113,250	188,450	160,250
Èrlián	80,050	131,350	111,650
Hohhot	118,150	166,650	

Ulaanbaatar–Russia Train Fares
The costs (in tögrög) for destinations in Russia from Ulaanbaatar:

DESTINATION	2ND CLASS	1ST CLASS
Naushki	42,250	66,750
Ulan-Ude	64,150	99,050
Irkutsk	97,850	146,950
Krasnoyarsk	142,750	220,350
Omsk	183,450	301,650
Yekaterinburg	216,350	359,950
Perm	226,350	373,950
Moscow	266,250	445,050

DOMESTIC TRAINS DEPARTING ULAANBAATAR

TRAIN (NUMBER)	FREQUENCY	DEPARTURE	DURATION (HR)	FARE (SEAT/HARD SLEEPER/ SOFT SLEEPER)
Darkhan (271)	daily	10.50am	7	5450/13,750/19,950
Sainshand (286)	daily	9.15am	10	8300/17,600/26,500
Sükhbaatar (263)	daily	8.25pm	9	7200/16,000/23,500
Sükhbaatar (271)	daily	10.50am	9	7200/16,000/23,500
Zamyn-Üüd (22; fast)	Thu, Sun	8.50pm	12	-/-/38,750
Zamyn-Üüd (276)	daily	5.20pm	14	10,950/21,150/32,750
Zamyn-Üüd (34; fast)	Mon, Fri	8.50pm	12	-/-/38,750
Zamyn-Üüd (44; fast)	Tue, Wed, Sat	8.50pm	12	-/-/38,750

BUS & MINIVAN

Minivans and buses heading for destinations in the north and west leave from the **Dragon Bus Stand** (☑ 7017 4902) on Peace Ave 7km west of Chinggis Khaan Sq. The **Bayanzürkh Avto Vaksal** (Баянзүрх Авто Вокзал; ☑ 7015 3386), 6km east of Chinggis Khaan Sq, has buses leaving to eastern cities and Dalanzadgad. Most buses depart between 7.30am and 8am; it's best to buy a ticket one or two days in advance. If you turn up and can't get a ticket, some private minivan drivers wait at the station and travel to the same destinations, departing when full. An online schedule (in Mongolian) of buses can be found at www.transdep.mn – click the box on the left side of the homepage that shows a Greyhound bus drawing.

❶ Getting Around

From the train station to the city centre it's about a 25-minute walk (about 2km). As international trains arrive in the early morning when the city is still quiet, the walk into town is fairly pleasant. Alternatively, metered taxis charge a standard T800 per kilometre (check the current rate as this increases regularly); most taxi drivers are honest and will use their meters. If there's no meter, make sure the driver sets the odometer to zero. Expect to pay around T5000 from the station to Chinggis Khaan Sq. Agree on a price before setting off, write it on a piece of paper and show to the driver to avoid confusion.

A taxi from the airport should be around US$15 to US$20. Bus 11 or 22 runs from the airport every 20 minutes to the Bayangol Hotel (T500, 25 minutes). However, it doesn't come to the terminal; it stops on the highway outside the airport. It's much better to organise a pick-up from your hotel.

For trips around town, you can hail a local taxi for T800 per kilometre, although drivers rarely speak English and may not know your destination. There are occasional horror stories of tourists getting ripped off or robbed by taxi drivers.

A good and safe option is **Help Taxi** (☑ 9965 2371; www.help-tours.com), which charges T5000 for the first 5km and then T1000 per kilometre.

Around Ulaanbaatar

Mongolia's real attraction lies in the untouched beauty of the countryside, its exhilarating wide open spaces and rich nomadic culture. Fortunately, these aspects are within in reach on day trips or overnights from Ulaanbaatar.

Mandshir Khiid Мандшир Хийд

Just over 50km south of Ulaanbaatar, the historic monastery **Mandshir Khiid** (Мандшир Хийд; GPS: N 47°45.520', E 106°59.675'; admission T5000; ⊙9am-sunset) is set in a stunning location amid cliffs and pine trees. The monastery was established in 1733 and once contained more than 20 temples and housed 350 monks. Destroyed during the 1930s, the main temple has been restored and now functions as a museum, but the other temples remain in ruins.

The monastery itself is not as impressive as Gandan Khiid in Ulaanbaatar, but the forest setting is exquisite. Behind the main temple, climb up the rocks to discover some **Buddhist rock paintings**.

There are a couple of ger camps in the area if you want to stay the night, including

Mandshir Ger Camp (☑01272-22535; 4-bed ger T40,000), just 200m up from the car park or the more secluded Ovooni Enger Ger Camp (☑7027 2011; per ger T80,000-100,000, mains T5000-7000), a bit past the park gate and off to the right.

From UB, take one of the hourly minibuses from Dragon Bus Stand to the town of Zuunmod (T1500, one hour) and then walk the 5km to the monastery or take a taxi.

There's a popular hike from Mandshir Khiid, over the Bogd Khan Mountain and back to Ulaanbaatar. The hike takes eight to 10 hours; with a very early start you could do it in a day but otherwise plan on camping on the mountain. The trail starts from the left side of the mountain. It is marked with paint on the trees but the markers can be hard to follow so bring a compass or GPS. Be well prepared with extra food, warm clothing and rain gear. Let someone in UB know where you are going and when you will be back.

Terelj Тэрэлж

Although it's somewhat overrun by ger camps, Terelj, about 80km northeast of UB and part of the **Gorkhi-Terelj National Park** (per person T3000), is still a beautiful and relaxing place to head to. There are many opportunities for hiking, rock climbing, swimming (in icy water), rafting and horse riding (T12,000 to T20,000 per day) in the alpine hills.

The most popular destination for hiking or horseriding is **Frog Rock** (Melkhi Khad), which most Ulaanbaatar expats mistakenly call Turtle Rock. It's easily spotted along the main road through the park. From here it's less than an hour's hike up to the picturesque Buddhist meditation retreat of Aryapala.

Terelj is a great place to go camping, or guesthouses can arrange accommodation in the park – sometimes staying in real gers with local families. Most of the tourist ger camps in Terelj offer similar facilities and prices – about US$30 per person, including three hearty meals, or US$15 without food. Among the better ones are **Buuveit** (☑11-322 870; www.tsolmontravel.com; per person with/without meals US$45/20), which has a beautifully secluded location, and the friendly **Guru Camp** (☑9909 6714; per person with meals US$45), 14km along the main road from the park entrance.

CHINGGIS KHAAN STATUE

The 40m-tall Chinggis Khaan Statue is a new local landmark and popular day trip for people from Ulaanbaatar. The statue features an enormous silver-plated Chinggis on horseback, holding his famed golden whip. There is an elevator rising up the tail with steps to the horse's head.

The complex includes a museum and six-minute film that describes how the statue was built. For an extra T1000 you can dress up in Mongol battle gear and pose for photos near a giant Mongol boot. The statue is located by the main eastern highway, 23km east of Nalaikh.

For the slightly more adventurous, there is the **Ecotourism Ger Camp** (☑9973 4710; bergroo@hotmail.com; GPS: N 47°58.722'; E 107°28.907'; per person with meals €35), run by a Dutchman named Bert. It's a 40-minute horse ride from the UB-2 Hotel at Terelj village. Call ahead and Bert can meet you at the hotel or provide walking directions. Bert can organise horse-riding trips of the area and can show you his cheese-making operation.

A bus (T2500) for Terelj village (passing Frog Rock) leaves at noon and 4pm in summer or 3pm in winter (1 October to 15 May) from Peace Ave in Ulaanbaatar, opposite the Narantuul Hotel. They may charge you T5000 but this includes the park-entry fee. Have a Mongolian speaker call ahead to the bus conductor **Ms Nara** (☑9665 4818) for more details. Otherwise, hire a taxi for about T70,000 one way.

Khustain National Park Хустайн Нуруу

This park (Khustain Nuruu, Birch Mountain Range; ☑21-245 087; www.hustai.mn; admission T10,000, Mongolians free), located about 100km southwest of Ulaanbaatar, is a 506-sq-km reserve set up to protect the reintroduced *takhi* or Przewalski's horse, a sub-species of horse that was never domesticated.

Due to poaching and overgrazing, the Przewalski's horse became extinct in the wild by the late 1960s, but the animals had been preserved in zoos in Europe and Australia. A reintroduction program started in the 1990s brought some back to Mongolia and they have been thriving in Khustain Nuruu. More than 300 horses now occupy the park, along with wolves, gazelle, boars and lynxes.

Horse riding (per hour/day 7000/42,000), hiking, mountain biking (per hour/day T4000/16,000) and jeep excursions (per kilometre T1400) are a few of the activities available here.

You can stay at the **Hustain Tourist Camp** (per person with 3 meals T82,500, with breakfast only T32,000) near the entrance to the park or at **Moilt Camp** (per person with 3 meals T82,500, with breakfast only T32,000) inside the park. For reservations contact the **Hustai National Park office** (☑21-245 087; www.hustai.mn; Hustai Bldg, 2nd khoroo, Bayangol District).

To get to the park, travel 100km west of Ulaanbaatar, then 13km up a dirt road off the main highway. Guesthouses and tour operators offer trips here, or contact the Park Trust for transport options.

Ikh Nartiin Chuluu Их Нартын Чулуу

A splendid area of rocky outcrop in the desert, **Ikh Nartiin Chuluu Nature Reserve** (Ikh Nart; www.ikhnart.com), can give you a good taste of the Gobi without venturing too far off the Trans-Mongolia.

Wildlife watching is a popular activity here, as the reserve is home to argali sheep, ibex and other creatures of the desert. An international team of wildlife biologists operate in the area and their conservation efforts have helped to boost the number of argali sheep.

Several ancient **burial mounds** (GPS: N 45°75.546', E 108°65.454') and **petroglyphs** (GPS: N 45°60.787', E 108°57.201'; N 45°60.237', E

CHANGING THE BOGIES

As in Russia, Mongolia's trains run on a 5ft (1.5m) gauge, which is slightly wider than the standard gauge used in much of the rest of the world. Before the train can continue its journey, it must make a stop at the bogie-changing shed, where the carriages are raised and the bogies are replaced with the appropriate size. The bogies are changed with the passengers still on board the train and you can see the operations happening around you.

108°55.959'; N 45°59.175', E 108°61.397') can also be found throughout the park. The petroglyphs are found on rocky outcrops and take the form of Buddhist prayers written in Tibetan script.

Red Rock Ger Camp (☑11-328 737; www. nomadicjourneys.com; GPS: N 45°39.830', E 108°39.204'; per night US$95, 4 days & 3 nights with meals per person US$350) ✍, operated by Nomadic Journeys, is a high-end ger camp in the reserve. The caretakers can organise guided walks in the reserve and transport to/from the camp. Pick-ups are available from Shivee Gobi, Choir or Dalanjargalan (Tsomog), all towns on the Trans-Mongolian Railway line. The train journey to any of these towns is about five hours, then a driver from Red Rock will shuttle you one hour to the camp. Make prior arrangements with Nomadic Journeys (p265).

Sainshand   Сайншанд

☑01522 / POP 19,820 / TIME MOSCOW + 5HR

Sainshand (Good Pond) is a sleepy, wind-raked Gobi town with a decent hotel, a few restaurants and sweeping views of the empty desert. It might not look like much now but authorities have big plans for Sainshand, with the city tapped to become an industrial hub to process coal and copper extracted from the mineral-rich Gobi Desert. Until that happens, the main reason to come to Sainshand is to visit the nearby 'Energy Centre' and Khamaryn Khiid, a popular monastery in the desert south of the city.

The town is divided in two sections, the area around the train station, and the more developed city centre 2km to the south.

Sainshand has an interesting **Aimag Museum** (☑01522-22657; admission T2000; ◷9am-1pm & 2-6pm) that houses stuffed Gobi animals, fossils and ethnographic items. It's across the street from the main square.

More unique is the **Museum of Danzan Ravjaa** (☑01522-23221; www.danzanravjaa.org; admission T1000; ◷9am-1pm & 2-6pm), dedicated to the life and achievements of the fifth Gobi Saint, Danzan Ravjaa (1803–56). Well-known for his artwork, poetry, music and theatre productions, Ravjaa retains almost mythical status in the Gobi and locals can tell you tales of his legendary feats. The museum curator Altangerel is the caretaker of Danzan Ravjaa's possessions, a hereditary honour passed on through five family generations. It's on the main square.

THE GOBI DESERT

The world's northernmost desert straddles the border between Mongolia and China, an immense, barren plateau the size of Western Europe. The Mongolians say that there are 33 different types of Gobi, but only about 2% of it is *Lawrence of Arabia*–style sand dunes. Most of the land is dry gravel plains, an occasional mountain range, and some sandstone cliffs.

The harsh climate sees the temperature shift from minus 30°C in winter to above 40°C in summer. Still, some hardy nomads manage to eke out an existence here, raising camels, goats and other livestock. They have recently been joined by an army of entrepreneurs, prospectors, geologists and others seeking to cash in on Mongolia's booming mining sector, based largely in the south Gobi.

The Gobi was brought into the consciousness of the Western world thanks largely to the explorations of Roy Chapman Andrews, the head of New York's Museum of Natural History. In the 1920s Andrews made five trips into the Gobi (with both camels and Dodge trucks sent across the Pacific), where he collected an enormous amount of dinosaur skeletons, fossils and dinosaur eggs.

Contrary to popular belief, the Gobi is home to a significant amount of wildlife, including *khavtgai* (wild camels), *hulan* (wild asses), *zeer* (gazelles), *argal* (argali sheep), *yangir* (ibex), *irbis* (snow leopards) and *mazaalai* (Gobi bears).

In the Gobi the locals have a lot of time on their hands, and can spin yarns about other legendary beasts of the desert, including the *allegorhoi horhoi* ('death worm'), which sprays poisonous venom from its mouth and discharges a powerful electric shock from its tail. Another Gobi resident is the Almas, a sort of Bigfoot or Yeti that locals describe as a 'marmot-eating half-ape.' Both creatures have inspired *National Geographic*–style search expeditions in recent years. So far both have remained elusive.

Dornogobi Hotel (☎ 7052 3657; tw T55,000-88,000; 🛜) is the landmark circular building on the northwest corner of the main square. Rooms are clean and comfortable and showers are reliably hot. There is a generous 6pm checkout for travellers that need to wait for the evening train back to Ulaanbaatar.

Altan Urag (meals T4000-4500; ⊘ 9am-11pm) serves Chinese and Mongolian dishes in large portions. It's on the main road, about 200m east of the Museum of Danzan Ravjaa.

❶ Getting There & Away

At least two trains per day pass through Sainshand (we have listed the most convenient). Departure times here are based on the summer schedule (May to September) and are subject to slight variations each year.

Sainshand to UB (northbound trains):

Train 285 departs 8.25pm daily; arrives in UB 7am.

Train 275 (originates in Zamyn-Üüd); departs Sainshand 11.40pm daily; arrives in UB 8.55am.

Sainshand to Zamyn-Üüd (southbound trains):

Train 276 (originates in Ulaanbaatar); departs daily 2.25am; arrives in Zamyn-Üüd 7.20am.

Around Sainshand

Although the desert in this part of the Gobi is typically flat and featureless, it is worth hiring a vehicle for a day to explore the attractions outside of town. Negotiate a trip with the drivers at Sainshand's jeep stand.

The highlight of the area is **Khamaryn Khiid** and the nearby Shambhala (also known as the Energy Centre). The monastery was founded by legendary poet-monk Danzan Ravjaa in the 1820s and for decades after it flourished as a cultural institution. Danzan Ravjaa organised opera here, wrote poetry and music and practised traditional medicine. After he died his followers maintained the institutions he founded and tall tales spread about his magical feats.

The monastery was destroyed in 1937 but many of his possessions were hidden and protected. In 1990 a new monastery was founded here and it has been growing in popularity as a pilgrim destination.

About 2km from the monastery is **Shambhala**, where pilgrims arrive in large numbers to lay flat on the ground and absorb the energy of this sacred spot. The site is surrounded by 108 stupas and special ceremonies are held here on 10 September.

MONGOLIA–CHINA BORDER CROSSINGS

This border crossing takes about five hours no matter which direction you are travelling in. Most trains cross the border at night, which guarantees that you won't get much sleep. In Zamyn-Üüd, Mongolian customs officials board the train and collect paperwork from passengers. In Èrlián, Chinese customs and passport officials repeat the process (or start it, if you're travelling west). You must fill out customs forms and departure/arrival cards.

You'll spend about an hour on the Mongolian side and about three hours on the Chinese side; it's on the Chinese side where the bogies are changed. The Èrlián station is usually quite lively, even at night. Once your passport is returned, catch some fresh air and explore the station and surroundings where you can change money or get something to eat. If you do get off, you will not have a chance to get back on the train for about two hours while the bogies are changed.

Alternative Routes to/from Běijīng

In the week leading up to Naadam, with thousands of visitors heading to Mongolia, it's practically impossible to score last-minute reservations on the direct trains and flights to Ulaanbaatar. After Naadam there is a reverse migration and it can be difficult to get tickets out of the country. If you haven't booked well in advance, all is not lost as there are alternatives.

Train tickets are often available on the twice-weekly service between Ulaanbaatar and Hohhot (China). Another option is to take an international train to Èrlián then continue by local bus or train to your destination. A slightly cheaper option is to train to Zamyn-Üüd on the Mongolian side and cross the border by jeep.

Around 23km northwest of the monastery is **Bayanzürkh mountain**, another sacred site associated with Danzan Ravjaa, where visitors make the short but blustery hike to the top of the mountain to utter three wishes at the wishing *ovoo* (stone cairns).

If you want to sleep out in the desert, **Gobi Sunrise Tavan Dohio** (☑9908 0151; GPS: N 44°45.418', E 110°11.236'; with/without meals US$45/25) is a well-maintained ger camp with flush toilets and hot showers. A taxi here from town is T20,000.

To see the monastery, Shambhala and mountain, you can organise a taxi in Sainshand and pay by kilometre (around T800 to T1000). Drivers wait around the market. The Danzan Ravjaa museum curator Altangerel (☑9909 0151) speaks some English and may be able to organise a ride.

Zamyn-Üüd   Замын-Үүд

☑02524 / POP 13,500 / TIME MOSCOW +5HR

The last stop (or first depending on your direction) of the Trans-Mongolia line before it plunges into China is this small, otherwise insignificant border village in the Gobi Desert. Most of the town's activity can be found around the square in front of the train station. The chief attractions here are the disused water fountain, some outdoor pool tables and grabbing a bite at one of the many eateries that cater to transit travellers killing time.

If you miss the train to UB and need to spend the night, the **Zamyn Uud Hotel** (☑7052 7032; tw T35,000) at the northern end of the train-station platform has clean rooms with attached bathroom.

Dàtóng, China   大同

☑0352 / POP 3.3 MILLION / TIME MOSCOW +5HR

Its coal-belt setting and socialist-era refashioning have robbed Dàtóng of much of its charm. The city has, however, ploughed mountains of cash – an estimated ¥50 billion – into a colossal renovation program of its old quarter. But even without its pricey facelift, Dàtóng still cuts it as a coal-dusted heavyweight in China's increasingly competitive tourist challenge. The city is the gateway to the awe-inspiring Yungang Caves, one of China's most outstanding Buddhist treasures, and close to the photogenic Hanging Monastery, the world's oldest wooden pagoda, and crumbling earthen sections of the Great Wall.

If you're headed south, the daily Ulaanbaatar to Zamyn-Üüd train arrives in the early morning and there is a scramble to get into a 4WD (¥50 to ¥80) to cross the border. Buses are also available; tickets are sold on the second floor of the Ulaanbaatar train station (buy at least one day before departure). Once you reach Èrlián you can quickly move on by bus. (There are only a handful of trains from Èrlián each week and most leave late at night.) There is one morning bus to Dàtóng (¥136, five hours), three afternoon buses to Běijīng (¥180 to ¥220, 10 hours) and six buses to Hohhot (¥95, six hours), the first at 8am.

For those headed north, there are two daily buses to Zamyn-Üüd (¥50) at 1.30pm and 3pm. It's also possible to take a 4WD across the border; these gather at the bus station and the markets around town. There is no use getting a taxi to the border to look for a 4WD as all vehicles will be full to capacity. Taxi drivers in Èrlián are notorious for overcharging foreigners, so always agree on a price beforehand, or better yet, use the meter.

Once you reach Zamyn-Üüd you'll have to wait for the 5.35pm train (275) to Ulaanbaatar. Three times a week there is also an evening train. Tickets for Ulaanbaatar often sell out, so it's best to get over the border as early as possible to get in line. If you're in a hurry (and don't mind spending more for your transport), it's usually possible to buy a ticket at the station in Èrlián for Ulaanbaatar-bound trains; prices are ¥656/914/1009 for hard sleeper/soft sleeper/deluxe.

Whichever way you're travelling, you have to cross the border in a vehicle. The border is open daily from 8.30am to 5.30pm.

⊙ Sights

Much of Dàtóng's **old town** (老城区; *lǎochéngqū*) has been levelled to restore what was there before. Illogical for sure, but this is China. The area around the **Drum Tower** (鼓楼; Gǔ Lóu) has emerged as 'Ye Olde Qing Quarter', version 2.0.

Buildings rebuilt from the ground up include the **mosque** (清真大寺; Qīngzhēn Dà Sì), a Taoist temple and many former courtyard houses, while portions of Huayan Jie, Da Beijie and Da Nanjie have become pedestrian-only shopping streets.

Huáyán Temple   BUDDHIST TEMPLE
(华严寺, Huáyán Sì; Huayan Jie; admission ¥80; ⊙8am-6.30pm; 🚌38) Built by the Khitan during the Liao dynasty (AD 907–1125), this temple faces east, not south (it's said the Khitan were sun worshippers) and is divided into two separate complexes. One of these is an active monastery (upper temple), while the other is a museum (lower temple).

Dating to 1140, the impressive main hall of the **Upper Temple** (上华严寺; Shàng Huáyán Sì) is one of the largest Buddhist halls in China with Ming murals and Qing statues within. The rear hall of the **Lower Temple** (下华严寺; Xià Huáyán Sì) is the oldest building in Dàtóng (1038), containing some remarkable Liao-dynasty wooden

sculptures. Side halls contain assorted relics from the Wei, Liao and Jin dynasties. Bus 38 runs here.

Nine Dragon Screen   WALL
(九龙壁, Jiǔlóng Bì; Da Dongjie; admission ¥10; ⊙8am-6.30pm) With its nine beautiful multicoloured coiling dragons, this 45.5m-long, 8m-high and 2m-thick Ming-dynasty spirit wall was built in 1392. It's the largest glazed-tile wall in China and an amazing sight; the palace it once protected belonged to the 13th son of a Ming emperor and burnt down years ago.

Shànhuà Temple   BUDDHIST TEMPLE
(善化寺, Shànhuà Sì; Nansi Jie; admission ¥50; ⊙8am-6pm) Originally constructed in AD 713; Shànhuà was rebuilt by the Jin. The grand wooden-bracketed rear hall contains five beautiful central Buddhas and expressive statues of celestial generals in the wings. Look out for an impressive five-dragon screen out the front.

🛏 Sleeping

Fly By Knight Datong Highrise Hostel   HOSTEL $
(夜奔大同客栈; Yèbēn Dàtóng Kèzhàn; 📞130 4109 5935; datongfbk@gmail.com; 22nd fl, Unit 14, 15 Yingbin Xijie, 迎宾西街15号22楼14室 (桐城中央); dm ¥80-140, s & tw shared bath ¥150-180,

Dàtóng

N 0 — 500 m
0 — 0.25 miles

★ **Garden Hotel** HOTEL $$$
(花园大饭店, Huāyuán Dàfàndiàn; ☏586 5888; www.gardenhoteldatong.com; 59 Da Nanjie, 大南街59号; d & tw incl breakfast ¥1080-1380; ❀❈@☎) The large impeccable rooms at this hotel feature goose-down quilts, carved rosewood bed frames, reproduction antique furnishings and superb bathrooms. It has an attractive atrium, Latin American and Chinese restaurants, plus excellent staff. The impressive breakfast spread includes good espresso coffee. Significant discounts (even in high season) knock prices as low as ¥310, making it one of the best-value hotels in China.

✗ Eating

The inhouse Chinese restaurant at the Garden Hotel has a picture menu and serves excellent food. You'll also find plenty of restaurants and street stalls in the area near the Garden Hotel.

Dōngfāng Xiǎo Miàn NOODLES $
(East Wheat, 东方削面; Yingze Jie, 迎泽街; noodles from ¥7; ⊙7am-10pm) Forgive the chainstore decor and bear the long queues and you'll soon be in noodle heaven. Steaming bowls of the humble Shānxī speciality is the star here; have it with pork, beef or lamb and pair it with a variety of side dishes such as sliced cucumbers. A beer will help top it all off.

If you're still hungry, you can grab charcoal-grilled lamb skewers (¥3) from the street stall just outside, come evening time.

---

d en suite ¥200; ☎) China's (possibly) priciest hostel is housed within a modern apartment located 1.5km west of the old town. Neat Ikea-furnished bedrooms have been converted into dorms and private rooms. Bathrooms are clean and the English-speaking staff are friendly. The hostel is a ¥10 cab ride from the bus station and old town, and ¥15 from the train station.

Today Hotel HOTEL $$
(今日商务酒店, Jīnrì Shāngwù Juǐdiàn; ☏537 9800; 1029 Weidu Dadao; 魏都大道1029号; d & tw ¥219; ❈☎) This chain hotel located opposite the train station has large and spotless rooms with wooden-panelled flooring (no icky carpets), good bathrooms and is a great spot to decamp after you stumble out of the train station from an overnight journey. Get a room on the higher floor to escape the street noise.

ℹ Information

Industrial and Commercial Bank of China
(ICBC; 工商银行; Gōngshāng Yínháng; Weidu Dadao)

Public Security Bureau (PSB, 公安局出入境接待处, Gōng'ānjú Chūrùjìng Jiēdàichù; ☑206 1833; 11 flr, Hualin Xintiandi, Weidu Dadao, 花林新天地, 11楼, 魏都大道; ☺9am-noon & 3-5.30pm Mon-Fri)

ℹ Getting There & Away

There are frequent train services between Dàtóng and Běijīng (hard seat/sleeper ¥54/108, six hours) but sleeper cars tend to sell out fast so you still need to book ahead. From the south bus station (新南站), located 9km from the train station, buses to Běijīng (¥128, four hours) depart hourly from 7.10am to 4.10pm.

If you're heading north to Mongolia your options are the K3 and K23 (running three days a week in summer), which can be purchased at the train station in Dàtóng. It's best if you can buy this ticket ahead of time at the CITS office in Běijīng, so that you can be assured of a ticket. If tickets are unavailable in Dàtóng, take a bus to Èrlián, cross the border and continue by rail to Ulaanbaatar.

ℹ Getting Around

Bus routes are being readjusted owing to the massive construction all around town so expect changes. Bus 4 and 15 runs from the train station to the main bus station. Bus 30 (30 minutes) runs from the train station to the new south bus station. Buses 27 and 35 go to the old town from Weidu Dadao. Taxi flagfall is ¥7.

Around Dàtóng

Yungang Caves 云冈石窟

One of China's best examples of Buddhist cave art, these 5th-century caves (Yúngāng Shíkū; ☑0352-302 6230; admission ¥150; ☺8.30am-5.30pm summer) are impressive in scope. With 51,000 ancient statues, they put virtually everything else in the Shānxī shade.

Carved by the Turkic-speaking Tuoba, the Yungang Caves drew their designs from Indian, Persian and even Greek influences that swept along the Silk Road. Work began in AD 460, continuing for 60 years before all 252 caves, the oldest collection of Buddhist carvings in China, had been completed.

Some caves contain intricately carved square-shaped pagodas, while others depict the inside of temples, carved and painted to look as though made of wood. Frescos are in abundance and there are graceful depictions of animals, birds and angels, some still brightly painted, and almost every cave contains the 1000-Buddha motif (tiny Buddhas seated in niches).

Eight of the caves contain enormous Buddha statues; the largest can be found in Cave 5, an outstanding 17m-high, seated effigy of Sakyamuni with a gilded face. The frescos in this cave are badly scratched, but note the painted vaulted ceiling. Bursting with colour, Cave 6 is also stunning, resembling a set from an *Indiana Jones* epic with legions of Buddhist angels, bodhisattvas and other figures.

Caves 16 to 20 are the earliest caves at Yungang, carved under the supervision of monk Tanyao. Examine the exceptional quality of the carvings in Cave 18; some of the faces are perfectly presented. Cave 19 contains a vast 16.8m-high effigy of Sakyamuni.

Past the last set of caves is a new museum (9.30am to 4.50pm) detailing the Wei kingdom.

Most of the caves come with good English captions, but there's also an audio guide in English (¥30 with ¥100 deposit). Note that photography is permitted in some caves but not in others.

ℹ Getting There & Away

Take the 云冈 double decker bus (¥2, 45 minutes) from outside the train station to its terminus. Buses run every 10 to 15 minutes. A taxi is ¥40 each way.

The Trans-Manchurian Route

Route Info

➡ Distance: 2790km

➡ Duration: Two days, eight hours

➡ Time zones: Moscow +7, Moscow +9

Best Places to Stay & Eat

➡ Lungmen Grand Hotel (p293)

➡ Fēngzéyuán Lǔdiàn (p289)

➡ Sōngyuàn Hotel (p297)

➡ Kazy International Youth Hostel (p293)

➡ Katusha (p294)

➡ Orient King of Eastern Dumplings (p294)

Why Go?

For connoisseurs of obscure rail routes, the Trans-Manchurian Railway ranks high on the wish list. It's not on the main line to Vladivostok, nor does it take the 'tourist route' via Mongolia; rather, the weekly Vostok (19/20) chugs through China's rust belt, where foreign faces are few and far between. From Chita the railway heads toward the Chinese border at Mǎnzhōulǐ, sweeps through the grasslands of Inner Mongolia and passes through Hā'ěrbīn (Harbin) before carrying on towards the megalopolis that is Běijīng. The highlight is fascinating Hā'ěrbīn, where elements of turn-of-the-century Russia still poke through the surface of a thoroughly modern Chinese city. Bullet trains speed south from Hā'ěrbīn to Běijīng, but there's plenty to see along the way. Jumping-off points include Chángchūn, one-time capital of Japanese-occupied Manchukuo; Shěnyáng, with well-preserved relics of the Manchu era; and Shānhǎiguān, where the Great Wall meets the sea.

When to Go

Hā'ěrbīn

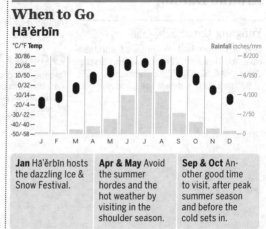

Jan Hā'ěrbīn hosts the dazzling Ice & Snow Festival.

Apr & May Avoid the summer hordes and the hot weather by visiting in the shoulder season.

Sep & Oct Another good time to visit, after peak summer season and before the cold sets in.

❶ The Route

In Russia the kilometre markers show the distance from Moscow. Once in China they show the distance to Hā'ěrbīn (Harbin); south of Hā'ěrbīn, they show the distance to Běijīng.

CHITA TO ZABAIKALSK

6199km from Moscow

There's a 20-minute stop at Chita, where you can stagger off the train and forage for snacks at the small shops near the platform.

6293km

The next major stop is Karymskaya, from where it's 12km down the line to Tarskaya, the official start of the Trans-Manchurian route; here the train crosses the Ingoda River and heads southeast.

6444km

There's a short stop at Olovyannaya, then the train crosses the Onon River, a tributary of the Ingoda. This area is said to be the birthplace of Chinggis (Genghis) Khaan.

6543km

The train makes another 10-minute stop at Borzya. A little-known spur line heads south from here to Mongolia; it was built to move military equipment into eastern Mongolia during the Japanese invasion of 1939.

6666km

A few hours are taken for the bogies to be changed in the Russian border town of Zabaikalsk before the train can travel into China. Passably edible meals are available at a cafe across from the station (take the bridge over the tracks and turn left). An ATM inside the station dispenses roubles.

MĂNZHŌULĬ TO HĀ'ĚRBĪN

935km (to Hā'ěrbīn)

Chinese border town Mǎnzhōulǐ, established in 1901 as a stop for the train, is booming thanks to cross-border trade.

749km

Next along the line is Hǎilā'ěr, the northernmost major town in Inner Mongolia, where the train stops for about 10 minutes. This is a great place to experience the Mongolian grasslands at Jīnzhànghán Grasslands, Shì Wěi or Ēnhé.

650-560km

The train enters the Greater Hinggan Mountains. Some trains make stops at towns such as Mianduhe (634km), Yilick Ede (574km) and Xinganling (564km). From here the train descends on the eastern side of the range.

539km

Shortly after the 15-minute halt at Boketu, the train leaves Inner Mongolia and enters the province of Hēilóngjiāng, meaning Black Dragon River. Known in Russian as the Amur River, it marks the border with Russia in northeastern China. At this point you can sense a changing climatic and topographic shift as you leave the steppes behind and enter the steamy Manchurian lowlands.

159km

The train makes a brief stop in Dàqìng at the centre of a large oilfield; look out for the 'nodding donkeys' pumping crude oil out of the ground.

1388km (to Běijīng)

The final stretch before Hā'ěrbīn, the capital of Hēilóngjiāng province, offers excellent views, especially as you cross the 1km-long bridge over the Sōnghuā River.

HĀ'ĚRBĪN TO BĚIJĪNG

1146km (to Běijīng)

The train stops for 10 minutes in the industrial city of Chángchūn, capital of Jílín province.

841km

Heading south, the train plies China's blighted rust belt towards Shěnyáng, where the Vostok halts for 15 minutes. This industrial city of 3.5 million people was a Mongol trading centre from the 11th century, becoming the capital of the Manchu empire in the 17th century.

THE TRANS-MANCHURIAN ROUTE

TRANS-MANCHURIAN ROUTE PLANNER

The following is a suggested itinerary for covering the main sights along the Trans-Manchurian route in the area:

Day 1 Leave Chita; overnight train to Zabaikalsk (10 hours); cross border, explore Mǎnzhōulǐ.

Day 2 From Mǎnzhōulǐ, take the overnight train to Hā'ěrbīn.

Day 3 Explore Hā'ěrbīn and overnight.

Day 4 See more of Hā'ěrbīn, then train to Chángchūn.

Day 5 Explore Chángchūn, then train to Shěnyáng.

Day 6 Tour Shěnyáng, then continue to Shānhǎiguān.

Day 7 Enjoy Shānhǎiguān, then travel to Běijīng.

Trans-Manchurian Route Highlights

1 Hanging out with Russian traders in the prosperous border town of **Mǎnzhōulǐ** (p288)

2 Experiencing the unique fusion of historic Russia and modern China on the cobblestone streets of Hā'ěrbīn's **Dàolǐqū district** (p292)

3 Viewing some majestic felines at the **Siberian Tiger Park** (p291), just outside Hā'ěrbīn

4 Delving into Hā'ěrbīn's unique Semitic past at **Hā'ěrbīn New Synagogue** (p293), which recounts the experience of 20,000 Jews on Chinese soil

5 Braving the cold to see the spectacular ice sculptures carved at Hā'ěrbīn's legendary **Ice & Snow Festival** (p292)

6 Going on the trail of Puyi, the last emperor of China, at Chángchūn's **Imperial Palace of the Manchu State** (p296)

7 Following the **Great Wall** (p299) to where it meets the sea at Shānhǎiguān

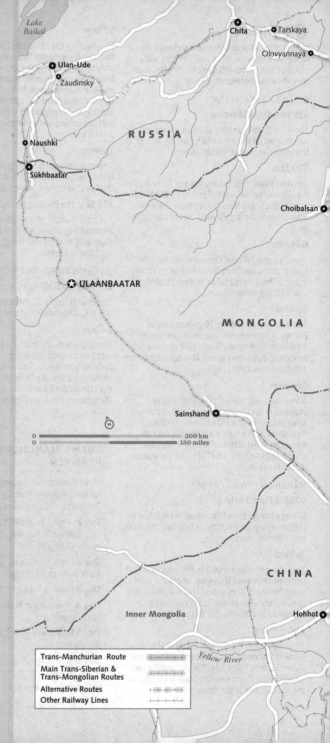

Lake Baikal

Ulan-Ude

Zaudinsky

Chita

Tarskaya

Olovyannaya

RUSSIA

Naushki

Sükhbaatar

Choibalsan

ULAANBAATAR

MONGOLIA

Sainshand

0 300 km
0 180 miles

CHINA

Inner Mongolia

Hohhot

Yellow River

Trans-Manchurian Route
Main Trans-Siberian &
Trans-Mongolian Routes
Alternative Routes
Other Railway Lines

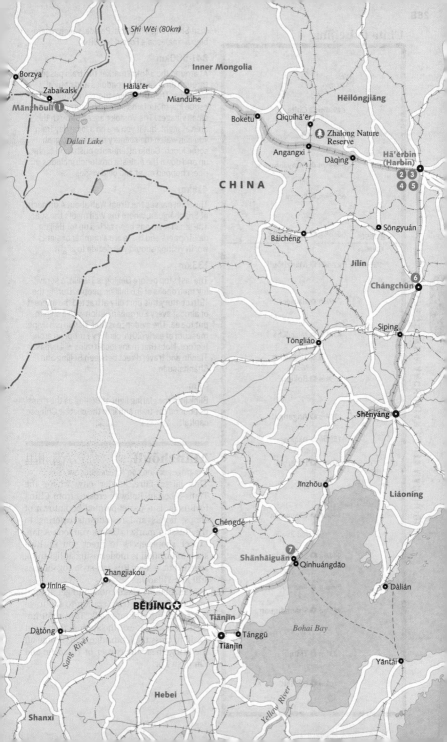

Chita to Běijīng

West to Moscow

6199km ● Chita

5hr

6444km ● Olovyannaya

2hr

6543km ● Borzya

2hr, 30min

To Vladivostok (Trans-Siberian)

RUSSIA 6666km ● Zabaikalsk

CHINA

935km to Hā'ěrbīn ● Mǎnzhōulǐ

2hr, 15min

749km ● Hǎilāěr

1hr, 30min

634km ● Mianduhe

1hr

564km ● Xinganling

30min

539km ● Boketu

3hr, 30min

270km ● Angangxi

40min

159km ● Dàqìng

40min

0km, 1388km to Běijīng ● Hā'ěrbīn

5hr

1146km ● Chángchūn

3hr, 25min

841km ● Shěnyáng

2hr, 30min

599km ● Jǐnzhōu

2hr

415km ● Shānhǎiguān

3hr, 35min

133km ● Tiānjīn

2hr

0km ● BĚIJĪNG

Visit Shěnyáng's Imperial Palace, which resembles a small-scale Forbidden City.

841-500km

At around the 545km marker the train passes through an area of rice paddies and natural wetlands. Then at 528km there are some picturesque low mountains flanked by cornfields and small villages. The Vostok passes through this area at night, but if you are on a local day train you can watch the scenery pass by and grab some lunch. Cabin attendants push food carts up and down the aisles; a box lunch includes rice, chopped meat and cold vegies.

415km

The train passes the Great Wall about 4km north of Shānhǎiguān, where the Wall meets the sea. The small town has been tarted up for Běijīng day-trippers and there are a number of sights worth visiting should you decide to alight.

133km

The last stop before Běijīng is Tiānjīn, a sprawling metropolis of 9.6 million people. During the 19th century this port city attracted the interest of almost every European nation with a ship to put to sea. The evidence is that Tiānjīn is a living museum of early-20th-century European architecture. Note that many local trains will bypass Tiānjīn and travel direct between Běijīng and Shānhǎiguān.

0km

Blink into the glaring light of Běijīng as the masses pour off the train and into the chaotic Chinese capital.

Mǎnzhōulǐ 满洲里

☎ 0470 / POP 300,000 / TIME MOSCOW +5HR

This laissez-faire border city, where the Trans-Siberian Railway crosses from China to Russia, is a pastel-painted boomtown of shops, hotels and restaurants catering to the Russian market. Unless you look Asian, expect shopkeepers to greet you in Russian. Mǎnzhōulǐ is modernising at lightning speed, but a few Russian-style log houses still line Yidao Jie.

Mǎnzhōulǐ is small enough to get around on foot. From the train station to the town centre, it's a 10-minute walk. Turn right immediately as you exit the station, then right again to cross the footbridge. You'll come off the bridge near the corner of Yidao Jie and Zhongsu Lu.

◉ Sights

Hūlún Lake
LAKE

(呼伦湖; Hūlún Hú; admission ¥30) One of the largest lakes in China, Hūlún Lake is called Dalai Nuur (Ocean Lake) in Mongolian. It unexpectedly pops out of the grasslands like an enormous inland sea. You can hire a horse (¥100 per 30 minutes) or a quad bike (¥100 per 20 minutes), take a boat ride (¥10 per 20 minutes) or simply stroll along the rocky lakeshore.

Russian Doll Park
PARK

(套娃广场, Tàowá Guǎngchǎng; ⊙8am-6pm) **FREE** This bizarre park is filled with giant Russian *matryoshka* dolls, many with portraits of famous historical figures, from Albert Einstein to Michael Jordan. The largest doll is a Russian-style restaurant. Next to the park is a **museum** of Russian art (admission ¥20). Bus 6 (¥1.50) runs along Liudao Jie past the bus station and the doll park before terminating at the Russian border area, **Guómén** (国门).

🛏 Sleeping

There are a huge number of hotels and guesthouses in Mǎnzhōulǐ. There are Chinese and Russian signs – гостиница (pronounced 'gastinitsa') is the Russian word for 'hotel'. Likewise, there are plenty of restaurants (pectopah in Russian).

Fēngzéyuán Lǚdiàn
GUESTHOUSE $

(丰泽源旅店; ☑225 4099, 139 4709 3443; Yidao Jie, 一道街; tw ¥200; @🛜) Located inside a restored Russian log cabin (painted yellow and green), this friendly (and cheap, for Mǎnzhōulǐ) guesthouse has large, clean rooms. Coming off the pedestrian bridge from the train station, it's the first building in front of you, next to the statue of Zhou Enlai. Prices fall to ¥50 in low season.

Shangri-La
HOTEL $$$

(香格里拉大酒店, Xiānggélǐlā Dàjiǔdiàn; ☑396 8888; www.shangri-la.com; 99 Liudao Jie, 六道街 99号; d¥1388, ste¥4588; ❀✳@🛜✸) Nothing indicates Mǎnzhōulǐ's soaring status more than this outpost of the Shangri-La chain; it's surely the most remote of its hotels in China if not Asia! The very comfortable rooms offer views over the surrounding grasslands, and there are Chinese and Russian restaurants, a swimming pool and a spa. The efficient staff will drum up someone who can speak English.

✗ Eating

Huāyàng Jiǎozi
DUMPLINGS $

(花样饺子; Yidao Jie 一道街; dumplings from ¥13; ⊙10am-10pm) This popular eatery opposite Fēngzéyuán Lǚdiàn serves up all manner of dumplings and cold beer. There's a picture menu on the wall detailing a huge variety of Chinese dishes if you are tired of dumplings.

Bèijiā'ěr Hú Xī Cāntīng
RUSSIAN $$

(贝加尔湖西餐厅; 23 Zhongsu Lu; 中苏路23 号; near Wudao Jie; dishes from ¥28; ⊙24hr) The name of the restaurant translates as 'Lake Baikal Western Restaurant', giving some indication of its target audience. Rub shoulders with Russians who come for robust Chinese-style Russian dishes such as borsch and steaks set to a Russian soundtrack. The set meals (from ¥60) let you sample the best dishes and are great paired with cold draught beer. Picture menu available.

ℹ Information

Industrial and Commercial Bank of China (ICBC; 工商银行; Gōngshāng Yínháng; cnr Yidao Jie & Zhongsu Jie)

China International Travel Service (CITS, 中 国国际旅行社, Zhōngguó Guójì Lǚxíngshè; ☑622 8319; 35 Erdao Jie; ⊙8-11.30am & 2-4pm Mon-Fri) Sells train tickets for Chinese cities and one-day tours (¥270) to the local sights. Located on the 1st floor of Guójì Fàndiàn (International Hotel).

China Post (中国邮政, Zhōngguó Yóuzhèng; cnr Haiguan Jie & Sidao Jie)

Public Security Bureau (PSB, 公安局; Gōng'ānjú; cnr Sandao Jie & Shulin Lu)

ℹ Getting There & Around

There are trains to/from Hǎilā'ěr (¥26, 2½ hours), Hā'ěrbīn (hard/soft sleeper ¥230/348, 12 to 16 hours) or Qíqíhā'ěr (hard/soft sleeper ¥180/265, 11 hours).

Mǎnzhōulǐ has a small airport on the edge of town with daily flights to Běijīng (¥1250, 2¼ hours) and, in summer, to Hohhot (¥1250, 2½ hours). A taxi from town costs ¥40 (15 minutes).

There are 10 buses a day to Hǎilā'ěr (¥47, three hours, 6.30am to 5.30pm) from the main bus station on Wudao Jie. Taxis charge ¥10 for most trips around town.

Hā'ěrbīn

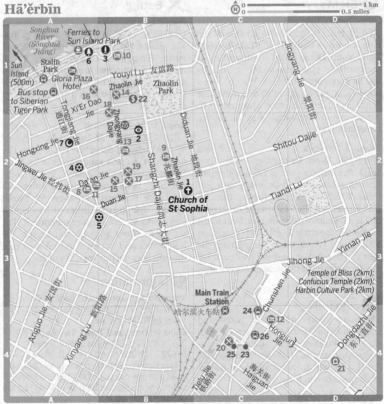

Hā'ěrbīn 哈尔滨

☑ 0451 / POP 4.59 MILLION / TIME MOSCOW +5HR

For a city of its size, Hā'ěrbīn (Harbin) is surprisingly easygoing. Cars (and even bicycles) are barred from Zhongyang Dajie, the main drag of the historic Dàolǐqū district, where most of Hā'ěrbīn's historic buildings can be found. The long riverfront also provides sanctuary for walkers, as does Sun Island on the other side.

The city's sights are as varied as the architectural styles on the old street. Here, temples, old churches and synagogues coexist. Hā'ěrbīn's rich Russian and Jewish heritage makes it worth visiting at any time of year, but winter is tops with the world-class ice-sculpture festival turning the frosty riverfront, and other venues, into a multicoloured wonderland.

History

In 1896 Russia negotiated a contract to build a railway line from Vladivostok to Hā'ěrbīn, then a small fishing village, and Dàlián (in Liáoníng province). The subsequent influx of Russian workers was followed by Russian Jews and then by White Russians escaping after the 1917 Russian Revolution.

These days, Hā'ěrbīn, whose name comes from a Manchu word meaning 'a place to dry fishing nets', is an ever-expanding, largely industrial city, and while Chinese are the majority, because Russia is so close, foreign faces are still common on the streets.

◉ Sights

★ Church of St Sophia   CHURCH
(圣索菲亚教堂, Shèng Suǒfēiyà Jiàotáng; cnr Zhaolin Jie & Toulong Jie; admission ¥20; ⊙8.30am-5pm) The red-brick Russian Orthodox Church of St Sophia, with its distinctive

Hā'ěrbīn

green onion dome and roosting pigeons, is Hā'ěrbīn's most famous landmark. Built in 1907, the church has traded religion for photographs of Hā'ěrbīn from the early 1900s. Its unrestored interior and dusty chandeliers evokes a faded glamour of yesteryear.

The church is fronted by a large square replete with fountains and sketch artists, and is a popular spot for locals and tourists alike.

Stalin Park
PARK

(斯大林公园, Sīdàlín Gōngyuán) This tree-lined promenade, dotted with statues, historic buildings, playgrounds and cafes, runs along a 42km-long embankment built to curb the unruly Sōnghuā River and is a pleasant spot to escape the hubbub of the city. The **Flood Control Monument** (防洪胜利纪念塔; Fánghóng Shènglì Jìniàntǎ) from 1958 commemorates the thousands of people who died in years past when the river overflowed its banks.

Boats rides along the river and to/from Sun Island also depart from various points along the park.

Sun Island Park
PARK

(太阳岛公园, Tàiyángdǎo Gōngyuán; cable car one way/return ¥50/80; ⊙ cable car 8.30am-5pm) Across the river from Stalin Park is Sun Island Park, a 38-sq-km recreational zone with landscaped gardens, a 'water world', a 'Russian-style' town, and various small galleries and museums. It's a pleasant place to have a picnic, walk or bike (¥60 per hour), though as usual you need to pay extra to get into many areas (too kitsch and not worth the money in our opinion).

★ Siberian Tiger Park
WILDLIFE RESERVE

(东北虎林园, Dōngběihǔ Línyuán 松北街88号; 88 Songbei Jie; admission ¥100; ⊙ 8.30am-4.30pm, last tour 4pm; 🚍 13, 122) Here, visitors get the chance to see one of the world's rarest animals (and largest felines) up close via safari-style tour buses which do a circuit of the enclosures. Finish your visit by walking around large fenced spaces where tigers roam freely. The centre has successfully bred over 1000 cats and watching them play, sleep and mate is fascinating.

The park is 15km north of the city. A taxi from the city centre costs ¥30 to ¥40 one way. A tourist shuttle (¥10 return, hourly) leaves from the top of Tongjiang Jie (at the bus stop before the cable car to Sun Island) and does a loop to/from the park.

The squeamish should avoid buying (live!) chickens (¥60) and even cows (¥2800) to throw to the animals. Chinese visitors also take absolute pleasure in dangling strips of meat (¥20) for tigers to jump up and grab at. While the tigers live in decent conditions with plenty of space to roam, other animals including a lion and liger (a cross between a tiger and lion), live in less-than-stellar enclosures.

Old Hā'ěrbīn

The **Dàolǐqū district**, in particular the brick-lined street of **Zhongyang Dajie**, is the most obvious legacy of Russia's involvement with Hā'ěrbīn. Now a pedestrian-only zone, the street is lined with buildings that date back to the early 20th century. Some are imposing, others distinctly dilapidated, but the mix of architectural styles is fascinating. Other nearby streets lined with handsome old buildings include **Shangzhi Dajie** and **Zhaolin Jie**.

Elsewhere in the city, **Hongjun Jie**, heading south from the train station, and **Dongdazhi Jie**, also feature rows of stately old buildings, including a few churches. The latter street, and some of its arteries, also have the dubious reputation of sporting some heady postmodern Russian-style architecture of questionable taste.

In all of these areas, the city has erected plaques on the most worthy buildings giving short English and Chinese descriptions of the date of construction, the architect and the former usage.

Temples

A number of temples are within walking distance of each other in the **Nángàng district**. The first sits off a pedestrian-only street reachable by taxi from the Dàolǐqū district for ¥10. For the Confucius Temple, look for an arch down to the right at the start of the pedestrian street. Pass through this and then a second arch on the left. The temple is a 10-minute walk along Wen Miao Jie.

Temple of Bliss   BUDDHIST TEMPLE
(极乐寺, Jílè Sì; 9 Dongdazhi Jie 东大直街9号; admission ¥10; ⊙8.30am-4pm) Hēilóngjiāng's largest temple complex has an active Buddhist community in residence, giving it a genuine religious atmosphere despite the ticket sales. There are many large statues here, including Milefo (Maitreya, the Buddha yet-to-come) and the Sakyamuni Buddha. The **Seven-Tiered Buddhist Pagoda** (七级浮屠塔; Qījí Fútú Tǎ) dates from 1924. The entrance to the temple is on the left at the start of the pedestrian street.

Hā'ěrbīn Confucius Temple CONFUCIAN TEMPLE
(文庙, Wén Miào; 25 Wenmiao Jie; 文庙街25号; ⊙9am-3.30pm, closed Wed) FREE This peaceful temple complex was first built in 1929 and is said to be the largest Confucian temple in northeastern China. Most of what you see now, though, is from a recent restoration. The site also houses the fascinating **Minority Cultures Museum** replete with photos and artefacts focusing on indigenous tribes such as the Ewenki. You need a passport to enter.

★ Festivals & Events

Harbin Ice & Snow Festival   ICE SCULPTURE
(冰雪节, Bīngxuě Jié; ☑8625 0068; day/evening ticket ¥150/300; ⊙9.30am-9.30pm) Hā'ěrbīn's main claim to fame these days is this festival. Every winter, from December to February (officially the festival opens 5 January), Zhàolín Park (照林公园) and Sun Island Park (p291) become home to extraordinarily detailed, imaginative and downright wacky snow and ice sculptures. They range from huge recreations of iconic buildings, such as the Forbidden City and European cathedrals, to animals and interpretations of ancient legends. At night they're lit up with coloured lights to create a magical effect.

It might be mind-numbingly cold and the sun disappears mid-afternoon, but the festival, which also features figure-skating shows and a variety of winter sports, is Hā'ěrbīn's main tourist attraction – and prices jump accordingly.

The festival takes place in multiple locations. The main venue, Harbin Ice and Snow World, is on Sun Island. The Ice and Snow World exhibits are held in the west end of the island on the north bank of the Sōnghuā River. They are best seen at night, so note that the half-price daytime ticket (good from 9am to noon) does not grant admission to the venue at night.

The Ice Lantern Venue is held in Zhàolín Park and many consider it the least interesting venue. If you do go, go at night when the lanterns are lit.

Hotels and hostels also organise reasonably priced group transport to/from festival locations. Taxis are expensive and hard to flag down during the festival times but you can ride horse carriages, or even use your own feet: the Sun Island venues are actually reachable by crossing the frozen Sōnghuā River (plan on one to two hours). Note that prices for the festival have been skyrocketing recently so don't be surprised if they are even higher than quoted here.

JEWISH HĀ'ĚRBĪN

The Jewish influence on Hā'ěrbīn was surprisingly long lasting; the last original Jewish resident of the city died in 1985. In the 1920s Hā'ěrbīn was home to some 20,000 Jews, the largest Jewish community in the Far East at the time. Tongjiang Jie was the centre of Jewish life in the city till the end of WWII, and many of the buildings on the street are from the early 20th century.

Hā'ěrbīn New Synagogue (哈尔滨犹太新会堂; Hā'ěrbīn Yóutài Xīnhuìtáng; 162 Jingwei Jie 经纬街162号; admission ¥25; ☉ 8.30am-5pm) This synagogue was built in 1921 by the city's Jewish community, the vast majority of whom had emigrated from Russia. Restored and converted into a museum in 2004, the 1st floor is an art gallery with pictures and photos of old Hā'ěrbīn. The 2nd and 3rd floors feature photos and exhibits that tell the story of the history and rich cultural life of Hā'ěrbīn's Jews.

Hā'ěrbīn Main Synagogue (哈尔滨犹太会堂; Hā'ěrbīn Yóutài Huìtáng; 82 Tongjiang Jie, Yóutài Jiùhuìtáng 通江街82号) The beautiful old Main Synagogue, built in 1909, was being refurbished at the time of writing and might reopen as a museum. Close by is the former Jewish Middle School.

Jewish Middle School (犹太中学; Yóutài Zhōngxué; Tongjiang Jie; 通江街) This was the first Jewish middle school in the Far East and most recently housed a Korean (!) school. It has since been immaculately restored as part of a shared compound with the original synagogue.

Turkish Mosque (土耳其清真寺; Tǔ'ěrqí Qīngzhēn Sì; Tongjiang Jie 通江街) Built in 1906, this mosque is no longer operating and is closed to visitors, but you can take a peek from the outside.

🛏 Sleeping

The most convenient places to stay are along Zhongyang Dajie in Dàolǐqū district or in one of the many hotels that surround the train station. During the Ice & Snow Festival hotel prices to go up by at least 20%.

Kazy International Youth Hostel HOSTEL $ (卡兹国际青年旅舍; Kǎzī Guójì Qīngnián Lǔshě; ☎ 8469 7113; kazyzcl@126.com; 27 Tongjiang Jie, 通将街27号; dm/s/tw with shared bathroom ¥50/60/80, d/tw with bathroom ¥180/160; ⊛; 🖥 13) It may have lost its enviable location in the Main Synagogue up the road, but this hostel still scores points for its cosy lounge area and friendly staff who are a great source of travel information for the city and province. The eight-bed dorms are better value than the musty (some are windowless) private rooms. The hostel is popular with Chinese travellers, so book ahead. A taxi will cost you ¥12.

Ibis Hotel HOTEL $$ (宜必思酒店; Yíbìsī Jiǔdiàn; ☎ 8750 9999; www.ibis.com; 92 Zhaolin Jie 兆麟街92号; d & tw ¥209; ⊛@⊛) The spotless rooms and handy location, minutes up the road from the Church of St Sophia and Zhongyang Dajie, make up for the surly, unhelpful front-desk staff.

Book online for deals with free (but unspectacular) breakfast.

Jīndì Bīnguǎn HOTEL $$ (金地宾馆; ☎ 8461 8013; 16 Dongfeng Jie, 东风街16号; s & d ¥218-298, tw ¥458; ⊛@⊛) If you're looking for a river view on the cheap, then this is the place. The owners are friendly, rooms are spacious and there's wi-fi available, with computers in the more expensive twins. To get to the hotel, turn right at the very end of Zhongyang Dajie past the Gloria Plaza Hotel. Discounts of up to 30% available.

Hàolín Business Hotel HOTEL $$ (昊琳商务连锁酒店; Hàolín Shāngwù Liánsuǒ Jiǔdiàn; ☎ 8467 5555; 26 Tongjiang Jie, 通将街26号; d & tw ¥268-368; ⊛@) In the centre of Jewish Hā'ěrbīn, a neighbourhood now full of restaurants and barbecue stalls at night, is this business-style express hotel with surprisingly comfortable rooms sporting high ceilings, bright interiors and good modern bathrooms. It's a two-minute walk to Zhongyang Dajie. Expect discounts of 30%.

★ Lungmen Grand Hotel HISTORIC HOTEL $$$ (龙门贵宾楼酒店; Lóngmén Guìbīn Lóu Jiǔdiàn; ☎ 8317 7777; 85 Hongjun Jie, 红军街85号; d/tw ¥580/680; ⊛@) With its turn of the century old-world styling almost entirely intact (including the marble staircase, dark wood-panelled hallways and the copper revolving door), the Lungmen is one of the most atmospheric top-end options in town. Across from the train station, the hotel lobby opens onto Hongjun Jie and its rows of heritage buildings. A quick walk up the street's wide pavements takes you into the shopping heart of Hā'ěrbīn. Discounts available.

Modern Hotel
HISTORIC HOTEL **$$$**

(马迭尔宾馆, Mǎdié'ěr Bīnguǎn; ☑8488 4000; www.madieer.cn; 89 Zhongyang Dajie, 中央大街89号; r incl breakfast from ¥980; ✳@☎✉) While hardly 'modern', this 1906 construction impressively features some of its original marble, blond-wood accents and art nouveau touches. Spend some time checking out the lobby bar's display of hotel memorabilia before retiring to (thankfully) modern rooms. Note that the entrance to the hotel is around the back. Discounts of up to 30% available.

🍴 Eating

Hā'ěrbīn dishes tend to be heavy, with thick stew-like concoctions commonly found on the picture menus of a thousand eateries. You'll also find delicious hotpot, barbecued meats and Russian dishes in the tourist areas. Zhongyang Dajie and its side alleys are full of small restaurants and bakeries. Tongjiang Jie has fruit stands, sit-down restaurants and an abundance of outdoor barbecue stalls (with ad hoc seating) set up in the evenings.

In summer the streets off Zhongyang Dajie come alive with open-air food stalls and beer gardens, where you can sip a Hāpí (the local beer), while chewing squid on a stick, or *yángròu chuàn* (lamb kebabs) and all the usual street snacks.

The year-round indoor **food market** (吃城, Xīchéng; 96 Zhongyang Dajie; ◷8.30am-7.30pm) has stalls selling decent bread, smoked meats, sausages, wraps and fresh dishes, as well as nuts, cookies, fruits and sweets. It's a great place to grab a quick breakfast or to stock up on food for a long bus or train ride.

Just south of the market, on the opposite side of the street, look for the underground **Lóngjiāng Xiǎochī Jiē** (龙江小吃街; Zhongyang Dajie; dishes ¥8-15; ◷9am-6pm), a clean modern food court with a range of inexpensive noodle and rice dishes, as well as kebabs.

★ Orient King of Eastern Dumplings
DUMPLINGS **$**

(东方饺子王, Dōngfāng Jiǎozi Wáng; 81 Zhongyang Dajie 中央大街81号; dumpling plate ¥12-38; ◷10.30am-9.30pm; ☎) It's not just the cheap *jiǎozi* (饺子; stuffed dumplings) that are good at this always-busy chain restaurant: there are also plenty of tasty vegie dishes and draught beer on tap. There's another location near the train station in the Kunlun Hotel. Picture menu available.

Láifù Biǎndan Chóngqìng Xiǎo Miàn
SICHUAN **$**

(来负扁担重庆小面; 134-1 Youyi Lu; noodles ¥8-16; ◷9am-10pm) A cute hole-in-the-wall eatery serving fiery Sìchuān noodles to a steady stream of customers. Pull up a rustic wooden chair and slurp down sweat-inducing *xiǎo miàn* (小面; spicy soup noodles) plain or with *niú ròu* (牛肉; beef). If you can't take the heat, order *qīng tāng* (清汤; clear soup noodles) instead. No one will notice... they're too busy eating!

Old Chang's Spring Rolls
SNACKS **$**

(老昌春饼, Lǎo Chāng Chūnbǐng; 180 Zhongyang Dajie 中央大街180号; dishes ¥12-38; ◷10.30am-9pm) At this well-known basement spring roll shop, order a set of roll skins (per roll ¥2), a few plates of meat and vegetable dishes, and then wrap your way to one enjoyable repast.

Katusha
RUSSIAN **$$**

(☑139 4566 6905; 261 Zhongyang Dajie 中央大街261号; dishes ¥20-78; ◷11am-9.30pm) A popular Russian-Western restaurant decked out in kitsch Chinese decor. Feast on a range of Russian and Western favourites such as borsch, bliny and steak. Russian vodka and beer? Yes and yes. Located diagonally across from the Flood Control Monument (p291) next to the Jīndì Bīnguǎn hotel.

Cafe Russia
RUSSIAN **$$**

(露西亚咖啡西餐厅, Lùxīyà Kāfēi Xī Cāntīng; 57 Xitoujiao 西头到街57号; dishes ¥20-78; ◷10am-midnight) Step back in time at this ivy-covered teahouse-cum-restaurant and cafe. Black-and-white photos illustrating Hā'ěrbīn's Russian past line the walls, while the old-school furniture and fireplace evoke a different era. Sadly, staff seem more interested in napping than serving their signature Russian fare such as borsch and *pirozhki* (cabbage, potato and meat puffs). Russian vodka is available, too. The restaurant is off Zhongyang Dajie in a little courtyard.

🍷 Drinking & Nightlife

Hā'ěrbīn has the usual collection of karaoke (KTV) joints. If communal singing isn't your bag, there are a few bars on and off Zhong-yang Dajie and Tiandi Lu. Zhongyang Dajie and Stalin Park (p291) also have beer gardens in the summer with cheap draughts and plenty of snack food to enjoy as you watch sports on the big screens. Nightclubs come and go, so you're best off asking for the latest when you arrive.

🛍 Shopping

Shops along Zhongyang Dajie flog imitation Russian and Chinese souvenirs. But there are also department stores, boutiques and many Western clothes chains here. Souvenir shops selling Russian knick-knacks, dolls, binoculars, and also vodka and other spirits can be found all over the city.

Locals head to Dongdazhi Jie for their shopping needs, as well as the **Hóngbó Century Square** (红博世纪广场, Hóngbó Shìjì Guǎngchǎng; ⏰6.30am-5pm), a huge subterranean shopping complex for men's and women's clothing.

ℹ Information

There are ATMs all over town. Most large hotels will also change money. Many midrange and top-end hotels have travel services that book tickets and arrange tours throughout the province.

Bank of China (中国银行, Zhōngguó Yínháng; Xi'er Daojie) Has a 24-hour ATM and will cash travellers cheques. Easy to spot on a side road as you walk up Zhongyang Dajie.

Harbin Modern Travel Company (哈尔滨马迭尔旅行社, Hā'ěrbīn Mǎdié'ěr Lǚxíngshè; 89 Zhongyang Dajie) This travel agency on the 2nd floor of the Modern Hotel offers one- and two-day ski trips to Yàbùlì and can handle flight tickets to Mòhé and other regions.

ℹ Getting There & Away

TRAIN

Hā'ěrbīn is a major rail transport hub with routes throughout the northeast and beyond. If you don't want to brave the lines in the **main station** (哈尔滨站, Hā'ěrbīn zhàn; 1 Tielu Jie, 铁路街1号), buy tickets at the nearby **train booking office** (铁路售票处, Tiělù Shòupiàochù; Tielu Jie; ⏰7am-9pm) to the left of Dico's (fast food restaurant). Note that the fast D and G trains leave from **Hā'ěrbīn West Station** (西站; Xīzhàn), 10km from town. A taxi will cost ¥30 to ¥40.

Běijīng hard seat/sleeper ¥159/293, 10 to 16 hours, eight daily

Běijīng (D train) seat ¥284, nine hours, four daily

Chángchūn (D/G train) seat ¥73/111, two/one hour, regular

Shěnyáng hard seat/sleeper ¥78/149, six to seven hours

Shěnyáng (D/G train) seat ¥161/245, three/two hours, five daily

AIR

Harbin Taiping International Airport (哈尔滨太平国际机场, Hā'ěrbīn Tàipíng Guójì Jīchǎng) has flights to Russia and South Korea as well as the following domestic routes:

Běijīng ¥800, 2 hours

Dàlián ¥700, 1½ hours

BUS

The main **long-distance bus station** (长途客运站, chángtú kèyùn zhàn) is directly opposite the train station. Buy tickets to most destinations in the surrounding provinces on the 2nd floor.

Chángchūn ¥78, four hours, five daily (noon, 1pm, 2pm, 3pm and 4pm)

ℹ Getting Around

PUBLIC TRANSPORT

Buses 101 and 103 run from the train station to Shangzhi Dajie, dropping you off at the north end of Zhongyang Dajie (the old street). Buses leave from a stop across the road and to the left as you exit the train station (where Chunshen Jie and Hongjun Jie meet).

Hā'ěrbīn's long-awaited metro has a single line that doesn't serve any of the tourist sights. Construction for further lines are underway.

TO/FROM THE AIRPORT

Hā'ěrbīn's airport is 46km from the city centre. From the airport, shuttle buses (¥20, one

---

ℹ BORDER CROSSING: GETTING TO RUSSIA

Trains no longer depart from Hā'ěrbīn East to Vladivostok. Trains do run as far as Suífēnhé, however, from where you can make an onward connection to Vladivostok.

Travellers on the Trans-Siberian Railway to or from Moscow can start or finish in Hā'ěrbīn (six days). Contact the **Hā'ěrbīn Railway International Travel Service** (哈尔滨铁道国际旅行社, Hā'ěrbīn Tiědào Guójì Lǚxíngshè; ☑5361 6721; www.ancn.net; Kunlun Hotel, 7th fl, 8 Tielu Jie; ⏰9am-5pm) for information on travelling through to Russia.

EXPLORING THE CHINA–RUSSIA FRINGE

Travellers who choose to get off the main line will be rewarded with some of the more unsung sights along the Trans-Manchurian route. From Hǎilā'ěr, the northernmost major town in Inner Mongolia, head out past rolling grasslands towards Shì Wěi and Ēnhé. The former is a small Russian-style village of log cabins located right on the É'ěrgǔnà River, which marks the border with Russia. Spend some time gazing at the Russian village on the opposite bank. Look for wooden stages on both sides of the river: each country used to host performances for their neighbours!

The township of Ēnhé, located 70km north of Lābùdálín en route to Shì Wěi, is one of the area's unsung villages brimming with atmosphere. Surrounded by hills and acres of lush grass, the village has only just opened to tourism and there's still a very low-key vibe here. Many residents are of Chinese-Russian origin; some could easily pass for Russians. Here, herders milk their cows outside their properties when they aren't taking them out to pasture. Sample boiled milk at your accommodation. You can ride a horse for ¥60 (a bargain in Inner Mongolia!), hire a bicycle (¥10 per hour) or go for hikes. The mosquitoes are killer in summer, so bring plenty of repellent. You'll find lots of homestays and local restaurants in both villages. Rooms start from ¥100.

From Hǎilā'ěr, buses travel to Lābùdálín (拉布达林; ¥38, two hours, half hourly, 6.40am to 5.30pm). From Lābùdálín (sometimes called É'ěrgǔnà) there are two daily direct buses (¥44, four hours) at 9.30am and 3.30pm to Shì Wěi and direct buses (¥27, two hours) at 12.10am and 2.30pm to Ēnhé. The Shì Wěi bound buses also stop on the main road leading to Ēnhé, from where it's a 1.5km walk into town. You can flag onward buses to Shì Wěi from the main road at around 11.15am and 5.15pm. From Shì Wěi, buses return to Lābùdálín at 8am and 1pm but do buy your ticket in advance. From Ēnhé, buses return to Lābùdálín at 8.30am and 9.30am.

hour) will drop you at the railway station. To the airport, shuttles leave every 30 minutes from a stand just beside Dico's opposite the train station from 5.30am to 7.30pm. A taxi (¥100 to ¥125) takes 45 minutes to an hour.

TAXI

Taxis are fairly plentiful though they fill up quickly when it's raining. Taxi flag-fall is ¥8.

Chángchūn 长春

📞 0431 / POP 7.64 MILLION / TIME MOSCOW +5HR

The Japanese capital of Manchukuo between 1933 and 1945, Chángchūn was also the centre of the Chinese film industry in the 1950s and '60s. Visitors expecting a Hollywood-like backdrop of palm trees and beautiful people will be disappointed, though. Chángchūn is now better known as China's motor city, the largest automobile-manufacturing base in the country.

But for people on the trail of Puyi, China's last emperor, it's an essential stop. There are also a fair few historic buildings dating back to the early 20th century, mostly along and off Renmin Dajie.

Chángchūn sprawls from north to south. The long-distance bus station and the train station are at the north end of the city and

surrounded by budget hotels. If you plan on more than an overnight in Chángchūn, however, the southern end is by far a more pleasant neighbourhood to stay in.

◉ Sights

★ Imperial Palace of the Manchu State
MUSEUM

(Puppet Emperor's Palace, 伪满皇宫博物院, Wěimǎn Huánggōng Bówùyuàn; 5 Guangfu Lu 光复北路5号; admission ¥80; ⊙8.30am-4.20pm, last entry 40min before closing) This is the former residence of Puyi, the Qing dynasty's final emperor. His study, bedroom, temple, his wife's quarters and opium den, as well as his concubine's rooms, have all been elaborately re-created. His American car is also on display, but it's the exhibition on his extraordinary life, told in part with a fantastic collection of photos, that is most enthralling. An English audio guide costs ¥20. A taxi from the train station to the palace costs ¥7.

In 1908, at age two, Puyi became the 10th Qing emperor. His reign lasted just over three years, but he was allowed to remain in the Forbidden City until 1924. He subsequently lived in Tiānjīn until 1932, when the Japanese installed him at this palace as the 'puppet emperor' of Manchukuo. After Japan's defeat in 1945, Puyi was captured by Russian troops. In 1950 he was returned to China, where he spent 10 years in a re-education camp before ending his days as a gardener in Běijīng. Puyi died in 1967; his story later became the basis for the Bernardo Bertolucci film *The Last Emperor*.

Chángchūn World Sculpture Park SCULPTURE
(长春世界雕塑公园, Chángchūn Shìjiè Diāosù Gōngyuán; Renmin Dajie 人民大街; admission ¥20; ⊙8am-5pm; 🚍66) Nestled amidst 90 hectares of parklands in the far south of the city, the Chángchūn World Sculpture Park hosts an impressive array of sculptures from Chinese and international artists. The park is an unsung sights and worth sniffing out. A taxi from People's Sq will cost ¥25 to ¥30.

Bānruò Temple BUDDHIST
(般若寺, Bānruò Sì; 137 Changchun Lu 长春路137号; 🚍281, 256) One of the largest Buddhist temples in northeast China, Bānruò is a lively place of worship for locals and pilgrims alike. After touring the inner grounds, wander the back alleys to observe the merchants peddling charms, statues and shrines.

🛌 Sleeping

There are half-a-dozen budget hotels within walking distance of the train station, with broadband-enabled rooms going for between ¥140 and ¥180.

Home Inn HOTEL $
(如家快捷酒店, Rújiā Kuàijié Jiǔdiàn; 🕿8986 3000; 20 Changchun Lu, 长白路20号; r ¥159-209; ⊛❄@) If you need a nonsmoking option near the train station, this branch of the well-run, spotlessly clean nationwide chain is a good choice. Rooms have broadband internet and there's also a computer in the lobby for guest use.

★ Sōngyuàn Hotel HOTEL $$$
(松苑宾馆, Sōngyuàn Bīnguǎn; 🕿8272 7001; www.songyuanhotel.com; 1169 Xinfa Lu, 新发路1169号; d & tw ¥498-998; ❄@🛜) Set in its own park grounds, the Sōngyuàn hosts tourists in plush, well-decorated rooms. Friendly staff and several good in-house restaurants (Japanese and international) seal the deal. The downside is a slightly inconvenient location. A taxi from the train station costs ¥7.

🍴 Eating & Drinking

Tongzhi Jie (and all the radiating lanes) between Longli Lu and Ziyou Lu are some of the most popular parts of Chángchūn. The streets are packed with inexpensive restaurants, music and clothing shops, while tree-lined Xikang Lu (west of Tongzhi Jie) is now an unofficial cafe street. Most of the dozen or so cafes have wi-fi and most offer sandwiches and other simple meals. Guilin Lu is lined with cheap eateries and snack stalls.

M+M NOODLES $
(面面, Miàn Miàn; 2447 Tongzhi Jie 同志街2447号; noodles ¥18-20; ⊙10am-10pm) You can slurp down your moreish noodles hot or cold, dry or in soup, with meat or without, at this popular 2nd-floor eatery overlooking busy Tongzhi Jie. Beer is ¥5.

Shinza Restaurant KOREAN $$
(延边信子饭店, Yánbiān Xìnzǐ Fàndiàn; 728 Xikang Lu 西康路728号; dishes ¥12-38; ⊙9am-midnight) This comfortable dining establishment offers Korean classics such as *shíguō bànfàn* (石锅拌饭; *bibimbap;* rice, vegetables and eggs served in a clay pot) as well as dumplings and filling cold noodle dishes. Korean beers are also available and there's a picture menu to help you order.

ℹ️ Information

There are 24-hour ATMs all over town and in the north bus station. Changchun Live (www.changchunlive.com) is a useful site started by long-term expats.

Civil Aviation Administration of China (CAAC, 中国民航, Zhōngguó Mínháng; 🕿8298 8888; 480 Jiefang Dalu) For air tickets and shuttle buses to the airport. It's in the CAAC Hotel.

ℹ️ Getting There & Away

TRAIN

The following leave from Chángchūn's **main railway station** (长春火车站; Chángchūn huǒchē zhàn; avoid getting tickets for the west station; *xī zhàn*):

Běijīng (D train) seat ¥227, seven hours, seven daily

Běijīng hard seat/sleeper ¥130/224, nine to 14 hours

Hā'ěrbīn (D train) seat ¥72, two hours, five daily

Shěnyáng (D train) seat ¥88, 2½ hours, 12 daily

BUS

The **long-distance bus station** (长途汽车站, chángtú qìchēzhàn; 226 Renmin Dajie) is two blocks south of the train station. Buses to Hā'ěrbīn leave from the **north bus station** (客运北站, kèyùn běi zhàn) behind the train station. Facing

THE TRANS-MANCHURIAN ROUTE CHÁNGCHŪN

CROSSING THE RUSSIA–CHINA BORDER

Rail

Expect to spend at least half a day crossing from Zabaikalsk (后贝加尔, Hòubèijiāěr) to Mǎnzhōulǐ and vice versa, with time eaten up by customs procedures on the Russian side, and the need to change the bogies on the train to match the narrower gauge used in China. This will likely be the case for travellers on the Vostok (19/20) or the Mǎnzhōulǐ–Chita train (Friday and Sunday from Mǎnzhōulǐ, Thursday and Saturday from Chita). If you arrive in Zabaikalsk on the train from Irkutsk and it's Friday or Sunday morning, it may be possible to buy a ticket (R80) for the Chita–Mǎnzhōulǐ train. However, this train is usually full by the time it gets to Zabaikalsk, so scoring a ticket at the station may be difficult.

In Mǎnzhōulǐ the international terminal is the yellow building next to the main station. This is where international travellers heading to Russia go through customs and passport control. However, international tickets are not sold here: you'll need to go to the China International Travel Service (p289) (CITS) branch at the Guójì Fàndiàn (International Hotel). Services to Chita leave on Monday at 7pm, Friday at 2pm and Sunday at 2pm; *platskart* (3rd-class) tickets may only be available (¥70).

There are daily overnight trains connecting Zabaikalsk and Chita (*platskart/kupe* R1855/2600, 12 hours); if these are full you can also take a train to Borzya and connect with a slower train to Zabaikalsk from there. Hǎ'ěrbīn and Mǎnzhōulǐ are also connected by four overnight trains (hard/soft sleeper ¥230/348, 12 to 16 hours), departing between 6pm and 9pm.

the station, head left and take the underpass just past the 24-hour KFC (not to be confused with the non-24-hour KFC to the right of the train station, or the two across the street).

Hǎ'ěrbīn ¥76, 3½ hours, 8.30am, 10am and noon

Shěnyáng ¥83, 4½ hours, 10am and 2pm

ⓘ Getting Around

Bus 6 follows Renmin Dajie from the train station bus stop all the way to the south part of town. Buses 62 and 362 travel from the train station to the Chongqing Lu and Tongzhi Jie shopping districts.

The airport is 20km east of the city centre, between Chángchūn and Jílín. Shuttle buses to the airport (¥20, 50 minutes, every 30 minutes from 6am to 7pm) leave from the **CAAC Hotel** (民航宾馆, Mínháng Bīnguǎn; 480 Jiefang Dalu) on the east side of town. Taxi fares to the airport are ¥80 to ¥100 for the 40-minute trip.

Taxi fares start at ¥5.

Shānhǎiguān   山海关

📞 0335 / POP 19,500 / TIME MOSCOW +5HR

The drowsy walled town of Shānhǎiguān marks the point where the Great Wall snakes out of the hills to meet the sea. Hugely popular with domestic tourists, Shānhǎiguān has, in recent years, sold some of its soul for a rebuild of the old town's central sections.

The effect has been to render it more than a little sterile in places, although thankfully a few pockets of original buildings remain in the alleys running off the main streets. Likewise, the ticketed sections of the Great Wall here have been heavily restored (and in some cases completely rebuilt), but there is still an accessible stretch of original earthen Great Wall here that can be explored.

History

Guarding the narrow plain leading to northeastern China, the Ming garrison town of Shānhǎiguān and its wall were developed to seal off the country from the Manchu, whose troublesome ancestors ruled northern China during the Jin dynasty (AD 1115–1234). This strategy succeeded until 1644, when Chinese rebels seized Běijīng and General Wu Sangui opted to invite the Manchu army through the impregnable pass to help suppress the uprising. The plan worked so well that the Manchus took over the entire country.

◉ Sights

Great Wall Museum   MUSEUM
(长城博物馆, Chángchéng Bówùguǎn; Diyiguan Lu 第一关路; ⊙9am-4pm Tue-Sun) FREE This impressive museum provides a comprehensive history of the Wall in this region and includes interesting scale models of the walled town and surrounding Great Wall locations.

The train ride between Zabaikalsk and Mǎnzhōulǐ takes about 10 minutes. There's a sort of rivalry at the border: each country has built an enormous arch over the railway line as if they were trying to outdo each other. You'll need to be quick with your camera as the train does not linger on the border for long.

Bus

There are frequent buses travelling between the Zabaikalsk bus station and the Mǎnzhōulǐ bus station. From Zabaikalsk to China it costs R400 and from Mǎnzhōulǐ to Russia it's ¥92 (five hours, eight daily between 7.40am and 1.30pm). There's also one daily bus from Mǎnzhōulǐ to Chita (¥380), departing at 6.40pm.

The crossing in either direction is slow, taking up to five hours. Going from China to Russia usually takes longer because the Russian border guards spend a lot of time checking travellers for contraband. Private vehicles driven by Russians tend to get through faster, so one option is to negotiate a ride with a Russian driver either in town or at the border 9km from town.

At the Chinese border post you'll have to pay ¥10 departure tax: do this at the door left of the entrance and then give the receipt to the immigration officials as they stamp you out of the country.

There's an exchange office in the Russian customs hall where your immigration card will be registered.

Plenty of photos and artefacts, as well as OK English captions.

First Pass Under Heaven   HISTORIC SITE
(天下第一关, Tiānxià Dìyī Guān; cnr Dong Dajie & Diyiguan Lu; entrance ¥50; ☉7am-5.30pm) The town wall's East Gate, which the Great Wall once linked up with, has been tarted up for tourism. This was Shānhǎiguān's principal watchtower – two storeys with double eaves and 68 arrow-slit windows – and is a towering 13.7m high. Several other watchtowers can also be seen and a *wèngchéng* (enceinte) extends out east from the wall. You can walk along a small stretch of the wall here.

★ Jiǎo Shān   GREAT WALL
(角山; admission ¥30, cable car one-way/return ¥10/20; ☉7am-sunset) Albeit a heavily restored section of the Great Wall, Jiǎo Shān does nevertheless offer an excellent opportunity to hike up the Wall's first high peak; a telling vantage point over the one-time invasion route for northern armies. The views are fabulous on a clear day. It's a steep 20-minute clamber from the base, or a cable car (索道; *suǒdào*) can yank you up for ¥10. To leave behind the crowds, continue beyond the cable car station, to Qīxián Monastery (栖贤寺; Qīxián Sì) or even further to Sweet Nectar Pavilion (甘露亭; Gānlù Tíng).

Bus 5 (¥2) goes here from the **train station** (天津站; Tiānjīn Zhàn), but it's an easy,

3km-walk (or cycle) north of town. Just follow the road straight on from Shānhǎiguān's North Gate.

More fun than just following the road, though, is to approach Jiǎo Shān on an original, overgrown stretch of **earthen Great Wall**, which still creeps its way through farmland from Shānhǎiguān to Jiǎo Shān. Most of its Ming brickwork has long since been pillaged, but there's still a scattering of bricks. To take this route, walk straight on from the North Gate and then, after the bridge that goes underneath the highway, take the first right and follow the road for a couple of hundred metres. Turn left up the pathway beside the iron bridge and clamber up the wall beside you wherever you feel you're able to – there's at least one overgrown path that leads up to the top. You can walk on this earthen wall all the way to Jiǎo Shān, where you'll have to clamber down to the ticket office to enter the restored section.

Old Dragon Head   WALL
(老龙头, Lǎolóngtóu; admission ¥60; ☉7.30am-6.30pm) Famous across China (although a little over-hyped if we're being honest), Old Dragon Head, 4km south of Shānhǎiguān, is where the Great Wall meets the sea. It's photogenic for sure, but bear in mind that what you see now was reconstructed in the late 1980s – the original wall crumbled away

long ago. It acts more like a small beach resort these days. In fact, you can jump in and actually swim around the Great Wall here. The water is filthy, though, so it's not surprising that the speedboat rides (¥80 per person) are more popular. Bus 25 (¥1) goes here from Shānhǎiguān's South Gate.

🛏 Sleeping

Almost no hotels in Shānhǎiguān are allowed to accept foreigners including all the cheap guesthouses (旅馆; *lǚguǎn*) inside the town walls, which used to make staying here so much fun. Luckily, there are still a handful that do welcome foreign guests.

Jǐngshān Hotel HOTEL **$**
(景山宾馆; Jǐngshān Bīnguǎn; ☑0335 513 2188/46; 1 Dong Dajie, 东大街1号; tw/tr from ¥220/240; ❋ 🛜) The cheapest place in town that accepts foreigners, and it's decent value. Housed in a pleasant, reconstructed, two-storey courtyard complex, rooms are neat and comfortable and come with private bathrooms. There's wi-fi in the lobby. Not much English spoken.

Shānhǎi Holiday Hotel HOTEL **$$$**
(山海假日酒店, Shānhǎi Jiàrì Jiǔdiàn; ☑0335 535 2888; www.shanhai-holiday.com; Bei Madao, 北马道; d & tw ¥880, discounted to ¥480; ❋ @ 🛜) A newly built, traditional-style four-star hotel with attractive rooms, restaurant and a bar.

🍴 Eating

Èrtiáo Xiǎoxiàng Jiǎoziguǎn DUMPLINGS **$**
(二条小巷饺子馆; Ertiao Xiaoxiang, off Nan Dajie; 南大街二条小巷; dumplings per portion ¥20; ⊙7am-7pm) Housed in a simple, 200-year-old residential *píngfáng* (平房, bungalow), this small, family-run dumpling joint does delicious golden-fried dumplings (煎饺; *jiānjiǎo*) with a range of fillings, including pork and cabbage (白菜猪肉; *báicài zhūròu*), egg and chives (韭菜鸡蛋; *jiǔcài jīdàn*), pork and courgette (角瓜猪肉; *jiǎoguā zhūròu*), egg and courgette (角瓜鸡蛋; *jiǎoguā jīdàn*) and pork and fennel (茴香猪肉; *huíxiāng zhūròu*). No English, but a friendly welcome. If walking south from the Drum Tower look for the sign saying "饺子馆" (meaning dumpling restaurant) pointing down the first alley on the left.

Lánzhōu Zhèngzōng Niúròu Lāmiàn NOODLES **$**
(兰州正宗牛肉拉面; Nan Dajie; 南大街; noodles ¥8-20; ⊙7am-9pm) Does a range of tasty noodle dishes, including pulled noodles with beef (牛肉拉面; *niúròu lāmiàn*), with lamb (羊肉拉面; *yángròu lāmiàn*), with Chinese cabbage (青菜拉面; *qīngcài lāmiàn*), with egg (鸡蛋拉面; *jīdàn lāmiàn*); braised beef noodles (红烧牛肉面; *hóngshāo niúròumiàn*) and knife-sliced beef fried noodles (牛肉炒刀削面; *niúròu chǎo dāoxiāomiàn*). Has photos of much of the menu. No English.

ℹ Information

Bank of China (中国银行, Zhōngguó Yínháng; Nanhai Xilu; ⊙8.30am-5.30pm) Foreign exchange facility.

Hēimǎ Chēxíng (黑马车行; 12-1 Nan Dajie; 南大街12-1号; ⊙6am-7pm) Rents bicycles for ¥20 per day.

Public Security Bureau (PSB, 公安局, Gōng'ānjú 第一关路; ☑505 1163; Diyiguan Lu) Opposite the entrance to First Pass Under Heaven (p299), on the corner of a small alleyway.

ℹ Getting There & Away

TRAIN

There are a number of G- and D-class bullet trains (and many more slower ones) linking Běijīng and Shānhǎiguān (¥93, 2½ hours). Four leave from Běijīng Main Station between 7am and 10am. Another leaves Běijīng South at 8.42am. There are also three or four afternoon fast trains. Among the many trains going back to Běijīng, there are seven high-speed trains between 5pm and 9pm. Alternatively, even more high-speed trains go from Běijīng to the nearby city of Qínhuángdǎo (秦皇岛; ¥90, 2½ hours regularly from 7am to 9pm), 18km from Shānhǎiguān. Buses from Běijīng's Bāwángfén station also run to Qínhuángdǎo (¥110, 4 hours).

BUS

Qínhuángdǎo's coach station, where long-distance buses arrive, is diagonally opposite its train station. From outside the train station, take Bus 8 (¥1) a couple of stops to Ba San Dong Li (三东里) bus stop, then take Bus 33 (¥2, 30 minutes) to Shānhǎiguān's South Gate.

There's no long-distance bus station in Shānhǎiguān, so you need to use Qínhuángdǎo coach station. Buses from there leave for Běijīng's Bāwángfén station (¥110, 4 hours) at 7am, 8am, 9am, 10am, 12pm, 2pm and 3.30pm, and for Běijīng Capital Airport (¥140, 4½ hours) on the hour every hour from 5am to 3pm, and at 5pm. There are also numerous direct buses from Qínhuángdǎo to Chéngdé (¥110, 3 hours), although most of them leave before noon, and there's one bus to Dàlián (¥150, 10am, 7 hours).

ℹ Getting Around

Taxis in Shānhǎiguān are ¥5 flag fall. Motor-rickshaws cost ¥2 to ¥3 for trips within town.

Běijīng

Best Places to Stay

➜ Great Wall Box House
(p328)

➜ Jīngshān Garden Hotel
(p316)

➜ Courtyard 7 (p317)

➜ Qiánmén Hostel (p314)

➜ Orchid (p316)

Best Places to Eat

➜ Little Yúnnán (p319)

➜ Bǎihé Vegetarian
Restaurant (p319)

➜ Dàlǐ Courtyard (p319)

➜ Crescent Moon Muslim
Restaurant (p318)

➜ Qiánmén Quánjùdé Roast
Duck Restaurant (p318)

Why Go?

For weary Trans-Siberian travellers, Běijīng (北京) will feel like the figurative pot of gold at the end of the rainbow. The 2008 Olympics were instrumental in transforming the Chinese capital, and perhaps for the first time since the Mongol invasion, Běijīng feels like a true international city, brimming with overseas business, cuisine of every kind, daring modern architecture and a thriving arts scene.

Despite its headlong rush into the future, though, the best of Běijīng lies in its links to the past. Magnificent historical sights such as the Forbidden City, Temple of Heaven Park, the Summer Palace and, of course, the Great Wall, will keep you busy for days. And ducking into the fast-disappearing *hútòng* (narrow alleyway) neighbourhoods is a magical experience, and the best way to discover Běijīng at its most intimate.

Come evening, choose from a million or so drinking spots and shout *'gān bēi!'* (bottoms up!) as you toast the end (or beginning) of your epic cross-continental journey.

When to Go
Běijīng

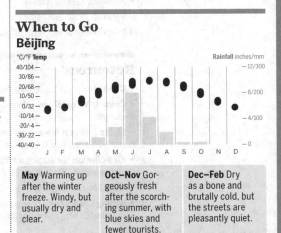

May Warming up after the winter freeze. Windy, but usually dry and clear.

Oct–Nov Gorgeously fresh after the scorching summer, with blue skies and fewer tourists.

Dec–Feb Dry as a bone and brutally cold, but the streets are pleasantly quiet.

MEDIA

Pick up the free monthly listings magazines *The Beijinger* (www.the beijinger.com), *TimeOut* (www.timeoutbeijing. com) and *City Weekend* (www.cityweekend.com. cn) from expat bars and restaurants around the city. *China Daily* is the main English-language newspaper.

Běijīng Basic Costs

➡ Subway ticket: ¥2

➡ Taxi rate (first 3km): ¥13

➡ Hostel bed: ¥70 to ¥100

➡ Private room: ¥200 upwards

➡ Bowl of noodles: ¥10

➡ Local beer from a shop/ bar: ¥4/20

Fast Facts

➡ Telephone code: ☑010

➡ Population: 20 million

➡ Time zone: Moscow +5

Getting Around

To/from the train station All three major train stations are connected to Běijīng's easy-to-use subway system.

To/from the airport The Airport Express (机场快轨; jīchǎng kuàiguǐ; 30 minutes; ¥25) links up with the subway system and is the easiest way to get into town. There are also various shuttle-bus routes (¥16 to ¥24). A taxi costs ¥80 to ¥100 – use the official taxi rank to avoid getting scammed.

CLIMATE & HOLIDAYS

Winter travel has its pros and cons. On the plus side, the city is relatively quiet and, if you're lucky the tree-lined *hútòng* (alleys) will be brushed with snow. On the down-side it's glacial outside (dipping as low as -20°C).

In summer, temperatures can surge over 35°C, and heavy downpours are common. This is also peak sea-son for domestic tourists, so the well-known sights are packed.

Air pollution can be very harsh in both summer and winter.

Spring (mid-April to mid-May) and autumn (Octo-ber to early November) are the best times to visit, but avoid the national holidays in the first week of May and October.

Train Categories in China

Bullet Trains

➡ C (*chéngjì gāosù*; 城际高速) ultra-high-speed express

➡ D (*dòngchē*; 动车, *héxiè hào*; 和谐号) high-speed express

➡ G (*gāotiě*; 高铁) high-speed

Ordinary Trains

➡ K (*kuàisù*; 快速) fast train

➡ T (*tèkuài*; 特快) express

➡ Z (*zhídá tèkuài*; 直达特快) direct express

Resources

➡ **Ctrip** (www.english.ctrip.com) Hotel and flight bookings.

➡ **China DIY Travel** (www.china-diy-travel.com) Train-ticket bookings.

➡ **Sinica Podcast** (www.popupchinese.com) Uncensored current-affairs podcast based in Běijīng.

➡ **Air Pollution** (www.aqicn.org/city/beijing) Real-time Air Quality Index (AQI) readings for Běijīng (and other cities).

➡ **MDBG** (www.mdbg.net) Online Chinese dictionary.

➡ **Běijīng Cream** (www.beijingcream.com) Lighthearted Běijīng-based blog covering China-wide current affairs.

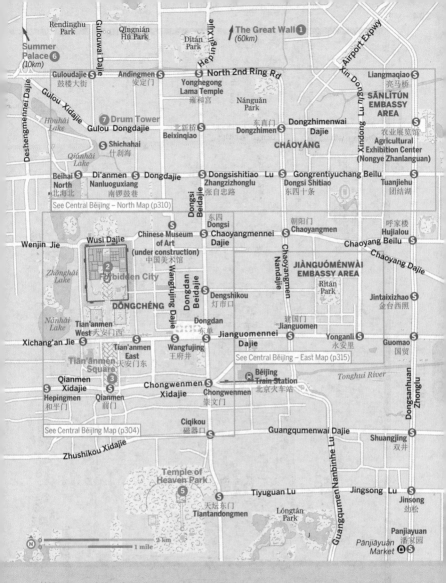

Běijīng Highlights

1 Hiking along China's most famous icon, the **Great Wall** (p327), then bunking up for the night in a village guesthouse

2 Marvelling at the splendour of the **Forbidden City** (p307), the world's largest palace complex

3 Rising at dawn to catch the flag-raising ceremony at iconic **Tiān'ānmén Square** (p308)

4 Cycling deep into the **hútòng** (p313), historic alleyways that crisscross the city centre

5 Soaking up the serenity of Běijīng's splendid **Temple of Heaven Park** (p308)

6 Enjoying a taste of imperial high life in the sumptuous gardens and pavilions of the **Summer Palace** (p314)

7 Climbing the magnificent **Drum Tower** (p312) and looking over the grey-tiled rooftops in the alleys below

BĚIJĪNG

Central Běijīng

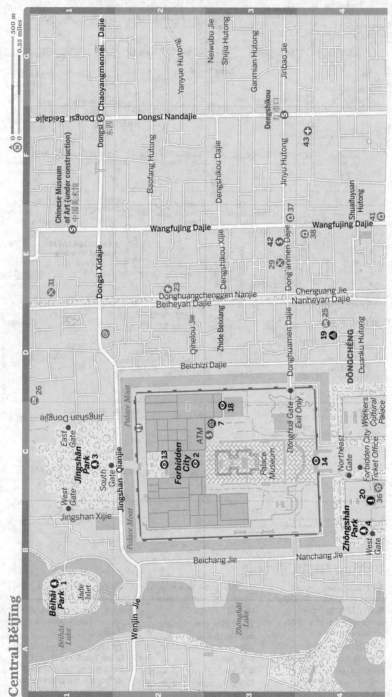

500 m
0.25 miles

Chinese Museum
of Art (under construction)
中国美术馆

Dongsi Beidajie
东四

Dongsi Chaoyangmennei Dajie

Dongsi Nandajie

Yanyue Hutong

Neiwubu Jie

Shijia Hutong

Ganmian Hutong

Jinbao Jie

Baofang Hutong

Dengshikou Dajie

Dengshikou
灯市口

43

Dongsi Xidajie

Wangfujing Dajie

Dengshikou Xijie

Jinyu Hutong

37

Wangfujing Dajie

38

Shuaifuyuan Hutong

41

31

Donghuangchenggen Nanjie
Beiheyan Dajie

23

Zhide Beixiang

29

42

Dong'anmen Dajie

Qihelou Jie

Chenguang Jie
Nanheyan Dajie

Beichizi Dajie

Donghuamen Dajie

19 25

DŌNGCHÉNG

Duanku Hutong

26

Jingshan Dongjie

Palace Moat

East
Gate

Jingshan
Park

3

South
Gate

West
Gate

Jingshan Qianjie

13

Forbidden
City

ATM

2

18

7

Palace
Museum

Donghua Gate
Exit Only

Workers
Cultural
Palace

Northeast
Gate

14

Jingshan Xijie

Palace Moat

Beichang Jie

Nanchang Jie

20

36

Forbidden City
Ticket Office

Běihǎi
Park

1

Jade
Islet

Beihǎi Lake

Wenjin Jie

Jingshan Jie

Zhōngshān
Park

West
Gate

4

Zhōnghǎi
Lake

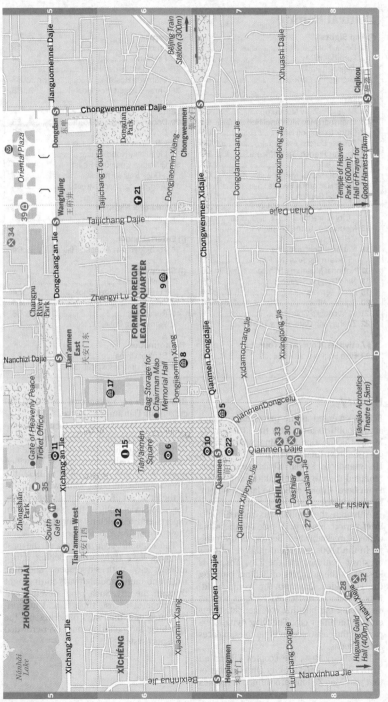

BĔIJĪNG

Nánhǎi Lake

ZHŌNGNÁNHǍI

XĪCHÉNG

Xichang'an Jie

Tian'anmen West 天安门西

South Gate

Zhōngshān Park

Gate of Heavenly Peace Ticket Office

Xijiaomin Xiang

Qianmen Xidajie

Hepingmen 和平门

Beixinhua Jie

Nanxinhua Jie

Liulichang Dongjie

Tíanshà Xiàjiē

Húguǎng Guild Hall (400m)

DASHILAR

Qianmen Xiheyan Jie

Dazhalan Jie

Meishi Jie

Dashilar

Qianmen Dajie

Qianmen 前门

Qianmen Dongdajie

Qianmen Dongcelu

Xidamochang Jie

Xixinglong Jie

Tiánqiáo Acrobatics Theatre (1.5km)

Tian'anmen Square 天安门

Bag Storage for Chairman Mao Memorial Hall

Dongjiaomin Xiang

FORMER FOREIGN LEGATION QUARTER

Zhengyi Lu

Changpu River Park

Nanchizi Dajie

Tian'anmen East 天安门东

Dongchang'an Jie

Dongan 东单

Wangfujing 王府井

Taijichang Dajie

Taijichang Toutiao

Dongjiaomin Xiang

Chongwenmennei Dajie

Dongdan Park

Chongwenmen Xidajie

Chongwenmen 崇文门

Dongdamochang Jie

Dongxinglong Jie

Xihuashi Dajie

Ciqikou 磁器口

Qianian Dajie

Temple of Heaven Park (600m); Hall of Prayer for Good Harvests (1km)

Beijing Train Station (300m)

Oriental Plaza

● 11
◎ 15
● 6
● 10
● 22
● 5
● 8
🏛 9
↑ 21
● 34
39
35
🏛 17
◎ 12
◎ 16
🏛 33
● 30
🏛 24
● 40
● 27
● 28
● 32

Central Běijīng

History

Běijīng emerged as the preeminent cultural and political force with the 13th-century Mongol occupation of China, when Chinggis (Genghis) Khaan descended on the city. His grandson, Kublai Khaan (c 1215–94), renamed the city Khanbalik (Khan's town). From here, Kublai ruled the largest empire in world history.

Although the capital was moved for a brief period, Emperor Yongle (of the Ming dynasty) reestablished Běijīng as the capital in the 1400s and spent millions of taels of silver refurbishing the city. Yongle is known as the architect of Běijīng, building the Forbidden City and the iconic buildings in Temple of Heaven Park, as well as developing the bustling commercial streets outside the inner city. The Qing dynasty expanded the construction of temples, palaces and pagodas.

In January 1949, the People's Liberation Army (PLA) entered the city. On 1 October of that year Mao Zedong proclaimed a 'People's Republic' to an audience of some 500,000 citizens in Tiān'ānmén Square.

Like the emperors before them, the communists significantly altered the face of Běijīng to suit their own image. Whole city blocks were reduced to rubble to widen major boulevards. From 1950 to 1952, the city's magnificent outer walls were levelled in the interests of traffic circulation. Before the Sino-Soviet split of the 1960s, Russian experts and technicians poured in, leaving their own Stalinesque touches.

The capitalist-style reforms of the past 25 years have transformed Běijīng into a modern city, with skyscrapers, shopping malls and multi-lane highways cutting right through the city. Such rapid development has come at a cost, though, and authorities must now find ways of addressing the appalling air pollution and over-crowded transport systems.

◉ Sights

◉ Forbidden City 紫禁城

Ringed by a 52m-wide moat and enclosed within towering walls at the very heart of Běijīng, the **Forbidden City** (紫禁城; Zǐjīn Chéng; Map p304; ☑ 8500 7114; www.dpm.org.cn; admission Nov-Mar ¥40, Apr-Oct ¥60, Clock Exhibition Hall ¥10, Hall of Jewellery ¥10, audio tour ¥40; ⊘ 8.30am-4pm May-Sep, 8.30am-3.30pm Oct-Apr, closed Mon; ⑤ Tian'anmen West or Tian'anmen East) is China's largest and best-preserved collection of ancient buildings, and the largest palace complex in the world.

So called because it was off limits to most people for 500 years, this was the reclusive home to two dynasties of imperial rule until the Republic overthrew the last Qing emperor. Today, the Forbidden City is prosaically known as the **Palace Museum** (故宫博物馆; Gùgōng Bówùguǎn), although most Chinese people simply call it *Gùgōng* (故宫; ancient palace).

Tourists must enter the complex through the south gate, known as the **Meridian Gate** (午门; Wǔ Mén; Map p304) although you can exit via the south, east or north gates. Audio guides are available in several languages, and are usually preferable to one of the many actual guides who hustle for work by the entrance.

The complex is enormous – give yourself at least half a day here (there are cafes and restaurants) – and is made up of a series of courtyards, gateways and imperials halls, the largest and most impressive of which run along the central north–south axis. These were largely ceremonial, whereas the smaller, more intimate courtyards and buildings, in the east and west of the complex, were more commonly used in the everyday life of the imperial court. These side courtyards are usually quieter, so can be more fun to explore.

Many buildings inside the complex house museum exhibitions, showcasing priceless artefacts from Imperial China (paintings, jade, porcelain etc). Some are extraordinarily impressive. Don't miss the **Nine Dragon Screen** (九龙壁; Jiǔlóng Bì; Map p304) (which is inside an area known as the Treasure Gallery), or the **Clock Exhibition Hall** (钟表馆, Zhōngbiǎo Guǎn; Map p304; admission ¥10; ⊘ 8.30am-4pm summer, 8.30am-3.30pm winter) (which you reach just before the Treasure Gallery entrance), both of which are in the eastern section of the complex, about halfway up.

The **Imperial Garden** (御花园; Yù Huāyuán; Map p304) at the back of the complex leads

---

BĚIJĪNG IN...

Two Days

Ease yourself into day one by strolling around the incense-smoke-filled courtyards of the **Lama Temple** (p312) before hopping over the road to the even more laid-back **Confucius Temple** (p312). Grab a coffee and lunch at **Cafe Confucius** (p321) before walking through the *hútòng* alleys to the ancient **Drum Tower** (p312) and **Bell Tower** (p313) and finishing off the day with a meal in **Dàlǐ Courtyard** (p319).

Get up at dawn on day two to enjoy **Temple of Heaven Park** (p308) at its magical, early-morning best: filled with opera-singing locals rather than photo-snapping tourists. Grab dumplings at **Dūyīchù** (p318) before walking via **Tiān'ānmén Square** (p308) to the **Forbidden City** (p307). Finish the day by tucking into Běijīng's signature dish – Peking duck (p318).

Four Days

Follow the itinerary above, but save plenty of energy for the trip of a lifetime on day three; your journey to the **Great Wall** (p327). There are plenty of options; the adventurous could try hiking at **Gǔběikǒu** (p328) or **Jiànkòu** (p327), while **Mùtiányù** (p327) is a good option for families. Pack a picnic and don't expect to get back to the city until nightfall.

Hop on the subway on day four to visit the **Summer Palace** (p314). You could spend the whole day here, or else save the afternoon for a trip to **798 Art District** (p314). Return to the city centre for an early evening meal so you have time to catch a show – **Peking Opera** (p321) or **acrobatics** (p321) – on your final evening.

TEMPLE OF HEAVEN PARK

A 20-minute walk southeast of Tiān'ānmén Square, **Temple of Heaven Park** (天坛公园, Tiāntán Gōngyuán; ☑ 6701 2483; Tiantan Donglu; admission park/through ticket high season ¥15/35, low season ¥10/30, audio tour ¥40 (deposit ¥100); ⊙ park 6am-8pm, sights 8am-5.30pm Apr-Oct, park 6am-8pm, sights 8am-5pm Nov-Mar; Ⓢ Tiantandongmen) is a tranquil oasis of peace and methodical Confucian design, and is the city's standout park.

The largest of Běijīng's imperial parks, Temple of Heaven not only assumes an important place in the history of China's capital, it's also a fabulous place in which to appreciate how Beijingers spend their free time.

It's impossible not to be bowled over by the architectural perfection of the **Hall of Prayer for Good Harvests** (祈年殿, Qínián Diàn; admission ¥20) even though the one you'll see is an 1890 replica of the original Ming-dynasty structure, which burned down after being struck by lightning.

Immediately south of this is the **Imperial Vault of Heaven** enclosed within **Echo Wall** – so named because its unusual acoustic properties allow people standing at opposite ends of its circular courtyard to talk to each other without shouting – and the **Round Altar**, all of which played important roles in the winter solstice ceremony carried out by the emperor each year.

He, and his enormous entourage, would travel in silent procession from the Forbidden City to the altars here, where animal sacrifices would be made as the emperor sought good harvests, divine clearance and atonement for the sins of the people.

The rest of the park is covered in groves of ancient cypresses, flower gardens and pleasant open spaces, including some well-tended lawns, where locals come to exercise, play music or just hang out. The area between the east gate and the north gate is prime kite-flying space. There's a huge exercise park in this area too, while nearby **Long Corridor** is a popular spot for occasionally animated games of cards.

Tiantandongmen subway station is beside the park's east gate.

to the north-gate exit, which pops you out opposite the south gate of Jǐngshān Park. Watch out for rickshaw and taxi touts here, who frequently cheat tourists with massively overpriced rides; instead, catch a bus (124 to the Drum Tower, or 专1 to Tiān'ānmén Sq) or walk a block away and hail a passing cab.

⊙ Tiān'ānmén Square & Around
天安门广场

Flanked to the east and west by stern 1950s Soviet-style buildings and ringed by white perimeter fences that channel the hoi polloi towards security checks and bag searches, **Tiān'ānmén Square** (天安门广场; Tiān'ānmén Guǎngchǎng), the world's largest public square (440,000 sq metres), is a vast desert of paving stones at the heart of Běijīng.

It's also a poignant epitaph to China's hapless democracy movement, which got a drubbing from the People's Liberation Army (PLA) in June 1989, and the stringent security and round-the-clock monitoring hardly makes it the most relaxing of tourist sights. Such, though, is its iconic status that few visitors leave Běijīng without coming here; and

for Trans-Sib travellers, a visit is a ritual of sorts – it's fascinating to size up Tiān'ānmén against your experience in Moscow's Red Square.

If you get up early you can watch the **flag-raising ceremony** at sunrise, performed by a troop of PLA soldiers drilled to march at precisely 108 paces per minute, 75cm per pace. The same ceremony in reverse is performed at sunset. Although the square is the symbolic centre of the Chinese universe, what you see today is a modern creation, conceived by Mao Zedong to project the enormity of the Communist Party. His giant portrait still hangs over the **Gate of Heavenly Peace** (天安门, Tiān'ānmén Sq; Map p304; admission ¥15, bag storage ¥2-6; ⊙ 8.30am-4.30pm; Ⓢ Tian'anmen West or Tian'anmen East) at the northern end of the square, flanked by the slogans 'Long Live the People's Republic of China' and 'Long Live the Unity of the Peoples of the World'.

At the square's southern end, **Front Gate** (前门, Qián Mén; Map p304; admission ¥20, audio guide ¥20; ⊙ 9am-4pm Tue-Sun; Ⓢ Qianmen) is a remnant of the wall that guarded the ancient Inner City as early as the 15th century.

It actually consists of two gates: the **Arrow Tower** (正阳门箭楼; Zhèngyángmén Jiànlóu; Map p304) to the south and the **Main Gate** to the north. Arrow Tower cannot be climbed, but the Main Gate contains a fascinating exhibition of old-Běijīng photographs.

Just north of Front Gate is the **Chairman Mao Memorial Hall** (毛主席纪念堂; Máo Zhǔxí Jìniàntáng; Map p304; Tiān'ānmén Sq; bag storage ¥2-10, camera storage ¥2-5; ⊙ 7.30am-1pm Tue-Sun; Ⓢ Tian'anmen West, Tian'anmen East or Qianmen) **FREE**, where you can join the masses of domestic tourists who shuffle past Mao's mummified corpse each day. It's free to enter, but all belongings must be left in a building over the road. Just north of the hall is the **Monument to the People's Heroes** (人民英雄纪念碑; Rénmín Yīngxióng Jìniànbēi; Map p304; Tiān'ānmén Sq; Ⓢ Tian'anmen West, Tian'anmen East or Qianmen), a 37.9m-high obelisk commemorating various patriotic and revolutionary events.

The National People's Congress, China's rubber-stamp legislature, sits on the western side of the square in the monolithic and intimidating **Great Hall of the People** (人民大会堂; Rénmín Dàhuìtáng; Map p304; adult ¥30, bag deposit ¥2-5; ⊙ 8.30am-3pm (times vary); Ⓢ Tian'anmen West). Further to the west,

the bulbous, titanium-and-glass **National Centre for the Performing Arts (NCPA)** (国家大剧院; Guójiā Dàjùyuàn; Map p304; ☑6655 0000; www.chncpa.org/ens; admission ¥30, concert tickets ¥100-400; ⊙ 9am-5pm Tue-Sun; Ⓢ Tian'anmen West) could be mistaken for an alien mothership that has landed to refuel.

A slight detour east of the square brings you to the **Former Foreign Legation Quarter**, a cluster of legation buildings (some elegantly restored) towards the west end of Dongjiaomin Xiang (东交民巷). A few of the iconic buildings on this road include, at number 40 the **Dutch Legation** (Map p304), at number 19 the **French Post Office** (Map p304) and at number 11 **St Michael's Church** (Map p304).

National Museum of China　　MUSEUM
(中国国际博物馆; Zhōngguó Guójì Bówùguǎn; Map p304; en.chnmuseum.cn; Guangchangdongce Lu, Tiān'ānmén Sq, 天安门，广场东侧路; audio guide ¥30; ⊙ 9am-5pm Tue-Sun, last entry 4pm; Ⓢ Tian'anmen East) **FREE** Běijīng's premier museum is housed in an immense 1950s building on the eastern side of Tiān'ānmén Sq, and is well worth visiting. The **Ancient China** exhibition on the basement floor is outstanding. You could easily spend a couple of hours in this exhibition alone. It contains dozens and dozens of stunning pieces, from prehistoric China through to the Qing dynasty, all displayed beautifully in modern, spacious, low-lit exhibition halls.

★ **Zhōngshān Park**　　PARK
(中山公园; Zhōngshān Gōngyuán; Map p304; adult ¥3, Spring Flower & Tulips Show ¥10; ⊙ 6am-9pm; Ⓢ Tian'anmen West) Named after Sun Zhongshan (Sun Yat-sen), the father of modern China, this peaceful park sits at the southwest corner of the Forbidden City and partly looks out onto the palace's moat (you can rent pedal-boats here) and towering walls. A refreshing prologue or conclusion to the magnificence of the Forbidden City, the park was formerly the sacred Ming-style Altar to the God of the Land and the God of Grain (Shèjìtán), where the emperor offered sacrifices. The **Square Altar** (wǔsè tǔ; Map p304) remains, bordered on all sides by walls tiled in various colours

Near the park's south entrance stands a towering dark-blue-tiled *páilou* (traditional Chinese archway) with triple eaves that originally commemorated the German

---

DAZZLING DESIGNS SHAPING MODERN BĚIJĪNG

History-rich Běijīng is also home to some of the world's most dazzling, state-of-the-art architectural designs:

➜ **CCTV Building** (央视大楼; Yāngshì Dàlóu; 32 Dongsanhuan Zhonglu; Ⓢ Jintaixizhao) The twisted overhang of 'Big Underpants' seems to defy gravity.

➜ **National Centre for the Performing Arts (NCPA)** Like a giant mercury bead from another planet.

➜ **Galaxy Soho** (Map p315) Deliciously curvy, space-station lookalike retail centre.

➜ **Bird's Nest & Water Cube** (国家体育场、国家游泳中心; Guójiā Tǐyùchǎng & Guójiā Yóuyǒng Zhōngxīn; Bird's Nest ¥50, Water Cube ¥30; ⊙ 9am-5pm Nov-Mar, 9am-6.30pm Apr-Oct; Ⓢ Olympic Sports Centre) The skeletal National Stadium, and its bubbly neighbour, the Water Cube, are particularly dazzling when lit up at night.

Central Běijīng – North

Central Běijīng – North

Foreign Minister Baron von Ketteler, killed during the Boxer Rebellion in 1900. Just off to the right (east) is the 100-year-old **Láijīnyǔxuān Teahouse** (来今雨轩茶社; Láijīnyǔxuān Cháshè; Map p304; inside Zhōngshān Park; 中山公园, Zhōngshān Gōngyuán; tea from ¥38 per cup, biscuit-cakes per serving ¥20; ⊙9am-9pm). North of here, also in the eastern section of the park, is the **Forbidden City**

Concert Hall (中山公园音乐堂, Zhōngshān Gōngyuán Yīnyuè Táng; Map p304; ☑ 6559 8285; Zhōngshān Park, 中山公园内; tickets ¥30-880; ⊙performances 7.30pm; ⑤Tian'anmen West). As with Jǐngshān Park, April and May is a beautiful time to visit thanks to the hugely colourful Spring Flower and Tulips Show. The northeast exit of the park brings you out by Meridian Gate, from where you can en-

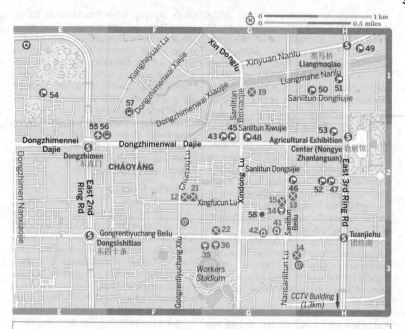

ter the Forbidden City. The south exit brings you out near Tiān'ānmén Sq. There is also a west gate.

Běijīng Railway Museum MUSEUM
(北京铁路博物馆, Běijīng Tiělù Bówùguǎn; Map p304; ☏6705 1638; 2a Qianmen Dongdajie, 前门东大街2a号; admission ¥20; ⊙9am-5pm Tue-Sun; Ⓢ Qianmen) Located in the historic for-mer Qiánmén Railway Station, which once connected Běijīng to Tiānjīn, this museum offers an engaging history of the develop-ment of the capital and China's railway sys-tem, with plenty of photos and models. Its lack of space, though, means it doesn't have many actual trains, although there is a life-size model of the cab of one of China's high-speed trains to clamber into (¥10).

Hard-core trainspotters should make tracks to the China Railway Museum (中国铁道博物馆; Zhōngguó Tiědào Bówùguǎn; ☑ 6438 1519; 1 Jiuxianqiao Bei Lu, Chaoyang District; 朝阳区酒仙桥北路1号院北侧; admission ¥20; ⊙ 9am-4pm Tue-Sun; ☐ 403) on the far northeastern outskirts of Běijīng, which is vast and has far more loco action.

◉ North of the Forbidden City

★ Lama Temple   BUDDHIST TEMPLE

(雍和宫; Yōnghé Gōng; Map p310; 28 Yonghegong Dajie; admission ¥25, English audio guide ¥50; ⊙ 9am-4.30pm; Ⓢ Yonghegong Lama Temple) This exceptional temple is a glittering attraction in Běijīng's Buddhist firmament. If you only have time for one temple (the Temple of Heaven isn't really a temple) make it this one, where riveting roofs, fabulous frescoes, magnificent decorative arches, tapestries, eye-popping carpentry, Tibetan prayer wheels, Tantric statues and a superb pair of Chinese lions mingle with dense clouds of incense.

The most renowned Tibetan Buddhist temple outside Tibet, the Lama Temple was converted to a lamasery in 1744 after serving as the former residence of Emperor Yong Zheng. Today the temple is an active place of worship, attracting pilgrims from afar, some of whom prostrate themselves in submission at full length within its halls.

Resplendent within the Hall of the Wheel of the Law (Fǎlún Diàn), the fourth hall you reach from the entrance, is a substantial bronze statue of a benign and smiling Tsong Khapa (1357–1419), founder of the Gelugpa or Yellow Hat sect, robed in yellow and illuminated by a skylight.

The fifth hall, the Wànfú Pavilion (Wànfú Gé), houses a magnificent 18m-high statue of the Maitreya Buddha in his Tibetan form, clothed in yellow satin and reputedly sculpted from a single block of sandalwood. Each of the bodhisattva's toes is the size of a pillow. Behind the statue is the Vault of Avalokiteshvara, from where a diminutive and blue-faced statue of Guanyin peeks out. The Wànfú Pavilion is linked by an overhead walkway to the Yánsuí Pavilion (Yánsuí Gé), which encloses a huge lotus flower that revolves to reveal an effigy of the Longevity Buddha.

Don't miss the collection of bronze Tibetan Buddhist statues within the Jiètái Lóu, a small side hall. Most effigies date from the Qing dynasty, from languorous renditions of

Green Tara and White Tara to exotic, Tantric pieces (such as Samvara) and figurines of the fierce-looking Mahakala. Also peruse the collection of Tibetan Buddhist ornaments within the Bānchán Lóu, another side hall, where an array of dorje (Tibetan sceptres), mandalas and Tantric figures are displayed along with an impressive selection of ceremonial robes in silk and satin.

The street outside the temple entrance heaves with shops piled high with statues of Buddha, talismans, Buddhist charms, incense and keepsakes, picked over by a constant stream of pilgrims.

Confucius Temple & Imperial College   CONFUCIAN TEMPLE

(孔庙、国子监; Kǒng Miào & Guózǐjiàn; Map p310; 13 Guozijian Jie; adult ¥30, audio guide ¥30; ⊙ 8.30am-5.30pm; Ⓢ Yonghegong Lama Temple) An incense stick's toss away from the Lama Temple, China's second-largest Confucian temple had a refit in recent years, but the almost otherworldly sense of detachment is seemingly impossible to shift. A mood of impassiveness reigns and the lack of worship reinforces a sensation that time has stood still. However, in its tranquillity and reserve, the temple can be a pleasant sanctuary from Běijīng's often congested streets – a haven of peace and quiet.

★ Drum Tower   HISTORIC SITE

(鼓楼; Gǔlóu; Map p310; Gulou Dongdajie; admission ¥20, both towers through ticket ¥30; ⊙ 9am-5pm, last tickets 4.40pm; Ⓢ Shichahai or Guloudajie) Along with the older-looking Bell Tower, which stands behind it, the magnificent red-painted Drum Tower used to be the city's official timekeeper, with drums and bells beaten and rung to mark the times of the day; effectively the Big Ben of Běijīng.

Originally built in 1272, the Drum Tower was once the heart of the Mongol capital of Dàdū, as Běijīng was then known. That structure was destroyed in a fire before a replacement was built, slightly to the east of the original location, in 1420. The current structure is a Qing-dynasty version of that 1420 tower.

You can climb the steep inner staircase for views of the grey-tiled rooftops in the surrounding hútòng alleys. But, you can't view the Bell Tower as the north-facing balcony has been closed. It's well worth climbing the tower, though, especially if you can time it to coincide with one of the regular drumming performances, which are played out on reproductions of the 25 Ming-dynasty watch drums, which used to sound out across this part of the city. One of the original 25 drums, the Night Watchman's Drum (更鼓; Gēnggǔ), is also on display; dusty, battered and worn. There is also a replica of a Song-dynasty water clock, which was never actually used in the tower, but is interesting nonetheless. The times of the drumming performances, which only last for a few minutes, are posted up by the ticket office.

Bell Tower
HISTORIC SITE

(钟楼, Zhōnglóu; Map p310; Gulou Dongdajie; admission ¥20, both towers through ticket ¥30; ⊙9am-5pm, last tickets 4.40pm; ⑤Shichahai or Guloudajie) The more modest, grey-stone structure of the Bell Tower (钟楼; Zhōnglóu) is arguably more charming than its resplendent other half, the Drum Tower, after which this area of Běijīng is named. It also has the added advantage of being able to view its sister tower from a balcony.

★ Běihǎi Park
PARK

(北海公园, Běihǎi Gōngyuán; Map p304; ☑6403 1102; admission high/low season ¥10/5, through ticket high/low season ¥20/15; ⊙park 6am-9pm, sights until 5pm; ⑤Xisi or Nanluogu Xiang) Běihǎi Park, northwest of the Forbidden City, is largely occupied by the North Sea (běihǎi), a huge lake that freezes in winter and blooms with lotuses in summer. Old folk dance together outside temple halls and come twilight, young couples cuddle on benches. It's a restful place to stroll around, rent a rowing boat in summer and watch calligraphers practising characters on paving slabs with fat brushes and water.

The site is associated with Kublai Khaan's palace, Běijīng's navel before the arrival of the Forbidden City. All that survives of the Khan's court is a large jar made of green jade in the Round City (团城; Tuánchéng), near the southern entrance. Also within the Round City is the Chengguang Hall (Chéngguāng Diàn), where a white jade statue of Sakyamuni from Myanmar (Burma) can be found, its arm wounded by the allied forces that swarmed through Běijīng in 1900 to quash the Boxer Rebellion. At the time of writing, the Round City was closed to visitors.

Attached to the North Sea, the South (Nánhǎi) and Middle (Zhōnghǎi) Seas to the south lend their name to Zhōngnánhǎi (literally 'Middle and South Seas'), the heavily-guarded compound less than a mile south of the park where the Chinese Communist Party's top leadership live.

Topping Jade Islet (琼岛; Qióngdǎo) on the lake, the 36m-high Tibetan-style White Dagoba (白塔; Báitǎ) was built in 1651 for a visit by the Dalai Lama, and was rebuilt in 1741. Climb up to the dagoba via the Yǒng'ān Temple (永安寺; Yǒng'ān Sì).

Xītiān Fánjìng (西天梵境; Western Paradise), situated on the northern shore of the lake, is a lovely temple (admission to which is included in the park ticket). The nearby

BĚIJĪNG'S HÚTÒNG

Běijīng's medieval genotype is most discernible down the city's leafy *hútòng* (胡同; narrow alleyways). The spirit and soul of the city lives and breathes among these charming and ragged lanes where a warm sense of community and hospitality survives.

After Chinggis (Genghis) Khaan's army reduced the city of Běijīng to rubble, the new city was redesigned with *hútòng*. By the Qing dynasty more than 2000 such passageways riddled the city, leaping to around 6000 by the 1950s; now the figure has drastically dwindled to somewhere above 1000.

Old walled *sìhéyuàn* (courtyards) are the building blocks of this delightful universe. Many are still lived in and hum with activity. From spring to autumn, men collect outside their gates, drinking beer, playing chess, smoking and chewing the fat. Inside, scholar trees soar aloft, providing shade and a nesting ground for birds. Flocks of pigeons whirl through the Běijīng skies overhead, bred by locals and housed in coops often buried away within the *hútòng*. More venerable courtyards are fronted by large, thick red doors, outside of which perch either a pair of Chinese lions or drum stones.

To savour Běijīng's courtyard ambience, enjoy a coffee at **Irresistible Cafe** (p320), a beer at **Great Leap Brewing** (p320) or a meal at **Dàlǐ Courtyard** (p319), before sleeping it all off at **Courtyard 7** (p317). Alternatively, **Bike Běijīng** (p326) does guided cycle tours of *hútòng* areas.

Nine Dragon Screen (九龙壁; Jiǔlóng Bì), a 5m-high and 27m-long spirit wall, is a glimmering stretch of coloured glazed tiles depicting coiling dragons, similar to its counterpart in the Forbidden City. West, along the shore, is the pleasant **Little Western Heaven** (小西天; Xiǎo Xītiān), a further shrine.

★**Hòuhǎi Lakes**   LAKES
(后海, Hòuhǎi; Map p310; Ⓢ Shichahai, Nanluoguxiang or Jishuitan) FREE Also known as Shíchàhǎi (什刹海) but mostly just referred to collectively as 'Hòuhǎi', the Hòuhǎi Lakes are compromised of three lakes: Qiánhǎi (Front Lake), Hòuhǎi (Back Lake) and Xīhǎi (West Lake). Together they are one of the capital's favourite outdoor spots, heaving with locals and out-of-towners in the summer especially, and providing great people-spotting action.

★**Jǐngshān Park**   PARK
(景山公园, Jǐngshān Gōngyuán; Map p304; Jingshan Qianjie; adult ¥2, in summer ¥5; ⏰6am-9.30pm; Ⓢ Tian'anmen West, then bus 5) The dominating feature of Jǐngshān – one of the city's finest parks – is one of central Běijīng's few hills; a mound that was created from the earth excavated to make the Forbidden City moat. Called Coal Hill by Westerners during Legation days, Jǐngshān also serves as a feng shui shield, protecting the palace from evil spirits – or dust storms – from the north. Clamber to the top for a magnificent panorama of the capital and princely views over the russet roofing of the Forbidden City.

◉ City Outskirts

★**Summer Palace**   HISTORIC SITE
(颐和园, Yíhé Yuán; 19 Xinjian Gongmen; ticket ¥20, through ticket ¥50, audio guide ¥40; ⏰7am-7pm, sights 8am-5pm summer, 8.30am-4.30pm winter; Ⓢ Xiyuan or Beigongmen) As mandatory a Běijīng sight as the Great Wall or the Forbidden City, the Summer Palace was the playground for emperors fleeing the suffocating summer torpor of the old imperial city. A marvel of design, the palace – with its huge lake and hilltop views – offers a pastoral escape into the landscapes of traditional Chinese painting. It merits an entire day's exploration, although a (high-paced) morning or afternoon exploring the temples, gardens, pavilions, bridges and corridors may suffice.

798 Art District   GALLERIES
(798 艺术新区, Qī Jiǔ Bā Yìshù Qū; cnr Jiuxianqiao Lu & Jiuxianqiao Beilu; 酒仙桥路; ⏰galleries 10am-6pm, most closed Mon; 🚌403 or 909) A vast area of disused factories built by the East Germans, 798 Art District, also known as Dà Shānzi (大山子), is Běijīng's main concentration of contemporary art galleries. The industrial complex celebrates its proletarian roots in the communist heyday of the 1950s via the retouched red Maoist slogans decorating gallery walls and statues of burly, lantern-jawed workers dotting the lanes. The giant former factory workshops are ideally suited to multimedia installations and other ambitious projects.

You could easily spend half a day wandering around the complex. There are signboards with English-language maps to guide you around.

Highlights include **BTAP** (Ceramics Third Street; ⏰10am-6pm, Tue-Sun), one of 798's original galleries; **UCCA** (798 Road; ⏰10am-7pm Tue-Sun), a big-money gallery with exhibition halls, a funky shop and a cinema screening films most days; **Pace** (797 Road; ⏰10am-6pm Tue-Sun), a wonderfully large space holding some top-quality exhibitions; **Galleria Continua** (just south of 797 Road; ⏰11am-6pm, Tue-Sun), another giant space, below a towering, hard-to-miss brick chimney.

From Exit C of Dongzhimen subway station, take Bus 909 (¥2) for about 6km northeast to Dashanzi Lukou Nan (大山子路口南) bus stop, where you'll see the big red 798 sign. Buses run until 8.30pm.

🛏 Sleeping

Běijīng has a tremendous range of places to stay, including some excellent hostels. The most atmospheric hotels are those built in the courtyards of the old *hútòng* neighbourhoods.

🛏 Tiān'ānmén Square & Around
天安门广场

★**Qiánmén Hostel**   COURTYARD HOSTEL $
(前门客栈, Qiánmén Kèzhàn; Map p304; ☎6313 2370, 6313 2369; www.qianmenhostel.net; 33 Meishi Jie, 煤市街 33号; 6-8 bed dm ¥70, 4-bed dm ¥80, with/without bathroom d & tw ¥280/240, tr ¥380/300; ✴@⏰; Ⓢ Qianmen) A five-minute trot southwest of Tiān'ānmén Sq, this heritage hostel with a cool courtyard offers a relaxing environment with able staff. The rooms are simple and not big but, like the

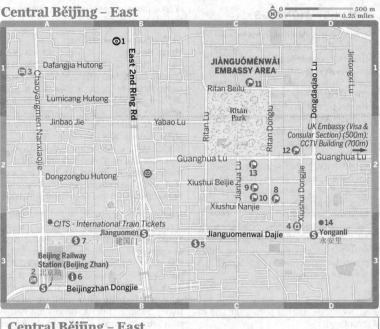

Central Běijīng – East

dorms, they are clean, as are the shared bathrooms, and all were being upgraded at the time of writing. There's a decent cafe to hang out in, too.

Three-Legged Frog Hostel   HÚTÒNG HOSTEL **$**
(京一食青年旅舍; Jīngyī Shí Qīngnián Lǚshè; Map p304; ☑6304 0749; 3legs@threeleggedfroghostel.com; 27 Tieshu Xiejie, 铁树斜街 27号; 6-bed dm with bathroom ¥65, 10-bed dm ¥55, d & tw ¥220, tr ¥270, f ¥339; ❄@☎; ⓢ Qianmen) The name is a mystery but the decent-sized six-bed dorms with bathrooms are an excellent deal, while the rooms are compact but clean. All are set around a cute courtyard that's pleasant in the summer. It has a helpful owner – it's

geared to foreign travellers – and a communal area out front that does Western breakfasts and evening beers.

Feel Inn   HÚTÒNG HOSTEL **$**
(非凡客栈; Fēifán Kèzhàn; Map p304; ☑6528 7418, 139 1040 9166; beijingfeelinn@gmail.com; 2 Ciqiku Hutong, off Nanheyan Dajie; 南河沿大街，磁器库胡同2号; dm ¥50-80, tw ¥240-300; ❄@☎) A small, understated hostel with a hidden, backstreet location, Feel Inn is tucked away amongst the alleys containing the little-known Pǔdù Temple, and yet is just a short walk from big-hitters such as the Forbidden City, Tiān'ānmén Sq and the shops on Wangfujing Dajie. Has simple,

TRAIN-STATION DIGS

Trans-Siberian-Mongolian trains leave from, and arrive at Běijīng Train Station (p324). If you can't be bothered to lug your heavy rucksack to nicer parts of town, then consider staying at **Běijīng City Central International Youth Hostel** (北京城市国际青年旅社, Běijīng Chéngshì Guójì Qīngnián Lǚshè; Map p315; ☑6525 8066, 8511 5050; www.centralhostel.com; 1 Beijingzhan Jie, 北京站街1号; 4-8 bed dm ¥60, s/d with shared bathroom ¥138/178, d ¥298-348; ☻❄@☎; Ⓢ Beijing Railway Station), ahead of you and to the left as you exit the train station. Rooms are basic but clean and there's a large bar-cafe area with free wi-fi, internet terminals, pool tables and Western food. The rooms with shared bathrooms are in the hostel proper, while those with private bathrooms are in the attached hotel (same reception).

clean rooms, a small bar-restaurant, and wi-fi throughout.

Emperor
HOTEL $$$

(皇家驿站, Huángjiā Yìzhàn; Map p304; ☑6701 7791; www.theemperor.com.cn; 87 Xianyukou St, Qianmen Commercial Centre, 前门商业区鲜鱼口街87号; r ¥1200; ❄☎❄; Ⓢ Qianmen) Brand new, this modernist hotel comes with a spa and a roof-top pool that enables you to laze in the sun while enjoying fine views over nearby Tiān'ānmén Sq. The cool, all-white rooms aren't huge, but the price is reasonable for a hotel of this quality and the location is perfect. Service is attentive and the atmosphere laid-back.

North of the Forbidden City

Běijīng Downtown Backpackers
HÚTÒNG HOSTEL $

(东堂客栈, Dōngtáng Kèzhàn; Map p310; ☑8400 2429; www.backpackingchina.com; 85 Nanluogu Xiang, 南锣鼓巷85号; dm ¥75-85, s ¥160, tw 160-210, ste ¥300; ❄@☎; Ⓢ Beixinqiao) Downtown Backpackers is Nanluogu Xiang's original youth hostel and it hasn't forgotten its roots. Rooms are basic, therefore cheap, but are kept clean and tidy, and staff members are fully plugged in to the needs of Western travellers. Rents bikes (per day ¥20) and runs recommended hiking trips to the Great Wall

(¥280), plus a range of other city trips. Rates include breakfast.

Běijīng Saga International Youth Hostel
HÚTÒNG HOSTEL $

(北京实佳国际青年旅社, Běijīng Shíjiā Guójì Qīngnián Lǚshè; Map p315; ☑6527 2773; www.sagayouthhostelbeijing.cn; 9 Shijia Hutong, 史家胡同9号; dm ¥70, d with/without bathroom from ¥259/200, tr ¥319; ❄@☎; Ⓢ Dengshikou) Enjoying an interesting location on historic Shijia Hutong, this friendly hostel is a grey block, but the inside compensates with some character and staff members are helpful towards travellers. Rooms are basic but well kept, and it has a decent restaurant-cum-bar. Rents bikes (¥50) and does Great Wall trips.

Nostalgia Hotel
HOTEL $

(时光漫步怀旧主题酒店; Shíguāng Mànbù Huáijiù Zhǔtí Jiǔdiàn; Map p310; ☑6403 2288; www.sgmbhotel.com; 46 Fangjia Hutong; 安定门内大街, 方家胡同46号; r summer ¥388-408, winter ¥360-380) A good-value option if you don't fancy staying in a youth hostel, this funky hotel is housed in a small arts zone on trendy Fangjia Hutong. Rooms are dotted with retro knicknacks, and have a different hand-painted mural in each. The bathrooms sparkle. Staff on reception speak English, and there's lift access, but no restaurant. To find it, enter the small arts zone named after its address (46 Fangjia Hutong) and walk to the far left corner of the complex.

⭐ Jīngshān Garden Hotel
COURTYARD HOTEL $$

(景山花园酒店; Jīngshān Huāyuán Jiǔdiàn; Map p304; ☑8404 7979; www.jingshangardenhotel.com; 68 Sanyanjing Hutong, off Jingshan Dongjie; 景山东街, 三眼井胡同68号; r ¥650-750; ❄@☎) This delightful, unfussy, two-storey guesthouse has bright spacious rooms surrounding a large, peaceful, flower-filled courtyard. First-floor rooms are pricier, but brighter than the ground-floor ones, and some have views of Jīngshān Park from their bathrooms. Walking down Sanyanjing Hutong from the direction of Jīngshān Park, turn right down the first alleyway, and the hotel is at the end.

⭐ Orchid
COURTYARD HOTEL $$

(兰花宾馆, Lánhuā Bīnguǎn; Map p310; ☑8404 4818; www.theorchidbeijing.com; 65 Baochao Hutong, 鼓楼东大街宝钞胡同65号; d ¥700-1200; ❄@☎; Ⓢ Gulouda jie) Opened by a Canadian guy and a Tibetan girl, this place may lack the history of other courtyard hotels, but it's been renovated into a beautiful space, with a peaceful courtyard and some rooftop seating with distant views of the Drum and Bell Towers. Rooms are doubles only, and are small, but are tastefully decorated and come with Apple TV home entertainment systems. They also do Great Wall tours, and can organise taxis for city tours (half/full day ¥400/600) or Great Wall trips (¥700). Hard to spot, the Orchid is down an unnamed, shoulder-width alleyway opposite Mr Shi's Dumplings.

★ **Courtyard 7**　　　COURTYARD HOTEL $$$
(四合院酒店, Sìhéyuàn Jiǔdiàn; Map p310; ☑ 6406 0777; www.courtyard7.com; 7 Qiangulouyuan Hutong, 鼓楼大街南锣鼓巷前鼓楼苑胡同7号, off Nanluogu Xiang; r ¥900-1500; ❉ @; Ⓢ Nanluoguxiang) Immaculate rooms, decorated in traditional Chinese furniture face onto a series of different-sized, 400-year-old courtyards, which over the years have been home to government ministers, rich merchants and even an army general. Despite the historical narrative, rooms still come with modern comforts such as underfloor heating, broadband internet, wi-fi, and cable TV.

✖ **Eating**

Běijīng has a staggering array of restaurants, covering every type of Chinese cuisine. You'll also find plenty of international restaurants here. For breakfast, pop into any small restaurant you see with bamboo steamers piled high at the entrance; this indicates that they're open early for dumplings!

✖ **Tiān'ānmén Square & Around**
天安门广场

Liú Family Noodles　　　NOODLES $
(刘家人刀削面, Liú Jiārén Dāoxiāomiàn; Map p304; 6 Tieshuxie Jie, 铁树斜街6号; noodles from ¥8; ⏱ 11am-3pm & 5-10pm; Ⓢ Qianmen) A rarity in this area: a restaurant that welcomes foreigners without trying to overcharge them. On the contrary, the prices couldn't be much lower, while the friendly owner is keen to practise her (limited) English. Choose from a selection of tasty noodle and cold dishes. To find it, look for the black sign with 'Best Noodles in China' written in English.

Dōnghuámén Night Market　STREET FOOD $
(东华门夜市, Dōnghuámén Yèshì; Map p304; Dong'anmen Dajie, 东安门大街; snacks ¥5-15; ⏱ 4-10pm; Ⓢ Wangfujing) A sight in itself, the bustling night market near Wangfujing Dajie is a veritable food zoo: lamb, beef and chicken skewers, corn on the cob, smelly *dòufu* (tofu), cicadas, grasshoppers, kidneys, quail eggs, snake, squid, fruit, porridge, fried pancakes, strawberry kebabs, bananas,

BĚIJĪNG EATING

HOME COMFORTS

If you're pining for a taste of home, head to the Sānlǐtún area in Cháoyáng District for a huge choice of international cuisine.

Carmen (卡门, Kǎmén; Map p310; ☑ 6417 8038; Nali Patio north side, 81 Sanlitun Lu, 三里屯路那里花园北外81层; mains from ¥70; ⏱ noon-1am; Ⓢ Tuanjiehu) One of the best options for tapas.

O'Steak (欧牛排法式餐厅, Ōu Niúpái Fàshì Cāntīng; Map p310; ☑ 8448 8250; 55-7 Xingfucun Zhonglu, 幸福村中路55-7杰座大厦底层; steaks from ¥88; ⏱ 11am-11pm; Ⓢ Dongsi Shitiao) High-quality French cuisine.

Bocata (Map p310; ☑ 6417 5291; 3 Sanlitun Lu, 三里屯北路3号; sandwiches from ¥28, coffee from ¥22; ⏱ 11.30am-midnight; ⏰; Ⓢ Tuanjiehu) Popular cafe with decent Western food.

Bookworm (书虫, Shūchóng; Map p310; ☑ 6586 9507; www.beijingbookworm.com; Bldg 4, Nansanlitun Lu, 南三里路4号楼; mains from ¥60; ⏱ 9am-midnight; ⏰; Ⓢ Tuanjiehu) Cafe-cum-library and a centre for cultural events.

Indian Kitchen (北京印度小厨餐厅, Běijīng Yìndù Xiǎo Chú Cāntīng; Map p310; ☑ 6462 7255; 2f, 2 Sanlitun Beixiaojie, 三里屯北小街2号二楼; mains ¥45-88; ⏱ 11am-2.30pm & 5.30-11pm; Ⓢ Agricultural Exhibition Center) One of the best Indian restaurants in town.

Purple Haze (紫苏庭, Zǐsū Tíng; Map p310; ☑ 6413 0899; 55 Xingfu Yicun, off Gongrentiyuchang Beilu, 工人体育场北路幸福一村55号; mains from ¥48; ⏱ 11.30am-10.30pm; ⏰; Ⓢ Dongsi Shitiao) Long-standing favourite for Thai cuisine.

Big Smoke (Map p310; ☑ 6416 5195; 1/F Lee World Bldg, Xingfucun Zhong Lu, 幸福村中路57号利世商务楼一层; dishes from ¥36; ⏱ 11am-midnight; Ⓢ Dongsi Shitiao) Combines some excellent craft beers with southern-US-inspired barbecues.

SELF-CATERING

For picnic supplies (or long train-journeys) head to large, outdoor food markets such as **Rùndélì Food Market** (润得立菜市场; Rùndélì Càishìchǎng; 4 Sihuan Hutong, off Deshengmennei Dajie; 德胜门内大街四环胡同; ☺7am-7pm) or **Xīnmín Food Market** (新民菜市场, Xīnmín Càishìchǎng; Jiugulou Waidajie, 就鼓楼外大街; ☺5am-noon). Pocket-sized delicatessen **Chez Gérard** (Map p310; 40 Jianchang Hutong, off Guozijian Jie, 国子监街, 箭厂胡同40号; ☺10am-10.30pm) has Western goodies.

Inner Mongolian cheese, stuffed eggplants, chicken hearts, pita bread stuffed with meat, shrimps – and that's just the start.

It's not a very authentic Běijīng experience, but the vendors take great glee in persuading foreigners to try such delicacies as scorpion on a stick. Expect to pay ¥5 for a lamb skewer; more than you would pay for the same snack from a *hútòng* vendor. More exotic skewers cost up to ¥50. Noodles or savoury pancakes (*jiānbing*) will set you back about ¥10. Prices are all marked and in English.

Dùyīchù
DUMPLINGS $$

(都一处; Map p304; ☑6702 1671; 38 Qianmen Dajie, 前门大街38号; dishes from ¥32; ☺6.30am-9.30pm; ⓢQianmen) Now back on the street where it opened during the mid-Qing dynasty, Dùyīchù specialises in the delicate dumplings called *shāomài* (¥42 to ¥52). The shrimp-and-leek and vegie ones are especially good, and are presented very nicely, but it also does a nice line in seasonal variations, such as sweet corn and bean in the summer, or beef and yam in the winter.

Qiánmén Quánjùdé Roast Duck Restaurant
PEKING DUCK $$$

(前门全聚德烤鸭店, Qiánmén Quánjùdé Kǎoyādiàn; Map p304; ☑6701 1379; 30 Qianmen Dajie, 前门大街30号; roast duck ¥296; ☺11am-1.30pm, 4.30-8pm; ⓢQianmen) The most popular branch of Běijīng's most famous destination for duck – check out the photos of everyone from Fidel Castro to Zhang Yimou. The duck, while not the best in town, is roasted in ovens fired by fruit-tree wood, which means the birds have a unique fragrance, as well as being juicy, if slightly fatty.

✕ North of the Forbidden City

★ Crescent Moon Muslim Restaurant
XINJIANG $

(新疆弯弯月亮维吾尔穆斯林餐厅, Xīnjiāng Wānwānyuèliàng Wéiwú'ěr Mùsīlín Cāntīng; Map p310; 16 Dongsi Liutiao Hutong, 东四六条胡同16号, 东四北大街; dishes from ¥18; ☺11am-11pm; ⓢDongsi Shitiao) You can find a Chinese Muslim restaurant on almost every street in Běijīng. Most are run by Huí Muslims, who are Han Chinese, rather than ethnic-minority Uighurs from the remote western province of Xīnjiāng. Crescent Moon is the real deal – owned and staffed by Uighurs, it attracts many Běijīng-based Uighurs and people from Central Asia, as well as a lot of Western expats. It's more expensive than most other Xīnjiāng restaurants in Běijīng, but the food is consistently good, and it has an English menu. The speciality is the barbecued leg of lamb (¥128). The lamb skewers (¥6) are also delicious, and there's naan bread (¥5), homemade yoghurt (¥12) and plenty of noodle options (¥18 to ¥25). You can also get Xīnjiāng tea (¥30 per pot), beer (¥15) and wine (¥95).

Zuǒ Lín Yòu Shè
BEIJING $

(左邻右舍褡裢火烧; Map p310; 50 Meishuguan Houjie, 美术馆后街50号; dumplings per liang ¥6-7, dishes ¥10-30; ☺11am-9.30pm; ⓢNational Art Museum) This small, no-frills restaurant focuses on Běijīng cuisine. The speciality is *dālian huǒshāo* (褡裢火烧), golden-fried finger-shaped dumplings stuffed with all manner of savoury fillings; we prefer the pork ones, but there are lamb, beef and vegie choices too. They are served by the *liǎng* (两), with one *liǎng* equal to three dumplings, and they prefer you to order at least two *liǎng* (二两; *èr liǎng*) of each filling to make it worth their while cooking a batch.

Other specialities include the pickled fish (酥鲫鱼; *sū jì yú*), the spicy tofu paste (麻豆腐; *má dòufu*) and the deep-fried pork balls (干炸丸子; *gān zhá wánzi*), while filling bowls of millet porridge (小米粥; *xiǎo mǐ zhōu*) are served up for free. No English sign (look for the wooden signboard), and no English spoken, but most parts of the menu have been translated into English.

Yáng Fāng Lamb Hotpot
MONGOLIAN HOTPOT $

(羊坊涮肉, Yáng Fāng Shuàn Ròu; Map p310; 270 Gulou Dongdajie, 鼓楼东大街270号; broth ¥8-15, dips & sauces ¥2-5, raw ingredients ¥6-25; ☺11am-11pm; ⓢShichahai) There are two main types of hotpot in China: the ridiculously spicy one that comes from the fire-breathing southwestern city of Chóngqìng, and the milder version which is cooked in an unusual conical brass pot and which originally hails from Mongolia, but has been adopted as a Běijīng speciality. Yáng Fāng is a salt-of-the-earth version of the latter, and is a real favourite with the locals round here.

First order the broth you want in your pot – clear (清汤锅底; *qīng tāng guōde;* ¥8), or spicy (辣锅底; *là guōde;* ¥15); clear is more common. Then ask for some sesame-paste dipping sauce (小料; *xiǎo liào;* ¥5); each person should have one. And, if you fancy it, order some freshly prepared chilli oil (鲜榨辣椒油; *xiān zhá là jiāo yóu;* ¥2) to mix into your dipping sauce; one bowl is enough for everyone to share.

Finally, select the raw ingredients you want to cook in your broth. Our favourites include wafer-thin lamb slices (鲜羊肉; *xiān yáng ròu;* ¥26), lotus root slices (藕片; *ǒu piàn;* ¥6), tofu slabs (鲜豆腐; *xiān dòufu;* ¥6), sweet potato (红薯; *hóng shǔ;* ¥6) and spinach (菠菜; *bō cài;* ¥6). No English sign; no English menu; no English spoken.

Jiānbǐng Savoury Pancake Vendor
STREET FOOD **$**

(煎饼; Map p310; 154 Yonghegong Dajie; 雍和宫大街154号; ¥5 to ¥6; ⏱7am-7pm) Hole-in-the-wall stall selling jiānbǐng (煎饼; savoury pancakes).

★ Little Yúnnán
YUNNAN **$$**

(小云南; Xiǎo Yúnnán; Map p304; ☑6401 9498; 28 Donghuang Chenggen Beijie; 东皇城根北街28号; mains ¥20-60; ⏱10am-10pm) Run by young, friendly staff and housed in a cute courtyard conversion, Little Yúnnán is one of the more down-to-earth Yúnnán restaurants in Běijīng. The main room has a rustic feel to it, with wooden beams, flooring and furniture. The tables up in the eaves are fun, and there's also some seating in the small open-air courtyard by the entrance.

Dishes include some classic southwest China ingredients, with some tea-infused creations as well as river fish, mushroom dishes and *là ròu* (腊肉; cured pork – south China's answer to bacon). They also serve Yúnnán rice wine and the province's local Dali Beer. Has an English sign and a well-translated English menu.

★ Bǎihé Vegetarian Restaurant
CHINESE, VEGETARIAN **$$**

(百合素食, Bǎihé Sùshí; Map p310; 23 Caoyuan Hutong, 东直门内北小街草园胡同甲23号; mains ¥25-60, tea per cup/pot from ¥16/45; ⏱11am-10pm; Ⓢ Dongzhimen or Beixinqiao) This peaceful, tastefully furnished, courtyard restaurant, which also serves as a delightful teahouse, has a wonderful air of serenity – it's not uncommon to see monks from nearby Lama Temple coming here for a pot of tea. The all-vegetarian menu (with English translations) includes imaginative mock-meat dishes as well as more conventional vegetable dishes and a range of tasty noodles.

Stuff'd
WESTERN **$$**

(塞; Sāi; Map p310; 9 Jianchang Hutong, off Guozijian Jie, 国子监街，箭厂胡同9号; sausages ¥50, pies ¥60, pizza ¥60, home-brewed ale ¥40; ⏱11.30am-2.30pm & 6-10pm, closed Tue) Handmade sausages and home-brewed beer. What more could you want? This cute little sister branch of nearby Vineyard Cafe has a more rustic feel to it; almost like an English pub, only housed in a restored Chinese *píngfáng* (bungalow). Lunchtimes are all about the sausages and ale, but the evening menu also includes pies and pizza.

Xù Xiāng Zhái Vegetarian Restaurant
VEGETARIAN **$$**

(叙香斋; Xù Xiāng Zhái; Map p310; 26 Guozijian Jie, 国子监街26号; buffet ¥68, mains ¥30-80; ⏱buffet 11.30am-2pm & 5.30-9pm, a la carte 1.30-3.30pm & 7.30-9pm; Ⓢ Yonghegong Lama Temple) The lunchtime and early-evening set-price buffet is very popular here, and good value. There's an elaborate selection of beautifully presented mock-meat creations, plus other standard vegetable dishes, representing vegetarian cuisine from across China. And it's all served in an elegant dining hall on the historic *hútòng* Guozijian Jie. The à la carte menu is in English and is also decent value.

Dàlǐ Courtyard
YUNNAN **$$$**

(大理, Dàlǐ; Map p310; ☑8404 1430; 67 Xiaojingchang Hutong, Gulou Dongdajie, 鼓楼东大街小经厂胡同67号; set menu ¥150; ⏱midday-2pm & 6-10.30pm; Ⓢ Andingmen) The charming *hútòng* setting in a restored courtyard makes this one of Běijīng's more pleasant places to eat, especially in summer (in winter they cover the courtyard with an unattractive temporary roof). It specialises in the subtle flavours of Yúnnán cuisine. There's

A NIGHT OUT IN SĀNLĬTÚN

It's sleazy in places, and expensive, but if you want a really big night out, Sānlǐtún (三里屯) in Cháoyáng District is your best bet. Rooftop Migas Bar (米家思, Mǐ Jiā Sī; Map p310; ☑5208 6061; 6th fl Nali Patio, 81 Sanlitunbei Lu, 三里屯北路81号那里花园6层; beer from ¥30, cocktails from ¥60, mains from ¥98; ⊙noon-2.30pm & 6-10.30pm, bar 6pm-late; ☎; ⑤Tuanjiehu) is a good place to start. It's on the sixth floor of a complex known as Nali Patio (那里花园), which also houses the excellent cocktail bar Apothecary (酒术, Jiǔ Shù; Map p310; ☑5208 6040; www.apothecarychina.com; 3rd fl Nali Patio, 81 Sanlitunbei Lu, 三里屯北路81号那里花园3层; cocktails from ¥65; ⊙6pm-late; ☎; ⑤Tuanjiehu). For DJs and dancefloors, head to nearby Workers Stadium, where two nightclubs, Vics (威克斯, Wēikèsī; Map p310; ☑5293 0333; Workers Stadium, North Gate, Gongrentiyuchang Beilu, 工人体育场北路，工人体育场北门; entry Sun-Thu ¥50, Fri & Sat ¥100; ⊙8.30pm-5am; ⑤Dongsi Shitiao) and Mix (克斯, Mǐkèsī; Map p310; ☑6530 2889; Workers Stadium, North Gate, Gongrentiyuchang Beilu, 工人体育场北路，工人体育场北门; entry Sun-Thu ¥30, Fri & Sat ¥50; ⊙8pm-6am; ⑤Dongsi Shitiao), vie for the attention of late-night revellers.

no menu. Instead, you pay ¥150 (drinks are extra), and enjoy whatever inspires the chef that day. He rarely disappoints.

🍷 Drinking & Nightlife

Sānlǐtún is the best area for a wild night out, while the lakes at Hòuhǎi (p314) are lined with fun, but noisy, neon-lit bars. For something more chilled, try some of the following, which are tucked away down Běijīng's *hútòng*.

★ Great Leap Brewing   BAR, BREWERY

(大跃啤酒, Dàyuè Píjiǔ; Map p310; www.great-leapbrewing.com; 6 Doujiao Hutong, 豆角胡同6号; beer per pint ¥25-50; ⊙2pm-midnight; ⑤Shichahai) Běijīng's original microbrewery, this refreshingly simple courtyard bar, run by American beer enthusiast Carl Setzer, is housed in a hard-to-find, but beautifully renovated, 100-year-old Qing-dynasty courtyard and serves up a wonderful selection of unique ales made largely from locally sourced ingredients. Sip on familiar favourites such as pale ales and porters or choose from China-inspired tipples like Honey Ma, a brew made with lip-tingling Sìchuān peppercorns.

If   BAR

(如果酒吧, Rúguǒ Jiǔbā; Map p310; 67 Beiluogu Xiang, 北锣鼓巷67号; beers from ¥20; ⊙1pm-2am; ⑤Guloudajie) The first bar to open on Beiluogu Xiang, quirky If (or Siif, as some people call it because of its sign out front, which incorporates the Spanish and the English for the word 'if') is housed on three small levels fitted with strange-shaped furniture, cheese-like wall panelling punctured with holes, and floors with rather disconcerting glass sections that allow you to view the level below.

El Nido   BAR

(号酒吧, Wǔshíjiǔ Hào Jiǔbā; Map p310; 59 Fangjia Hutong, 方家胡同59号; beers from ¥10; ⊙6pm-late; ⑤Andingmen) Friendly pint-sized bar, with more than 100 types of imported beer. There's no drinks menu; just dive into the fridge and pick out whichever bottles take your fancy. Prices for the foreign beers start at ¥30, while Harbin beer costs just ¥10 a bottle. There's also some imported liquor, including a number of different types of absinthe.

Mao Mao Chong Bar   BAR

(毛毛虫, Máo Máo Chóng; Map p310; 12 Banchang Hutong, 板厂胡同12号; beers from ¥35, cocktails ¥40-50; ⊙7pm-midnight, closed Mon & Tue; ⑤Nanluoguxiang) This small but lively expat favourite has a rustic interior, good-value cocktails and a no-smoking policy. Its pizzas (¥40 to ¥65) also get rave reviews.

Mado   BAR

(麻朵, Má Duǒ; Map p310; 60 Baochao Hutong, 宝抄胡同60号; beers from ¥15; ⊙summer 2pm-2am, winter 7pm-2am; ⑤Shicahai or Guloudajie) Friendly, no-frills bar with good-priced drinks and a large roof terrace.

Irresistible Cafe   CAFE

(诱惑咖啡厅, Yòu Huò Kāfēitīng; Map p310; 14 Mao'er Hutong, 帽儿胡同14号; ⊙11am-midnight, closed Mon & Tue; ☎) Large courtyard. Czech beers. Good, healthy food.

Cafe Confucius CAFE

(秀冠咖啡, Xiù Guàn Kāfēi; Map p310; 25 Guozijian Jie, 国子监街25号; ☉8.30am-8.30pm; 🛜) Friendly, Buddhist-themed cafe with good coffee and roadside seating.

☆ Entertainment

Peking Opera

Húguǎng Guild Hall PEKING OPERA

(湖广会馆, Húguǎng Huìguǎn; ☎6351 8284; 3 Hufang Lu, 虎坊桥路3号; tickets ¥180-680, opera museum ¥10; ☉performances 8pm, opera museum 9am-5pm; ⑤Caishikou) The most historic and atmospheric place in town for a night of Peking opera. The interior is magnificent, coloured in red, green and gold, and decked out with tables and a stone floor, while balconies surround the canopied stage. Opposite the theatre there's a very small opera museum displaying operatic scores, old catalogues and other paraphernalia.

Acrobatics

Tiānqiáo Acrobatics Theatre ACROBATICS

(天桥杂技剧场, Tiānqiáo Zájì Jùchǎng; ☎6303 7449; 95 Tianqiao Shichang Lu Jie, 天桥市场街 95号; tickets ¥180-380; ☉performances 5.30pm & 7.15pm; ⑤Taranting) West of the Temple of Heaven Park, this 100-year-old theatre offers one of Běijīng's best acrobatic displays, a one-hour show performed by the Běijīng Acrobatic Troupe. Less touristy than the other venues, the theatre's small size means you can get very close to the action. The highwire display is awesome. The entrance is down the eastern side of the building.

Live Music

★ Jiāng Hú LIVE MUSIC

(江湖酒吧, Jiāng Hú Jiǔbā; Map p310; 7 Dongmianhua Hutong, 东棉花胡同7号; admission ¥30-50; ☉7pm-2am, closed Mon; ⑤Nanluoguxiang) One of the coolest places to hear Chinese indie and rock bands, Jiāng Hú, run by a trombone-playing, music-loving manager, is housed in a small courtyard and packs in the punters on a good night. Intimate, cool, and a decent spot for a drink in a courtyard, even when no bands are playing. Beers from ¥25.

★ East Shore Jazz Café JAZZ

(东岸, Dōng'àn; Map p310; ☎8403 2131; 2 Shichahai Nanyan, 地安门外大街 什刹海南沿2号楼 2层, 地安门邮局西侧, 2nd fl; beers from ¥30, cocktails from ¥45; ☉3pm-2am; ⑤Shichahai) Cui Jian's saxophonist, whose quartet play here, opened this chilled venue just off Di'anmen Waidajie and next to Qiánhǎi Lake. It's a place to hear the best local jazz bands, with live performances from Wednesdays to Sundays (from 10pm), in a laid-back, comfortable atmosphere. There's a small roof terrace open in summer with a nice view of the lake. No cover charge.

🔒 Shopping

Cháoyáng district has some of the swankiest malls in town, many of which can be found in the eye-catching, ultra-modern shopping zone known as **Sānlǐtún Village** (Map p310; 19 Sanlitun Lu, 三里屯路19号; ☉10am-10pm; ⑤Tuanjiehu). Cháoyáng is also home to two of the city's most popular (and crowded) multi-floor clothing-and-souvenir markets, the **Silk Market** (秀水市场, Xiùshuǐ Shìchǎng; Map p315; 14 Dongdaqiao Lu, 东大桥路14号; ☉9.30am-9pm; ⑤Yong'anli) and **Sānlǐtún Yashow Clothing Market** (三里屯雅秀服 装市场, Sānlǐtún Yǎxiù Fúzhuāng Shìchǎng; Map p310; 58 Gongrentiyuchang Beilu, 工体北路58号; ☉10am-8.30pm; ⑤Tuanjiehu), both of which will test your bartering skills, and your patience, to the full.

DON'T MISS

PĀNJIĀYUÁN ANTIQUES MARKET

Hands down the best place to shop for *yìshù* (arts), *gōngyì* (crafts) and *gǔwán* (antiques) is **Pānjiāyuán Market** (潘家园古玩市场, Pānjiāyuán Gǔwán Shìchǎng; West of Panjiayuan Qiao, 潘家园桥西侧; ☉8.30am-6pm Mon-Fri, 4.30pm-6pm Sat & Sun; ⑤Panjiayuan). Some stalls open every day, but the market is at its biggest and most lively on weekends, when you can find everything from calligraphy, Cultural Revolution memorabilia and cigarette ad posters, to Buddha heads, ceramics, Qing dynasty-style furniture and Tibetan carpets.

Pānjiāyuán hosts around 3000 dealers and up to 50,000 visitors a day, all scoping for treasures. The market is chaotic and can be difficult if you find crowds or hard bargaining intimidating. Make a few rounds to compare prices and weigh it up before forking out for something.

To get there, come out of Exit B at Panjiayuan subway station (Line 10), then walk west for 200 metres.

CAMPING EQUIPMENT

For good-quality camping equipment, try **Sanfo** (三夫户外, Sānfū Hùwài; ☑6201 1333; www.sanfo.com; 3-4 Madian Nancun, 北三环中路马甸南村4之3—4号; ⊗9am-9pm). This location, by the north 3rd ring road, has three outlets side by side, as well as some cheaper camping shops next door. Turn right out of Exit D of Jiandemen subway station (Line 10) and walk south for about 800m, then cross under the 3rd ring road and the camping shops will be on your right.

Locals and out-of-towners haunt **Wangfujing Dajie** (王府井; Map p304; ⑤Wangfujing), a prestigious, partly pedestrianised shopping street with slick shopping malls, such as **Oriental Plaza** (东方广场, Dōngfāng Guǎngchǎng; Map p304; ☑8518 6363; 1 Dongchang'an Jie, 东长安街1号; ⊗10am-10.30pm; ⑤Wangfujing) and **Běijīng apm** (新东安广场; Xīndōng'ān Guǎngchǎng; Map p304; ⊗9am-10pm), as well as plenty of tacky souvenir outlets. You'll also find the well-stocked **Foreign Languages Bookstore** (外文书店, Wàiwén Shūdiàn; Map p304; 235 Wangfujing Dajie, 王府井大街235号; ⊗9.30am-9.30pm; ⑤Wangfujing) here.

The wildly popular *hútòng* **Nanluogu Xiang** (南锣鼓巷; Map p310; ⑤Nanluoguxiang), and the many lanes branching off it, contain an eclectic mix of clothes and gifts, sold in trendy boutique shops. It can be a pleasant place to shop for souvenirs, but avoid summer weekends when the shopping frenzy reaches fever pitch and you can hardly walk down the street for the crowds.

Ruìfúxiáng   SILK
(瑞蚨祥丝绸店, Ruìfúxiáng Sīchóudiàn; Map p304; ☑6303 5313; 5 Dazhalan Jie,大栅栏街5号; ⊗9.30am-8pm; ⑤Qianmen) Housed in a historic building on Dashilar, this is one of the best places in town to browse for silk. There's an incredible selection of Shāndōng silk, brocade and satin-silk. The silk starts at ¥168 a metre, although most of the fabric is more expensive. Ready-made, traditional Chinese clothing is sold on the 2nd floor.

Ruìfúxiáng also has an outlet at **Dianmenwai Dajie** (瑞蚨祥, Ruìfúxiáng; Map p310; 50 Di'anmen Waidajie, 地安门外大街50号; ⊗10am-8.30pm; ⑤Shichahai).

Mǎliándào Tea Market   TEA
(马连道茶城, Mǎliándào Cháchéng; ☑6334 3963; 11 Maliandao Lu, 马连道路11号; ⊗8.30am-6pm; ⑤Běijīng West Railway Station) Mǎliándào is the largest tea market in northern China and home to if not all the tea in China, then an awful lot of it. There are brews from all over the country here, including *pu'er* and oolong, while Maliandao Lu has hundreds of tea shops, where prices for tea and tea sets are lower than in tourist areas.

The market is 1km south of Běijīng West Train Station; walk south out of the subway station, turn left at the main road, then right onto Maliandao Lu and it will be on your right just after the crossroads.

ⓘ Information

EMERGENCY
Ambulance (☑120)
Fire (☑119)
Police (☑110)

INTERNET ACCESS
Internet cafes (网吧; *wǎngbā*) are everywhere (we've marked some on our maps), but signs for them are rarely in English. They are usually open 24/7. Expect to pay ¥3 to ¥5 per hour. Bring your passport with you. Apart from five-star hotels, which charge an extortionate daily rate, most hotels and hostels have free wi-fi, as do most cafes, bars and, increasingly, restaurants too. Most hostels also have a computer or two for internet use (¥10 to ¥20 per hour).

MAPS
English-language maps of Běijīng can be bought across town, including at the airport, train station newspaper kiosks, and the Foreign Languages Bookstore. Note, the scale on most maps is too large to be used to navigate the narrow lanes in Beijing's *hútòng* districts.

MEDICAL SERVICES
Pharmacies (药店; *yàodiàn*) are identified by a green cross and are widespread.
Běijīng Union Hospital (协和医院, Xiéhé Yīyuàn; Map p304; ☑6915 6699, emergency 6915 9180; 53 Dongdan Beidajie, Dōngchéng; ⊗24hr) A recommended hospital, open 24 hours and with a full range of facilities for inpatient and outpatient care, plus a pharmacy. Head for **International Medical Services** (国际医疗部, Guójì Yīliáo Bù; ☑6915 6699), a wing reserved for foreigners which has English-speaking staff and telephone receptionists.
Běijīng United Family Hospital (和睦家医疗, Hémùjiā Yīliáo; ☑4008 919191, 24hr emergency hotline 5927 7120; www.united-familyhospitals.com; 2 Jiangtai Lu, Cháoyáng;

VISAS FOR ONWARD TRAVEL

Mongolia

Many nationals can visit Mongolia visa-free, but if you do need a visa, obtaining one at the Mongolian Embassy in Běijīng is straightforward. Fill in a simple application form, which you can download (www.beijing.mfa.gov.mn) or pick up at the embassy, and hand that in with a passport photo and your passport.

The embassy is open for visa drop-off from 9am to noon, Monday to Friday. Visa pick-up is 4pm to 5pm.

To pay for the visa, you need to take the payment slip the embassy gives you to a specific branch of **Bank of China** (中国银行; Zhōngguó Yínháng; Map p315; 24 Jianguomenwai Dajie; 建国门外大街24号) nearby. Standard visas cost ¥270 (available in five working days) or ¥495 (available in one working day).

Russia

You can only obtain a Russian tourist visa in Běijīng if you have a residence permit for China.

If you're on a Chinese tourist visa, you can, however, get a 10-day Russian transit visa in Běijīng, but you will need to show your train tickets for the entire journey through Russia, and if you intend to stop-off in Mongolia the embassy advises you to apply for your Russia visa in Ulaanbaatar.

If at all possible, apply in your home country. Consular hours are Monday to Friday from 9:30am to noon.

⊘24hr) Can provide alternative medical treatments, along with a comprehensive range of inpatient and outpatient care. There is a critical care unit. Emergency room staffed by expat physicians.

MONEY

Carry Chinese cash with you at all times as credit cards are much less widely accepted than you'd expect. ATMs (取款机; qǔkuǎnjī) taking international cards are in abundance, including at the airport. Foreign currency and travellers cheques can be changed at large branches of most banks, at the airport and in top-end hotels. For international money transfers, branches of **Western Union** (☏800 820 8668; www.westernunion.com) can be found at post offices across town.

Bank of China (中国银行; Zhōngguó Yínháng; Map p304; ☏6513 2214; 19 Dong'anmen Dajie, 东城区东安门大街19号, Dōngchéng District) By the Dōnghuámén Night Market, this is one of dozens of branches around Běijīng with money-changing facilities.

HSBC (汇丰银行; Huìfēng Yínháng; Map p315; ☏6526 0668, nationwide 800 820 8878; www.hsbc.com.cn; 1st fl, Block A, COFCO Plaza, 8 Jianguomennei Dajie, Dōngchéng; ⊘9am-5pm Mon-Fri, 10am-6pm Sat) One of 12 branches in the capital.

POST

Most post offices (邮局; yóujú) are open daily between 9am and 6pm. We've marked some on our Běijīng maps. Letters and parcels marked 'Poste Restante, Běijīng Main Post Office' will arrive at the **International Post Office** (国际邮电局, Guójì Yóudiàn Jú; Map p315; ☏6512 8114; Jianguomen Beidajie, Cháoyáng; ⊘8.30am-6pm).

Outgoing and incoming packages are almost always opened and inspected, so if you're sending a parcel, don't seal the package until it's been looked at.

Express Mail Service (EMS; 快递; kuàidì) is available for registered deliveries to domestic and international destinations from most post offices. Prices are very reasonable.

TOURIST INFORMATION

Hotels often have tourist information desks, but the best travel advice for independent travellers is usually dished out at youth hostels.

Běijīng Tourist Information Centers (北京旅游咨询, Běijīng Lǚyóu Zīxún Fúwù Zhōngxīn; ⊘9am-5pm) have branches across town, including at **Běijīng Train Station** (Map p315; ☏6528 4848; 16 Laoqianju Hutong) and the **Hòuhǎi Lakes** (Map p310; 49 Di'anmenxi Dajie, 地安门西大街49号, Hòuhǎi Lakes). English skills are limited and information is basic, but you can grab free maps. The detailed map of the hútòng surrounding Hòuhǎi Lakes, which is given out at the Hòuhǎi branch, is particularly useful.

VISA EXTENSIONS

The Foreign Affairs Branch of the **Public Security Bureau (PSB)** (北京公安局出入境管理处, Běijīngshì Gōng'ānjú Chūrùjìng Guǎnlǐchù; Map p310; ☏8402 0101, 8401 5292; 2 Andingmen Dongdajie, Dōngchéng; ⊘8.30am-4.30pm Mon-

Sat) handles visa extensions. The visa office is on the 2nd floor. First-time extensions of 30 days are generally issued on any tourist visa, but further extensions are harder to get. Expect to wait up to five days for processing.

ⓘ Getting There & Away

TRAIN
International Tickets

Moscow, Ulaanbaatar and Hā'ěrbīn (Harbin) trains depart from, and arrive at **Běijīng Train Station** (北京站; Běijīng Zhàn; ☎ 5101 9999),

2km east of Tiān'ānmén Sq. **Běijīng West Train Station** (北京西站; Běijīng Xī Zhàn; ☎ 5182 6253) has trains for Hong Kong and Vietnam. Both these train stations are connected to the subway system, as is the airport.

International tickets to Ulaanbaatar and Moscow are sold at the helpful office of the state-owned **CITS** (China International Travel Service; Zhōngguó Guójì Lǚxíngshè; Map p315; ☎ 6512 0507; 9 Jianguomennei Dajie, Běijīng International Hotel, Dōngchéng; ⊙9am–noon & 1.30–5pm Mon-Fri, 9am–noon Sat & Sun), housed round the back of the left-hand side of the lobby

INTERNATIONAL TRAINS DEPARTING BĚIJĪNG

DESTINATION	TRAIN NUMBER	DEPARTURE DAY	DEPARTURE TIME	DURATION
Hanoi***	T5	Thu & Sun	3.57pm	40hr
Moscow (via Ulaanbaatar)	K3	Wed	11.22am****	4 days, 16 hrs (arrives Monday 1.58pm); Ulaanbaatar 27hr
Moscow (via Hā'ěrbīn)	K19	Sat	11pm	5 days (arrives Friday 5.58pm)
Pyongyang	K27 & K28	Mon, Wed, Thu, Sat	5.27pm	26hr
Ulaanbaatar	K23 (year round)*	Tue**	11.22am	27hr
Ulaanbaatar	K23 (summer only extra train)*	Mon or Sat***	11.22am	27hr

*Train 23 passes through Jíníng at around 5pm, Èrlián at 9.50pm and Zamyn-Üüd at 1.30am.

**The K23 changes its departure day each year (depending on whether it's run by China or Mongolia railway). The Chinese train typically departs Běijīng on Tuesday, while the Mongolian train typically departs Běijīng on Saturday. Note that the Chinese and Mongolians switch operating duties in May.

***The K23 summer train is an extra train put on for the summer holiday season (it usually runs from June to September). When operated by Mongolia it usually departs Běijīng on a Monday, when run by China it usually departs Běijīng on Saturday.

****Departure time from Běijīng varies slightly in some years.

*****Departs from Běijīng West Station.

International Train Fares from Běijīng

The costs (in *yuán*) for international destinations from Běijīng:

DESTINATION	HARD SLEEPER (4-BERTH)	SOFT SLEEPER (4-BERTH)	DELUXE (2-BERTH)
Hanoi (河内; Hénèi)	-	2081	-
Moscow (莫斯科; Mòsīkē) – K3	3496	5114	5604
Moscow (莫斯科; Mòsīkē) – K19	3891	-	6044
Pyongyang (平壤; Píngrǎng)	1017	1476	-
Ulaanbaatar (乌兰巴托; Wūlánbātuō)	1222	1723	1883

SELECTED NORTHBOUND DOMESTIC TRAINS DEPARTING BĚIJĪNG

DESTINATION	DEPARTURE TIME	DURATION (HR)	FARE (HARD SEAT/ SLEEPER)
Dàtóng	3 daytime departures (10.55am, 3.38pm & 11.42pm	6½	¥55/105
Èrlián (K23)	11.22am, Sat	10½	¥130 (hard seat only)
Èrlián (K3)	11.22am, Tue & Wed	10½	¥130 (hard seat only)
Hā'ěrbīn (D-class bullet train)	3 daily (10.02am, 1.51pm & 3.15pm)	7½	¥307 (2nd-class seat)
Hā'ěrbīn (G-class bullet train)	1 daily (8am, from Běijīng South)	7	¥540 (2nd-class seat)
Hā'ěrbīn (K-class sleeper)	4 daily (11am, 1.57pm, 8.43pm & 11pm)	16-19	¥153/271
Mǎnzhōulǐ	10.17am, daily	34	¥243/429

of the **Běijīng International Hotel** (北京国际饭店; Běijīng Guójì Fàndiàn), one block north of Běijīng Train Station.

If you want to stop in Dàtóng on the way to Ulaanbaatar, it is possible to buy a Dàtóng–Ulaanbaatar ticket from CITS, then go to the Běijīng train station and buy a separate ticket for Běijīng to Dàtóng. It can be difficult to snag sleeper tickets, but hard-seat tickets can usually be bought. Alternatively, there are frequent bus services to Dàtóng from Liùlǐqiáo Long-distance Bus Station.

If you want to avoid the headache of buying multiple rail tickets, contact experienced travel agent Monkey Business (p40), which has an office in Běijīng's Sānlǐtún district, as well as in Hong Kong. They specialise in Trans-Siberian journeys and can arrange tickets if you plan to make the journey in stages. They can also provide visa support and tours to Mongolia.

For Vietnam, buy tickets at the office of **CRTS** (China Railway Travel Service, 中国铁道旅行社, Zhōngguó Tiědào Lǚxíngshè; ☎5182 6541; 20 Beifengwo Lu, 北蜂窝路20号; ⊙9am-4pm). There's no English sign, but it's opposite the easy-to-spot Tiānyòu Hotel (天佑大夏; Tiānyòu Dàxià). Walk straight out of Exit C1 of Military Museum subway station, take the first right and CRTS will be on your left (10 minutes).

For help with booking a tour to North Korea, Běijīng's leading tour company to the area is **Koryo Tours** (www.koryogroup.com).

Domestic Tickets

Běijīng has three major train stations, but most trains for destinations along the Trans-Mongolian/Manchurian routes leave from Běijīng Train Station (one bullet train to Hā'ěrbīn leaves from Běijīng South Train Station, and a few night-time trains to Dàtóng leave from Běijīng West Train Station).

There are no longer special ticket counters for foreigners, so you'll have to join the masses in the ticket queues at the station; arm yourself with some key Chinese phrases, and plenty of patience.

Now that tickets can be bought online (www.12306.cn; in Chinese), it's almost impossible to buy sleeper tickets on the day of departure, so try to buy your tickets in advance (they can be bought up to 20 days in advance). Hard-seat tickets, and seats on bullet trains, are easier to get, but it's still advisable to buy them in advance.

Youth hostels and hotels usually offer a ticket-buying service, for a commission of around ¥50 per ticket. Alternatively, try the reliable **China DIY Travel** (www.china-diy-travel.com), which, for a US$10 commission, will pre-book tickets for you to pick up at the train station in person.

AIR

Běijīng's Capital Airport has direct air connections to most major cities in the world and every major city in China. Use **www.ctrip.com** or **www.elong.net** to book flights.

BUS

No international buses leave from Běijīng, but you can catch a sleeper bus to the Mongolian border at Èrlián (二连).

Numerous buses (¥180, 12 hours) leave at around the same time (between 4pm and 5pm) from **Mùxīyuán Bus Station** (木樨园汽车站; Mùxīyuán qìchēzhàn; Dahongmen Lu; 大红门路); turn left out of Exit D of Liujiayuan subway station and keep walking straight for about 1km. Just before the road goes under Mùxīyuán Bridge, bear left, then left again down Dahongmen Lu and the bus station will be on your right after 500m.

You can't pre-book tickets, but turning up anytime before 3pm should guarantee you a berth.

From Èrlián Bus Station you can catch a bus (¥50, 1.30pm and 3pm) or a shared jeep or minivan (same price) over the border to Zamyn-Üüd, from where you can catch a train to Ulaanbaatar (5.35pm and, on some days, 9.25pm).

Arriving into Běijīng from the Mongolian border (usually in the early hours of the morning), buses will drop you near, but not in Mùxīyuán Bus Station. From the drop off, it's a 1.5km walk to Liujiayuan subway station; walk down the steps in front of you and turn right along the main highway. The first subway of the day is at 5.45am. If you need to take a taxi, avoid the black cabs that hustle passengers at the bus drop-off (they won't use meters), and hail a genuine blue-and-yellow painted taxi from the main road. At night, using the meter, it should cost around ¥40 to get to the Drum Tower from here.

ℹ Getting Around

Each of Běijīng's three major train stations has its own subway station, but note that for Běijīng Train Station (which Trans-Mongolian and Trans-Siberian trains arrive at) you have to exit the train station to find the separate entrance to the subway (directly in front of you).

TO/FROM THE AIRPORT

The **Airport Express** (机场快轨, jīchǎng kuàiguǐ; Map p310; one way ¥25), also written as ABC (Airport Běijīng City), is quick (30 minutes) and convenient and links Terminals 2 and 3 to Běijīng's subway system at Sanyuanqiao station (Line 10) and Dongzhimen station (Lines 2 and 3). Train times are as follows: Terminal 3 (6.21am to 10.51pm); Terminal 2 (6.35am to 11.10pm); Dongzhimen (6am to 10.30pm).

There are 11 different routes for the **airport shuttle bus** (机场巴士, jīchǎng bāshì; one way ¥15 to ¥24), including those listed here. They all leave from all three terminals and run from around 5am to midnight.

Line 3 To Běijīng Train Station (北京站; Běijīng Zhàn), via Dōngzhímén (东直门), Dōngsì Shítiáo (东四十条) and Cháoyángmén (朝阳门)

Line 7 To Běijīng West Train Station (西站; xīzhàn)

Line 10 To Běijīng South Train Station (南站; nán zhàn)

A taxi should cost ¥80 to ¥100 from the airport to the city centre (including a ¥10 highway toll). Ignore taxi touts who may approach you as you exit customs. Go to the official taxi rank instead. Have the name of your hotel written down in Chinese characters to show the driver. Very few drivers speak any English.

BICYCLE

To get around the city in true Běijīng style, consider renting a **bicycle** (自行车; zìxíngchē). Your youth hostel will probably rent them. Alternatively, **Bike Běijīng** (康多自行车租赁, Kāngduō Zìxíngchē Zūlìn; Map p304; ☑6526 5857; www.bikebeijing.com; 34 Donghuangchenggen Nanjie, 东皇城根南街34号; ⊙9am-6pm; ⑤China Museum of Art) rents good-quality bikes and organises guided bike tours, including ones to the Great Wall. For cheap, secondhand bike hire (per day ¥30), try **Jīnsè Fēilún Bike Shop** (金色飞轮自行车商行; Jīnsè Fēilún Zìxíngchē Shāngháng; Map p310; 35 Gulou Dongdajie; 鼓楼东大街35号; ⊙8am-10pm).

PUBLIC TRANSPORT

Běijīng's **subway** (地铁; dìtiě) is cheap, extensive and easy to use. Tickets were a flat-rate ¥2 at the time of research, but are expected to change to a distance-based price system.

Public **buses** (公交车; gōngjiāochē) are also cheap and extensive, but harder to navigate for non-Chinese speakers as few signs are in English. Tickets are a flat-rate ¥1, but are expected to become distance-based, too.

TAXI

Taxis (出租车; chūzūchē) are everywhere, although finding one can be a problem during rush hour, rainstorms and between 8pm and 10pm – prime time for people heading home after eating out. Flag fall is ¥13, and lasts for 3km. After that it's ¥2 per kilometre. Drivers also add a ¥1 fuel surcharge. Rates increase slightly at night.

Drivers rarely speak any English so it's important to have the name and address of where you

---

CAR HIRE & DRIVERS

Miles Meng (☑137 1786 1403; www.beijingtourvan.blog.sohu.com) Friendly, reliable, English-speaking driver. See his blog for prices.

Mr Sun (孙先生, Sūn Xiānsheng; ☑136 5109 3753) Only speaks Chinese but is reliable and can find other drivers if he's busy. Round trips to the Wall from ¥600.

Hertz (赫兹, Hèzī; Map p315; ☑5739 2000, 800 988 1336; www.hertz.cn; ⊙8am-8pm Mon-Fri, 9am-6pm Sat-Sun) Has an office at Terminal 3 of Běijīng airport. Self-drive hire cars (自驾; zìjià) from ¥230 per day, with ¥10,000 deposit. Car with driver (代驾; dàijià) from ¥660 per day.

want to go written down in Chinese characters. Remember to keep your hotel's business card on you so you can get home at the end of the night.

Most Běijīng taxi drivers are honest and use the meter (打表; *dǎbiǎo*). If they refuse, get out and find another cab. The exception is for long, out-of-town trips to, say, the Great Wall, where prices are agreed (but not paid for!) beforehand.

AROUND BĚIJĪNG

Great Wall of China   长城

China's most famous landmark, and one of the world's superlative manmade sights, the Great Wall snakes its way across northern China for almost 9000km, but nowhere beats Běijīng as a base for mounting your assault. Scattered throughout the municipality are more than a dozen fragmented stretches, from the perfectly chiseled to the charmingly dilapidated. You can get to them by bus, by train, by taxi...even by bicycle. And the adventurous can hike along it for days. The question isn't whether to see the Great Wall; it's how.

History

China's first sovereign emperor, Emperor Qin Shihuang, is credited with the 'original' construction of the Great Wall between 221 and 207 BC. He accomplished this feat by reconstructing and linking the ruins of older walls, which had been built by the vassal states under the Zhou dynasty in the 7th century BC. The result was a magnificent 4800km stretch of wall, which was meant to keep out the marauding nomads in the north (Huns, Turks and Mongols). The effort required hundreds of thousands of workers, many of them political prisoners.

By the collapse of the Qin, the Great Wall had already started to crumble due to years of neglect. Emperor Han Wu-Di once again undertook the task of rebuilding the existing wall, and extending it 480km further west into the Gobi Desert. During this period, the wall served mainly as an elevated highway, along which men and equipment could be transported across mountainous terrain.

The stronger, bricked wall that you see today is largely a product of the Ming dynasty (1368–1644).

Mùtiányù   慕田峪

Mùtiányù (慕田峪; adult/student ¥45/25; ☉7am-6.30pm, winter 7.30am-5.30pm) is a hugely handsome, recently renovated, 3km-stretch of wall, which sees a lot of tourists but is fairly easy to reach. It's also well set up for families. Famed for its Ming-era guard towers and excellent views, the wall here can get crowded, but most souvenir hawking is reserved to the lower levels.

From the ticket office, there are three or four stepped pathways leading up to the wall, plus a **cable car** (缆车; lǎn chē; one way/return ¥60/80, children half price), a **chairlift** (索道; suǒdào; combined ticket with toboggan ¥80) – called a 'ropeway' on the signs here – and a very popular **toboggan ride** (滑道, huádào; one-way ¥60).

The adventurous can continue hiking beyond the renovated sections of Mùtiányù (turn left when you hit the wall and keep going) towards a long and winding stretch of 'wild wall', known as **Jiànkòu** (剪扣), which snakes off to the west for several kilometres. You could camp on the wall out here (although strictly speaking it's not allowed). Take great care hiking here as the wall is crumbling away in places.

🛏 Sleeping & Eating

There's a cluster of village guesthouses, with English signs, about 1km downhill from the Mùtiányù entrance. Expect to pay around ¥100 for a room. For something more comfortable, reserve a room at the lovely **Brickyard Eco Retreat** (瓦厂; Wǎ Chǎng; ☎6162 6506; www.brickyardatmutianyu.com; Běigōu Village, Huáiróu District 怀柔区渤海镇北沟村; r ¥1480-1980, ste ¥3990; ❋ 🛜) 🅿, about 2km away.

ⓘ Getting There & Away

From **Dongzhimen Wai bus stand** (Map p310), bus 867 makes a special detour to Mùtiányù twice every morning (¥16, 2½ hours, 7am and 8.30am, 15 March to 15 November only) and returns from Mùtiányù twice each afternoon (2pm and 4pm). Otherwise, go via Huáiróu: from **Dongzhimen Transport Hub** (Map p310) (Dōngzhímén Shūniǔzhàn) take bus 916快 (the character is 'kuài', and means 'fast') to Huáiróu (¥12, one hour, 6.30am to 7.30pm). Get off at Mingzhu Guangchang (明珠广场) bus stop, then take the first right to find a bunch of minivans waiting to take passengers to Mùtiányù (per person ¥10 to ¥20, 30 minutes). Note, after around 1pm, you'll probably have to charter your own minivan (¥60 one-way). The last 916快 back to Běijīng leaves Huáiróu at around 7pm.

In a taxi, a return day trip from Běijīng costs around ¥600 to ¥700.

Gǔběikǒu 古北口

The historic, far-flung village of Gǔběikǒu was once an important, heavily guarded gateway into Běijīng from northeast China. The village, split into two sections by a ridge, with the Great Wall running along it and a small tunnel running through it, contains plenty of old courtyard homes and half-a-dozen small **temples** (¥20 combined ticket). Various stretches of unrestored Wall meet in and around the village in a kind of Great Wall crossroads that gives you lots of rugged hiking options. One short stony stretch of wall dates from the far-off Northern Qi dynasty (AD 550–577). The other stretches are Ming.

There are two main sections of Wall: the **Coiled Dragon** (蟠龙; Pán Lóng; admission ¥25), which runs along the ridge that cuts Gǔběikǒu Village in two and which eventually leads to Jīnshānlǐng Great Wall (a seven-hour hike), and **Crouching Tiger Mountain** (卧虎山; Wò Hǔ Shān), on the other side of the Cháo Hé River (walk through the tunnel, cross the river bridge, and follow the steps you'll soon see on your right). Both make for fabulous hiking, although Crouching Tiger is extraordinarily steep.

🛏 Sleeping & Eating

All the tourist accommodation is in the recently redeveloped southern half of the village (before the Gǔběikǒu Tunnel), now called the **Folk Customs Village** (it's less twee than it sounds). Get off the bus immediately before the tunnel (if you miss the stop, you can walk back through the tunnel from the next stop), and walk through the archway on the right. There are dozens of *nóngjiāyuàn* (农家院; village guesthouses), so there's no need to book anything (unless you want to stay at Great Wall Box House).

Just turn up and look for one you like. They all have English signage, but very little English is spoken. Expect to pay ¥80/120/150 for a single/double/triple occupancy in a simple room with bathroom. All guesthouses also do food (mains ¥20 to ¥40).

★**Great Wall Box House** GUESTHOUSE **$$** (团园客栈; Tuán Yuán Kèzhàn; ☑ 8105 1123; http://en.greatwallbox.com; No 18 Dongguan, Gǔběikǒu Village; 古北口镇东关甲18号; weekday/weekend, incl dinner dm ¥180/200, s ¥200/220, tw ¥500/550) Run by a young, friendly, English-speaking Chinese couple called Joe and Sophie, this wonderful place is housed in a 100-year-old courtyard building that was an abandoned chessboard factory before being lovingly renovated by Joe. Rooms surround a long, well-tended garden-courtyard, and are large (the dorm is enormous), bright and spotlessly clean. Incredibly, a small, over-grown section of the Great Wall runs along one side of the property.

The shared bathroom is modern (with sit-down toilets), there's a small kitchen-dining area, and 12 adorable cats. Joe and Sophie dish out reliable hiking advice and rent mountain bikes (per hour/day ¥10/40). They also do tasty vegetarian meals. Get off the bus just before the Gǔběikǒu Tunnel and, instead of walking through the archway, walk along the lane to the south of the village stream. You'll see the Box House sign after about 500m.

ℹ Getting There & Away

Take bus 980快 from Dongzhimen Transport Hub to its terminus at Mìyún Bus Station (密云汽车站; Mìyún qìchēzhàn; ¥15, 90 minutes, 6am-7pm). The 快 (*kuài*) means fast. Come out of Mìyún bus station, cross the road and turn right to find the bus stop for bus 密25. The 密 (Mì) stands for Mìyún. Then take bus 密25 to Gǔběikǒu (¥9, 70 minutes). The last 密25 back to Mìyún leaves at 5.30pm. The last 980 back to Dongzhimen is at 7pm.

In a taxi, a return day trip from Běijīng costs around ¥1000 to ¥1200.

Understand Your Journey

History of the Railway

Spurred initially by the political whims and expansionist policies of Imperial Russia, the facts of how the Trans-Siberian Railway became a reality are but the prelude to an epic history that spans not only the great expanses of Siberia and the Russian Far East but monumental events of the 20th century including revolution, civil and world wars, the Gulag and the highs and lows of the Soviet Union and modern-day Russia.

Rail historian Christian Wolmar's *To The Edge of The World* (2013) focuses on the development of the Trans-Siberian and BAM lines, and is a pacy, fact-packed read summing up the route's construction and impact.

Birth of Russia's Railways

A latecomer to the Industrial Revolution, Russia had long been dominated by a bloated autocratic state tied to an obsolete, landowning aristocracy. By the mid-19th century, Russia was slipping from the ranks of Europe's great powers. In 1857 Tsar Alexander II issued a railway decree, through which the state determined to reinvigorate the economy's pre-industrial infrastructure with modern railway routes.

The new railroads connected the central industrial region to the raw materials of the Ural Mountains and the agricultural products of the Black Earth region. Moscow became the hub of the national rail system, serving as the terminus of nine different lines. This spurt of construction was mostly confined to European Russia, but fear of British encroachment from the Indian subcontinent prompted the construction of a trans-Caspian line, which penetrated deep into Central Asia in the 1880s. Much to the chagrin of Siberian nationalists, some of whom believed that forces in the capital were even deliberately trying to hinder their region's development, Siberia remained a distant, exotic land whose potential was not fully realised.

The Lure of the East

In the 1840s, a geological expedition discovered that the Chinese had left the Amur River region unsettled and unfortified. Shortly thereafter, Tsar Nicholas I appointed the ambitious and able Nikolay Muravyov as the governor-general of Eastern Siberia. Unlike his predecessors, Muravyov was not another corrupt official, but a strong advocate of developing the Siberian Far East. With the tsar's approval, he collected some Cossacks

TIMELINE	Early 1580s	1601	1619
	Yermak Timofeevich and his Cossack brigands capture Isker, the capital of the Turkic khanate Sibir, beginning Russia's expansion into Siberia.	A customs house is erected at Verkhoturye in the Ural Mountains, and this town becomes the only legal entry and exit point for those crossing the Ural Mountains to and from Siberia.	The Northern Sea Route along Siberia's north coast is closed completely to hinder the British and Dutch, whose search for a new sea route to Asia rouses territorial concerns.

and cruised the Amur, establishing towns for Russia and provoking fights with China. Preoccupied with foreign encroachment along the eastern seaboard, China was in no mood for hassles over Siberian forests. Without bloodshed, Muravyov was thus able to redraw the border with China along the Amur River in the north and the Ussuri River in the east in exchange for some cash and a promise of mutual security. At the tsar's request, Muravyov henceforth attached the sobriquet 'Amursky' to his name.

Muravyov-Amursky continued to pursue his vision of Siberian colonisation, becoming a leading advocate of a railway that would connect European Russia to the Far East. He attracted a long line of suitors from Russia, England and the USA, offering their own proposals for a railroad to the Pacific. Nothing came of the proposals, however, until the late 19th century when centralism, the prestige of territorial possessions and a nationalist spirit that infused the Age of the Industrial Empire became cornerstones of the new tsar Alexander III's policies.

In March 1891 the tsar officially proclaimed the building of a Trans-Siberian Railway, from the Ural Mountains to the Pacific, and dispatched his son and heir apparent, Nicholas, to lay the first stone at Vladivostok.

The Russian word for station (*vokzal*) comes from London's Vauxhall – either the station itself, which Russia's railway planners visited in the 19th century, or the area's pleasure gardens. The same name was given to gardens created near the tsar's new railway to Tsarskoe Selo.

Witte's State Within a State

The task of building the Trans-Siberian Railway fell to one of Imperial Russia's most industrious and talented statesmen, Sergei Witte (1849–1915). Son of a colonial bureaucrat in the Caucasus and a graduate in mathematics, Witte had risen from lowly ticket-seller in Odesa's Southwest Railway Company to stationmaster and then company director. His power grew so strong that even the foreign minister of the day remarked that Witte had built his own 'state within a state'.

Witte's only problem was finding the cash for his 'state'. He implemented a host of financial policies and did some sharp manoeuvring, including issuing bonds, raising taxes and taking out foreign loans. Finally, he triggered a wave of inflation by resorting to the printing presses to produce extra roubles to cover the soaring costs. 'Better to lose money than prestige', he explained to the concurring tsar.

The Trans-Siberian Railway also provided Witte with the opportunity to play diplomat, when he proposed to build a 560km shortcut across Manchuria, rather than follow the northern bend in the Amur to Vladivostok. Already besieged with foreigners, the Chinese emperor rejected the proposal.

A determined Witte changed tactics. He bought the influence of senior Chinese statesmen, offered a generous loan to the close-to-bankrupt Chinese government and repackaged his proposal to look like a Chinese-Russian joint venture. The result was an 80-year lease agreement over a

1628–39	1649–51	1689	1730
Russian pioneers reach the Lena River in 1628, establish the fort of Yakutsk in 1637 and, two years later, sail out of the Ulya River into the Sea of Okhotsk.	Siberian explorer Yerofei Khabarov leads 150 men from Yakutsk towards the Amur River, which he reaches in the winter of 1650, ruthlessly subduing Daur tribes and encroaching on Chinese territory.	Russia and China sign the Treaty of Nerchinsk, defining the Sino-Siberian frontier and halting Russia's expansion east of the Amur. Russia gains right of passage to Běijīng for its traders.	Work begins on a full-scale Siberian Post Road, the only means of travel across Siberia to the Mongolian border. Over the centuries the route is gradually redirected south to Yekaterinburg.

corridor of territory for the railway. The Manchurian diversion led to the formation of the East Chinese Railway Company and the Russo-Chinese Bank, which were both in fact fronts for the Russian Ministry of Finance.

In 1898 Witte negotiated further territorial concessions, allowing Russia to build a Southern Manchurian line to a warm-water outlet at Port Arthur (Dàlián), located on the southern tip of the Liaodong Peninsula, west of the Korean Peninsula. The minister of finance, in effect, became the tsar's chief envoy to the Far East.

Building the Trans-Siberian Railway

Construction on the railway began almost immediately after the tsar's decree was issued in 1891. Beginning at Chelyabinsk, in the southern Ural Mountains, the line would run parallel to the old post road as far as Irkutsk, from where an iron trail would blaze onwards through the untamed Baikal, Amur and Ussuri regions to Vladivostok, the eastern terminus on the Pacific.

This route was selected for the south's warmer weather conditions and more arable lands, which would hopefully encourage new agricultural settlements. But it didn't please local industrialists and merchants, since it bypassed many larger mining colonies and river towns in the north. The line was later altered to accommodate these influential economic lobbies by including Perm, Yekaterinburg and Tyumen.

Building the railroad across a formidable landscape posed ongoing challenges of engineering, supply and labour. The route cut through thick forests, crossed countless rivers, scaled rocky mountains and traversed soggy quagmires. Work brigades were poorly outfitted, using shovels and picks, and horses (and humans) for the hauling.

Workers were recruited, or conscripted, from all over the empire as well as from abroad. Some of these were Siberian prisoners, others labour recruits from China or Italian stonemasons, who worked on the tunnels. They toiled from dawn to dusk in the sweltering heat and freezing cold, and were preyed on by deadly diseases, forest bandits and hungry tigers. The construction work was divided into territorial segments, starting simultaneously from the eastern and western terminus points.

Worth tracking down is the out-of-print *To the Great Ocean* by Harmon Tupper, a well-researched, lively and interesting take on the construction of the Trans-Siberian Railway.

Western Siberian: 1892–96

From Chelyabinsk in the west (which is no longer part of the official Trans-Siberian route), the railway ran through Omsk and on to the Ob River, the site of present-day Novosibirsk. The Western Siberian section was 1440km long and the easiest to build. For the engineers, the main challenge was spanning the many rivers that fed the Ob Basin. The crossings for the Irtysh and Ob Rivers both required the building of bridges that were almost 1km long.

1833–35	1837	1851	1857
Father and son mechanics EA and ME Cherepanov construct Russia's first steam locomotives, based on British technical knowledge. One of the engines is sent to St Petersburg.	On 30 October, Russia's first passenger railway, the 24km Tsarskoe Selo line connecting St Petersburg with Pavlovsk, is opened in order to illustrate the value of railways to the country.	On 1 November the first passenger train on the 649.7km St Petersburg–Moscow railway, Russia's second such transport line, departs on a journey of 21 hours and 45 minutes to Moscow.	Tsar Alexander II issues a railway decree to build a Russian rail network, the same year in which American Perry McDonough Collins proposes an Amur Railroad between Chita and Irkutsk.

Ussuri: 1891–97

Meanwhile, construction was under way in the east on the Ussuri section of the railway. Beginning in Vladivostok, the line ran northward through the Ussuri River valley to Khabarovsk, a distance of about 800km. The forest terrain was more difficult for the engineers. Moreover, after the first tracks had been laid, it was discovered that the Amur rose as much as 10m during the spring, which meant redrawing the route and starting again.

The builders faced severe labour shortages in this remote corner of the Far East. Despite initial misgivings, the construction brigades recruited over 8000 workers from the local Korean population and migrant Chinese labourers, over one-half of the total workforce for this section. They received lower wages than the Russian workers because, the foremen said, their work was inferior (though it may have been because they did not run tabs in the company canteen).

The builders of the Ussuri line introduced convict labour to the railroad, when 600 prisoners destined for incarceration on Sakhalin Island were instead ordered to start digging. Some prisoners escaped from their

RUSSIA'S EARLY RAILS

In 1833, inspired by newfangled steam technology from overseas, EA Cherepanov and his son ME Cherepanov invented Russia's first steam railway locomotive at Nizhny Tagil in the Ural Mountains (there's a model of it in Yekaterinburg, opposite the railway station). The locomotive and first Russian rail line, just 2km long, were built to support the Ural Mountains' mining industry, although the Cherepanovs also sent one of their engines to Tsar Nicholas I in St Petersburg.

It was here in St Petersburg that Russia's first public railway opened in 1836. Built by Austrian engineer Franz Anton von Gerstner and operating with British-built locomotives, it was a 24km line connecting the imperial capital to the tsar's summer residence, Tsarskoe Selo. Nicholas I was so impressed with this new form of transport that plans were quickly made to roll out a rail network across European Russia.

Legend has it that in 1850, when the tsar commanded that a 650km rail line be built between Moscow and St Petersburg, he accidentally drew around his own finger on the ruler as he traced out a straight line between the cities. Engineers, too afraid to point out the error, duly incorporated the kink into the plans, which became a 17km bend near the town of Novgorod.

The truth is somewhat more prosaic. The curve was actually built to circumvent a steep gradient that Russian steam locomotives of the time were not powerful enough to climb. In 2001, the line was closed for 24 hours so that workers could finally straighten it out.

1860	1876	1886–89	Early 1890s
The Treaty of Peking sees China cede to Russia all territory east of the Ussuri and south to the Korean border, including Vladivostok, the newly founded port.	China's first railroad, the Woosung Railway, connects Shànghǎi with Woosung (now Baoshan District). However, the private project, constructed without government approval, is demolished the following year.	Following Tsar Alexander III's approval of the idea of a Trans-Siberian Railway, topographical surveys are taken along part of the proposed route between Tomsk and Sretensk, and around Vladivostok.	Russian playwright Anton Chekhov and American journalist George Kennan travel along the Trakt, the rough road across Siberia and the Far East, inspecting the penal colonies of the region.

SIBERIA & THE EXILES

Siberia's reputation as a 'House of the Dead' for exiles and convicts has its beginnings in the mid-17th century, when a formal system of exile to the region was introduced. However, even before that, political exiles and criminals had been dispatched across the Ural Mountains. Siberia's first exile is often considered to be the Uglich bell, which was publicly flogged and dispatched to Siberia during the 16th-century 'Time of Troubles'.

Often, being exiled was the soft part of the punishment, and beforehand you might be flogged or mutilated, for instance having the septum of your nose ripped out for illegally using snuff. Gradually, though, Siberia itself and performing various degrees of hard labour came to be seen as punishment enough.

Nineteenth-century political reformists like the Decembrists (exiled after an uprising in 1825) or the Petrashevsky Circle (Russia's famous writer Fyodor Dostoevsky was exiled for being a member of this group) were among the best-known waves of exiles. The Decembrists' wives who followed their husbands into exile did much for Siberia's cultural and academic life.

By the time the US author George Kennan travelled to Siberia to write a series of damning articles about the exile system, the main types of exiles were *katorzhniki* (the ones serving hard labour), *poselentsy* (someone in a penal colony), *ssylny* (banished but they were able to return afterwards), and those who went voluntarily to be with their exiled spouse or relative. Later, communist revolutionaries such as Lenin, Stalin and Sverdlov were all exiled in Siberia along different stretches of the Yenisey River.

After a brief respite following the Russian Revolution of 1917, a new system of exile took shape under Stalin: the Gulag camp. This 'archipelago' of brutal forced labour camps strung across the country – but in Siberia in particular – exploded in number during Stalin's purges and drive to industrialise in the 1930s and 1940s, continuing to exist until just after his death in 1953, when the camps were slowly disbanded. Today the best-preserved memorial is the Perm-36 Gulag camp located in the Ural Mountains.

inexperienced handlers and went on a local crime spree. The project as a whole eventually employed nearly 15,000 convicts and exiles, with far better results. Convicts could work time off their sentences, and the living conditions were a small improvement on the tsar's prisons.

Central Siberian: 1893–98

The Central Siberian section covered a distance of 1920km from the Ob River through Krasnoyarsk and on to Irkutsk, west of Lake Baikal. The work of the engineers became more complicated on this leg, because of the mountainous terrain and the steep river valleys. The Yenisey River required a steel bridge nearly 1km in length. The earth – frozen until July and then swampy after the thaw – was less than ideal for digging. Water

1891	1892–96	1893–99	1895
Following a grand tour of Greece, Egypt, India, Indo-China and Japan (where he escaped assassination), Nicholas II lays the first stone in Vladivostok for the Ussuri line to Khabarovsk.	Almost at the same time, construction of the Western Siberian segment from the tea-trading city of Chelyabinsk in the southern Ural Mountains to the Ob River (present-day Novosibirsk) begins.	Mountainous terrain and the steep river valleys of central Siberia prove the chief challenges for the construction of the segment from the Ob River to Lake Baikal, via Krasnoyarsk.	Construction starts on the Trans-Baikal line from Lake Baikal to Sretensk. Two years later torrential flooding washes away over 300km of the track and 15 bridges, wrecking another two irreparably.

from the drained bogs collected in stagnant pools, which bred swarms of bloodthirsty mosquitoes around work sites.

Supply and labour became chronic. Unlike on the plains, there were few settlements to tap for workers (particularly those skilled with stone) or provisions. The builders advertised throughout the empire, offering higher wages and bonuses to entice fresh forces. In August 1898 the first train rolled into the station at Irkutsk.

Trans-Baikal: 1895–1900

The Trans-Baikal section ran from the eastern shore of Lake Baikal past Ulan-Ude and Chita, then on to Sretensk on the Shilka River. For the engineers, this section of 1072km of dense forest was nearly as daunting as the Circumbaikal section was a few years later, and would prove more frustrating. The railroad had to scale the Yablonovy Mountains, rising 5630m above sea level. The rivers were not so wide, but they ran in torrents and cut steep valley walls. The tracks were laid on narrow beds along high mountain ledges. Harsh weather, including summer droughts and heavy rains, exacerbated the difficulties. The great flood of 1897 washed away over 300km of laid track and 15 completed bridges.

East Chinese: 1897–1901

In 1894 Russia secured an agreement from the weakened Chinese that allowed for a Manchurian section of the Trans-Siberian Railway. From Chita, the 1440km-long East Chinese Railway turned southeast, crossing the Argun River and rolling through Hā'ěrbīn (Harbin) to Vladivostok. It sliced over 600km off the journey and, after a one-sided negotiation, the Russian wide gauge was laid across the terrain of flat steppe lands, broad mountain passes and fertile river valleys.

In 1898–1901 the East Chinese Railway was extended in a branch line south from Hā'ěrbīn to the ice-free harbour of Port Arthur, which Russia was leasing from China. Sergei Witte vehemently opposed building this branch, saying it would inflame Chinese nationalism. He was right. In 1899 Chinese nationalism mobilised into a rancorous anti-foreigner movement, the self-proclaimed 'Fists of Higher Justice'. Better known as the Boxer Rebellion, the movement quickly spread to Manchuria and the Russian-controlled railway. Stations and depots were set ablaze, 480km of track were torn up and besieged railroad workers took flight. The main East Chinese line was only able to return to service after the Russian military intervened, and in 1901 the entire main line and branch to Port Arthur came into service. Both were later integrated into the fully-fledged Trans-Manchurian Railway used today.

General History Books

A History of Russia (Nicholas Riasanovsky)

A Traveller's History of China (Stephen Haw)

The Modern History of Mongolia (Charles Bawden)

Siberian History Books

Russia's Frozen Frontier (Alan Wood)

A History of the Peoples of Siberia (James Forsyth)

East of the Sun (Benson Bobrick)

HISTORY OF THE RAILWAY BUILDING THE TRANS-SIBERIAN RAILWAY

1896	1898	1900	1901
China grants Russia a concession to build the Chinese Eastern Railway (the Manchurian line) from Chita to Vladivostok via Hā'ěrbīn in Manchuria, avoiding the difficult terrain of Russia's Amur region.	Work begins on the South Manchurian Railway 550km from Hā'ěrbīn to the ice-free, deep-water port at Port Arthur (Lüshun Port, present-day Dàlián) near the tip of the Liaodong Peninsula.	The first Trans-Siberian services go into operation, using the train-ferry Baikal to transport passengers across Lake Baikal. It's later supplemented by the Angara ferry, transporting passengers and freight only.	With ferries proving a less than successful solution to crossing Baikal, the decision is taken to construct the Circumbaikal line along the southwestern shore of the lake.

Circumbaikal: 1901–04

Heading east from Irkutsk, the builders encountered their most formidable obstacle: Lake Baikal. No previous experience prepared the engineers for the frigid lake's steep and rocky cliffs, which dominated the shoreline.

Engineers initially decided that construction of a railroad line around the lake would be impossibly expensive. Instead, the steamship *Baikal,* strong enough to smash through ice and big enough to carry train carriages, was commissioned from Britain. From April 1900, it transported trains and passengers between Port Baikal and Mysovaya (now Babushkin), while more passengers followed on the *Angara* – now moored in Irkutsk. However, the ships proved less than efficient, being prey to severe storms and sometimes impassable ice. This hindrance became a national security threat in 1904 – when Russia needed to transport troops and supplies to the front during the Russo-Japanese War, temporary tracks were actually laid across the ice in an attempt to expedite the military movement. Tragically, the first train to attempt this crossing sank through the cracked ice into Baikal's depths.

The decision was made in 1901 to construct a railway line that would skirt the southern edge of the lake, connecting Port Baikal and Mysovaya. The cliffs around the lake made this the most challenging section of all to build. Tsar Alexander III brought in Armenian and Italian masons to design the portals and arched bridges. The pride of Mother Russia at the time, this section was nicknamed 'the Tsar's Jewelled Buckle'.

In the 1950s the Angara River was dammed, raising the level of Lake Baikal by about 1.5m and submerging the railway line between Irkutsk and Port Baikal. A shortcut bypassing this flooded section was built between Irkutsk and Slyudyanka – today's Trans-Siberian main line. The remaining 94km of the Circumbaikal became a neglected branch line, along which a few weekly minitrains still chug, much to the delight of train buffs.

The Circumbaikal consumed four times as much stone as the entire Trans-Baikal section. Workers chiselled 39 tunnels into the lake's craggy capes and erected over 100 bridges and viaducts.

Amur: 1907–16

The 2080km-long Amur section presented similar engineering, supply and labour challenges. The Amur required some of the longest and most complicated bridges, including a span of almost 2km across the Amur. The builders relied heavily on convict labour, supplemented by army units and Chinese migrants. Building materials, including iron rails, had to be imported from British and North American suppliers.

The Amur was the last section of the Trans-Siberian Railway built, going into operation in 1916. The railway's first travellers transferred into boats at Sretensk for a long river voyage down the Amur to Khabarovsk, where they reboarded. The completion of the East Chinese Railway in 1898 bypassed the Amur, diverting passengers through northern China.

An exquisite miniature version of a Trans-Siberian train, with luxury carriages and church car, was created in 1900 to go inside one of the jewelled eggs made by Fabergé for the tsar; today it's at the Armoury of Moscow's Kremlin.

1904	1905	1906	1907
Port Arthur comes under attack from the Japanese, provoking the Russo-Japanese War. The Trans-Siberian Railway buckles under the strain of transporting troop reinforcements to the Far East.	The Russian fleet is annihilated in the Tsushima Straits in May and Russia signs the Treaty of Portsmouth, turning southern Manchuria over to Japan; Russia keeps the East Chinese Railway.	Japan founds the South Manchurian Railway Company within Japanese-controlled southern Manchuria. The railway runs to Hă'ĕrbīn where it connects to the Chinese Eastern Railway.	To protect Russia's Pacific access and territory in the Far East, Russia decides to construct the Amur line from Sretensk to Khabarovsk, the final portion of the Trans-Siberian Railway.

The Promise of Luxury

At the dawn of the 20th century, Russia was ready to launch its engineering achievement to the world. Prince Mikhail Khilkov, the communication minister, made arrangements with a Belgian company to create 'an ambulant palace of luxury' and had promotional brochures printed up in four languages proclaiming how it would now only 'take 10 days to cover the 5500 miles between Moscow and Vladivostok, or Port Arthur'.

To further press home the Trans-Siberian Railway's advantages, a 'Palace of Russian Asia' pavilion was constructed at the Exposition Universelle in Paris in 1900. Inside the pavilion, visitors were treated to images of Siberia's pristine rugged landscape and exotic native cultures – including, incongruously, stuffed polar bears clinging to papier mâché icebergs. Luxurious, mock 1st-class sleepers offered comfortable and commodious compartments decorated with French Empire and Chinese-style furnishings.

The imitation dining car served caviar, sturgeon and other Russian delicacies, while allowing visitors to admire moving Siberian scenery through the window, as recreated by a complex, multilayered painted panorama. The exhibit also featured a handsome smoking car, a music salon with piano, a well-stocked library, a fully equipped gymnasium and a marble and brass bath.

Trans-Siberian Reality

Travel along the early Trans-Siberian Railway, however, did not live up to its luxurious billing. East of Baikal, the train routinely ran out of food. 'Today we did not eat until 3pm, and then it was vile', wrote one cranky American traveller in 1902. 'There was one wretched little eating room filled with Russians. You may stand around and starve for all they care.'

Nor did the hastily constructed Trans-Siberian succeed in providing a more expeditious route to the Far East. Travellers experienced frequent delays, sometimes lasting days. The Trans-Siberian had the highest accident rate of any line in the empire. Ties splintered, bridges buckled and

> Russian Railways have crafted a virtual Trans-Sib to Vladivostok from Moscow to Vladivostok with a choice of views from different carriages and an audio soundtrack – view it at http://eng.rzd.ru/vtour/index.html

> Before the Trans-Siberian Railway was built, it was quicker to travel from St Petersburg to Vladivostok by crossing the Atlantic, North America and the Pacific than by going overland.

RELIGION ON THE RAILS

The original pre-1917 Trans-Siberian trains included a Russian Orthodox church car, complete with icons, bells and a travelling priest. At stations along the route where a church had yet to be built, the church car was used to hold services for the locals, railway workers and any interested passengers.

Jump forward a century to April 2005, when the Russian Orthodox Church signed an agreement with Russian Railways to cooperate on, among other things, restoring chapels and mobile carriage chapels to the railway transport system.

1908	1914–21	1915	1916
China's last emperor, two-year-old Puyi, ascends the throne. As new railways are financed and built in Chinese territory by foreigners, an anti-Qing dynasty Railway Protection Movement is born.	About 60% of Russia's railway network, 90% of its locomotives and 80% of the country's railway carriages are destroyed during WWI and the civil war.	Having declared its independence from the dying Manchu empire in 1911, Mongolia signs the Treaty of Kyakhta with China and Russia, and is granted limited autonomy.	The completion of the 2.6km Khabarovsk Bridge (the longest Trans-Siberian bridge) over the Amur River allows the opening of the 1920km Amur line, establishing the modern-day Trans-Siberian route.

rails warped. The locomotives chugged along at no more than 25km/h because of the risk of derailment.

One passenger bound for Běijīng scribbled in resignation: 'A traveller in these far eastern lands gradually loses his impatience and finally ceases to care whether his train goes fast or slowly, or does not go at all. Certainly we have been two hours at this station for no apparent reason' – an observation that may still ring true for many contemporary Trans-Siberian travellers.

The 'Track of the Camel'

The completion of the Trans-Siberian Railway and its glamorous unveiling at the Paris Exhibition lured many a curious traveller onto the rails to Siberia. Among Russians it became known as the 'track of the camel', because it wound around and bypassed so many towns and ran through the middle of nowhere. A principal goal of the railway, however, was not to satisfy a craving for luxury among a travelling elite intent on sipping champagne in a spectacular wilderness. It was to facilitate the resettlement of Russian peasants to Siberia.

Restrictions on internal migration had been lifted in the 1800s, but a modest 500,000 people resettled to Siberia between 1860 and 1890. Once the train came on line, this turned into a raging torrent. Between 1891 and 1914, over five million new immigrants sought a better future there. Station halls were packed with hundreds of waiting peasants sleeping on the floor. One could travel for more than 3200km on the Trans-Siberian for less than R20 in 3rd class. These wagons dispensed with any pretension of style or comfort. A 1st-class rider observed: 'The 3rd-class passengers are packed like sardines. Their cars hold nothing save wooden bunks, two tiers thereof, and each has four and sometimes six. One's health would certainly be jeopardised by a passage through them. I notice that our car is constantly guarded. I am not surprised, and do not object in the least.'

It's believed that Russia adopted the wider 5ft gauge track for its railways, as opposed to the 4ft 8.5in track favoured by the rest of Europe and American railways, to stop foreign invaders being able to use standard-width rolling stock.

It's estimated that by the time the Trans-Siberian Railway was completed in 1916 it had cost around R1400 million, over four times its original estimated cost of R300 million.

War & Revolution

Alexander III saw the Trans-Siberian Railway as the means for Russia to become a Far East power. Under his less able successor, Nicholas II, the construction of the railway instead provoked confrontations that exposed the many weaknesses of Imperial Russia.

The Russo-Japanese War

The East Chinese Railway involved Russia in the multilateral dismemberment of the Chinese empire. In the subsequent grab for territorial and commercial concessions in Manchuria, Russia came into direct conflict with imperial Japan. Witte was always inclined towards diplomacy

1918	1918–20	1920	1926
Following the October Revolution, Lenin pulls Russia out of WWI and moves the capital to Moscow. Civil war ensues. Nicholas II and his family are executed in Yekaterinburg.	The Czechoslovak Legion, a volunteer army who fought with Britain, France and Russia in WWI, seizes control of large parts of the Trans-Siberian Railway.	Admiral Kolchak, leading the counter-revolutionary White Army, is defeated by the Red Army at Omsk. He retreats to Irkutsk where he's executed. The civil war ends two years later.	US correspondent Junius B Wood reports that the railway is falling apart and rarely punctual. In the dining car he finds 'pre-cooked cauliflower warmed with a sauce of unknown texture'.

in Russia's Far Eastern policy, but Nicholas was poorly advised: 'What Russia really needs,' the minister of interior opined, 'is a small victorious war'.

The tsar's aggressive stance in the Far East provoked Japan to attack Port Arthur in February 1904. The overconfident Nicholas was dazed by the rapid string of defeats. Japanese forces quickly seized the advantage over Russia's outnumbered troops, while the reinforcements remained stalled at Lake Baikal. The single-track, light-rail Trans-Siberian was simply inadequate. The tsar dispatched his prized Baltic fleet. In May 1905 the war concluded when – upon reaching the Tsushima Straits – the fleet was annihilated in just one afternoon.

Nicholas summoned Witte to salvage Russia's dignity in the peace negotiations. Under the Treaty of Portsmouth, Russia vacated southern Manchuria, but managed to hold on to the main East Chinese Railway line. Almost all of the branch line south to Port Arthur fell to the Japanese and was upgraded into the so-called South Manchurian Railway.

The 1905 Revolution

Russia's woeful performance in war unleashed a wave of anti-tsarist protest at home that culminated in the 1905 Revolution. Railroad workers were quick to join the protest movement, with 27 different lines experiencing strikes in the first two months of 1905. In April they coordinated their efforts by forming an All-Russia Union of Railroad Workers. At first they demanded economic concessions, such as higher wages and shorter hours, but soon their demands became more political, such as the rights to organise and strike.

The government attempted to impose martial law over the railway system, and striking rail workers sparked a nationwide general strike.

The Bolshevik Revolution

Radical railroad workers also played a crucial role in the Bolshevik Revolution of 1917. Exhausted by its involvement in WWI, the tsarist regime fell to street demonstrators in February 1917. Nicholas' abdication created a power vacuum in the capital. The liberal provisional government was hesitant in dealing with the war issue, which swung public sentiment towards the more radical political parties.

In an attempt to restore order, General Kornilov ordered his troops at the front to march on St Petersburg, with the intention of declaring martial law. Radicals and liberals alike took cover. But Kornilov's men never made it. Railroad workers went on strike, refusing to transport them, and the putsch petered out. Within weeks, Vladimir Ilych Lenin and the Bolsheviks staged a palace coup, deposed the provisional government and declared themselves rulers of Russia.

Trains buffs can flick through evocative historic and more contemporary images of past Trans-Siberian locos and carriages at Trains-World Expresses (http://trains-worldexpresses.com).

Published in 1897, *Roughing it in Siberia* by Robert Louis Jefferson is an amusing account of the eccentric English adventurer's journey on the Trans-Siberian as far as Krasnoyarsk and then by road to Minusinsk.

HISTORY OF THE RAILWAY WAR & REVOLUTION

1929	1930s	1931	1934
Electrification of the Trans-Siberian line begins as part of the first of Stalin's five-year plans, designed to centralise the economy, boost heavy industry and make the USSR a superpower.	Slave labour from Siberia's Gulag system is used to start constructing the Baikal-Amur Mainline (BAM), an ambitious project to provide a backup Trans-Siberian Railway.	A turn-of-the-century proposal to connect the Trans-Siberian Railway with the tsarist-built Trans-Caspian Railway is realised with the opening of the Turkestan–Siberian line from Novosibirsk to Lugovoy, in Kazakhstan.	The *Asia Express* plies the South Manchurian Railway between Dàlián and Hsinking, capital of Japanese-controlled Manchuria. Reaching a speed of 134km/h, it's the world's fastest scheduled train of its day.

The Russian Civil War

The Bolsheviks' claim on power was soon challenged. In the spring of 1918, as the war in Europe continued without Russia, a legion of Czech POWs tried to return home to rejoin the fighting. Unable to cross the front line in the west, they headed east. Along the way, they provoked a confrontation with the Bolsheviks. When the White Army, hostile to the Bolsheviks, came to support the Czechs, the Russian Civil War began.

The Czech legion seized control of the western half of the Trans-Siberian Railway; in the meantime, the Japanese, who had landed in Vladivostok, took control of the railway east of Baikal. A separatist Siberian Republic was formed in Omsk, until tsarist naval officer Admiral Kolchak overthrew the Omsk government and was declared supreme ruler of Siberia. Another former tsarist general reigned over the East Chinese Railway in Manchuria. Cossacks menaced the Trans-Baikal and Amur regions. Siberia had returned to the era of warlords.

It took the Bolsheviks more than three years to secure complete control over the Trans-Siberian Railway and to establish Soviet power across Siberia. Kolchak was arrested, tried and shot in Irkutsk.

WWII

In WWII, Nazi Germany's blitzkrieg invasion was an unintended impetus for Siberia's industrial development, when the industrial stock of European Russia was hastily evacuated to safer interior locations. Cities like Yekaterinburg, Tyumen, Novosibirsk, Barnaul (south of the Trans-Siberian) and Krasnoyarsk received an industrial boost, and Lenin's body was removed from its mausoleum in Moscow and freighted to Tyumen for safe-keeping. During the German occupation, the Trans-Siberian Railway served as a lifeline, furnishing the front with reinforcements and equipment.

Development of Siberia

While the Trans-Siberian Railway had brought Russia's peasants flocking to Siberia to share in a better life, it also meant increased demand for materials to feed the railway and helped spur a period of tremendous optimism on the subcontinent. A second track was built alongside the original single line and the light rails were replaced with heavier, more durable rails. Wooden bridges and supports were replaced with iron and steel.

From the late 1920s, the Soviet leader Josef Stalin (1878–1953) abandoned the New Economic Policy (NEP) begun by Lenin – who before his death in 1924 had set about liberalising sectors to bolster a stagnating economy – and put economic control firmly back into state hands with his First Five Year Plan. This was aimed at industrialising Russia's

Robert Service is the author of a biography of Vladimir Ilych Lenin and *A History of Twentieth Century Russia*, both excellent introductions to the dawn and progress of the Soviet era.

Seventeen Moments in Soviet History (http:// soviethistory. macalester.edu) is a well-designed and highly informative website that covers all the major events that occurred during the life of the USSR.

1935	1937	1939	1941
Russia sells the East Chinese Railway in Manchuria to Japan for ¥170 million (around US$48.3 million), the year Mao Zedong is recognised as the head of the Chinese Communist Party.	Russia's railways, including the Trans-Siberian, are revived. The largest plant east of the Ural Mountains for building and repairing locomotives and rolling stock goes into operation in Ulan-Ude.	Japan invades Mongolia from Manchuria in May. With help from the Soviet Union, and after heavy fighting, the Mongols defeat Japan in September – just as WWII starts in Europe.	In June, Hitler invades the Soviet Union in Operation Barbarossa, beginning the 'Great Patriotic War'. During WWII, much Russian industry is transferred to Siberia.

THE RAILROAD OF DEATH

It's impossible to tally the human toll of building railways across Siberia's wilderness, but one section of track in the far north of the region was so perilous that it was known as the Railroad of Death. The 1297km railway between Salekhard and Igarka was planned under Stalin's rule for three reasons: to aid the export of nickel from Norilsk; to connect the ports of Salekhard and Igarka with Russia's railway network; and as work for the thousands of prisoners herded into the Gulag system of forced-labour camps.

Construction started in 1949 but was immediately hampered by terrible weather and permafrost. Poorly treated workers died in droves. Only Stalin's death in 1953 put a halt to the railway's construction, by which time 699km of track had been laid, at a cost of nearly R42 billion. After construction ceased, the elements quickly finished off what was left of the railway. All that remains today is the ghostly presence of abandoned villages, rusting rails and machinery and rotting sleepers amid dense forests.

regions, especially Siberia, but it also foresaw collectivisation of agriculture, the breaking down of what it saw as 'backward' indigenous lifestyles by shifting children of the small nationalities of the north into boarding schools, and resulted in political paranoia and purges.

Stalin's drive for industrialisation was enormously successful, but it was also to a large extent achieved on the backs of prisoners of the Gulag camps, who were worked to death in slave labour camps.

In the 1950s and 1960s, oil and gas discoveries energised Siberia. While these deposits were in the north, they promoted development in the cities along the railway.

Stalin's reform-minded successor, Nikita Khrushchev, denounced his former boss and liberated millions of labour-camp inmates. Meanwhile, incentive-laden offers lured new workers to the region, and the Siberian population became highly skilled. A uniquely planned academic community was created near Novosibirsk. Military industry flourished in secret cities, sheltering well-tended scientists and technicians. By 1970, 13 Siberian cities had populations of 250,000 or more.

During this time, Siberia's native populations were increasingly assimilated into the lifestyle and culture of Soviet Russian society. In 1900 native peoples accounted for more than 15% of Siberia's total population but, by 1970, this number was less than 4%. Simultaneously, Siberia's development was having detrimental effects on the environment.

Anne Apple-baum's Pulitzer Prize–winning *Gulag: A History* is the definitive account of the forced labour camps of Russia's most desolate regions.

For a very personal history of China through the 20th century read *Wild Swans* by Jung Chang. She followed this epic tale in 2005 with her collaborative warts-and-all portrait of Mao Zedong, *Mao: The Unknown Story*, cowritten with Jon Halliday.

Branching Out

The Soviet regime continued to develop overland rail access to the Eurasian continent so that travellers could reach ever more remote corners of

1945	1947–49	1950–52	1956
The USSR declares war against Japan. Soviet troops occupy Manchuria. When Japan surrenders, the Manchurian Railway is placed under Sino-Russian administration.	Construction of the Trans-Mongolian line begins in 1947, with an extension from Ulan-Ude south towards the border town of Naushki. In 1949 the line reaches Mongolia's capital of Ulaanbaatar.	In 1950 the USSR signs a treaty with the People's Republic of China, shifting its support from the Nationalists to Mao's communists. In 1952 China receives Manchuria's East Chinese Railway.	The Gobi Desert is spanned as the Trans-Mongolian Railway connects Moscow with Běijīng via Ulaanbaatar. Due to different gauges, bogies have to be changed at the China–Mongolia border.

the Far East. The construction and operation of branch lines throughout the Far East were entangled in the politics of the region for most of the 20th century.

The Trans-Manchurian

The Trans-Manchurian line connects Běijīng to the Trans-Siberian at Chita, via the Russian-built East Chinese Railway and also the section leading down to Port Arthur. The latter section was later known as the South Manchurian Railway, and had fallen to Japan as spoils of war in 1905. At this time, American railroad baron EH Harriman made several generous bids to buy these routes from their respective operators. He saw a rare opportunity to realise his ambition of building a railroad line that circumnavigated the globe. Harriman's offers, however, were rebuffed.

From 1917 until the early 1920s, revolution and civil war had thrown the Soviet Union into chaos. Gradually, however, the country recovered. Although Russia was good to its promises to renounce its privileges in Manchuria, it baulked at handing over its main-line segment of the East Chinese Railway across northern Manchuria. Instead it negotiated a temporary joint custody of the line, stacked positions with its own people and stalled all attempts by China to get it back.

The Russians had to continuously defend their (partial) claim to the railway line. During the 1920s the Russian managers were arrested by a Manchurian warlord and again by Chiang Kai-shek (leader of the Kuomintang, the Chinese Nationalist Party), both of whom seized control of the railroad. In each case the aggressors were forced to relinquish their prizes and prisoners. In 1932 the Japanese took control of Manchuria, renaming it Manchukuo and installing the last Manchu emperor, Puyi, as a puppet ruler. Under pressure, Russia sold her interest in the main-line segment of the East Chinese Railway to the new rulers in 1935.

This was not the proverbial end of the line, however. According to the secret protocols negotiated at Yalta, Winston Churchill and Franklin D Roosevelt conceded back to Stalin the East Chinese and South Manchurian rail lines as part of the price of Soviet entry into the Pacific War. The lines were given back to China in 1952 as a Soviet goodwill gesture to the new Chinese communist regime.

By the mid-1960s relations between China and Russia had soured and the border was closed, thus stopping the Trans-Manchurian service. The low point was reached in 1969 when armed clashes occurred over Damansky Island in the Ussuri River, part of the border between the two communist neighbours. The so-called Sino-Soviet Split lasted until the early 1980s, and since this time Russian-Chinese relations have warmed considerably, allowing the Trans-Siberian to be reconnected to the Trans-Manchurian, giving us the route you follow today.

Bernardo Bertolucci's The Last Emperor (1987) is a lavish, epic-scale story of Puyi, China's last imperial ruler. The film tells the story through the eyes of Puyi, using flashbacks to his childhood and days heading a Japanese puppet regime.

In 1999 a 2612m combined road and rail bridge over the Amur River replaced the original 18 span, 2568m-long construction – the longest such bridge on the Trans-Siberian Railway.

1961	1961–63	1965	1969
Mongolia is admitted to the UN as an independent country, but the Soviet Union continues to occupy Mongolia with troops and run it as a satellite state.	The Trans-Siberian Railway is used to transport cosmonaut hardware to Baikonur (in present-day Kazakhstan). The first man in space, Yury Gagarin, blasts off in 1961.	Oil begins to flow in Siberia as Prime Minister Alexey Kosygin tries to shift the Soviet economy over to light industry and consumer goods. Leonid Brezhnev's opposition brings economic stagnation.	Political relations between China and Russia deteriorate and armed clashes erupt along the Ussuri River. The Trans-Mongolian and Trans-Manchurian routes into China are suspended.

The Trans-Mongolian

Tracing the route travelled by the ancient tea caravans, from Běijīng through Mongolia to Ulan-Ude, the 2080km Trans-Mongolian line was built piecemeal, a direct result of fluctuations in the relationship between Russia and China.

During the late 19th century, Mongolia was formally part of the Chinese Manchu empire. After centuries of neglect, China's officials became more interested in the region, much to the irritation of the Mongolians. Plans were made to construct a railroad from Běijīng to Örgöö (Ulaanbaatar). Instead, the Chinese empire collapsed in 1911.

Mongolia was very eager to be rid of its Chinese overlord but was too weak to fend for itself. Russia emerged conveniently as a protective patron of Mongolian independence. The Soviet Union consolidated its influence in 'independent' Mongolia and in 1936 a short rail route was announced, linking Mongolia and Soviet Buryatiya, whose peoples shared close ethnic ties. This new line between Ulan-Ude and Naushki was completed in 1940, and in 1949, it was extended to the capital, Ulaanbaatar.

In the early 1950s, relations between the Soviet Union and communist China relaxed somewhat, allowing the Chinese to finally begin work on the long-planned railroad connecting Běijīng with Ulaanbaatar. Although train service began on this line in 1956, the Sino-Soviet Split in the 1960s closed the border. Like the Trans-Manchurian, the Trans-Mongolian line was reopened in the 1980s.

The Baikal-Amur Mainline

The 4234km Baikalo-Amurskaya Magistral (Baikal-Amur Mainline, or BAM) begins west of Irkutsk and passes north of Lake Baikal on its way east to the Pacific coast. The route was first considered as an option for the Trans-Siberian line in the 1880s, but it would not be until the 1930s that work actually started on its construction, beginning at Tayshet.

Although parts of the far-eastern end of the line were built from 1944 (partly using Japanese and German POWs as labour), the project was put on indefinite hold in 1953 after the death of Stalin. Its resumption, amid much fanfare, came in 1974, when Leonid Brezhnev hailed it the 'Hero Project of the Century'. The call went out to the youth of the Soviet Union to rally to the challenge of constructing the BAM.

Even though the project employed 100,000 workers, including 20,000 communist youth league 'volunteers' it was poorly coordinated and badly mismanaged. It had to overcome Siberia's swamps, its seven mountain ranges, its seemingly infinite number of rivers and, in particular, its vast swath of permafrost. Lacking adequate housing and electricity, few workers reenlisted and others simply deserted.

In 2005 China and Russia settled a post-WWII dispute over 2% of their 4300km common border. For the first time, the whole border was legally defined.

One of the most interesting and readable accounts of the BAM railway is *Brezhnev's Folly* by Christopher Ward. The author goes against the grain of most researchers and believes, despite political stagnation, that the Brezhnev era can also be seen as a dynamic period.

1974	1980s	1990	1991
As work resumes on the long-abandoned BAM, the railroad is styled by party general secretary Leonid Brezhnev as a huge Komsomol (communist youth league) project with completion scheduled for 1982.	Following a thaw in international relations between Russia and China, the Trans-Mongolian and Trans-Manchurian lines reopen for business and travellers begin writing about the routes again.	Democracy demonstrations occur in Ulaanbaatar. Soviet troops begin withdrawing, and in the first free, multiparty elections the Mongolian People's Revolutionary Party wins 85% of the vote.	The BAM's second official opening is overshadowed by an attempted coup against USSR president Mikhail Gorbachev, and the demise of the Soviet Union. Boris Yeltsin becomes Russia's president.

The line was officially opened in 1991, when it became possible to travel the whole length from Tayshet to Sovetskaya Gavan on the Pacific coast. However, the BAM's 15.34km Severomuysky tunnel, the longest in Russia, was only completed in 2003. The official cost of the project (US$11 billion) hardly covers the true bill. As Christian Wolmar notes in *To The Edge of the World*, 'It was the most expensive project ever undertaken in the Soviet Union and, probably, anywhere in the world in the 20th century.'

The AYaM (Amuro-Yakutsk Mainline or Amuro-Yakutskaya Magistral) is a branch line that already extends south from Tynda on the BAM to Bamovskaya on the Trans-Siberian line, and will eventually terminate in the north at Yakutsk, capital of the Sakha Republic. At the time of writing, passenger trains went as far as the coal mining town of Neryungri on the AYaM.

The Russian railway system, covering 85,500km of track, is the second largest in the world after the USA's 228,464km of track.

Future Developments

London to New York by train via a tunnel beneath the Bering Strait is an idea almost as old as the Trans-Siberian Railway itself, but now engineers believe it's possible. Today, the cost is reckoned (conservatively) to be US$65 billion for the Russian side and tunnel alone, which would be about 103km, twice the length of the Channel Tunnel linking Britain with continental Europe. Legislators in Russia have given a green light to the project and, in May 2014, the *Guardian* reported that the Chinese are also keen to join the railway building party, envisioning a grand 'China-Russia-Canada-America' line.

In the meantime Russia continues to expand its high-speed services. In time for the FIFA World Cup to be hosted by Russia in 2018, it's planned that high-speed services will be extended from Nizhny Novgorod, where they currently terminate, to Kazan and Yekaterinburg. Efforts are also underway to upgrade the BAM with Vladimir Putin pledging 'a complex modernisation of its infrastructure' in July 2014.

China is also getting serious about a railway that might eventually connect Běijīng with Singapore. Starting from Kunming in southwest China's Yunnan province, the railway will travel south through neighbouring Laos and then into Thailand, extending all the way to Singapore, via Malaysia. However, don't plan your Singapore–London train journey quite yet; 154 bridges and 76 tunnels alone will be required just for the 420km section from the Laos–China border to Laos' capital Vientiane.

1992	2002	2005	2011
A third route from Russia to China is established via a railway from Ürümqi to Kazakhstan, connecting with a line completed in 1960 to Aktogay, between Almaty and Semey.	The electrification of the Trans-Siberian line, started in 1929, is finally completed. Train weights can be doubled to 6000 tonnes on this route covering one-sixth of the globe.	The private *Golden Eagle* luxury train service begins service between Vladivostok and Moscow, making a detour on some services to Ulaanbaatar in Mongolia, complementing the private *Tsar's Gold* service.	The Russian government approves a plan to extend the railway from Yakutsk (yet to be reached by the AYaM line) to the Bering Strait and build a bridge or tunnel on to Alaska.

Siberian & Far East Travellers

The magnetic lure of Siberia, the Russian Far East, Mongolia and China has tempted many an adventurer and hardy traveller to battle their way through the taiga long before the railway made the going a hell of a lot easier. Vivid accounts of these journeys, provided by writers as great as Dostoevsky and Chekov, make for fascinating reading before or during a contemporary Trans-Siberian trip.

Zhang Qian & the Silk Road

Although he travelled only to Siberia's fringes, Chinese explorer Zhang Qian (195–114 BC) was the most influential of the early explorers of northern and Central Asia. He brought back to China the first descriptions of Central Asia, leading to the development of the ancient trading routes that became the Silk Road.

The northern Silk Road through Samarkand would have a considerable impact on Siberia; even prior to Russian colonisation, traders from Bukhara (in modern-day Uzbekistan) provided a trade lifeline between the towns of the khanate of Sibir and the Silk Road. The Bukharans also conducted the religious education of the Tatar khans of Sibir. Once the Russians arrived, the Bukharan trade caravans and their wares were a common sight at Siberian markets and in the Tatar quarters of towns such as Tobolsk.

The Real Siberia: Together With an Account of a Dash Through Manchuria (1902) by John Foster Fraser describes Siberia during its boom years and avoids many of the prejudices of the period.

Yermak's Conquest of Siberia

At the forefront of Russia's concerted expansion into Siberia was the Volga brigand and Cossack Yermak Timofeevich, who was later glorified in a series of religious stories known as the *Siberian Chronicles,* compiled over later centuries. Some historians liked to colour him as a Russian Hernán Cortés, the conquistador of South America.

From 1563, Sibir began raiding what were then Russia's easternmost flanks on the cusp of the Ural Mountains. Funded and given firearms by the Stroganov industrial family, Yermak led his group of 840 Cossacks into the khanate of Sibir. He marched and sailed the rivers into Siberia, probably armed only with the tacit agreement of Ivan the Terrible, taking Tyumen (on the Trans-Siberian line today) as his first major possession. In late 1582 or 1583 (dates are conflicting) Yermak reached an abandoned Isker (the capital of Sibir, buried in the river meadows near today's Tobolsk), triggering what would later become Russia's extraordinary drive across Siberia to the Pacific, culminating in Russians reaching Alaska by the 1730s.

In Xanadu (1989) by William Dalrymple is the best of a bunch of books following in the footsteps of Marco Polo, who travelled from Jerusalem to Shàngdū (about 280km north of Běijīng), better known in the West as Xanadu, the summer residence of Kublai Khaan.

A Fine Place for a Freak

Siberia has long attracted freak travellers. One of the more unusual was the Briton James Holman (1786–1857), who edged across Siberia as blind as a proverbial badger and recorded his journey, writing with mechanical help, in *Travels through Russia, Siberia, Poland, Austria, Saxony,*

Prussia, Hanover, etc. undertaken during the years 1822, 1823, and 1824, while suffering from total blindness, and comprising an account of the author being conducted a state prisoner from the eastern parts of Siberia (1825).

In Irkutsk, Holman was led by the Cockney-born widow of a deceased British adventurer to the tomb of St Innocent and had tincture rubbed into his eyes in an attempt to cure his blindness. While awaiting near-impossible permission to exit Siberia at the Mongolian border, Holman was arrested and expelled as a spy (explaining his moniker 'the Blind Spy').

The American John Ledyard (1751–89), who had been on Captain James Cook's third voyage of the Pacific in the late 1770s (the one that ended with Cook being eaten in Hawaii), aimed to walk across Siberia and sail to North America via Asia. He kept a journal of the trip from 1787, sprinkled with dubious theories about Siberia's native peoples, published in selected form by Jared Sparks in 1828 as *The Life of John Ledyard, the American Traveller*.

On reaching Irkutsk, Ledyard encountered the Third Kamchatka Expedition, led by another crew member of Cook's, Joseph Billings, who took Ledyard under his wing. According to one expedition member, Ledyard repaid the kindness by abusing everyone. Eventually, back in Irkutsk, Russian authorities solved everybody's problem with Ledyard by arresting him on the pretence of being a French spy and deporting him.

> In *Strange Siberia, Along the Trans-Siberian Railway* (1911), Marcus Lorenzo Taft (1850–1936) mentions arriving in Glasgow, located across the Angara River in Irkutsk.

China's First Embassy to Russia

The first full-scale embassy from Manchu China through Mongolia to Russia took place in 1712, when the ambassador of the Qing dynasty, Túlǐshēn (1667–1741), travelled on a roundabout route through Russia to negotiate with the Kalmyks on the Volga. Túlǐshēn records the journey in his *Yìyùlù*, first published in English translation by George Thomas Staunton as *Narrative of the Chinese Embassy to the Khan*

TRAVELLING THE TRAKT

The Sibirsky Trakt, the post road leading across Siberia (really nothing more than a rough track), was the main route across the subcontinent before the advent of today's Trans-Siberian Railway. Siberia had been colonised by its rivers, with short portages between them, but once construction of a post road was stepped up in the 1730s, travellers, explorers and settlers often followed routes between isolated post stations set about 30km to 40km apart and housing a postmaster, his family, and the *yamshchiki*, the drivers you hired along with horses and a *telega* (a rudimentary one-horse cart without suspension).

During the travels of George Kennan, the American who surveyed a proposed telegraph route across Siberia in the 1860s and later wrote *Tent Life in Siberia* (1877), the post road connected Yekaterinburg with the Amur River, petering out on the border to Mongolia almost 5000km later.

Kennan says he used to feel ashamed waking up a driver in the dead of night to be driven across dangerous country for a pittance. Sometimes the drivers were so drunk or tired that they toppled off the carts, and travelling in a *telega* often meant holding on tight with your legs dangling over the sides. Even so Kennan called the transport along the *trakt* 'the most perfectly organised horse express service in the world'.

Travellers could also use the hired horses – usually a *troika* (group of three) and driver for their own vehicles. Anton Chekhov travelled to Sakhalin Island in his own *tarantass* – the most comfortable vehicle because it was fully enclosed and had suspension – and another option was the *kibitka*, which resembled a baby's rocking cradle on wheels and had struts jutting out on each side to prevent a complete capsize. In winter the *kibitka* and *tarantass* were adapted into sleds.

of the Tourgouth Tartars, in the years 1712, 13, 14, and 15, by the Chinese Ambassador, and published by the Emperor's Authority, at Peking (1821).

After crossing the Russia–Mongolia border, Túlǐshēn and his attendants met a messenger sent by the governor of the Selenga district, who was taking an active interest in the (self-proclaimed) 'imperial ambassadors and heavenly messengers of his most excellent majesty, emperor of China'. The governor arranged accompaniment and the embassy was taken in boats on the Selenga River to Lake Baikal, where Túlǐshēn wrote: 'The Baykale Lake is surrounded by mountains; its banks are overgrown with reeds, and upon its surface thick fogs and noxious vapours collect from the vast forests and deserts in the vicinity. It is a great expanse of waters, extending further than the eye can reach, and its waves are like those in the ocean.'

18th- & 19th-Century Travellers

Some of the best travel writing is from the early 18th century, a time when travellers were less susceptible to nationalist prejudices. Standing out among the early crop is the Scottish-born physician John Bell (1691–1780), who travelled with an embassy to Běijīng in 1719. Bell's embassy was typically large, consisting of guards, valets, footmen, interpreters, clerks and even musicians – anything between 60 and 100 people. His recollections, published in 1763 as *Travels from St. Petersburg in Russia, to Diverse Parts of Asia,* are refreshing and interesting.

The retinue received camels on the Mongolian border to complement their horses. Later, once in China itself, Bell described the turreted post houses he saw, set about 2.5 miles apart and within sight of each other. Each post house was guarded by several soldiers, part of a network of stations for running messages across Qing China and which also served to keep highway robbers at bay. After passing the Great Wall, Bell was met by the former Chinese ambassador, Túlǐshēn. Once in Běijīng, the Russian ambassador and Bell were granted an audience with the ageing Emperor Kangxi (1654–1722), who received gifts in the name of Peter the Great – furs, clocks, watches set in diamonds, and mirrors.

In 1890, even though he was ill with tuberculosis, the 30-year-old Russian playwright Anton Chekhov embarked on an 11-week journey across Siberia to Sakhalin Island to witness and later describe prison conditions there in *Sakhalin Island.* Some modern-day editions of this title are published along with an account of his Siberian journey and letters penned on the way, including the ones in which he described Tomsk as 'dull' and his visit to a brothel in Blagoveshchensk.

Early Trans-Siberian Railway Travellers

The advent of the Trans-Siberian Railway generated enormous interest in Siberia and produced a flood of books about rail travel. The best are insightful, the worst are culturally jaundiced or xenophobic. Mrs John Clarence Lee's *Across Siberia Alone: An American Woman's Adventures* (1913) is both, but interesting for a take on the Trans-Manchurian.

The New York politician and engineer Lindon Bates Jr (1883–1915) had the misfortune to perish in 1915 on the *Lusitania,* a British passenger ship, but his *The Russian Road to China* (1910) remains a nice blend of history, railway description and travel with occasional literary glimpses of life on the train ('Darkness may be ahead, behind, and beside, but within there is light – enjoy it!').

In the 1896 title *The New Siberia* (partly about the penal colonies), Harry de Windt (1856–1933), a rail and road traveller, journeyed much of the way on a *telega* (an open cart without any suspension). De Windt reckoned he could hardly keep a cigarette between his teeth because of the jolting, adding that he had blisters from trying to hold on.

Frostbitten and broken by a mock execution in St Petersburg, Fyodor Dostoevsky (1821–81) shuffled across Siberia in shackles in the mid-19th century, pausing in Tobolsk and Omsk, and reworked his hardships into the novel *The House of the Dead* (1862).

In *A Ribbon of Iron,* Annette Meakin, the first Englishwoman to circumnavigate the globe by rail in 1900, recounts her generally favourable impression of the early Trans-Siberian services.

SIBERIAN & FAR EAST TRAVELLERS 18TH- & 19TH-CENTURY TRAVELLERS

20th- & 21st-Century Travellers

In late 1973 Paul Theroux boarded the Trans-Siberian for the first time on the final leg of his global train odyssey for *The Great Railway Bazaar* (1975). The train was delayed and he ended up spending Christmas on it 'miserable and homesick'. He would tackle the route again in the late 1980s as a prelude to covering China's rail network in *Riding the Iron Rooster* (1988) and, once again, found it wanting: 'The experience of the Trans-Siberian is both monotony and monkish beauty'. It clearly didn't put him off as a third Trans-Siberian trip appears in *Ghost Train to the Eastern Star* (2008), by which time Theroux had graduated to travelling in soft class.

Enjoying himself much more was Eric Newby, whose classic *The Big Red Train Ride* (1978) stands out for being hilarious and a vivid snapshot of the Soviet era when minders dogged a traveller's every step and where disembarking at many Siberian locations was banned (even the train during this era started and terminated its journey in Nakhodka rather than Vladivostok).

Opting instead for the Baikal-Amur Mainline (BAM), Irish octogenarian Dervla Murphy penned two books on her travels around Siberia in the early 21st century (*Through Siberia by Accident* and *Silverland*). *Platskart* (3rd class) was the only way to roll for the famously frugal 'Irish babushka', as she dubbed herself. Travelling alone and speaking not a

Journey Into the Mind's Eye by Lesley Blanch is a semi-autobiographical tale about a romantic obsession with Russia and the Trans-Siberian Railway, which the author eventually travels along in the 1960s.

IAN FRAZIER – IN THE FOOTSTEPS OF KENNAN

Published in 2010, Ian Frazier's *Travels in Siberia* almost immediately took its place among the best travel books on Siberia. The book recounts the author's travels during several visits to Russia.

What does Siberia mean for you personally? I'd done a book about my family, who come from Norwalk in Ohio, and the most famous man in that town was the traveller George Kennan. In 1866 Kennan travelled to Siberia and wrote *Tent Life in Siberia,* and later he returned and wrote about the prisons. When *Siberia and the Exile System* appeared in the 1890s everybody read it – people like Tolstoy and Chekhov. The personal connection is that when Kennan went to Siberia the first time he wrote letters back to the local newspaper, which was edited by my great-great-great grandfather. So an ancestor was Kennan's first publisher. I wanted to retrace George Kennan's route as much as I could.

What was it like travelling through the contemporary Siberian landscape? The landscape was overwhelmingly big, and quite monotonous. There's a wonderful phrase from the French traveller Marquis de Custine, who I think wrote the best book on Russia by a foreigner [*Empire of the Czar: A Journey through Eternal Russia*]. He said monotony is the divinity of Russia – it's really true. I love the American West 'big sky country'. Well this is 'bigger sky country', scenery beyond conception.

Much of the time you travelled by road, with Russians as guides. How do you find travelling with guides? Oh, it's awful. If you read de Custine's *Empire of the Czar* you see that somebody was sent with him. He had the same vexed relationship as I did. You feel manipulated by them, condescended to, pushed around, and later I realised I was wounding my guides in the same way with my arrogance and my will. It's a clash of wills.

What's your experience of the Trans-Siberian? I haven't had good experience of the Trans-Siberian. I was in a railway car with no windows and sat in our vehicle [inside a vehicle transport carriage between Chernyshevsk and Magdagachi on the Moscow to Vladivostok line]. It was a passenger railway car with all the seats taken out – dim, there were little cracks at the tops where the windows used to be, and at night it was totally dark. Still, it was pretty. You would go out in the space between the railroad cars and see the landscape.

BOWIE ON THE TRANS-SIBERIAN

Could there have been a more vivid culture shock experience – for both Russians and the Brixton-born musician at its centre – than David Bowie's trip on the Trans-Siberian in 1973? For years rumours of this near mythical event circulated across Russia, including ones that had Bowie and Iggy Pop tearing up the streets of Vladivostok. The truth, as documented in Geoffrey MacCormack's *From Station to Station* (www.genesis-publications. com), a memoir and photo book about life on tour with Bowie, is both less fanciful and way more bizarre.

Apparently, Bowie took the train following the end of his Ziggy Stardust tour in Japan because he was afraid of flying. To get to Russia, Bowie and MacCormack sailed on the Soviet cruise ship the *Felix Dzerzhinsky* to the port of Nakhodka. During the voyage, Bowie thrilled passengers and crew with an impromptu concert including his hit 'Space Oddity'. The henna-haired pop star later charmed the Trans-Siberian *provodnitsas* Danya and Nadya by singing songs for them. 'They sat with big smiles on their faces, sometimes for hours on end, listening to my music, and at the end of each song they would applaud and cheer', Bowie later wrote.

In Khabarovsk the singer was joined on the train by veteran UPI correspondent Robert Muesel (read his fascinating account of the trip on www.5years.com/jtswdb.htm). A week later, by the time Bowie & Co reached Moscow, they were greeted like the Spiders from Mars. 'We were every inch the freakiest show in town', wrote MacCormack. 'Everywhere we went people stared in amazement, but few had the courage to approach us.'

word of Russian, Murphy brought out the best in Siberian people, whose hospitality she describes as nothing short of legendary.

Dedicated to a carbon-friendly, organic lifestyle, ferociously anti-war and an avowed technophobe and critic of today's gadget-obsessed world, Murphy mixes colourful vignettes about her travels with evocative landscape descriptions and riveting historical asides about the BAM and Siberia in general. She also excels at bringing to life the Cossack 'heroes' who conquered and ruled these unforgiving lands centuries ago.

Colin Thubron's *In Siberia* (1999) details the 24,000km journey from the Ural Mountains to Magadan; it captures the bleak majesty of the landscape and the pain of Siberian existence with poetic force.

Russia Today

The controversies surrounding the jailing of Pussy Riot members, the Sochi Winter Olympics, the annexation of Crimea and the shooting down of the Malaysia Airlines flight MH-17 have meant that recently Russia has seldom been far from international headlines. And the face most readily associated with the country is that of Vladimir Putin, who polarises opinion between those who see him as the leader of a party of 'crooks and thieves', and those who hail him as the president of an economically and politically resurgent Russia.

Best on Film

Transsiberian This 2008 Hollywood thriller starring Woody Harrelson and Ben Kingsley includes a cameo by a Lonely Planet guidebook.

The Edge (Kray) Alexey Uchitel's 2010 post–WWII adventure features classic stream trains in the Siberian taiga; Oscar-nominated.

Pussy Riot: A Punk Prayer Directed by Mike Lerner and Maksim Pozdorovkin, this 2013 documentary covers the trial of the Pussy Riot trio.

A Winter Journey Sergei Taramaev and Lubov Lvova directed this 2013 award-winning feature, which has been shunned in Russia because of its gay love theme.

Best in Print

Russia – A Journey with Jonathan Dimbleby A BBC series, this is a revealing snapshot of a multifaceted country by one of the UK's top broadcasters.

The Last Man in Russia Oliver Bullough's spot-on portrait of modern Russia, told through the tumultuous and tragic life of an Orthodox priest.

Lost Cosmonaut and **Strange Telescopes** Daniel Kalder's books explore some of Russia's quirkiest and least visited locations.

Controversial Olympics

The most famous of recent Siberian prisoners – Maria Alyokhina and Nadezhda Tolokonnikova of feminist punk collective Pussy Riot, and the former oligarch Mikhail Khodorkovsky – were among 25,000 people released in an amnesty granted by Putin in December 2013. Shortly after her release, with the Olympics approaching, Tolokonnikova stated that she had been released only because of the approaching Olympic Games, which Putin did not want ruined.

Indeed, as the most expensive Olympics ever with a budget of more than US$51 billion, the sporting event was hyped as Russia's chance to turn around world opinion on the country, often still seen in the harsh light of the Soviet and Yeltsin years of decline. Was it money well spent? Well, Russia did top the medals table and the event was mostly hailed an organisational success.

However, the 2014 Olympics also acted as a lightning rod for disaffected Russians. The LGBT community protested the introduction of a controversial law banning the distribution of 'propaganda of nontraditional sexual relationships' and increased homophobia in the country. Environmentalists were angered by the detrimental effects of construction for the event.

Taking Back Krushchev's Gift

With the Olympics barely over, the focus shifted abruptly to Crimea. This peninsula on the north coast of the Black Sea had been transferred to Ukraine in 1954 by the Supreme Soviet as a symbolic gesture of the country's 300-year union with Russia. However, nearly 60% of its population are ethnic Russians and Russia's Black Sea Fleet had been based at Sevastapol since the 18th century, underlining the peninsula's key strategic value.

With the pro-Russian Ukrainian president Viktor Yanukovych having fled Kyiv for Moscow, Crimea's

Russia-backed, self-proclaimed government organised a 'referendum' on 16 March. The new leaders claimed that 97% 'voted' in favour of Crimea joining Russia; a few days later Moscow rubber-stamped the decision by incorporating the region into the Russian Federation. State Duma representative and Putin supporter Vyacheslav Nikonov justified the annexation by comparing it to the Cuban Missile Crisis in reverse, with Russia forced to defend its interests against an overly aggressive West. Detractors instead compared it to Hitler's move into the Sudetenland in 1938.

Putin's Endgame

At the time of writing, ethnic Russian–dominated areas of southern Ukraine were mired in conflict. International sanctions have been imposed on Russia following the MH-17 disaster, prompting Russia to issue its own sanctions against the West. No wonder many are labelling this the start of a new cold war.

None of this has dented Putin's popularity ratings. A poll conducted in August 2014 by the Levada Center found that the Russian President had an approval rating of 87%, a six-year high and an increase of more than a third since the beginning of 2014. This is against a background where Russia's opposition media is finding it tougher than ever to get its message heard above pro-Kremlin views. Laws have been introduced to regulate the use of public wi-fi hotspots and popular blogs on the internet.

However, there is ample evidence of how damaging the crisis has been to Russia's economy, which has been hit by capital flight (thought to exceed $60 billion in the first three months of 2014), a depressed stockmarket and a devalued rouble. In May, the IMF reported that Russia was in recession, slashing its growth forecast for 2014 for the country to 0.2%.

Asian Overtures

Meanwhile, at the Asian end of Russia's empire, Putin has been buddying up with China, conducting joint military exercises in the East China Sea in May 2014 and angling to boost trade (most notably for gas exports) with its economically powerful neighbour.

Siberians and Russian Far Easterners have had to contend with major floods during the summer months over the last couple of years. But their plight has not been ignored by Moscow; in April 2013, Prime Minister Dmitry Medvedev ordered the government to devise a $16 billion Far East Development Program for Siberia and its environs by 2018, saying it was a top priority for Russia.

POPULATION: **143.8 MILLION**

AREA: **17,098,242 SQ KM**

GDP: **US$2.092 TRILLION**

INFLATION: **7.2% (FORECAST FOR END OF 2014)**

UNEMPLOYMENT: **4.9% (MAY 2014)**

if Russia were 100 people

.80 would be Russian   1 would be Bashkir
4 would be Tatar   1 would be Chuvash
2 would be Ukrainian   12 would be other

belief systems
(% of population)

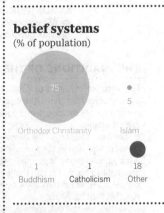

75 Orthodox Christianity
5 Islam
1 Buddhism
1 Catholicism
18 Other

population per sq km

RUSSIA   UK   USA

♦ = 8 people

Russian Culture & Cuisine

Russia's multiethnic society is the result of imperial expansion, forced movements, migration and the mingling of ethnic groups over many thousands of years. Within the Russian Federation, one's 'nationality' refers to one's ethnicity rather than one's passport – and Russia has over 160 nationalities. Despite such enormous ethnic and cultural variation, there is much that Russian citizens have in common.

The Russian People

The Smithsonian National Museum of Natural History in Washington, DC, (www.mnh. si.edu/arctic/ features/croads) provides a virtual exhibition on the native peoples of Siberia and Alaska.

The overwhelming majority of Russia's population – about 80% – have Slavic European–Russian roots. Almost 4% are Tatars who descend from the Mongol armies of Chinggis (Genghis) Khaan, his successors and from earlier Hunnic, Turkic and mostly Finno-Ugric settlers.

The remainder of Russia's population consists of smaller ethnic groups such as Ukrainians (2%), Muslim Bashkirs (1.2%) and Orthodox Christian Chuvash (about 1.15%). In Siberia the largest ethnic groups are the ethnic Mongol Buryats (445,000), who speak a language closely related to Mongolian, and the peoples who speak languages with Turkic roots or Turkic influences: Yakuts or Sakha (444,000), Tuvans (243,000), Khakass (76,000) and Altai (67,000). In addition, there are the so-called small-numbered Peoples of the North – Siberians mostly spread across Siberia's northern regions.

THE TRADITIONS OF THE BANYA

For centuries, travellers to Russia have commented on the particular (in many people's eyes, peculiar) traditions of the *banya* (bathhouse). To this day, Russians make it an important part of their week and you can't say you've really been to Russia unless you've visited a *banya*.

The main element of the *banya* is the *parilka* (steam room). Here, rocks are heated by a furnace, with water poured onto them using a long-handled ladle. A few drops of eucalyptus or pine oils (sometimes even beer) are often added to the water, creating an aroma-filled burst of steam that's released into the room. You'll note that even though people are naked in the *banya,* some wear a *chapka* (felt cap) to protect their hair from the effects of the heat.

As they sweat it out, some bathers grab hold of a *venik* (a tied bundle of birch branches) and beat themselves or each other with it. Though it can be painful, the effect can also be pleasant and cleansing: the birch leaves (sometimes oak or, agonisingly, juniper branches) and their secretions are supposed to help rid the skin of toxins. After the birch-branch thrashing, bathers run outside and, depending on their nerve, plunge into the *basseyn* (ice-cold pool) or take a cooling shower. The whole process is then repeated several times for up to two hours.

Russia's big cities all offer *banya* complexes with Moscow's Sanduny Baths being the most luxurious (and expensive). Grab any chance to try a traditional countryside *banya*: nearly all the guesthouses on Olkhon Island in Lake Baikal have them.

Russian Lifestyle

There is a vast difference in the quality of life of urban and rural Russians. Sochi-style redevelopments are far from the norm, with many areas of Russia seemingly unchanged from the days of the USSR – as witnessed in any of the preserved-in-Soviet-formaldehyde towns along the Baikal-Amur Mainline (BAM).

This said, some common features of contemporary life across Russia stand out, such as the Soviet-era flats, the dacha (country home), education and weekly visits to the *banya* (bathhouse). Cohabitation remains less common than in the West, so when young couples get together, they get married just as often as not.

As the economy has improved so too has the average Russian's lifestyle, with more people than ever before owning a car, a computer and a mobile phone, and taking holidays abroad. The lives of Russian teenagers today couldn't be more different from those of their parents, who just a generation ago had to endure shortages of all kinds of goods on top of the ideology of Soviet communism. It's not uncommon to come across young adults who have only the vaguest, if any, idea of who Lenin or Stalin are.

This has to be balanced against the memories of those who knew the former Soviet leaders all too well and are now suffering as the social safety net that the state once provided has been largely withdrawn.

Indigenous Peoples of Siberia

Russians who ventured across the Ural Mountains before the 16th century returned with colourful reports of an endless forest rich in fur-bearing sable, but also told of bizarre people who didn't stop short of hacking up their own children to feed a guest (an unlikely form of hospitality) or who died each winter because water trickled out of their noses and caused their feet to freeze to the ground.

The rumours were fanciful; the reality, however, was that Orthodox Russians had begun to weave themselves into a complex cultural region and dominate it. This region included the Turkic-speaking Tatars (but also other Turkic-speaking groups, such as the peoples of Altai), Mongol-speaking Buryats, as well as Khanty and Mansi peoples who inhabited the plains and taiga of Western Siberia, spoke a Finno-Ugric language and lived off of hunting, fishing and sometimes reindeer herding.

In the north of Siberia, Orthodox Russians encountered clans of Samoyeds along a vast stretch of tundra and taiga from the Ural Mountains region to the Lena River in Eastern Siberia. So-called Samoyeds included Nenets (today centred on the capital, Salekhard, in Western Siberia), Enets, Nganasans and other tundra peoples whose lifestyle was often based around reindeer herding, hunting and fishing. Small related groups of Selkups (earlier known as Yenisey Ostyaks or Ostyak Samoyeds) lived south in forests around the

RUSSIAN HISTORY

862
The legendary Varangian (Scandinavian) Rurik of Jutland gains control of the village Staraya Ladoga near Novgorod and Rus, the infant version of Russia, is born.

10th–11th Centuries
Oleg of Novgorod shifts the centre of Rus to Kyiv (Kiev) in the early 10th century, where the powerful Kyivan Rus reach their zenith, eventually uniting Kyiv with the Novgorod principality.

1223
Chinggis Khaan's defeat of the Russian princes at the Battle of Kalka River sparks Mongol incursions into Rus territory, followed by Batu Khaan's massive invasion from 1236 to 1240.

1552–56
Ivan IV (aka 'the Terrible' for his fearsome temper) defeats the splinter khanates of Kazan (once Batu's headquarters) and Astrakhan. The Volga region also falls to Russia; Siberia beckons.

Early 1580s–1613
Yermak Timofeevich and his Cossacks cross the Ural Mountains and capture Tyumen and Isker, the capital of the surviving khanate of Sibir based in Western Siberia. The Romanov dynasty begins in 1613.

1660
Nikon, Patriarch of the Orthodox Church, enacts reforms and creates a schism, leading to his being deposed. Many 'Old Believers', who reject the reforms, flee to Siberia and form communities.

Yenisey River, and even further south Russians met upon descendants of the Kets, some of whom even lived on houseboats similar to the sampans of China.

Further east across the north of Siberia were peoples such as the reindeer-herding Chukchi, seafaring Aleuts, reindeer-herding Koryaks, and Koryaks and Itelmeni of Kamchatka who mostly hunted and fished. In the southern regions of the Far East lived over half a dozen ethnic groups of fishing or hunting peoples such as the Nivkhi of Sakhalin Island.

In terms of land area, the most widespread ethnic group in Siberia comprised the Evenki (and Evens, together often called Tungusi), who populated pockets of Western Siberia, a vast heartland of Central Siberia and the north that took in Central Siberia, a large swath of Yakutia and even parts of the Pacific seaboard. In the south, Tungusi populated large portions of the Lake Baikal and Amur River regions, and even the northern fringes of Mongolia and China, where they adopted Mongolian equestrian culture. Most Tungusi, however, were forest people who hunted and fished. Many were reindeer people; they revered bears and practised shamanism like almost all of the Siberian peoples, and they lived in groups of a couple of families, or up to a dozen in summer. Today there are about 35,000 Evenki, mostly living in Russia.

Many of these peoples make up the 'small-numbered people of the North', 40 indigenous groups throughout Russia's taiga and tundra who number less than 50,000. There are another five that are also viewed as indigenous but number over 50,000 – notably, the Yakuts.

In *Arctic Mirrors,* the historian Yuri Slezkine gives a detailed account of relations between European Russians and the 'small-numbered peoples of the North' since colonisation. *The Reindeer People* by Piers Vitebsky is a poetic and informative description of life among reindeer herders of the north.

Peoples of the Borderlands

For the Trans-Siberian traveller, the Lake Baikal and Amur regions are especially interesting as it's here that one enters a historical and contemporary conflux of Russian, Mongolian and Chinese cultures.

While Russia was expanding eastwards, China, ruled by the Manchus of the Qing dynasty, was gradually expanding into present-day Mongolia. As James Forsyth wryly notes in his *A History of the Peoples of Siberia,* when Russia and China encountered each other in the Amur region, the arrogance of the 'Great Lord, Tsar and Grand Duke of All Russia' met with Manchu China's 'son of Heaven' and 'Celestial Emperor of the Middle Kingdom'.

With the Treaty of Kyakhta in 1727, many Khalkh Mongolians – a tribe that makes up about 86% of all Mongolians today – were stranded on the Russian side, became integrated into Buryat culture and had an enormous influence on Buryatiya.

The Amur region was traditionally inhabited by Mongol-speaking Daurs, and further east of the Daurs were the Jurchen, a group related to the Tungusi and the Manchus. Beyond these were various other Manchu-Tungusi peoples, including the predecessors of today's 16,000-strong

Top Siberian Churches

....

Church of the Blood, Yekaterinburg

....

Trinity Monastery, Tyumen

....

St Sofia & Intercession cathedrals, Tobolsk

....

Znamensky Monastery, Irkutsk

CHURCH-GOING RULES

➡ Working churches are open to everyone.

➡ As a visitor you should take care not to disturb any devotions or offend sensibilities.

➡ On entering a church, men bare their heads and women cover theirs.

➡ Shorts on men and miniskirts on women are considered inappropriate.

➡ Hands in pockets or crossed legs or arms may attract frowns.

➡ Photography is usually banned, especially during services; if in doubt, ask permission first.

community of Nanai (also known as Goldi) who live around both the Amur and the Ussuri rivers and across the Amur in Hēilóngjiāng province in China. In China the Amur is known as the Black Dragon River.

Religion

One of the most noticeable phenomena in Russia following the end of the atheist Soviet Union is the resurgence of religion. Since 1997 the Russian Orthodox Church has been legally recognised as the leading faith, but Russia also has anything between six and 20 million Muslims (depending on whether you define this by practice or ethnicity), 250,000 Jews and about 1.5 million Buddhists, as well as various smaller groups that adhere to shamanism.

Russian Orthodox Church

The Orthodox Church flourished until 1653, when it was split by reforms of Patriarch Nikon (1605–81), who insisted on a new translation of the Bible to bring it closer to the Greek original and that the sign of the cross be made with three fingers. This led to a schism, with many of the persecuted Starovery (Old Believers) fleeing. A large number settled in remote pockets of Siberia and Central Asia.

For the most part, Soviet leaders dealt blow after blow to the Church, but today about 90% of Russians identify with the Orthodox Church, even if only about 15% to 20% practise Orthodoxy.

Islam

Muslim history dates back about 1000 years in Russia. The majority of Muslims live in the Caucasus region. Kazan, situated on the Volga River, is the capital of the Tatarstan Republic, where about 48% of the population is Tatar and 43% Russian. Other cities on the middle Volga with large Muslim populations are Ulyanovsk, Samara and Nizhny Novgorod, while significant communities also live in Moscow and St Petersburg. Tyumen, Tobolsk, the Baraba Steppe and Tomsk in Siberia have significant Muslim Tatar populations.

Buddhism

The Kalmyks (from the Republic of Kalmykia north of the Caspian Sea) form the largest group of Russian Buddhists. These are Gelugpa or 'Yellow Hat' Buddhists, as in Tibet. The Gelugpa sect reached eastern Buryatiya via Mongolia in the 18th century, but only in the 19th century did it really take root. Stalin's ideologues and henchmen destroyed hundreds of *datsany* (Buddhist temples) in the 1930s, and executed or exiled thousands of peaceable lamas. At the end of WWII two *datsany* were opened – a new one at Ivolginsk near Ulan-Ude, which houses Russia's largest collection of Buddhist texts, and another at Aginskoe (southeast of Chita). The glorious 1820 Tsugol Datsan is the only other Siberian *datsan* to survive virtually intact.

1689
Russia and China sign the Treaty of Nerchinsk. Russia withdraws from the Amur Basin; it retains the Trans-Baikal and trade caravans receive rights of passage to travel to Běijīng.

1696–1725
Peter I ('the Great') becomes sole tsar after a period co-ruling with his half-brother. Under Peter the Great, St Petersburg is founded and Russia modernises and becomes more European.

1812–14
Napoleon's invasion of Russia (1812) culminates in his ill-fated march on Moscow, when Muscovites burn two-thirds of the capital rather than see it occupied. Russians briefly occupy Paris in 1814.

1904–05
The Russo-Japanese War results in Russia's defeat. Abysmal social and political conditions lead to the revolution of 1905, when Russia nominally becomes a constitutional monarchy, but reform remains patchy.

1914–18
WWI rages. In February 1917 Nicholas II abdicates; in October Bolsheviks seize power. In 1918 Lenin pulls Russia out of WWI and Nicholas II is murdered during Russia's civil war.

1922–53
Stalin rules over an era that brings brutal collectivisation, purges and Gulag camps. Russia industrialises and liberates parts of Europe in WWII, but it establishes a stifling hegemony over Eastern Europe.

THE SOVIET SUN GOD

Soviet authorities liked to depict shamans in propaganda as forces of evil. In practice, shamans were simply a threat to the Soviet ideologists' own influence over the native peoples. But in an interesting turn of events, the ideologists even tried to win hearts and minds by depicting Lenin and Stalin as *über*-shamans who battled evil spirits.

In his book *The Peoples of the Soviet Far East,* Walter Kolarz mentions a 'Nanai' tale in which Lenin is depicted as a kind of sun god who resides far away and spreads light into the darkness and upon the oppressed of the land. With the death of Lenin, evil seems to triumph, but no, along comes an omniscient Stalin, Lenin's great friend, who sees and hears everything (the propagandists were almost right about that): 'Nobody can equal the strength of that hero. He sees everything that goes on on Earth. His ears hear everything people say. His brain knows all that people think.'

Shamanism & Animism

One of the best books about shamanism is *The Shaman's Coat* by Anna Reid. This combines journeys to native communities with histories and accounts of shaman practices in traditional and modern life.

Many cultures, from the Finno-Ugric Mari and Udmurts to the nominally Buddhist Mongol Buryats, retain varying degrees of animism. This is often submerged beneath, or accepted in parallel with, other religions. Animism is a primal belief in the presence of spirits or spiritual qualities in objects of the natural world. Peaks and springs are especially revered and their spirits are thanked with token offerings. This explains (especially in Tuva and Altai) the coins, stone cairns, vodka bottles and abundant prayer ribbons that you'll commonly find around holy trees and mountain passes. Spiritual guidance is through a medium or shaman – a high priest, prophet and doctor in one. Animal skins, trance dances and a special type of drum are typical shamanic tools, though different shamans have different spiritual and medical gifts. Siberian museums exhibit many shamanic outfits.

The Arts

With 19th-century composers such as Modest Mussorgsky (1839–81) and Pyotr Tchaikovsky (1840–93), later greats like Sergei Rachmaninov (1873–1943) and Dmitry Shostakovich (1906–75), and the contemporary soprano star Anna Netrebko (b 1971), Russia has a lot to offer the classical-music buff. Understandably, Moscow and St Petersburg take the lead role in stage, music and theatre in Russia, and galleries like the Tretyakov Gallery or the Pushkin Museum of Fine Arts in Moscow and the Hermitage in St Petersburg are absolute highlights.

Recent Siberia Films

How I Ended this Summer (Kak ya provyol etim letom; 2010)

Sibir. Monamur (2011)

The Edge (Kray; 2010)

Moscow's Rerikh Museum contains works by the artist and spiritualist Nikolai Rerikh (known internationally as Nicholas Roerich). The Tretyakov has a large collection of paintings by the Krasnoyarsk-born painter Vasily Surikov (1848–1916), including details of his *The Conquest of Siberia by Yermak*. The full-scale painting is in the Russian Museum in St Petersburg.

In Siberia itself, Surikov's house in Krasnoyarsk is a splendid inner-city retreat, and there are Rerikh works in the State Art Museum in Novosibirsk. In Irkutsk's Art Gallery are a couple of works by Ilya Repin (1844–1930) and Ivan Shishkin (1832–98). Both are closely tied to the Peredvizhniki (Wanderers) movement, a 19th-century breakaway group that began staging exhibitions at temporary locations and focused on national and Slavic themes in its paintings.

The regional museums across Siberia are excellent places to learn about indigenous arts and crafts.

Near Irkutsk, the Taltsy Museum of Wooden Architecture is supurb for traditional Russian-European wooden designs, including original

17th-century structures from the Ilimsk fort. Further east, just outside Ulan-Ude, the Ethnographic Museum has Old Believer houses and Buryat artefacts. In Listvyanka, check out the small artists colony with a picture gallery *(kartinaya galeriya)* in the side valley at Chapaeva 76 (a sign points to it).

In literature, Valentin Rasputin (b 1937) has written some evocative and thought-provoking works about Siberia and was associated early on with the Village Prose movement, which focused on traditional Russian values. Siberia, with its abundance of villages, was a perfect locus for the movement. Another Siberian of national and international acclaim is Vasily Shukshin (1929–74), who wrote *Stories from a Siberian Village*. Shukshin was a famous Soviet-era director, screenwriter and writer who hailed from the Altai region.

Russian Cuisine

Russia has a great food heritage enriched by influences from the Baltic to the Far East as well as pan-European trends. One of the healthiest culinary highlights of a rail journey through Russia will be the freshwater fish of Lake Baikal, and in Moscow or St Petersburg don't forgo a meal in a good Georgian restaurant. Russians like to eat till late, and they also like to enjoy a crossover of eating, drinking, dancing and entertainment (often karaoke these days) in one session. So while the traditional Slavic kitchen might lack the culinary peaks of, say, French or Italian cooking, a night out in a restaurant in Russia can be a splendid 'universal' experience.

Staples

A typical *zavtrak* (breakfast) will include bliny (pancakes) with savoury or sweet fillings, various types of *kasha* (porridge), and *syrniki* (cottage-cheese fritters), delicious with jam, sugar and the universal Russian condiment, *smetana* (sour cream). Russians excel in dairy products such as *tvorog* (soft curd) and dairy drinks, so make sure you sample these.

Lunch or dinner usually starts with *zakuski* (appetisers) then progresses to soup – often served with piles of bread and a thick dollop of sour cream – such as borsch, made with beetroot and mostly beef; *lapsha* (chicken noodle); *solyanka* (a thick broth with meat, fish and a host of vegetables); *Ukho* (fish soup) and shchi (cabbage soup).

Main dishes often come with a small salad garnish, and side dishes are almost always ordered separately on the menu as *garniry*. Lamb from the steppes of Kalmykia and beef from Altai are excellent. *Pelmeni* (ravioli) has been elevated to an art form in Siberia; it has various fillings and is commonly eaten in a broth or fried in butter.

During summer, outdoor pizza and shashlyk (kebab) stalls pop up all over the place – in Krasnoyarsk you will find an enormous row of shashlyk stands and beer tents along the Yenisey River. Not to be missed are *pirozhki* (pies) with a range of fillings.

In most Russian cities it's common to find restaurants serving set three-course *biznes* lunches from noon to 4pm Monday to Friday; these cost as little as R200 (up to R400 in Moscow and St Petersburg).

RUSSIAN CULTURE & CUISINE RUSSIAN CUISINE

1953–82

Nikita Khrushchev becomes first secretary and condemns Stalin's brutal policies. The years from 1964 under successor Leonid Brezhnev are marked by stagnation. Siberian oil discoveries hide Soviet economic flaws.

1985–91

Mikhail Gorbachev is elected first secretary and initiates *perestroika* (restructuring) and *glasnost* (openness) reforms. A failed coup in August 1991 causes the collapse of the USSR and the rise of Boris Yeltsin.

1990s

Yeltsin uses force in 1993 to crush dissenters in parliament; the decade brings civil freedoms but also powerful oligarchs, crime, poverty, and war in breakaway Chechnya. Yeltsin resigns in 1999.

2000–present

A 'tandem' of Vladimir Putin and Dmitry Medvedev ruling variously as president and prime minister oversee relative re-stabilisation of Russia. Power is re-centralised, but many Russians seek greater civil freedoms.

Russkiy Mir (www.russkiymir.ru) was created by the Russian government in 2007 as an organisation to preserve and promote the Russian language and culture throughout the world.

Sweet-toothed Russians adore *morozhenoe* (ice cream) and gooey *torty* (cream cakes), often decorated in lurid colours. *Pecheniye* (pastries) are eaten at tea time in the traditional English style and are available at any *bulochnaya* (bakery). Locally made chocolate and *konfetki* (sweets) are also excellent and, with their colourful wrappings, make great presents.

Specialities

The following are among the variety of regional food specialities you'll find along the rail routes.

Kasylyk (dried horsemeat sausages) and *zur balish* (meat pies) – both from Tatarstan, where *chek chek* (honey-drenched, macaroni-shaped pieces of fried dough) are also an essential part of celebrations.

Manti (steamed, palm-sized dumplings) – known as *buuz* or *buuzy* in Buryatiya and *pyan-se* (a peppery version) in the Russian Far East.

Oblyoma (dried, salty fish found in the Volga) – most often eaten as a snack food with beer.

Omul (a cousin of salmon and trout) – endemic to Lake Baikal and considered a great delicacy. *Kharius* (grayling) is also delicious.

Vegetarians & Vegans

Russian restaurants are tough on vegetarians, Georgian ones less so. Salmon is widespread for those who eat fish. *Zakuski* include quite a lot of meatless ingredients, such as eggs and mushrooms. Failing that, a Greek salad with feta cheese is fairly widespread in cities. If you're travelling during Lent, many restaurants have special nonmeat menus.

Drinks

Russia produces hundreds of different brands of vodka, including ones that you'll certainly have heard of such as Stolichnaya and Smirnoff. Also look out for Moskovskaya, Flagman and Gzhelka. As well as 'plain' vodka you'll find *klyukovka* (cranberry vodka, one of the most popular kinds), *pertsovka* (pepper vodka), *starka* (vodka flavoured with apple and pear leaves), *limonnaya* (vodka with lemon), and *okhotnichya* (meaning 'hunter's vodka', with about a dozen ingredients, including peppers, juniper berries, ginger and cloves).

The local market leader in beer is Baltika, making 10 brews; No 3, the most common, is a very quaffable lager.

Most wines drunk in Russia are foreign, and although you will find some decent ones, there will be little unique about drinking wine in Russia. The word for 'dry' is *sukhoe*. Russian *konyak* (brandy) from the Caucasus is generally a very pleasant surprise.

Kvas is fermented rye-bread water, and in summer is dispensed on the street from big wheeled tanks. It tastes not unlike ginger beer, and is a wonderfully cool and refreshing drink. *Mors,* a fruit drink made from cranberries and other fruits, is popular in summer.

Russians are world-class tea drinkers, and this partly explains the samovars at the end of every railway carriage. In Russian homes, the traditional brewing method is to make an extremely strong pot, pour small shots of it into glasses and fill the glasses with hot water from the kettle. Putting jam, instead of sugar, in tea is quite common.

Coffee comes in small cups, and unless you buy it at kiosks or stand-up eateries, it's usually quite good. There's been an explosion of Starbucks-style cafes all across Russia's bigger cities – cappuccino, espresso, latte and mocha are now as much a part of the average Russian lexicon as elsewhere.

Other drinks, apart from the ubiquitous canned soft drinks, include *sok* (juice) and *kefir* (yogurt-like sour milk).

In *A Year of Russian Feasts,* Catherine Cheremeteff Jones recounts how Russia's finest dishes have been preserved and passed down through the feast days of the Russian Orthodox Church.

Mongolia Today

Mongolia may be no more than a little fish in the big pond of globalisation, but its importance on the world stage has only just started to grow. Pundits have dubbed the country 'Mingolia', a nod to its enormous mineral wealth. Mongolians are stepping cautiously ahead, wary of the fact that other natural-resource-rich countries have been ruined by corruption and mismanagement. The government has set up checks to ensure transparent accounting of mining revenue, but whether or not the bonanza is spent wisely is something only time will tell.

Best on Film

The Story of the Weeping Camel (2003) Docu-drama that follows a camel herder family in the Gobi.
Mongol (2007) Dramatic depiction of the rise of Chinggis (Genghis) Khaan.
Tracking the White Reindeer (2009) Docu-drama on reindeer herders, available online.

Best in Print

Genghis Khan and the Making of the Modern World (Jack Weatherford; 2005) Groundbreaking book and a bestseller on the Mongol Empire.
When Things Get Dark (Matthew Davis; 2010) Raw examination of life in Tsetserleg from an American teacher.
Hearing Birds Fly (Louisa Waugh; 2003) Recollections of a year spent in remote Bayan-Ölgii by a British teacher.
Dateline Mongolia (Michael Kohn; 2006) Three years in the life of a young reporter in Ulaanbaatar who worked for the local media.
Mörön to Mörön (Tom Doig; 2013) Wacky adventures of two Kiwis making their way across Mongolia on pushbikes.

The Great Leap Forward

The economic growth driver is the US$6.6 billion Oyu Tolgoi copper and gold mine, developed by the Anglo-Australian company Rio Tinto, but 34% owned by the Mongolian government. While the relationship between the shareholders has erupted in periodic disputes, the company did manage to start copper concentrate exports in 2013. At full production (sometime after 2018), the mine is expected to account for one-third of the country's total GDP. The hope is that this single world-class deposit will lift the whole country up by the bootstraps.

China is a ready market for Mongolia's raw materials and the government is rapidly trying to build up its infrastructure to deliver the goods. New rail and road links to China are being built, and in a bid to diversify its markets, Mongolia is also planning a 1000km railway from Ömnögov all the way to Russia (via Choibalsan).

Mongolia's political leaders seem keenly aware of the need to invest their newfound wealth back into the country. A copper smelter, oil refinery and coal washing plants are a few of the planned factories. A new international airport is expected to open in 2016 and the government is also planning to build a new university and IT campus outside of Ulaanbaatar.

Democrats Sweep to Power

Mongolians went to the polls in June 2012 and gave the Democratic Party (DP) a narrow victory over the rival Mongolian People's Party (MPP). A year later President Elbegdorj Tsakhia was re-elected, giving the DP control of all top political positions until 2016.

Calling itself the 'Reform Government', the DP made some surprisingly progressive political decisions soon after taking office.

Ulaanbaatar Mayor Bat-Uul Erdene kicked things off with a new traffic system in the capital (banning cars from driving on certain days based on their licence plate number). Another popular move was a strict ban on smoking in all public areas. A provision in the law forced vendors to stop selling cigarettes if they were located 500m from a school.

The DP announced grand plans to modernise Ulaanbaatar, including the redevelopment of ger areas and the construction of highways. Rural areas are also tapped for development and billions in debt have been raised to pay for it all. The DP is attempting to make these changes at the grassroots level, by putting funds in the hands of local governments to spend money on projects as they see fit.

More controversially, the president put his foot down on corruption, resulting in the jailing of dozens of officials from MIAT employees right up to former president Nambar Enkhbayar. Critics pointed out that few of the convicted felons came from the president's own party, the DP.

The Future

For Mongolia, the challenge lies largely in the task of sustainable nation building. Even as the nation's infrastructure improves, planners face the challenge of protecting the land from overzealous mining companies and real estate developers.

From a cultural point of view, Mongolia has established a new path of fierce nationalism fused with Western influences. Urban youth flash *soyombo* (the national symbol) tattoos, musicians play rock music with Mongolian instruments and rappers write lyrics that praise the eternal blue skies.

Yet life on the ground remains rough for many, with social problems like poverty and alcoholism still prevalent, particularly in Ulaanbaatar's ger districts. Work, housing, education and good healthcare remain elusive for many, while a small segment of the population continues to profit through shady business deals and political connections.

There has been some trickle-down effect and the beginning of a middle class, but the future still depends on the fragile economy, which itself largely hangs on external factors such as the price of minerals and China's continued growth. What seems more certain is that Mongolia's passion for democracy will preserve it as one of the freest countries in the region.

POPULATION: 3 MILLION (2014)

GDP: US$3900 PER CAPITA (2014)

VOTER TURNOUT (2012): **65%**

NUMBER OF LIVESTOCK: **41 MILLION**

INFLATION: **13.7%**

if Mongolia were 100 people

95 would be Mongol (mostly Khalkh)
5 would be Turkic (mostly Kazakh)

belief systems
(% of population)

80
Mahayana Buddhism

5
Islam

5
Christianity

10
Atheism

population per sq km

MONGOLIA   RUSSIA   USA

 ≈ 2 people

Mongolian Culture & Cuisine

Nomadic herders speed over the steppes on motorcycles to herd their flocks while Buddhist monks tap away at iPhones between prayer sessions – these are some of the paradoxes that visitors frequently come across in Mongolia. It's a constant battle here to keep the traditional lifestyle alive amid the advances of modern society. And yet Mongolia is pulling it off, even fusing traditional and modern music, food and spiritual beliefs. This uncanny ability to adapt to changing times has helped usher in the new era of democracy.

The Mongolian People

Mongolians, no matter how long they may have lived in a city, are nomads at heart. The nomadic way of life was born out of necessity, as herders were forced to move their animals over the harsh landscape in search of fresh pasture. This lifestyle has shaped Mongolians' psyche, worldview, philosophy, ethics and relationship with their neighbours.

Livestock, especially horses, play a crucial role in Mongolian culture. It was the horse that allowed ancient tribesman to spread across the steppes and cover great distances as they tended their animals. Later it was the horse that carried Mongol warriors across Asia as they built their empire. An old Mongolian proverb says: 'A man without a horse is like a bird without wings'.

Nomadic peoples are greatly affected by the climate and other natural forces. Because good pastures are a requirement for the survival of the herds (and therefore the people), traditional beliefs eschew mining, construction or other development of the land. Throughout the ages, Mongolians have believed that nature is not something to be tamed or dominated but something that's better left untouched. These traditional beliefs are now giving way to other considerations as politicians and businesspeople seek to develop mines and other infrastructure.

Seasons also shape Mongolian life. Spring in particular is a crucial time. Because the country's rainy season

209–174 BC

Reign of Modun, as *shanyu* of the Huns; the first great steppe empire of Mongolia stretches from Korea to Lake Baikal and south into northern China.

AD 552–744

Succession of two Turkic empires; the greatest ruler is Bilge Khan. Following his death in 734 a monument is erected near Lake Ögii.

744–840

The Uighur empire occupies central Mongolia until expelled by the Kyrgyz tribe; the Uighur move south into western China and control the Silk Road for nearly 1000 years.

1162

Birth of Temujin, the child destined to become Chinggis (Genghis) Khaan, near the Onon River. According to legend, Temujin emerges with a blood clot clutched in his fist.

1206

Chinggis Khaan calls a massive conclave at Kherlen Gol and creates his empire, which he names the Great Mongol Nation.

1368

Yuan dynasty collapses in China but the Mongol government returns to Mongolia refusing to submit to the newly created Ming dynasty. They continue ruling as the 'Northern Yuan'.

1585

Founding of Erdene Zuu, first Buddhist monastery in Mongolia, at the site of the Mongol capital, Karakorum (modern Kharkhorin).

comes towards the end of summer, spring is dry, dusty, windy and un-forgiving. This is the time when the weaker animals die and, it is said, when people die. Despite the severe temperatures, it's during winter that Mongolians feel most comfortable. After a difficult summer filled with chores and moving around the herds, winter is a time to relax inside a ger (yurt) and fatten up against the cold.

Mongolia's vast, open steppes and great distances have made hospital-ity a matter of sheer necessity rather than simply a social obligation. It would be difficult for anyone to travel across this immense, sparsely pop-ulated country without the hospitality that has developed, as each ger is able to serve travellers as a hotel, restaurant, pub and repair shop. As a result, Mongolians are able to travel rapidly over long distances without the weight of provisions.

Life on the steppes is by no means easy or idyllic. Constant work is re-quired to care for the animals, cook food and collect dung and water. It's also a precarious life: a harsh winter can kill millions of head of livestock, as happened in 2009. The government can resupply some herders who lose animals in a severe storm, but many herders have ended up jobless in the sprawling suburbs around Ulaanbaatar.

In the capital, urban Mongolians have developed their own unique blend of Mongolian and Western lifestyles. You'll see young people wear-ing the latest European or American fashions, sporting mohawks, hoop earrings, gangsta garb and iPhones. Materialism is apparent in all the flashy SUVs bounding around the city. But talk to some young locals and you'll soon realise that their hopes and dreams lie not only in the West but also in the future of Mongolia, its success and prosperity and the continuation of its unique culture.

Nearly all nomadic families have a short-wave radio to get national and world news. Many receive satellite TV and certainly everyone reads newspapers when they're available (98% of Mongo-lians are literate).

Religion

Spirituality in Mongolia comes in many forms, with many day-to-day rituals rooted in Mongolia's shamanic past. The ancient animist beliefs of the Siberian and steppe tribes who worshipped the sun, earth and sky are still very much alive, woven intimately into the fabric of modern Mongolia.

CHINGGIS KHAAN

Known to the world as a bloodthirsty conqueror, Chinggis (Genghis) Khaan is remem-bered by Mongolians as the great lawgiver and they proudly refer to him as the 'Man of the Millennium' (a title bestowed on him by the *Washington Post* in 1995). His laws de-rived from practical considerations more than ideology or religion.

After the abduction of his wife Borte, Chinggis Khaan recognised the role of kidnap-ping in perpetuating feuds among clans and outlawed it. Similarly, he perceived religious intolerance as being a source of violence in sedentary society and so decreed religious freedom for everyone and exempted religious scholars and priests from taxes.

To promote trade and communications, Chinggis Khaan built an international network of postal stations that also served as hostels for merchants. He decreased and standard-ised taxes on goods so that they would not be repeatedly taxed. Under these laws the Mongol Empire formed the first intercontinental free-trade zone.

In an era when ambassadors served as hostages to be publicly tortured or killed dur-ing times of hostilities, Chinggis Khaan ordered that every ambassador be considered an envoy of peace. This law marked the beginning of diplomatic immunity and international law. Today, nearly every country accepts and promotes, at least in theory, the ideas and policies behind the 'Great Law of Chinggis Khaan'.

Shamanism

Mongolians have long believed in the spirit world as their shamans described it to them. Their cosmic view of the universe did not differentiate between the worlds of the living and the dead, nor did they consider themselves any greater than other creatures in this or other worlds. Any imbalance between the human and natural worlds could cause calamity.

Shamanism centres on the shaman – called a *bo* if a man or *udgan* if a woman – who has special medical and religious powers. One of a shaman's main functions is to cure any sickness caused by the soul straying, and to accompany the soul of a dead person into the afterlife. Shamans act as intermediaries between the human and spirit worlds, and communicate with spirits during trances, which can last up to six hours.

Sky worship is another integral part of shamanism and you'll see Mongolians leaving blue scarves (representing the sky) on *ovoos* (piles of stones built to honour earth spirits). Sky gods are likewise honoured by flicking droplets of vodka into the air before drinking.

Buddhism

The Mongols had limited contact with organised religion before their great empire of the 13th century. It was Kublai Khaan who first found himself with a court in which all philosophies of his empire were represented, but it was a Tibetan Buddhist, Phagpa, who wielded the greatest influence on the khaan.

In 1578 Altan Khaan, a descendant of Chinggis Khaan, met the Tibetan leader Sonam Gyatso, was converted, and subsequently bestowed on Sonam Gyatso the title Dalai Lama (*dalai* means 'ocean' in Mongolian). Sonam Gyatso was named as the third Dalai Lama and his two predecessors were named posthumously.

Mass conversions occurred under Altan Khaan. As Mongolian males were conscripted to monasteries, rather than the army, the centuries of constant fighting seemed to wane (much to the relief of China, which subsequently funded more monasteries in Mongolia).

Buddhist opposition to needless killing reinforced strict hunting laws already set in place by shamanism. Today, Buddhist monks are still influential in convincing local populations to protect their environment and wildlife.

Buddhism in Mongolia was nearly destroyed in 1937 when the young communist government, fearing competition, launched a purge that wiped out nearly all of the country's 700 monasteries. Up to 30,000 monks were massacred and thousands more sent to Siberian labour camps. Freedom of religion was only restored in 1990 following Mongolia's peaceful democratic revolution.

Islam

The country has a significant minority of Sunni Muslims, most of them ethnic Kazakhs who live primarily in Bayan-Ölgii. Because of Mongolia's great isolation and distance from the major Islamic centres of the Middle East, Islam has never been a major force in Bayan-Ölgii.

MONGOLIAN CULTURE & CUISINE RELIGION

1639
Zanabazar, a direct descendent of Chinggis Khaan and the greatest artist in Mongolian history, is recognised as the first Jebtzun Damba, the supreme religious leader of Mongolia.

1696
The Manchus defeat Galdan Khaan of Zungaria and claim western Mongolia for the Qing dynasty, but some western Mongolians continue to resist for several generations.

1911
Mongolia declares independence from China and sets up religious leader Bogd Khan as the head of state.

1915
Treaty of Kyakhta is signed by Mongolia, China and Russia, granting Mongolia limited autonomy.

1924
The Bogd Khan, the eighth reincarnation of the Jebtzun Damba, dies; the People's Republic of Mongolia is created on 26 November.

1937
Choibalsan's Buddhist purge leaves 700 monasteries destroyed and 27,000 monks and civilians dead. Purge victims include former prime minister P Genden.

1939
Japan invades Mongolia from Manchuria in May. With help from the Soviet Union, and after heavy fighting along the Khalkh Gol, the Mongols defeat Japan by September.

However, most villages have a mosque and contacts have been established with Islamic groups in Turkey. Several prominent figures in the community have been on a hajj to Mecca. A small population of Kazakhs live in the city of Nalaikh, 35km southeast of Ulaanbaatar.

Christianity

The fastest-growing religion in Mongolia is Christianity. A whole spectrum of mainstream and fundamentalist sects have set up shop in Ulaanbaatar, each of them competing to convert a nation whose native faith is not well supported. In 1990 the number of Christians was negligible. Today there are an estimated 65,000 Christians and more than 150 churches.

Nestorian Christianity was part of the Mongol Empire long before Western missionaries arrived. The Nestorians followed the doctrine of Nestorius (358–451), patriarch of Constantinople (428–31), who proclaimed that Jesus exists as two separate persons: the man Jesus and the divine son of God.

> Because of his failing health, Ögedei Khaan (a son of Chinggis) was advised to halve the number of cups of alcohol he drank per day. Ögedei readily agreed, then promptly ordered that his cups be doubled in size.

The Arts

From prehistoric oral epics to the latest movie from MongolKino film studios in Ulaanbaatar, the many arts of Mongolia convey the flavour of nomadic life and the spirit of the land.

Music

Traditional Mongolian music, which can be heard at concerts in Ulaanbaatar, is usually played on a *morin khuur* (horsehead fiddle), a two-stringed vertical violin and a lute. These instruments are also used by some of Mongolia's popular rock bands, including Altan Urag and Boerte Ensemble.

There are also several unique traditional singing styles. The enigmatic *khöömei* – throat singing – has the remarkable effect of producing two notes simultaneously – one low growl and the other an ethereal whistling. Translated as 'long songs', *urtyn-duu* use long trills to relate traditional stories about love and the countryside.

There is a thriving contemporary music scene in Ulaanbaatar and you can hear live music at many downtown bars like River Sounds or Grand Khaan Irish Pub. Popular music genres include pop, rap and hip-hop, as

---

THE MAD BARON

Throughout their history the disparate countries of Mongolia, Russia and China have had few agreements. It was only in 1920 that the three found themselves facing a common enemy – one Baron Roman Nikolaus Fyodirovich von Ungern-Sternberg, aka the Mad Baron.

A renegade White Russian officer who believed he was the reincarnation of Chinggis (Genghis) Khaan, the Baron was described by his contemporaries as a psychotic killer whose army consisted of escaped convicts and bandits.

In the summer of 1920 the Baron led his 6000-strong army on an assault of Ulaanbaatar, chasing out the Chinese army that occupied the city. The Baron declared himself emperor of Mongolia and Russia, and then sent his men on a three-day orgy of looting, burning and killing.

After only a few months, the Bolshevik advance across Siberia forced the Baron to abandon Urga. Out on the steppes, his own followers tried to kill him by shooting him in his tent, but he managed to escape. He was eventually captured by the Bolsheviks, deported to Novosibirsk and shot on 15 September 1921.

well as a totally Mongolian brand of folklore-rock fusion music that includes drums and guitars along with traditional instruments.

For folklore-rock, Altan Urag (www.altanurag.mn) is regarded as one of the best. Their mash-ups of Western percussion and Mongolian string instruments will have you entranced. We are also fans of the Boerte Ensemble, which fuses all sorts of instruments into a mellow sound good for long road trips. Their videos are available on YouTube. Another band enjoying some success is Khusugtun (www.khusugtun-group.com).

The recent breakout in Mongolian rap has not gone unnoticed. Australian filmmaker Benj Binks has documented the phenomena in Mongolian Bling (www.mongolianbling.com). Not to be outdone, American Lauren Knapp created Live From UB (www.livefromub.com) a documentary exploring Mongolian rock music.

Theatre & Film

Mongolia's best-known modern poet and playwright is Dashdorjiin Natsagdorj (1906–37), regarded as the founder of Mongolian literature. His dramatic nationalist poems and plays are still performed in Mongolian theatres today. There's also been a revival in Mongolian cinema, its brightest star being director Byambasuren Davaa. Her best-known films, *The Story of the Weeping Camel* (2003) and *The Cave of the Yellow Dog* (2005), depict nomadic life, the simplicity of the steppes and Mongolia's transition into the 21st century.

Visual Arts

Many of Mongolia's visual arts are religious in nature. Religious scroll paintings, depicting deities and their enlightened qualities, can be found on family altars in many homes. Another traditional style of painting is *zurag* – landscape storytelling. These landscapes include intricate sketches depicting every aspect of Mongolian life. Balduugiyn Sharav (1869–1939) is Mongolia's best-known painter in this style. The sculptor Zanabazar (1635–1723) is one of Mongolia's most revered artists, as well as a religious and political leader. He is known primarily for his cast-bronze statues, which are now on display in monasteries and museums around Ulaanbaatar.

Ulaanbaatar has a vibrant modern-art scene. The best place to see contemporary art is in the Tsagaandarium Art Gallery, near Zaisan Monument.

Mongolian Cuisine

Mongolian cuisine evolved from nomadic traditions and the types of food available on Mongolia's barren steppes. Livestock (which offer meat and milk) have long been in plentiful supply. Fruit, vegetables, nuts, herbs and spices are mostly absent, due to the fact that nomadic people move frequently and crops do not. Mongolians have long traded for goods such as rice and flour, but more perishable products rarely made it north of the Gobi.

1956
Trans-Siberian railroad through Mongolia is completed, connecting Běijīng with Moscow.

1961
Mongolia is admitted to the UN as an independent country, but the USSR continues to occupy Mongolia with troops and run the country as a satellite state.

1990
Democracy demonstrations in Ulaanbaatar. In June the first free, multiparty elections are held, with the Mongolian People's Revolutionary Party (MPRP) winning 85% of the vote.

1996
The Democratic Coalition becomes the first non-communist government to win an election (although a series of scandals causes the fall of four successive governments).

1998
S Zorig, the leader of the 1990 democratic revolution, is assassinated in his apartment on 2 October. The killers are never found.

2008
In hotly contested parliamentary elections the MPRP narrowly defeats the Democratic Coalition. Protestors allege vote rigging, and subsequent riots end with four people shot dead and hundreds arrested.

2013
Production of copper concentrate begins at Oyu Tolgoi, Mongolia's biggest ever infrastructure project. By 2018 the mine could become one of the top five copper mines in the world.

The 2010 documentary *Babies* featured four newborns from different corners of the globe: Namibia, San Francisco, Tokyo and Mongolia. Watching the film gives unique insight into the life of a typical Mongolian rural family.

Mongolian food tends to be seasonal. In the summer months, when animals provide milk, dairy products become the staple. Meat (and fat) takes over in winter, supplemented with flour (in some form) and potatoes or rice if these are available.

Almost any Mongolian dish can be created with meat, rice, flour and potatoes. Most meals consist of *talkh* (bread) in the towns and cities and *bortzig* (fried unleavened bread) in the gers, and the uncomplicated *shölte khool* (literally, soup with food) – a meal involving hot broth, pasta slivers, boiled mutton and a few potato chunks. Nowadays, you can find plenty of international cuisine in the capital.

Buuz (steamed meat dumplings) and *khuushuur* (deep-fried meat pancakes) are two of the most popular menu options you'll find in restaurants. Miniature *buuz*, known as *bansh,* are usually dunked in milk tea. If you are travelling north from Běijīng, *buuz* may seem familiar – they are distant cousins of Chinese *bāozi.*

The classic Mongolian dinner staple is referred to simply as *makh* (meat) and consists of boiled sheep bits (bones, fat, various organs and the head) with some sliced potato, served in a plastic bucket. This meal does not require silverware; just trawl around the bucket of bones until a slab catches your fancy. There'll be a knife to slice off larger chunks.

The other main highlight of Mongolian cuisine is *khorkhog,* made by placing hot stones from an open fire into a pot or urn with chopped mutton, some water and sometimes vodka. The container is then sealed and left on the fire. When eating this meal, it's customary to pass the hot, greasy rocks from hand to hand, as this is thought to be good for your health.

In summer you can subsist as Mongolians do on *tsagaan idee* (dairy products; literally 'white foods'): yoghurt, milk, delicious fresh cream, cheese and fermented milk drinks. When you visit a ger you will be offered dairy snacks such as *aaruul* (dried milk curds), which are as hard as a rock and often about as tasty.

Finally, if you get a chance, don't miss the opportunity to try blowtorched marmot (prairie dog), a delicacy of the steppes.

Meals are occasionally interrupted for a round of vodka. Before taking a swig, a short ritual is employed to honour the sky gods and the four cardinal directions. There is no one way of doing this, but it usually involves dipping the left ring finger into the vodka and flicking droplets into the air four times before wiping your finger across your forehead.

WHAT'S YOUR DRINK?

Mongolians are big tea drinkers and will almost never start a meal until they've had a cup of tea, as it's thought to aid digestion.

Süütei tsai, a classic Mongolian drink, is milk tea with salt. If you can't get used to the salty brew, try asking for *khar tsai* (black tea), which is like European tea, with sugar and no milk.

Alcoholic drinks are readily available and Mongolians can drink you under the table if you challenge them. There is much social pressure to drink, especially on males – those who refuse to drink *arkhi* (vodka) are considered wimps.

Locally produced beer labels include Mongol, Chinggis, Borigo and Khan Brau. Popular vodkas include the very smooth Chinggis black label, which costs just US$8 a bottle.

While it may not seem obvious at first, every countryside ger doubles as a tiny distillery. One corner of the ger usually contains a tall, thin jug with a plunger that is used for fermenting mares' milk. The drink, known as *airag* or *koumiss,* has an alcohol content of about 3%. Go easy on the *airag* from the start or your guts will pay for it later.

China Today

A highly idiosyncratic mix of can-do entrepreneurs, inward-looking Buddhists, textbook Marxists, overnight millionaires, the out-of-pocket, leather-faced farmers, unflagging migrant workers and round-the-clock McJobbers, China today is as multifaceted as its challenges are diverse. From the outside, China's autocratic decision-making may suggest national uniformity, but things are actually more in a state of controlled, and not so controlled, chaos.

Best in Print

Country Driving: A Chinese Road Trip (Peter Hessler) Hessler's amusing and insightful journey at the wheel around the highways and byways of China.

Tiger Head, Snake Tails (Jonathan Fenby) Compelling account of contemporary China's myriad challenges and contradictions.

Diary of a Madman & Other Stories (Lu Xun) Astonishing tales from the father of modern Chinese fiction.

Best on Film

Still Life (Jia Zhangke; 2005) Bleak and hauntingly beautiful portrayal of a family devastated by the construction of the Three Gorges Dam.

Raise the Red Lantern (Zhang Yimou; 1991) Exquisitely fashioned tragedy from the sumptuous palette of the Fifth Generation.

In the Mood for Love (Wong Kar-Wai; 2000) Seductive, stylishly costumed and slow-burning Hong Kong romance.

New Superpower or the Next Japan?

Tipped to overtake the US economy sometime before 2020, China can readily seem to be assuming the mantle of superpower. The rash of books trumpeting China's ascendancy echoes the glut of titles in the late 1980s that celebrated the rise of its island neighbour. While the Chinese economy effortlessly streaked past Japan's in 2010 and today gradually fills the United States' rear-view mirror, the unstoppable juggernaut of the Chinese economy could be hitting some hefty potholes, if not nearing the end of the road. Some financial analysts foresee China slewing into a long era of stagnation similar to that which depressed Japan after its asset bubble burst in the early 1990s. A combination of bad debt accumulation, imbalanced growth, downward property prices, a burdensome overcapacity and overdependence on exports could commence a persistent squeeze to the brakes on economic growth. Resolving bad debt and sorting out the shaky banking sector and the deeply undercapitalised financial system may be central to any long-term resolution but a real estate slump could limit options, while inequality in China remains among the most severe in the world.

To Boldly Go

In December 2013, the Chang'e 3 probe landed on the surface of the moon, marking the first lunar landing since 1976. Carrying the Yutu (Jade Rabbit) lunar rover, the mission also marked China's coming of age as a space power. Since the 1960s, moon landings have been a superpower hallmark: China's foray into the ether is as much about national standing as it is about scientific research. Rivalries notwithstanding – India's unmanned Mars probe achieved Martian orbit in 2014 – China wants to show the world it has both the ambition and the sophistication to pull a (jade) rabbit from its hat. The space program also casts China as an exploratory power that is willing to take risks, in an arena littered with noble failures. China also has a working space station – the Tiangong-1, a precursor to a much larger station in the pipeline – and plans to put a man on the moon and a rover on Mars (despite a Chinese probe to the Red Planet ending in failure in 2011).

Troubled Waters & Restive Borderlands

China's dazzling economic trajectory over the last two decades has been watched with awe by the West and increasing unease by the Middle Kingdom's neighbours. By virtue of its sheer size and population, a dominant China has been ruffling some East Asian feathers. A growing – and seemingly intractable – spat over the contested and uninhabited Diaoyu Islands (Senkaku Islands to the Japanese) has soured relations between China and Japan. Close to shipping lanes, surrounded by well-stocked fishing grounds and near to the Chunxiao gas field, the islands have aggravated Chinese and Japanese nationalism and overseen a growing mutual antipathy. Occasionally violent anti-Japanese protests in China have been the result. A festering dispute has also seen growing tensions between China and Vietnam, the Philippines and other nations over the control of waters, islands, reefs, atolls and rocky outcrops in the South China Sea.

While keeping an eye on maritime issues, at home President Xi Jinping has to deal with growing unrest in Xīnjiāng province, which has led to terror attacks in both Yúnnán and in front of the Gate of Heavenly Peace in Běijīng, as well as a spate of brazen bombings and attacks in Xīnjiāng itself. The rising Uighur disquiet has prompted an increasingly harsh security clampdown from Běijīng, which may threaten to inflame sentiments further.

POPULATION: **1.35 BILLION**

GDP PER CAPITA: **$9800**

LABOUR FORCE: **797.6 MILLION**

UNEMPLOYMENT: **4.1%**

HIGHEST POINT: **MT EVEREST (8848M)**

if China were 100 people

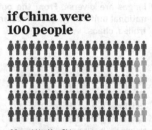

92 would be Han Chinese
8 would be ethnic minorities, eg Zhuang, Manchu, Uighur etc

belief systems
(% of population)

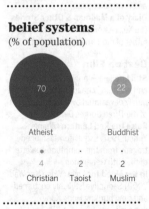

70 — Atheist
22 — Buddhist
4 — Christian
2 — Taoist
2 — Muslim

population per sq km

BĚIJĪNG KŪNMÍNG SHÀNGHǍI

≈ 300 people

Chinese Culture & Cuisine

Powerful links connect the Chinese of today with their ancestors 5000 or 6000 years ago, making this the longest-lasting complex civilisation on earth. No wonder then that China, home to roughly one-fifth of humanity, is custodian of one of the world's richest cultural and artistic legacies.

The People

The Chinese Character

Shaped by Confucian principles, the Chinese are thoughtful and discreet, subtle but also pragmatic and practically minded. Conservative and somewhat introverted, they favour dark clothing over bright or loud colours while their body language is usually reserved and undemonstrative, yet attentive.

The Chinese (apart from the Shanghainese, some Chinese insist) are particularly generous. Don't be surprised if a person you have just met on a train invites you for a meal in the dining carriage; they will insist on paying, in which case do not try to thwart their efforts. The Chinese also adore children and delight in showing them affection.

Particularly diligent, the Chinese are inured to the kind of hours that may prompt a workers' insurrection elsewhere. This is partly due to a traditional culture of hard work but is also a response to inadequate social-security safety nets and an expression of anxiety regarding economic and political uncertainties. The Chinese impressively save much of what they earn, emphasising the virtue of prudence. Despite this restraint, however, wastefulness can be astounding when 'face' is involved: mountains of food are often left on restaurant dining tables, particularly if important guests are present.

The Chinese are also a very dignified people. They are proud of their civilisation and history, of their written language and of their inventions and achievements. This pride rarely comes across as arrogance or self-assurance, however, and may be tinged with a lack of confidence. The Chinese may, for example, be very gratified by China's newfound world status, but may squirm at the mention of food safety and hygiene.

CHINESE HISTORY

c 4000 BC

Archaeological evidence for the first settlements along the Yellow River (Huáng Hé).

551 BC

Birth of Confucius. Collected in the *Analects,* his ideas of an ethical, ordered society that operated through hierarchy and self-development would dominate Chinese culture until the early 20th century.

214 BC

Emperor Qin indentures thousands of labourers to link existing city walls into one Great Wall, in hope of reducing attacks on his country by nomadic warriors from Mongolia.

c 100 BC

Buddhism arrives in China from India. This religious system ends up thoroughly assimilated into the culture and becomes more powerful in China than in its country of origin.

1215

Chinggis (Genghis) Khaan conquers Běijīng as part of his creation of a massive Eurasian empire under Mongol rule.

1368

Zhu Yuanzhang founds the Ming dynasty and tries to impose a rigid Confucian social order on the population. However, China is too commercialised for the policy to work.

1842

The Treaty of Nánjīng concludes the first Opium War. China is forced to hand over Hong Kong island to the British and open up five Chinese ports to foreign trade.

CHINA'S ONE-CHILD POLICY

The 'one-child policy' (actually a misnomer, as the policy allows many exceptions and ethnic minorities are exempt) came into effect in 1979 in a bid to keep China's population to one billion by the year 2000; the latest government estimate is that the population will peak at 1.5 billion in 2033. The policy was originally harshly implemented, but rural revolt led to a softer stance; nonetheless, it has generated much bad feeling between local officials and the rural population.

Rural families were later allowed two children if the first child was a girl, but some couples have upwards of three or four kids. Additional offspring can result in fines and families having to shoulder the cost of education themselves, without government assistance. Official stated policy opposes forced abortion or sterilisation, but allegations of coercion continue as local officials strive to meet population quotas. Families who do abide by the one-child policy often go to great lengths to make sure their child is male, which has resulted in a lopsided male-to-female ratio of 111 boys to 100 girls.

In November 2013, China announced the decision to relax the one-child policy. Under new rules, families can now have two children if one parent is an only child.

The modern Chinese character has been shaped by recent political realities, and while Chinese people have always been reserved and circumspect, in today's China they can appear even more prudent. Impressive mental gymnastics are performed to detour contentious domestic political issues, which can make the mainland Chinese appear complicated, despite their reputation for being straightforward and down-to-earth.

Fǎlún Gōng is a quasi-religious lifestyle philosophy that gained so much traction in the 1990s that it was labelled a cult by Chinese authorities, and subsequently outlawed. Its followers at the time numbered between 60 and 70 million.

Ethnic Groups

When we think of China, we think of the world's most populous nation, dominated by the Han Chinese. While 92% of the population is Han, China is also home to 55 other ethnic minorities, including Tibetans, Uighurs and Mongols. Most of the minorities live on China's borderlands. In the northeast, near Hǎilāěr, there are small pockets of Evenki (reindeer herders) and even ethnic Russians who speak Mandarin as their native tongue.

But it is indeed the Han Chinese who dominate, not only in the population figures but in every aspect of life in China – including writing, the arts, literature, sport and politics. For the minorities, the ability to operate comfortably in Han culture and language is essential for moving ahead in society.

The Han are distributed throughout the country but predominantly concentrate along the Yellow River, Yangzi River and Pearl River basins. These core areas are but a small fraction of the total area of China – the colossal areas of Tibet, Qīnghǎi, Xīnjiāng, Inner Mongolia and the northeast (Manchuria) are historically non-Han areas but were slowly brought into the motherland following centuries of warfare and occupation.

Religion

Far West China (www.farwestchina.com) is a useful website and blog covering the people, culture and landscapes of Xīnjiāng, in China's northwest.

Religion in China has been influenced by three streams of thought: Taoism, Confucianism and Buddhism. All three have been inextricably entwined in popular Chinese religion along with ancient animist beliefs. The founders of these traditions have been deified; the Chinese worship them and their disciples as fervently as they worship their own ancestors and a pantheon of gods and spirits.

The Chinese communist government professes atheism. It considers religion to be base superstition, a remnant of old China used by the ruling classes to maintain power. Nevertheless, in an effort to improve relations with the Muslim, Buddhist and Lamaist minorities, in 1982 the

Chinese government amended its constitution to allow freedom of religion. However, only atheists are permitted to be members of the Chinese Communist Party (CCP). Since almost all of China's 55 minority groups adhere to one religion or another, this rule precludes most of them from party membership.

Muslims and Christians are believed to be the largest identifiable religious groups still active in China today, each numbering perhaps 3% to 5% of the nation's population. The government has not published official figures of the number of Buddhists – hardly surprising given the ideological battle it has been waging with Tibetan Buddhists, who have been fighting for decades to preserve their culture and their nation. It's impossible to determine the number of Taoists, but the number of Taoist priests is very small.

Traditional Chinese religious beliefs took a battering during the Cultural Revolution when monasteries were disbanded, temples were destroyed and the monks were sometimes killed or sent to the fields to labour. Since Mao's death, the Chinese government has allowed many temples (sometimes with their own contingent of monks and novices) to reopen as active places of worship. All religious activity is firmly under state control and many of the monks are caretakers within renovated shells of monasteries, which serve principally as tourist attractions and are pale shadows of their former selves.

The Arts

China is the custodian of one of the world's richest cultural and artistic legacies. Until the 20th century, China's arts were deeply conservative and resistant to change; in the last hundred years, revolutions in technique and content have fashioned a dramatic transformation. Despite this evolution, China's arts – whatever the period – remain united by a common aesthetic that taps into the very soul of the nation.

In reflection of the Chinese character, Chinese aesthetics have traditionally been marked by restraint and understatement, a preference for oblique references over direct explanation, vagueness in place of specificity. These guiding principles compellingly find their way into virtually every Chinese art form.

Calligraphy & Painting

Perhaps the most iconic of China's arts is calligraphy. However, it can be tricky for Westerners to comprehend calligraphy as an art form, unless they have a sound understanding of written Chinese. This is because the characters represent both an image of beauty as well as a description or concept. Less 'insider' knowledge is needed, however, to appreciate Chinese traditional painting. There may be subtle meanings behind the work, but in general Chinese landscapes are accessible to any eye and have long been treasured in the West for their beauty.

CHINESE CULTURE & CUISINE THE ARTS

1898
The New Territories adjoining Kowloon in Hong Kong are leased to the British for 99 years, eventually being returned, along with the rest of Hong Kong, in 1997.

1904–05
The Russo-Japanese War is fought entirely on Chinese territory. Japan's victory is the first triumph by an Asian power over a European one.

1911
Revolution spreads across China as local governments withdraw support for the Qing dynasty, and instead support a republic under the presidency of Sun Yat-sen.

1931
Japan invades Manchuria, provoking an international crisis and forcing Kuomintang leader Chiang Kai-shek to consider anti-Japanese as well as anti-communist strategies.

1949
Mao Zedong stands on top of the Gate of Heavenly Peace in Běijīng on 1 October and announces the formation of the People's Republic of China, saying 'The Chinese people have stood up'.

1962
Mao initiates the Great Leap Forward; at least 20 million people starve when his plan to industrialise the country causes a collapse in agriculture.

1966
The Cultural Revolution breaks out, and Red Guards demonstrate in cities across China. The movement is marked by a fetish for violence as a catalyst for transforming society.

The five fundamental brushstrokes necessary to master calligraphy can be found in the character 永 (yǒng), which means eternal or forever.

Visual Arts

China turned an artistic corner of sorts after 1949, when artists eschewed washes on silk in favour of oil on canvas. The Chinese obsession with the mysterious and the ineffable made way for attention to detail and realism. By the 1970s, Chinese artists aspired to master the skill of socialist-realism. Saturated with political symbolism and propaganda, the blunt artistic style was produced on an industrial scale. Traditional Taoist and Buddhist philosophy was overturned; humans were now the masters of nature, which would bend to their will.

Mao's death ended the era of 'art for the masses' and a new school of artists began exploring a variety of themes, largely influenced by the Western art world. After the Tiān'ānmén Square protests in 1989 the Chinese art world turned cynical, with many works mocking Chinese consumerism and political ideology. Today there is a vast array of subjects as Chinese artists have moved away from overtly political work towards more universal concerns.

Ceramics

One of China's biggest art exports is ceramics, for which it has been developing techniques for thousands of years. Some of the best pieces date from the Yuan dynasty, when the 'blue-and-white' (qīnghuā) porcelain, made with cobalt-blue paint from Persia, was developed. The porcelain became famous the world over, eventually acquiring the name 'China' whether the pieces were produced in China or not.

Sculpture

Ai Weiwei: Never Sorry (2012) is an acclaimed documentary that chronicles three years in the life of the outspoken Chinese artist and activist Ai Weiwei.

Sculpture in China reached its zenith after the arrival of Buddhism, when artists across the land were commissioned to carve enormous statues of the Buddha. Early concepts for Buddhist sculpture came from India, so it's not surprising that some of China's most spectacular Buddhist statues are found along the Silk Road west of Xī'ān.

Dàtóng, on the train line from Běijīng to Ulaanbaatar, is home to one of China's four most celebrated sites of Buddhist sculptures; the magnificent Yungang Caves.

ANCESTORS, GHOSTS & KITCHEN GODS

Beliefs about ancestor worship permeate almost every aspect of Chinese philosophy. Many homes have their own altar, where family members pay their respects to deceased relatives by burning spirit money and providing offerings. It's believed that a person possesses two 'souls' – a guǐ (literally 'ghost'), which is yin and represents everything dark, damp and earthly, and a shén (literally 'spirit'), which is yang, and represents light, goodness and strength. When a person dies the two souls go in separate directions – the shén to heaven and the guǐ to the underworld. If a person has suffered a tragic death or if the body is neglected the guǐ lingers on earth, often seeking revenge.

Closely tied to ancestor worship is popular religion, which consists of an immense celestial bureaucracy of gods and spirits, from the lowly but all-important kitchen god (zào jun) to the celestial emperor himself (tiāndì). Each god has a particular role to fulfil and can be either promoted or demoted depending on his or her performance. Lower-ranking gods who protect homes, doors and neighbourhoods from evil spirits (guǐ) are of particular interest, and in pre-communist China tiny altars and shrines were a ubiquitous sight. Offerings to the gods consisted not only of food and incense but also opera performances, birthday parties (to which the other local gods were invited) and the occasional procession around town.

Architecture

Balance and symmetry are important features of traditional Chinese architecture and can be found in all types of buildings, from humble farmhouses to great imperial palaces. Another common feature is the idea of enclosure. Whereas contemporary Western architectural practices typically involve surrounding a building by an open yard or garden, traditional Chinese architecture involves constructing buildings that take up an entire property but enclose open spaces within themselves. These enclosed spaces come in two forms; the courtyard (more common in north China, including Běijīng) and the 'sky well' (more common in the south).

Classical Chinese buildings, especially those of the wealthy, are built with an emphasis on breadth rather than height, featuring an enclosed heavy platform and a large roof that floats over this base, with the vertical walls not well emphasised. This contrasts with Western architecture, which tends to grow in height and depth.

The halls and palaces in Běijīng's Forbidden City, for example, have relatively low ceilings when compared to equivalent stately buildings in the West, but their external appearances suggest the all-embracing, sweeping nature of Imperial China; a concept you can visualise yourself when you stand on top of Coal Hill, in Jǐngshān Park and look out over the vast Forbidden City below you.

Along the Trans-Manchurian route the architecture is distinct from much of the rest of China, primarily as a result of foreign influences in the region. At the turn of the 20th century, much of Manchuria was occupied – either economically or militarily – by Russia, Japan and various European powers, all of whom left their mark on the cities in this region. The best example is Tiānjīn, which contains quarters once dominated by Austro-Hungarians, Belgians, Germans, Italians and Japanese. In Dàolǐqū, the oldest part of Hā'ěrbīn (Harbin), onion domes and ornamental facades reveal the city's Russian roots.

If modern architecture in China is defined as anything post-1949, then China has ridden a roller-coaster ride of styles and fashions. In Běijīng, stand between the Great Hall of the People and the National Centre for the Performing Arts (NCPA) and weigh up how far China has travelled in 50 years. Interestingly, neither building has clear Chinese motifs. The same applies to the complex form of Běijīng's CCTV Building, where a continuous loop through horizontal and vertical planes required some audacious engineering.

Many of the top names in world architecture – IM Pei, Rem Koolhaas, Norman Foster, Herzog & de Meuron – have designed at least one building in China in the past decade. Other impressive examples in Běijīng include the National Stadium (aka the 'Bird's Nest'), the National Aquatics Centre (aka the 'Water Cube') and Běijīng South Train Station.

1976
Mao Zedong dies, aged 83. The Gang of Four (a faction led by Mao's wife Jiang Qing) are put on trial, blamed for all the disasters of the Cultural Revolution.

1979
The one-child policy is introduced as a means of reducing the population but it imposes unprecedented control over women's personal liberty.

1989
Hundreds of civilians are killed by Chinese troops in the streets around Tiān'ānmén Square. No official reassessment has been made, but rumours persist of deep conflict within the party.

2008
Běijīng hosts the 2008 Summer Olympic Games and Paralympics. The Games go smoothly and are widely considered to be a great success in burnishing China's image overseas.

2008–09
Violent riots erupt in Tibet and Xīnjiāng, evidence that Běijīng's policy of development in Western regions is not enough to quell local demands for greater autonomy and limited Han migration.

October 2013
A car crashes into crowds beside Tiān'ānmén Square, in what police describe as a terrorist suicide attack. Five people die: the three inside the vehicle, plus two tourists.

March 2014
Malaysia Airlines flight MH370 from Kuala Lumpur to Běijīng is declared missing, sparking the largest and most expensive multinational search-and-rescue effort in history.

HALLMARK NORTHERN DISHES

PINYIN	SCRIPT	ENGLISH
Běijīng kǎoyā	北京烤鸭	Peking duck
jiāo zhá yángròu	焦炸羊肉	deep-fried mutton
qīng xiāng shāo jī	清香烧鸡	chicken wrapped in lotus leaf
shuàn yángròu	涮羊肉	lamb hotpot
mántou	馒头	steamed buns
jiǎozi	饺子	dumplings
ròu bāozi	肉包子	steamed meat buns
sān měi dòufu	三美豆腐	sliced bean curd with Chinese cabbage
yuán bào lǐ jí	芫爆里脊	stir-fried pork tenderloin with coriander
zào liū sān bái	糟溜三白	stir-fried chicken, fish and bamboo shoots

Chinese Cuisine

China is a gastronome's paradise. Cooking is a way of life here and first-time visitors will find a feast far greater than what is on offer in Chinatowns the world over. Food plays a prominent role in the national psyche – work, play, romance, business and family life all revolve around it. When people meet, a common greeting is '*nǐ chīfàn le ma?*' ('have you eaten yet?'). The food in China varies greatly by region and is influenced by the topographical and climatic disparities that exist across this vast nation. Naturally, seafood is plentiful near the coast and meat dominates in interior regions like Inner Mongolia. Likewise, grains are more prevalent in the north, while rice is the staple in the south.

The Northern School

The northern school of cooking is what you'll experience when travelling along the Trans-Mongolian and Trans-Manchurian railway lines, although big cities like Běijīng and Hā'ěrbīn will also have restaurants that represent the southern, eastern and western schools.

The northern school has a reputation for being bland and unsophisticated, but it's filling, appetising and well suited to the harsh winter climate. There's a particular accent on millet, sorghum, maize, barley and wheat rather than rice (which requires a lot of water). The spectrum of flavours is somewhat muted compared to southern cooking, as salt is preferred to spice.

Roasting meat is also more common in the north than in other parts of China. Meats in northern China are braised until they're falling off the bone, or brushed with spices and barbecued until smoky. Pungent garlic, chives and spring onions are used with abandon and are also used raw.

Culinary Influences

The influence of Manchurian cooking and the cold climate of the northeastern provinces have left a legacy of rich and hearty stews, dense breads and dumplings. The cooking of the nomadic Mongolians has also left a pronounced mark on northern meat cooking, especially in the development of northern hotpot. Milk from nomadic herds of cattle, goats and horses has also made its way into northern cuisine, as yoghurts for example. In Běijīng it's common to spot small clay jars of yoghurt being sold at streetside stalls.

China Statistics

Population: 1.35 billion

Birth rate: 12.17 births per 1000 people

Percentage of people over 65 years of age: 9.4%

Urbanisation rate: 2.7%

Life expectancy: 73.2 years

Landscapes & Wildlife

One of the attractions of the Trans-Siberian routes is the opportunity to experience the vast changes in landscape across the three countries. Much of the wildlife is naturally shy, hidden from view or too distant to be observed well from the train itself, so the best way to appreciate nature in Russia, Mongolia and China is to alight and spend a few days exploring the countryside.

Taiga

The most prevalent of the vegetation zones traversed by the railway is the iconic Russian taiga, a dense forest belt running from Scandinavia across Siberia to the Pacific coast. Hints of the vast taiga lying ahead can be found even as Trans-Siberian trains crawl across European Russia, but train travellers get a sense of what writer Anton Chekhov called the true Siberian taiga once they have crossed the Yenisey River at Krasnoyarsk. The Baikal-Amur Mainline (BAM) route (from Tayshet) is wall-to-wall taiga for days on end.

True taiga is coniferous forest, particularly Siberian pine *(Pinus sibirica)*, but you will often find mixed conifer and deciduous forest, and in some places completely deciduous forest. Silver firs, spruce, larch and birch often mingle with maple and aspen, while willows and poplars dominate the innumerable rivers, lakes and ponds. Typically, as you cross Siberia, the mixed and coniferous forest is broken by clearings or farmland, which in turn are punctuated by Siberian towns, villages and settlements. In Eastern Siberia and the Far East the landscape folds and rises in parts into forested mountains, such as the Barguzin Mountains that flank the eastern shore of Lake Baikal.

The Gobi Desert is encroaching on Běijīng at a rate of 2km per year. To stop it the Chinese government is trying to create a 5700km long 'green wall' by paying farmers to plant trees.

Ussuriland

Towards the far eastern end of the main Trans-Siberian route you will encounter Ussuriland. This unique environment is largely covered by a monsoon forest filled with an exotic array of flora and fauna, many species of which are found nowhere else in Russia. The topography is dominated by the Sikhote-Alin Range, which runs for more than 1000km in a spine parallel to the coast. Unlike the sparsely vegetated woodland floor of the taiga, the forests of Ussuriland have a lush undergrowth, with lianas and vines twined around trunks and draped from branches.

The Wild Russia website (www.wild-russia.org) belongs to the US-based Center for Russian Nature Conservation, which assists and promotes nature conservation across Russia and publishes the English-language journal *Russian Conservation News*.

Steppe

As the Trans-Mongolian Railway crosses Mongolia, it passes through the pastures of the Selenga Gol (Selenga River) Valley. Gradually, however, the landscape changes to steppe. The steppe (some of it mountain forest steppe) spans the continent from the plains north of the Black Sea across Central Asia through Mongolia to the western edge of China. This gently rolling and – in its driest form – semiarid grassland is often unsuitable for cultivation, but it provides sufficient vegetation to support large herds of grazing animals.

SIBERIAN LANDSCAPES & BELIEFS

Landscapes, perhaps more than anything else, shape the lives and beliefs of human beings.

In Russia, the countryside is imbued with aspects of both Christian and traditional lifestyles. After the Cossack Yermak drowned in the Irtysh River near Tobolsk during a Tatar ambush, his corpse was described in the early semi-religious *Siberian Chronicles* as being too miraculous to be touched even by birds. Almost a century later, the exiled Old Believer Archpriest Avvakum (1621–82) was flogged and tormented across Siberia and on reaching Lake Baikal he described it as a paradise on earth, where everything was larger than life. Later still, in 17th-century Russia, the Daur region in the Amur Basin was widely seen by Cossacks as a land of milk and honey to which they could flee and where they might find refuge from brutal masters. For Russian peasants as a whole, Siberia stood for freedom from serfdom.

In the 18th century, a bizarre castrati sect (called Skoptsy in Russian) established itself in Siberia and several other regions, according to which males were (as the name suggests) castrated. Even today, sects and gurus are attracted to Siberia, the most famous being the neo-Jesus Vissarion (aka Sergei Torop), whose Abode of Dawn community is tucked away in a forest near the town of Abakan, south of Krasnoyarsk. If one religious movement would seem to be without a future, however, it was the castrati. Bizarrely, it later spawned an offshoot 'neo-castrati' sect in the Balkans.

South of the Trans-Siberian at Novosibirsk, in the Altai Republic, the Russian painter and mystic Nikolai Rerikh (known internationally as Nicholas Roerich) sought the mythical, heavenly kingdom of Shambhala, and today ordinary Russians popularly perceive the picturesque Altai as a 'sacred' place imbued with spiritual energy.

The tie between landscape and shamanism among Buryats of the regions around Lake Baikal is very similar to those of Mongolians across the border. The sky is an integral aspect of shamanist belief, and in Mongolia blue scarves are placed on *ovoos* (stone cairns) to represent it. Mongolians also flick droplets of vodka into the air before they drink, in order to honour the sky gods.

In China a special role is played by its sacred mountains. Beyond Tibet, there are four sacred Buddhist mountains, each one the home of a specific bodhisattva, an enlightened being or source of enlightenment. The two most famous are Wǔtái Shān and Éméi Shān, respectively ruled over by Wenshu and Puxiang.

To the south, the steppe becomes arid and gives way to the deserts of Central Asia. The Gobi Desert in Mongolia and China retains a thin grass cover that sustains some of the hardier herbivores. The section traversed by the Trans-Mongolian south of Choir gets grass in a good year.

Mongolia's Wild Heritage by Christopher Finch, written in collaboration with the Mongolian Ministry of Nature and Environment, is an outstanding book on Mongolia's fragile ecology and has excellent photos.

Rivers & Lakes on the Routes

Russia has six of the world's 20 longest rivers. The east-flowing Amur (2824km) forms the China–Russia border, while the Lena (4400km), Yenisey (3487km), Irtysh (4248km) and Ob (3650km) all flow north across Siberia ending up in the Arctic Ocean.

Beautiful Lake Baikal itself is the world's deepest lake, holding nearly one-fifth of all the globe's unfrozen fresh water. Formed by rifting tectonic plates, Baikal is also the world's oldest lake, dating back 25 million years. The rift, which widens by about 2cm per year, is thought to be 9km deep, of which 7km of depth is covered by sediment.

Europe's longest river, the Volga (3690km), rises northwest of Moscow and flows via Nizhny Novgorod and Kazan into the Caspian Sea.

National Parks & Reserves

Along or close by the Trans-Siberian routes you'll find easily reached national parks and reserves.

➡ Perm, Kungur and Yekaterinburg are good springboards into the Ural Mountains' landscapes and parks.

➡ Irkutsk (Listvyanka) provides access to spectacular walking trails, whereas Ulan-Ude is best for the Barguzin National Reserve within Zabaikalsky National Park.

➡ Krasnoyarsk has the unusual Stolby Nature Reserve.

➡ Close to Ulaanbaatar, you'll find Gorkhi-Terelj National Park and Khustain Nuruu National Park.

Wildlife

Wildlife flourishes in the taiga; the indigenous cast includes squirrels, chipmunks (which dine on pine-cone seeds), voles and lemmings, as well as small carnivores such as polecats, foxes, wolverines and, less commonly, the sable – a weasel-like creature whose luxuriant pelt played an important role in the early exploration of Siberia.

The most common species of large mammal in the taiga is the elk, a large deer that can measure over 2m at the shoulder and weighs almost as much as a bear. The brown bear itself is also a Siberian inhabitant that you may come across, despite the Russian penchant for hunting it. Other taiga-dwelling animals include deer, wolves and lynx.

Ussuriland's animal life includes wolves, sables, Asian black bears (tree-climbing, herbivorous cousins to the more common brown bears, also found here), as well as the rare Siberian or Amur tiger. The largest of all wild cats, the Siberian tiger can measure up to 3.5m in length. They prey on boar, though they've been observed to hunt and kill bears, livestock and even humans.

Ussuriland is also home to the Amur leopard, a big cat significantly rarer than the tiger, though less impressive and consequently less well known. Around 30 of these leopards roam the lands bordering China and North Korea. Sadly, both the leopard and tiger are under threat from constant poaching by both Chinese and Russian hunters. For more about this beautiful animal see ALTA Amur Leopard Conservation (www.amur-leopard.org).

One of the best places to spot waterfowl is on the Baraba Steppe between Omsk and Novosibirsk. Part of this is an outlier of the Vasyugan Swamp, the largest swamp in the northern hemisphere.

WCS Russia (www.wcsrussia.org) estimates that of the 400 Siberian tigers left in the wild, 95% of them live in the Russian Far East.

LANDSCAPES & WILDLIFE NATIONAL PARKS & RESERVES

SPECIES UNDER THREAT

The largest of all wild cats, the Siberian tiger can measure up to 3.5m in length. There are currently estimated to be only about 400 tigers in Russia's Ussuriland, but their genetic diversity is so low that the effective number is just 14 animals. Across the border in China the situation is even less rosy – there is thought to be no more than 50 or 60 Siberian tigers living there freely. Though protected by Chinese law and recognised as one of the world's most endangered species, the animals' survival hangs by a thread due to urban encroachment on its territory and a lucrative poaching industry. Tiger bones are prized in traditional Chinese medicine, while tiger skins also fetch a hefty price on the black market.

In response to the tigers' plight, the Chinese government set up a number of breeding centres, including the Siberian Tiger Park outside Hā'ěrbīn (Harbin). The centres aim to restore the natural tiger population by breeding and reintroducing them into the wild. While this might seem like a good idea in theory, in practice the need for minimal human contact and 'natural' conditions is at odds with the busloads of tourists snapping photos of big cats munching on cows and chickens at the park.

Lake Baikal

Lake Baikal's wildlife is unique. Thanks to warm water entering from vents in the bottom of the lake, and the filtering action of countless millions of minute crustaceans called epischura, the water is exceptionally clear and pure. Over 1700 species of plants and animals live in the lake (nearly all endemic), including over 200 types of shrimp and 80 types of flatworm; one species of flatworm is the world's largest and eats fish.

The many kinds of fish include the endemic *omul,* Baikal's main commercial fish. A remarkable species, the *omul* (a white fish of the salmon family) is reputed to emit a shrill cry when caught. It spawns in the Selenga River, but its main food source is the endemic Baikal alga, *melosira,* which has declined drastically because of pollution.

The *golomyanka* – a pink, translucent oilfish with large pectoral fins – is endemic to Baikal. It's unusual in having no scales and being viviparous – giving birth to live young, about 2000 at a time. It is the lake's most common fish, although its numbers have been depleted by pollution. By day it lives in the deep, dark depths; at night it rises close to the surface.

Golomyanka is the preferred food of the *nerpa* (Baikal seal, *Phoca siberica*), the world's only freshwater seal, with no relatives nearer than the ringed seal of the Arctic. The *nerpa* is an attractive, gentle creature with unusually large eyes set in a round, flat face, enabling it to hunt down to at least 1500m below the surface – even at night. Despite their size (less than 1.5m, making them the world's smallest seal), they have particularly strong claws for forcing their way through winter ice and keeping their breathing holes open. Pups are born in late winter. At the top of the food chain, Baikal seals have been greatly affected by pollution and are still harvested by local people. According to research by Greenpeace, the seal population hovers around the 60,000 mark – not sufficient for the animal to be endangered but on the brink as it is under threat from excessive hunting.

There is plenty of other wildlife around the lake. The huge delta, nearly 40km wide, formed by the sediment brought down to the lake by the Selenga River, is a great attraction to wild fowl and wading birds. In summer such beautiful and rare species as the Asiatic dowitcher and white-winged black tern nest in the delta, while in autumn vast numbers of waterfowl from the north use the mudflats and marshes to rest and feed on their migration south. It's a sort of international bird airport, with many birds overwintering there, too.

Vast numbers of caddis flies and other insects hatch and swarm on the lake in summer, providing a rich and vital food source for all kinds of wildlife from fish to birds. Despite their lack of visual impact for the Trans-Siberian traveller, these tiny insects, along with the microscopic plant and animal organisms, form the base of the pyramid of wildlife that graces this unique area.

China has an incredibly diverse range of natural escapes scattered across the country. Since the first nature reserve was established in 1956, around 2000 more parks have joined the ranks, protecting about 14% of China's land area, offering the traveller a wonderful variety of landscapes and diversity of wildlife.

Survival Guide

Directory A–Z

Accommodation

For much of your Trans-Siberian journey your bed will be on the train, but at either end of your journey and most likely at points along it you'll be looking for more traditional accommodation.

➡ Listed prices are generally for a standard twin or double room in the high season (summer), including breakfast, and with a private bathroom.

➡ Big discounts on rack rates can be had for online bookings on sites such as www.booking.com.

➡ It's a good idea to book a few nights in advance for big cities in each country, but elsewhere it's usually not necessary.

Russia

➡ Make bookings by email or fax rather than telephone so you get a written copy of your reservation.

➡ A few old Soviet-style hotels charge a booking surcharge *(bron)* which can be up to 50% of the first night's accommodation rate.

➡ For cheaper places to stay, head for the smaller towns or consider a homestay or serviced apartment; many travel agencies can arrange these.

➡ Occasionally, twin rooms are cheaper than singles, but you may end up sharing with a stranger unless you make it clear that you'd prefer single occupancy.

➡ Types of accommodation include hotels, hostels, B&Bs, homestays and apartments.

➡ Resting rooms *(komnaty otdykha)* are found at all major train stations and several of the smaller ones as well as at a few larger bus stations. Generally, they have basic (but usually clean) shared accommodation, mostly with communal facilities. The beds can be rented by the half day (around R1000) or for a 24-hour (from R16550) period. Some will ask to see your train ticket before allowing you to stay.

➡ *Kempingi* (organised camping grounds) are rare and usually only open from June to September. Camping is generally not allowed in the wild – check with locals if you're in doubt. *Turbazy*, tourist bases with shared bungalows or sometimes space for tents, are good alternatives.

China

➡ Options include rustic homesteads, homestays, youth hostels, student dormitories, guesthouses, courtyard lodgings, boutique hotels and five-star towers.

➡ Dorms in hostels usually cost between ¥50 and ¥100 around the centre of Běijīng. Doubles or twin rooms in Běijīng hostels start at around ¥200 with a shared bathroom.

ACCOMMODATION PRICES

SYMBOL	MAJOR RUSSIAN CITIES	REST OF RUSSIA	ULAANBAATAR/ REST OF MONGOLIA	CHINA
$	<R3000	<R1500	<T112,000/30,000	<¥400
$$	R3000-8000	R1500-4000	T112,000-192,000/30,000-60,000	¥400-1000
$$$	>R8000	>R4000	>T192,000/60,000	>¥1000

➡ Useful accommodation websites include **Asia Hotels** (www.asiahotels.com) and **Ctrip** (www.english.ctrip.com).

Mongolia

➡ Mongolia has excellent campsites everywhere, even near Ulaanbaatar in places such as Terelj. Camping is the better option if you are travelling in the countryside, considering the lack of hotels and the expense of ger (yurt) camps.

➡ A tourist ger camp is a 'camping ground' with traditional ger, a separate building for toilets and showers, and a restaurant-bar. The gers are furnished with two to four beds. Toilets and bathrooms, which are shared, are usually clean. Most ger camps in Terelj are open from June to September. In the Gobi Desert, they are open from May to October.

➡ Ger camps typically charge US$20 to US$40 per person per night, including three hearty meals, but prices are negotiable and may drop considerably if you bring your own food. Tour agencies and travel agencies in Ulaanbaatar can arrange visits.

➡ Ulaanbaatar (UB) has an abundant range of guesthouses targeting foreign backpackers. Most guesthouses are in apartment blocks and have dorm beds as well as private rooms.

➡ At US$20 to US$30 per day, an apartment is much better value than Ulaanbaatar's hotels, which are decent but overpriced.

➡ Dorm beds at UB guesthouses cost around US$5, private rooms around US$10.

Activities

Below is a brief overview of when a permit is required.

HOMESTAYS

As well as the following agencies which can arrange homestays in Russia and China, there are growing Couchsurfing, Airbnb and Homestay (www.homestay.com) participants in both countries providing rooms or even whole homes for short-term rent. Rates start from as little as US$15 a day but more commonly US$38 to US$76, depending on the location and the quality of accommodation.

Russia

International Homestay Agency (www.homestayagency.com/homestay/russia.html)

Host Families Association (www.hofa.ru)

Worldwide Homestay (www.worldwidehomestay.com/Russia.htm)

China

China Homestay (www.chinahomestay.org)

China Study Abroad (www.chinastudyabroad.org)

Parks, Reserves & Protected Areas

Most tourist destinations can be entered without special permits, but you will usually have to pay an admission/permit fee at the entrance.

Fishing

Russia and Mongolia are the two places you are likely to go fishing.

Russia Anglers will take you out onto the waters (or the winter ice) of Lake Baikal. Rules on when you can fish, how and for what species vary from region to region and the time of year; the local boat operator or tour company can take care of permits where required.

Mongolia The situation with permits is very strict. If you fish illegally you risk a fine of about US$40 (or jail, depending on the mood of the ranger). While it's relatively easy to get a fishing permit in a national park in Mongolia, buying one for other areas is much more difficult. Anglers must have a special permit authorised by the **Ministry of Environment and Green Development** (☎051-266 286; www.mne.mn; Negdsen Undestnii Gudamj 5/2, Government Bldg II, Ulaanbaatar), which costs US$120 a week.

Activities in Border Regions

Russia Designated border zones throughout Russia can only be entered with a permit from the local Federalnaya Sluzhba Bezopasnosti (FSB), the Russian Federal Security Service (formerly known as the KGB). No special permits are required for most tourist rail routes and the border crossings. Nor do you usually need one if you are transiting on a main road, but for side trips or deeper exploration inside border regions, such as the Mongolia–Russia border zone in the Altai Republic or Tuva, you certainly will require one.

China Much of the northeastern border between China and Siberia follows the Black Dragon River (Hēilóng Jiāng), known to the Russians as the Amur River. At the time of writing, you didn't need permits to visit any areas along the border, but it would be good to check with the **Public Security Bureau** (PSB, 公安局, Gōng'ānjú; 26 Duan Jie; ☉8.40am-noon & 1.30-4.30pm Mon-Fri) in Hā'ěrbīn.

Mongolia If you are travelling to border areas such as Altai Tavan Bogd National Park in Bayan-Ölgii, the **General Office of Border Protection** (☑011-454 142; Border Defence Bldg; ◷10am-12.30pm & 2-5pm Mon-Fri), in the east of UB, is the place to go for permits. You must send a Mongolian on your behalf to apply with a passport photocopy and a map showing your route.

Children

Travelling in Russia, China or Mongolia with children can be a breeze as long as you come well prepared with the right attitudes, equipment and patience.

Practicalities

➡ Baby-changing rooms are uncommon.

➡ Public toilets are often in poor condition.

➡ Nappies (diapers), powdered milk and baby food are widely available except in rural areas.

➡ Finding English-language kids' publications is difficult; toy shops are plentiful.

➡ Some Russian *firmeny* (premium) trains (including the 1/2 and 9/10) have a staff carriage for children in which the *provodnitsa* (carriage attendant) is also a child-minder; there is also a shower and films and toys for children.

➡ If you are travelling alone with a child on a train, carriage attendants will briefly watch over children while you use the toilet.

➡ Lonely Planet's *Travel with Children* contains useful advice on how to cope with kids on the road and what to bring to make things go more smoothly.

Customs Regulations

Russia

➡ Searches beyond the perfunctory are quite rare, but clearing customs when you leave Russia by a land border can be lengthy.

➡ Visitors are allowed to bring in and take out up to US$10,000 (or its equivalent) in currency, and goods up to the value of €10,000 and weighing less than 50kg, without making a customs declaration.

➡ Fill in a customs declaration form if you're bringing into Russia major equipment, antiques, art works or musical instruments (including a guitar) that you plan to take out with you – get it stamped in the red channel of customs to avoid any problems leaving with the same goods.

➡ If you plan to export anything vaguely 'arty' – instruments, coins, jewellery, antiques, antiquarian manuscripts and books (older than 50 years) or art (also older than 50 years) – it should first be assessed by the **Ministry of Culture** (Коллегия экспертизы; ☑499-391 4212; ul Akademika Korolyova 21, bldg 1, office 505, 5th fl; price R350; ◷11am-5pm Mon-Fri; ⓂVDNKh) in Moscow; it is very difficult to export anything over 100 years old. Bring your item (or a photograph, if the item is large) and your receipt. If export is allowed, you'll be issued a receipt for tax paid, which you show to customs officers on your way out of the country.

China

➡ Chinese customs officers generally pay tourists little attention.

➡ There are no restrictions on foreign currency, but you should declare any cash exceeding US$5000 (or its equivalent in another currency).

➡ Objects considered to be antiques (basically anything made before 1949) require a certificate and red seal to clear customs. To get these, your antiques must be inspected by the **Relics Bureau** (Wénwù Jiàndìng; ☑010-6401 9714, no English spoken).

Mongolia

➡ To export antiques you must have a receipt and customs certificate from the place you bought them; most reliable shops in Ulaanbaatar provide this, otherwise you'll need one from UB's **Centre of Cultural Heritage** (☑7011 0877). You'll need to fill in a form giving your passport number, details of where the antique was purchased and two photos of the antique itself.

➡ If you have anything that even *looks* old, it is a good idea to get a document to indicate that it is not an antique. That goes for Buddha images and statues as well.

Discount Cards

Full-time students and people aged under 26 can sometimes (but not always) get a discount on admissions – flash your student card or International Student Identity Card (ISIC) before paying. If you're not a student but are under 26, ask a student

---

BOOK YOUR STAY ONLINE

For more accommodation reviews by Lonely Planet authors, check out http://lonelyplanet.com/hotels/. You'll find independent reviews, as well as recommendations on the best places to stay. Best of all, you can book online.

agency at home for an ISIC Youth Card (www.isic.org).

Senior citizens also *might* get a discount, but no promises: carry your pension card or passport anyway.

Electricity

→ Electrical power in Russia, China and Mongolia is 220V, 50Hz.

→ Sockets in Russia and Mongolia are designed to accommodate two round prongs in the European style. Chinese plugs come in at least four designs: three-pronged angled pins as used in Australia; three-pronged round pins as in Hong Kong; two-pronged flat pins as in the USA; or two narrow round pins as in Europe.

Embassies & Consulates

Russia

IRKUTSK

Mongolian Consulate
(☏3952-342 447; ul Lapina 11)

KHABAROVSK

Chinese Consulate
(☏4212-302 590; www.china-consulate.khb.ru/rus; Southern Bldg, Lenin Stadium 1; ☉11am-1pm Mon, Wed & Fri)

Japanese Consulate
(☏4212-413 044; www.khabarovsk.ru.emb-japan.go.jp; ul Turganeva 46)

MOSCOW

Australian Embassy
(Посольство Австралии; Map p66;☏495-956 6070; www.russia.embassy.gov.au; Podkolokolny per 10a/2; ⓂKitay-Gorod)

Belarusian Embassy
(Посольство Беларуси; Map p66;☏495-777 6644; www.embassybel.ru; ul Maroseyka 17/6; ⓂKitay-Gorod)

Canadian Embassy
(Посольство Канады; Map p70;☏495-925 6000; http://russia.gc.ca; Starokonyushenny per 23; ⓂKropotkinskaya)

PRACTICALITIES

Russia

→ English-language newspapers include the **Moscow Times** (www.moscowtimes.ru) in Moscow and the weekly **St Petersburg Times** (www.sptimes.ru) in St Petersburg. Also see the online **Siberian Times** (http://siberiantimes.com).

→ Russia follows the metric system.

Mongolia

→ English-language newspapers include the **UB Post** (http://ubpost.mongolnews.mn).

→ Mongolia follows the metric system.

China

→ The standard English-language newspaper is the **China Daily** (www.chinadaily.com.cn). China's largest Chinese-language daily is the **People's Daily** (Rénmín Rìbào).

→ Although China officially subscribes to the metric system, ancient Chinese weights and measures persist. Fruit and vegetables are sold by the *jin,* which is 0.5kg (1.32lb). Tea and herbal medicines are usually sold by the *liang,* which is 37.5g (1.32oz).

Chinese Embassy
(Посольство Китая; ☏consular 499-951 8435; http://ru.chineseembassy.org/rus; ul Druzhby 6; ⓂUniversitet)

Finnish Embassy
(Посольство Финляндии; ☏495-787 4174; www.finland.org.ru; Kropotkinsky per 15/17; ⓂPark Kultury)

French Embassy
(Посольство Франции; Map p70;☏495-937 1500; www.ambafrance-ru.org; ul Bolshaya Yakimanka 45; ⓂOktyabrskaya)

German Embassy
(Посольство Германии;☏495-937 9500; www.germania.diplo.de; Mosfilmovskaya ul 56; ☐119; ⓂUniversitet)

Irish Embassy (Посольство Ирландии; Map p66;☏495-937 5911; www.embassyofireland.ru; Grokholsky per 5; ⓂProspekt Mira)

Japanese Embassy
(Посольство Японии; Map p66;☏495-229 2550; www.ru.emb-japan.go.jp; Grokholsky per 27; ⓂArbatskaya)

Mongolian Embassy
(Посольство Визовый отдел; Map p66;☏495-690 6792; Borisoglebsky per 11; ⓂArbartskaya) Visa section (Посольство Монголии (Визовая отдель); Map p66; ☏499-241 1548; Spasopeskovsky per 7/1; ⓂSmolenskaya)

Netherlands Embassy
(Посольство Королевства Нидерландов; Map p66;☏495-797 2900; www.netherlands-embassy.ru; Kalashny per 6; ⓂArbatskaya)

New Zealand Embassy
(Посольство Новой Зеландии; ☏495-956 3579; www.nzembassy.com/russia; Povarskaya ul 44; ⓂArbatskaya)

UK Embassy (Посольство Великобритании; Map p66;☏495-956 7200; www.gov.uk/government/world/russia; Smolenskaya nab 10; ⓂSmolenskaya)

Ukrainian Embassy
(Посольство Украины; Map p66; ☑495-629 9742; http://russia.mfa.gov.ua; Leontevsky per 18; Ⓜ Pushkinskaya)

US Embassy (Посольство США; Map p66; ☑495-728 5000; http://moscow.us embassy.gov; Bol Devyatinsky per 8; Ⓜ Barrikadnaya)

NOVOSIBIRSK

German Consulate (☑383-231 0020; www.nowosibirsk.diplo.de; Krasny pr 28)

ST PETERSBURG

Belarusian Consulate (☑812-274 7212; ul Bonch-Bruevicha 3a; Ⓜ Chernyshevskaya)

Chinese Consulate (Посольство Китая; Map p98; ☑812-713 7605; http://saint-petersburg.chineseconsulate.org/rus/; nab kanala Griboyedova 134; Ⓜ Sadovaya, Sennaya Ploshchad)

Finnish Consulate (Map p98; ☑812-331 7600; www.finland.org.ru; Preobrazhenskaya pl 4; Ⓜ Chernyshevskaya)

French Consulate (Map p94; ☑812-332 2270; www.ambafrance-ru.org/-Consulat-Saint-Petersbourg; 5th fl, Nevsky pr 12; Ⓜ Admiralteyskaya)

German Consulate (Map p98; ☑812-320 2400; www.germania.diplo.de; Furshtatskaya ul 39; Ⓜ Chernyshevskaya)

Japanese Consulate (☑812-314 1434; nab reki Moyki 29; Ⓜ Nevsky Pr)

UK Consulate (Map p98; ☑812-320 3200; pl Proletarskoy Diktatury 5; Ⓜ Chernyshevskaya)

US Consulate (Map p98; ☑812-331 2600; stpetersburg.usconsulate.gov; Furshtatskaya ul 15; Ⓜ Chernyshevskaya)

ULAN-UDE

Mongolian Consulate (Посольство Монголии; ☑3012-215 275; ul Profsoyuznaya 6)

VLADIVOSTOK

Australian Consulate (☑4232-446 782; ul Krasnogo Znameni 3)

Chinese Consulate (☑4232-495 037; Hotel Gavan, ul Krygina 3)

Japanese Consulate (☑4232-267 573; ul Verkhneportovaya 46)

South Korean Consulate (☑4232-267 573; ul Pologaya 19)

US Consulate (☑4232-300 070; ul Pushkinskaya 32)

YEKATERINBURG

German Consulate (☑343-359 6399; www.germania.diplo.de/Vertretung/russland/ru/03-jeka/0-gk.html; ul Kuybysheva 44)

UK Consulate (☑343-253 5600; ul Gogolya 15A)

US Consulate (☑343-379 4691; http://russian.yekaterinburg.usconsulate.gov; ul Gogolya 15)

China

BĚIJĪNG

There are two main embassy compounds in Běijīng: Jiànguóménwài and Sānlǐtún. Embassies are open from 9am to noon and 1.30pm to 4pm Monday to Friday, but visa departments are usually only open in the morning.

Australian Embassy (澳大利亚大使馆; ☑010-5140 4111; www.china.embassy.gov.au; 21 Dongzhimenwai Dajie)

Canadian Embassy (☑010-5139 4000; www.canadainternational.gc.ca; 19 Dongzhimenwai Dajie)

French Embassy (法国大使馆; ☑010-8532 8080; www.ambafrance-cn.org; 3 Sanlitun Dongsanjie)

German Embassy (Map p310; ☑010-8532 9000; www.china.diplo.de; 17 Dongzhimenwai Dajie, 东直门外大街17号)

Indian Embassy (☑010-8531 2515; www.indianembassy.org.cn; 5 Liang Ma Qiao Bei Jie)

Irish Embassy (☑010-8531 6200; www.embassyofireland.cn; 3 Ritan Donglu)

Kazakhstan Embassy (☑010-6532 6182; 9 Sanlitun Dongliujie)

Mongolian Embassy (蒙古大使馆; Ménggǔ Dàshǐguǎn; Map p315; ☑010-6532 1203; 2 Xiushui Beijie) There is a separate visa section (Map p315; ☑010-6532 6512; ⏰ 9am-11am Mon-Fri).

Netherlands Embassy (☑010-8532 0200; www.hollandinchina.org; 4 Liangmahe Nanlu)

New Zealand Embassy (☑010-8531 2700; www.nzembassy.com/china; 3 Sanlitun Dongsanjie)

North Korean Embassy (Map p315; ☑010-6532 1186; 11 Ritan Beilu)

Pakistan Embassy (Map p310; ☑010-6523 3504; www.pakbj.org.pk; 1 Dongzhimenwai Dajie)

Russian Embassy (俄罗斯大使馆; Èluósī Dàshǐguǎn; Map p310; ☑010-6532 1381; www.russia.org.cn; 4 Dongzhimen Beizhongjie, 东直门内大街东直门北中街4号, off Dongzhimennei Dajie)

UK Embassy (Map p315; ☑010-5192 4000; www.gov.uk/government/world/china; 11 Guanghua Lu)

US Embassy (美国大使馆; ☑010-8531 3000; http://beijing.usembassy-china.org.cn; 55 Anjialou Lu)

Vietnamese Embassy (越南大使馆, Yuènán Dàshǐguǎn; Map p315; ☑010-6532 1155; http://vnemba.org.cn; 32 Guanghua Lu, 光华路32号)

HOHHOT

Mongolian Consulate (蒙古领事馆, Měnggǔ Língshìguǎn; 5 Dongying Nanjie, 东影南街5号; ⏰ 9am-noon Mon, Tue & Thu)

ÈRLIÁN (ERENHOT)

Mongolian Consulate (☑151-6497-1992; Youyi Lu; ⏰ 9am-noon & 3-5pm Mon-Fri)

Mongolia

Note that the German embassy also looks after the

interests of Dutch, Belgian, Greek and Portuguese citizens. The British embassy handles normal consular duties for most Commonwealth countries.

ULAANBAATAR

Canadian Embassy (Map p258; 011-332 500; www.canadainternational.gc.ca/mongolia-mongolie; Central Tower 6th fl, Peace Ave)

Chinese Embassy (Map p258; 011-323 940; http://mn.china-embassy.org; Zaluuchuudyn Örgön Chölöö 5) The consular section is actually on Baga Toiruu.

French Embassy (Map p258; 011-324 519; www.ambafrance-mn.org; Peace Ave 3)

German Embassy (Map p258; 011-323 325; www.ulan-bator.diplo.de; Negdsen Undestnii Gudamj 7)

Japanese Embassy (011-320 777; www.mn.emb-japan.go.jp; Olympiin Gudamj 6)

Kazakhstan Embassy (011-345 408; kzemby@mbox.mn; Zaisan Gudamj, Khan Uul District) The embassy is located on the way to Zaisan; take the last right turn before the bridge, into an alley with hideous-looking villas. Look for the Kazakh flag on the right.

Russian Embassy (Map p258; 011-327 191, 011-312 851; www.mongolia.mid.ru/en; Peace Ave A6)

UK Embassy (011-458 133; www.british-embassy.net/mongolia.html; Peace Ave 30)

US Embassy (7007 6001; http://ulaanbaatar.usembassy.gov; Denver St 3)

Food

For more on Chinese food, see p374.
For more on Mongolian food, see p365.
For more on Russian food, see p357.

Restaurant hours:
China 10am to 10pm
Mongolia 10am to 10pm

MEAL PRICES

The following meal prices are for two courses plus a non-alcoholic drink:

SYMBOL	MOSCOW & ST PETERS-BURG/REST OF RUSSIA	MONGOLIA	CHINA
$	<R500/R300	<T7000	<¥40
$$	R500-1000/R300-800	T7000-T14,000	¥40-100
$$$	>R1000/R800	>T14,000	>¥100

Russia noon to midnight

Gay & Lesbian Travellers

Russia

➡ Russia is a conservative country and being gay is generally frowned upon. LGBT people face stigma, harassment and violence in their everyday lives.

➡ Homosexuality isn't illegal, but promoting it (and other LGBT lifestyles) is. What constitutes promotion is at the discretion of the authorities.

➡ There are active and relatively open gay and lesbian scenes in both Moscow and St Petersburg. Elsewhere, the gay scene tends to be underground.

➡ For a good overview, visit http://english.gay.ru, which has up-to-date information, good links and a resource for putting you in touch with personal guides for Moscow and St Petersburg. Also see http://comingoutspb.ru/en/en-home, the site of a St Petersburg support organisation.

China

Despite China's florid homosexual traditions, the puritanical overseers of the Chinese Communist Party (CCP) have worked tirelessly to suppress gays. Even in urban areas, gay and lesbian visitors should not be too open about their sexual orientation in public. **Utopia** (www.utopia-asia.com/tipschin.htm) has tips on travelling in China and a complete listing of gay bars nationwide.

Mongolia

Mongolia is not a gay-friendly place, nor one to test local attitudes towards homosexuality. Ulaanbaatar has a small gay community that will occasionally convene at a tolerant restaurant or bar, but it moves around every few months, so you'll need to quietly tap into the scene and ask. Insight can be found at www.utopia-asia.com/tips-mong.htm and www.gay.mn.

Insurance

It's wise to take out travel insurance to cover theft, loss and medical problems. There are many policies available, so check the small print for things such as ambulance cover or an emergency flight home. Worldwide travel insurance is available at www.lonelyplanet.com/travel_services. You can buy, extend and claim online any time – even if you're already on the road.

Internet Access

Most hotels and many cafes and restaurants in big cities along the Trans-Siberian routes have in-room broadband or wi-fi connections.

Russia

Internet access is cheapest at the main post office or telephone office (typically around R30 to R40 an hour). Wi-fi is common, particularly in Moscow and St Petersburg and other large cities, where many bars, cafes, restaurants and hotels have it. Often access is free but you may have to ask for a password (*parol*) to get online. A few hotels have high-speed link via broadband cables; if so they can usually provide the connection cords if you don't have one.

China

Despite massive usage, China's clumsy tango with the internet continues to cause some headaches for travellers. Wi-fi accessibility in hotels, cafes, restaurants and bars is generally good. The best option is to bring a wi-fi equipped smartphone, tablet or laptop or use your hotel computer or broadband internet connection.

The Chinese authorities remain mistrustful of the internet and censorship is heavy-handed. Around 10% of websites are blocked; sites like Google may be slow, while social-networking sites such as Facebook and Twitter are blocked (as is YouTube). Gmail is often inaccessible, as is Google Drive, so plan ahead. Newspapers such as the *New York Times* are also blocked, as is Bloomberg. Users can get around blocked websites by using a VPN (Virtual Private Network) service such as Astrill (www.astrill.com).

Internet cafes are of limited use; many only accept customers with Chinese IDs, barring foreigners. In large cities and towns, the area around the train station generally has internet cafes (网吧; *wǎngbā*) if you want to try your luck.

Mongolia

You'll find internet cafes on nearly every street in downtown Ulaanbaatar. Expect to pay between T400 to T800 per hour for online access, double or triple that for hotel business centres.

Wi-fi access is widespread in Ulaanbaatar. Wi-fi in rural areas is still uncommon. Many apartment rentals offer internet access of some kind, either wi-fi or with a cable hook-up. If you don't mind a slow connection you can even use dial-up – a card that will last for 10 hours is available from the Central Post Office for T3000.

Legal Matters

In Russia, and to a lesser extent in Mongolia, it's generally best to avoid contact with the police. It's not uncommon for Russian police to bolster their puny incomes by extracting sham 'fines' from the unaware; you always have the right to insist to be taken to a police station (we don't recommend this) or that the 'fine' be paid the legal way through Sberbank. If you do need police assistance (ie you've been the victim of a robbery or an assault) go to a station with a Russian for both language and moral support.

Note anyone caught smoking in a public place in Russia can be subjected to fines of up to R1500, according to a law that came into force in 2014. This includes bars, restaurants, children's playgrounds, station platforms or at the end of carriages on long-distance trains.

If you are arrested, the police in all three countries are obliged to inform your embassy or consulate immediately and allow you to communicate with it without delay. Although you can insist on seeing an embassy or consular official straight away, you can't count on the rules being followed, so be polite and respectful towards officials and hopefully things will go far more smoothly for you.

Maps

Maps of all the major cities along the route are on sale in each city.

➡ **Russia** City and regional maps for Russia are available from bookshops and map shops in Moscow or St Petersburg. Magazine kiosks at larger Russian train stations usually sell city maps.

➡ **China** In Běijīng, English-language maps of the city are available for free at most big hotels and branches of the Běijīng Tourist Information Center.

➡ **Mongolia Conservation Ink** (www.conservationink.org) produces maps (US$8) using satellite images combined with useful information on culture, wildlife and tourist facilities. The national park series includes Gorkhi-Terelj and Khustain Nuruu.

Money

The Russian currency is the rouble (рубль), abbreviated as 'ру' or 'р'. There are 100 kopeks in a rouble and these come in coin denominations of one (rarely seen), five, 10 and 50. Also issued in coins, roubles come in amounts of one, two, five and 10, with banknotes in values of 10, 50, 100, 500, 1000 and 5000 roubles.

In Russia, it is illegal to make purchases in any currency other than roubles. When you run into prices quoted in euros or dollars (or the pseudonym 'units', often written as 'ye' – the abbreviation for *uslovnye yedenitsy*, conventional units) in expensive restaurants and hotels, you will still be presented with a final bill in roubles.

The Chinese currency is the renminbi (RMB), or 'people's money'. The basic unit of RMB is the yuán (元; ¥), which is divided into 10 jiǎo, which is again divided into 10 fēn. Colloquially, the yuán is referred to as *kuài* and jiǎo as *máo*. The fēn has so little value these days that it is rarely used.

The Bank of China issues RMB bills in denominations of one, two, five, 10, 20, 50 and 100 yuán. Coins come in denominations of one yuán, five jiǎo, one jiǎo and five fēn.

The Mongolian unit of currency is the tögrög (T), which comes in notes of T5, T10, T20, T50, T100, T500, T1000, T5000, T10,000 and T20,000 (T1 notes are basically souvenirs).

ATMs

➺ **Russia** Use your credit or debit card as you would in ATMs at home and you can obtain cash as you need it – usually in roubles, but sometimes in dollars or euros, too. You're rarely a block or so from an ATM: look for signs that say *bankomat* (БАНКОМАТ).

➺ **China** Bank of China and the Industrial & Commercial Bank of China (ICBC) 24-hour ATMs are plentiful, and you can use Visa, MasterCard, Cirrus, Maestro Plus and American Express to withdraw cash. All ATMs accepting international cards have dual language ability.

➺ **Mongolia** Golomt, Trade & Development Bank, Khan Bank and Khas Bank all have ATMs in their Ulaanbaatar and countryside branches. These ATMs accept Visa and MasterCard and work most of the time, allowing you to withdraw up to T600,000 per day.

Cash

Any currency you bring should be in pristine condition: banks and exchange bureaus do not accept old,

tatty bills with rips or tears. Wrap notes in plastic if you're carrying them anywhere sweaty.

There are no official facilities for exchanging money on the train but some *provodnitsas* or the restaurant staff will accept foreign cash at very poor exchange rates – don't count on this. Stock up at your major stops, where you should find ATMs. There are usually exchange places at border-town train stations.

Get rid of your tögrög before you leave Mongolia, as almost no one will want to touch them once you are outside the country.

Credit Cards

Credit cards are accepted in Russian cities and towns, but don't rely on them in more rural areas. When using a credit card at Russian stations to buy tickets, say so early on by showing it. Cash is usually required for train tickets in China and Mongolia. Most sizable cities in Russia have banks or exchange bureaus that will give you a cash advance on your credit card, but be prepared for paperwork in the local language. Always carry enough cash for a night in a hotel – hand-held card machines in Russian hotels may suffer communication breakdown.

In Mongolia credit cards are often accepted at top-end hotels, the expensive souvenir shops, airline offices and travel agencies, but usually with an additional 3% charge. Banks can give cash advances off credit cards, often for no charge if you have Visa, but as much as 4% with MasterCard.

In China credit cards are useful for withdrawing money at ATMs, but are much less useful for buying goods and services.

Tipping

➺ **Russia** Common in restaurants – about 10% is good. Tip your guide, if you have one, a similar amount

of their daily rate; a small gift is appropriate if service is especially good.

➺ **China** Neither required nor expected, except for porters in upmarket hotels.

➺ **Mongolia** Optional; if you round up the bill, then your server will be satisfied.

Travellers Cheques

Use only as backup if you are going to be getting off the train in large cities. In descending order of acceptance, the favourites are American Express, Thomas Cook and Visa; you'll have little or no luck with other brands.

Opening Hours

Russia

Museum hours are not uniform. They close one day a week and there will be one extra 'sanitary' day per month when the facility is closed for cleaning.

Banks	9am-6pm Mon-Fri, some open 9am-5pm Sat
Restaurants & bars	noon-midnight, bars usually until 3am Fri & Sat
Businesses & shops	10am-9pm Mon-Fri, 10am-7pm Sat & Sun

Mongolia

Many museums and tourist attractions have shorter hours and more days off in winter.

Banks	9am-6pm Mon-Fri, 10am-3pm Sat
Government offices	9am-5pm Mon-Fri
Restaurants	10am-10pm
Shops	10am-8pm

China

Banks	9am–noon & 2-5pm Mon-Fri
Restaurants	10.30am-11pm
Shops	10am-10pm

Photography

For more professional tips on taking some decent photos, read Lonely Planet's *Travel Photography*, by Richard I'Anson.

Equipment & Backup All major towns have photographic shops for digital burning to CD, printing and film purchases. Slide film is not widely sold.

Photographing People Always ask before photographing someone, especially on the train (including the *provodnitsa*). In Russian, 'May I take a photograph of you?' is *'Mozhno vas sfotografirovat?'*; in Mongolian it is *'Bi tany zurgiig avch bolokh uu?'*. Remember that many people will be touchy if you photograph 'embarrassments' such as drunks, run-down housing and other signs of social decay.

Restrictions

Sensitive Infrastructure In all three countries (but especially in Russia), be particularly careful about taking photographs of stations, official-looking buildings and any type of military/security structure. Sometimes over-eager police in Russia will stop you taking a platform photo.

Museums and Galleries Many forbid flash pictures, some ban all photos and most will charge you extra to snap away. Some caretakers in historical buildings and churches charge mercilessly for the privilege of using a still or video camera.

Religious Buildings Taking photos inside churches and in monasteries and temples is discourteous or, in the case of the latter in Mongolia, forbidden; you may photograph building exteriors and monastery grounds.

Post

The postal service in all three countries is generally reliable, although Russia can still be a problem zone. Allow at least a couple of weeks for letters and postcards to arrive home from Mongolia, more like four or five from Russia (although it can be quicker), and about five to 10 days from China. The major Russian cities, plus Běijīng and Ulaanbaatar, have international private courier firms such as **FedEx** (www.fedex.com), **UPS** (www.ups.com), **DHL** (www.dhl.com) and **TNT Express** (www.tnt.com).

For receiving post along the Trans-Mongolian, Běijīng and Ulaanbaatar central post offices are useful for poste restante (in Russia there's no poste restante, and embassies and consulates won't hold mail for transient visitors).

Ulaanbaatar Central Post Office ('Poste Restante, Central Post Office, Ulaanbaatar') seems to work quite well; bring along your passport as proof of identification. Don't even think about using poste restante anywhere else in the country.

Běijīng International Post Office ('Poste Restante GPO, Beijing') Costs ¥3 and letters are held for a maximum one month. Take your passport for collection.

Public Holidays

Russia

Many businesses are closed from 1 to 7 January. Another widely celebrated holiday is Easter Monday.

New Year's Day 1 January

Russian Orthodox Christmas Day 7 January

Defender of the Fatherland Day 23 February

International Women's Day 8 March

International Labour Day/ Spring Festival 1 May

Victory Day (1945) 9 May

Russian Independence Day (when the Russian republic of the USSR proclaimed its sovereignty in 1991) 12 June

Unity Day 4 November

China

The 1 May holiday kicks off a three-day holiday, while National Day marks a week-long holiday from 1 October, and the Chinese New Year is also a week-long holiday for many. It's not a great idea to arrive in China or go travel-

---

RUSSIAN STREET NAMES

We use the Russian names of all streets and squares to help you when deciphering Cyrillic signs and asking locals the way. To save space, the following abbreviations are used:

bul – bulvar бульвар – boulevard

nab – naberezhnaya набережная – embankment

per – pereulok переулок – side street

pl – ploshchad площадь – square

pr – prospekt проспект – avenue

sh – shosse шоссе – road

ul – ulitsa улица – street

Please also note that some of the Soviet-era names for streets and places have been changed back to their prerevolutionary names or to new names.

ling during these holidays as things tend to grind to a halt. Hotel prices in China rapidly shoot up during these holiday periods.

New Year's Day 1 January

Chinese New Year (Spring Festival) Usually February

International Women's Day 8 March

International Labour Day 1 May

Youth Day 4 May

International Children's Day 1 June

Birthday of the Chinese Communist Party 1 July

Anniversary of the Founding of the People's Liberation Army 1 August

National Day 1 October

Mongolia

Note that Constitution Day, Women's Day and Mongolian Republic Day are generally normal working days.

Shin Jil (New Year's Day) 1 January

Constitution Day 13 January

Tsagaan Sar January/February; a three-day holiday celebrating the Mongolian New Year

Women's Day 8 March

Mother & Children's Day 1 June; a great time to visit parks

National Day Celebrations (Naadam Festival) 11–12 July

Mongolian Republic Day 26 November

Safe Travel

Russia, China and Mongolia are generally safe countries and crime against foreigners is rare.

Trains On the whole the trains are reasonably safe, but it always pays to take simple precautions with your luggage. If you've got the compartment to yourself, ask the carriage attendant to lock it when you leave for the restaurant car or get out at the station platforms.

Traffic Your biggest danger in all three countries – always keep your wits about you.

Stray Dogs A problem especially in rural areas in Russia and Mongolia. An often effective defence against dogs (and potential muggers) is a loud whistle.

Pickpockets Exercise caution, especially in Ulaanbaatar on Peace Ave, between the post office and the State Department Store.

Alcoholism A problem in Mongolia and Russia; you are bound to encounter drunks in both the city and countryside. On the trains, the carriage attendant can sort out difficulties.

Hotels Generally, hotels are quite safe, but leaving valuables lying around your room is tempting providence. Always take precautions at youth hostels and guesthouses, where other travellers may be trying to subsidise their journeys.

Taxis Use an official taxi – as opposed to a private vehicle – late at night in Ulaanbaatar. The same goes for Russia, and even with official taxis in Russia it's usually better to agree on a price before you get in; whenever possible, store your luggage on the back seat, where you can easily retrieve it, not in the boot. While the risk is greater outside of cities, even in Běijīng taxi drivers have been known to take passengers to remote areas and rob them.

Manipulation of ATMs Use ATMs in carefully guarded public places such as at banks, major hotels and restaurants as manipulation that allows thieves to read credit card and PIN details is common.

Mosquitoes & Ticks These are the great bane of summer throughout the region. Mostly, they're an annoyance, but in rural areas of Siberia they can be a grave health threat. From May to July, tick-borne encephalitis and lyme disease are problems in Russia.

Border Zones & Regulated Areas Official border crossings aside, Russia's borders are usually off limits. Being caught near borders could result in a large fine at best and deportation at worst. The same

goes for Russia's **closed cities** (usually associated with the military in some way). You will also need permission from the FSB to enter **regulated areas** (Зоны с Регламентированным Посещением Иностранных Граждан), mainly wilderness zones scattered across Russia. These are not obvious and rarely marked – if you are planning any serious backcountry exploration it's worth checking first what official permits you may need, to avoid incurring fines or deportation.

Scams

Russian Police They want to see your documents, find fault (such as not being registered, even when it's not necessary) and want you to pay a 'fine' to get the documents back. It's ransom, and fortunately it's happening less often these days. The only course of action is to remain calm, polite and stand your ground. Show copies, not originals, whenever possible. Try to enlist the help of a passer-by to translate for you (or at least witness what is going on).

Běijīng Airport Taxis A well-established illegal taxi operation at the airport attempts to lure weary travellers into a ¥300-plus ride to the city, so be on your guard. If anyone approaches you offering a taxi ride, ignore them and insist on joining the queue for a taxi outside.

Pretty-Woman Scam On Běijīng's Wangfujing Dajie, well-dressed girls flock to drag single men to expensive cafes or Chinese teahouses, leaving them to foot monstrous bills.

Racism & Discrimination

Sadly, racism is a problem in Russia. Frightening reports of racial violence appear from time to time in the media, and it's a sure thing that if you are non-Caucasian you'll be targeted with suspicion by many (the police, in particular).

Telephone & Fax

In all three countries faxes can be sent from most post offices and upmarket hotels.

Russia

⇒ The country code for Russia is ☑7.

⇒ Local calls from homes and most hotels are free.

⇒ To make a long-distance call from most phones first dial ☑8, wait for a second dial tone, then dial the city code and number.

⇒ To make an international call dial ☑8, wait for a second dial tone, then dial ☑10, then the country code etc. Some phones are for local calls only and won't give you that second dial tone. From mobile phones, just dial ☑+ followed by the country code to place an international call.

MOBILE PHONES

There are several major networks, all offering pay-as-you-go deals.

Beeline (http://moskva.beeline.ru)

Megafon (http://moscow.megafon.ru)

MTS (www.mts.ru)

Skylink (http://skylink.ru)

Reception is available right along the Trans-Siberian Railway and increasingly in rural areas. MTS probably has the widest network. Our researchers found Beeline to be pretty reliable.

To call a mobile phone from a landline, the line must be enabled to make paid (ie nonlocal) calls. SIMs and phone-credit top-up cards are available at any mobile phone shop or kiosk across cities and towns (you'll usually find them in the airport arrival areas and train stations). They cost as little as R300 and can be slotted into your regular mobile phone handset during your stay (assuming it is unlocked). Call prices are very low within local networks, but charges for roaming larger regions can mount up; cost-conscious locals switch SIM cards when crossing regional boundaries.

Topping up your credit can be done either via prepaid credit cards bought from kiosks or mobile phone shops or, more commonly, via certain ATMs (look for phone logos on the options panel) and the brightly coloured QIWI Cash-in paypoint machines found in all shopping centres, metro and train stations and the like. Choose your network, input your telephone number and the amount of credit you'd like, insert the cash and it's done, minus a small fee for the transaction. Confirmation of the top-up comes via a text message to your phone.

PAY PHONES

Taksofon (pay phones, ТАКСОФОН) are located throughout most cities. They're usually in working order but don't rely on them. Most take prepaid phone-cards. There are several types of card-only phones, and not all cards are interchangeable. Card phones can be used for either local and domestic calls, or for international calls.

PHONECARDS & CALL CENTRES

Local phonecards (телефонная карта) in a variety of units are available from shops and kiosks – they can be used to make local, national and international calls.

Sometimes a call centre is better value for international calls – you give the clerk the number you want to call, pay a deposit and then go to the booth you are assigned to make the call. Afterwards, you either pay the difference or collect your change. Such call centres are common in Russian cities and towns – ask for *mezhdunarodny telefon* (международный телефон).

China

⇒ The country code for China is ☑86.

⇒ To call internationally from China, drop the first zero of the area or city code after dialling the international access code, and then dial the number you wish to call.

⇒ Local calls from hotel-room phones are generally cheap (and sometimes free), although international phone calls are expensive; it's best to use a phonecard.

MOBILE PHONES

If you have an unlocked GMS phone, you can use it with a SIM card from **China Mobile** (www.chinamobileltd.com), which will cost from ¥60 to ¥100 depending on the phone number (Chinese avoid the number four as it sounds like the word for death) and will include ¥50 of credit. When this runs out, you can

top up the number by buy-
ing a credit-charging card
(*chōngzhí kǎ*) from China
Mobile outlets and some
newspaper stands.

PAY PHONES

If making a domestic call,
look out for very cheap public
phones at newspaper stands
(报刊亭; *bàokāntíng*) and
hole-in-the-wall shops (小
卖部; *xiǎomàibù*); you make
your call and then pay the
owner. Domestic and international long-distance phone
calls can also be made from
main telecommunications
offices and 'phone bars' (话
吧; *huàbā*). Cardless international calls are expensive
and it's far cheaper to use an
IP card.

PHONECARDS

If you wish to make international calls, it is much
cheaper to use an IP card.
You dial a local number, then
punch in your account number, followed by a pin number
and finally the number you
wish to call. English-language
service is usually available.
IP cards can be found at
newspaper kiosks, hole-in-
the-wall shops, internet cafes
and from any China Telecom
office, although in some
cities they can be hard to
find. Some IP cards can only
be used locally, while others
can be used nationwide, so it
is important to buy the right
card (and check the expiry
date).

Mongolia

➡ The country code for
Mongolia is ☎976.

➡ Ulaanbaatar has several
area codes; ☎11 is the most
widely used. If a phone
number begins with a 23, 24
or 25, then the area code is
☎21. If the phone number
begins with a 26, the code
is ☎51.

➡ If you are calling out of
Mongolia and are using an
international direct dial
(IDD) phone, just dial ☎00
and then your international
country code. On non-IDD

TIME ZONES

Moscow	Noon	(GMT/UTC +3 hours)
San Francisco	1am	(GMT/UTC -8 hours)
New York	4am	(GMT/UTC -5 hours)
London	9am	(GMT/UTC +0 hours)
Paris, Berlin	10am	(GMT/UTC +1 hour)
Helsinki	11am	(GMT/UTC +2 hours)
Krasnoyarsk, Tuva	4pm	(GMT/UTC +7 hours)
Irkutsk, Ulan-Ude	5pm	(GMT/UTC +8 hours)
Běijīng, Ulaan-baatar, Perth	5pm	(GMT/UTC +8 hours)
Vladivostok, Sydney	7pm	(GMT/UTC +10 hours)

phones you can make direct
long-distance calls by dialling
the international operator
(☎106), who may know
enough English to make the
right connection (but don't
count on it).

➡ The cost of calls from the
central Telecom offices in
any city are reasonable:
T560 per minute to the USA
and UK, T820 per minute to
Australia. To make the call,
you need to pay a deposit
in advance (a minimum
equivalent of three minutes).
A couple of the top-end
hotels have Home Country
Direct dialling, where the
push of a button gets you
through to international
operators in the USA, Japan
and Singapore. You can then
make a credit-card, charge-
card or reverse-charge
(collect) call.

MOBILE PHONES

If you bring an unlocked GSM
phone, it will work with the
SIM cards from **Mobicom**
(www.mobicom.mn) and **Uni-
tel** (www.unitel.mn). Make
sure you buy a SIM card
appropriate for your phone,
as the companies **G-Mobile**
(www.gmobile.mn) and **Skytel**
(www.skytel.mn) are both
on the CDMA network. The
process is simple –
just go to a mobile-phone
office (a good one is the Tedy
Centre on Baruun Selbe
Gudamj), buy a SIM card
(around T7000), and top up
with units as needed.

To call a mobile-phone
number in Mongolia from
abroad, just dial the country
code (☎976) without the
area code. Note that you
drop the '0' off the area code
if dialling an Ulaanbaatar
number *from* a mobile phone
but you retain the '0' if using
other area codes.

PHONECARDS

Pre-paid international phone
cards are available at the
Central Post Office, starting
from T2000. You can use
these when calling from a
landline.

Time

One of the most disorienting
aspects of a Trans-Siberian
trip is working out what
time it is. The important
thing to remember is that
all long-distance trains run
on Moscow time – so check
carefully when you buy a ticket exactly what time *locally*
you should be at the station.
Once inside the station and
on the train all clocks are set
to Moscow time.

Mongolia is divided into
two time zones: the three
western aimags of Bayan-
Ölgii, Uvs and Khovd are one
hour behind Ulaanbaatar and
the rest of the country. Since
1949, China has had only one
time zone, which is the same
as the time in Ulaanbaatar.
Russia has 11 time zones,
nine of which are covered by

the Trans-Siberian routes in this guide.

Russia, China and Mongolia do not change clocks to daylight-saving time.

In this guide we try to list how far major cities and towns are ahead of Moscow time, eg 'Moscow + 5hr' means five hours ahead.

Toilets

It's rare that paper will actually be available in the stalls of public toilets, so always bring a supply of toilet paper or tissue with you. Plumbing systems in all three countries often have problems digesting toilet paper. If there is a rubbish basket next to the toilet, this is where the paper should go.

Russia

Pay toilets are identified by the words платный туалет (platny tualet). In any toilet Ж (zhensky) stands for women's, while M (muzhskoy) stands for men's.

In cities, you'll now find clusters of temporary plastic toilet cubicles in popular public places, although other public toilets are rare and often dingy and uninviting. A much better option are the loos in major hotels or in modern food outlets. In all public toilets, the attendant who you pay your R10 to can provide miserly rations of toilet paper.

China & Mongolia

Public toilets in hotels, ger camps and restaurants are usually European-style, with moderately clean facilities. In contrast, public facilities in parks, stores and train stations usually require that you squat over a smelly hole. In China you'll also come across toilets without doors and separated only by a low partition, making it easy to strike up a conversation with the person squatting next to you.

Toilets along the Route

➡ On Russian and Mongolian trains the toilets are of the Western variety. The bowl on older toilets is designed to allow you to squat. The carriage attendants generally do a good job of keeping them clean, particularly on the more prestigious class of trains.

➡ Before and after any major stops, and along any densely populated stretches of the line, the toilets will be locked; a timetable for this is usually posted on the toilet door.

➡ On Chinese trains (but not train 3/4) toilets are often of the squat variety.

Tourist Information

Russia

Tourist offices like you may be used to elsewhere are few and far between in Russia. Along the Trans-Siberian routes the only places we've found them are St Petersburg, Perm, Kazan and Irkutsk. Elsewhere you're mainly dependent for information on the moods of hotel receptionists and administrators, service bureaus and travel firms. The latter two exist primarily to sell accommodation, excursions and transport – if you don't look like you want to book something, staff may or may not answer questions.

Overseas, travel agencies specialising in Russian travel are your best bet.

China

While Běijīng's tourist information structure is improving, on the whole tourist information facilities in China are rudimentary and of little use for travellers. The fallback position is the China International Travel Service (CITS), with branches in all major towns and cities. There

is usually a member of staff who can speak English and may be able to answer questions and offer some travel advice, but the main purpose of CITS is to sell you an expensive tour.

Mongolia

Ulaanbaatar has a reasonably good tourist information centre.

Travellers with Disabilities

Russia, China and Mongolia can be difficult places for disabled travellers. Most buildings, buses and trains are not wheelchair accessible. In China and Russia, crossing busy streets often requires using underground walkways with many steps. Uneven pavements in the cities and rough roads in the countryside make for uncomfortable and potentially dangerous travel.

For a list of Russian Railways trains with wheelchair accessible carriages see http://eng.rzd.ru/statice/public/en?STRUCTURE_ID=132. Failing these, travellers in wheelchairs will have to be carried on and off the train and into their compartments and will have difficulty with the toilets, which are utterly unfriendly for wheelchairs.

Some useful organisations are:

Australia

Nican (☎1800-806 769, 02-6241 1220; www.nican.com.au; Unit 5, 48 Brookes St, Mitchell, ACT 2911)

Germany

Mare Nostrum (☎030-4502 6454; www.mare-nostrum.de; Oudenarder Strasse 7, Berlin 13347)

UK

Tourism For All (☎0845-124 9971; www.tourismforall.org.uk; 7A Pixel Mill, 44 Appleby Rd, Kendal, Cumbria LA9 6ES)

USA

Accessible Journeys
(☎800-846 4537; www.disabili-tytravel.com; 35 West Sellers Ave, Ridley Park, PA 19078)

Mobility International USA
(☎541-343 1284; www.miusa.org; 132 East Broadway, Suite 343, Eugene, Oregon, 97401)

Visas

For information about obtaining, registering and extending visas for Russia, China and Mongolia, see p41.

Women Travellers

Russian women are very independent and, in general, you won't attract attention by travelling alone.

That said a woman alone should certainly avoid private taxis at night. Never get in any taxi with more than one person – the driver – already

in it. You're unlikely to experience sexual harassment on the streets in most parts of Russia, though sexual stereotyping remains strong. In rural areas, revealing clothing will probably attract unwanted attention (whereas on hot days in Moscow women wear as little as possible).

On the train consider buying a *platskart* ticket (*platskartny;* open carriage) rather than one in a *kupe* (*kupeyny;* compartmentalised carriage), to avoid the risk of getting stuck in a closed compartment with three shady male characters. Some Russian trains offer a female (*zhensky*) compartment. If you travel *kupe* and don't like your cabin mates, tell the conductor, who will more than likely find you a new place. If a drunk starts accosting you, especially on trains or in minibus taxis, simply do what Russian women do: ignore him and avoid eye contact.

China is probably among the safest places in the world for foreign women to travel alone. Women are generally treated respectfully, because principles of decorum are ingrained deeply in the culture.

Mongolia doesn't present too many problems for foreign women travelling independently. The majority of Mongolian men behave in a friendly and respectful manner. However, you may come across an annoying drunk or the occasional macho idiot. The phrase for 'Go away!' is *'Sasha bel'*.

There are occasional incidents of solo female travellers reporting being harassed by their male guide. If your guide is male, it is best to keep in touch with your tour agency in Ulaanbaatar, perhaps making contingency plans with them if things go awry. Better yet, take a female guide whenever possible.

Transport

GETTING THERE & AWAY

Most travellers will start their Trans-Siberian or Trans-Mongolian trip in either Moscow or Běijīng. It's also possible to fly into or out of other major gateways, such as St Petersburg, Irkutsk, Vladivostok or Ulaanbaatar.

Flights, tours and rail tickets can be booked online at lonelyplanet.com/bookings.

Air

Airports & Airlines

Moscow's **Sheremetyevo** (www.svo.aero/en) and **Domodedovo** (www.domodedovo.ru) airports host the bulk of Russia's international flights. There are also many daily international services to St Petersburg's **Pulkovo** (www.pulkovoairport.ru) airport.

Plenty of other trans-Siberian cities have direct international connections, including Irkutsk, Kazan, Khabarovsk, Nizhny Novgorod, Novosibirsk, Perm, Ulan-Ude and Yekaterinburg.

Běijīng's **Capital Airport** (http://en.bcia.com.cn) is served by both international and domestic connections, as is Ulaanbaatar's **Chinggis Khaan Airport** (www.airport.mn).

Airlines flying internationally to/from Mongolia are Aeroflot, Aero Mongolia, Air China, Korean Air, MIAT and Turkish Airlines. From continental Europe, the best connection is MIAT's Berlin–Ulaanbaatar twice-weekly flights via Moscow for one-way/return €790/1340 (at the time of research).

The choice of airlines for Russia and China is much greater, and tickets are usually cheaper.

Tickets

Use any fares quoted here as a guide only. Quoted airfares do not necessarily constitute a recommendation for the carrier. Some agencies specialise in tours and may offer discount fares.

The peculiarity about flying to and from the railheads for travel on the Trans-Siberian routes is that you will probably be flying in and out of two different cities on one-way tickets, and perhaps using two different airlines.

The cheapest tickets to Hong Kong and China can often be found in discount agencies in Chinatowns around the world.

Land

Listed train fares for trips to/from Russia are usually for a 2nd-class *kupe* ticket in a four-berth compartment. Most routes also offer cheaper *platskart* (3rd-class open carriage) fares. See Russian Railways for a complete list of international services (http://eng.rzd.ru – click on 'Passengers').

Border Crossings
RUSSIA–MONGOLIA

The border crossed by the Trans-Mongolian trains is at Naushki (Russia) and Sükhbaatar (Mongolia). It's also possible to cross borders by minivan or local train. In addition, there are three road crossings between Russia

CLIMATE CHANGE & TRAVEL

Every form of transport that relies on carbon-based fuel generates CO_2, the main cause of human-induced climate change. Modern travel is dependent on aeroplanes, which might use less fuel per kilometre per person than most cars but travel much greater distances. The altitude at which aircraft emit gases (including CO_2) and particles also contributes to their climate change impact. Many websites offer 'carbon calculators' that allow people to estimate the carbon emissions generated by their journey and, for those who wish to do so, to offset the impact of the greenhouse gases emitted with contributions to portfolios of climate-friendly initiatives throughout the world. Lonely Planet offsets the carbon footprint of all staff and author travel.

and Mongolia: Tashanta–Tsagaannuur in Bayan-Ölgii aimag; Kyakhta–Altanbulag in Selenge; and Solovyevsk–Ereentsav in Dornod. As a rule, crossings are open from 9am to noon and 2pm to 6pm daily except holidays. The Mondy–Khankh border in northern Khövsgöl is not open to third-country nationals.

MONGOLIA–CHINA
The border crossing is at Zamyn-Üüd and Ereen (Érliàn or Erenhot in Chinese). Don't be concerned if you get off at Ereen (on the Chinese side of the border) and the train disappears from the platform. About an hour is spent changing the bogies (wheel assemblies) because the Russians (and, therefore, the Mongolians) and the Chinese use different railway gauges.

RUSSIA–CHINA
The Trans-Manchurian train crosses the border at Zabaikalsk (Russia) and Mǎnzhōulǐ (China). The bogies are changed here to account for the different rail gauges.

Buses to/from Zabaikalsk (¥65), on the Russian side of the border, depart eight times daily between 7.50am and 1.30pm, but they tend to be much slower than the private cars (because the Chinese traders on your bus will take ages to get through customs). In Mǎnzhōulǐ you could ask around for a ride from a Russian trader (Russians get through faster).

Otherwise, take a taxi to the border (¥20), 9km from town, and get a ride across from there with a Russian driver.

Belarus
TRAIN
Minsk is connected by train with Moscow (R3500, eight to 12 hours, eight daily) and St Petersburg (R4670, 13 to 14 hours, three daily) as well as several other Russian cities.

BUS
At least two buses a week go from Minsk to Moscow and one a week to St Petersburg.

CAR & MOTORCYCLE
There are six main road routes into Russia from Belarus, the recommended one being the E30 highway that connects Brest and Minsk with Smolensk and finishes up in Moscow.

Estonia
The nearest border crossing from Tallinn is at Narva. There are daily trains between Tallinn and Moscow (R8680, 15 hours) and St Peterbsrug (R1720 *platskartny*, six hours 20 minutes). By bus you can connect to/from Tallinn with St Petersburg (from €20, 7½ hours, seven daily) and Kaliningrad (€32, 16 hours, two daily).

Finland
TRAIN
High-speed Allegro trains (from R2300, 3½ hours, four daily) connect St Petersburg

and Helsinki. The daily 31/34 Leo Tolstoy service between Moscow and Helsinki (R6000, 14 hours) also passes through St Petersburg (R4000, seven hours).

BUS
There are many daily buses between Helsinki and St Petersburg.

CAR & MOTORCYCLE
Highways cross at the Finnish border posts of Nuijamaa and Vaalimaa (Brusnichnoe and Torfyanovka, respectively, on the Russian side).

Kazakhstan
There are trains on even days between Moscow and Almaty (R11,500, three days and seven hours) and a few times a week from Astrakhan to Atyrau (R17,300, 12 hours) in addition to several services from Siberia.

Roads into Kazakhstan include those south from Chelyabinsk and Omsk.

Latvia
Overnight trains run daily between Rīga and Moscow (R7000, 15 hours 40 minutes) and St Petersburg (R5200, 15 hours).

Rīga is connected by bus to St Petersburg (€33, 11 hours, six to 11 daily).

The M9 Rīga–Moscow road crosses the border east of Rezekne (Latvia). The A212 road from Rīga leads to Pskov, crossing a corner of Estonia en route.

Lithuania

Trains from Vilnius include Moscow (R4000, 14 to 15 hours, three daily) and St Petersburg (R5900, 13½ hours, two daily). The St Petersburg trains cross Latvia and the Moscow ones cross Belarus, for which you'll need a Belarus visa or transit visa.

Poland

Warsaw is connected with Moscow (from R5400, 17 to 18 hours, two daily). The Moscow trains enter Belarus near Brest, so you'll need a Belarus visa or transit visa.

UK & Western Europe

Travelling overland by train from the UK or Western Europe takes a minimum of two days and nights.

There are no direct trains from the UK to Russia. The cheapest route you can take is on the **Eurostar** (www.eurostar.com) to Brussels, and then via Cologne and Warsaw to Moscow, a journey that also passes through Minsk (Belarus). The total cost can be as low as £207 one way. See www.seat61.com/Russia.htm for details of this and other train services to Moscow.

From Moscow and St Petersburg there are also regular international services to European cities including Amsterdam, Berlin, Budapest, Nice, Paris, Prague and Vienna.

For European rail timetables check www.railfaneurope.net, which has links to all of Europe's national railways.

Ukraine

At the time of research parts of southeastern Ukraine were dangerously volatile – this has affected border crossings and transport services to and from Russia in this region.

TRAIN

Trains from Kyiv to Moscow cross at the Ukrainian border town of Seredyna-Buda.

Trains on this route are as follows (specific numbers are for the best southbound/northbound services):

Moscow–Kyiv *firmeny* R4200, 9½ hours, daily, 1/2

Moscow–Kyiv R3700, 12 to 14 hours, nine daily

Moscow–Lviv R5000, 23 hours, two daily via Kyiv

Moscow–Odesa R5200, 23 hours, daily via Kyiv, 23/24

St Petersburg–Kyiv R6500, 22½ hours, one daily, 53/54

St Petersburg–Lviv R7000, 37½ hours, daily, 47/48

St Petersburg–Odesa R7300, 35 hours, one daily, 19/20

There are also many trains on the Moscow–Kharkiv line, all of which pass through Kharkiv (from R3800, 12 hours) and proceed to southern Ukrainian destinations such as Donetsk (from R4670, 18 hours). While the situation in southeastern Ukraine and Crimea remains unstable it's advisable to make enquiries about safety before proceeding into or out of the country in this direction.

BUS

A handful of weekly buses travel from Kharkiv across the border into Russia on the E95 (M2) road. The official frontier crossing is 40km north of Kharkiv and is near the Russian border town of Zhuravlevka. Check the security situation carefully before arranging to cross into or out of Russia on this route.

CAR & MOTORCYCLE

The main auto route between Kyiv and Moscow starts as the E93 (M20) north of Kyiv, but becomes the M3 when it branches off to the east some 50km south of Chernihiv. At the time of research this was the main safe border crossing for vehicles between Ukraine and Russia.

River & Sea

St Petersburg Between early April and late September, international passenger ferries connect with Stockholm, Helsinki and Tallinn.

Vladivostok Year-round DBS Cruise Ferry (www.dbsferry.com) has connections with Donghae in South Korea, continuing onto Sakaiminato in Japan.

Khabarovsk There are daily ferries across the Amur River to Fŭyuǎn in China.

Travel Agencies & Organised Tours

See Booking Tickets (p33) for listings of travel agencies who offer organised tours on the Trans-Siberian routes and who can also arrange individual tickets and itineraries.

GETTING AROUND

For most, if not all, of your Trans-Siberian journey you're going to be getting around on the train, but sometimes you might need or want to take an internal flight, a boat or a bus.

Air

Unless you plan to explore destinations off the main Trans-Mongolian and Trans-Manchurian railways in China and Mongolia, it is unlikely you will need to fly within those countries. Russia is a different matter, as flights can shorten a route or may be necessary to return from, say, Vladivostok to Moscow.

Russia

Major Russian airlines allow you to book over the internet. Otherwise it's no problem buying a ticket at ubiquitous *aviakassa* (ticket offices). Generally speaking, you'll

AIRLINE SAFETY IN RUSSIA

Deadly lapses in Russian airline safety are frighteningly common. A string of accidents involving Tupolevs – including one near Smolensk (April 2010) which killed 96 people, including the Polish president, and near Petrozavodsk (June 2011) which killed 44 – has raised particular concerns about the continued use of these vintage planes. Then there was the November 2013 crash of a Boeing 737 Tatarstan Airlines flight at Kazan, which killed all 50 people on board.

If you're worried about airline safety, the good news is that for many destinations in Russia, getting there by train or bus is practical and often preferable (if you have the time). But in some cases – where you're short of time or where your intended destination doesn't have reliable rail or road connections – you will have no choice but to take a flight.

Industry experts recommend taking the following factors into account when deciding whether an airline is safe to fly with in Russia:

➡ Where there's a choice stick to airlines that are member of the International Air Transport Association – these include Aeroflot, Transaero, S7 and UTAir.

➡ A Class 1 Russian airport, which has more than 7 million passengers per year, is much more likely to be safe to fly in and out of than a Class 5 airport, which serves less than 100,000 passengers a year.

➡ Fly an airline with regularly scheduled flights, not a charter. The accident rate for charter flights is about three times higher than for regular flights.

➡ Fly off-season. Accidents in Russia tend to peak in busy travel season, when pilots and ground crews are more likely to be overworked and excessively tired.

➡ Check aviation-safety.net or airport.airlines-inform.ru to see the number of accidents and incidents at an airport and read traveller reviews.

do better booking internal flights once you arrive in Russia, where more flights and flight information are available, and where prices may be lower.

Most internal flights in Moscow use either Domodedovo or Vnukovo airports; if you're connecting to Moscow's Sheremetyevo-2 international airport, allow a few hours to cross town. It's a good idea to reconfirm your flight at least 24 hours before takeoff.

China & Mongolia

➡ **China** The Civil Aviation Administration of China (CAAC; Zhōngguó Mínháng) is the authority for numerous airlines, including **Air China** (www.airchina.com.cn), **China Eastern Airlines** (www.ce-air.com) and **China Southern Airlines** (www.cs-air.com). Check timetables at www.elong.net.

➡ **Mongolia** Dirt airstrips are the norm, and almost all destinations are served from Ulaanbaatar. If you plan to fly in one direction and travel overland in another, try to book and fly from Ulaanbaatar, as flying from rural towns can mean waiting several days for a seat, especially in summer. See www.flyeznis.com and www.aeromongolia.mn for inland routes and ticket purchases.

Train

For more information on train travel see Choosing Your Route (p24).

Russia

The trains of **Russian Railways** (RZD, РЖД; www.eng.rzd.ru) are generally comfortable and punctual. Bookings open 45 days before the date of departure. On the Trans-Siberian main line try to book at least a few days ahead for the cheapest places. Tickets for key trains on the busy Moscow–St Petersburg route can be difficult to come by at short notice if you are not flexible.

If you speak Russian, the nationwide free information service ☏8-800-775 0000 can be useful.

At the station you'll be confronted by several ticket windows. Some are special windows reserved exclusively for use by the elderly or infirm, heroes of the Great Patriotic War or members of the armed forces. All will have different operating hours and generally non-English-speaking staff.

The sensible option, especially if there are long queues, is to use the service centre (сервис центр) found at most major stations. Here you'll encounter helpful, sometimes English-speaking staff who, for a small fee

READING A TRAIN TIMETABLE

Russian train timetables vary from place to place but generally list a destination, train number, category of train, frequency of service, and time of departure and arrival in Moscow time, unless otherwise noted.

Trains in smaller city stations generally begin somewhere else, so you'll see a starting point and a destination on the timetable. For example, when catching a train from Yekaterinburg to Irkutsk, the timetable may list Moscow as the point of origin and Irkutsk as the destination. The following are a few key points to look out for.

Number

Номер (nomer). The higher the number of a train, the slower it is; anything over 900 is likely to be a mail train.

Category

Скорый (Skory), Пассажирский (Passazhirsky), Почтово-багажный (Pochtovo-bagazhny), Пригородный (Prigorodny) – and various abbreviations thereof. These are train categories and refer, respectively, to fast, passenger, post-cargo and suburban trains. There may also be the train's name, usually in quotation marks, eg 'Россия' (Rossiya).

Frequency

Ежедневно (yezhednevno, daily), чётные (chyotnye, even-numbered dates), нечётные (ne-chyotnye, odd-numbered dates), отменён (otmenyon, cancelled). All of these can appear in various abbreviations, notably еж, ч, не and отмен.

Days of the week are listed usually as numbers (where 1 is Monday and 7 Sunday) or as abbreviations (Пон, Вт, Ср, Чт, Пт, С and Вск are, respectively, Monday to Sunday). Remember that time-zone differences can affect these days. So in Chita (Moscow +6hr) a train timetabled at 23.20 on Tuesday actually leaves 5.20am on Wednesday.

In months with an odd number of days, two odd days follow one another (eg 31 May, 1 June). This throws out trains working on an alternate-day cycle so if travelling near month's

(typically around R200), can book your ticket.

Tickets for suburban trains are often sold at separate windows or from an automatic ticket machine (автомат). A table beside the machine tells you which price zone your destination is in.

LEFT LUGGAGE

Many train stations have a left-luggage room (камера хранения, kamera khranenia) or left-luggage lockers (автоматические камеры хранения, avtomaticheskiye kamery khranenia). These are generally secure, but make sure you note down the room's opening and closing hours and, if in doubt, establish how long you can leave your stuff for. Typical costs are around R120 per bag per day (according to size) or R130 per locker.

Here is how to work the left-luggage lockers (they're generally the same everywhere). Be suspicious of people who offer to help you work them, above all when it comes to selecting your combination.

➡ Put your stuff in an empty locker.

➡ Decide on a combination of one Russian letter and three numbers and write it down or remember it.

➡ Set the combination on the inside of the locker door.

➡ Close the locker.

➡ Pay the attendant the fee.

To open the locker, set your combination on the outside of your locker door. Note that even though it seems as if the knobs on the outside of the door should correspond directly with those on the

inside, the letter is always the left-most knob, followed by three numbers, on both the inside and the outside. After you've set your combination, wait a second or two for the electrical humming sound and then pull open the locker.

China

Although carriages can be crowded, trains are the best way to get around the country in reasonable speed and comfort.

The following classes are available on Chinese trains:

Hard seat (硬座; yìngzuò) Generally padded, but this class can still be hard on one's sanity – it can be dirty, noisy and crowded. You may or may not have a seat reservation.

Soft seat (软座; ruǎnzuò) Less crowded, on some shorter routes.

end pay special attention to the hard-to-decipher footnotes on a timetable. For example, '27/V – 3/VI Ч' means that from 27 May to 3 June the train runs on even dates. On some trains, frequency depends on the time of year, in which case details are usually given in similar abbreviated small print: eg '27/VI – 31/VIII Ч; 1/IX – 25/VI 2, 5' means that from 27 June to 31 August the train runs on even dates, while from 1 September to 25 June it runs on Tuesday and Friday.

Arrival & Departure Times

Corresponding trains running in opposite directions on the same route may appear on the same line of the timetable. In this case you may find route entries such as время отправления с конечного пункта (vremya otpravlenia s konechnogo punkta), or the time the return train leaves its station of origin. Most train times are given in a 24-hour time format, and almost always in Moscow time (Московское время, Moskovskoye vremya). But sub urban trains are usually marked in local time (местное время, mestnoe vremya). From here on it gets tricky (as though the rest wasn't), so don't confuse the following:

➡ время отправления (vremya otpravleniya) Time of departure.

➡ время отправления с начального пункта (vremya otpravleniya s nachalnogo punkta) Time of departure from the train's starting point.

➡ время прибытия (vremya pribytiya) Time of arrival at the station you're in.

➡ время прибытия на конечный пункт (vremya pribytiya v konechny punkt) Time of arrival at the destination.

➡ время в пути (vremya v puti) Duration of the journey.

Distance

You may sometimes see the расстояние (rastoyaniye) – distance in kilometres from the point of departure – on the timetable as well. These are rarely accurate and usually refer to the kilometre distance used to calculate the fare.

Hard sleeper (硬卧; yìngwò) Doorless compartments with half a dozen bunks in three tiers; sheets, pillows and blankets are provided.

Soft sleeper (软卧; ruǎnwò) Four comfortable bunks in a closed compartment; on Z-class trains (the best) you'll also have your own TV. Z-class trains also have luxury two-berth compartments with their own shower and toilet facilities. It does very nicely as an overnight hotel.

Once you are on the train, the conductor may be able to upgrade your ticket if space is available in other carriages. The cost of the upgraded ticket is pro rata to the distance travelled in the higher class.

For tips on reading tickets, see http://cnvol.com/read-china-train-ticket.htm. For more info on China's railways and trains, consult the following sites:

Duncan Peattie's Chinese Railways Home Page (www.chinatt.org) English-language timetable information for trains in China.

Man in Seat 61 (www.seat61.com/china.htm)

Railways of China (www.railwaysofchina.com)

Mongolia

Note that you can't use the Trans-Mongolian Railway for domestic transport. If you're travelling from Ulaanbaatar, it is important to book a soft seat well in advance – this can be done up to 10 days before departure. There may be a small booking fee. In general, booking ahead is a good idea for any class, though there will always be hard-seat tickets available.

There are usually three classes on domestic passenger trains:

Hard seat Padded bunks, but none are assigned, nor is there any limit to the amount of tickets sold; carriages are always crowded and dirty.

Hard sleeper (platzkartnuu) Looks just like the hard seat but everyone gets their own bunk and optional sheets and a blanket (T1000). Upgrades available to soft seat.

Soft seat Compartments with four assigned beds. If you travel at night, clean sheets are provided for about T1100; a wise investment since some of the quilts smell of mutton.

Boat

Russia

In summer it's possible to travel long distances across Russia on passenger boats. You can do this either by taking a cruise, which you can book through agencies at home or in Russia, or by using scheduled river passenger services. The season runs from late May through to mid-October, but is shorter on some routes.

Numerous boats ply routes between Moscow and St Petersburg, many stopping at some of the Golden Ring cities on the way; and along the Volga River from Moscow to other Trans-Siberian cities such as Nizhny Novgorod and Kazan. In Siberia and the Russian Far East there are services along the Ob and Irtysh Rivers (between Omsk and Tobolsk), the Yenisey from Krasnoyarsk, the Lena from Ust-Kut via Lensk to Yakutsk, as well as across Lake Baikal from Irkutsk to Nizhneangarsk.

Beware that boat schedules can change radically from year to year (especially on Lake Baikal) and are only published infuriatingly close to the first sailing of each season.

Bus

Long-distance buses generally serve areas with no railway or routes on which trains are slow, infrequent or overloaded.

Russia

Most cities have a main intercity *avtovokzal* (автовокзал; bus station). Tickets are sold at the station or on the bus. Fares are normally listed on the timetable and posted on a wall. As often as not you'll get a ticket with a seat assignment, scribbled almost illegibly on a till receipt. Buses are cheaper than trains and often faster. You need to pay a baggage fee for items that are too large for racks.

Marshrutky (just a diminutive form of *marshrutnoye taksi,* meaning a fixed-route taxi) are minibuses that are quicker than the rusty old buses and rarely cost much more. Where roads are good and villages frequent, *marshrutky* can be twice as fast as buses, and well worth the double fare.

China

Chángtú gōnggòngqìchē (long-distance buses) are one of the best means of getting around China. On popular long-haul routes, *wòpù qìchē* (sleeper buses) may cost around double the price of a normal bus service. Some have comfortable reclining seats, while others have two-tier bunks. Watch out for your belongings on them, however.

In many cities, the train station forecourt doubles as a bus station. Tickets are easy to purchase and often you can just turn up at the bus station and buy them. Booking in advance, however, can secure you a better seat, as many buses have numbered seats; the earlier you buy your ticket, the closer to the front of the bus you will sit.

Car & Motorcycle

A useful general site for motorcyclists, with some information on Russian road conditions, is www.horizonsunlimited.com.

In all countries, vehicles are driven on the right-hand side of the road, in theory. In practice, a Russian, for instance, will drive on footpaths whenever the need arises.

Russia

Siberian roads are atrocious, with potholes large enough to consume an entire vehicle – which is why vehicle workshops with puncture repair services (шиномонтаж; *shinomontazh*) are everywhere in cities. If you are driving, this will be the most useful word to learn.

You'll need to be 18 years old and have an International Driving Permit with a Russian translation of your licence, or a certified Russian translation of your full licence (you can certify translations at a Russian embassy or consulate).

Don't forget your vehicle's registration papers, proof of insurance (be sure it covers you in Russia) and a customs declaration promising that you will take your vehicle with you when you leave. To get the exact details on all this it's best to contact your automobile association (eg the AA or RAC in the UK) at least three months before your trip.

See the US consulate website in Vladivostok (http://vladivostok.usconsulate.gov/acsdriving.html) for some useful tips.

China

Road conditions in China should abolish any remaining desire to drive. Bilingual road signs are making a slow appearance along some highways, but much remains to confuse would-be drivers from abroad.

Both Běijīng's Capital Airport or Shànghǎi's Pǔdōng International Airport have a Vehicle Administration Office (车管所; *chēguǎnsuǒ*) where you can have a temporary three-month driving licence issued. This involves checking your driving licence and a simple medical exam (including an eyesight test). You will need this licence before you can hire a car from reputable companies.

Wikitravel (http://wikitravel.org/en/Driving_in_China) has useful information.

Mongolia

Travellers can use an International Driving Permit to drive any vehicle in Mongolia. The roads are worse than atrocious. Accidents occur frequently. Try to avoid travelling at night, when unseen potholes, drunk drivers and wildlife can wreak havoc. Driving in the dark is also a great way to get completely and utterly lost in Mongolia.

What look like main roads on the map are often little more than tyre tracks in the dirt, sand or mud, and there is hardly a signpost in the whole country. Remote tracks quickly turn into eight-lane dirt highways devoid of any traffic, making navigation tricky – some drivers follow the telephone lines when there are any, or else ask for directions at gers along the way. Towns with food and water are few and far between, and very few people in the countryside will speak anything but Mongolian or, if you are lucky, Russian.

Hitching

Hitching is never entirely safe in any country in the world, and Lonely Planet doesn't recommend it. Travellers who hitch should understand that they are taking a small but potentially serious risk.

Russia

Hitching in Russia is a very common method of getting around. Hitching in cities in private vehicles is becoming less of a necessity these days but in the countryside, especially in remote areas not well served by public transport, it's a major mode of transport. You are expected to pitch in for petrol; paying what would be the normal bus fare for a long-haul ride is appropriate.

China

Hitching in China is more difficult. Sometimes even a moderate, agreed-upon price can be inflated by the driver on arrival. Unless you travel into extremely remote regions, there is little reason to hitch, as it's neither cost-saving nor necessary.

Mongolia

Because the country is so vast, public transport so limited and the people so poor, hitching (usually on trucks) is a recognised – and, often, the only – form of transport in the countryside. Hitching is seldom free and often no different from just waiting for public transport to turn up. It is *always* slow – with stops, a truck can take 48 hours to cover 200km.

Hitching is not generally dangerous personally, but it is still hazardous and often extremely uncomfortable. Don't expect much traffic in remote rural areas; you might see one or two vehicles a day on many roads, and sometimes nobody at all for several days. The best place to wait is a petrol station on the outskirts of town, where most vehicles stop before any journey. Pay truck drivers about T3000 per hour travelled.

Local Transport

Russia & Mongolia

In Russia and Mongolia, using buses and minibuses is easier than in China. For a taxi in Ulaanbaatar, just flag down any driver and agree on a price – T400 per kilometre was the rate at the time of writing.

In Russia, flagging down any driver and agreeing on a price is still a method in some cities, but official taxis are common. Some drivers use meters (the number on the meter must be multiplied by the multiplier listed on a sign that should be on the dashboard or somewhere visible), but generally it's better to haggle a price. Depending on your haggling skills and the city, this will be about R200 to R500 for a short city ride.

Most Russians book taxis. Normally, the dispatcher will ring you back or send a text message within a few minutes to provide a description and licence number of the car. If you don't have a phone or speak Russian, duck into the nearest large hotel and ask them to order for you. Restaurant staff will often help if you eat there.

Whenever possible avoid putting luggage in the trunk of the taxi in Russia and Mongolia, as the driver can hold it for ransom.

China

Navigation on buses can be tricky for non-Chinese speakers as Chinese without Pinyin appears on stops. Taxis (出租汽车; *chūzū qìchē*) are cheap, plentiful and easy to find. Taxi drivers rarely speak any English so have your destination written down in characters. To use the same driver again, ask for his card (名片; *míngpiàn*). Taxi rates per kilometre are clearly marked on a sticker on the rear side window of the taxi, and there's a flagfall. China also has motorcycles, motor tricycles and pedal powered tricycles, all mustering outside train and bus stations. Agree on prices first for these.

Health

Russia, Mongolia and China present few serious health problems. If you are dependent upon strong or finely dosed medication, you should consult your doctor about dosages due to the changes in time zones. Apart from injury due to a traffic accident on the busy streets and bad drivers, the main dangers are ticks in some regions, bacteria in drinking water and coping with heat or cold. HIV infection is a serious problem, especially in Siberia – *always* take precautions.

BEFORE YOU GO

➡ Pack medications in their original, clearly labelled containers.

➡ Double your vital medication needs in case of loss or theft.

➡ Western medicine can be in short supply in Mongolia; bring whatever you think you might need from home.

➡ Take a signed and dated letter from your physician describing any medical conditions and medications (using generic names).

➡ If carrying syringes or needles, ensure you have a physician's letter documenting their medical necessity.

➡ If you have a heart condition, bring a copy of your ECG taken just prior to travelling.

➡ Get your teeth checked before you travel.

➡ If you wear corrective lenses, take a spare pair and your prescription.

Insurance

Make sure you are covered for all regions and activities and find out in advance what is excluded and how payment is arranged. If your health insurance does not cover you for medical expenses abroad, consider supplemental insurance. (Check the Lonely Planet website at www.lonelyplanet.com/travel-insurance for more information.) Make copies of your policy (a digital photograph uploaded into an email account is useful for all documentation). Declare any pre-existing conditions.

Medical Checklist

Following is a list of items you should consider including in your medical kit – consult your pharmacist for brands available in your country.

➡ Antibacterial cream (eg Muciprocin).

➡ Antibiotics (prescription only) – for travel well off the beaten track; carry the prescription with you in case you need it refilled.

➡ Antifungal cream or powder (eg Clotrimazole) – for fungal skin infections and thrush.

➡ Anti-nausea medication (eg Prochlorperazine).

➡ Antiseptic (such as povidone-iodine) – for cuts and grazes.

➡ Aspirin or paracetamol (acetaminophen in the USA) – for pain or fever.

➡ Bandages, Band-Aids (plasters) and other wound dressings.

➡ Calamine lotion, sting-relief spray or aloe vera – to ease irritation from sunburn and insect bites or stings.

➡ Cold and flu tablets, throat lozenges and nasal decongestant.

➡ Insect repellent (DEET-based).

➡ Loperamide or diphenoxylate – 'blockers' for diarrhoea.

➡ Multivitamins – consider them for long trips, when dietary vitamin intake may be inadequate.

➡ Rehydration mixture (eg Gastrolyte) – to prevent dehydration, which may occur during bouts of diarrhoea (particularly important when travelling with children).

➡ Scissors, tweezers and a thermometer – note that mercury thermometers are prohibited by airlines.

➡ Sunscreen, lip balm, face cream (against cold) and eye drops.

➡ Water purification tablets or iodine (iodine is not to be used by pregnant women or people with thyroid problems).

Websites

Centers for Disease Control & Prevention (CDC; www.cdc.gov)

Lonely Planet (www.lonely planet.com)

MD Travel Health (www.mdtravelhealth.com) Provides complete travel health recommendations for every country; updated daily.

World Health Organization (WHO; www.who.int/ith) Publishes the excellent *International Travel & Health*, revised annually and available online at no cost.

Further Reading

Lonely Planet's *Healthy Travel – Asia & India* is a handy pocket size, and is packed with useful information. Also recommended is *Traveller's Health*, by Dr Richard Dawood, and *Travelling Well* (www.travellingwell.com.au), by Dr Deborah Mills.

IN RUSSIA, CHINA & MONGOLIA

Availability & Cost of Health Care

Medical care is readily available across Russia but the quality can vary enormously. The biggest cities and towns have the widest choice of places, with both Moscow and St Petersburg well served by international-style clinics. In remote areas, the standard of care is lower and care should always be taken to avoid the risk of hepatitis B and HIV transmission via poorly sterilised equipment.

Good clinics catering to travellers can be found in major cities in China. They are more expensive than local clinics. These clinics usually have a good understanding of the best local hospital facilities and close contacts with insurance companies.

Mongolia suffers from a serious lack of medical facilities. Health care is readily available in Ulaanbaatar, but choose your hospital and doctor carefully. Ordinary Mongolians won't know the best place to go, but a reputable travel agency or top-end hotel might. The best

---

REQUIRED & RECOMMENDED VACCINATIONS

Ask your doctor for an International Certificate of Vaccination (otherwise known as the yellow booklet), which will list all of the vaccinations you have received, and take it with you. If travelling from a yellow fever zone within six days of entering China, proof of vaccination is required. The following vaccinations are recommended.

➡ **Adult Diphtheria & Tetanus**

➡ **Hepatitis A**

➡ **Hepatitis B**

➡ **Measles, Mumps & Rubella (MMR)** Two doses are recommended unless you have had the diseases.

➡ **Typhoid**

➡ **Varicella** If you haven't had chickenpox, discuss this vaccination with your doctor.

Depending on circumstances and age, the following are worth keeping in mind:

➡ **Influenza A** Especially for those over 65 years of age or with underlying medical conditions.

➡ **Pneumonia** A single injection with a booster after five years is recommended for all travellers over 65 years of age or with underlying medical conditions that compromise immunity.

➡ **Rabies** Three injections are required. A booster after one year will then provide 10 years' protection.

➡ **Tuberculosis (TB)** A complex issue. It's usually recommended that high-risk adult long-term travellers have a TB skin test before and after travel, rather than a vaccination. Only one vaccine is given in a lifetime.

➡ **Japanese B Encephalitis** Consider vaccination if spending a month or longer in parts of the Russian Far East and Siberia, in China, or if making repeated trips to at-risk areas.

DRINKING WATER

The quality of drinking water varies greatly from region to region, so it's best to play it safe:

➡ Never drink tap water.

➡ Check that the seal on bottled water is intact on purchase.

➡ Avoid ice and fresh juices if you suspect they have been watered down.

➡ Boiling water is the most efficient method of purifying it. Trains have a samovar (hot-water heater) in every carriage. (Never use the tap in the train toilet for drinking water or washing vegetables.)

➡ The best chemical purifier is iodine. It should not be used by pregnant women or those with thyroid problems.

➡ Water filters should also filter out viruses. Ensure your filter has a chemical barrier such as iodine and a small pore size, eg less than four microns.

advice will come from your embassy. In rural areas the availability of health services is generally poor. You may be better off travelling on to Běijīng.

Apart from the chief *provodnitsa* (female carriage attendant) probably having a first-aid box, there is no medical assistance available on the train itself.

Infectious Diseases

Rabies

This is a problem in all three countries. It is spread through bites or licks on broken skin from an infected animal. It's always fatal unless treated promptly. Vaccination is advisable for those travelling to remote areas where a reliable source of postbite vaccine is not available within 24 hours. A simple precaution against dog attack is to carry a high-pitched whistle.

Tick-borne Encephalitis & Japanese B Encephalitis

Tick-borne encephalitis is spread by tick bites and is a serious infection of the brain; vaccination is advised for those in risk areas who are unable to avoid tick bites (such as campers, forestry workers and walkers). The risk is highest in spring and summer, when ticks are active. The Ural Mountains, Siberia and the Far East and China's north are particular problem zones. Two doses of vaccine will give a year's protection, three doses will last up to three years.

Typhoid & Hepatitis A

Spread through contaminated food (particularly shellfish) and water, typhoid can cause septicaemia (blood poisoning); hepatitis A causes liver inflammation and jaundice. Neither is usually fatal but recovery can be delayed if you don't see your doctor immediately.

Traveller's Diarrhoea

Treatment for diarrhoea consists of staying well hydrated; rehydration solutions such as Gastrolyte are best. Antibiotics such as norfloxacin, ciprofloxacin or azithromycin will kill the bacteria quickly. Loperamide is just a 'stopper' and doesn't cure the problem; it can be helpful, however, for long rides. Don't take loperamide if you have a fever, or blood in your stools. Seek medical attention quickly if you do not respond to an appropriate antibiotic.

➡ Don't drink the tap water on the trains or in any of the countries unless it's been boiled (eg in the samovar).

➡ Brush your teeth using bottled water.

➡ In all three countries avoid ice, and unpeeled fruit and vegetables that have been washed in tap water.

➡ Check use-by dates of food sold on train platforms.

➡ If a restaurant is full of locals, the food is probably safe.

Environmental Hazards

The temperatures on the trains are generally kept at a comfortable level, but once out in the wide open spaces of Russia, Mongolia and China the main environmental hazards to be careful of are heat exhaustion in summer and frostbite in winter.

Heat Exhaustion & Heatstroke

Heat exhaustion is best avoided by drinking water on a constant basis. Train carriages can get hot in summer and be overheated in winter, so make sure you have sufficient bottled water with you.

Heat stroke is much more serious, resulting in

irrational and hyperactive behaviour and eventually loss of consciousness and death. Rapid cooling by spraying the body with water and fanning is ideal. Emergency fluid and electrolyte replacement by intravenous drip is recommended.

Hypothermia & Frostbite

Winters are cold on the Trans-Siberian routes and proper clothing will reduce the risks of getting hypothermia. Make sure you have a heavy coat ready for station stops. Don't overdo outdoor sightseeing if you are not well-prepared against the cold.

Frostbite is caused by freezing and subsequent damage to bodily extremities. As it develops, the skin blisters and then becomes black. Adequate clothing, staying dry, keeping well hydrated and ensuring adequate calorie intake will help prevent frostbite. Treatment involves rapid rewarming. Avoid refreezing and rubbing the affected areas.

Ticks & Mosquitoes

Ticks can transmit Lyme disease, an infection that may be acquired throughout the region. The illness usually begins with a spreading rash at the site of the tick bite, accompanied by fever, headache, extreme fatigue, aching joints and muscles, and mild neck stiffness. It is essential that you receive medical treatment as serious long-term complications can arise.

Always check all over your body after hiking or outdoor activities. The best way to remove a tick is to use dedicated plastic or metal tweezers designed to grip the head of the tick. Rotate it out of the skin. Ordinary tweezers can also be used.

Mosquitoes are a problem in summer all across Russia. From May to September in the rural areas bordering Mongolia, China and North Korea, take extra-special care as mosquito bites can cause Japanese encephalitis. If visiting rural areas you should consider being immunised.

Travelling with Children

Children should be encouraged to avoid and mistrust any dogs or other mammals because of the risk of rabies and other diseases. Any bite, scratch or lick from a warm-blooded, furry animal should immediately be thoroughly cleaned. If there is any possibility that the animal is infected with rabies, immediate medical assistance should be sought.

Women's Health

Emotional stress, exhaustion and travelling through different time zones can all contribute to an upset in the menstrual cycle.

Travelling along the Trans-Siberia routes while pregnant is possible but not really advisable because emergency treatment can be patchy in remote segments. Always consult your doctor before planning your trip. The most risky times for travel are during the first 12 weeks of pregnancy and after 30 weeks.

Language

In this chapter, we're providing some basic travel words and phrases in Mandarin, Mongolian and Russian that might come in handy during your travels.

MANDARIN

Pinyin & Pronunciation

In 1958 the Chinese adopted a system of writing their language using the Roman alphabet. It's known as Pinyin. The original idea was to eventually do away with Chinese characters. However, tradition dies hard, and the idea has been abandoned. Pinyin, which we've provided alongside the Mandarin script in this chapter, is often used on shop fronts, street signs and advertising billboards. Don't expect all Chinese people to be able to use Pinyin, however. In the countryside and the smaller towns you may not see a single Pinyin sign anywhere, just Chinese characters. Below are some basic guidelines as to how to pronounce Pinyin sounds (in blue in this chapter):

a	as in 'father'
ai	as in 'aisle'
ao	as the 'ow' in 'cow'
e	as in 'her', without audible 'r' sound
ei	as in 'weigh'
i	as the 'ee' in 'meet' (or like a light 'r' as in 'Grrr!' after c, ch, r, s, sh, z, zh)
ian	as the word 'yen'
ie	as the English word 'yeah'
o	as in 'or', without audible 'r' sound
ou	as the 'oa' in 'boat'
u	as in 'flute'
ui	as the word 'way'
uo	like a 'w' followed by 'o'
yu/ü	like 'ee' with lips pursed
c	as the 'ts' in 'bits'
ch	as in 'chop' *
h	as in 'hay', but articulated from further back in the throat
q	as the 'ch' in 'cheese'
sh	as in 'ship' *
x	as in 'ship'
z	as the 'ds' in 'suds'
zh	as the 'j' in 'judge'*

* but with the tongue curled up and back

In Pinyin, the only consonant sounds that occur at the end of a syllable are n, ng and r. Also, apostrophes are occasionally used to separate syllables in order to prevent ambiguity, eg the word píng'ān can be written with an apostrophe after the 'g' to prevent it being pronounced as pín'gān.

Finally, Mandarin is a language with a large number of words with the same pronunciation but a different meaning. The only thing that distinguishes these words are tones – the raising and the lowering of pitch on certain syllables. Mandarin has four tones (high, rising, falling-rising and falling), indicated by accent marks over the vowels. The word ma, for example, has four different meanings according to tone:

high tone	mā (mother)
rising tone	má (hemp, numb)
falling-rising tone	mǎ (horse)
falling tone	mà (scold, swear)

There's a fifth 'neutral' tone (without accent mark) that you can all but ignore.

WANT MORE?

For in-depth language information and handy phrases, check out Lonely Planet's *Mandarin, Russian, Mongolian or China Phrasebooks*. You'll find them at **shop. lonelyplanet.com**.

Basics

When asking a question it is polite to start with qǐng wèn – literally, 'may I ask?'.

Hello	你好。	Nǐhǎo.
Goodbye	再见。	Zàijiàn.
Excuse me		
(to get attention)	劳驾。	Láojià.
(to get past)	借光。	Jièguāng.
Sorry	对不起。	Duìbùqǐ.
Yes./No	是。/不是。	Shì./Bùshì.
Please ...	请……	Qǐng ...
Thank you	谢谢你。	Xièxie nǐ.
You're welcome	不客气。	Bù kèqi.

What's your name?
你叫什么名字？ Nǐ jiào shénme míngzi?

My name is ...
我叫…… Wǒ jiào ...

Do you speak English?
你会说英文吗？ Nǐ huìshuō Yīngwén ma?

I don't understand
我不明白。 Wǒ bù míngbái.

Accommodation

Do you have a single/double room?
有没有（单人/ Yǒuméiyǒu (dānrén/
套）房？ tào) fáng?

How much is it per night/person?
每天/人多少钱？ Měi tiān/rén duōshǎo qián?

air-con	空调	kōngtiáo
bathroom	浴室	yùshì
bed	床	chuáng
campsite	露营地	lùyíngdì
guesthouse	宾馆	bīnguǎn
hostel	招待所	zhāodàisuǒ
hotel	酒店	jiǔdiàn
window	窗	chuāng

Directions

Where's (a bank)?
（银行）在哪儿？ (Yínháng) zài nǎr?

What's the address?
地址在哪儿？ Dìzhǐ zài nǎr?

Could you write the address, please?
能不能请你 Néngbunéng qǐng nǐ
把地址写下来？ bǎ dìzhǐ xiě xiàlái?

Please show me on the map where it is.
请帮我找它在 Qǐng bāngwǒ zhǎo tā zài
地图上的位置。 dìtú shàng de wèizhi.

behind	背面	bèimiàn
far	远	yuǎn
in front of ...	……的前面	... de qiánmian
near	近	jìn
next to	旁边	pángbiān
opposite	对面	duìmiàn
turn left	左转。	Zuǒ zhuǎn.
turn right	右转。	Yòu zhuǎn.

Eating & Drinking

What would you recommend?
有什么菜可以 Yǒu shénme cài kěyǐ
推荐的？ tuījiàn de?

What's in that dish?
这道菜用什么 Zhèdào cài yòng shénme
东西做的？ dōngxi zuòde?

I don't eat (red meat)
我不吃(牛羊肉)。 Wǒ bùchī (niúyángròu)

Cheers!
干杯！ Gānbēi!

That was delicious!
真好吃！ Zhēn hǎochī!

The bill, please
买单！ Mǎidān!

Key Words

appetisers	凉菜	liángcài
bar	酒吧	jiǔbā
bottle	瓶子	píngzi
bowl	碗	wǎn
bread	面包	miànbāo
breakfast	早饭	zǎofàn
butter	黄油	huángyóu
cafe	咖啡屋	kāfēiwū
children's menu	儿童菜单	értóng càidān
(too) cold	(太)凉	(tài) liáng
dinner	晚饭	wǎnfàn
dish (food)	盘	pán
egg	蛋	dàn
food	食品	shípǐn
fork	叉子	chāzi
glass	杯子	bēizi
halal	清真	qīngzhēn
herbs/spices	香料	xiāngliào
highchair	高凳	gāodèng
hot (warm)	热	rè
knife	刀	dāo
kosher	犹太	yóutài
local specialities	地方小吃	dìfāng xiǎochī

lunch	午饭	wǔfàn
main courses	主菜	zhǔ cài
market	菜市	càishì
menu (in English)	(英文) 菜单	(Yīngwén) càidān
noodles	面条	miàntiáo
nuts	果仁	guǒrén
pepper	胡椒粉	hújiāo fěn
plate	碟子	diézi
restaurant	餐馆	cānguǎn
rice (raw/cooked)	大米/米饭	dàmǐ/mǐfàn
salt	盐	yán
soy sauce	酱油	jiàngyóu
(too) spicy	(太)辣	(tài) là
spoon	勺	sháo
sugar	砂糖	shātáng
tofu	豆腐	dòufu
vegetable oil	菜油	càiyóu
vegetarian food	素食食品	sùshí shípín
vinegar	醋	cù
yoghurt	酸奶	suānnǎi

Meat & Fish

beef	牛肉	niúròu
chicken	鸡肉	jīròu
duck	鸭	yā
fish	鱼	yú
lamb	羊肉	yángròu
pork	猪肉	zhūròu
poultry	家禽	jiāqín
seafood	海鲜	hǎixiān

Fruit & Vegetables

apple	苹果	píngguǒ
banana	香蕉	xiāngjiāo
bok choy	小白菜	xiǎo báicài
carrot	胡萝卜	húluóbo
cucumber	黄瓜	huángguā

'dragon eyes'	龙眼	lóngyǎn
fruit	水果	shuǐguǒ
grape	葡萄	pútáo
green beans	扁豆	biǎndòu
guava	石榴	shíliu
lychee	荔枝	lìzhī
mango	芒果	mángguǒ
mushroom	蘑菇	mógū
onion	洋葱	yáng cōng
orange	橙子	chéngzi
pear	梨	lí
pineapple	凤梨	fènglí
plum	梅子	méizi
potato	土豆	tǔdòu
radish	萝卜	luóbo
spring onion	小葱	xiǎo cōng
sweet potato	地瓜	dìguā
vegetable	蔬菜	shūcài

Drinks

beer	啤酒	píjiǔ
Chinese spirits	白酒	báijiǔ
coffee	咖啡	kāfēi
(orange) juice	(橙)汁	(chéng) zhī
milk	牛奶	niúnǎi
mineral water	矿泉水	kuàngquán shuǐ
red wine	红葡萄酒	hóng pútáo jiǔ
rice wine	米酒	mǐjiǔ
soft drink	汽水	qìshuǐ
tea	茶	chá
(boiled) water	(开)水	(kāi) shuǐ
white wine	白葡萄酒	bái pútáo jiǔ

Emergencies

Help!	救命!	Jiùmìng!
Go away!	走开!	Zǒukāi!
I'm lost	我迷路了。	Wǒ mílù le.

There's been an accident!
出事了! Chūshì le!

Call a doctor!
请叫医生来! Qǐng jiào yīshēng lái!

Call the police!
请叫警察! Qǐng jiào jǐngchá!

I'm ill
我生病了。 Wǒ shēngbìng le.

It hurts here
这里痛。 Zhèlǐ tòng.

Where are the toilets?
厕所在哪儿? Cèsuǒ zài nǎr?

SIGNS – MANDARIN

入口	Rùkǒu	**Entrance**
出口	Chūkǒu	**Exit**
问讯处	Wènxùnchù	**Information**
开	Kāi	**Open**
关	Guān	**Closed**
禁止	Jìnzhǐ	**Prohibited**
厕所	Cèsuǒ	**Toilets**
男	Nán	**Men**
女	Nǚ	**Women**

1	一	yī
2	二/两	èr/liǎng
3	三	sān
4	四	sì
5	五	wǔ
6	六	liù
7	七	qī
8	八	bā
9	九	jiǔ
10	十	shí
100	一百	yībǎi
1000	一千	yīqiān

Shopping & Services

I'd like to buy ...
我想买…… Wǒ xiǎng mǎi ...

How much is it?
多少钱？ Duōshǎo qián?

Can you lower the price?
能便宜一点吗？ Néng piányi yīdiǎn ma?

There's a mistake In the bill
帐单上有问题。 Zhàngdān shàng yǒu wèntí.

ATM	自动取款机	zìdòng qǔkuǎn jī
credit card	信用卡	xìnyòng kǎ
internet cafe	网吧	wǎngbā
market	市场	shìchǎng
post office	邮局	yóujú
supermarket	超市	chāoshì
tourist office	旅行店	lǚxíng diàn

Time, Dates & Numbers

What time is it?
现在几点钟？ Xiànzài jǐdiǎn zhōng?

morning	早上	zǎoshang
afternoon	下午	xiàwǔ
evening	晚上	wǎnshàng
yesterday	昨天	zuótiān
today	今天	jīntiān
tomorrow	明天	míngtiān

Monday	星期一	xīngqī yī
Tuesday	星期二	xīngqī èr
Wednesday	星期三	xīngqī sān
Thursday	星期四	xīngqī sì
Friday	星期五	xīngqī wǔ
Saturday	星期六	xīngqī liù
Sunday	星期天	xīngqī tiān

January	一月	yīyuè
February	二月	èryuè
March	三月	sānyuè
April	四月	sìyuè
May	五月	wǔyuè
June	六月	liùyuè
July	七月	qīyuè
August	八月	bāyuè
September	九月	jiǔyuè
October	十月	shíyuè
November	十一月	shíyīyuè
December	十二月	shí'èryuè

Transport

boat	船	chuán
bus (city)	大巴	dàbā
bus (intercity)	长途车	chángtú chē
plane	飞机	fēijī
taxi	出租车	chūzū chē
train	火车	huǒchē
tram	电车	diànchē

I want to go to ...
我要去…… Wǒ yào qù ...

Does it stop at (Hāěrbīn)?
在(哈'ěrbīn)能下车吗？ Zài (Hā'ěrbīn) néng xià chē ma?

What time does it leave?
几点钟出发？ Jǐdiǎnzhōng chūfā?

What time does it get to (Hángzhōu)?
几点钟到(杭州)？ Jǐdiǎnzhōng dào (Hángzhōu)?

Can you tell me when we get to (Hángzhōu)?
到了(杭州)请叫我，好吗？ Dàole (Hángzhōu) qǐng jiào wǒ, hǎoma?

I want to get off here
我想这儿下车。 Wǒ xiǎng zhèr xiàchē.

When's the ... (bus)?	……(车)几点走？	... (chē) jǐdiǎn zǒu?
first	首趟	Shǒutàng
last	末趟	Mòtàng
next	下一趟	Xià yītàng

A ... ticket to (Dàlián).	一张到(大连)的……票。	Yīzhāng dào (Dàlián) de ... piào.
1st-class	头等	tóuděng
2nd-class	二等	èrděng
one-way	单程	dānchéng
return	双程	shuāngchéng

aisle seat	走廊的座位	zǒuláng de zuòwèi
buy a ticket	买票	mǎi piào
cancelled	取消	qǔxiāo
delayed	晚点	wǎndiǎn
hard-seat	硬席/硬座	yìngxí/yìngzuò
hard-sleeper	硬卧	yìngwò
one ticket	一张票	yìzhāng piào
platform	站台	zhàntái
soft-seat	软席/软座	ruǎnxí/ruǎnzuò
soft-sleeper	软卧	ruǎnwò
ticket office	售票处	shòupiàochù
timetable	时刻表	shíkè biǎo
train station	火车站	huǒchēzhàn
two tickets	两张票	liǎngzhāng piào
window seat	窗户的座位	chuānghu de zuòwèi

MONGOLIAN

Mongolian is a member of the Ural-Altaic family of languages, and as such it is distantly related to Turkish, Kazakh, Uzbek and Korean. It has around 10 million speakers worldwide. The traditional Mongolian script (cursive, vertical and read from left to right) is still used by the Mongolians living in the Inner Mongolia Autonomous Region of China. In 1944 the Cyrillic alphabet was adopted and is in use in Mongolia and two autonomous regions of Russia (Buryatiya and Kalmykia). We've used the Cyrillic script in this chapter. The only difference between Mongolian and Russian Cyrillic is that the Mongolian version has two added characters (θ and γ).

It's well worth the effort to familiarise yourself with the Cyrillic alphabet so that you can read maps and street signs. Mongolian pronunciation is also explained in the Cyrillic alphabet table, but if you just read the coloured pronunciation guides given next to each word as if they were English, you'll be understood.

Just remember to pronounce double vowel letters as long sounds, because vowel length can affect meaning. In our pronunciation guides the stressed syllables are in italics.

Basics

Hello	Сайн байна уу?	sain bai·na uu
Goodbye	Баяртай.	ba·yar·tai
Excuse me	Уучлаарай.	uuch·laa·rai
Sorry	Уучлаарай.	uuch·laa·rai
Yes	Тийм.	tiim
No	Үгүй.	ü·güi

CYRILLIC ALPHABET

Cyrillic		Sound (Mongolian)
А а	a	as the 'u' in 'but'
Г г	g	as in 'get'
Ё ё	yo	as in 'yonder'
И и	i	as in 'tin'
Л л	l	as in 'lamp'
О о	o	as in 'hot'
Р р	r	as in 'rub'
У у	u	as in 'rude'
Х х	kh	as the 'ch' in the Scottish *loch*
Ш ш	sh	as in 'shoe'
Ы ы	y	as the 'i' in 'ill'
Ю ю	yu	as the 'yo' in 'yoyo'
	yū	long, as the word 'you'
Б б	b	as in 'but'
Д д	d	as in 'dog'
Ж ж	j	as in 'jewel'
Й й	i	as in 'tin'
М м	m	as in 'mat'
Θ θ	ö	long, as the 'u' in 'fur'
С с	s	as in 'sun'
Y y	ū	long, as the 'o' in 'who'
Ц ц	ts	as in 'cats'
Щ щ	shch	as in 'fresh chips'
Ь ь		'soft sign' meaning the preceding consonant is pronounced with a faint y after it.
Я я	ya	as in 'yard'
В в	v	as in 'van'
Е е	ye	as in 'yet'
	yö	as the 'yea' in 'yearn'
З з	z	as the 'ds' in 'suds'
К к	k	as in 'kit'
Н н	n	as in 'neat'
П п	p	as in 'pat'
Т т	t	as in 'tin'
Ф ф	f	as in 'five'
Ч ч	ch	as in 'chat'
Ъ ъ		'hard sign' meaning the preceding consonant is pronounced without a faint y after it.
Э э	e	as in 'den'

Thank you	Баярлалаа.	ba·yar·la·laa
You're welcome	Зугээр.	zü·geer

What's your name?
Таны нэрийг хэн гэдэг вэ? — ta·ny ne·riig khen ge·deg ve

My name is ...
Миний нэрийг ... гэдэг. — mi·nii ne·riig ... ge·deg

Do you speak English?
Та англиар ярьдаг уу? — ta an·gliar yair·dag uu

I don't understand
Би ойлгохгүй байна. — bi oil·gokh·güi bai·na

Accommodation

I'd like a single/double room
Би нэг/хоёр хүний
өрөө авмаар байна.
bi neg/kho·yor khü·nii ö·röö av·maar bai·na

How much is it per night/week?
Энэ өрөө хоногт/
долоо хоногт ямар
үнэтэй вэ?
e·ne ö·röö kho·nogt/ do·loo kho·nogt ya·mar ün·tei ve

air-con	агааржуулалт	a·gaar·juul·alt
bathroom	угаалгын өрөө	u·gaal·gyn ö·röö
cot	хүүхдийн ор	khüükh·diin or
dormitory	нийтийн байр	nii·tiin bair
hotel	зочид буудал	zo·chid buu·dal
window	цонх	tsonkh
youth hostel	залуучуудын байр	za·luu·chuu·dyn bair

Directions

Where's ...?
... хаана байна вэ? ... khaan bai·na ve

How can I get to ...?
... руу би яаж очих вэ? ... ruu bi yaj o·chikh ve

Can you show me on the map?
Та газрын зураг
дээр зааж өгнө үү?
ta gaz·ryn zu·rag deer zaaj ög·nö üü

address	хаяг	kha·yag
after	ард	ard
before	урд	urd
behind	хойно	khoi·no
in front of	өмнө	öm·nö
straight ahead	чигээрээ урагшаа	chi·gee·ree u·rag·shaa
to the left	зүүн тийш	züün tiish
to the right	баруун тийш	ba·ruun tiish

Eating & Drinking

Can I have a menu, please?
Би хоолны цэс авч
болох уу?
bi khool·nii tses avch bo·lokh uu

What food do you have today?
Өнөөдөр ямар хоол
байна вэ?
ö·nöö·dör ya·mar khool bai·na ve

I'd like to have this
Би энэ хоолыг авья. bi en khoo·lyg a·vi

I don't eat (meat)
Би (мах) иддэггүй. bi (makh) id·deg·gui

We'd like to drink some koumiss
Бид айраг уух
гэсэн юм.
bid ai·rag uukh ge·sen yum

Cheers!
Эрүүл мэндийн төлөө! e·rüül men·diin tö·löö

The bill, please
Тооцоогоо бодуулъя. too·tsoo·goo bo·duu·li

Key Words

appetisers	хүйтэн зууш	khüi·ten zuush
bottle	шил	shil
bread	талх	talkh
breakfast	өглөөний хоол	ög·löö·nii khool
butter	цөцгийн тос	tsöts·giin tos
cake	бялуу	bya·luu
camel yogurt	хоормог	khoor·mog
canteen	гуанз	guanz
cold	хүйтэн	khüi·ten
cheese	бяслаг	byas·lag
cream	өрөм	ö·röm
cup	аяга	a·yag
(dried) curds	ааруул	aa·ruul
dairy	цагаан-идээ	tsa·gaan i·dee
dessert	амтат зууш	am·tat zuush
dinner	оройн хоол	o·roin khool
dining room	зоогийн газар	zoo·giin ga·zar
dumplings	банштай	ban·shtai
egg	өндөг	ön·dög
food	хоол	khool
fork	сэрээ	se·ree
fried	шарсан	shar·san
fried food	хуураг	khuu·rag
glass	шилэн аяга	shi·len a·yag
honey	зөгийн бал	zö·giin bal
hot	халуун	kha·luun
ice cream	зайрмаг	zair·mag
jam	жимсний чанамал	jims·nii cha·na·mal
knife	хутга	khu·tag
lunch	үдийн хоол	ü·diin khool
market	зах	zakh
menu	хоолны цэс	khool·ny tses
noodle soup	гоймонтой шөл	goi·mon·toi shöl
pasta	хөндий гоймон	khön·diin goi·mon
pepper	поваарь	po·vaair
plate	таваг	ta·vag
restaurant	ресторан	res·to·ran

rice	цагаан будаа	tsa·gaan bu·daa
salad	ногоон зууш	no·goon zuush
salt	давс	davs
set dish	бэлэн хоол	be·len khool
soup	шөл	shöl
sour cream	тараг/цөгцгий	ta·rag/tsöts·gii
spoon	халбага	khal·bag
tea shop	цайны газар	tsai·ny ga·zar
sugar	чихэр	chi·kher
vegetarian	ногоон хоолтон	no·goon khool·ton
with rice	будаатай	bu·daa·tai

Meat & Fish

antelope	цагаан зээр	tsa·gaan zeer
beef	үхрийн мах	ü·khriin makh
carp	булуу цагаан	bu·luu tsa·gaan
chicken	тахианы мах	ta·khia·ny makh
duck	нугас	nu·gas
fillet	гол мах	gol makh
fish	загас	za·gas
goat	ямаа	ya·maa
kebab	шорлог	shor·log
marmot	тарваг	tar·vag
meat	мах	makh
(fried) meat pancake	хуушуур	khuu·shuur
meat with rice	будаатай хуураг	bu·daa·tai khuu·rag
mutton	хонины мах	kho·ni·ny makh
mutton dumplings	бууз	buuz
patty	бифштекс	bif·shteks
perch	алгана	al·gan
pike	цурхай	tsurh·kai
pork	гахайн мах	ga·khain makh
salmon	омуль	o·mul
sausage	хиам/зайдас/ сосик	khiam/zai·das/ so·sisk
sturgeon	хилэм	khi·lem
antevenison	бугын мах	bu·gyn makh
wild boar	бодон гахай	bo·don ga·khai

Fruit & Vegetables

apple	алим	a·lim
cabbage	байцаа	bai·tsaa
carrot	шар лууван	shar luu·van
cucumber	өргөст хэмэх	ör·göst khe·mekh
fruit	жимс	jims
onion	сонгино	son·gin
potato	төмс	töms
radish	улаан лууван	u·laan luu·van
salad	салат	sa·lad

tomato	улаан лооль	u·laan loo·il
turnip	манжин	man·jin
vegetable	ногоо	no·goo

Drinks

beer	пиво	piv
coffee	кофе	ko·fi
(buckthorn) juice	(чацарганы) шүүс	(cha·tsar·ga·ny) shüüs
koumiss	айраг	ai·rag
lemonade	нимбэгний ундаа	nim·beg·nii un·daa
milk	сүү	süü
milk tea	сүүтэй цай	süü·tei tsai
milk with rice	сүүтэй будаа	süü·tei bu·daa
mineral water	рашаан ус	ra·shaan us
tea	цай	tsai
vodka	архи	a·rikh
wine	дарс	dars

Emergencies

Help!	Туслаарай!	tus·laa·rai
Go away!	Зайл!	zail
I'm lost	Би төөрчихлөө.	bi töör·chikh·löö

There's been an accident
Осол гарчээ. o·sol gar·chee

Call a doctor/the police!
Эмч/Цагдаа дуудаарай! emch/tsag·daa duu·daa·rai

I'm ill
Би өвчтэй байна. bi övch·tei bai·na

It hurts here
Энд өвдөж байна. end öv·döj bai·na

Where is the toilet?
хорлон хаана байна вэ? jor·long khaan bai·na ve

Shopping & Services

I'd like to buy ...
Би ... авмаар байна. bi ... av·maar bai·na

How much is it?
Энэ ямар үнэтэй вэ? en ya·mar ün·tei ve

Can you reduce the price?
Та үнэ буулгах уу? ta ün buul·gakh uu

exchange rate	мөнгөний ханш	möng·nii khansh
post office	шуудан	shuu·dan
public phone	нийтийн утас	nii·tiin u·tas
signature	гарын үсэг	ga·ryn ü·seg
travellers check	жуулчны чек	juulch·ny chek

Time, Dates & Numbers

What time is it?

Хэдэн цаг болж байна?		khe·den tsag bolj bai·na

morning	өглөө	ög·löö
afternoon	өдөр	ö·dör
evening	орой	o·roi
yesterday	өчигдөр	ö·chig·dör
today	өнөөдөр	ö·nöö·dör
tomorrow	маргааш	mar·gaash

Monday	даваа	da·vaa
Tuesday	мягмар	myag·mar
Wednesday	лхагва	lkha·vag
Thursday	пүрэв	pü·rev
Friday	баасан	baa·sang
Saturday	бямба	byamb
Sunday	ням	nyam

Remember to add the word cap sar (literally 'month', 'moon') after the following words:

January	нэгдүгээр	neg·dü·geer
February	хоёрдугаар	kho·yor·du·gaar
March	гуравдугаар	gu·rav·du·gaar
April	дөрөвдүгээр	dö·röv·dü·geer
May	тавдугаар	tav·du·gaar
June	зургадугаар	zur·ga·du·gaar
July	долдугаар	dol·du·gaar
August	наймдугаар	naim·du·gaar
September	есдүгээр	yes·dü·geer
October	аравдугаар	a·rav·du·gaar
November	арваннэг-дүгээр	ar·van·neg·dü·geer
December	арванхоёр-дугаар	ar·van·kho·yor·du·gaar

1	нэг	neg
2	хоёр	kho·yor
3	гурав	gu·rav
4	дөрөв	dö·röv
5	тав	tav
6	зургаа	zur·gaa
7	долоо	do·loo
8	найм	naim
9	ес	yös
10	арав	ar·av
100	зуу	zuu
1000	мянга	myang·ga

Transport

What times does the ... leave/arrive?

... хэдэн цагт явдаг/ирдэг вэ?		... khe·den tsagt yav·dag/ir·deg ve

bus	Автобус	av·to·bus
plane	Нисэх онгоц	ni·seh on·gots
train	Галт тэрэг	galt te·reg
trolleybus	Троллейбус	trol·lei·bus

I want to go to ...

Би ... руу явмаар байна.   bi ... ruu yav·maar bai·na

Can you tell me when we get to ...?

Бид хэзээ ... хүрэхийг хэлж өгнө үү?	bid khe·zee ... khu·re·hiig helj ög·nö uu

I want to get off!

Би буумаар байна!   bi buu·maar bai·na

1st class	нэгдүгээр зэрэг	neg·dü·geer ze·reg
2nd class	хоёрдугаар зэрэг	kho·yor·du·gaar ze·reg
one-way ticket	нэг талын билет	neg ta·lyn bi·let
return ticket	хоёр талын билет	kho·yor ta·lyn bi·let

first	анхны	ankh·ny
next	дараа	da·raa
last	сүүлийн	süü·liin

airport	нисэх онгоцны буудал	ni·sekh on·gots·ny buu·dal
bus stop	автобусны зогсоол	av·to·bus·ny zog·sool
platform	давцан	dav·tsan
ticket office	билетийн касс	bi·le·tiin kass
timetable	цагийн хуваарь	tsa·giin khu·vaair
train station	галт тэрэгний буудал	galt te·re·ge·nii buu·dal

RUSSIAN

Russian belongs to the Slavonic language family and is closely related to Belarusian and Ukrainian. It has more than 150 million speakers within the Russian Federation and is used as a second language in the former republics of the USSR, with a total number of speakers of more than 270 million.

Russian is written in the Cyrillic alphabet (see the next page), and it's well worth the effort familiarising yourself with it so that you can read maps, timetables, menus and street signs. Otherwise, just read the coloured pronunciation guides given next to each Russian phrase in this chapter as if they were English, and you'll be understood. Most sounds are the same as in English, and the few differences in pronunciation are explained in the alphabet table. The stressed syllables are indicated with italics.

Basics

Hello	Здравствуйте.	zdrast·vuy·tye
Goodbye	До свидания.	da svi·da·nya
Excuse me	Простите.	pras·ti·tye
Sorry	Извините.	iz·vi·ni·tye
Yes/No	Да./Нет.	da/nyet
Please	Пожалуйста.	pa·zhal·sta
Thank you	Спасибо.	spa·si·ba
You're welcome	Пожалуйста.	pa·zhal·sta

What's your name?
Как вас зовут?   kak vas za·vut

My name is ...
Меня зовут ...   mi·nya za·vut ...

Do you speak English?
Вы говорите   vi ga·va·ri·tye
по-английски?   pa·an·gli·ski

I don't understand
Я не понимаю.   ya nye pa·ni·ma·yu

Accommodation

Do you have a ... room?	У вас есть ...?	u vas yest' ...
single	одноместный номер	ad·na·myest·nih no·mir
double	номер с двуспальней кроватью	no·mir z dvu·spal'·nyey kra·va·tyu
How much is it for ...?	Сколько стоит за ...?	skol'·ka sto·it za ...
a night	ночь	noch'
two people	двоих	dva·ikh
boarding house	пансионат	pan·si·a·nat
campsite	кемпинг	kyem·ping
heating	отопление	a·ta·plye·ni·ye
hot water	горячая вода	ga·rya·cha·ya va·da
hotel	гостиница	ga·sti·ni·tsa
youth hostel	общежитие	ap·shi·zhih·ti·ye
light	свет	svyet

Directions

Where is ...?
Где ...?   gdye ...

What's the address?
Какой адрес?   ka·koy a·dris

Could you write it down, please?
Запишите,   za·pi·shih·tye
пожалуйста.   pa·zhal·sta

Can you show me (on the map)?
Покажите мне,   pa·ka·zhih·tye mnye
пожалуйста   pa·zhal·sta
(на карте).   (na kar·tye)

behind ...	за ...	za ...
far	далеко	da·li·ko
in front of ...	перед ...	pye·rit ...
near	близко	blis·ka
next to ...	рядом с ...	rya·dam s ...
opposite ...	напротив ...	na·pro·tif ...
straight ahead	прямо	prya·ma

Eating & Drinking

What would you recommend?
Что вы рекомендуете?   shto vih ri·ka·min·du·it·ye

What's in that dish?
Что входит в это   shto fkho·dit v e·ta
блюдо?   blyu·da

I don't eat (meat).
Я не ем (мяса).   ya nye yem (mya·sa)

To your health!
За ваше здоровье!   za va·shih zda·rov·ye

That was delicious!
Было очень вкусно!   bih·la o·chin' fkus·na

Please bring the bill
Принесите,   pri·ni·sit·ye
пожалуйста счёт.   pa·zhal·sta shot

Key Words

bottle	бутылка	bu·tihl·ka
bowl	миска	mis·ka
bread	хлеб	khlyep
breakfast	завтрак	zaf·trak
cheese	сыр	sihr
cold	холодный	kha·lod·nih
dinner	ужин	u·zhihn
dish	блюдо	blyu·da
egg	яйцо	yeyt·so
fork	вилка	vil·ka
glass	стакан	sta·kan
honey	мёд	myot

hot (warm)	жаркий	*zhar*·ki
knife	нож	nosh
lunch	обед	ab·*yet*
menu	меню	min·*yu*
nut	орех	ar·*yekh*
oil	масло	*mas*·la
pasta	паста	*pa*·sta
pepper	перец	*pye*·rits
plate	тарелка	tar·*yel*·ka
restaurant	ресторан	ris·ta·*ran*
rice	рис	ris
salt	соль	sol'
spoon	ложка	*losh*·ka
sugar	сахар	*sa*·khar
vinegar	уксус	*uk*·sus
with	с	s
without	без	byez

Meat & Fish

beef	говядина	gav·ya·di·na
caviar	икра	i·*kra*
chicken	курица	*ku*·rit·sa
duck	утка	*ut*·ka
fish	рыба	*rih*·ba
herring	сельдь	syelt'
lamb	баранина	ba·*ra*·ni·na
meat	мяса	*mya*·sa
oyster	устрица	*ust*·rit·sa
pork	свинина	svi·*ni*·na
prawn	креветка	kriv·*yet*·ka
salmon	лососина	la·sa·*si*·na
veal	телятина	til·*ya*·ti·na
turkey	индейка	ind·*yey*·ka

Fruit & Vegetables

apple	яблоко	*yab*·la·ka
bean	фасоль	fa·*sol'*
cabbage	капуста	ka·*pu*·sta
capsicum	перец	*pye*·rits
carrot	морковь	mar·*kof'*
cauliflower	цветная капуста	tsvit·*na*·ya ka·*pu*·sta
cucumber	огурец	a·gur·*yets*
fruit	фрукты	*fruk*·tih
mushroom	гриб	grip
onion	лук	luk
orange	апельсин	a·pil'·*sin*
peach	персик	*pyer*·sik
pear	груша	*gru*·sha

plum	слива	*sli*·va
potato	картошка	kar·*tosh*·ka
spinach	шпинат	shpi·*nat*
tomato	помидор	pa·mi·*dor*
vegetable	овощ	*o*·vash

CYRILLIC ALPHABET

Cyrillic	Sound (Russian)
А а	a	as in 'father' (in a stressed syllable); as in 'ago' (in an unstressed syllable)
Б б	b	as in 'but'
В в	v	as in 'van'
Г г	g	as in 'get'
Д д	d	as in 'dog'
Е е	ye	as in 'yet' (in a stressed syllable and at the end of a word);
	i	as in 'tin' (in an unstressed syllable)
Ё ё	yo	as in 'yore' (often printed without dots)
Ж ж	zh	as the 's' in 'measure'
З з	z	as in 'zoo'
И и	i	as the 'ee' in 'meet'
Й й	y	as in 'boy' (not transliterated after ы or и)
К к	k	as in 'kind'
Л л	l	as in 'lamp'
М м	m	as in 'mad'
Н н	n	as in 'not'
О о	o	as in 'more' (in a stressed syllable);
	a	as in 'hard' (in an unstressed syllable)
П п	p	as in 'pig'
Р р	r	as in 'rub' (rolled)
С с	s	as in 'sing'
Т т	t	as in 'ten'
У у	u	as the 'oo' in 'fool'
Ф ф	f	as in 'fan'
Х х	kh	as the 'ch' in 'Bach'
Ц ц	ts	as in 'bits'
Ч ч	ch	as in 'chin'
Ш ш	sh	as in 'shop'
Щ щ	shch	as 'sh-ch' in 'fresh chips'
Ъ ъ	–	'hard sign' meaning the preceding consonant is pronounced as it's written
Ы ы	ih	as the 'y' in 'any'
Ь ь		'soft sign' meaning the preceding consonant is pronounced like a faint y
Э э	e	as in 'end'
Ю ю	yu	as the 'u' in 'use'
Я я	ya	as in 'yard' (in a stressed syllable);
	ye	as in 'yearn' (in an unstressed syllable)

SIGNS – RUSSIAN

Вход	Entrance
Выход	Exit
Открыт	Open
Закрыт	Closed
Справки	Information
Запрещено	Prohibited
Туалет	Toilets
Мужской (М)	Men
Женский (Ж)	Women

Drinks

beer	пиво	pi·va
'soviet-brand' champagne	советское шампанское	sav·yet·ska·ye sham·pan·ska·ye
coffee	кофе	kof·ye
(orange) juice	(апельсин-овый) сок	(a·pil'·si·na·vih) sok
milk	молоко	ma·la·ko
tea	чай	chey
(mineral) water	(минеральная) вода	(mi·ni·ral'·na·ya) va·da
vodka	водка	vot·ka
(home-made) vodka	самогон	sa·ma·gon
wine	вино	vi·no

Emergencies

Help!
Помогите! — pa·ma·gi·tye

Leave me alone!
Приваливай! — pri·va·li·vai

I'm lost
Я заблудился/ — ya za·blu·dil·sa/
заблудилась. (m/f) — za·blu·di·las'

There's been an accident
Произошёл — pra·i·za·shol
несчастный случай. — ne·shas·nih slu·chai

Call a doctor!
Вызовите врача! — vih·za·vi·tye vra·cha

Call the police!
Вызовите милицию! — vih·za·vi·tye mi·li·tsih·yu

I'm ill
Я болен/больна. (m/f) — ya bo·lin/bal'·na

It hurts here
Здесь болит. — zdyes' ba·lit

Where are the toilets?
Где здесь туалет? — gdye zdyes' tu·al·yet

Shopping & Services

I need ...
Мне нужно ... — mnye nuzh·na ...

How much is it?
Сколько стоит? — skol'·ka sto·it

That's too expensive
Это очень дорого. — e·ta o·chen' do·ra·ga

There's a mistake in the bill
Меня обсчитали. — min·ya ap·shi·ta·li

bank	банк	bank
market	рынок	rih·nak
post office	почта	poch·ta
telephone office	телефонный пункт	ti·li·fo·nih punkt

Time, Dates & Numbers

What time is it?
Который час? — ka·to·rih chas

Is this Moscow time?
Это московское — e·ta ma·skof·ska·ye
время? — vryem·ya

Is this local time?
Это местное — e·ta myes·na·ye
время? — vryem·ya

morning	утро	ut·ra
afternoon	после обеда	pos·lye ab·ye·da
evening	вечер	vye·chir

yesterday	вчера	vchi·ra
today	сегодня	si·vod·nya
tomorrow	завтра	zaft·ra

Monday	понедельник	pa·ni·dyel'·nik
Tuesday	вторник	ftor·nik
Wednesday	среда	sri·da
Thursday	четверг	chit·vyerk
Friday	пятница	pyat·ni·tsa
Saturday	суббота	su·bo·ta
Sunday	воскресенье	vas·kri·syen·ye

January	январь	yan·var'
February	февраль	fiv·ral'
March	март	mart
April	апрель	ap·ryel'
May	май	mai
June	июнь	i·yun'
July	июль	i·yul'
August	август	av·gust
September	сентябрь	sin·tyabr'

October	октябрь	ak·*tyabr'*
November	ноябрь	na·*yabr'*
December	декабрь	di·*kabr'*

1	один	a·*din*
2	два	dva
3	три	tri
4	четыре	chi·*tih*·ri
5	пять	pyat'
6	шесть	shest'
7	семь	syem'
8	восемь	*vo*·sim'
9	девять	*dye*·vyat'
10	десять	*dye*·syat'
100	сто	sto
1000	тысяча	*tih*·si·cha

Transport

A ... ticket (to Novgorod).	Билет ... (на Новгород).	bil·*yet* ... (na *nov*·ga·rat)
one-way	в один конец	v a·*din* kan·*yets*
return	в оба конца	v *o*·ba kan·*tsa*
arrival	прибытие	pri·*bih*·ti·ye
baggage	багаж	ba·*gash*
bus	автобус	af·*to*·bus
conductor/ carriage attendant	проводник	pra·*vad*·nik
departure	отправление	at·prav·*lye*·ni·ye
first	первый	*pyer*·vih
last	последний	pas·*lyed*·ni
map	карта	*kar*·ta
metro token	жетон	zhi·*ton*
platform	платформа	plat·*for*·ma
(bus) stop	остановка	a·sta·*nof*·ka
ticket	билет	bil·*yet*
ticket office	билетная касса	bil·*yet*·na·ya *ka*·sa
timetable	расписание	ras·pi·*sa*·ni·ye
train	поезд	*po*·ist
tram	трамвай	tram·*vai*
trolleybus	троллейбус	tra·*lyey*·bus

I want to go to ...
Я хочу ехать в ... — ya kha·*chu* ye·*khat'* v ...

Does it stop at ...?
Поезд останавливается в ...? — *po*·yist a·sta·*nav*·li·va·yit·sa v ...

When does it leave?
Когда отправляется? — kag·*da* at·prav·*lya*·it·sa

When is the next train?
Когда следующий поезд? — kag·*da* slye·du·yu·shi *po*·ist

Which platform does the train leave from?
С какой платформы отходит поезд? — s ka·*koy* plat·*for*·mih at·*kho*·dit *po*·ist

How long does it take to get to ...?
Сколько времени нужно ехать до ...? — *skol'*·ka *vrye*·mi·ni *nuzh*·na ye·*khat'* da ...

What station is this?
Какая эта станция? — ka·*ka*·ya e·ta *stant*·sih·ya

What's the next station?
Какая следующая станция? — ka·*ka*·ya slye·du·yu·sha·ya *stant*·sih·ya

Please stop here
Остановитесь здесь, пожалуйста! — a·sta·na·*vit*·yes' zdyes' pa·*zhal*·sta

I need (assistance)
Мне нужна (помощь). — mnye nuzh·*na* (*po*·mash)

I'd like to buy an SV/kupe/platstkartny ticket for train number ... to ...
Я хотел/хотела бы купить билет для СВ/для купе/ в плацкарте на поезд номер ... до ... (m/f) — ya kha·*tyel*/kha·*tye*·la bih ku·*pit'* bil·*yet* dlya es ve/dlya ku·*pe*/ f plats·*kar*·tye na *po*·ist *no*·mir ... na ...

RUSSIAN TRAIN TALK

Passports, please!
Предъявите паспорт! — prid·yi·*vit*·ye *pas*·part

There's no train today
Сегодня не будет поезда. — si·*vod*·nya nye *bu*·dit pa·iz·*da*

The train is full
Все билеты на этот поезд проданы. — fsye bil·*ye*·tih na *et*·at *po*·ist *pro*·da·nih

There are no SV/kupe/platskart tickets left for the train
Билеты для СВ/ для купе/ в плацкарте уже все распродались. — bil·*lye*·tih dlya es ve/ dlya ku·*pe*/ f plats·*kar*·tye u·*zhye* vsye ras·pra·*da*·lis'

Tickets for that service aren't on sale until ...
Билеты на этот город будут на продаже с ... — bil·*ye*·tih na e·tat *go*·rat *bu*·dut na pra·*da*·zhye s ...

You're at the wrong ticket window
Вы стоите не в том месте. — vi sta·*i*·tye nye f tom *myes*·tye

Please go to window ...
Обращайтесь к окошку ... — a·bra·*shai*·tyes k a·*kosh*·ku ...

GLOSSARY

This glossary is a list of Russian (R), Chinese (C) and Mongolian (M) terms you may come across during your Trans-Siberian journey. See p357, p366 and p374 for words that will help you while dining.

aimag (M) – province or state within Mongolia

airag (M) – fermented mare's milk

apteka (R) – pharmacy

arkhi (M) – the common term for homemade vodka

aviakassa (R) – air-ticket office

avtomat (R) – automatic ticket machine

avtovokzal (R) – bus terminal

AYaM (R) – Amur-Yakutsk Mainline, in Russian Amuro-Yakutskaya Magistral

babushka (R) – grandmother

BAM (R) – Baikal-Amur Mainline, in Russian Baikalo-Amurskaya Magistral

bankomat (R) – ATM

banya (R) – bathhouse

bei (C) – north

bilet (R) – ticket

bīnguǎn (C) – tourist hotel

bolnitsa (R) – hospital

bulvar (R) – boulevard

CAAC (C) – Civil Aviation Administration of China, which controls most of China's domestic and foreign airlines

CCP (C) – Chinese Communist Party

Chángtú gōnggōngqìchē (C) – long-distance buses

CIS (R) – Commonwealth of a Independent States; an alliance of independent states comprising the former USSR republics, with the exception of the three Baltic countries

CITS (C) – China International Travel Service

CTS (C) – China Travel Service

dacha (R) – country cottage, summer house

dajie (C) – avenue

datsan (R) – Buddhist monastery

detsky (R) – child's, children's

dom (R) – house

dong (C) – east

duma (R) – parliament

dvorets (R) – palace

elektrichka (R) – also *prigorodny poezd*; suburban train

fen (C) – a 10th of a *jiao*, in Chinese currency (which makes it minuscule)

firmeny poezda (R) – trains with names (eg *Rossiya*); these are usually of a higher standard

FSB (R) – Federalnaya Sluzhba Bezopasnosti, the Federal Security Service, the successor to the KGB

gavan (R) – harbour

ger (M) – traditional, circular felt *yurt*

gol (M) – river

gorod (R) – city, town

gostiny dvor (R) – trading arcade

gudamj (M) – street

Gulag (R) – Glavnoe Upravlenie Lagerey (Main Administration for Camps); the Soviet network of concentration camps

hú (C) – lake

hútòng (C) – narrow alleyway

Inner Mongolia (M) – a separate province within China

Intourist (R) – the old Soviet State Committee for Tourism, now hived off, split up and in competition with hundreds of other travel agencies

izba (R & M) – traditional wooden cottage

jiao (C) – a 10th of a *yuán*, in Chinese currency

jie (C) – street

kassa (R) – ticket office, cashier's desk

Kazakh (M) – Turkic ethnic group from Central Asia, also found in the west of Mongolia; people from Kazakhstan

KGB (R) – Komitet Gosydarstvennoy Bezopasnosti; Committee of State Security; now the *FSB*

khaan (M) – a king or chief

Khalkh (M) – the major ethnic group living in Mongolia

khiid (M) – Buddhist monastery

khram (R) – church

kino (R) – cinema

kladbishche (R) – cemetery

komnaty otdykha (R) – literally 'resting rooms'; cheap lodgings in Siberian train stations

kray (R) – territory

kreml (R) – kremlin, a town's fortified stronghold

Kuomintang (C) – Chiang Kaishek's Nationalist Party, the dominant political force after the fall of the Qing dynasty; now Taiwan's major political party

kupeyny (R) – *kupe*; compartmentalised carriage; 4-berth compartment

lama (M) – Tibetan Buddhist monk or priest

lavra (R) – senior monastery

living Buddha (M) – common term for reincarnations of Buddhas; Buddhist spiritual leader in Mongolia

lu (C) – road

lyuk (R) – 2-berth compartment

lyux (R) – a *lyux* room in a hotel is a kind of suite, with a sitting room in addition to the bedroom and bathroom

Mafia (R) – anyone who has anything to do with crime, from genuine gangsters to petty criminals

magazin (R) – shop

Manchus (C) – non-Chinese ethnic group from Manchuria (present-day northeast China) that took over China and established the Qing dynasty

manezh (R) – riding school

marshrutky (R) – minibus that runs along a fixed route

matryoshka (R) – set of stacking, painted wooden dolls

mestnoe vremya (R) – local time

militsia (R) – police

more (R) – sea

morin khuur (M) – horsehead fiddle

most (R) – bridge

MPRP (M) – Mongolian People's Revolutionary Party, now called the Mongolian People's Party

muzey (R) – museum; also some palaces, art galleries and nonworking churches

muzhskoy (R) – men's (toilet)

naadam (M) – game

naberezhnaya (R) – embankment

nan (C) – south

novy (R) – new

nuruu (M) – mountain range

oblast (R) – region

obshchiy (R) – 4th-class train compartment

okrug (R) – district

örgön chölöö (M) – avenue

ovoo (M) – shamanistic collection of stones, wood or other offerings to the gods, usually placed in high places

ozero (R) – lake

Paskha (R) – Easter

pereryv (R) – break (when shops, ticket offices, restaurants etc close for an hour or two during the day)

pereulok (R) – lane or side street

Pinyin (C) – the system of writing the Chinese language in the Roman alphabet, adopted by the Communist Party in 1958

PLA (C) – People's Liberation Army

platskartny (R) – *platskart*, also *zhyosky*; 3rd class (or hard seat) in an open carriage of a train

ploshchad (R) – square

poezd (R) – train

posolstvo (R) – embassy

PRC (C) – People's Republic of China

prichal (R) – landing, pier

prigorodny poezd (R) – also *elektrichka*; suburban train

prospekt (R) – avenue

provodnik/provodnitsa (R) – male/female carriage attendant on a train

PSB (C) – Public Security Bureau; the arm of the police force that deals with foreigners

rayon (R) – district

rechnoy vokzal (R) – river terminal

Renminbi (C) – literally 'people's money', the formal name for the currency of China; shortened to RMB

Rozhdestvo (R) – Christmas

sad (R) – garden

samovar (R) – urn with an inner tube filled with hot charcoal, used for heating water for tea

selo (R) – village

sever (R) – north

shosse (R) – highway

siheyuan (C) – traditional house with courtyard

skory (R) – fast

spalny vagon (R) – also SV; sleeping wagon

stupa (M) – Buddhist religious monument composed of a solid hemisphere topped by a spire, containing relics of the Buddha; also known as a pagoda, or *suburgan* in Mongolian

süm (M) – Buddhist temple

taiga (R) – northern pine, fir, spruce and larch forest

teatr (R) – theatre

tögrög (M) – unit of currency in Mongolia

troika (R) – vehicle drawn by three horses

Tsagaan Sar (M) – 'White Moon' or 'White Month'; a festival to celebrate the start of the lunar year

tualet (R) – toilet

UFMS (R) – Upravleniye Federalnoy Migratsionnoy Slyzhby (Federal Migration Service), often shortened to UFMS or FMS. It's likely you'll hear the old acronyms PVU and OVIR used for this office.

ulitsa (R) – street

urtyn-duu (M) – traditional singing style

uul (M) – mountain

vokzal (R) – station

vostok (R) – east

xi (C) – west

yezhednevno (R) – daily

yuán (C) – the Chinese unit of currency, also referred to as RMB

yurt (R) – nomad's portable, round tent-house made of felt or skins stretched over a collapsible frame of wood slats

zheton (R) – token (for metro etc)

Behind the Scenes

SEND US YOUR FEEDBACK

We love to hear from travellers – your comments keep us on our toes and help make our books better. Our well-travelled team reads every word on what you loved or loathed about this book. Although we cannot reply individually to postal submissions, we always guarantee that your feedback goes straight to the appropriate authors, in time for the next edition. Each person who sends us information is thanked in the next edition – the most useful submissions are rewarded with a selection of digital PDF chapters.

Visit **lonelyplanet.com/contact** to submit your updates and suggestions or to ask for help. Our award-winning website also features inspirational travel stories, news and discussions.

Note: We may edit, reproduce and incorporate your comments in Lonely Planet products such as guidebooks, websites and digital products, so let us know if you don't want your comments reproduced or your name acknowledged. For a copy of our privacy policy visit lonelyplanet.com/privacy.

OUR READERS

Many thanks to the travellers who used the last edition and wrote to us with helpful hints, useful advice and interesting anecdotes: Ask Gudmundsen, Chris Fray, Elisabeth Tacke, Ercan Tatar, Gaston Hourcade, Hanna Sarkimaa, Hannah Leupold, Jay Phang, Julia Simon, Michael Omota, Olivier Ordóñez, Patrice Etienne, Piet van den Heuvel, Saori Komuro, Siegfried Schwab, Sonja Minkus, Stef Russell, Thomas Sarosy,

AUTHOR THANKS

Simon Richmond

Many thanks to my fellow authors and Brana at HQ; Sasha & Andrey for a lovely place to stay, the ever knowledgable Peter Kozyrev, Chris Hamilton, Adelya Dayanova, Polina Adrianova, Dimitri Ozerkov, Vladimir Stolyarov, Yegor Churakov, Oksana, Maxim Pinigin, Alexander Kim, Maria Isserlis, Yevgenia Semenoff and Polina at the Street Art Museum.

Greg Bloom

Thanks to Dima for the hospitality in Sheregesh. Thanks to Rita for the Altai advice and for hooking me up with several contacts. Thanks to Vladimir, my crazy cab driver, for the colourful language and Chuysky Trakt anecdotes. Thanks to Russian Railways for being so damn punctual.

Thanks to *kalyan*. Thanks to the peeps of Western Siberia for being good souls.

Marc Di Duca

Huge *dyakuyu* goes to Kyiv parents-in-law Mykola and Vira for looking after sons Taras and Kirill while I was in Siberia. Big thanks to Alex in Chita, Denis and Marina in Ulan-Ude, Andriy and Anya in Slyudyanka, Zhenya in Irkutsk, Igor, Lena and Georgy in Tayshet, the Maryasovs of Severobaikalsk, Anatoliy and Alex in Krasnoyarsk, Real Russia in London for their hassle-free visa service and, of course, my wife Tanya, for suffering my long absences from our home in Sandwich, Kent.

Anthony Haywood

Thanks to those who helped out with local knowledge, mostly anonymously, along the way, but especially to Katya Y in Kazan and Katya P in Perm. In Yekaterinburg I'd like to thank Konstantin and Olga Brylyakov for sharing their knowledge (and delicious cream cake!), and Luba Suslyakova for her expert opinions and good company over dinner. Thanks also to the staff at Lonely Planet, especially Anna Tyler and Brana Vladisavljevic.

Michael Kohn

Many thanks to Molly and Baigalmaa for their companionship on the tour to northern Mongolia. A round of thanks is owed to Daniel,

Densmaa and Gustavo Correa, Susan Fox, Surendra Kumar Bansal, Andrea Prégnan, Toroo and Degi, Sabine Schmidt, Lhagva Erdene, Altangerel at the Danzan Ravjaa Museum and Mogi Badral.

Shawn Low

As always thanks to the DE, Brana, for steadying the Trans-Siberian ship and for your friendship. Cheers also to CA: Simon (yet another one done and dusted!). Thanks to the Lonely Planet crew who are working on this: eds, cartos, LDs etc. I've been behind the scenes and know how hard you all work. Thanks also to new friends and old friends on the ground: too numerous to list but I promise to buy you all beers when our paths cross again. Otherwise, we'll catch up on WeChat!

Tom Masters

Huge thanks to my many friends in St Petersburg, but especially Anatoliy Buzinskiy at Dozhd, Biblioteka Gogolya and Letovpitere for making such huge efforts to help me with contacts and introductions. Thanks to my old friend and tireless Petersburger Simon Patterson, his wife Olga Dmitrieva and their amazing children for making me feel at home during my stay, and also for organising my accommodation. Thanks also to such reliable comrades as Nikita Yumanov, Gena Bogolepov, Alexei Dmitriev, Alexei Chernov, Nikita Slavich, Dima Dzhafarov, Sasha & Andrey, Peter Kozyrev and Nastya Makarova. At Lonely Planet big thanks to Simon Richmond, Anna Tyler, Brana Vladisavljevic and all the in-house eds and cartos for their hard work on this title.

Daniel McCrohan

Huge thanks to my uncle, Dave Campos, for being brave enough to join me on my latest Trans-Mongolian adventure; if only that jeep had been as comfortable as the train! Thanks too to fellow authors, David Eimer and Mike Kohn for their help with research in Běijīng and Mongolia respectively. A big nǐhǎo to all my family and friends back in the UK. But most of all, to Taotao and the kids: 我爱你们！

Leonid Ragozin

Many thanks to my wife Masha Makeeva for bearing with my absences and for accompanying me on the Yaroslavl section of this trip. Huge thanks to my Lonely Planet colleague Branislava Vladisavljevic for her patience and helping with numerous issues that were coming up in the course of research. It was also great to catch up with fellow authors – Simon Richmond, Anthony Haywood and Mara Vorhees – in Moscow. Good to see you again!

Regis St Louis

Thanks go to Anna Kaminski and Greg Bloom for helpful tips on the Far East; Martha Madsen for her hospitality and many tips in Yelizovo; Irina and Sasha for a warm welcome in Esso; Yelena for loads of info at Omega Plus in Yuzhno-Sakhalinsk; Anastasia for Vladivostok insight; Sasha for the Russky Island excursion; Yegor Makarov for Sakha lore, and Aita, Illary, Elena and expats for all the help in Yakutsk. Hugs to Cassandra and daughters Magdalena and Genevieve for a warm homecoming.

Mara Vorhees

Самое болшое спасибо to my friend and co-author, Leonid Ragozin, who is a pleasure to work with and fontanka of information about his hometown. Thanks to Tim O'Brien (of course), Marc Bennetts, Simon Richmond and Andrei Muchnik for lots of ideas. As always, thanks to my little guys S&V, for challenging me to see familiar destinations from new perspectives, and to Daddio, for, well, everything.

ACKNOWLEDGMENTS

Climate map data adapted from Peel MC, Finlayson BL & McMahon TA (2007) 'Updated World Map of the Köppen-Geiger Climate Classification', *Hydrology and Earth System Sciences*, 11, 163344.

Illustrations p60-1 and p92-3 by Javier Zarracina

Cover photograph: Lake Baikal, Tony Wheeler©

THIS BOOK

This 5th edition of Lonely Planet's *Trans-Siberian Railway* guidebook was researched and written by Simon Richmond, Greg Bloom, Marc Di Duca, Anthony Haywood, Michael Kohn, Shawn Low, Tom Masters, Daniel McCrohan, Leonid Ragozin, Regis St Louis and Mara Vorhees. The previous edition was written by Greg Bloom, Marc Di Duca, Anthony Haywood, Michael Kohn, Tom Masters, Leonid Ragozin, Mara Vorhees and Marc Bennetts. This guidebook was produced by the following:

Commissioning Editor Anna Tyler

Destination Editor Brana Vladisavljevic

Product Editor Tracy Whitmey

Book Designer Wendy Wright

Senior Cartographer Valentina Kremenchutskaya

Assisting Editors Kellie Langdon, Anne Mulvaney, Jenna Myers, Rosie Nicholson, Christopher Pitts

Cover Researcher Naomi Parker

Thanks to Sasha Baskett, Megan Eaves, Ryan Evans, Larissa Frost, Claire Naylor, Karyn Noble, Dianne Schallmeiner, Samantha Tyson, Lauren Wellicome, Amanda Williamson

Index

NOTES

Map Legend

Sights

- Beach
- Bird Sanctuary
- Buddhist
- Castle/Palace
- Christian
- Confucian
- Hindu
- Islamic
- Jain
- Jewish
- Monument
- Museum/Gallery/Historic Building
- Ruin
- Shinto
- Sikh
- Taoist
- Winery/Vineyard
- Zoo/Wildlife Sanctuary
- Other Sight

Activities, Courses & Tours

- Bodysurfing
- Diving
- Canoeing/Kayaking
- Course/Tour
- Sento Hot Baths/Onsen
- Skiing
- Snorkelling
- Surfing
- Swimming/Pool
- Walking
- Windsurfing
- Other Activity

Sleeping

- Sleeping
- Camping

Eating

- Eating

Drinking & Nightlife

- Drinking & Nightlife
- Cafe

Entertainment

- Entertainment

Shopping

- Shopping

Information

- Bank
- Embassy/Consulate
- Hospital/Medical
- Internet
- Police
- Post Office
- Telephone
- Toilet
- Tourist Information
- Other Information

Geographic

- Beach
- Hut/Shelter
- Lighthouse
- Lookout
- Mountain/Volcano
- Oasis
- Park
- Pass
- Picnic Area
- Waterfall

Population

- Capital (National)
- Capital (State/Province)
- City/Large Town
- Town/Village

Transport

- Airport
- Border crossing
- Bus
- Cable car/Funicular
- Cycling
- Ferry
- Metro/MRT/MTR station
- Monorail
- Parking
- Petrol station
- Skytrain/Subway station
- Taxi
- Train station/Railway
- Tram
- Underground station
- Other Transport

Note: Not all symbols displayed above appear on the maps in this book

Routes

- Tollway
- Freeway
- Primary
- Secondary
- Tertiary
- Lane
- Unsealed road
- Road under construction
- Plaza/Mall
- Steps
- Tunnel
- Pedestrian overpass
- Walking Tour
- Walking Tour detour
- Path/Walking Trail

Boundaries

- International
- State/Province
- Disputed
- Regional/Suburb
- Marine Park
- Cliff
- Wall

Hydrography

- River, Creek
- Intermittent River
- Canal
- Water
- Dry/Salt/Intermittent Lake
- Reef

Areas

- Airport/Runway
- Beach/Desert
- Cemetery (Christian)
- Cemetery (Other)
- Glacier
- Mudflat
- Park/Forest
- Sight (Building)
- Sportsground
- Swamp/Mangrove

Michael Kohn

Trans-Mongolian Route, Mongolian Today, Mongolian Culture & Cuisine Michael first rode the Trans-Mongolia Railway in 1997, stepping off the train in Ulaanbaatar on a chilly -30°C December day. That was the start of an extended stay in Mongolia, where he worked for an English-language newspaper and various international media. He has since chugged along most northeast Asia's rail routes, including the remote train journey from Choibalsan to the Russian border. Michael has updated four editions of Lonely Planet's *Mongolia* guide and three editions of Lonely Planet's *China*. He is currently based in Ulaanbaatar.

Shawn Low

Trans-Manchurian Route Shawn grew up in hot, humid, food-crazy Singapore but later made his way further south to less hot, less humid, food-crazy Melbourne (Australia, not Florida). He's spent the last eight years working for Lonely Planet: as an editor, commissioning editor, author, TV host and travel editor. This time, Shawn travelled along the unsung Trans-Manchurian line through grand Chinese-Russian cities, China's rust belt, and the lush Inner Mongolian grasslands before sweeping into bustling Beijing. Hey, it's a hard job but someone's gotta do it right? He's on Twitter @shawnlow.

Tom Masters

St Petersburg Tom first came to St Petersburg in 1996 while studying Russian at the School of Slavonic & East European Studies, part of the University of London. He loved the city so much that he came back after graduating and worked as a writer and editor at the *St Petersburg Times,* a job that allowed him to get to know the city in intimate detail. While since living in London and Berlin, Tom has always retained a strong link with the city, authoring the last three editions of Lonely Planet's *St Petersburg* guide. You can see more of Tom's work at www.tommasters.net.

Read more about Tom at:
lonelyplanet.com/members/tommasters

Daniel McCrohan

Běijīng, China Today, Chinese Culture & Cuisine Daniel has been living in Běijīng for more than a decade, trying in vain to perfect his ropey Chinese, whilst developing a taste for raw garlic (there's no better accompaniment to a bowl of noodles, apparently). He is the creator of the iPhone app, *Beijing on a Budget*, a co-host for the TV series, *Best in China*, and has worked on more than 20 Lonely Planet guidebooks, including *China* and *Mongolia*. During his time in Běijīng, Daniel has travelled the Trans-Mongolian route by train, bus, jeep and bicycle, although has yet to make it past Ulaanbaatar; he blames the incredible Mongolian hospitality. Contact him through danielmccrohan.com.

Read more about Daniel at:
lonelyplanet.com/members/danielmccrohan

Regis St Louis

Ulan Ude to Vladivostok An early fan of Gogol and Dostoevsky, Regis spent his university years in America and Moscow immersed in the world of Rus, in pursuit of a rather impractical degree in Slavic Languages and Literatures. On this trip across the vast Far East, Regis dined on frozen fish and fermented mare's milk in Yakutsk, searched for secret hot springs in Kamchatka and spent far too many hours on overnight trains. A full-time travel writer since 2003, Regis has contributed to more than 40 Lonely Planet titles. He lives in Brooklyn, New York.

Read more about Regis at:
lonelyplanet.com/members/regisstlouis

Mara Vorhees

Moscow Mara's first visit to Moscow was in 1990, when the lines inside GUM were dwarfed only by the lines outside Lenin's Tomb. She witnessed the post-communist transition from her vantage point in the Ural Mountains. Nowadays, she often travels with her twins (who celebrated their 4th birthday in Moscow). Follow their adventures at www.havetwinswilltravel.com.

Read more about Mara at:
lonelyplanet.com/members/mvorhees

Contributing Author

Leonid Ragozin contributed to the Moscow to Yekaterinburg chapter. He spent 12 years voyaging through different parts of the BBC, with a break for a four-year stint as a foreign correspondent for the Russian Newsweek. Leonid is currently a freelance journalist, largely focusing on the war in Ukraine, a country he has also covered for Lonely Planet.

OUR STORY

A beat-up old car, a few dollars in the pocket and a sense of adventure. In 1972 that's all Tony and Maureen Wheeler needed for the trip of a lifetime – across Europe and Asia overland to Australia. It took several months, and at the end – broke but inspired – they sat at their kitchen table writing and stapling together their first travel guide, *Across Asia on the Cheap*. Within a week they'd sold 1500 copies. Lonely Planet was born.

Today, Lonely Planet has offices in Franklin, London, Melbourne, Oakland, Beijing and Delhi, with more than 600 staff and writers. We share Tony's belief that 'a great guidebook should do three things: inform, educate and amuse'.

OUR WRITERS

Simon Richmond

Coordinating author Simon first visited Russia in 1994, spending time in St Petersburg and Moscow and travelling by train from there to Central Asia. He's since travelled the breadth of the nation from Kamchatka in the Far East to Kaliningrad in the far west, stopping off at many points between. An award-winning travel writer and photographer, Simon has co-authored the last four editions of the *Russia* guide for Lonely Planet as well as the first three editions of the *Trans-Siberian Railway* guide. He's contributed to many other titles for the company, ranging from Cape Town to Korea. Read more about his travels at www.simonrichmond.com

Read more about Simon at:
lonelyplanet.com/members/simonrichmond

Greg Bloom

Yekaterinburg to Krasnoyarsk Greg cut his teeth in the former Soviet Union as a journalist and later editor-in-chief of the *Kyiv Post*. He left Ukraine in 2003, but returns frequently to the region. In the service of Lonely Planet, he has been detained in Uzbekistan, taken a shlagbaum to the head in Kyiv, swam in the dying Aral Sea, snowboarded down volcanoes in Kamchatka and hit 100km/h in a Latvian bobsled. These days Greg divides his time between Cambodia and the Philippines. Read about his trips at www.mytripjournal.com/bloomblogs.

Read more about Greg at:
lonelyplanet.com/members/gbloom4

Marc Di Duca

Lake Baikal: Krasnoyarsk to Ulan Ude, Baikal-Amur Mainline Marc has spent over two decades crisscrossing the former communist world, half of that time as a travel guide author. Stints on previous editions of Lonely Planet's *Russia* and *Trans-Siberian Railway* were preceded by other guides to Moscow, St Petersburg and Lake Baikal. Stalking Decembrists across four million square kilometres, ice fishing on frozen Lake Baikal, and munching through cholesterol-elevating amounts of Buryat buuzy all formed part of research on the Trans-Sib this time round.

Read more about Marc at:
lonelyplanet.com/members/madidu

Anthony Haywood

Moscow to Yekaterinburg After studying literature and later Russian language at university, Anthony travelled to Moscow during the post-Soviet, pre-anything days of January 1992. Journeys in Russia since that chaotic time have taken him to many different regions, including Siberia to research his book *Siberia, A Cultural History*, as well as Moscow, St Petersburg, and to the Volga Region and Urals to research various editions of this book. He coordinated the 4th edition of this guidebook. Find out more at www.anthonyjhaywood.com

EAGLE VALLEY LIBRARY DISTRICT
P.O. BOX 240   600 BROADWAY
EAGLE, CO 81631   (970) 328-8800

Read more about Anthony at:
lonelyplanet.com/members/anthonyhaywood

OVER PAGE MORE WRITERS

Published by Lonely Planet Publications Pty Ltd
ABN 36 005 607 983
5th edition – Apr 2015
ISBN 978 1 74220 740 7
© Lonely Planet 2015   Photographs © as indicated 2015
10 9 8 7 6 5 4 3 2 1
Printed in China